ISAAC ASIMOV

ON THE ——

HUMAN BODY
AND THE
HUMAN BRAIN

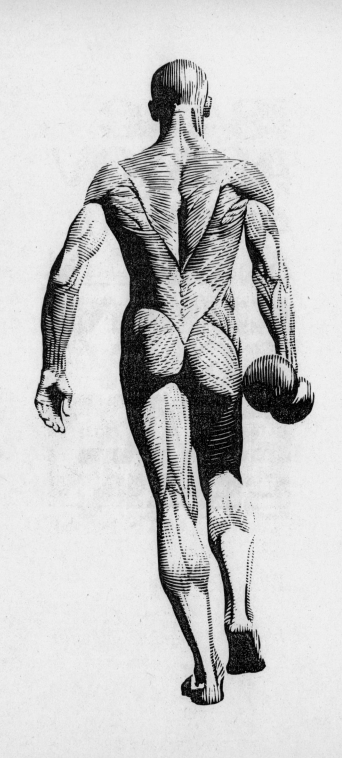

ISAAC ASIMOV
ON THE
HUMAN BODY
AND THE
HUMAN BRAIN

TWO VOLUMES IN ONE

By Isaac Asimov

Illustrated by Anthony Ravielli

BONANZA BOOKS
New York

This 1985 edition is published by Bonanza Books, distributed by Crown
Publishers, Inc., by arrangement with Houghton Mifflin Company.

Originally published in two separate volumes under the titles
The Human Body and *The Human Brain*.

Manufactured in the United States of America

Library of Congress Cataloging in Publication Data

Asimov, Isaac, 1920–
    Isaac Asimov on the human body and human brain.

    Reprint (1st work). Originally published: The human body. Boston :
Houghton Mifflin, 1963.
    Reprint (2nd work). Originally published: The human brain, its
capacities and functions. Boston : Houghton Mifflin, c1963.
    Includes index.
    1. Brain. 2. Body, Human, I. Asimov, Isaac, 1920–   Human brain,
its capacities and functions. 1984. II. Title.
QP376.A83 1984   612   84-24199
ISBN: O-517-459981

h g f e d c b a

CONTENTS

Part I
The Human Body

1 Our Place

DISTINCTIONS	1
THE PHYLA	4
THE DEVELOPMENT OF PHYLA	8
THE CHORDATES	12
THE VERTEBRATES	17

2 Our Head and Torso

THE VERTEBRAL COLUMN	27
THE VERTEBRAE AND RIBS	32
THE SKULL	40
THE TEETH	49

3 Our Limbs and Joints

THE ARMS	56
THE LEGS	63
CELLS	71

BONE STRUCTURE   76
TOOTH STRUCTURE   82
BONE MOVEMENT   84

4   *Our Muscles*
LIVING MOTION   89
MUSCLE CONTRACTION   92
STRIATED MUSCLE   95
TENDONS   105
MUSCLES IN ACTION   110
SOME INDIVIDUAL MUSCLES   114

5   *Our Lungs*
THE ENTRANCE OF OXYGEN   120
THE NOSE AND THROAT   126
THE VOICE   135
THE BRONCHIAL TREE   140
BREATHING   145

6   *Our Heart and Arteries*
THE INNER FLUID   152
THE CIRCULATION   156
THE HEARTBEAT   167
BLOOD PRESSURE   174

7   *Our Blood*
THE LIQUID TISSUE   182
THE ERYTHROCYTE   187

ANEMIA 191

LEUKOCYTES AND THROMBOCYTES 199

LYMPH 205

8 *Our Intestines*

FOOD 211

THE MOUTH 215

THE STOMACH 219

THE PANCREAS AND LIVER 227

ABSORPTION 235

THE COLON 241

9 *Our Kidneys*

CARBON DIOXIDE AND WATER 246

THE EXCRETORY SYSTEM 252

URINE 260

10 *Our Skin*

SCALES AND EPIDERMIS 266

PERSPIRATION 275

HAIR 281

11 *Our Genitals*

REPRODUCTION 291

THE EGG 296

THE PLACENTA 301

THE HUMAN FEMALE 305

THE HUMAN MALE 313

Postscript: Our Longevity   319

Part II
The Human Brain

Introduction   331

1   *Our Hormones*
    ORGANIZATION   337
    SECRETIN   340
    AMINO ACIDS   344
    STRUCTURE AND ACTION   349
    MORE POLYPEPTIDE HORMONES   354

2   *Our Pancreas*
    DUCTLESS GLANDS   359
    INSULIN   364
    INSULIN STRUCTURE   369
    GLUCAGON   374
    EPINEPHRINE   376

3   *Our Thyroid*
    IODINE   381
    THYROXINE   387

THYROID-STIMULATING HORMONE   391
PARATHYROID HORMONE   395
POSTERIOR PITUITARY HORMONES   398

4   *Our Adrenal Cortex*
CHOLESTEROL   402
OTHER STEROIDS   406
CORTICOIDS   412
ACTH   417

5   *Our Gonads and Growth*
PLANT HORMONES   423
GROWTH HORMONE   428
METAMORPHOSIS   431
ANDROGENS   434
ESTROGENS   439
GONADOTROPHINS   444

6   *Our Nerves*
ELECTRICITY AND IONS   448
THE CELL MEMBRANE   453
POLARIZATION AND DEPOLARIZATION   457
THE NEURON   461
ACETYLCHOLINE   468

7   *Our Nervous System*
CEPHALIZATION   475
THE CHORDATES   479

THE PRIMATES   485

APES AND MEN   490

8   *Our Cerebrum*

THE CEREBROSPINAL FLUID   497

THE CEREBRAL CORTEX   504

ELECTROENCEPHALOGRAPHY   513

THE BASAL GANGLIA   519

THE HYPOTHALAMUS   524

9   *Our Brain Stem and Spinal Cord*

THE CEREBELLUM   531

THE CRANIAL NERVES   540

THE SPINAL NERVES   545

THE AUTONOMIC NERVOUS SYSTEM   550

10   *Our Senses*

TOUCH   556

PAIN   563

TASTE   571

SMELL   575

11   *Our Ears*

HEARING   579

THE EXTERNAL AND MIDDLE EAR   584

THE INTERNAL EAR   592

ECHOLOCATION   598

THE VESTIBULAR SENSE   601

12   *Our Eyes*

LIGHT   605
THE EYEBALL   611
WITHIN THE EYE   619
THE RETINA   624
COLOR VISION   630

13   *Our Reflexes*

RESPONSE   634
THE REFLEX ARC   638
INSTINCTS AND IMPRINTING   643
CONDITIONING   648

14   *Our Mind*

LEARNING   654
REASON AND BEYOND   660
PSYCHOBIOCHEMISTRY   667
A FINAL WORD   674

Index   679

Part I

THE HUMAN BODY

Its Structure and Operation

1

OUR PLACE

DISTINCTIONS

In writing a book about the human body there is the great advantage that all the readers know what a human body is. They can recognize it at a glance and distinguish it, let us say, from a rock or from a cypress tree, from an oyster or frog, from a dog, even from a chimpanzee. What is more, we all know the prominent external features of the human body to begin with and even have some idea as to its internal features. We know something about its more obvious ways of functioning.

In a sense, this is a disadvantage too, for there is always the temptation to assume all this knowledge and to plunge into the description and discussion of the human body without as much as a sideward glance. And yet man does not exist in isolation: he is a small part of the domain of life and, in a still larger sense, is an even smaller part of the totality of all things.

There is profit to be gained, now and then, in viewing the structure and workings of the human body, not in isolation, but against this background of life and the universe, and it will be helpful therefore if we pretend an ignorance we do not really have. Let's concern ourselves with the definition of what, exactly, we mean by the human body.

One way of doing this logically and systematically is to try to divide all things into two or more classifications by making some reasonable distinction among them, and then to place man in one of those classifications. Concentrating on the classification into which we have placed him, we can divide that further by making finer distinctions, place him anew, and so proceed as far as is necessary for the purposes of this book.

To begin with, for instance, we can say that a rock is not a man. A rock does not feed, grow, and multiply; it does not sense its environment and respond to it in an adaptive way (that is, in a way designed to protect its existence). A man, however, does all these things. In this way, we distinguish not only a rock from a man, but all nonliving things from all living things. We make the first clear-cut distinction leading to the proper placing of man by stating that he is alive.*

If we restrict ourselves next to living things, we can go on to say with great confidence that it is easy to distinguish a cypress tree or a cactus from man. The former are rooted in the ground and are incapable of rapid voluntary motion. Important portions of their surface are green. A man, on the other hand, is not rooted, can move rapidly, possesses no green parts of any significance, and so on. A great many other distinctions can easily be made which will divide living things into the two grand divisions of the *Plant Kingdom* and the *Animal Kingdom*, with ourselves clearly a member of the latter. (Some biologists define a third and even a fourth kingdom, but these involve microscopic creatures only and need not concern us.)

When we confine ourselves to animal life and try to restrict man into a still narrower group, things cease to be quite so easy. It is almost automatic to try to make the kind of distinction that

* The difference between life and nonlife, under the circumstances ordinarily encountered, is sufficiently great for even the casual observer to find words sufficiently exact to make the distinction easily. As we study simpler and simpler forms of life, however, matters become less clear and, at the simplest levels, the distinction becomes difficult to express. This book is not the place to work out the necessary concepts and phraseology, but if you are curious, you will find this in another book of mine, *Life and Energy* (1962).

will divide a heterogeneous group in two. That is the simplest form of classification and I have already done this twice: nonlife and life; plant and animal. There were bound to be attempts to continue this binary classification.

The Greek philosopher Aristotle (who lived in the 4th century B.C.) classified all animals into those with blood and those without blood, and man, of course, came into the former group. Yet almost all animals have blood of one sort or another, and even if we restrict ourselves to red blood (which is what Aristotle undoubtedly meant) the division is erratic and gives rise to two quite heterogeneous groups, neither of which can be easily studied as a whole.*

In modern times another attempt was made, one closer to the mark. The French naturalist Jean Baptiste Lamarck, in 1797, divided animals into *vertebrates* and *invertebrates*. The vertebrates include those animals possessing a backbone made up of a series of individual bones called "vertebrae." The invertebrates, very naturally, include all other animals. According to this system man would be a vertebrate.

In one respect this is good. The vertebrates make up a comparatively close-knit group of animals. In another respect it is not so good, for the invertebrates are such a wide range of animals with such fundamental differences among themselves that they cannot be studied as a unified whole. To the average man, far more interested in himself than in any other animal, the term invertebrate is good enough, however, and Lamarck's division is still widely used in popular writing. After all, among the invertebrates are bugs, worms, jellyfish, starfish, and other creatures

---

* I should pause here to point out that in drawing distinctions and making classifications, mankind is usually imposing artificial divisions of his own choosing upon a universe that is, in many ways, "all one piece." The justification for doing so is that it helps us in our attempted understanding of the universe. It breaks down a set of objects and phenomena too complex to be grasped in its entirety into smaller realms that can be dealt with one by one. There is nothing objectively "true" about such classifications, however, and the only proper criterion of their value is that of their usefulness.

of little moment to the layman and they can be dismissed easily enough. To the zoologist, intent on classifying *all* animal life in a reasonable fashion, matters cannot be dismissed so easily. It early became evident that no simple line could be drawn clear across the Animal Kingdom. Rather a number of lines must be drawn. The first to do so with marked success was the 18th-century Swedish botanist Carolus Linnaeus. In 1735 he published a book in which the forms of life were classified into divisions and subdivisions along lines that have been broadly adhered to ever since.

THE PHYLA

It was not Linnaeus, however, who gave the modern name to the broadest groups that can be included within the Animal Kingdom. This feat fell to the French naturalist, Georges Léopold Cuvier, a contemporary of Lamarck. In 1798 he divided the Animal Kingdom into four major branches and called each of these branches a *phylum* (fy'lum; plural, *phyla*), from a Greek word meaning a tribe or race.*

As time went on and zoologists studied the Animal Kingdom more closely and in greater detail, Cuvier's four phyla seemed overmodest. At the present time, there are roughly twenty phyla accepted. I say "roughly," because all such classifications, being man-made, depend upon the individual judgment of the classifier. There are borderline cases where a group of animals is classed with a particular phylum by one investigator but is judged sufficiently different by another to be given a phylum all to itself.

* I intend, whenever it seems advisable, to give the pronunciation and derivation of technical terms. It seems to me this ought to help invest an otherwise nutcrackerish term with familiarity and perhaps lessen its terrors. Thus, a phylum may mean nothing to us, but we all know what a tribe is, and once we can pronounce phylum there is no further reason to be concerned about it. Since most scientific terms are derived from either Latin or Greek, I shall save space by putting the literal meaning in parenthesis with an L or G added: *phylum* ("tribe" G). Where other languages are involved, or where the derivation is of particular interest, I shall of course go into greater detail.

Each phylum (at least in the intent of the classifier) includes all animals that follow a certain basic plan of structure that is quite different, in important ways, from the one followed by all other animals. The best way to explain what is meant by that is to give some examples. This will tell us, in the end, what the basic plan of structure of the human body (as well as the bodies of related animals) is. Almost as important, it will tell us what the basic plan of structure of the human body is not. Finally, it will give us a framework to which we can refer later in the book from time to time.

The phylum *Protozoa* (proh-toh-zoh'ah; "first animals" G) includes all animal organisms consisting of a single cell. (I'll have more to say about cells later, but I shall assume now that you have heard enough about cells for the statement to have meaning for you.) That the phylum consists only of single-celled organisms is quite distinctive, for all the remaining animal phyla are made up of organisms that consist of a number of cells (*multicellular organisms*).

Consider, as another example, a pair of phyla — *Brachiopoda* (bray'kee-op'oh-duh; "arm-leg" G) and *Mollusca* (muh-lus'kuh; "soft" L).* The animals of both phyla possess hinged double-shells constructed of calcium carbonate (limestone). In this they are unique. To be sure, there are creatures outside these phyla that have calcium carbonate shells — as, for instance, the corals. The calcium-carbonate shells of corals and other outsiders, however, are in one piece and are not composed of two hinged halves. You might wonder why, then, the animals with hinged double-shells of similar chemical composition are nevertheless

---

* Each name is poor if the meaning of the word is taken literally. The name Brachiopoda was suggested because the naturalist who first studied the creatures assumed that certain structures served them as both arms and legs. This proved not to be so. The animals in the phylum Mollusca are not particularly soft. In fact, most have hard shells. Internally, of course, they are soft, but no softer than other animals. Nevertheless, as long as zoologists agree on a particular name it serves a useful function even when the literal meaning is wrong. And the derivation is always of historical interest, too.

divided into two phyla. Well, among the mollusks one half of the shell is formed beneath the animal and the other half above, and the two are generally unequal in size. Among the brachiopods the halves of the shell are formed to the left and right of the animal and are roughly equal in size.

These are by no means the only important differences among the two groups, but even alone they would be considered sufficient by zoologists to make two phyla mandatory. (Just to indicate that matters are not really simple, there are mollusks with more than two shells, with only one shell, and with no shell at all. These nevertheless belong in the phylum on the basis of other qualifications.)

The phylum *Echinodermata* (ee-ky'noh-dur'muh-tuh; "spiny skin" G), although among the more complex of the phyla as far as most of its structure is concerned, can be differentiated from all other phyla of similar complexity by its possession of radial symmetry. This is a primitive characteristic; one, in other words, that is ordinarily associated with quite simple organisms.

Most phyla have bilateral symmetry. That is, an imaginary plane can be drawn through the body which will divide it into two halves that are mirror images of each other. There is thus a distinct left and right, and, if no other plane of symmetry can be drawn, there is also a distinct front and back, or, if you prefer, a distinct head and tail. The human being is clearly a member of a bilaterally symmetric phylum. His paired organs — eyes, ears, nostrils, arms, legs, and so on — are placed symmetrically on either side of a midplane running from head to feet. His single organs — nose, mouth, navel, anus, and so on — are placed at the midplane.

In radial symmetry no such unique plane can be drawn. Instead, there is a central point around which structures radiate. In the case of the echinoderms, there are usually five equivalent structures radiating out from the center, a fact that is most evident in the starfish, which is the best-known echinoderm.

Two phyla, *Annelida* (a-nel'i-duh; "little ring" L) and *Arthropoda* (ahr-throp'oh-duh; "jointed feet" G), display a plan of structure that is shared by a third phylum, which I shall discuss later. This plan is that of segmentation; the organism is divided into a number of sections of similar structure, something like a railroad train made up of similar passenger cars. This is obvious in the best known of the annelids, the earthworm, where the

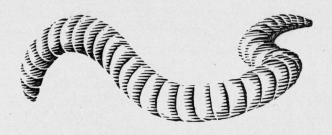

creature is divided into clearly marked off sections. The result resembles successive little rings of tissue and it is from this that the name of the phylum is derived. In some arthropods, such as centipedes, the existence of segments is as clear as it is in the earthworm. In others, the segmentation may be rather masked but it still shows up as a repetition of structures along the length of a creature; as, for example, the series of legs of the lobster. The two phyla, although sharing this very fundamental characteristic of segmentation, are clearly distinguished from each other by the fact that the annelids have no hard tissues, whereas the arthropods have a shell. (There are also additional distinguishing qualifications, of course.)

Nor is the arthropod shell to be confused with those of either the mollusks or the brachiopods. The arthropod shell is made of *chitin* (ky'tin), from a Greek word for a type of garment. Chitin is an organic substance built up of complex sugar molecules. It is tough, light, and flexible, whereas the stony calcium carbonate of the other phyla is hard, heavy, and brittle.

But the human being is also segmented. It is not as obvious in the human as in the earthworm or in the lobster, but he is. Does this make him a member of either Annelida or Arthropoda? Not necessarily. As we have seen in the case of Mollusca and Brachiopoda, resemblance in one respect is not enough. The human being, in addition to being segmented, has an elaborate internal skeleton. This no annelid and no arthropod possesses, and the difference is sufficiently fundamental to debar the human being from membership in either of these phyla.

THE DEVELOPMENT OF PHYLA

It is the opinion of biologists that the various phyla have not been independent throughout the past but that all have been descended from a common ancestor. Unfortunately, the order in which the phyla have arisen, and the exact manner in which one developed from another are not definitely known, though reasonable speculations may be and have been advanced.

The past history of living things is obtained most clearly from fossil records, the petrified remnants of creatures long dead, uncovered in deep-lying rocks. The earliest fossils that clearly show animal structure are found in the rocks of the Cambrian Period (named for Cambria, the Roman name for Wales, where these rocks were first studied). The rocks of the Cambrian Period date back half a billion years and more, and at that time all the phyla but one were already clearly established in advanced form so that the connections among them were no longer obvious.

Decisions as to the detailed evolution of the phyla must be based, therefore, on indirect information. For instance, since the arthropods and annelids both possess segmentation, and since the arthropods are, on the whole, the more complex in structure, it sounds reasonable to suppose that long ago, more than a half-billion years ago certainly, a group of annelids developed a chitinous shell and became the first arthropods.

This assumption, reasonable in itself, is strengthened by the existence, today, of an animal called *peripatus* (pee-rip'uh-tus; "walking about" G, because of the quickness of its scurrying). It is classified as an arthropod but is clearly the most primitive of the arthropods and possesses some characteristics that zoologists would ordinarily expect to find among the annelids. It is a "missing link," therefore; the descendant of a line of creatures that may have been annelids once and had not yet become complete arthropods.

What would interest zoologists most of all, of course, would be the establishment of a clear line of descent for the phylum that includes man. This phylum I have not (deliberately) yet mentioned.

The phyla I have mentioned clearly differ from man in very fundamental ways and he cannot be included in any of them. Unlike protozoans, we are made up of many cells. Unlike brachiopods, mollusks, and arthropods, we have no shell of any kind. Unlike annelids, we do have hard tissues. Unlike echinoderms, we are bilaterally symmetrical.

And yet our phylum must have been developed from one of the others. Our lack of knowledge as to how this occurred is particularly frustrating since it happens, so to speak, in front of our eyes. I said that by the Cambrian Period all the phyla but one had already been established. That one, not yet established, is our own; and its manner of establishment has left no record that has yet been found. By the time very shortly after the Cambrian Period when the first fossils of animals of our own phylum make their appearance, they are already as far advanced as many creatures now living. The origin is lost or, at best, is as yet uncovered.

Nevertheless, all hope is not gone. There is indirect evidence. In the muscles of animals of our phylum, there is a compound called *creatine phosphate* (kree'uh-teen) which plays an important part in the chemistry of muscle contraction. In all other phyla (with one exception) creatine phosphate does not exist, but a similar role is taken by an allied compound called *arginine phosphate* (ahr'jih-neen). The one exception is the echinoderm phylum, some members of which also use creatine phosphate.

This is curious. Can we be descended from the echinoderms? Their radial symmetry makes them seem to differ from ourselves more than the animals of almost any other phylum.

Then, too, our phylum consists of segmented animals. To be sure, this is well masked in most cases, but you can verify this on your own body by running your hand down your backbone. You will clearly feel a series of similar bones, one to each segment, a repetition of structure as characteristic of segmentation as the repeated tissue rings of an earthworm or the repeated legs of a lobster. Since this is so, is it possible that our phylum, like that of the arthropods, is descended from the annelids?

But similarities cannot always be used to argue descent. It often happens in the course of evolutionary development that two quite different groups develop marked similarities even though they are not closely related. Thus, whales have developed a fishlike form but they are far more closely related (on the basis of other criteria) to man than to fish. Again, bats have developed wings but are far more closely related to man than to birds. This development of similarities on the part of animals not closely related (usually through the pressure of exposure to similar environments) is called *convergence*.

It may be then that man's phylum is descended from the annelids and that the use of creatine phosphate by both ourselves and some of the echinoderms is an example of convergence. On the other hand, we may be descended from the echinoderms and the existence of segmentation in ourselves as well as in annelids and arthropods may be the result of convergence. Or we could be descended in another fashion altogether, and creatine phosphate and segmentation may represent convergence all around.

Fortunately, there is further evidence to help us decide.

It often happens that the very early stages of the development of an individual animal show structures that resemble those of far distant ancestors. For instance, even the most advanced multicellular animals begin life as a single cell, which can be taken to signify the ultimate descent of all the multicellular phyla from the protozoa.

As this single cell divides into numerous daughter cells, the mass of cells eventually forms a cup-shaped structure consisting of two layers. The outside layer is the *ectoderm* (ek'toh-durm; "outer skin" G) and the layer facing the inside of the cup is the *endoderm* (en'doh-durm; "inner skin" G). There is a phylum of creatures with bodies that consist essentially of elaborations of this cup-shaped structure. This phylum is *Coelenterata* (seelen'tur-ay'tuh; "hollow gut" G, because digestion takes place in the interior of the cup, which thus becomes a gut).

In all phyla more complicated than the coelenterates, however, a third layer of cells is formed, lying between the two original layers and therefore called the *mesoderm* (mee'soh-durm; "middle skin" G). In some phyla the mesoderm arises at the point of junction of ectoderm and endoderm, and in others it arises at several different points of the endoderm only.

This difference in the manner of origin of the mesoderm is felt to be extremely fundamental by zoologists. It seems logical to suppose that from primitive two-layered coelenterates, a billion years ago or more, two new phyla arose, each of which independently developed the mesoderm in its own fashion. From each of these original three-layered phyla, a number of modern phyla developed. The phyla containing mesoderm are therefore divided into two superphyla, each representing a line of common descent far far back in time.

As it happens, the echinoderms and the annelids, the two candidates for the honor of representing our ancestry, are in different superphyla which, in fact, are named for them. In the echinoderm superphylum, which is much the smaller of the two, the mesoderm develops from several points in the endoderm.

In the annelid superphylum, the mesoderm develops from the ectoderm-endoderm junction.

It is a relatively easy task now to decide to which of the superphyla our own phylum belongs by studying the manner in which the mesoderm develops. The answer is, quite clearly and definitely, that our phylum belongs to the echinoderm superphylum. Of all the phyla, then, Echinodermata must be most closely related to our own.

THE CHORDATES

But what, then, of radial and bilateral symmetry?

A clue can be obtained from the young of the echinoderms. In the case of a number of animals, the creature, as it hatches from the egg, has a structure quite different from that of the adult. In the course of its life it undergoes a radical change in order to became an adult. The most familiar example is the caterpillar that becomes a butterfly.

Such a young form, differing radically from the adult, is a *larva,* which is a Latin word for a kind of ghost. Just as a ghost arises from a man but does not have the form and structure of a man, so a larva arises from the eggs laid by the mother but lacks the form and structure of the mother. Sometimes (but not always) the larva will possess structure and function that we have reason to believe were characteristic of the creatures from which it descended, while the adult form is a later specialization.

For instance, many of the echinoderms, brachiopods, and mollusks spend most of their life fixed to some one position or are at best capable of but slow movement. The larval form of such creatures is, however, capable of free motion; and this is useful — it can select a spot for itself upon which to settle down. Were it as motionless as its parent, all the offspring would grow up about the parent and the competition for food might insure the death of all. It is reasonable to suppose, then, that these sessile creatures were descended from free-moving ancestors and to search in the larvae for possible other characteristics of those ancestors.

Well, the echinoderm larvae are not only capable of free motion; they are also bilaterally symmetrical. It is only after conversion into the adult form that radial symmetry appears. The radial symmetry would thus appear to be a secondary development, which may not have existed at all in the very earliest days of the echinoderms.

In fact, we can imagine that when the echinoderm superphylum arose from the primitive coelenterates, two general types arose. One of them developed radial symmetry and gave rise to the modern echinoderms and the other developed certain distinctive features that were characteristic of no other phylum, thus developing into creatures that were not echinoderms at all. The distinctive features were three in number (excluding the retention of bilateral symmetry, which is not distinctive but is shared with many other phyla): These three distinctive features are worth attention because remnants are retained in all members of the phylum, including man. In other words, we will be talking about structures we possess at least in rudimentary form and during at least part of our lives.

First, the creatures of the new phylum possessed a hollow nerve cord that ran along the back of the organism — a *dorsal cord* ("back" L). In all other phyla the central nerve cord, if it existed at all, was solid and ran along the abdomen — a *ventral cord* ("belly" L).

Second, the creatures of the new phylum possessed an internal rod made of a tough, light, and flexible gelatinous substance. Such internal stiffening does not exist in other phyla except for a gristle-like substance in the most advanced mollusks. Even there it does not exist in the form of a rod. Because, in its most distinctive form, the gelatinous rod runs the length of the animal just under the dorsal nerve cord, the rod is called the *notochord* (noh'toh-kord; "back-string" G).

Third, the creatures of the new phylum possess a throat which is perforated by a number of *gill slits*. As water passes into the mouth and out these slits, food can be strained.

Any one of these three unique characteristics is sufficient to mark off a separate phylum, and it is to this phylum that we belong. The phylum is named after the presence of the noto-chord and is therefore *Chordata* (kawr-day'tuh).

The original chordates are lost (perhaps irrevocably) in the past, as are the original echinoderms. All we have today are living specimens of each phylum, specimens that have been develop-ing through hundreds of years of time and have lost all apparent similarity. Yet there are examples of primitive chordates even today that have not altogether lost touch with the echinoderms. Biologists are particularly interested in them not only for their own sake but because they outline what may well have been the course of evolution from some primitive sea urchin to the com-plex group of animals of which man is a member. Thus, to begin with, there is a sea-dwelling wormlike creature, discovered about 1820, with a head that ends in a proboscis shaped vaguely like a tongue or an acorn. Behind this is a collar-like structure that seems to resemble a barnacle. It is called *balanoglossus* (bal'an-oh-glos'us; "barnacle tongue" G). The interesting thing about the balanoglossus, wormlike though it seems, is that behind the collar is a series of gill slits, a fact which alone spells "chordate." Furthermore, in the region of the collar there is a definite hollow dorsal nerve cord and, sticking into the proboscis, a short length of cartilage that seems to be a piece of notochord.

This and a few allied species represent the most primitive chordates known. And the crucial point is that the larva of the balanoglossus is so like the larvae of the echinoderms that when the balanoglossus larva was first discovered it was classified as an echinoderm. Surely the proof of our echinoderm descent is overwhelming.

The larva of another type of primitive chordate is not like that of an echinoderm but is shaped like a small tadpole. In its tail there is a hollow dorsal nerve cord and a notochord. In the forepart are the gill slits. A chordate beyond question. However, this creature in undergoing the change to the adult form discards its tail (as a tadpole does), losing in the process all its notochord and all but a tiny scrap of the nerve cord. What is left of the creature adopts a sessile habit — that is, it is fixed to the surface — and develops a thick, tough covering called a tunic, so that the creatures are referred to as *tunicates*.

Viewed as adults they seem to have nothing of the chordate about them at all, except for the fact that they do retain numerous gill slits through which water is sucked so that food might be filtered out. The filtered water is squirted through an opening in the side, and the creature is also called a "sea squirt."

So far the chordates seem to be doing very little with the notochord, but let's go back to the larva of the tunicates.

There is sometimes a tendency among animals to retain the larval form for extended periods. It may happen that the larva is better adapted to a particular set of environmental conditions than the adult so that it becomes advantageous to lay stress upon this form. Among some insects, for instance, the larvae are relatively long lived (living for a number of years on occasion) and the adult form is very short lived indeed. The adult form may have as its sole function the quick laying of eggs out of which another extended larval form might hatch. Those adults may even lack mouth parts, since in their ephemeral life span there would be no necessity for them to eat.

If the larva develops the last special ability retained by the adult form, that of reproducing itself, the adult form may be eliminated altogether and the larval form can become all there is. This is actually observed to happen among certain salamanders and the phenomenon is called *neoteny* (nee-ot'i-nee; "new stretch" G, that is, a new creature developed through stretching out the larval stage). This tendency also exists among the tunicates: there are small creatures within the group in which the tail of the larva persists throughout life.

In the long-ago Cambrian Period, then, it was possible that some primitive tunicate underwent neoteny and the tail portion of the animal took on a greater importance until a new type of creature arose that was all tunicate tail.

There is a small creature existing today that could conceivably be the descendant of an early tunicate-tail. It is about two inches long and is vaguely fishlike in appearance. Its head end has a circular opening surrounded by bristles which sweep a current of water into the mouth and out the gill slits behind the head. Both head and tail come to a relatively sharp point and the creature is therefore called *amphioxus* (am'fee-ok'sus; "equally-sharp" G). Because it also resembles a tiny lance in shape it is called a *lancelet*.

The amphioxus has a hollow dorsal nerve cord and beneath it a notochord running the full length of the body from end to end. This is the simplest living creature in which an internal

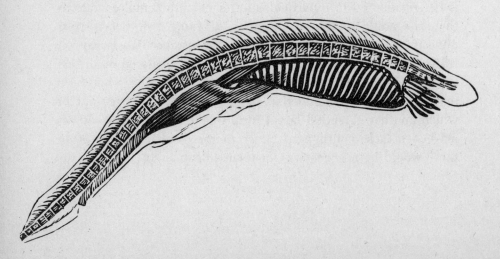

rod can actually act as a stiffening agent throughout life. The amphioxus also clearly shows segmentation. The mere existence of a series of repeated structures such as the gill slits is sign enough that segmentation is a fundamental characteristic of all chordates, but in the amphioxus one can see, through its semi-transparency, that its muscles are arranged in segments.

These three groups of organisms — balanoglossus, the tunicates, and amphioxus — are so different that although all are chordates they are nevertheless placed in three separate *subphyla*. Balanoglossus is *Hemichordata* (hem'ee-kawr-day'tuh; "half-cord" G); the tunicates are in *Urochordata* (yoo'roh-kawr-day'tuh; "tail cord" G); and amphioxus is in *Cephalochordata* (sef'uh-loh-kawr-day'tuh; "head cord" G). Some zoologists consider Hemichordata a small phylum in its own right.

THE VERTEBRATES

By and large, the chordates as described so far are not a successful phylum. The number of species they include are few and obscure and the lives they lead are passive and backward. Yet there is great potentiality here. The notochord is the beginning of an internal bracing to which muscles may be attached. Such internal bracing is much lighter and more efficient than the external bracing of a shell. Then, too, the gill slits can be adapted to extracting oxygen as well as food from the water, so that respiration can be more efficient than in other phyla. Finally, the dorsal nerve cord proved itself in the course of some hundreds of millions of years to be capable of elaboration and development beyond that possible for any ventral nerve cord.

But all of this remains potential, rather than actual, in the small and unsuccessful trio of subphyla so far described. There remains, however, a fourth subphylum which might conceivably have developed from the ancestors of amphioxus, the one primitive group with a notochord lasting through life. It is to this fourth subphylum that man belongs, and, in fact, most of the familiar animals about us as well.

What happened was that the notochord, a continuous and unsegmented rod, took on the segmentation of the rest of the body. It was gradually replaced by a series of discs of *cartilage* ("wickerwork" L), one to each segment. Not only did this supply the new creature with a rod that was springier and more flexible, but the individual segments grew to enclose the dorsal nerve cord so as to offer that key portion of the organism important protection from shocks and buffets. Strips of cartilage also lined the gill slits, stiffening them and forming the *gill arches.*

The individual discs into which the notochord had been converted are called *vertebrae* (vur'ti-bree; singular, *vertebra*), for reasons I will explain later. Creatures with such vertebrae make up all the rest of the Chordata and are included in the fourth and last of its subphyla, *Vertebrata* (vur'ti-bray'tuh). It is this subphylum which includes the "vertebrates" of Lamarck.

All vertebrates possess the hollow dorsal nerve cord characteristic of chordates, enclosed by the vertebrae. (We ourselves do, which makes man a member of Chordata and of Vertebrata.) However, the vertebrates, having gained the vertebrae, have lost the notochord. Should this give them the status of a separate phylum? Perhaps it might, if the notochord had really been lost, but it hasn't. To qualify as a chordate, it is only necessary that an organism possess a notochord at some time in its life, as the tunicate does in its larval stage.

Now a vertebrate such as man has no larval form in the usual sense, but he does develop in stages from the original fertilized ovum. From the time of the fertilization of the ovum to the time of actual birth, a period of some nine months elapses. During that time the human being is systematically developing within the mother's body as an *embryo* (em'bree-oh; "inner swelling" G).

The human embryo has not been studied as well as have embryos of other creatures more available for experimentation and dissection, but the main line of development is clear. During the third week of development, for instance, there is an unmistakable notochord present in the human embryo. As the days pass, the tissues about it segment, and form blocks which absorb and replace the notochord, forming vertebrae instead. However, the notochord was there for a while and man (as well as all other members of Vertebrata) is therefore a full-fledged chordate.

25-DAY
EMBRYO

The subphylum Vertebrata is divided into a total of eight narrower classifications called *classes,* and these are in turn grouped by fours into two *superclasses.* If we describe the nature of these classes briefly, we shall continue to get glimpses of the evolution of man; of the manner in which little by little structural refinements were added and extended until we ourselves existed on the face of the earth.

The first of the two superclasses of Vertebrata is *Pisces* (pis'eez; "fish" L) and includes all the vertebrates that are primarily water-dwelling creatures. The most primitive of the four classes of Pisces must have included the amphioxus-like creatures that first developed cartilaginous nerve-enclosing vertebrae. Like amphioxus, they retained a circular mouth opening without the type of jaw that can open and close. For that reason, the class is called *Agnatha* (ag'nuh-thuh; "no jaws" G).

The original agnaths must have been harmless filter-feeders like the modern amphioxus, but the few agnaths that remain in existence today have learned new tricks. The best known is the lamprey, its circular mouth equipped with hard little rasps, which attaches itself to a fish and plays the role of vampire.

The original agnaths, half a billion years ago, went on to develop a second improvement. In a number of phyla, as I have explained, protection was introduced by means of a hard outer shell and the agnaths fell back on this same device. One group of the creatures developed a shell over the head and forebody and are therefore termed the *ostracoderms* (os'truh-koh-durms; "shell-skin" G).

These agnath shells were not just another set of shells, however. They represented a vital new departure. Instead of being composed of calcium carbonate, as were those of the mollusks, they were composed of calcium phosphate. The calcium phosphate structures produced by ostracoderms is called "bone" and it is a substance unique to the vertebrates. It is found nowhere else in the domain of life. The advantage of bone as compared with shells of other materials lay in its uncommon toughness and strength. A section of bone that is one square inch in diameter has a tensile strength of almost six tons; it would take that much force to pull it in half.

The next step, once the vertebrates were so efficiently defended, was to furnish equipment for possible aggression. The first of the gill arches, the one nearest the circular opening that served the agnaths as a mouth, gradually bent in two and, hinged at the middle, became a primitive jaw. This was enough of a change to warrant placing the newly jawed creatures into a separate class. Since they retained the bony foreshell of the ostracoderms, the new class is called *Placodermi* (plak'oh-durm'eye; "plated-skins" G). The Placodermi could, with the development of teeth, seize food, tear it into bits, and swallow it. The gill slits lost their food-straining properties and began to specialize for breathing only.

The placoderms are now extinct, the only class of Vertebrata to have no living representatives at all. They were successful in their time, but they gave rise to new classes of Pisces that replaced them. The new classes did away, by and large, with the external armor, and relied on maneuverability and speed rather than passive defense. In evolutionary progress as in human warfare, this is often a good move. The ostracoderms are also extinct, but some of the unarmored varieties of Agnatha — just a few species — are still in existence today.

From the placoderms were developed the remaining two classes of Pisces. In both classes the external armor was abandoned as such. Some was discarded altogether and the rest was overgrown with skin so that it became an internal protection enclosing the fore end of the nerve cord, which had grown and specialized into a primitive brain.

These two classes further developed movable, paired fins. The agnaths and placoderms possessed fins (sometimes a considerable number of them) along the midline of the body. They served as balancing organs and kept them right side up when swimming. They were stiffened by cartilaginous fin-rays.

The new classes converted these into two paired fins, located on either side of the midline, one pair just behind the head and the other just before the tail. These were stiffened not only by cartilaginous rays but by internal stiffening rods extending down from the vertebrae. To these supports muscles could be attached which could move the fins and convert them from passive balancing devices to oars that could help bring about rapid turns and all sorts of agile maneuvers. From the individual vertebrae, curved extensions were formed which stiffened the sides of the creature. The internal bracing that had begun with the simple rod of the notochord had thus become a complicated system including a jointed vertebral column with a brain-enclosing skull at one end, a set of ribs enclosing the body, and limb supports.

The two new classes differed in one important respect in their treatment of bone. One class retrogressed, abandoning bone altogether and forming a system of bracing entirely out of cartilage. This is the class *Chondrichthyes* (kon-drik'thee-eez; "cartilaginous fish" G), represented today by the various sharks. The second class, which makes up the last of the Pisces, retained the bone, shifting it inward. They even converted the cartilage of the vertebral column and its extensions into bone. This is the class *Osteichthyes* (os'tee-ik'thee-eez; "bony fish" G) and it is to this class that all the familiar fish of today belong.

The bony fish came into prominence in the Devonian Period (named for a region in southern England where rocks of that period were first studied) about 400,000,000 years ago. It took a hundred million years of chordate evolution to do it, but the phylum finally made its mark. The bony fish dominated the ocean and proliferated into a large number of species. The period is sometimes called the "Age of Fishes" in consequence. As far as the ocean is concerned, in fact, the Age of Fishes has never ended, for the bony fish still dominate the ocean today.

Most of the varieties of bony fish kept their paired fins largely in the form of thin fringes of ray-supported tissue. The bony supports were small and weak, only as strong, in fact, as was necessary to maneuver the fins as oars. It was not from these, the most successful fish, that man descended but from poor relations of these ray-finned fish.

Among these poor relations, the fleshy part of the fin, together with its bone and muscle, was expanded so that each of the four fins seemed to form a stubby extension of the body, a kind of fleshy lobe with but a thin extension of ray-supported fringe. These are the "lobe-finned fishes," or *crossopterygii* (kros-op'tuh-rij'ee-eye; "fringe-fins" G).

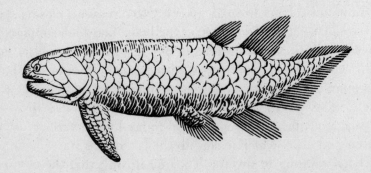

The lobe-finned fishes sacrificed swimming agility by this sort of fin formation and were far less successful than the other groups of bony fish. They were thought to have become extinct about 70,000,000 years ago, but in 1939 a living lobe-finned fish was netted in the waters off South Africa and several have been caught since World War II. This only means that a tiny remnant have managed to hang on through the ages. The lobe-finned fishes gained an advantage, however, in shallow, swampy water, where their stubby fins, poor at swimming, showed up well as supports. They could hobble out of a drying stretch of water into a deeper pool.

The limbs strengthened further, and with other adaptations, involving lungs and heart, developed into forms of life capable of living on dry land, first for extended periods and finally permanently. Thus, although the descendants of the lobe-finned fishes may have perished — or largely perished from the waters — other descendants invaded the dry land successfully and gave rise to the second superclass of Vertebrata, the superclass to which man belongs.

The members of this second superclass could no longer rely on water buoyancy to help their movements. They had to struggle against the full force of gravity. Their limbs became larger and stronger. Those remained four in number for the most part, though some members of the superclass, such as certain flightless birds, reduced them to only two functional ones, and others, such as the snakes, got rid of them altogether. Nevertheless these are exceptional and no land vertebrate ever developed a fifth limb. For this reason, the entire superclass is termed *Tetrapoda* (te-tra'-poh-duh; "four-footed" G). We make use of about the same term when we speak of the animals with which we are most familiarly acquainted as quadrupeds, which is Latin for "four-footed."

The tetrapods are divided into four classes, of which the first was developed from the crossopterygii about 300,000,000 years ago. This includes creatures that are not yet entirely emancipated from water. That is, they lay eggs in water and the larval forms that hatch out are rather fishlike, with finny tails and gills, but with no legs. Eventually these larvae undergo a radical change, substitute lungs for gills and legs for a tail. Their adult life they spend on land (but near water, usually). Since their life is spent both in water and on land, they make up the *Amphibia* (am-fib'ee-uh; "double life" G). The frogs, toads, and salamanders are the best known of still existing amphibia.

Eventually certain descendants of the amphibians developed eggs that could be laid on land and thus freed themselves of the waters. These were a second class of tetrapods, *Reptilia* (rep-til'ee-uh; "to creep" L, from the fact that the most spectacular of modern-day reptiles, the snakes, progress in that fashion). The amphibians and reptiles, though each witnessed a time when their members were the dominant forms of life on land, are today rather unsuccessful classes. They were replaced and supplanted by certain reptilian descendants that reached new heights of efficiency.

The reptiles and amphibians, together with all members of the superclass Pisces, and, indeed, with all members of all the phyla outside Chordata, are cold-blooded — their internal temperature tends to be that of the external environment. Descended from the reptiles, however, are two classes of animals which independently developed, about 150,000,000 years ago, the faculty of being warm-blooded; that is, of having an internal temperature kept constant at a point generally higher than that of the external environment. This was something new and unique, with advantages I shall discuss later in the book.

The first of these classes to come into existence was that of *Mammalia* (ma-may'lee-uh; "breast" L, so called because the members of the class possess milk-producing organs for feeding their young). The fourth and last class was that of *Aves* (ay'veez; "birds" L), a class commonly referred to as "birds." The easiest way of distinguishing between these two warm-blooded classes lies in their method of insulating their bodies

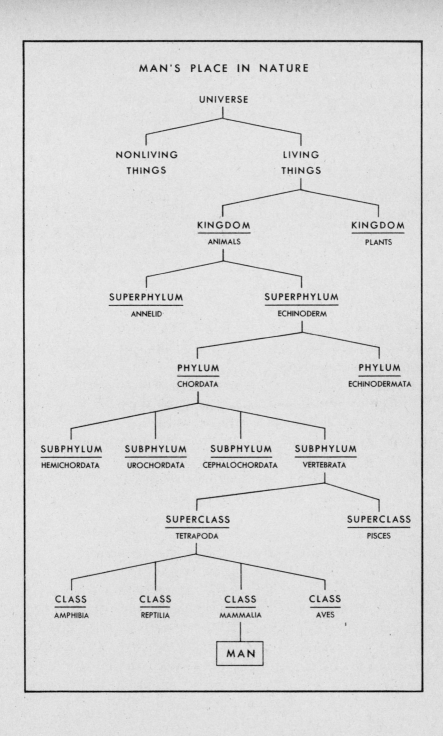

against the excessive loss of body heat. The birds use feathers for the purpose and the mammals use hair, and in both cases the structure is absolutely unique to the class possessing it. The fact that man possesses hair is therefore, in itself and alone, sufficient to tab him a mammal. In addition he possesses a number of other structures characteristic of the mammals.

To be sure, the tetrapods past the Amphibia lack gill slits and thus seem to have lost one of the three characteristic signs of the chordate phylum. It is not entirely lost if we take embryonic development into account. If we consider the human embryo, for instance: there is a period during the fourth week when it develops stiffening structures in the throat that are recognizably gill arches. Hollows even form between them as though the throat were going to be perforated and gill slits formed, but these "gill pouches" never actually break through. Nevertheless, this is enough to lend us the chordate mark, along with the notochord we momentarily possess as embryos, and with the hollow dorsal nerve cord all of us possess throughout life.

I shall have more to say about the development of the various tetrapod classes toward the end of the book, and I shall consider the question of which group of mammals man belongs to. For the present, it is sufficient to have defined man as a mammal and to show his place in nature according to the highly schematicized diagram on the preceding page.

2

OUR HEAD AND TORSO

THE VERTEBRAL COLUMN

That which makes man most clearly a vertebrate (even to the untutored eye), which most firmly knits him to other members of the subphylum, which most markedly sets him off from creatures outside the subphylum is his internal framework of bone. The initial chapter on man's place in nature would thus seem to lead us to this bony bracing as the logical place to start considering the human body.

The bones of our body (and, indeed, of any vertebrate body) make up the *skeleton* ("dried up" G, because a skeleton by itself has a resemblance to a completely dried up human being, a shriveled mummy with even the skin removed). In fact, the skeleton, which is the framework about which the "soft tissues" are molded, gives a clear indication of what the human form in its entirety is. The same can be said for other members of our subphylum and it is by finding fossilized skeletal remains of long-dead creatures that paleontologists are able to reconstruct the appearance of animals that lived hundreds of millions of years ago.

In the case of man, the grisly similarity of skeleton to body, the wide grin, the slitted ribs, the overlong fingers, at once showing the man, yet distorting him, lends the skeleton a frightening

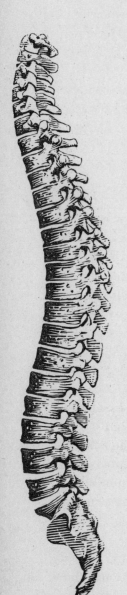

aspect to children and to unsophisticated adults. We ourselves shall, of course, proceed to view the skeleton unemotionally, and even statistically.

The skeleton makes up about 18 per cent of the weight of the human body; some 25 pounds, in other words; and is made up of a little more than 200 individual bones. Of these, the oldest, evolutionarily speaking, is the series of bones running the length of the back to form the central axis of the body — the bones that mark the original site of the notochord. The common name for this line of bones is *backbone,* which is descriptive enough but implies the existence of a single bone, whereas a family of more than two dozen bones actually is involved.

Each of these bones is irregularly shaped, with several projections pointed enough to resemble spiny outgrowths. If you bend your back forward, you will be able to feel a line of these projections. If you observe someone else's curved back, they will show up as a line of knobs. Since this is the most clearly visible characteristic of the backbone in living man, it is not surprising that another common name for it is the *spinal column* (that is, a column of spiny bones). Sometimes, this is shortened to *spine,* which saves breath but again mistakenly implies the existence of a single bone.

If the spinal column were indeed a single bone, the back would be rigid and unbending; just as the thigh, which is built about a long single bone, happens to be. It is because the column is a column and one built of separate bones that the trunk can bend forward, backward, to either side, or even go through small circular movements.

Furthermore, it does not bend sharply at some individual point, as the arm bends at the elbow, but only slightly at each of a number of points, forming a smooth concavity or convexity. In this way it retains something of the strength of a rigid bone and something of the flexibility of truly jointed bones. It is a very successful compromise.

The property of the spinal column which allows turning and bending in various directions gives it its most formal name, the *vertebral column* (vur'ti-brul; "to turn" L).* The individual bones of the column are therefore *vertebrae*, and that is how members of our subphylum come to be called *vertebrates*.

In the various sea creatures of the superclass Pisces the spinal column forms a straight line, running horizontally when the creature is in the usual swimming position. The individual vertebrae are very much alike.

In land animals such a simple arrangement is not practical. Whereas in sea creatures the body is supported at every point by water buoyancy, in tetrapods the body is supported on four legs, of which one pair are at the front end of the vertebral column and the other pair at the back end. From the stretch of column between forelegs and hindlegs are suspended various organs, pulled downward naturally by the force of gravity. If, under these conditions, the column were straight, the suspension of weight would inevitably lead to a downward curve — a "swayback." To prevent that, the spinal column in tetrapods is arched so that each vertebra rests partly on the bone immediately before or behind it. The pull of the suspended organs is transferred down the line of vertebrae to the forelegs and hindlegs.

In the tretrapod, moreover, the individual vertebrae begin to show differentiation; that is, they show differences in form that

---

* I must warn you that the derivation given is not necessarily a direct translation of the scientific term. Thus "vertebral" is from the Latin *vertebralis*, meaning "of the spine," but that in turn comes from the Latin *vertere*, meaning "to turn." In my derivations I shall, when necessary, skip the intermediate stages and get back to what seems to me to be the significant root.

suit them to differences in function. This might also be termed specialization, since the individual bones are modified to suit special functions.

After all, when a fish must turn, a flip of the tail will turn the whole body easily enough, suspended as it is in fluid. On land, a vertebrate is not so fortunate. To turn its body, it must initiate a series of complicated leg movements. When the turning is only for the purpose of bringing the sense organs (concentrated in the head) to bear in a new direction, it would be very convenient if the head were turned without involving the limbs.

The ability to do this was indeed developed, and for the purpose a narrowed neck region was evolved. This region formed about a section of the vertebral column that was specialized in form to allow a greater freedom of bending. The line of vertebrae in the neck region also curved upward to give the head greater height for vision over a greater area.

When a land vertebrate returns uncompromisingly to the sea, as the whales and porpoises have, these modifications for land life are done away with. In the whale and its relatives, the vertebral column is once again quite straight and the neck region has all but disappeared.

In man, there is a new change. When born, we have the two-curved vertebral column of the typical land vertebrate, a downward curve at the neck and an upward curve in the back. To get around, infants crawl quite handily in the usual tetrapod fashion. In the second year of life, however, the infant rises upon his hind legs and finds it increasingly comfortable and natural to remain so. In order to make that possible, the human vertebral column bends backward in the region of the hip, forming a new curve that is concave toward the back. The human vertebral column, although still perfectly straight when viewed from the back, displays a series of rather graceful curves, a kind of double S-shape, when viewed from the side.

Despite the fact that the human body seems to be precariously tipped upright, the curves of the vertebral column make the position a relatively easy one to maintain and lend us a springy balance. Other animals that are capable of rising to their hind legs, such as bears and gorillas, lack this vertebral curve in the hip regions and therefore cannot maintain the upright position for long. The gorilla, consequently, rarely is truly erect, but hunches forward for lack of the vertebral curve and supports itself partly on the knuckles of its hands.

To be sure, there are two-legged creatures, such as the kangaroos and birds, which retain an essentially horizontal vertebral column. They manage to retain balance by the development of a tail set far enough back so as to act as a counterweight for the forepart of the body. (The penguin is an exception, with a rather humorously manlike waddle.)

This tipping of the vertebral column in man raises certain difficulties in comparing positions in man with those in other animals. Anatomists use *dorsal* ("back" L) to mean "toward the back." Although this is really toward the back as far as the human being is concerned, it is toward the top in most other animals. (We run into the same thing in using expressions of Anglo-Saxon origin. We speak of riding "horseback" but the horse's back is not at the back of the animal but at the top.)

Again, there is *ventral* ("belly" L), which means "toward the belly"; that is, frontward in man, but downward in most other animals. The expressions *anterior* ("farther forward" L) and *posterior* ("farther backward" L), which mean toward the head and tail, respectively, when referring to positions in most animals, mean toward the belly and back where man is concerned.

Perhaps the safest way to avoid confusion is to forget about up, down, forward, and backward altogether and define the directions in terms of parts of the body. In most vertebrates dorsal is toward the vertebral column, ventral is toward the belly, anterior is toward the head, and posterior is toward the tail. In man, *superior* is toward the head, *inferior* toward the feet.

THE VERTEBRAE AND RIBS

Since the notochord originally lay ventral to the nerve cord, the main portion of the typical vertebra is still ventral. Here there is a solid cylinder of bone called the *centrum,* or *body,* of the vertebra. From it arises dorsally an arch of bone, enclosing a roughly circular space. The enclosed space is the *neural canal* (nyoo'rul; "nerve" G) and the bony arch that forms it is the *neural arch.* As you can guess from the derivation, the dorsal nerve cord runs through that ring. In fact, it runs through a whole series of rings, formed by successive vertebrae.

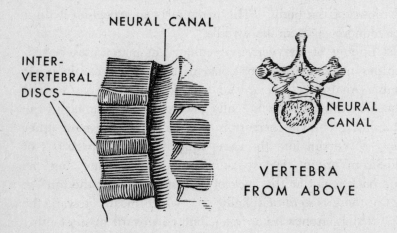

NEURAL CANAL

INTER-
VERTEBRAL
DISCS

NEURAL
CANAL

VERTEBRA
FROM ABOVE

The neural arch possesses three projections, or processes. One emerges dorsally (sometimes angled a bit downward) and it is the one you feel when you run your finger down the vertebral column. These being the "spines" you feel, it is called the *spinous process.* The other two emerge to either side and are the *transverse processes.* The word, transverse ("move across" L) implies a direction that is neither forward nor backward but sideways.

If you have ever nibbled at the neck of a chicken, you know

how irregular and sharp these processes can be. These irregularities are not useless ornaments, but serve an important purpose, for it is to these processes that various muscles are attached and to which other bones may join.

The human vertebrae are divided into differentiated groups. The seven most superior of them, for instance, are the *cervical vertebrae* (sur'vi-kul; "neck" L), which are, as the name implies, the vertebrae of the neck. The fact that there are seven of these cervical vertebrae is typical of the mammals. With the exception of a couple of species of sloths, all mammals, regardless of the length of the neck, possess just seven, no more and no less. In the case of the whale, which has no neck, the seven vertebrae are flattened to negligible size, yet there remain seven of those flattened discs. As for the giraffe, the full length of its neck contains but seven cervical vertebrae, though these have lengthened out until they look more like bones of the limbs than like vertebrae.

Birds, on the other hand, though not as rigid in the number of cervical vertebrae as mammals are, usually possess about twice the mammalian number. And so (a fact dear to the heart of "Believe It or Not" columnists) the sparrow has more bones in its neck than the giraffe does. It follows also that birds such as the swan or flamingo have much greater range and grace of movement in their long necks than the giraffe has. In fact, while to say a girl's neck is "swanlike" can be used as a great compliment, to say it is "giraffe-like" would be to invite disaster. (To point out that, anatomically, a girl's neck *is* giraffe-like and not swanlike would probably do no good, either. In fact I am sure it would just make matters worse.)

In man the first cervical vertebra has a specially modified shape to allow it to be connected with the bony structure of the head. It has no real centrum but is all neural arch. What's more, it is a large neural arch, for the nerve cord is at this point widening to become the brain.

When you nod your head, bending takes place chiefly between the skull and the first vertebra. Because in man the roughly globular structure of the skull rests upon the neural arch of this first vertebra, like the globe of the earth resting upon the shoulders of the giant Atlas in the Greek myth, this vertebra is called the *atlas*.

When you shake your head from side to side, the atlas moves with the skull, the motion taking place along the division between the first and second cervical vertebrae. The second vertebra possesses a special process, jutting upward. Over it, the atlas fits neatly, and it is about that anterior process as an axis that the head makes the gesture of *No*. The second vertebra is therefore commonly called the *axis*.

The spinous processes of the cervical vertebrae are rather sharp and are slightly forked just at the end.

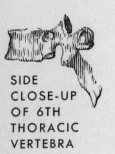

SIDE
CLOSE-UP
OF 6TH
THORACIC
VERTEBRA

Inferior to the cervical vertebrae are twelve *thoracic vertebrae* (thaw-ras'ik; "chest" L) which run down the length of the chest. (These are sometimes called the *dorsal vertebrae,* but this is a poor alternative, for all the vertebrae are dorsal, really.)

The thoracic vertebrae have somewhat longer than average transverse processes for to them are attached *ribs*.* There is one rib attached to each transverse process of each thoracic vertebra, making twelve pairs of ribs, or twenty-four in all.

Where the rib meets the vertebra, it extends two processes, one adjoining the transverse process of the vertebra and the other adjoining the centrum itself. Each rib curves in a downward semicircle, so that taken together a pair encloses the chest. Most of the pairs come together ventrally and join a flat bone extending down the midline of the front of the chest. This is the *sternum* ("chest" G), or the *breastbone*.

---

* One of the anatomical terms of Anglo-Saxon derivation, which I shall henceforth indicate, when it seems helpful, by a simple AS in parentheses.

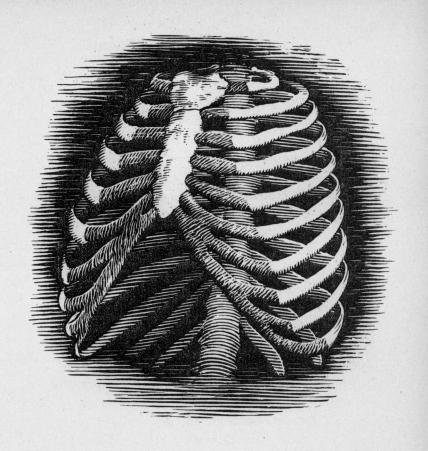

The first pair of ribs are comparatively short, but each of the next six pairs are successively longer. All seven pairs join the sternum directly and are sometimes called the "true ribs" in consequence. Pairs eight, nine, and ten are the "false ribs." They do not join the sternum directly but converge and join the seventh rib at a point before the sternum is reached. There is thus a sharp upward notch in the bony structure in front of your chest, which you can easily feel if you follow the line of your lower ribs. The eleventh and twelfth pairs of ribs do not complete their curve, but come to an end in midchest, so to speak. These are the "floating ribs." The ribs and breastbone, taken all together, can be referred to as the "rib cage."

The fact that the ribs occur in pairs is an evidence of our bilateral symmetry. For a bone to occur singly it must lie along the midline of the body. Examples are the various vertebrae and the sternum. Any bone that lies to one side of the midline possesses a sister bone, mirror image in shape, that lies on the other.

The vertebrae and ribs, taken together, are the most obvious indication of the fundamental segmentation of the human body. This sort of indication is much more dramatic in certain other vertebrates. Reptiles generally have ribs attached to every ver- tebra except those in the tail. A large python, with a couple of hundred vertebrae running the sinuous length of its body, has a couple of hundred pairs of ribs, and its skeleton gives the unmistakable impression of being a monstrous centipede.

Incidentally, it might be well to emphasize that the number of ribs in men and women are identical. Because of the story in the book of Genesis (2:21–22) to the effect that God made Eve out of a rib he withdrew from Adam's side, it is sometimes suggested that one rib is missing in the male. Not so. In fact, although anatomists can easily tell the skeleton of a male from that of a female because of the difference in the shape and pro- portion of some of the bones, neither sex has a bone that the other lacks.

But let's return to the vertebral column. Inferior to the thoracic vertebrae are five *lumbar vertebrae* (lum'bur; "loin" L). These lack ribs and form the narrow "waistline" of the skeleton. It is also because they lack ribs that some women can delight in a narrow waistline that accentuates the broader areas above and below.

The lumbar vertebrae are the largest and heaviest of the col- umn, because, thanks to man's upright posture, they support the weight of the entire upper half of the body. The spinous processes of these vertebrae are stubbier and set farther apart than are those of the cervical and thoracic vertebrae. This makes it possible for a person to bend backward at the waist through a considerable arc. Were the spinous processes similar to those of the thoracic vertebrae, their mutual interference would prohibit the backward bend.

Inferior to the lumbar vertebrae are five *sacral vertebrae* (say'krul; "sacred" L) which differ in several ways from all those I have described previously. In the first place, they are not named after their position in the body, in contrast to the previous groups of vertebrae which are named after neck, chest and loins. Actually, no one is certain why they are named as they are. The easiest assumption is that they had some special significance in Roman religious rites, but that is just an easy assumption, and it is not necessarily the truth.

Then, too, the five sacral vertebrae are separate in young children, but with age, the spaces between become ossified and they fuse into a single bone called the *sacrum* (say'krum). In adulthood all that remains to indicate the original separation are four transverse lines where the joining had taken place and four pairs of holes, one of each pair on either side of the midline. These holes are formed when the process of the adjoining sacral vertebrae fuse together. Holes such as these through a bone or through any otherwise continuous structure in the body are called *foramina* (faw-ram'i-nuh; "to pierce" L); the singular is *foramen* (faw-ray'men).

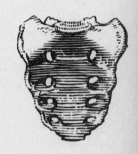

The case of the sacrum shows that it isn't possible to be too hard and fast in describing the body. The body is not a machine turned out by some known and unvarying process, but has its individual idiosyncrasies. It is easy to say, for instance, that there are 33 bones all told in the human vertebral column, but does the sacrum count as one bone or as five? It is clearly five in the infant, and as clearly one in the adult. If it is counted as one then there are only 29 bones in the human vertebral column. There are other cases where bones may or may not be fused in different individuals, so that in the end one ought only to speak approximately of the number of bones in the human body, as I did at the beginning of the chapter when I said there were a little more than 200. Sometimes the number is stated precisely as 206, but that is not always so.

The sacrum forms a strong bone to which the bones of the hips and hind legs can be securely attached. It is proportionately larger and stronger in man than in other mammals, because man's upright structure places considerable weight upon it. On the other hand, mammals that have adapted themselves to the sea to the point where they have no hind legs at all (as in the case of whales and sea cows) have no sacrum, either — merely a line of lumbar vertebrae running down to the tail. Since the sacrum is intimately connected with the bones of the hip and a woman's hips are proportionately wider than are those of a man, the sacrum in the female is likewise proportionately wider. Here, then, is one way in which an anatomist can tell the skeleton of a woman from that of a man.

The final, most inferior group of vertebrae are conspicuous indeed in most mammals, since they are the *caudal vertebrae* (kaw'dul; "tail" L). They are numerous in mammals with long tails. It might be thought that a human being, who clearly does not have a tail, would as clearly lack caudal vertebrae. But this is not so.

Below the human sacrum are four small vertebrae, each smaller than the one above, and each without a neural arch. These make up the remnant of what might have been a tail. (Some individuals may have five — another reason for not being too dogmatic about the number of bones in the human body.) Together these final vertebrae make up the *coccyx* (kok'siks; "cuckoo" G, so named because the whole seems to resemble the beak of a cuckoo in shape). As a result, the individual vertebrae are sometimes called *coccygeal vertebrae* (kok-sij'ee-ul).

If there is any doubt that the coccyx represents a tail and not something else entirely, the answer lies in the study of the developing human embryo. In the early stages a small but distinct tail region is formed. By the eighth week of development it is gone, but its evanescent existence would seem to make it clear that man descended from some creature with a tail, and that he still carries about with him, hidden below the skin, a last evidence of it. (It is interesting, by the way, that the gorilla seems to have moved farther from a presumably tailed ancestor than we have: the gorilla is down to three caudal vertebrae as opposed to our four.)

The vertebral column is not made up of bone alone. It also contains cartilage, the structure out of which the column of the first vertebrates was formed. A baby is born with its skeleton still largely in the cartilaginous stage, and ossification proceeds throughout all the years till maturity. As an example, those portions of the ribs adjacent to the sternum are actually bars of cartilage, called the *costal cartilages* ("rib" L). These costal cartilages are extensive in the infant, but become much shorter in length in the adult.

In the vertebral column particularly, the elasticity and flexibility of cartilage plays an important part. Between the individual vertebrae are stubby cylindrical discs of fiber and cartilage containing a gelatinous material in the center, which may be the last remnant of the original notochord. These discs are consequently spongy and compressible, and make possible the smooth bending of the vertebrae. They also act as shock absorbers, so that the column can take the sudden pressure changes that result, let us say, from jumping off a six-foot height or lifting a hundred pounds. In old age the discs lose the gelatinous center and become all cartilage. This is responsible for much of the characteristic stiffness of age.

The intervertebral discs have also gained a certain notoriety that stems, really, from the flaws inherent in our upright posture. The upright posture of man is extremely useful from the standpoint of freeing his arms and hands for purposes other than locomotion. It also gives him added height so that he might make more efficient use of his head-centered senses. Nevertheless, it remains a monstrous perversion of tetrapod structure.

For some hundreds of millions of years, the structure of land vertebrates has been designed to fit an internal skeleton consisting of a more or less horizontal (though arched) vertebral column set firmly on four supports. Over the space of a single million of years or less, various human and prehuman species have tipped the whole structure on end. While the ingenuity of the adjustment to such a change is impressive, it must be admitted that the vertebral column is not completely adjusted to the new situation.

It is possible, as the result of a momentary over-great stress, to cause one of the discs to protrude slightly from between the vertebrae. This is most likely to happen in the lumbar region where, thanks to upright posture, stresses can be almost unbearably concentrated. Such a "slipped disc" will, naturally, pinch the nearby nerves and can result in excruciating pain — the price we still pay (among others) for getting up on our hind legs some hundreds of thousands of years ago.

THE SKULL

The superior end of the spinal column is connected to the *skull* (AS), which makes up the bony framework of the head and face. The main portion of the skull is a nearly smooth, roughly ovoid structure called the *cranium* ("skull" L). It almost entirely encloses the brain, which is thus the only organ in the body to have such a close-fitting coating of bone. In fact, the brain can almost be viewed as enclosed in a shell. It should therefore not be surprising that the word "skull" may be cognate to "shell,"

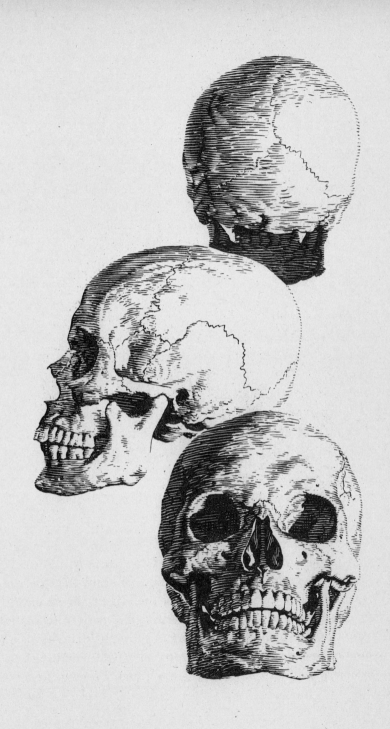

both coming from the Scandinavian word *skel*, meaning a sea-shell. A consonantal change in one direction and a vowel change in the other ended by giving us two words.

At the base of the skull is a hole called the *foramen magnum* ("large hole" L), which fits over the enlarged neural arch of the atlas, that is, the first vertebra. Knobs at the bottom of the skull, on either side of the foramen magnum, fit neatly into depressions in the atlas. Such a bony knob is called a *condyle* (kon′dil; "knuckle joint" G). Through the foramen magnum the thickening nerve cord makes its way, and within the cranium expands to form man's large brain. In a way, the skull may be looked upon as forming a gigantic dead-ended neural arch.

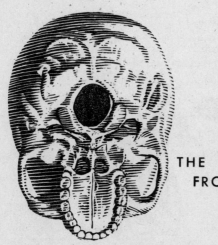

THE SKULL
FROM BELOW

This development of a specialized and quite intricate bony structure about the anterior end of the original nerve cord is the end product of a process that began quite early in evolutionary history. Once a multicellular organism with bilateral symmetry was developed (long, long before our fossil record begins), it became possible to have a preferred direction of movement. At one end of the plane of symmetry would be the head and at the other the tail, the head being defined as the end which lay in the direction in which the animal moved. This meant that it was the head that was always breaking new ground, so to speak, and advancing into a new and untried environment. Specialized organs for detecting changes in the environment were most useful if they were located in the head. In order to receive and correlate the impressions received by such "sense organs," the forward end of the nerve cord had a tendency to grow more complex.

This tendency to enrich the head with sense organs and to swell the forward end of the nerve cord is called *cephalization* ("head" G) and it is to be found in many phyla.

Chordata, by shifting the nerve cord to the dorsal position, seemed in a sense to have to begin all over. At least amphioxus (a chordate but not a vertebrate) is quite uncephalized. It has no advanced sense organs, no nerve-cord swelling; in fact, its very name indicates that it has no head to speak of but is "equally pointed" at both ends.

Cephalization did begin with the subphylum Vertebrata, however, and was here carried to the greatest extreme the realm of life can show. The agnaths, which first developed cartilaginous vertebrae to protect the nerve cord generally, also developed a cartilaginous box to enclose and protect the enlarged anterior end of it. In addition, the agnaths and their descendants, the placoderms, developed a bony shell to protect the precious and specialized head region.

Oddly enough, this bony shell, though it seemed to disappear with the extinction of the placoderms and the armored agnaths, has left its mark upon all their unshelled descendants, including ourselves. The proof of that lies in the manner in which the various bones develop in the embryo. Most bones of the body are produced by the ossification of previous cartilaginous structures, which, in this fashion, act as models for the final product.

These are "cartilage replacement bones," and the vertebrae, ribs, and sternum are all examples. The human skull, however, does not develop from such a cartilaginous model. Instead, the bones that make it up begin to form beneath the skin, as though harking back to a long-past time when such bone formed on the outside rather than the inside of the body. The skull is apparently a relic of the external armor of the placoderms which has been narrowed in function. Instead of enclosing the head and fore regions generally, it has been drawn within and set to work as a tight enclosure for the brain and as a specific protection for the most specialized and most vulnerable of the sense organs, the eyes and ears.*

In the lower vertebrates the skull tends to be quite complicated in structure. The evolutionary tendency has been in the direction of greater simplicity and fewer individual bones. Fish have more than 100 bones in the skull, some reptiles as many as 70, and primitive mammals as many as 40. In contrast to this, the human skull contains only 23 bones, and of those only 8 suffice to make up the cranium. There is sense to this because a bony structure, designed for protection, is naturally weakest at the joints; the fewer the joints, the stronger the structure.

Of the eight bones of the cranium, the most prominent is the *frontal bone,* a single bone making up the forehead and the forward half of the top of the skull. The frontal bone reaches down to the bony circle enclosing the eye, which is called the *orbit* ("circle" L), and to the top of the nose. Just above each eye there is a low ridge stretching across the frontal bone, which may originally have served as further protection for the eye. It is very pronounced in the apes and quite pronounced in early species of man. The ridge is still present in the adult male, but is virtually absent in children and in the adult female (which

---

* I shall not deal in this book with the brain, nerves, and sense organs except in passing. This is not because the subject is unimportant, but rather because it is of most particular importance. I am planning a companion volume to deal with the nervous system in detail.

is why the forehead of a woman is so attractively smooth).

Behind the frontal bone, forming the frame of the rest of the top of the skull, is a pair of bones that join at the midline of the top of the skull. These are the *parietal bones* (puh-ry'i-tul; "wall" L), which do indeed seem to be the walls of the brain. Still farther behind is a single bone forming the undersurface of the rear of the skull. This is the *occipital bone* (ok-sip'i-tul; "away from the head" L). This rearmost portion of the skull is sometimes called, even in common speech, the *occiput* (ok'si-put).

On either side of the skull, beneath the parietals, are the two *temporal bones*. These are located in the portion of the head usually referred to as the temples. Both "temporal" and "temple" come from a Latin word meaning "time." There are several theories as to the connection between time and this side portion of the skull. None of these sound completely convincing, but the most interesting one is that since hair tends to go gray at the temples first, that portion of the head most clearly marks the passing of time.

The six bones so far mentioned (frontal, occipital, two parietals, and two temporals) make up the main structure of the cranium. Two more bones remain, which are less evident because they are below the cranium and in life are hidden from us by the eyes. These are the *sphenoid bone* (sfee'noid; "wedge-shaped" G) and the *ethmoid bone* ("sieve-like" G).*

One might expect that with continued evolution, the number of bones in the skull might diminish further, and so they might. There seems nevertheless to be a limit to how far the decrease in number can go.

---

* The first giving of names to the parts of the body (and, indeed, scientific naming in general) was and is a tedious and difficult process; anatomists, both ancient and modern, do their best, however. Colorful images are found, as when the ethmoid bone is compared with a sieve because it contains a number of foramina. Or the particular shape of the bone is used as inspiration for the name, as in the wedge shape of the sphenoid.

The bones of the cranium of the newborn child are not joined. There are six sizable gaps, yet unossified, in the skull at birth. These are called *fontanelles* ("little fountain" L) because the pulse of blood vessels can be felt under the skin in those areas, so that doctors were reminded of the spurting of a fountain. In ordinary language they are the "soft spots," and the largest of these is at the top of the skull. Any parent is tenderly aware of the presence of that one, particularly in a first child.

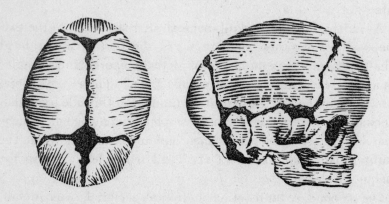

The presence of such a loose structure of the cranium in the newborn is essential to normal birth. The skull is the largest portion of the fetus, and if that passes through the birth canal the rest of the body can follow without trouble. For the skull to get through, a certain amount of distortion is often necessary and it is these spaces between the bone that make distortion possible.

After birth, ossification proceeds and by the second year even the largest fontanelle is closed. Yet complete ossification does not take place till maturity, a fact that is also vital, since only with the joints relatively open can the brain case increase in size and allow for the growth of the brain.

Nevertheless, once birth and growth are finished, the skull, having eaten its cake, metaphorically speaking, proceeds to have it also, since the various bones seal tightly together. The boundaries formed are ragged uneven lines, as though each bone tried to grow as far into its neighbor as possible and the battle were exactly even, with one having the upper hand at this point and the other at the next point. Such an intricate, meandering joint is a *suture* (syoo'tyoor; "seam" L). The interwedged line of the suture is such that the bones cannot be separated short of breaking them. The cranium in the adult is, therefore, to all intents, a single bone.

As for the face, though it possesses a smaller surface area than the cranium, it possesses more bones — almost twice as many. These include 7 pairs of bones, plus one that is unpaired, making 15 in all. To begin with, there are the two *nasal bones* ("nose" L) which form the bridge of the nose and meet at the midplane. Behind the nasal bones are the *vomer bones* (voh'mer; "plowshare" L), named for their shape, of course, but making a comparison that is lost on today's urbanized population. The vomers make up the bony portion of the tissues dividing the interior of the nose into two nostrils.

Such a partition is a *septum* ("partition" L). The lower portion of the septum is not bony, but is cartilaginous, as you can tell from the manner in which you can bend and twist it. The fact that the human skull contains nothing to indicate the portion of the nose we are most aware of, gives the skeleton a horridly snubbed appearance that lends it its ugliness — along with the empty eye sockets and the ghastly grin.

The rear of the nostrils is bordered by the *inferior nasal conchae* (kon'kee; "shell" L, because it has a spiral shape something like that of a snail's shell). There are also middle and superior nasal conchae; they are not separate bones, but, rather, are processes of the ethmoid ("inferior" refers, remember, to something which is below; "superior" to something above).

Behind the nasal bones, and making up part of the orbit, are the *lacrimal bones* (lak'ri-mul; "tear" L). These are so called because they are located in the neighborhood of the tear ducts.

Thus there are no less than eight bones making up the nose and its environs; the two nasals, the two vomers, the two lacrimals, and the two inferior nasal conchae.

Most of the front of the face from the eye to the upper jaw is stiffened by the *maxillary bones* (mak'si-ler'ee; "jaw" L). These bones meet at the midplane and make up the entire upper jaw, which is therefore referred to as the *maxilla* (mak'si-luh). It also makes up part of the upper border of the mouth, runs under the cheeks, and reaches up to the eye, forming part of the orbit. Behind the maxillaries in the roof of the mouth are the much smaller *palatine bones,* also meeting at midplane, so called because it makes up the palate — that is, the rear of the roof of the mouth. The *zygomatic bones* (zy'go-mat'ik; "yoke" L, another reference to a shape that is no longer familiar to many people) make up the sides of the face to the front of the sphenoid and temporal bones of the cranium. They form the bony overhang above the upper jaw and are therefore popularly called the "cheekbones." The zygomatics also reach to the border of the eye and make up part of the orbit. All told each orbit consists of portions of no less than seven bones of the face and cranium.

All the bones of the face I have mentioned so far are immovably joined to each other and to the cranium, so that the skull, down to the line of the upper jaw at least, is a single piece. But there is one more bone in the head and it is the one movable bone. Naturally, I refer to the lower jaw.

As I have said in Chapter 1, the vertebrate jaw was originally formed in the placoderm out of the first gill arch. Originally the jaw, so formed, was separate from the remaining skeleton of the head. It still is in the sharks. However, in the bony fish, the upper jaw fused with the cranium, and this is the situation with all their tetrapod descendants. The lower jaw remains hinged in the rear to the upper jaw and must remain movable, of course, if biting and chewing is to be kept in the realm of possibility.

Here, too, the evolutionary trend has been in the direction of a decrease in the number of bones and a consequent strengthening of structure. The numerous bones in the lower jaw of the reptiles were reduced to two, one on each side, in mammals and these two are fused into a single piece by the second year of life in the human being. This lone bone of the lower jaw is the *mandible* ("chew" L).

The human being (and mammals, generally) have not lost all trace of those other bones of the reptilian lower jaw. As the mandible expanded in size and virtually shoved the other bones backward, several ended in the middle ear as the *ossicles* ("little bones" L). These are six in number, one set of three being found in each middle ear. They are named for their shapes: *stapes* (stay′peez; "stirrup" L), *malleus* (mal′ee-us; "hammer" L), and *incus* (ing′kus; "anvil" L). Of these, the stapes is thought to be a remnant of the second gill arch rather than the first, of which almost all the jaw is formed.

The ossicles are not generally counted among the bones of the skull, and neither is another bone set at the base of the tongue, the *hyoid bone* ("U-shaped" G). This is also a remnant of the second gill arch. Although it is sometimes called the "tongue bone," it is not in the tongue itself; it lies between the mandible and the voice box, and is unusual in that it is jointed to no other bone and lies in isolation. In fish, the bone was an important link between the jaw and the rest of the cranium, but it has lost that function in us.

THE TEETH

Set in both upper and lower jaws in man are the various teeth. These are *not* bones. They are hard, to be sure (harder than bone, even), and are constructed chiefly of calcium phosphate.

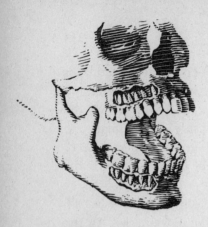

Nevertheless, the structure of teeth differs considerably from that of bone.

Teeth originated among the primitive sharklike fish and probably represented modified fish scales to begin with. At first, they were undifferentiated, all being of the same simple conical shape. There were many of them and they were replaced when worn down. The evolutionary tendency, however, was to reduce the number of teeth and the number of times they could be replaced. Furthermore, there was a change in the direction of greater efficiency through the specialization of groups of teeth for different functions.

Among the higher mammals, the number of teeth has been reduced to a maximum of 44; this maximum is found in dogs and pigs, for example, although in many other animals (and in man) the number is well below the maximum. Mammalian teeth fall into four different groups, all of which are represented in our own mouths.

In front of the mouth are the *incisors* ("to cut into" L). These are wedge-shaped teeth with the cutting edge compressed into a narrow line, so that when the incisors above and below meet they have a scissors action. To accomplish this most efficiently, when the jaw closes the lower incisors should come up just behind and in contact with the rear surface of the upper incisors. If the upper incisors are set too far forward, or the lower ones too far backward so that there is a gap between them when the jaw closes, most of their efficiency of action is destroyed. This is one of the more common varieties of *malocclusion* (mal'o-kloo'zhun; "bad closing" L).

Behind the incisors are the *canines* ("dog" L), conical tearing teeth that are the least specialized and most nearly resemble the ancestral shape. They are prominent in dogs, as one can deduce from the name. The canines of the upper jaw are often called "eye teeth," a name that arose in the mistaken impression that their roots were more or less intimately connected with the eye.

Next we have the *bicuspids* ("two-pointed" L), which have the appearance of double canines, since they seem to consist of two cones fused together. The double point that results gives them their name.

Finally, there are the *molars* ("millstone" L), the working edges of which have four or five blunt cusps, or points, that fuse into an uneven surface. These exert a grinding millstone-like action on food, since the lower jaw works from side to side. These teeth are often called "grinders" in common speech as a consequence. The bicuspids, coming before the molars, are very commonly called *premolars.*

Among the full 44 teeth possessed by higher mammals, 12 are incisors, 4 are canines, 16 premolars and 12 molars. The number of teeth are symmetrical on either side of the midplane of the face, so that in listing the teeth of any particular species it is only necessary to number them on one side of the mouth, the other side being presumed identical (barring loss of teeth through disease or accident, of course). However, the upper and lower jaws are not necessarily identical, so both are described. The numbers are placed in the order in which they occur in the mouth: incisor, canine, premolar, and molar. The dental formula for the dog or pig can be presented thus:

$$\frac{3 \cdot 1 \cdot 4 \cdot 3}{3 \cdot 1 \cdot 4 \cdot 3}$$

However, not only is the number of teeth reduced in many mammals but a varying emphasis is placed on one group or another. In rodents, the incisors are enlarged and are by far the most prominent teeth in the mouth. They are permanently growing, moreover, being replaced by new growth as fast as they are worn down by the gnawing activity of the animal. In carnivorous animals, the canines are much enlarged, forming, as an example, the "fangs" of a tiger. Again, in grazing animals such as cattle and horses, which must continuously grind coarse grains and grass, the molar teeth are much developed and have an exceedingly intricate grinding surface.

Specialization sometimes emphasizes teeth to almost grotesque extent, as in the tusks of elephants (which are overgrown upper incisors) or those of walruses (which are overgrown upper canines).

On the other hand, teeth that are not useful to an animal's way of life may be suppressed altogether. Cattle lack incisors and canines in the upper jaw, and the sperm whale entirely lacks teeth in the upper jaw. The narwhal possesses only two teeth all told, one of which (in the male) grows forward to form a spiral tusk up to eight feet long. Anteaters possess no teeth at all, and this is true of the entire class of Aves (birds).

The teeth of the human being are far less specialized than the teeth of most mammals, in the direction of either over- or under-development. (As a matter of fact, the structure of the human being is surprisingly primitive and unspecialized in comparison with that of most other animals. This is, perhaps, a clue to our success, for we have not committed ourselves too far in any one direction.)

To be sure, human teeth are small, considering our size and

weight, but that is part and parcel of the general shrinkage of man's face over a million years of evolution. In most animals the face is drawn forward into a "muzzle" so that the jaws may seize while allowing the eyes still to see. The jaws are therefore large enough to accommodate large teeth. The development in man (and in related creatures) of hands that can seize food and bring it up to the mouth made the muzzle unnecessary. Smaller jaws could accommodate only smaller teeth.

This is also one reason why the teeth of the human adult fall short of the full mammalian number by twelve. And yet, despite this loss, we have retained at least some of each variety of tooth, have emphasized none of them unduly, and have kept the number the same in upper and lower jaw. The dental formula for man is:

$$\frac{2 \cdot 1 \cdot 2 \cdot 3}{2 \cdot 1 \cdot 2 \cdot 3}$$

Mammals generally possess two sets of teeth in their lifetimes. The reason for this is clear. The jaw of the young mammal is simply too small to accommodate the size and number of teeth the adult will require. Nor can we expect teeth to erupt in small size and grow with the child, for once teeth have erupted, they lack the capacity for further growth.

The human child, for instance, makes out at first with 20 small teeth. These are variously called *deciduous teeth* ("to fall off" L, since that is what they will inevitably do), "temporary teeth" (which gives the same idea), "milk teeth" (because the infant gets the first of them when it is still very largely on a milk diet), and "baby teeth" (which is obvious).

At birth, these teeth are already forming within the gums, but the first of these, the two lower middle incisors, do not actually cut through the gums until the second half year of life. (The process is fairly painful and during the period of "teething" the child becomes fretful and a great trial to its parents.) When the child is two or two and one half, the process may be complete, at which point the dental formula is:

$$\frac{2 \cdot 1 \cdot 2 \cdot 0}{2 \cdot 1 \cdot 2 \cdot 0}$$

As you can see, the incisors, canines, and premolars are of the same number as in the adult. It is the 12 molars that are missing. Though the 8 rearmost baby teeth are called molars, they are replaced by adult premolars. The true adult molars come in fresh and without predecessors.

The first of the "permanent teeth" or "adult teeth" to come in are the first molars, at about the age of six. They enter behind the baby teeth, in a jaw which, by then, has grown large enough to have room for them. After that, the baby teeth begin falling out, starting at the front and working backward. There is usually a lapse of time between the going of the first teeth and coming of the second, which gives rise to the characteristically toothless smile of the six- or seven-year-old.

By the time the child is twelve, the first teeth are entirely replaced, and it is only in the teens that the second and third molars come in, the jaw by then having grown almost large enough to accommodate them. I say "almost" because, as a matter of fact, the human jaw does not generally grow large enough to accommodate the third and final set of molars comfortably. Eruption of these is commonly delayed until the age of 20 or even later, sometimes, as though to give the jaw a last chance, so to speak. For this reason, the third molars are popularly known as "wisdom teeth," since they make their appearance only at an age when the owner may be considered (optimistically) to have attained to years of wisdom.

On occasion, one or more — even all four — of the wisdom teeth may not erupt at all. This is no great loss, perhaps; on a modern human diet eight molars will do. Then, too, in jaws where the wisdom teeth do erupt, they are often uncomfortably crowded and may even be so firmly wedged ("impacted") between the jawbone and the second molar that their removal, when made necessary by the decay to which they are all too prone, becomes a matter of almost major surgery.

There is good reason to think that the wisdom teeth are on the way out and that in a relatively short time (evolutionarily speaking) man's teeth will be reduced in number to 28.

3

OUR LIMBS AND JOINTS

THE ARMS

The skull, vertebral column, ribs, and sternum, all taken together, represent the *axial skeleton,* forming as it does the axis of the body. Evolutionarily speaking, this was the original skeleton. The bones of the limbs and the structures related to them form the *appendicular skeleton* ("to hang from" L), since the limbs do indeed, in a manner of speaking, hang from the body proper. They are "appendages," in other words. Originally the appendicular skeleton was small in comparison with the axial skeleton, for, when first appearing in the late placoderms and early sharks, they were needed only for the bracing of stubby fins.

Among tetrapods the limbs had to become larger and stronger in order to support the body against gravity, and this tendency continued among mammals. Longer limbs raised the body, together with the head and sense organs, higher off the ground and made the field of vision larger and the opportunities for long-distance hearing and smelling greater. Furthermore, the longer the leg the faster the movement of the extremity for a given angular motion, so that a long-legged animal can run faster than a short-legged one, a matter of value both in pursuit and escape. (This holds true for nonflying birds as well — consider the long-legged ostrich.)

Man shares this tendency with the mammals generally so that our legs are longer than the torso itself and more bones are to be found in the appendicular skeleton than in the axial skeleton. It is to the bones of the legs moreover that the variations in human height are largely due. The human spine averages 28 inches in length in the male and 24 inches in the female, with surprisingly little variation from individual to individual. It is the length, or lack of it, in the bones of the legs that is responsible for most of the variation in height. You can see this for yourself if you observe a group of seated men who all stand up and suddenly become much more heterogeneous in height.

Among the various tetrapods, the limbs have undergone a variety of modifications suiting the way of life of the particular creature. In the case of mammals that have returned to aquatic life, the limbs have reverted to an almost fishlike stubbiness and have become paddles. (In whales and sea cows, the hind limbs have completely disappeared, at least as far as any external evidence is concerned.)

In the case of birds and bats, the forelimbs have been modified into wings, and in instances where birds have become flightless those wings shrink and (in at least one case, that of the New Zealand kiwi) have just about disappeared. Animals like the kangaroo that hop or jump as the favored means of locomotion developed oversized hind limbs and those that swing through the branches of trees, like the gibbon, have developed oversized forelimbs.

All, however, retain much the same basic bony plan. It is the basic similarity of the bones of the human arm, whale's flipper, bat's wing, and bear's leg which is one of the most striking manifestations of the close relationship among vertebrates. It is almost impossible to look at such a pattern of similarity without imagining a long gone ancestor that supplied the basic theme on which modern species only ring variations.

And in the case of limbs, as well as teeth, the human being

is comparatively unspecialized; except for the lengthening of some of the bones, the arms especially remain remarkably similar to what the original tetrapod limb must have been like.

The bones of the arm are connected to the axial skeleton by way

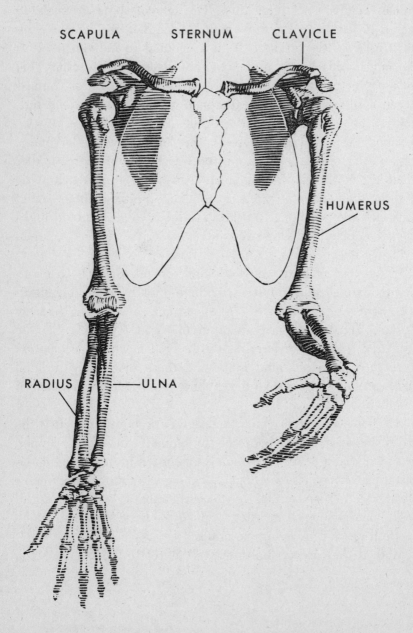

SCAPULA   STERNUM   CLAVICLE

HUMERUS

RADIUS ——— ULNA

of two pairs of bones in the upper torso, one in front and one in back. Those in back are the "shoulder blades," broad flat bones which, if you twist your arm behind your back, stand out under the skin like burgeoning wings. The formal name is the *scapula* (skap'yoo-luh; "to dig" G), because of the resemblance of the bone to the business end of a spade. The scapulae lie dorsal to the ribs but do not actually make contact with them, since there is a binding layer of muscle between.

The pair of bones in front, ventral to the rib cage and just above the first rib, are the "collarbones." You can feel them at the base of your neck just about where your collar is. They are long narrow bones, gently curved like an italic lower-case *f*. To some imaginations it is shaped like an old-fashioned key, a point commemorated by its formal name *clavicle* ("little key" L). The end of the clavicle near the midline of the body adjoins the upper end of the sternum; at the other end it adjoins the scapula. (The clavicle is important to the mythology of childhood, for in birds this pair of bones join firmly to form the familiar V-shaped "wishbone.")

If you were to look down at these bones from above, they would seem to form a double crescent almost encircling the upper part of the body. It is not a complete circle, since there is a short gap of about an inch between the two clavicles and a larger gap between the two scapulae. However, if you count the stretch of sternum and vertebrae between, you can consider the bones as a girdle, the *pectoral girdle* (pek'to-rul; "breast" L), in reality.

Adjoining the pectoral girdle are the bones of the arm itself. The arms are divided into three segments, an upper arm, a lower arm, and a hand. The leg and, actually, the tetrapod limb in general are similarly divided into three portions.

In describing the structure of the limbs, the adjectives *proximal* ("nearest" L) and *distal* (a word coined from "distant") become useful. That section of limb or of any extended structure which

is nearer the trunk or the midplane of the body is the proximal
part. The opposite end would be the distal part. Thus, the upper
arm is the proximal portion and the hand is the distal portion.
The lower arm is the intermediate portion.

In all tetrapods, the proximal portion of the limb contains a
single bone, while the intermediate part contains two. This is
certainly true of the human arm. As the limbs lengthened, these
bones lengthened and became the "long bones" of the body.

The upper arm contains one long bone, the *humerus* (hyoo'-
mur-us; "shoulder" G).* The lower arm contains the two long
bones, the *radius* ("ray" L) and the *ulna* ("elbow" L). A ray
obviously is something that radiates outward from a center and
the word was originally applied to the spokes of a wheel. The
radius of the lower arm apparently seemed straight enough to be
such a spoke; whence its name. The ulna is likewise appropriately
named — the bony portion of the elbow is indeed the end of
the ulna.

The distal end of the limb contains many bones; 27, as a matter
of fact. This situation dates back to the origin of the limbs when
their stubbiness was braced by a number of small, irregular bones.
There was a value to this. A single bone would have made a
flipper a stiff and inefficient oar. A single line of bones would
have allowed it to bend as our vertebral column bends but only
as a unit. A number of bones spread out in two planes — length-
wise and breadthwise — and able to slide past one another to a
limited degree, introduce a two-dimensional flexibility and allow
the delicacy of maneuver required for efficient steering. Three
of the bones lengthened out to form the upper and lower limbs
in the extended version required by tetrapod structure, but the
distal end of the limbs retained the remaining bones.

* It is almost irresistible to wonder if the humerus is by any chance the
"funny bone" which gives us that unpleasant tingling feeling when we jar our
elbow. To be sure, the humerus ends near the point we jar, but the source of
the sensation is not a bone at all, but a nerve, and the relationship between
"humerus," "humorous," and "funnybone" is merely coincidence.

When the first amphibians clambered onto the muddy tidal flats and took to living on land, they needed not only stronger support for their limbs but also a more splayed-out surface where limb met ground, to keep them from sinking into the mud — a sort of snowshoe effect. For this purpose, the small bones at the distal end of the limb spread out (probably with webs between), distributing body weight more widely and evenly upon the mud. Each limb developed a number of bone-braced digits and the primitive number was five on each limb. There seems no particular reason why the number should have been five, but that is what it was and no normal living tetrapod has more than five digits on any limb.

With the passage of time, the evolutionary tendency often lay in the direction of a reduction in the number of digits. On hard ground there is less necessity for a splayed-out limb. It is more important, instead, to develop a fleshy pad or horny sheath to absorb shocks and make possible the pounding that would accompany a fast run. Where the pad develops, the digits decrease in size and become mere claw-carrying devices; as in the cat. Where horny sheaths ("hoofs") develop, the number of digits tends to decrease so that the individual hoof can become larger and stronger. The rhinoceros has only three toes left; cattle, deer, and ruminants generally have only two; the horse and related creatures carry the process to its logical conclusion and have but one horn-sheathed toe on each leg.

It is the sign of the primitive character of the human arm that it retains five long, maneuverable digits. Of course, it is not for support on marshy ground that we need them. Rather, we have turned the hand into a superlative manipulative organ, incomparably the best thing of the sort in all the realm of life — with four limber fingers and an opposing thumb so that the whole can be used as a delicate pincer or firm grasper, a twister, bender, puller, pusher, and manipulator of piano and typewriter keys.

The bony condition of the original flipper persists in the wrist, where eight irregular bones in, roughly, two lines of four each (all in close contact) make for flexibility. The wrist can bend backward and forward easily and, to a more limited extent, to the left and right.

The eight bones as a group are the *carpal bones* ("wrist" L), and individually they are named after whatever it was that the particular bone seemed to resemble in the colorful fancy of early anatomists. They are the *navicular* (na-vik'yoo-ler; "boat-shaped" L), *lunate* ("crescent-shaped" L), *triquetrum* (try-kwee'-trum; "three-cornered" L), *pisiform* (py'si-form; "pea-shaped" L), *greater multangular* ("many-angled" L), *lesser multangular*, *capitate* ("head-shaped" L, that is, rounded), and *hamate* ("hooked" L).

The hand itself contains 19 bones, arranged in five rows. Four of the rows contain four bones, the fifth contains three. The five bones that adjoin the carpals are the *metacarpal bones* (met'uh-kahr'pul; "after the wrist" L). They are encased in soft tissue, and form the palm of the hand, but it is easy enough to feel the five separate bones under the skin of the back of the hand. The metacarpals are numbered one through five, beginning at the thumb. The second, third, fourth, and fifth metacarpals are virtually parallel and immovable; but the first is set at an angle and has limited mobility.

Adjoining the metacarpals are the "fingerbones," or *phalanges* (fuh-lan'jees), of which the singular is *phalanx* (fay'lanks). The phalanx in Greek history was a close array of soldiers side by side and back to front. The bones of the fingers, set in similar close array, was reminiscent of that, and this accounts for the name. Each finger, except the thumb, has three phalanges of decreasing size as one proceeds distally. The thumb has but two. Some anatomists feel that the thumb can be counted as having three phalanges, too, if the first metacarpal is considered a phalanx. If that were so, then the first phalanx of the thumb would connect with the carpals directly and there would be only four metacarpals instead of five.

(The absence of flesh in a skeleton allows the metacarpals to add their separateness to that of the phalanges, and this gives the skeletal hand its long-fingered aspect. What seems to be the palm in a skeleton is actually the wrist.)

Each finger has a formal anatomical name, by the way. The thumb is *pollex* ("strong" L) because it is stronger than the other fingers, as you recognize whenever you push a tack into a board with the thumb, rather than with any other finger; hence a "thumbtack." The other four fingers are, in order, *index* ("pointer" L), *medius* ("middle" L), *annularis* (an'yoo-lar'is; "ring" L), and *minimus* ("least" L).

THE LEGS

The legs, which in bipedal man bear the brunt of support and locomotion, are longer, stronger, and more specialized than the arms. Yet the similarities, indicating the common plan of all four limbs, are unmistakable. To begin with, just as there is a pectoral girdle so there is another girdle (far heavier and stronger), to which the structure of the leg is attached. This lower girdle consists of three pairs of bones: the *ilium* (il′ee-um; "groin" L), the *ischium* (is′kee-um; "hip" G), and the *pubis* (pyoo′bis; "adult" L). One of each of these is on either side of the mid-plane, and all together form the bony structure of the hips.

The ilium and ischium are flat, irregular bones — the ilium above (superior) and the ischium below (inferior). You can feel the crest of the ilium on either side of the body just below the waistline. It is upon the ischium, on the other hand, and on the muscles attached to it, that you sit.

In front, smaller than either ilium or the ischium, is the pubis. It joins the ischium in such a way as to form a pair of large holes at the bottom of the girdle which are very prominent when the skeleton alone is viewed. These are the *obturator foramina* (ob′tyoo-ray′ter; "stopped-up holes," because in actual life they are almost entirely covered by a membrane). The derivation of "pubis" from "adult" arises in the following manner. A common sign of adulthood, or at least of sexual maturity, is the appearance of hair in the genital region. Such hair is therefore the "pubic hair" ("adult hair") and the bone which is to be found just under that region came to share the name.

In the child these three bones are separate, but by the middle twenties, they are firmly fused into a single bone, which in common parlance is the "hipbone." A more formal name is *os coxae* (os kok′see; "hipbone" L). Before this rather obvious name, — for Latin-speakers — was accepted, the name most often used, and still much used, was *os innominata* (i-nom′i-nay′tuh; "nameless bone" L) because, though the three parts had names, all three together had not. ("Innominata" is also applied to other anatomical parts without names, so that the very namelessness becomes a name.)

The two os coxae meet in front, where the pubes join by way

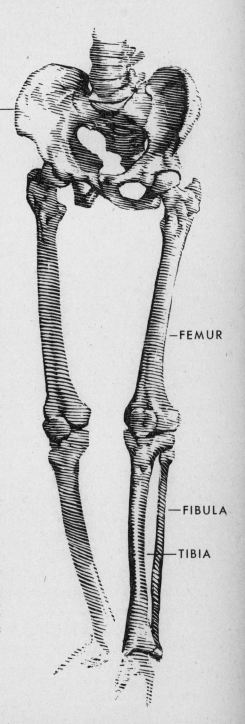

PELVIS—

—FEMUR

—FIBULA

—TIBIA

of a cartilaginous link something like those between vertebrae. This is the *pubic symphysis* (sim′fi-sis; "a growing together" G). Dorsally the two ilia do not meet. Rather, they join the sacrum, one on either side. (The fusion of the five sacral vertebrae thus makes for a stronger hip structure.) So neat and firm is the connection between sacrum and ilium that it is common to speak of them as though they were a single bone, the "sacroiliac." Because of man's troubles in the small of the back resulting from the imperfections of bipedal structure, the word has come to have most unpleasant connotations.

The hipbone and sacrum, taken together, form a complete bony girdle, stronger in proportion to man's size than are the similar structures in other mammals. (This is not surprising, in view of man's bipedal position.) Furthermore, in no other mammal do the hipbones form such a rounded and basin-like structure. Again, this is the consequence of bipedality. In a four-legged creature, the organs within the abdominal cavity are suspended from the backbone and rest on the ventral muscular wall of the abdomen. In man, the abdominal wall is vertical (or should be) and cannot serve as support. It is the hipbones that must do so and their basin-like shape is adapted to that function. In fact, the hip region is called the *pelvis* ("basin" L) and the ring of bone is the *pelvic girdle,* in recognition of its shape. Unfortunately, the pelvis is not perfectly adapted for the purpose. The basin tips forward (man has only been at bipedality some hundreds of thousands of years and it takes more time to adjust structure to so radical an innovation) and the support isn't entirely satisfactory.

The pelvic girdle, by the way, offers the easiest method of distinguishing the skeleton of the female from that of the male.

COMPARISON FROM ABOVE

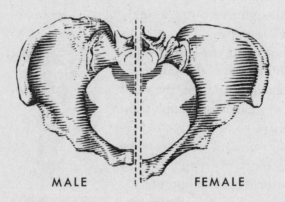

MALE   FEMALE

The female requires room in the abdomen for the development of an infant, and the bony ring formed by the pelvic girdle must be large enough to accommodate the extrusion of a baby weighing seven pounds or more. For that reason, the female pelvic girdle is on the average two inches wider than that of the male, although the bones themselves are thinner and lighter. This additional width is all the more obvious because of the generally smaller size of the rest of the skeleton of the female as compared with that of the male.

Further, the angle made by the meeting of the two pubic bones at the symphysis is much wider in the female, where it is about 90 degrees, than in the male, where it is only 70 degrees. The net result of all this is that the living female possesses prominent hips which may be a cause for concern to her at those times when slenderness is in fashion. They are, however, essential to the smooth functioning of her role as a mother, and, thanks to the inscrutable wisdom of Nature, prove attractive to the male of the species, whatever the fashion.

Adjoining the pelvic girdle is the *thigh* (AS), which is the proximal portion of the leg. This, like the proximal portion of the arm, contains one long bone. This "thighbone" or *femur* (fee'mur; "thigh" L) is the longest bone in the body, making up about 2/7 of the height of an individual. At its proximal end it has a very characteristic rounded head, which is set to one side and fits into a rounded depression, or socket, in the hipbone. This socket is the *acetabulum* (as'i-tab'yoo-lum), so called because of its resemblance to a round cup the Romans used for holding vinegar (*acetum*).

The intermediate section of the leg, again like that of the arm, contains two bones. However, whereas the two bones in the arm are nearly equal in size, those in the leg are quite unequal. The larger of the two is the *tibia* (tib'ee-uh; "flute" L; which in length and shape it seems to resemble). The tibia, commonly called the "shinbone," is the second longest bone of the body. It runs just under the skin in the forepart of the leg and you can easily feel it. Its distal end, at the ankle, forms a swelling, which you can feel as the bony protuberance at the inside of the ankle.

The smaller bone of the intermediate section is as long as the tibia but is much thinner, so that it is commonly called the "splint-bone," since it resembles a splinter broken off the main bone. It is, in fact, the thinnest bone, in proportion to its length, in the body. Its formal name, *fibula* (fib'yoo-luh; "pin" L), also indicates this: the implication is that its relation to the tibia resembles that of a pin to a brooch. For most of the length of its course, the fibula is well hidden under muscle and cannot be felt by probing fingers. At its distal end, however, it forms the bony prominence on the outside of the ankle.

The knee, which is the joint between the proximal and intermediate sections of the leg, differs from its analog, the elbow, in that it possesses a separate bone. This is the small, flat, triangular "knee bone," or *patella* (puh-tel'uh; "small pan" L). It protects an important joint which in the ordinary course of walking, and particularly of running, is constantly being pushed out ahead of the body. Like the hyoid bone, the patella is not directly connected to any other bone, although it is held in place by muscle attachments. If you relax your leg muscles so that the patella is not held firmly in place by them, you will find that you can move it about quite a bit in any direction.

The distal section of the leg contains the ankle and foot, which are analogous to the wrist and hand. The ankle, like the wrist, contains a series of irregular bones, though it possesses only seven as compared with the eight of the wrist. The ankle bones make up the *tarsus* ("wicker-basket" G, the name apparently being suggested by the fact that the separate bones in such close association, resembled the interwoven wicker strands of such a basket). One of the bones of the tarsus, the *calcaneus* (kal-kay'nee-us; "heel" L), does indeed, as the name implies, extend backward to form the heel. It is the largest bone of the tarsus.

This backward extension of the calcaneus would seem an attempt to make man's bipedal support more stable. Any object resting upon two narrow supports is at best in unstable equi-

librium, and any jar will topple it. By extending a heel backward, the support is propped up and even made somewhat
quadrupedal. A man stands not on two feet, but on two soles
and two heels. It is not much of an advance toward stability —
it is still easy for a man to fall (and, in fact, a baby learns to
walk only through an inevitable succession of falls) — but it
answers the purpose. A careful adult can go sometimes for years
without falling and yet without seriously limiting his locomotion,
either.

The remaining six bones of the tarsus are the *talus* (tay′lus;
"ankle" L), *cuboid* ("cube-shaped" L), *navicular* ("boat-shaped"
L), and the first, second, and third *cuneiform* (kyoo-nee′i-form;
"wedge-shaped" L). The calcaneus and talus bones are roughly
cube-shaped and so, of course, is the cuboid. The soldiers of
ancient Rome used such bones (obtained from horses, usually)
to hack out rough-and-ready dice. For this reason, the talus
in particular is sometimes called the *astragalus* (as-trag′uh-lus;
"die" L).

Just as the hand is made up of metacarpals and phalanges,
the foot proper is made up of the five parallel bones of the
metatarsus plus five sets of phalanges. As in the hand, the first
digit — the big toe, or *hallux* (hal′lux; "big toe" L) — has two
phalanges, the other digits three.

The foot is one of the more specialized portions of the human
skeleton. It has gained a heel and has lost those characteristics of
the hand that the feet of our early ancestors must have had.

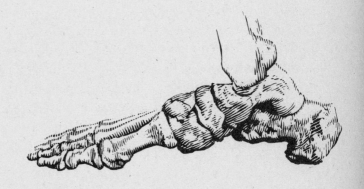

Living apes and monkeys still possess hind feet with much of the characteristics of hands. Those animals have opposable big toes, well separated from the other toes, so that the foot can be used to grasp. Indeed, the apes and monkeys are sometimes lumped together as the *Quadrumana* (kwod-roo'muh-nuh; "four-handed" L).

In man, as another token of specialization, the foot possesses a big toe that is parallel to the other digits and is not opposable. The phalanges have shrunk almost to nothing in the other toes so that the foot is almost one piece. In man, each pair of limbs has its special job; the hands are the graspers and the feet are the support; whereas in the other primates, both limbs compromise their function.

The use of two limbs alone as a support affects us in another way. Most mammals have cut into the support function of the legs by raising themselves to their toes, thus adding the length of their metatarsals to their height. Such creatures are *digiti-grade* (di'ji-ti-grayd'; "toe-walking" L), and the best-known examples are the cats and dogs. The additional height, with its advantages of better placement of the sense organs and greater speed, is counterbalanced by the smaller area of the feet touching the ground and the consequent increase in the stresses upon the feet. Apparently the advantages outweigh the disadvantages in their case.

The hoofed animals go further and lift all the phalanges but the distal one. They add two of the phalanges to the height and end up walking literally on the tips of their toes. This is all very well if you have four widely-spaced supports. It is possible to narrow the areas of contact. Man, with but two supports, can afford no such luxury. He must splay them out and keep phalanges and metatarsus firmly on the ground. If he must add to his height he must do so by lengthening only the long bones of the thigh and shin. He is *plantigrade* (plan'ti-grayd; "sole-walking").

There are other plantigrade mammals, too — notably the bear, which can take up an erect posture better than most tetrapods. Man goes the bear (and also other plantigrade mammals) one better by using the calcaneus, so that he actually walks on his ankles, in part.

The sole of man's foot is not straight for the same reason that the vertebral column of a tetrapod is not. We need an arch for strength, and we have it in the sole. Thus weight is transmitted to the heel and to the ball of the foot, and there is also an elasticity to absorb the shock of walking, when weight is constantly being shifted from foot to foot. (Here is another important specialization of the human foot. Apes do not have arches.) But here again, adjustment to bipedal postures is not perfect. The structures forming the arches can give under weight and flatten out. The "flat feet" that result lower the efficiency of walking and can make it downright painful after a while as the successive jars, relatively unabsorbed, are transmitted to the spinal column and the skull.

CELLS

So far I have been describing the external appearance of the bones and the position of each in the body. This gives a rather static impression of the bones as an inert framework and nothing more. To be sure, a hard mineral makes up 45 per cent of the weight of bone and this part is dead; but in life, bone is more than its mineral matter and is anything but inert. Within its mineral makeup, and within the structure of cartilage, too, are living cells.

The *cell* is the unit of living tissue. It received its name in 1665, when the English scientist Robert Hooke, one of the first microscopists, observed that a thin slice of cork showed a spongy structure and contained tiny, oblong, regularly-spaced holes. The name "cell," meaning a small room, seemed ideal for those holes.

The equivalent Greek word is *kytos* and this is often used in compound words as *cytology* (sy-tol'uh-jee),* meaning the study of cells.

However, the holes observed by Hooke were but dead remnants of a woody skeleton. In living tissue there is the same spongy structure but the cells are not empty. They are filled with a gelatinous material which in the early 19th century received the name of *protoplasm* ("first form" G).

The cells are complicated indeed in structure, but for purposes of this book only the barest description will be necessary. In the first place, cells are small. The largest cell in the human body is the egg cell produced by the female, about the size of a pinhead and just visible to the naked eye. Other cells in the body fall far below this in size and can be seen only by microscope.

Each cell has a boundary, a thin and delicate *cell membrane*. The membrane marks off the interior of the cell from the outer environment; and the chemical and physical structure of the regions on either side of the membrane are completely different. There is a natural tendency for structure and composition to equalize across the membrane; but it is the essential function of life to maintain the difference despite the equalizing tendency. The membrane is only about 10 millimicrons thick (a millimicron is one billionth of a meter, or 1/25,000,000 inch) and consists of only three or four layers of complex molecules. Nevertheless, it somehow serves as a selective and oneway passage for certain substances from environment to interior and for others from interior to environment. The mechanism by which this is done is by no means understood as yet.

Within the membrane the cell is divided into two major portions. A small central region called the *nucleus* ("little nut" L, because it resembles a small nut within a larger shell) is surrounded by its own *nuclear membrane*. The nucleus controls

* The Greek *k* becomes the Latin *c*, which is always hard but in English often becomes soft. Hence the switch from the Greek *k* sound to the English *s* sound.

cell division and contains the mechanism that ultimately dictates the nature of the cell's chemical machinery.* Between the nucleus and the cell membrane is the *cytoplasm*, which carries on the everyday work of the cell.

The cell is complicated enough to serve not only as a component of living tissue but as an independent organism. There are numerous species of one-celled organisms. Nevertheless, all plants and animals that we see about us with our unaided eye are made up of a number of cells. The human body contains more than 50,000,000,000,000 (50 trillion) cells.

In a multicellular organism the cells fall into specialized groups, each performing a particular function with particular efficiency, to the exclusion, sometimes, of adequate performance in other functions equally vital to life. This means that an individual cell from a multicellular organism cannot maintain its life independently but only as part of a complex group, where other cells make up its deficiencies and where a smoothly working organization unites and controls all the specialties. (The analogy of a modern society containing numerous highly specialized human beings who would quickly starve if marooned separately on uninhabited islands but who can get along perfectly well within the social structure, is irresistible.)

A particular tissue is made up of a mass of cells of similar specialization. Those cells which specialize in forming the various substances that in one way or another hold the body structure together make up *connective tissue.* The specialized function of the cells of the connective tissue is to manufacture about themselves those molecules that make up bone, cartilage, and other portions of the connecting framework of the body.

Many of the molecules so manufactured are *organic* in nature; that is, made up chiefly of the elements carbon, hydrogen, oxygen,

---

* This is a tremendous subject with which there is no room to deal in this book. If you are curious, you will find a rather detailed discussion of such matters in my book *The Wellsprings of Life* (1960).

and nitrogen, which constitute the major portion of all living tissue. Such molecules are in contradistinction to those which lack carbon (the key element of life) and which are similar in properties to the substances making up the nonliving air, sea, and rocks about us. These latter compounds are, very naturally, called *inorganic* ("not organic"). Despite the latter name, the body can and does make use of inorganic substances. Water is inorganic and so is the calcium phosphate that makes up the major portion of the bones.

The organic substances of the connective tissue fall into two classes: *protein* and *mucopolysaccharide* (myoo′koh-pol-ee-sak′-uh-ride). The proteins are particularly complex molecules, built up of long chains of smaller molecules called *amino acids* (a-mee′-noh). A single protein molecule will contain thousands of atoms, even millions sometimes, arranged in helical coils, like miniature spiral staircases. The importance of protein to life is indicated by the fact that "protein" comes from a Greek term meaning "of first importance." In connective tissue the protein molecules associate themselves into bundles of coils — tiny fibers, that is — which mat together to form a sturdy fibrous structure that can be reasonably elastic, if the coils are properly arranged. The cells that produce this fibrous connective tissue are called *fibroblasts* ("fibrobud" G). The two chief proteins existing in connective tissue are *collagen* (kol′uh-jen; "glue-producer" G, because it will produce a glue if boiling is prolonged) and *elastin* (ee-las′tin, so called because of its elasticity).

The mucopolysaccharides are also large molecules, but are built up of a series of units derived from the simple sugars. The "polysaccharide" portion of the name is from Greek words meaning "many sugars." A solution of mucopolysaccharide is gummy, viscous, and sticky, and the prefix comes from the similarly viscous material ("mucus") secreted by many parts of the body.

FIBROBLAST

In fact, mucus possesses its properties because it is a solution of mucopolysaccharide.

One particular mucopolysaccharide is *hyaluronic acid* (hy'al-yoo-ron'ik), which occurs almost universally between cells and helps hold them together. It is sometimes called "ground substance" or "intercellular cement" for that reason. Another molecule of this type, containing some sulfur atoms in the molecule in addition to the more usual types, is *chondroitin sulfate* (kon-droh'i-tin). Cartilage is rich in mucopolysaccharides, and the Greek word for cartilage (*chondros*) is the source for the name chondroitin sulfate.

Cartilage is formed by relatively large oval cells called *chondrocytes* (kon'droh-sites; "cartilage cells" G) which form collagen and chondroitin sulfate chiefly, and deposit those substances outside the cell. The chondrocytes are thus separated by the cartilage they form, although they tend to remain in groups. Though the cartilage between the cells is nonliving, the cells themselves are alive.

The most common type of cartilage is *hyaline cartilage* (hy'uh-lin; "glassy" G) because of its clear and translucent appearance. (The occurrence of hyaluronic acid in such cartilage accounts for part of the name of that mucopolysaccharide.) It is as hyaline cartilage that most of the skeleton is first formed, and some of the skeleton remains in that form into old age, as, for instance, is the case with the costal cartilages connecting ribs and sternum.

There is also *elastic cartilage,* which is yellow in color. (Both elasticity and yellowness are due to its content of elastin.) Such cartilage occurs, for example, in the framework of the ear.

Finally there is *fibrocartilage,* in which molecules are bound together to form a tough fibrous substance rather than a soft elastic one. It is this fibrocartilage that forms the intervertebral discs and joins the two hipbones at the pubic symphysis.

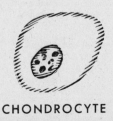

CHONDROCYTE

OSTEOCYTE

BONE STRUCTURE

Despite the hard, dry appearance of bones in a skeleton on display, it is important to remember that in life about 25 per cent of bone weight is water and another 30 per cent is organic material. The organic material is almost entirely collagen, with some mucopolysaccharide also present.

Like cartilage, bone contains living cells whose function it is to manufacture the connective material. The difference is that the *osteocytes* (os'tee-oh-sites; "bone cells" G) also bring about the formation of mineral matter, which is then deposited in the organic framework, hardening it and giving it strength.

The mineral matter is chiefly a basic calcium phosphate, in which calcium ions are surrounded by phosphate ions and hydroxyl ions* in a pattern that is by no means unique to life. There are common minerals that show the same pattern. The closest approach is that of *fluoroapatite* (floo'ur-roh-ap'uh-tite) which differs only in containing fluoride ion in place of hydroxyl ion. For this reason, the mineral structure of the bone is sometimes spoken of as *hydroxyapatite* (high-droks'ee-ap'uh-tite). When bone has been buried for long periods of time in the soil, there is a slow tendency to replace the hydroxyl ion by fluoride ion, so the age of fossil bones can sometimes be judged by their fluoride ion content.

Bone also contains calcium carbonate in fair amount, together with small quantities of compounds of magnesium, sodium, and potassium. It is — in addition to being the rigid framework of the body — a complex mineral reservoir, its components being continuously available to the body.

* In this book, I intend to involve myself as little as possible with chemistry. If you are acquainted with these ions, fine. If not, you can either find information on the subject in any elementary chemistry book or, if you prefer, you can ignore the matter and read on.

Bone is penetrated by narrow *Haversian canals* (ha-ver'zhun, after the English physician Clopton Havers, who first described them in 1691). It is through these canals that the blood vessels and nerves pass. The osteocytes, ovoid cells with numerous jagged processes, are arranged in concentric layers about the canals. A Haversian canal and its concentric layers of cells and mineral is called an *osteon* (os'tee-on) and a number of osteons fuse together, looking like adjoining tree trunks under the microscope, to form bone.

The layers of mineral may be laid down quite densely to form *compact bone,* or mineral matter may be laid down in a series of separated bony fibers forming a spongy latticework. This is called *cancellous bone* (kan'sel-us; "lattice" L).

The long bones of the limbs show both forms of bone. The outermost surface is a layer of compact bone; within is cancellous bone. Such bones are lighter than they would be if they were compact throughout, and yet their strength is scarcely

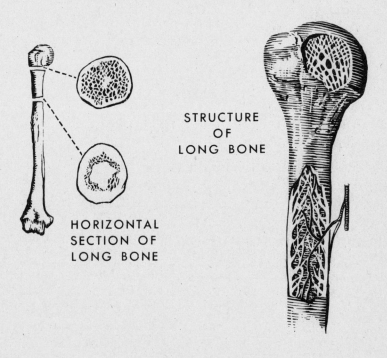

STRUCTURE
OF
LONG BONE

HORIZONTAL
SECTION OF
LONG BONE

decreased. In the first place, a hollow cylinder is surprisingly strong. (A sheet of ordinary writing paper, rolled into a loose cylinder and bound so by a rubber band, will support a fairly heavy textbook.) In addition, the bony bars and plates within the cancellous region act as reinforcing struts formed along the lines of the tension and pressure produced by the normal movements of the body.

The hollowness of human bones is not unqualified. They are filled with a soft, fatty material called *marrow* (AS). The marrow is lighter than bone itself, and a marrow-filled hollow bone is lighter than a solid one (and uses up less inorganic material). Where lightness is particularly necessary, however, true hollowness will be found. The elephant, as an example, needs a huge skull upon which to base the muscles required to manipulate his massive trunk and to hold up a head weighted down by both the trunk and his majestic tusks. In order to supply the surface of bone necessary for the muscles without negating the whole purpose by a prohibitive weight of bone, large hollows exist in the elephant's skull bones.

Similarly, flying birds must conserve weight and their bones are hollow and fragile to the point where they fulfill their function as supporting framework with very little room to spare. For many types of birds it is true that their coating of feathers weighs more than their bones.

In man, and in mammals, generally, however, there are few true hollows in the bone. This has its advantages too, for, as we shall see, there is good use for the bone marrow.

A bone grows or is repaired through the activity of two kinds of osteocytes with opposed functions: the *osteoblasts* ("bone bud" G) and the *osteoclasts* ("bone breaker" G). An osteoblast builds up bone (produces its buds, in other words) by putting out layers of hydroxyapatite. An osteoclast is a cell that breaks down bone, by gradually dissolving the hydroxyapatite and feeding it into the bloodstream.

Thus a bone grows in diameter through the activity of osteo-clasts within, which dissolve out the inner walls and make the interior hollow wider (but leave the strengthening struts along the lines of pressure and tension). Meanwhile osteoblasts are adding layers of hydroxyapatite on the outer surface. In repair-ing a break in the bone, osteoblasts lay down the minerals and osteoclasts polish off the rough edges, so to speak, and remove the excess.

A long bone consists of a shaft, or *diaphysis* (dy-af'i-sis), and knobby ends, each of which is an *epiphysis* (ee-pif'i-sis). The knobby epiphyses fit into appropriate spots in adjoining bones, are coated with cartilage, and in youngsters at least are separated from the bony parts of the diaphysis by a stretch of more car-tilage. Osteoblasts in the bony portion of the diaphysis contin-ually invade the cartilage in the direction of the epiphyses, laying down hydroxyapatite as they do so; and the cartilage continually grows away from the shaft itself, pushing the epiphyses on ahead. The net result is that the bone grows longer and longer.

Finally, somewhere in the middle or late teens, the relentless layering of bone catches up with the epiphyses and wipes out the cartilage between. The bones no longer lengthen and the youngster reaches his or her adult height. One of the reasons why women are generally shorter than men is that this completion of the process takes place at a younger age in their case.

The Greek meaning of "diaphysis" is "growth between" and of "epiphysis" is "growth upon." The epiphysis, in other words, is a piece of bone growing upon another bone but separated by cartilage from it, while the diaphysis is the growth between the epiphyses at the two ends.

This complicated layering and delayering of mineral substance and this careful race of bone and cartilage cannot, as you can well imagine, be left to the bone itself. There must be some central directing force handling all the bones in order that the growth of each bone continue in due proportion with that of every other bone, and with the soft parts of the body, too. Such central control is exerted, in part, through the action of *growth hormone,* a chemical released into the bloodstream in tiny quantities by a small organ just under the brain called the *pituitary gland* (pi-tyoo'i-ter-ee). The presence of growth hormone keeps cartilage ahead in the race, so to speak.*

When something goes wrong with the supply of growth hormone, the results can be drastic. An undersupply will bring about a quick overrunning of the cartilage. Such a rapid ossification can put an end to growth in early childhood and the result is the circus midget. (Where the long bones are particularly affected, so that head and torso are about normal in size and the arms and legs remain stubby, the result is a "dwarf.") On the other hand, an oversupply of growth hormone can put cartilage so far ahead that a youngster may shoot up with unusual rapidity and continue to do so into adulthood. A circus giant results. Men have been definitely known to have reached heights of almost nine feet, and some midgets have been less than two feet high as adults.

Occasionally, there is an abnormal production of growth hormone after a normal complete ossification has taken place. In this case, further growth is induced at the only places where growth remains possible, even under such stimulation — at the ends of the limbs and the tip of the lower jaw. Hands, feet, and jaw enlarge grotesquely, and this condition is known as *acromegaly* (ak'roh-meg'uh-lee; "large extremities" G).

Also involved in the production of bone is *vitamin D,* whose more formal name, *calciferol* (kal-sif'uh-role; "calcium-carrying") indicates its function. Children who for one reason or another happen to endure a shortage of vitamin D have bones that do not properly ossify. They remain soft and therefore deform under

---

* Except for passing mentions such as this one, I shall not discuss hormones and hormone action in this book. It will be more useful to leave such "chemical controls" to be dealt with along with the "electrical controls" of nerve, spine, and brain in the book I plan to write as a companion volume to this one.

stress, giving rise to bowlegs and a curved spine. The skull may be soft and misshapen, a condition known as *craniotabes* (kray'-nee-oh-tay'beez; "wasting of the skull" L). The disease, in general, is called *rickets* or *rachitis* (ra-kigh'tis; "spine" G, which, after all, is a portion of the body often affected). The effect of rickets is to be seen from the meaning of the adjective "rickety." Nowadays, with the widespread fortification of milk and bread with vitamin D, and the use of vitamin pills, rickets is not a serious threat, at least in the more developed portions of the world.

The vitamin D requirement of adults, once bone growth is over, is very low, and yet it may not be entirely zero. Mineral matter deposited in bone is not there permanently. It can always be mobilized by the body in case of need, so there must always be a mechanism to replace it when the need has passed. The lack of vitamin D may be one reason why adults sometimes suffer bone-softening, as mineral matter is removed from the bones and is not replaced. This condition is found in women more often than in men, particularly in the Orient. Usually it makes its appearance during pregnancy or lactation, when the mother's calcium supply is being stripped on behalf of the developing infant. This condition is called *osteomalacia* (os'tee-oh-muh-lay'shee-uh; "bone softness" G) and has symptoms similar to those of rickets.

Infection of the bone marrow, sometimes a serious disease that has required surgery, is *osteomyelitis* (os-tee-oh-my-uh-ly'tis; "inflammation of the bone marrow" G). (The suffix "-itis" has come, by general agreement among medical men, to be used to signify "inflammation of." You can see at once, then, what such common words as "tonsillitis" and "appendicitis" must mean.)

TOOTH STRUCTURE

Like the bones, the teeth are built up about central channels containing nerves and blood vessels, so that they too incorporate living parts. There is but one such channel in each tooth and it is the *pulp* (which contains the nerve). It is the sensitive portion of the tooth, as is graphically portrayed by the common phrase "hitting the nerve."

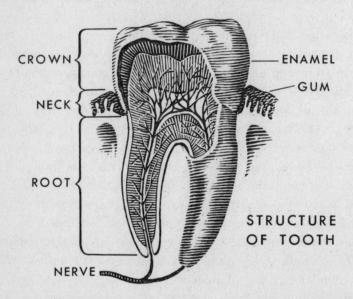

CROWN

NECK

ROOT

NERVE

ENAMEL

GUM

STRUCTURE OF TOOTH

Immediately about the pulp and making up the bulk of the tooth is *dentine* ("tooth" L), which is much more mineralized than bone. Dentine is up to 70 per cent inorganic salt, in place of the 45 per cent that makes up bone. Dentine is therefore harder than bone and also less active. It exchanges material with the bloodstream to only a tenth of the extent that bone does. The ivory used for billiard balls and piano keys is an example of virtually pure dentine when derived from elephant tusks.

The dentine of that portion of the tooth below the gumline (the *root*) is surrounded by a thin layer of *cementum* which serves, as the name would indicate, to anchor the tooth to the jaw. Cementum is itself quite like bone in composition.

On the other hand, the dentine of the portion of the tooth above the gumline is overlaid by *enamel*. Whereas cementum is less mineralized than dentine, enamel is more so. Enamel is actually up to 98 per cent inorganic and is almost entirely inert. It is the hardest substance in the human body.

The mineral of teeth differs from the mineral of bones in that the former contains a small but significant quantity of fluoride ions in place of some of the hydroxyl ions—provided such fluoride ions are available to the body. This closer approach to the fluoro-apatite structure produces, apparently, a tooth that is less amenable to bacterial decay. (It is rather ironical that the hardest and strongest structure in the body is the only one subject to decay while man is still alive — and yet perhaps it is not so surprising at that; being the most mineralized and therefore the least alive of tissues, it is most defenseless against the onslaught of bacteria. Tooth decay can be referred to as *caries* [kair'eez; "decay" L].)

The matter of the fluoride content of teeth poses a pretty problem. Food and water always contain minute amounts of fluoride ion, but not always quite enough. If the quantity is too low, say less than one part per million, little if any fluoride ions find their way into tooth structure and decay is prevalent except where heroic measures of mouth care are instituted. If the quantity of fluoride ion is too high, say over two parts per million, then the enamel displays a permanent yellow mottling that is not actually harmful but is certainly not pretty.

At about one part per million, the fluoride ion content reduces dental caries to one third its usual incidence (where no other change in oral hygiene is instituted) without any observable harm of any kind. (This last conclusion is based upon a quarter century of painstaking dental and medical research.) There is therefore a strong movement among the dental profession in favor of the addition of fluoride ion (*fluoridation*) to drinking-water supplies in order to bring the fluoride ion content up to the one-part-per-million level. It is estimated that dental bills could in this way be reduced by a billion dollars a year, with all the saving (not capable of being measured in money) in fear and pain that would imply.

Unfortunately, the reduction in caries would apply only to children during those ages when their teeth are forming and incorporating fluoride ions. Adults, with fully formed teeth, will no longer incorporate fluoride, but at least the new generation would be started off on the right foot.

BONE MOVEMENT

The skeleton is not merely a framework for the body, it is a movable framework. Since the bones themselves are rigid, the only possibility of motion comes at those points where two bones join. These points of joining are called, very obviously, *joints*. More ornately, they can also be called *articulations* ("to join" L). The existence of a joint does not by itself necessarily imply mobility. Some bones, such as those of the skull and of the hipbone, fuse together, as I explained earlier, into what is essentially a single structure, with no movement of any kind possible at the lines of joining.

Other joints allow a mere gliding movement, and not much of that. Examples include the joints between the vertebrae and those between the ribs and the thoracic vertebrae. These allow the limited motions involved in the bending of the back or the lifting of the rib cage during breathing. The small bones of the wrist and ankle can also glide one against the other. The joint motions with which we are most familiar, however, involve sharp and extreme changes in the relative positions of neighboring bones. These are most marked in the limbs, as when you bend your arm at the elbow or your leg at the knee. The motion there is virtually through an angle of 180 degrees.

With one bone moving so against another, one important concern (as it would be in an equivalent man-made apparatus) is to reduce friction. For this reason the portions of the bone that meet are lined with a smooth layer of cartilage. The bones are also held together by a capsule (*synovial capsule*) of connective tissue that encloses the joint and secretes a viscous liquid containing hyaluronic acid. The joints slide easily against this lubricating layer of *synovial fluid* (si-noh'vee-ul; "egg white," which it resembles in its smooth thickness). Joints about which more or less free movement is possible are, for this reason, referred to as *synovial joints*.

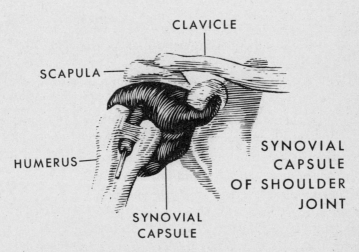

CLAVICLE

SCAPULA

HUMERUS

SYNOVIAL CAPSULE OF SHOULDER JOINT

SYNOVIAL CAPSULE

The type of movement allowed at a particular synovial joint depends upon its structure. As a consequence, motion is sometimes possible in one plane only, back and forth like a door upon its hinges, so that such a joint is a *hinge joint*. One example is at the elbow where the proximal epiphysis of the ulna just fits between the two epiphyses at the distal end of the humerus.

It can therefore move back and forth but not from side to side.

The knee joint is another hinge joint. So are the joints between the first and second phalanges of fingers and thumb, and between the second and third phalanges of the fingers. (This also holds true for the analogous joints in the toes, so that in the limbs there are 40 hinge joints in all.)

Some joints can allow motion in each of two axes. For instance, you cannot only bend your toes; you can also spread them apart. This is even truer of the fingers.

The lower jaw can be moved up and down and is mostly a hinge joint, but it can be moved somewhat from side to side and the normal action of chewing involves a rotary motion rather than a mere clashing of teeth. (Watch a cow chewing its cud if you want to see such rotary motion in slow and stately fashion.) The head itself is even more freely movable about its connection with the vertebral column, since it can be bent forward, backward, leftward, rightward, or rotated about a vertical axis.

The lower arm can be rotated through an angle of 180 degrees so that the palm of the hand can face either down or up, without motion at either elbow or shoulder. This is made possible by the manner in which the proximal epiphysis of the radius fits into a depression in the ulna. Within that depression the radius can pivot. If you hold out your arm before you, palm up, radius and ulna are parallel; turn the arm palm-down and the radius pivots and crosses the ulna. (The foot is much less versatile than the arm in this respect.)

When the epiphysis of one bone fits into a cup-shaped socket in another, you have a *ball-and-socket joint*. The most obvious case is that of the femur fitting into the acetabulum of the hipbone. This allows the freest possible motion so that the leg can be thrown into almost any position, especially with practice, thus making ballet dancing the graceful thing it is.

A similar ball-and-socket joint between the humerus and the

scapula involves even freer motion, since the socket is shallower in this case than in that of the hip. You can turn your arm through a complete circle at the shoulder and this joint is by all odds the most maneuverable in the body. (Watch a baseball pitcher in a complicated windup.) This is a good thing too, considering that the possession of arms and hands capable of almost infinitely versatile manipulation is one of the factors that is the making of the human being.

Violent movement about a joint can succeed in moving one bone out of alignment with another (*dislocation*), which results in making motion at that point impossible and attempted motion extremely painful. A ball-and-socket joint is more easily dislocated than any other kind and the shallow shoulder joint is most easily dislocated of all, with the hip joint next. The elbow is sometimes dislocated, as are the various phalanges. One misadventure that is almost humorous (to everyone but the victim) is the dislocation of the lower jaw as the result of a too vigorous yawn.

To prevent dislocations, as far as possible, it is not enough to depend on the synovial membranes or the pressure of surrounding muscles to keep the joints from coming unhooked. Neighboring bones at synovial joints are held together by strands of tough connective tissue called *ligaments* ("to tie" L). Ligaments help restrict motion at the joints to certain reasonable limits. However, those limits can be exceeded under extreme conditions so that ligaments can be torn, with or without dislocation of the joint itself. Such *sprains* occur most frequently at the wrist or ankle. The resultant pain and swelling are familiar to all of us for there are few, if any, who can avoid sprains altogether.

Ligaments may be either white or yellow. White ligaments are composed chiefly of collagen and are not elastic. Yellow ligaments contain elastin and are, therefore, elastic. The former are common but the latter are rare and are found only in the neck in man.

Strong white ligaments bind the bones of the foot in such a way as to curve them into an arch. It is the springy ligament that cushions the shocks of locomotion, and it is the giving of those ligaments that results in flat feet.

Despite all precautions, moving parts are a particular prey to disorder and are as vulnerable in the body as they would be in manufactured products. The knee (perhaps the most vulnerable joint in the body despite the added protection of the patella) may accumulate synovial fluid after injury; this condition is popularly known as "water on the knee." Or the synovial pouch, the membrane of connective tissue enclosing the joint, may grow inflamed and painful. This can happen when steady pressure is placed on the knee, as traditionally among housemaids, who were forever scrubbing floors (in the old days when floors were scrubbed and housemaids existed), so that the disorder came to be called "housemaid's knee." The synovial pouch is called a *bursa* ("purse" L, because it seems to enclose the joint as a purse would enclose its contents). Inflammation of the synovial pouch may therefore be called *bursitis*. It strikes often in the shoulder.

Any inflammation of the joints, for whatever reason, is a type of *arthritis* ("joint inflammation" G). The most serious and widespread variety is *rheumatoid arthritis*, the cause of which is unknown but which can attack anyone at any age, although it most often strikes between the ages of 30 and 45. (It is called "rheumatoid" because it has the symptoms once associated with what was called "rheumatism"; that is, pain at the joints.) In addition to the general pain and misery it brings on, the disease in its extreme manifestations may destroy the structure of a joint or even immobilize it permanently by fiber formation and the deposition of mineral matter. In this way, rheumatoid arthritis can, in effect, produce a bedridden patient.

4

OUR MUSCLES

Although the skeleton considered by itself clearly provides the possibility of motion — after all, it is jointed — it does not and cannot move of itself. The skeleton, when used as a fright-object for children in stories and in animated cartoons, is most terrifying when its lank bones stir in pursuit and its skinny arms stretch out in menace. However, it takes no more than the tiniest advance in sophistication to know that bones, even fresh bones with all their cells intact and alive, could no more move of their own accord than a plaster cast of those same bones could. For motion we must look elsewhere; if there is one characteristic we strongly associate with life, it is that of voluntary movement.

We associate such movement with animal life particularly, for a casual inspection would lead us to suppose that plants do not move except where motion is forced upon them by wind or water current. This is not entirely correct, of course. Plant stems will turn slowly in the direction of light and away from the pull of gravity, while plant roots will turn slowly in the direction of water and toward the pull of gravity. This slow motion depends, apparently, upon differential growth. That is, the cells on one side of the stem or root divide rapidly and the cells on the other side divide slowly so that the structure bends in

89

the direction of the nongrowing side. If light or humidity inhibits growth on the side of the structure it reaches, that structure will turn toward the light or water.

For more rapid motions, in response to touch or light, plants make use of water turgor, which means that certain cavities at the base of petals can be filled with fluid under pressure. When those bases stiffen, the petals are pulled open. When the cavities empty, the petals grow limp and close. This is a primitive device but animals are no stranger to it. The human body contains portions which, ordinarily flaccid, can swell and become rigid when spongelike cavities fill with blood under pressure. The best-known example is, of course, the male penis.

Nevertheless, none of this is what we usually think of when we think of life in motion. We think of antelopes, horses, cheetahs, ostriches (and, in a bumbling way, we ourselves) racing across the ground; we think of the flying of birds, bats, and insects; of the slithering of snakes; of the swimming of fish and porpoises; of the burrowing of moles; and so on. (Yet there are animals, such as clams and coral, which throughout most of their lives are scarcely less immovable than plants are.)

If we are to discover the mechanism of motion, we must turn to the cell, which is the biological unit of life. And we find that all cells — those of men, eagles, clams, and sycamore trees alike — show a capacity for internal movement. The protoplasm within the cell constantly circulates in a definite pattern. This is sometimes called *protoplasmic streaming* and, sometimes, *cyclosis* (sy-kloh'sis; "circulation" G).

The value of cyclosis for any cell is that of keeping its contents well distributed, of making sure that different parts spend a fair share of the time near the membrane where material can be picked up from the outside world or discharged into it. Also, material could be transported, by cyclosis, between the membrane and vital cell structures more or less permanently placed in the interior.

Such streaming can be modified so as to result in the bodily movement of a cell. The protoplasm of a cell can exist in one of two states: as a stiffish semisolid called a *gel* (short for "gelatin"), a protein that when properly mixed with water offers the best-known example of such a state; or as a freely moving fluid called a *sol* (short for "solution"). The balance between the two states is a delicate one, a small change sufficing to switch an area of protoplasm from gel to sol or from sol to gel.

Imagine the protoplasm along the central axis of a cell to be in the sol form, and the portion surrounding it gel. If the gel at the rear were somehow to contract, it would squeeze the sol forward like toothpaste out of a tube. The forward portion of the cell would bulge outward.

As the sol streamed forward, it would turn to gel along the walls, while some of the gel in the rear would turn to sol and in its turn be pushed forward. In this way the capacity for internal motion is channeled into movement forward and the entire cell creeps.

This form of movement has been most thoroughly studied in a one-celled animal called the *amoeba* (uh-mee'buh; "change" G) and is therefore called *amoeboid movement*. The very name of the creature arises from its mode of locomotion — as the cell bellies forward in this direction or that, forming *pseudopods* (syoo'doh-podz; "false feet" G), its shape is constantly changing.

Other one-celled creatures have, over the ages, developed specialized attachments that make more rapid movement possible. These are microscopic hairlike structures to lash the water and move the cell. The attachments may be few and comparatively long, in which case they are called *flagella* (fla-jell'uh; "whip" L), the singular being *flagellum*. The attachments may also be many and short, in which case they are *cilia* (sil'ee-uh; "eyelash" L), the singular being *cilium*.

Although these forms of motion may strike us as being adapted particularly for primitive cells, the lordly multicellular creatures that have developed over the eons have not abandoned them. Consider man, for instance. There are cells in our blood that exhibit amoeboid movement, crawling about within us by the old gel-sol interchange. The human sperm cell makes its way toward the egg cell by means of the lashing of a single flagellum. (The fact that it is called a "tail" doesn't make it less a flagellum.) Finally, there are ciliated cells in the respiratory system and in the female reproductive system, the whipping cilia of the first serving to brush foreign matter out of the lungs, and those of the latter serving to brush the egg cell from the ovary to the uterus.

It would seem that the flowing-forward of sol in amoeboid movement is the result of a contraction of the gel in the rear. It is also contraction that may be the cause of the motion of cilia and flagella. Both cilia and flagella are composed of eleven fine filaments, nine of which form a circle about a central pair. One theory as to the cause of their motion is that the filaments first on one side of the center and then on the other contract, bending the whole structure back and forth.

The contraction involved in amoeboid movement and in the whipping of cilia is only conjecture so far, but it seems quite reasonable that this ability to contract a part of itself is a very basic property of the animal cell. After all, quite early in the evolution of multicellular life, certain cells were developed which dedicated their lives, so to speak, to contraction. Their contraction is visible and unmistakable, and it is reasonable to suppose that such a specialty is not created out of nothing, but that it represents the extension and exaggeration of a property already existing, in more dilute form, in cells generally.

MUSCLE CONTRACTION

Cells specializing in contraction make up those portions of the body we call *muscles,* and the individual cells are, therefore, *muscle cells.* The word "muscle," according to one theory, comes from a Latin word meaning "little mouse," because a man can make his muscles ripple in such a fashion as to make it look as though a little mouse were running about under his skin. This seems a bit fanciful; another theory, which I like better, has the word arising from a Greek expression meaning "to enclose," because layers of muscle enclose the body.

There are several types of muscle tissue in the human body, which can be distinguished in a number of ways. Under the microscope, for instance, certain muscles are seen to consist of fibers that have a striped, or striated, appearance, with alternate bands of lighter and darker material. These are *striated muscles.* Another type of muscle, lacking these bands, is the *unstriated muscles,* or *smooth muscles.* (There is also a type of muscle, not quite like either, that makes up the structure of the heart, but this I will consider in a later chapter.)

It is striated muscle that has been most carefully studied in fine detail. Under polarized light, the darker stripes refract light in different ways, according to the direction of the light beam. Whenever the property of some structure varies with direction, it is said to be *anisotropic* (an-eye'soh-trop'ik; "turning unequally" G), so the darker stripes are *anisotropic bands* or, simply, *A bands.* The lighter stripes do not change properties with direction and are *isotropic* ("turning equally" G), so that they make up the *I bands.* The A band is divided in two by a thin line called the *H disc* (this being short for *Hensen's disc,* named for Victor Hensen, a German anatomist of the 19th century). Down the middle of each I band is a dark line called the *Z line.* Using the electron microscope, it would seem that the A band consists of a series of wide filaments, and the I band consists of a series of thin filaments anchored to the Z line. When the muscle fiber is relaxed, the overlapping is not complete and adjacent I band filaments do not meet. It is the gap between the I band filaments that make up the H disc.

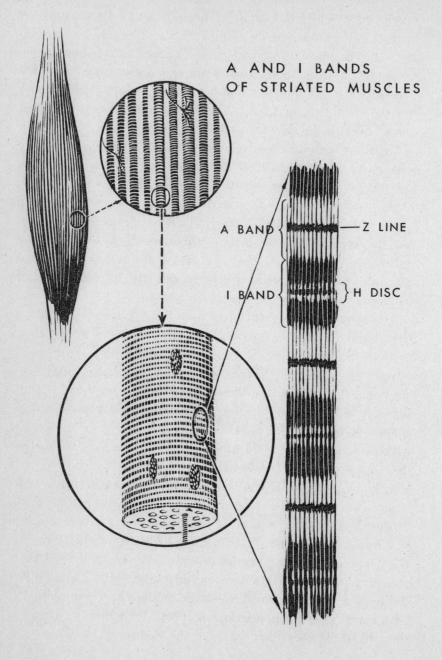

A AND I BANDS
OF STRIATED MUSCLES

A BAND — Z LINE

I BAND } H DISC

Now the stage is set for movement. A nerve impulse reaches the fiber and this sets into action a series of chemical changes that, among other things, liberate energy. Changes visible under the electron microscope make plain what happens as a result. The I band filaments inch toward each other, dragging the Z line anchor with them. The I bands meet each other between the A band filaments, wiping out the H disc.

The A band filaments remain essentially unchanged so that, to put it as simply as possible, the muscle fiber in relaxation is the full length of the dark bands plus light bands. In contraction, however, it is the length of the dark bands only.

What makes the I band filaments move as they do? This is not quite settled, but the most reasonable conjecture is that there are tiny extensions of the A band filaments which can connect at specific places with the I band filaments. The connection is at a backward angle and under the inflow of energy arising from the chemical changes induced by a nerve impulse, the bridge moves forward (through changes in intermolecular attractions, presumably) dragging the I band filaments together. The bridge then moves backward to a new connection, moves forward again, and repeats this process over and over.

It is this sort of ratchet arrangement which may account for the contraction of all muscles and consequently may explain virtually all the motions we are accustomed to witness in the animal world.

STRIATED MUSCLE

The striated muscles are organized for the purpose of quick and hard contraction. Toward this end the ratchet arrangements are multiplied and piled up until they become visible to the microscope-aided eye as bands of light and dark. Such muscles, designed for quick contraction, are most necessary for manipulating the bones of the skeleton, and the majority of them are attached to those bones for just that purpose. Those are the muscles involved in walking, jumping, grasping; in twisting the torso, nodding the head, expelling the breath, and so on. Because they are so involved with the skeleton, striated muscles are sometimes called *skeletal muscles*.

If such muscles are to be useful, they must react quickly to changes in the environment. A creature must be ready to move quickly at the sight of food or of an enemy, to maneuver without delay to accomplish whatever is needful. To put it as briefly as possible, such muscles must be activated through no more than an effort of will. This is so true that we can contract our muscles in such a way as to do ourselves harm if this is what we desire. Every deliberate suicide contracts muscles in such a way as to bring about the end of his own life, and though he may change his mind at any moment before the end, his muscles will not refuse to obey him if he doesn't change his mind. For this reason, striated muscles are also called *voluntary muscles*.

The smooth muscles, on the other hand, are poorer in the contracting filaments (poor enough to be unstriated, but, although they have not been well studied, it is assumed that they contract through the same mechanism striated muscles do). As a result, smooth muscles contract slowly and are restricted to organs where quick motion is not so vitally required. They are found making up the walls of the internal organs, such as those of the blood vessels, and the digestive tract. Since the internal organs are referred to as *viscera,* the smooth muscles are sometimes called *visceral muscles.*

The visceral muscles react relatively slowly to changes within the body and do so without the intervention of the will. The walls of the blood vessels contract or expand in response to certain chemicals in the blood or in response to the effects of temperature, but we cannot of ourselves deliberately cause them to do either in the same effortless way in which we lift our arm

or lick our lips. For this reason, smooth muscles are also called *involuntary muscles*.

On a cellular level, the differences are also meaningful. The individual cells of smooth muscle are cigar-shaped (they are usually described as spindle-shaped, but there are few people now alive who are intimately acquainted with spindles or know what they look like) and have but one nucleus. The striated muscles, on the other hand, are made up of cylindrical structures that differ from ordinary cells in having a number of nuclei placed here and there, as though a number of cells have been combined in order that the total force of contraction might be the greater and the better coordinated.

Muscle fibers contract on the "all-or-none principle." That is, a stimulus (which can be an electric current, the pressure of touch, the action of heat or of certain chemicals) either applied directly to the muscle or to the nerve that leads to it may be so weak that the muscle is not affected at all. If the stimulus is strengthened, a point is reached where the fiber responds, and it does this in the one way it knows — the complete contraction of which it is at that moment capable. There is no intermediate stimulus that will bring about an intermediate contraction. It is all or none.

This seems to be at variance with actual experience, for the muscle of our upper arm, to name the one with which we are most familiar (it is the one children contract to "make a muscle"), can be made to contract to any degree, from the barest twitch that just moves the lower arm a hairbreadth to a rapid and maximal flexure at the elbow.

This is no paradox but arises from the fact that an actual muscle is made up of many fibers which, to a certain extent, have the capacity for independent action. If only a few fibers of the muscle are activated, those few will contract all the way, but the net effect of those few "alls" against the background of the very many "nones" will result in only a slight total flexure. As more fibers respond to the stimulus, the overall contraction grows gradually greater.

The response of a fiber of striated muscle to a stimulus is quick and brief, lasting only a fraction of a second; only 1/40 of a second in some cases. This is followed by a quick relaxation. A single quick stimulus of this sort is called a "twitch" and does not normally occur in the body. More usual is the slower contraction of a whole muscle, or even its continued contraction over some reasonable period of time, this being produced and maintained by various fibers taking their turn at twitching. No one fiber is contracted for very long, but the muscle as a whole can be contracted for quite a while. It is, however, possible to induce a single twitch in a body muscle. The best example is the sharp blow under the knee which gives the familiar response of the "knee jerk."

It is possible to stimulate an isolated fiber so that it will respond by a series of twitches. If the stimuli are close enough together, each twitch will build on the one before it. That is, after one twitch, a muscle will not have time to relax completely before another twitch is called for. The second twitch, beginning at a state of greater tension, achieves a greater force, and the third twitch, hurrying on the heels of the second, a still greater one. By the time stimuli reach 50 per second the fiber is in a continuous tight contraction. This is called *tetany* (tet'uh-nee; "stretched" G — even though the muscle is contracted rather than stretched).

Tetany does not take place in the muscles of a well-organized body, but bodies are not always well organized. Even those capacities that are subject to our will can get out of control. Our body is a chemical machine and it remains obedient to us only when its chemistry is in order. As an example, the proper transmission of the nerve impulse to the muscle depends upon the proper concentration of certain metallic ions in the blood. One of these is calcium ion. If for any reason the calcium ion concentration sinks below a certain minimal level, the nerve starts to deliver rapid impulses and muscles respond by going into tetany. Death will follow if the condition is not relieved.

The calcium ion concentration in blood is well controlled by the body and is not likely to go wrong. Danger threatens more often from without. There is a bacterium called *Clostridium tetani* (klos-trid'ee-um; "spindle-shaped" G), which is all too common and can enter the body through any wound. It produces a *toxin* (anything poisonous may be called a "toxin" [from the Greek word for "arrow"] because of the old habit of poisoning arrow tips), which in turn causes muscles to go into tetany, with usually fatal results. The disease is called *tetanus* or, graphically and rather horribly, "lockjaw," because the earliest muscles affected are those of the jaws, which contract and lock firmly.

Tetanus was once one of the more deadly dangers that accompanied wounds that might not otherwise have been of much concern. Fortunately it has been found possible to treat the tetanus toxin chemically so as to alter it slightly and produce a *toxoid*. This toxoid will not induce tetany but will encourage the body to produce substances (*antibodies*) that will not only neutralize the molecules of toxoid but will also neutralize any molecules of the toxin itself that enter the body. In this way a series of well-spaced "shots" of tetanus toxoid will produce immunity to the disease. During World War II American soldiers were constantly being punctured to produce immunity to tetanus, and other diseases too, and although the procedure was the subject of many heartfelt jibes on the part of the victims of the needle, tetanus virtually disappeared. This is worth a needle.

Symptoms similar to that of tetanus, and with the same fatal result, are brought about by the drug *strychnine* (strik'nin; "deadly nightshade" G, the plant from which it is obtained). Exactly how either strychnine or the tetanus toxin produces its effect is not known.

Muscles will also stiffen and grow hard during the period from

12 to 36 hours after death, this being the *rigor mortis* ("death-stiffening" L) made famous by murder mysteries (which also did their bit in familiarizing the general public with strychnine). Rigor mortis is not due to a tetany but to the precipitation of ordinarily soluble proteins in muscle tissue. The effect is rather like that of hard-boiling an egg. As decomposition sets in, rigor mortis vanishes.

The price paid by skeletal muscle for its gifts of speed and force is fatigue. The chemical changes induced by nerve stimulation of muscle inevitably deplete the relatively small supply of energy-producing substances in the muscle cells. In one way or another these substances must be replaced as quickly as they are consumed, and this is usually done by means of other chemical reactions involving oxygen molecules brought to the muscle cells by the bloodstream, which in turn picks up those molecules at the lungs.

The visceral muscles, working slowly and in response to orderly changes in the internal environment, maintain a pace that matches their oxygen supply. They keep their energy-producing substances at the necessary level at all times and are immune to fatigue.

The skeletal muscles, however, are subject to levels of activity much higher than normal over extended periods of time. It might seem necessary, then, to see that the blood supply is correspondingly greater at all times "just in case," and yet it would be inefficient to design muscles for continuous work at ditch-digging level when most life activities are considerably less intense. Still, it is sometimes necessary to dig ditches or chop wood or run at top speed to escape a danger. For that matter, it sometimes seems desirable to play several sets of tennis. On such occasions, the body can adapt itself to the greater need for oxygen. Hard work or hard play results in an increase in both the rate and depth of breathing (we pant), and in the rapidity of the heartbeat (it pounds) and in the capacity of the blood vessels feeding the muscles (we flush). And yet survival may depend upon finding a way, at least temporarily, to go beyond all that lungs and heart and blood can do.

The muscle accomplishes this by obtaining a supply of energy (a limited supply, to be sure) at the expense of chemical changes that do not involve oxygen. In these chemical changes, a compound known as *lactic acid* is produced.* This dodge, which allows the muscle a possibly life-saving extra push, is not without its price. As lactic acid accumulates, it becomes more difficult for the muscle to contract, and the sensation we experience is that of fatigue. We slow down perforce, and eventually, even with life at stake, we must stop in utter exhaustion.

When fatigue stops us, we cannot recover entirely until the lactic acid is removed from the muscle. This requires oxygen — all the oxygen that would have been used up if the total effort expended had been at a rate slow enough for the oxygen-supplying capacity of the body to have kept up. We have incurred an "oxygen debt" that must be paid off. It is done by supplying the muscle with oxygen at top rate until the lactic acid is partially burned away and partially rebuilt into the original energy-producing substances. For this reason, we continue to pant and flush and our heart continues to pound for quite an interval after we have ceased our activity and crumpled exhausted onto the ground or into a chair.

Just as striated muscles are capable of harder and more intense work than visceral muscles and are therefore also capable of fatigue, so there are gradations among the striated muscles themselves. Those muscles designed for particularly quick and hard contraction are more easily fatigued than those not so designed. In general, the particularly quick and particularly easily fatigued muscles are paler in color than the slow but more enduring ones. The division is most plainly visible to us when we eat chicken or turkey. The breast muscles, intended for operating the

* See my book *Life and Energy* for the details.

wings and therefore designed for hard work, make up the "white meat." The leg muscles, intended for less intense work over longer-sustained intervals, make up the "dark meat."

In man, too, there are darker and lighter muscle fibers. When a man stands, the large muscles of the back are continually twitching him this way and that in order to maintain him in balance. (A two-legged stance is not very stable; when a man gets a trifle drunk, so that his muscular coordination is thrown off, it becomes all too easy for him to fall down.) These back muscles are of the dark slow-to-fatigue variety, and even though we eventually tire of standing we tire of digging much more quickly, let us say, where the quick-to-fatigue arm muscles come into play.

There is a long-term adaptation to the intense use of muscles which is designed to decrease the effect of fatigue. The muscle itself, under the stimulus of long continued use at strenuous levels (whether because of the necessity of physical labor or the whim of physical exercise), increases in size. This is called *hypertrophy* (hy-per'troh-fee; "growth beyond" G). The lumberjack or athlete has larger muscles than the storekeeper or file clerk and in those larger muscles can store greater supplies of energy-producing substances and find more room for lactic acid. Lungs of greater capacity and a heart of greater pumping force supply the large muscles with extra quantities of oxygen, and the result is to make possible greater force over more extended periods with less fatigue.

On the other hand, though lack of exercise keeps a muscle relatively weak and small, under ordinary conditions there is no danger that a muscle will lose its ability to function at reasonable levels, however sedentary a man's life. For one thing, the normal muscle maintains a weak contraction even when the body seems to be relaxing. This is called *muscle tone* and, in a sense, it means that we are constantly exercising.

Muscle tone serves to keep the individual muscles in greater

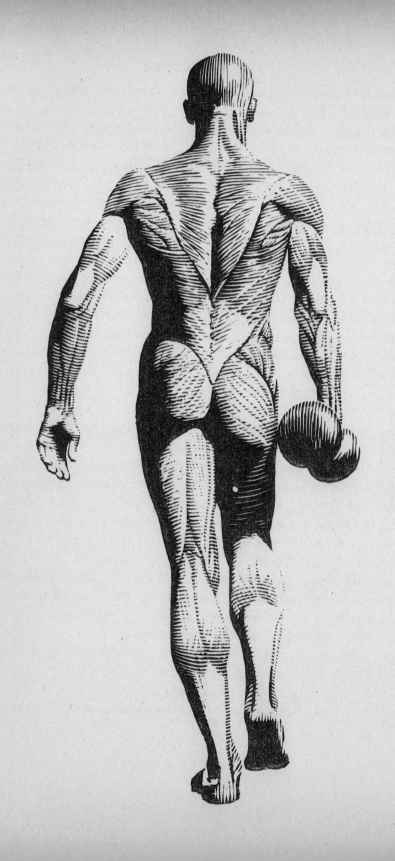

readiness for contraction at short notice. The muscles begin with a headstart, so to speak. People under nervous tension usually have a more intense muscle tone and require a smaller stimulus to set them off. For that reason, they twitch and are "jumpy." Nevertheless, the principle remains valuable, even if it can be overdone.

During sleep, muscle tone diminishes to minimal levels and muscles can experience periods of virtually complete relaxation; something they cannot experience during wakefulness. This imposed relaxation of muscle is undoubtedly one of the vital functions of sleep. It is one of the reasons why sleep is not only pleasant but is actually more necessary than food. (Sleeplessness is far worse torture than hunger, and a man will die for lack of sleep sooner than he will starve for lack of food.)

If muscle tone is removed permanently, as by cutting the nerve that leads to the muscle, then the muscle does indeed waste away. It undergoes *atrophy* (at'roh-fee; "no growth" G). If a nerve-destroying disease such as poliomyelitis paralyzes the legs, the leg muscles wither even though the rest of the body remains strong and well-developed.

The visceral muscles, on the other hand, retain their tone and therefore their usefulness even without nerve stimulation, so that they are not affected by polio. In fact, the greatest immediate danger of the disease is that it will paralyze the muscles that act to move the rib cage up and down. These muscles are striated and make breathing possible. When these are paralyzed, an "iron lung" becomes necessary; when a patient is in one, changes in air pressure will do for him what the muscles of the chest do for one not so unfortunate.

TENDONS

The muscles most familiar to us are those of the arms and legs, since we use our limbs freely and the muscles involved change

shape visibly in the course of limb movements. Consider the muscle of the upper
arm: it is thick in the middle (the "belly"
of the muscle) and narrows as it approaches
the bone. It stretches across the elbow joint
and is attached to each of the two bones
(the humerus and the radius, in this case)
meeting at that joint. When this muscle, or
any similar one, contracts, one of the bones
to which it is joined remains virtually stationary as a result of the steadying action of
other muscles ("fixation muscles") joined to
that bone. The point of junction of the
muscle with the stationary bone is the *origin*
of that muscle. When the muscle contracts,
then, it is the second bone that moves, pivot-
ing about the joint to approach the first
bone. The attachment of the muscle to
the bone that moves is its *insertion*.

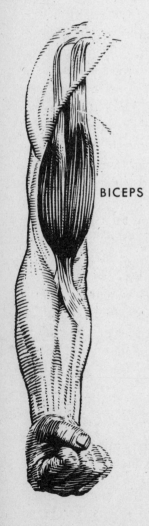

BICEPS

There can be more than one origin, as
is actually the case with the muscle of the
upper arm, where one origin is at the upper
end of the humerus near the shoulder joint,
and a second origin reaches above to the
scapula. This muscle is an example of a
biceps ("two heads" L) and is sometimes
called just that. Actually it is not the only
muscle with two origins so that its proper
name is *biceps brachii* (by'seps bray'kee-
eye; "two-heads of the arm" L). The insertion of the biceps brachii is at the upper
end of the radius near the elbow. When the
biceps brachii contracts, the humerus remains
motionless and the radius moves toward it.

The arm bends at the elbow in the familiar "making a muscle" gesture, and the "muscle" that is made is the contracted, thickened, and hardened belly of the biceps brachii.

Toward the point of insertion, a muscle usually narrows down to a strong tough cord of connective tissue, formed through a combination of the thin sheath of connective tissue surrounding each muscle fiber. This cord, attaching the muscle to the bone, is a *sinew* (AS), or *tendon* ("to stretch" G; because it stretches tightly from muscle to bone). Tendons are surprisingly strong, and in laboratory testing they have withstood a pull of as much as 9 tons per square inch before breaking. It can happen that in a violent muscular spasm the bone to which the muscle is attached will break sooner than the tendon connecting the muscle to the bone. To be specific: you can feel the tendon connecting the biceps brachii to the radius if you bend your arm into a right angle at the elbow and put your fingers at the inner angle of the joint.

Tendons serve to concentrate the full force of the muscle upon one spot on the bone. Naturally there are times when a group of bones must be moved and then the tendon must broaden and flatten out. For example, there is a muscle called *palmaris longus* (pal-may′ris long′gus; "long muscle of the palm" L) which has its origin at the humerus of the upper arm and its insertion at the *palmar fascia.* The term fascia (fash′ee-uh; "band" L) refers to sheets of fibrous tissue encircling the body under the skin and enclosing muscles and groups of muscles. The palmar fascia would be the section of that fibrous tissue which underlays the skin of the palm.

The action of the palmaris longus is to flex the wrist. If you hold your hand before you, palm upward, you will be making use of that muscle when you bend the wrist so that the palm faces you. If this muscle had an ordinary tendon attached at some particular point at the palmar fascia, tension would be greatest at that point and the relatively broad palm would be under uneven stress. For that reason, the tendon expands into a widening flat sheet that attaches across the width of the palm. Such a wide, flat tendon is called an *aponeurosis* (ap'oh-nyoo-roh'sis; "from a tendon," because before the point at which it begins to widen the tendon is of the ordinary shape).

Tendons also serve to allow action at a distance, so to speak, when it is impractical to have muscles themselves on the spot. Thus, the usefulness of the fingers lies in their slim maneuverability, and if you feel them they seem little more than skin and bone. If muscles were present in their structure, they would have to be built more thickly and softly and would lose much of their value. The muscles that do move them lie in the lower arm and palm. These possess tendons which run down the length of the fingers. The fingers are then flexed on the same principle that a puppet-master maneuvers his marionettes: by tightening strings. If you tense your fingers, claw fashion, you can feel tendons just under the skin of the back of your hands. You can see them, too, sometimes, especially where they pass over the knuckles. Similar tendons run across the top of the foot and along the toes.

As an example of a particularly long and stout tendon, consider the one attached to the large muscle in the back of the lower leg; you can feel it just below the knee. The lower leg bellies out at that point, and, as a matter of fact, the name of the muscle is *gastrocnemius* (gas'trok-nee'mee-us; "belly of the leg" G). It is commonly called the "calf muscle."

The muscle has two heads, both of them having their origin at the femur just above the knee. In the other direction it reaches down only to the middle of the lower leg (as you can see for yourself, if you tense it and look). Below is a long stout tendon with its point of insertion at the calcaneus, the bone of the heel. This tendon is called *tendo calcaneus* (ten'doh kal-kay'nee-us; "heel tendon" L) but a more common name is the "Achilles tendon." In Greek mythology, as you probably know, the warrior Achilles was dipped into the river Styx by his mother when he

was an infant. He was invulnerable
to weapons as a result. However, his
mother had held him by one heel as
she immersed him and had forgotten
to dip the heel separately afterward.
The result was that his heel remained
unprotected and Achilles was eventually killed by a poisoned arrow in the
heel — and left his name upon the
tendon.

The existence of the Achilles tendon means that although the calf is
powerfully muscled, the shin, ankles,
and feet are slim. In the case of certain animals designed for running,
such as horses, deer, and antelope,
the lower portion of the leg (corresponding to our ankle and foot) is
greatly lengthened. That section, as
in ourselves, remains without large
muscles. If you look at a horse you
will see that powerful muscles are
bunched at the top of the limb near
the torso, whereas the legs themselves,
equipped with tendons, are slim.
This is important in connection
with their ability to develop speed
— a small contraction of the distant muscle will swing the thin,
light leg through a large arc.

Another term for the tendo calcaneus of such animals is "hamstring,"
since it is the string (tendon) that
connects the lower portion of the

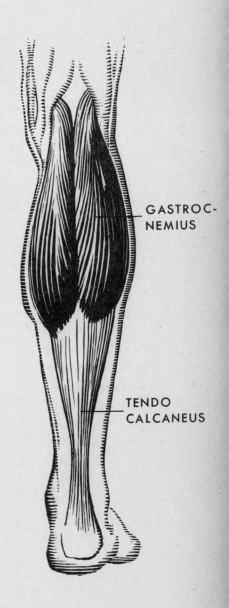

GASTROC-
NEMIUS

TENDO
CALCANEUS

limb with the uppermost portion, or "ham." The action of those upper muscles is essential to walking, and to cut the hamstring of an animal is to cripple it.

In man, the tendo calcaneus connects the heel to the calf of the leg and not to the ham (or back of the thigh). You can, nevertheless, feel two tendons behind your knee, one on either side, which represent the insertions into the tibia and fibula of several muscles running down the back of the thigh. These muscles bend the leg at the knee and it is these tendons that represent the hamstrings in man.

MUSCLES IN ACTION

The one function of a muscle is to contract. When it has finished contracting, it will do nothing further but simply relax. It cannot counteract or undo its earlier action. To give an example, if you contract your biceps, your arm will bend at the elbow. If you arrange your arm in such a way that the lower arm lies above and rests upon the upper, as a result of biceps contraction, and then relax the biceps, the lower arm will continue to lie there limply. If you shifted your upper arm properly, the force of gravity would pull your lower arm downward and your arm would then dangle, extended. But how could you extend your arm against gravity (as you can) if relaxing the biceps doesn't do it?

The answer lies in the existence of a second muscle whose contraction serves to produce a motion contrary to that of the biceps. Opposite the biceps is a second muscle called the *triceps brachii* ("three-headed arm muscle" L). It is so named because it has three origins, two on the humerus and one on the scapula. Its point of insertion is on the ulna, on the side opposite that of the point of insertion of the biceps.

When the triceps contracts, the lower arm, if bent to begin

with through biceps action, is straightened out. In fact, the bending of the arm is not the result of the action of either muscle on its own but is the well integrated action of both muscles simultaneously. The force of one muscle can be played out very slowly and smoothly by having the other muscle almost neutralize its force, but not quite. (It is like lowering a piano by a rope over a pulley system. The action of gravity alone would be disastrous, but by neutralizing most of the gravitational attraction through the counterforce applied by a man or group of men, the descent is made smooth.)

You can even contract the biceps strongly without moving the arm at all, if the triceps matches the pull evenly. Hold your lower arm at right angles to the upper and harden the biceps without moving your arm. You will feel the triceps on the other side of the humerus harden as well.

Muscles are always arranged at least in pairs, and usually in even more complex coordinating groups, so that one muscle or group of muscles will balance another. If there is a series of tendons acting to bend the fingers, a companion series on the other side of the fingers can act to straighten them.

Sometimes we can rely on gravity to undo the work of a muscle. One of the functions of the large gastrocnemius of the calf is to raise us on tiptoe. No equally large muscle on the other side of the tibia is required to bring us down from our tiptoe position.

TRICEPS

Gravity will serve the purpose. It is for this reason that the front part of the leg is relatively unmuscled and we can feel the tibia just under the skin all the way down.

The bones and the muscles attached to them act as a lever system. The simplest form of a lever is the seesaw, in which the fulcrum is at the center of the lever and two approximately equal weights (in the form, usually, of little boys or girls) are at either end. The only purpose is to change the direction of the force, so that when one child moves down the other moves up, and all that is accomplished is amusement.

More usefully, the fulcrum can be placed near one end of the lever, which is thus divided into a short shaft and a long one. A relatively small push downward at the end of the long shaft will then lift a relatively large weight upward at the end of the short shaft. Actually, the balance is such that the product of the force and the shaft length is the same at either end. If, for example, the long shaft is ten times as long as the short one, then a one-pound push downward at the long end will lift a ten-pound weight at the short end.

This seems a cheap way to lift ten pounds, but of course there is a price for everything. The payment one makes shows up in the distance through which the force must be exerted. If the one-pound push is carried downward through ten inches, the ten-pound weight is lifted upward only one inch. What is gained in force is lost in distance, and the total work (which is force times distance) is the same on both sides.

The lever, then, does not increase the work capacity but merely trades distance for force. When it is necessary to lift a heavy weight with a force inadequate for the task if applied directly, then a lever of the sort described is just the thing.

It is also possible for the fulcrum to be at one end of the lever and for both the force and weight to be on the same side rather than on opposite sides. If the weight is nearer the fulcrum than the force is, the situation remains the same. The force is smaller than the weight but must move through a greater distance.

Suppose that you want to stand on tiptoe. The gastrocnemius contracts and pulls your heel upward. The ball of the foot acts as a fulcrum, and the weight of the body is centered about half-way between the ball of the foot and the heel. If the weight of the body is 150 pounds, the gastrocnemius need only pull with a force of 75 pounds. To be sure, it has to lift the heel three inches to raise the body one and a half, but that might seem worth it to save 75 pounds of pull.

And yet it is not always desirable to multiply distance to save force. It is easy to imagine a "reverse-lever" which deliberately multiplies force. Such a lever would have a weight at the end of the long shaft with the force at the end of a short shaft. If the long shaft were ten times the length of the short one, we would have to push downward with a force of ten pounds in order to lift a weight of one pound.

This might seem a ridiculous arrangement, but we gain something too. The one-pound weight at the end of the long shaft moves up ten inches for every inch we push the end of the short shaft downward. Suppose that we tie a heavy weight to the end of the short shaft, a weight almost large enough to balance the small weight at the end of the long shaft. Now we add our own weight to the short shaft, so that the weight at the end of the long shaft lifts through a long arc, at a faster rate than we could move it by the direct application of force. We expend force to gain distance and we have a catapult. The same is true if the weight and force are on the same side of the fulcrum but with the weight farther from the fulcrum than the force is.

Consider the biceps again. When it contracts, it pulls up your lower arm. The bones of the lower arm form a lever with the fulcrum at the elbow. The biceps is attached to the radius about one quarter of the way from the elbow to the palm, so that the force to lift the arm is being applied perhaps three inches from the elbow-fulcrum. The weight that must be lifted, however, is in the palm about twelve inches from the fulcrum. For every pound placed in your palm which you must lift, the biceps must exert a force of four pounds. However, it need only contract one inch to lift the weight four inches, and by multiplying the force, it lends the hand a catapult-like action that makes it possible to develop considerable speed of motion.

It is by such catapult-like actions that a baseball pitcher can throw a fast ball, and horses can move their legs fast enough to race as they do.

The amount of force that can be exerted by muscle is quite astonishing. When you rise from a squatting position, the muscles straightening the knee must exert about ten pounds of force for every pound of weight lifted. Any man who can lift a 200-pound weight on his back (and this is not too hard for a good-sized man in trim condition), exerts a force of 2000 pounds as he straightens his legs, half a ton on each leg.

SOME INDIVIDUAL MUSCLES

Muscles make up about 40 per cent of the weight of a man and about 30 per cent of the weight of a woman. An average man, in other words, will have nearly 60 pounds of muscle and an average woman will have nearly 35 pounds of muscle. (This disparity in muscle weight is explanation enough for the fact that men are more powerful than women — at least in the brute-strength department.) This heavy weight of muscle is necessary in any creature that engages in rapid motion; but in the course of vertebrate evolution, there has been a profound change in muscle distribution, if not in muscle quantity.

Fish move through water by lateral movements of the body, with the tail slapping against the water from either side. The limbs are small and are used merely as balancing and turning organs rather than for propulsion. As a result, it is the musculature of the trunk that is important, and when we eat fish it is the trunk muscles we consume. (That would give us the chance to notice that those trunk muscles are clearly segmented.)

On land the chief means of propulsion is the push of the limbs against the ground, or, in the case of the birds, against the air. Consequently, the musculature of the limbs becomes important and the muscles of the trunk fade out. When we eat meat taken from birds and mammals, it is the limb musculature that we mainly consume, and this is not segmented.

It would be quite tedious to try to list all the muscles in the human body; there are some 650 of them (almost all in pairs), with complicated interrelationships. Nevertheless, it would be helpful to mention a few of the more noticeable muscles.

Starting at the head, there is the *masseter* (ma-see′tur; "chewer" G), which has its origin in the cheekbone and its insertion in the angle of the lower jaw. As the name implies, it is a muscle used in the chewing of food. You can feel it bunch just outside the teeth when you clench your jaw.

Among the many muscles that govern the motions of the head are the *trapezius* (tra-pee′zee-us; "four-sided" G) and the *sternocleidomastoid* (ster′noh-kly′doh-mas′toid; "sternum-clavicle-breast" L, so called because of the bones to which it is attached). The former runs down the back of the neck and pulls the head back, while the latter runs down the side of the neck and pulls the head to the side. Underneath the sternocleidomastoid is the *splenius* (splee′nee-us; "bandage" G, because of its appearance), which turns the head in a *no* gesture.

The muscle of the upper arm just under the outermost edge of the shoulder is the *deltoid* ("delta-shaped" G, which means "triangular" because the Greek capital-letter delta has the shape of a triangle). It has its origin in the clavicle and scapula and its insertion in the humerus. It is used to raise the arm away from the body. You can feel it harden when you do so.

Opposing the action of the deltoid is the *pectoral* ("breast" G), which underlies the skin of either breast. It has its origin along the clavicle and sternum, and its insertion is also in the humerus. It draws the arm in toward the body, and if you perform this action you will (if you are male) feel the muscle beneath the skin of the breast harden.

Running down the rib cage is a whole series of *intercostal muscles* ("between the ribs" L) stretching, as the name implies, from one rib to its neighbor. Their function is to expand and contract the rib cage in the course of breathing, and of all the muscles they most clearly show the segmentation common to all vertebrates.

Below the ribs is the abdomen, the largest area of the body to be unprotected by bone. In the average tetrapod this is not serious, for the abdomen is underneath and is the least exposed portion of the body; but in standing upright man has moved the tetrapod's "soft underbelly" into a position of vulnerability. It is vulnerable not only to enemy action but also in the sense that his internal design has worsened.

In the ordinary tetrapod posture the muscles of the abdomen acted as a floor for the intestines and other organs of the interior, and for this purpose it was well designed, with some hundreds of millions of years of evolutionary development behind it. When man rose on his hind legs, the floor became a wall (it is frequently called the "abdominal wall") and for that it is not so well designed. Unless the muscles are kept firm by constant exercise they will bulge flabbily outward and give rise to the unsightly (but very common) potbelly.

Among the muscles of the abdominal wall is the *rectus abdominis* (rek'tus ab-dom'i-nis; "upright of the abdomen" L), which runs from the pubis up to the middle ribs on either side of the midplane of the body. Between these two vertical muscles, a fibrous band runs the whole length of the abdomen, crossing the navel and marking the midplane of the body. It is the *linea alba* (lin'ee-uh al'buh; "white line" L). In lean and muscular men the linea alba can be seen as a shallow, vertical furrow, with the rectus abdominis bulging slightly on either side.

The *transversus abdominis* ("crosswise of the abdomen") runs under the rectus abdominis and at right angles to it, extending from the linea alba around either side of the body. The *obliquus externus abdominis* (ob-ly'kwus eks-ter'nus; "outer oblique of the abdomen") also lines the sides and flanks.

These muscles and others by no means make up an impervious wall. There is constant danger, made worse by man's upright posture and the consequent poor distribution of his internal organs, that a portion of those organs may come to protrude through some weakened section of the wall. The section may be weak congenitally or it may have weakened over the years. Some abnormal strain (lifting a heavy weight, or perhaps a convulsive cough) may finally bring on this situation, which is called a *rupture* (that is, of the integrity of the abdominal wall) or *hernia* ("rupture" L). Hernias usually involve protrusions of sections of intestine, and, although there are a number of possible locations, about 85 per cent are in the groin. These are the *inguinal hernias* (ing'gwin-ul; "groin" L).

At the hip are several large muscles. Among them are the *gluteus medius* (gloo'tee-us mee'dee-us; "middle of the buttock" L) and *gluteus maximus* ("largest of the buttock" L). Both muscles have their origin in the ilium and their point of insertion in the femur. The gluteus medius may be felt on the sides, just under the upper curve of the hipbone, and the gluteus maximus makes up the muscular bulk of the buttocks themselves. You can feel it harden when you pinch your buttocks together.

The gluteus medius has the ability to draw the thigh away from the midplane of the body. The gluteus maximus pulls the thigh into a straight line with the trunk. In other words, when you are sitting down and contract the gluteus maximus (upon which you are sitting), you stand up.

I have mentioned the gastrocnemius as one large muscle of the leg. Another, and even larger one is the *rectus femorus* (rek'tus fem'uh-rus; "upright of the thigh" L), a vertical muscle running from the ilium to the patella and tibia, down the front of the entire length of the thigh. It straightens the leg at the knee when it contracts.

The limbs are essentially solid objects — layers of muscle built about central shafts of bone. The torso, on the contrary, is differently planned. The bone structure is not central but is at the edges. The vertebral column runs along the dorsal edge, the ribs curve about the sides, and the sternum is at the ventral edge. The pectoral girdle bounds the anterior edge and the pelvic girdle the posterior. The muscles attached to those bones also confine themselves to the edges of the torso, filling the space between the bones and producing the abdominal wall as a further boundary at the ventral edge.

Within this muscle-and-bone enclosure is a space in which are to be found the internal organs of the body. In mammals, and in mammals only, the internal space is divided into two parts by a thin partition composed of muscle and tendon and called the *diaphragm* ("partition off" G). It is attached to the sternum in front, to the lower ribs along the sides, and to the vertebral column behind. It bellies upward in its middle stretch so that it divides the body space into a smaller superior cavity and a larger inferior one. The superior cavity is the *thorax* ("chest" G), the inferior one is the *abdomen.* As we shall see, the chief contents of the thoracic cavity are the lungs and heart; the chief contents of the abdominal cavity are the intestines, kidneys, and genital organs.

The diaphragm is not a hermetically sealed partition. A number of blood vessels, nerves, and even a portion of the digestive tract must cross it. It can also give way abnormally, so that abdominal organs may protrude through a weakened section to form a "diaphragmatic hernia."

Not all striated muscles, although called skeletal muscles, are attached to the skeleton. Some are attached to the fascia under the skin. The horse has many such muscles over its body, as we can see when we watch it shake the skin here and there in order to drive away insects. We have lost the capacity for this, but we still retain the use of many muscles under the skin of the face — to an extent more marked than in other animals. It is these facial muscles that make it possible for us to smile, frown, purse our lips, wrinkle our nose, and give our face all the mobile expressivity it has.

We even have small muscles originally intended to move the ear. In creatures such as dogs and horses, these are most useful in directing the outer trumpetlike portion of the ear in the direction of some sound. Our ears are no longer trumpets, and most men cannot use the ear muscles. There are individuals, however, who retain enough of their use to be able to wiggle their ears, an accomplishment that inspires unfailing admiration among those of us who can't.

Structures such as the muscles of the ear or, for that matter, the bones of the coccyx, which represent organs useful to our long-dead ancestors (with trumpet-shaped ears and long tails) but useless to us, are *vestigial organs* (ves-tij'ee-ul; "footprint" L). Like footprints, they indicate that something must once have passed that way.

5

OUR LUNGS

THE ENTRANCE OF OXYGEN

Muscle contraction, and almost all other life processes as well, are energy-consuming. The source of the energy lies in the chemical reactions that go on within the cells, and of these the most important, from the standpoint of energy, are those involving oxygen.

To be sure, current theories as to the origin of life strongly suggest that, to begin with, there was little or no free oxygen available for living organisms on this planet. However, the development of green plants introduced the process of photosynthesis, which uses the energy of solar radiation to break up water into hydrogen and oxygen. The hydrogen is used to convert carbon dioxide first into carbohydrates and then into all the other organic components of living tissue. The oxygen is liberated into the atmosphere and, after the green plants multiplied and covered the face of the earth, the atmosphere slowly filled with oxygen.

For at least a billion years, then, the earth's atmosphere has contained a considerable proportion of free oxygen (it is 21 per cent oxygen now). Cells have drawn on it freely during all that time, combining it with foodstuffs to produce energy, while green plants have continued to use solar energy to restore oxygen to the air. The result is a neat balance, which, we trust, will continue on into the indefinite future.

Of course, we think of oxygen mainly as a component of the atmosphere, but that is partly because we ourselves are land creatures living at the bottom of the air ocean and directly dependent on its oxygen content. From the standpoint of breathing, we think of water merely as something to drown in. Yet during most of the span of life upon this planet, the land surfaces were barren and even today not more than 15 per cent of the mass of living organisms dwells on land. All living organisms, not many hundreds of millions of years ago, and most living organisms even now, live in the sea and make no direct use of the oxygen of the atmosphere.

But the creatures of the sea are as dependent upon oxygen as we are. The fact that they live immersed in water means that they obtain oxygen out of the natural waters of the earth by methods for which they are designed and we are not.

Oxygen will dissolve in water. A liter of pure cold water will hold nearly 5 milliliters* of oxygen. Ocean water, which is not pure water, but contains $3\frac{1}{2}$ per cent dissolved solids, can do somewhat better and will hold 9 milliliters of oxygen per liter (0.8 per cent by volume); which through all the vast ocean comes to 10,000,000,000,000,000,000 liters of oxygen. Upon this dissolved oxygen the life of the ocean depends. In water from which the dissolved oxygen has been removed, a fish will drown as easily and as quickly as a man.

The first problem that faces any organism, as far as oxygen is concerned, is getting it out of the environment and into the cell. The cell membrane is semipermeable; that is, it will act to let

---

* A liter is equal to about 1.05 quarts. A milliliter is a thousandth of a liter. These are units of the metric system, used by all civilized nations except Great Britain, the United States, Canada, Australia, New Zealand, and South Africa. Even in these "English-speaking nations" scientists use the metric system in their work. If you are not familiar with the metric system, and want to be, you might try my book *The Realm of Measure* (1960).

some substances through and others not; it will even allow some substances through in one direction but not in the other. It is freely permeable in either direction, however, to most very small molecules which can be pictured as having no difficulty in slipping through the submicroscopic pores of the membrane. One of the small molecules with this privilege is the oxygen molecule; it *diffuses* ("pour out" L) across the membrane freely. But it diffuses freely in either direction, so it may seem that we have gained nothing. Surely for every oxygen molecule that pops into the cell one from the cell's interior pops out. This might well be the case if the oxygen remained oxygen within the cell.

However, any oxygen that diffuses into the cell is at once combined with the substances within the cell. The oxygen becomes part of molecules incapable of passing through the membrane and is thus trapped. None will diffuse outward. The result is that oxygen travels in one direction only: from the outer environment into the cell.

In general, whenever a substance moves from position A to position B and vice versa, the overall drift is from the point of high concentration to that of low. The difference in concentrations is the *concentration gradient*, and the higher the gradient, the more rapid the overall drift. In this particular case, oxygen travels from the environment where, in the case of the sea, it makes up 0.8 per cent of the volume, into the interior of the cell, where its concentration as free molecular oxygen is virtually zero.

All this is very well, of course, for organisms that consist of a single cell or of a relatively small number of cells, for then the membrane of each cell has environment on one side and protoplasm on the other and diffusion can be depended upon to maintain an adequate oxygen inflow. When we consider fairly large organisms new problems arise. The larger an organism, the larger the proportion of cells located well inside its structure and separated from direct contact with the environment by layers of other cells. The danger of oxygen starvation becomes more serious.

To put it another way, I cite what is called the "square-cube law": if an organism increases in dimensions but retains its shape, its surface will increase as the square of its length, while its volume increases as the cube of its length. To show what that means as simply as possible, let's suppose that a creature one centimeter long has a surface of one square centimeter and a volume of one cubic centimeter. A similar creature two centimeters long would have a surface of 2 times 2 or four square centimeters, but it would have a volume of 2 times 2 times 2 or eight cubic centimeters. We can set up a small table that will make it even plainer:

Length:	1	2	3	4	5	6	7
Area:	1	4	9	16	25	36	49
Volume:	1	8	27	64	125	216	343

The rate at which oxygen will diffuse into the cell depends upon the amount of surface exposed to its passage. But the number of cells that the oxygen must supply depends on the volume of the organism. If a square centimeter of surface can just barely supply a cubic centimeter of volume with the needful oxygen, then 49 square centimeters of surface will just barely supply 49 cubic centimeters of volume. If 49 square centimeters of surface are required to supply the necessary oxygen for 343 cubic centimeters of surface, the creature depending upon the fulfillment of such a requirement will die.

One solution is for an organism to change shape; to become longer and flatter, so that more surface is exposed per unit volume. After a certain point is reached, however, this produces new problems of its own, for the long thin creature becomes ungainly.

A better and more efficient solution is to specialize at least a portion of the body for the task of oxygen absorption. Oxygen would be absorbed at a greater rate and this in turn would make it possible for a given surface area to support a larger volume. The remainder of the creature's external surface can then divorce itself altogether from the task of gathering oxygen and can be made impermeable; it can be coated with horny scales, bony armor, stony shells.

To maintain a high rate of absorption of oxygen through the specialized area, it is also necessary to drive a current of water past it. Where water is stagnant, the concentration of oxygen in the water layers near the absorption area decreases as oxygen passes from those layers with the cell. This lowers the concentration gradient and the inflow of oxygen slows. If, however, the water layers next to the absorption area constantly change, the concentration gradient remains high at all times.

Thus the chordates made use of a scheme in which water was drawn in through the mouth and out through slits behind the head. On the way, the current of oxygen-rich water passed across membranes that presented a great deal of thin surface through which oxygen could be absorbed with special ease. These membranes are gills and the slits through which the water emerges are the gill slits. Between the gill slits are the skeletal supports called the gill bars. In sharks, the gill slits are separate and can be clearly seen as vertical clefts just behind the head on either side. In bony fish, there is a *gill cover* over the slits, with an opening behind.

Early in the game an auxiliary means of absorbing oxygen came into play. A buoyancy device is useful to any creature living under the surface of the sea. If a fish is heavier than water, he tends to sink and must work continuously and frantically to keep from doing so. If it were lighter than water, he would tend to rise and would have to work just as continuously and frantically to keep from doing that. It would be most useful if there were some way in which it could adjust its own density so that it could sink, rise or stay put with a minimum of muscular effort.

One answer lay in the development of an internal gas-filled *air bladder* or *swim bladder*. By increasing the gas volume within the bladder, the fish's overall density is decreased; while by decreasing the gas volume, its overall density is increased. The swim bladder opens into the throat region, so the simplest way of adjusting the gas supply in it is for a fish to stick its mouth out of water and swallow some air or discharge some.

But this raises an interesting possibility. The swim bladder is lined with a moist membrane and some of the oxygen in the gulped air will dissolve in the moisture. Such dissolved oxygen will unavoidably diffuse into the cells with which it is in contact and you have what can be called a "lung." This can be tremendously useful. If a fish is living in a body of water which for one reason or another is brackish and low in dissolved oxygen, any additional oxygen that the creature can gain by gulping air and absorbing it through the swim bladder is so much manna. In fact, there is good reason to believe that the bony fish developed in fresh water first, which proved often brackish, and that the swim bladder first became useful as a lung, and only secondarily came to serve as a buoyancy control.

Later fish, which migrated to the oxygen-rich oceans, converted the primitive lung into a pure swim bladder and used it for no other purpose. At least most of them did. Nevertheless, some fish which continued to live in brackish water retained and even refined the lung. There are several species of "lungfish" living today in Africa, Australia, and South America which can live in foul, muddy water, and even survive for considerable periods in dried mud, by switching from gills to lungs.

About 300,000,000 years ago certain varieties of lung-breathing fish developed into amphibia and during adult life at least abandoned gills altogether. The lungs of the amphibia were rather primitive devices, in comparison with those that developed later among their more advanced descendants. This can be seen plainly in the case of modern amphibia: the adult frog, although using his lung, still absorbs much oxygen directly through the skin — which represents, actually, a step backward.

THE NOSE AND THROAT

Above the mouth in fish is a pair of pits lined with cells equipped to test the chemical content of the water in which it is swimming. (We also possess the same type of cells and we call the sensations to which they give rise "smell.") Among some of the higher fish the nostrils extend backward and open into the rear of the mouth. In this way, food placed in the mouth can be both tasted and smelled, a sense combination more effective than either alone. This situation has persisted in all tetrapods, including ourselves, and what we think of as taste is in fact almost all smell. This proves itself whenever a cold blocks our air passages to the point where the sense of smell is lost. The sense of taste shrinks to almost nothing and meals become a woeful affair.

Once the connection is made between the pits and the mouth, it becomes possible to breathe with the mouth closed. Whereas fish must open and close their mouths constantly to drive water past the gills, a frog breathes with its wide lips closed.

The frog uses the bottom of its mouth as a pump. That area bulges downward and sucks air into its lungs via what were once mere smelling pits; and it squeezes upward to force the air out again. Reptiles and mammals use a more efficient pumping mechanism because they possess ribs, which modern amphibians do not. When the intercostal muscles lift and expand the rib cage, a partial vacuum is created within the chest and air enters from the outside. This is *inspiration* ("breathe in" L). Another set of intercostal muscles then contracts the rib cage, forcing air in an *expiration* ("breathe out" L). Both processes, repeated alternately over and over again, together are *respiration* ("breathe again" L).

In mammals, still another refinement is added in the form of the diaphragm. When the rib cage lifts in mammals, the dome-shaped diaphragm flattens out, further increasing the volume of the chest and hastening the influx of air. When the rib cage presses downward, the diaphragm bulges upward, helping to squeeze out the air.

As in the case of the frog, we can breathe with our mouth closed, the air entering the lungs through that prominent feature in the middle of the face, the *nose* (AS). It enters through twin openings in the nose, each of these being a *nostril* (AS). The nostril actually is an opening drilled into the nose, so to speak, a "nose-drill" — and that is the old meaning of the word. The Latin term for the nostrils is *nares* (nay′reez).

If the nose were nothing more than a mere air vent, there would seem no need for elaborating its structure. Thus, in whales, where it is no more than an air vent, it consists of a single opening (in some species, a double one) set flush with the top of the head, where it can be used for rapid emptying and refilling of the lungs. As far as breathing is concerned, a whale has no time for frills. Speed is of the essence, and his nasal vent, or vents, is called, dramatically, a "blowhole."

On the other hand, the patterns of life are versatile enough to turn any organ to subsidiary and sometimes surprising uses. A nose can thicken and swell, as in pigs, to become a rooting device. Or it can take on fleshy outgrowths, as in some moles, in order that it may form a delicate organ of touch to substitute for eyes in the dark underground. The nose may even vastly lengthen to become an organ of manipulation, as in the elephant, and become second in versatility and delicacy only to the primate hand.

In man, a compromise has been struck. The nose is still primarily an air vent and has no exotic uses. It nevertheless has a more complex structure than does the whale's simple blowhole; with us breathing is not the emergency it is with the whale. Our lungs can be filled in more leisurely fashion and our nasal passages are lengthened, narrowed, and made more complex in order that air might not only be allowed entrance but that it might be conditioned — moistened and warmed — on its way.

As a result of this lengthening of the passages, the nose forms a definite projection in the midface region. (The nose is one of the more variable of human features, and it contributes a great deal to fixing the general impression a face makes upon us.) Projecting as it does, the nose is in an exposed position, where it can be easily battered and broken by the buffets of the outer world. The septum dividing the nostrils (which ideally marks out an equal division) can be deformed so that a "deviated septum" will result. One or the other of the nasal cavities is narrowed and this can make breathing a bit more difficult.

Our own system of air-conditioning begins at the very entrance to the nostrils. The skin within the opening of the nostrils is hairy, as we can easily see for ourselves, and these hairs serve to strain out any coarse particles, small bugs or other impurities that may be swept in with the air flow. In adult males the hair on the upper lip might serve as an additional safeguard, but this cannot be very important, for women and children (to say nothing of clean-shaven men) lack the mustache and yet do not seem to suffer as a result.

Deeper within the nose subtler devices are used. The air passage takes on a horizontal direction and runs beneath the floor of the cranium in the direction of the throat. Along this horizontal portion of the passage are three bony projections, roughly horizontal and parallel to each other. They are rather intricate in shape and curve sufficiently to remind anatomists of seashells. They are examples of *turbinated bones* ("whirl" L) and are sometimes called simply *turbinates*. More dramatically, they are the *nasal conchae* (kon'kee; "seashell" L). The turbinates divide the air passageways on either side of the nose into three channels, each of which is called a *meatus* (mee-ay'tus; "passage" L). Between the uppermost of the turbinates and the base of the cranium is a recess that contains special cells equipped to give us the sensation of smell. These represent the original olfactory pits of the fish, drawn deep inside the nose.

The air, as it is drawn in through the nasal passages, must make its way through the various meatuses and, in continued contact with the warm, moist walls of the narrow passages, is itself warmed and moistened. Furthermore, because of the curving shape of the turbinates, the air is forced to change direction constantly. Any smaller particles that may have escaped the hairy trap at the nostrils cannot change direction quite as easily as the much lighter air molecules can and at one projection or another the particle is bound to make contact with the nasal lining.

This lining is always stickily moist because it contains *goblet cells*, which secrete a viscous liquid called *mucus* (myoo'kus). Because of this, the lining of the nasal cavities is an example of a *mucous membrane*. Particles making contact with the nasal lining adhere to and are entangled in the mucus. The nasal passages are further moistened by liquid draining from four pairs of hollows in the bones of the face. These are located in the frontal, ethmoid, sphenoid, and maxillary bones and they are called *sinuses* (a Latin term for any hollow with but one opening). The sinuses are lined with tiny cilia that act to swirl the liquid through the narrow openings that connect them with the nasal passages.

In the four-footed position of most mammals, the sinuses are so placed that drainage is downhill. When man tipped himself upright, however, the sinuses tipped with him and took up horizontal or even somewhat uphill positions. Drainage is inefficient and, particularly when the passage to the nasal cavity is blocked during a cold, fluid may accumulate in the sinuses and the pressure then gives rise to excruciating headaches. Anyone who has

experienced an attack of sinusitis can be certain that our two-
leggedness is not all gravy.

The mucous membrane of the nasal passages also contain ciliated cells. There is a constant beating of the cilia in the direction
opposed to the air flow, so that any particles that have escaped
all the traps laid for them are beaten back and made to run the
gantlet again. The accumulating mucus, with its trapped impurities, can be cleared out of the nasal passages by the force
of an explosive expiration of air: the sneeze. This is a reflex
action induced by any irritation of the nasal membrane and is
not under voluntary control, as you know if you have ever tried
to stop a sneeze at a time when a sneeze might have been

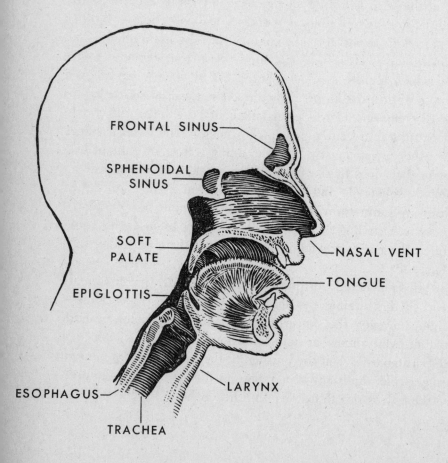

embarrassing. The net result is that the air (if reasonably unpolluted to begin with) enters the lungs in an amazingly clean state. Unfortunately, modern man's tendency to use the air as a disposal dump is too much even for our well-designed nose. Uncounted tons of dust and smoke hang over every large city and the lungs of a city dweller gradually blacken with time.

It is easier to condition the incoming air, by the way, in climates where the atmosphere is warm and moist to begin with. This may be one of the reasons why the Negroes of Africa have developed wide nostrils and a short nose. The inhabitants of Europe have developed narrow nostrils and a long nose, and the longer, narrower passage increases the efficiency of warming and moistening.

Naturally, since the nasal passages are open to the outside world and bear the brunt of its dangers, they are particularly subject to infection. As a result of exposure to wet or to cold or to sudden temperature changes or to a sneeze from an already infected person, the virus of the common cold or of influenza can begin to multiply in the nasal passages. The mucous membrane reacts by intensifying its protective functions to the point where they become more troublesome than helpful. A copious flow of mucus gives us the familiar "runny nose." This flow, together with a swelling of the numerous small blood vessels in the mucous membrane, blocks the passages and makes breathing through the nose difficult or impossible. Add to that the constant activation of the sneeze reflex, and the misery is complete.

The same set of unpleasant reactions may be in response not to a virus but to a foreign protein which in itself is harmless but to which the body may have developed a sensitivity. During the late summer and fall, for instance, the pollen of many plants floats in the atmosphere. Most of us are unaffected by this. The pollen particles are filtered out as any other particles would be, and there's an end to them. To those with "hay fever," however, contact with the pollen particles throws the respiratory system into a spasm of overprotection. (This is an example of an allergic reaction.) Just as in the case of a cold, there is the runny nose, the congestion of the passages, and the frequent sneezing.

The nasal passage joins the food canal just behind the mouth in the region called the *throat* (AS), or *pharynx* (far'inks; "throat" G). The union of the two passageways at this point makes it possible to breathe with reasonable comfort through the mouth. In fact, when the nasal passages are blocked through a cold or through allergy, it is either breathe through the mouth or die. Nevertheless, the two forms of breathing are not equivalent. The mouth does not possess the adaptations necessary for the proper purification of the air and, except where necessity dictates, it is desirable to breathe through the nose at all times.

Though the two canals join in the throat, they do not remain joined but separate again. Unfortunately, in doing so, they cross. That is, the air passage enters the throat from behind, but below the throat it lies in front of the food canal. This crossing makes it that much easier for either food or air to take a wrong turning. In the case of air, this would not be serious. In the first place, air is not likely to go wrong — it moves naturally in the direction of lower pressure, which means toward the expanding lungs. And then, even if some did find its way into the food canal, it would at the most produce a mild and temporary feeling of discomfort. The matter of food is much more important. Unless there are special precautions, food or drink could be sucked into the air passage by the pull of a low-pressure area just as air could. And with even a small quantity of solid or liquid matter finding its way into the air passages, breathing could be seriously blocked — even to the point of suffocation.

Special precautions against this are, however, indeed taken. The opening of the air passage lies behind and below the tongue and is called the *glottis* ("tongue" G). Just above the glottis is a flap of cartilage attached to the root of the tongue and called the *epiglottis* ("on the tongue" G). In the act of swallowing, when food or water must move through the throat, the glottis automatically moves under the epiglottis, a tight seal being formed. Only one passageway remains open and it is taken by the swallowed material, which moves down toward the stomach and not toward the lungs. You can experience this for yourself, if you begin to swallow and stop at the midpoint; you will find it is impossible to breathe at that stage.

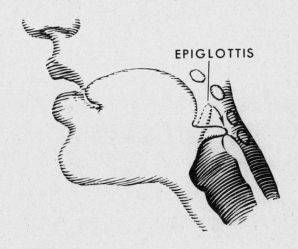

EPIGLOTTIS

The epiglottis and diaphragm combine to produce a sound familiar to all of us. The diaphragm is sometimes subject to periodic spasms of contraction that enlarge the lung cavities and lead to a quick inrush of air. The epiglottis claps down over the glottis to stop the flow, and the air, so suddenly set into motion and so suddenly stopped, makes the sharp noise we call a *hiccup* (AS). The word is spelled to imitate the sound, but by analogy to "cough" it is often written "hiccough," though it is still pronounced "hiccup."

The body does not entirely depend on the perfect functioning of the epiglottis; the matter is too vital. The passageway below the epiglottis is lined with cilia which lash upward to force back and out any tiny impurities that may enter. In addition, any contact of a sizable liquid or solid particle with the glottis sets off an explosive expulsion of air that will blow it out again. This, of course, is a *cough* (AS). When for some reason the epiglottis doesn't get across the glottis in time and we "swallow the wrong way," we go into a strangled fit of coughing that is surely among the unpleasant memories all of us share.

We associate the cough most often with infection, however. The inflammation of the throat that often accompanies a cold causes the mucous membrane of the region to overproduce mucus. The situation is made worse by mucus entering the throat from the inflamed nasal passages above ("post-nasal drip"). The spasmodic coughing that accompanies a cold is the body's attempt to get rid of the mucus.

It is also possible, after swallowing, for food and water to enter the nasal passages above. This would mean motion against gravity, so it is not as likely a misadventure as that of entering the air passages below. Nevertheless, the body guards against this by pressing a flap of tissue against the upper air passage, during swallowing, just as the epiglottis closes the lower air passage. The flap of tissue guarding the upper air passage is an extension of the roof of the mouth, or *palate* (a word of uncertain derivation). Since the roof of the mouth is underlaid by bone, it is the *hard palate*. Behind that hard portion is a soft, rearward extension, the *soft palate,* and at its end is the guarding flap of tissue. You can see that flap if you open your throat wide and look into the mirror. It hangs downward from the top center of the back of the mouth. Because of a fancied resemblance to a grape, it is called the *uvula* (yoo'vyoo-luh; "little grape"). The uvula gives us the curse of the snore. A current of air passing it can cause it to vibrate raspingly. When awake, we automatically keep the passage wide enough to prevent this from happening. At night, some of us do not — as most of us have discovered to our regret.

THE VOICE

Anything that moves is likely to set up the air vibrations we sense as sound. For that reason sound can be an attribute of the inanimate world, as when waves crash against the shore. Or it can be imposed upon living organisms from without, as when the leaves of a tree rustle in the wind. Life itself is distinguished by a variety of noises, from the cricket's strident chirp to the elephant's trumpet.

Noise has its inconvenient side. If it heralds an approach it may prove a warning to an intended prey, so the cat walks on padded toes in order that the sound of its footfall be deadened. More frequently, sound is put to use as psychological warfare, as a code of signals, or, perhaps most important of all, as a mating call. (Considering that an organism must find a member of the opposite sex of its own species from among a swarming myriad of creatures of other species, anything that will increase the chance of discovery and the speed of recognition is useful.)

In mammals a portion of the air passage has been modified for the production of sound. In man this specialized area is found immediately below the glottal opening. It is protected by the *thyroid cartilage* ("shieldlike" G) that nearly encircles it. (The thyroid cartilage is so called because it possesses a downward nick on top of its ventral surface, like a Greek shield of Homeric times. You can feel the nick easily with your fingers if you place them in front of the neck just under the chin.) Immediately beneath the thyroid cartilage is another stiff ring, the *cricoid cartilage* (kry'koid; "ringlike" G).

Across the glottis are two folds of tissue called the *vocal cords*, and the space between them is the *rima glottidis* (ry'muh glot'i-

dis; "glottal fissure" L). The vocal cords are attached in front
to the midpoint of the thyroid cartilage. In back, each is attached
to one of a pair of small cartilages called *arytenoid cartilages*
(ar'i-tee'noid; "ladle-shaped" G). The cords and cartilages together make up the *voice box,* or, to use a Greek term of uncertain derivation, the *larynx.*

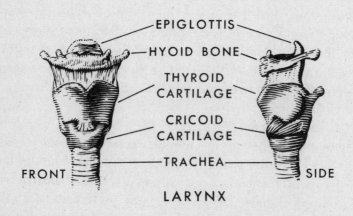

EPIGLOTTIS

HYOID BONE

THYROID
CARTILAGE

CRICOID
CARTILAGE

TRACHEA

FRONT   SIDE

LARYNX

Small muscles can rotate the arytenoid cartilages in such a
fashion that the vocal cords are moved away from each other,
forming a V with the apex forward. When this is done, the rima
glottidis is wide enough so that air passes up and down without
affecting the cords. A rotation in the opposite direction, however,
brings the vocal cords close together and parallel. Only a narrow
passage is left for air, and as the air current moves past it sets
up a vibration in the vocal cords. This is what you are doing
when you hum.

VOCAL
CORDS

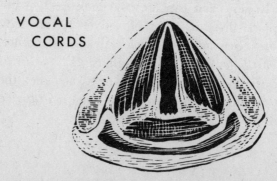

The faster and more forcefully air is expelled past the cords, the louder the hum. Furthermore, it is possible to put the vocal cords under varying degrees of tension. The tenser the cords, the higher the pitch of the hum. We are not aware that we are tightening or relaxing the cords, but that is what we are doing when we sing.

Although with training a singer can learn to do amazing things with his vocal cords in the way of controlled variations of pitch, there is a limit to the extremes he can reach, since he can only tense or relax the cords so far. In general, short cords will produce higher tones than long cords will, and that is why the male voice is generally lower than the female voice. Whereas the rima glottidis in man is up to an inch in length, in women it is only about o.6 inches.

In children, obviously, the vocal cords are shorter still, accounting for their high-pitched voices and the piercing shrillness of the childish scream. The larynx suddenly increases in size in boys at the beginning of adolescence so that the boyish soprano can become a baritone in rather short order. The change, in fact, may take place faster than the boy can learn to adjust the muscular movements involved in controlling the tension of the cords. The adolescent will find himself, consequently, passing through a period in which his "voice is changing" and he speaks in bursts of baritone and tenor ludicrously interspersed. It is one of the dreadful embarrassments of the early teens. The ultimate size of the adult larynx is not necessarily closely related to the size of the body. A large, strapping athlete may speak in a squeaky tenor and a short, slight man may possess a resonant baritone.

The male larynx is apt to make a prominent pointed bulge in front of the neck, marking the apex of the thyroid cartilage, this being most noticeable in lean men. In women, where the larynx in the first place is smaller and there is a more uniform fatty layer beneath the skin to soften the body outlines, such a bulge is small and not very noticeable.

In swallowing, as the epiglottis moves over the glottis, the glottis (and the larynx that surrounds it) rises in response. When the swallowing is done, the glottis and larynx drop again. The effect, where the bulge of the thyroid cartilage is visible, is a clear (and somewhat humorous) bobbing motion. This motion is visible for the most part in men only, and gives the impression of something swallowed but stuck midway in the neck. This resulted in the legend that when Adam swallowed his bite of the apple in Eden he couldn't quite get it down, and that the mark of this effort is present in all his male descendants in the form of the larynx. This legend, completely unbiblical and unrealistic, is mentioned only because it accounts for the fact that the bulge of the larynx is so commonly referred to as the "Adam's apple."

The nasal passages, the mouth, and the chest all act as a resonating chamber for the sounds produced by the vocal cords. The vocal cords alone would set up a relatively simple and faint sound, and it is to the resonating chambers that we owe the ability to shout. (Some primates, called "howler monkeys," have developed their resonating chambers to the point where their cries can be heard for a mile and more.)

The resonating chamber, moreover, adds a complication of overtones that lend the voice its "quality" or "timbre." Since no two people have nose, mouth, throat, and chest of precisely the same shape, no two people have voices exactly alike in quality. Our ears are designed to detect delicate differences in timbre and it is because of this that we can recognize the voice of a friend or loved one at once, even when it is imperfectly reproduced by the telephone and even when we have not heard it for a long period of time. It is because of this, too, that a mother can quickly recognize the loud cry of her own youngster from the very similar cries of other youngsters in the neighborhood, so that she will react violently and at once to the one, while remaining unmoved by the others.

Man is blessed with an unusually well developed larynx. (In

most amphibians and reptiles, in comparison, the larynx is quite crude. In birds, the larynx is present, but the characteristic bird calls are made by another organ, the *syrinx*, lower in the air passages.) It is not man's good larynx that is crucial in the development of human speech but his ability, thanks to the development of his brain and nervous system, to control numerous delicate muscles that alter the condition of the vocal cords and the nature of the resonating chamber.

In particular, the mouth is easily, quickly, and delicately changed in shape by motions of the lips, tongue, and cheeks. The quality of the voice can be changed to produce different sounds. If the air passage remains uninterrupted, the various vowels can be produced. (If you will make various vowel sounds, you will note the manner in which you change the shape of the mouth without blocking the air passage.) If air is forced to make its way through narrow openings, as when you make the sound of *f* or *s*, or is temporarily stopped altogether as when you make the sound of *p* or *k*, consonants are formed. By changing the shape of the mouth continuously and rapidly, a whole spectrum of shifting sounds can be produced in form complicated enough to act as a communication code. In this manner, abstract thoughts can be expressed with remarkable clarity.

Other animals communicate and some do so not even by sound. (Bees communicate by dancing, and other insects may possess a "mating call" that depends on the sense of smell.) Nevertheless, no land creature but man* can communicate in so complicated a fashion. Even a chimpanzee cannot learn to say more than a few fuzzy, garbled words. Some birds may be able to mimic human sounds and develop a small vocabulary, but they produce the words in a different manner. They tweet them rather than say them, and of course don't understand what they say.

---

* There is growing reason to think that dolphins and related creatures, with brains that are larger and more complicated than our own, may be able to duplicate man's speaking ability.

As adults we are not aware of the tremendously complicated muscular movements involved in speech, but this is only because long use has made the whole procedure second nature. Those of us who have reared a child know the years required to learn satisfactory speaking ability.

Infections of the throat and nasal passages will alter the shape of the resonating chambers and change the sound of the voice; roughening it so that we are hoarse. When the membranes of the larynx are themselves affected (*laryngitis*) our speech may be reduced to a whisper. (In whispering, the vocal cords are not involved and use is made of tissue folds, sometimes called "false vocal cords," that lie just above the vocal cords themselves.)

THE BRONCHIAL TREE

Below the larynx is a vertical tube lying just under the ventral surface of the neck. It is about 4½ inches long and is somewhat under an inch in diameter. It is important that this tube be kept open at all times: if the air supply to the lungs is cut off for even a few minutes death will result. For that reason the tube is fitted with C-shaped rings of sturdy cartilage to stiffen the front and sides of the tube. There are 16 to 20 of these rings, separated by fibrous connective tissue. The rings can be tightened by muscles connecting the open ends of the *C*, so that the diameter of the tube can be altered slightly when this is desirable. If you tilt your head back you can feel the tube as you run your fingers down the front of your neck. You will also feel the ridges produced by the alternation of cartilage and fibrous tissue, giving the tube a feeling of roughness. It is therefore called the *trachea* (tray'kee-uh; "rough" G), though a more graphic and less classical word is *windpipe* (AS).

Despite the cartilaginous stiffening, it is still possible to close the windpipe by force. To do this by hand takes considerable effort, however, and the windpipe must be kept closed for several minutes against wild struggling if a victim is to be choked in this fashion. It is not an easy way to commit murder.

A little below the point where the neck meets the trunk, the trachea divides into two branches called *bronchi* (bron′keye; "windpipe" G). The singular form is *bronchus*. Each bronchus leads to a separate lung, and in doing so divides and subdivides into continually smaller, finer, and more numerous tubes, something in the fashion of the branches of a tree. For this reason, the whole structure is sometimes called the *bronchial tree*. In the larger branches there also is stiffening by rings of cartilage, but as the branches get smaller the cartilage becomes less prominent and finally drops out altogether. When a cold or other infection extends its ravages as far down as the bronchi (*bronchitis*) the coughing spasms that result are particularly agoniz-

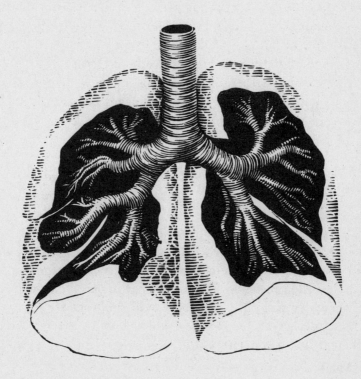

ing. It is the "cold in the chest" of popular speech as opposed to the "cold in the throat." Bronchitis can very easily become chronic, particularly where the continuous irritation of smoking exists.

The smaller branches of the bronchial tree (*bronchioles*) are themselves a possible source of another sort of unpleasantness. The fine subdivisions of the air passages are lined by circular muscles which through contraction or relaxation can alter the diameter, thus helping to control the air capacity of the lungs. Sometimes, as a result of infection or an allergic reaction to some foreign substance, there is a spasmodic contraction of the small muscles and a swelling of the mucous membrane of the bronchioles. The air passages narrow and the lung capacity is cut down. What follows amounts to a partial strangulation, and although rarely fatal an attack of *asthma* ("to breathe hard" G) can certainly crush out the joy of life.

Surrounding the bronchial tree that stems from each of the main bronchi are the *lungs* (AS). These extend from the collarbone to the diaphragm, one on the right side of the body and one on the left. Taken together, they fill almost all of the thoracic cavity. The two lungs are not quite mirror images of each other. The right lung, which is slightly the larger of the two, is partially divided into three lobes; the left lung is divided only into two. These lobes are, to a certain extent, self-contained. That is, it is possible for one lobe to be suffering a serious disorder and the other lobes to remain normal. In that case the infected lobe itself can be removed, leaving the rest of the lobes to possible normality for the indefinite future. Nor does the removal of a lobe seriously hamper breathing. In many organs there is a built-in "safety factor" where the total work capacity is greater than necessary. In such instances the loss of part of an organ will leave the remainder still able to carry a load sufficient for all reasonable purposes.

The maximum capacity of the lung averages about 6500 cubic

centimeters, or about 1.7 gallons. However, what counts in absorbing air is not the volume of the lungs but the area of surface that it presents. Air can only be absorbed at the surface and a quantity of air somewhere in the center of the lungs that happened to be out of touch with the surface could not be absorbed. The fact that it was inside the lungs would make no difference. It might as well be in Africa, for all the absorption it would undergo.

This would indeed be a serious consideration if the lungs were a simple pair of balloon-like organs holding air in a hollow interior lined by smooth walls. If that were the case, the lung surface that would be exposed to the air would amount to something like 2000 square centimeters, or 2 square feet. Lungs are, indeed, more or less simple sacs in lungfish, amphibia, and reptiles, but these are cold-blooded creatures (that is, creatures with body temperatures approximating that of their environment). Cold-blooded creatures, if not necessarily sluggish, can fade into sluggishness when conditions are right.

Birds and mammals, on the contrary, are warm-blooded creatures. Their body temperature is maintained in the neighborhood of 100 degrees Fahrenheit (the normal figure for man is usually given as 98.6 when temperature is measured by mouth) whatever the outside temperature. Not only is this perpetual maintenance of warmth in defiance of the arctic blast energy-consuming, but it keeps our chemical machinery moving at a rapid rate. (All chemical reactions increase in rate with rise in temperature.) To keep the chemical machinery racing, a far larger supply of oxygen is needed than will suffice a cold-blooded creature of similar weight.

For this reason, a lung that is a mere sac would not do for us. Two square feet of surface is not enough. To increase surface area, one must divide and subdivide the interior of the lung, and this is exactly what the bronchi and bronchioles do. The walls of the bronchi and larger bronchioles are far too thick to absorb air but as the bronchioles get smaller and finer, their walls get thinner, until finally, in the smallest bronchioles of all, absorption is possible. These *respiratory bronchioles* lead into several ducts, each of which ends in a cluster of air sacs, each cluster resembling a tiny bunch of grapes. The air sacs end in tiny air cells called *alveoli* (al-vee'oh-leye; "small cavity" L), the singular being *alveolus*.

This whole thin-walled structure, including the respiratory bronchiole, the ducts (usually called *alveolar ducts*), the air sacs, and the alveoli, is called a *lung unit*. It can also be referred to, more dramatically, as the "leaf" of the bronchial tree. The walls of the alveoli are cell membranes, and across those thin membranes oxygen can pass freely. It can pass freely in both directions of course, but the body tissues themselves contain virtually no free oxygen and the air in the alveoli contains a good deal, so that the direction of flow is from the interior of the lungs into the body itself. (Please remember that although the lungs are inside the body the air within the lungs is not. That air is connected by an unobstructed passage to the air outside your nostrils and it is not any more inside your body than the air in the hole of a doughnut is inside the doughnut itself. It is only when the oxygen crosses the alveolar membrane that it enters the body.)

With the volume of the lung broken up completely into lung units, the lung can no longer be considered a sac; it is, rather, a vastly complex sponge. (Because air is retained in this spongy mass even after death, the lungs removed from slaughtered animals are light enough to float on water — the only organs to do so. In butcher-parlance they are therefore referred to as *lights*. The very word "lung" may be distantly derived from the same source as "light." Nevertheless, the human lungs do weigh from 2 to 2½ pounds in adults.)

It is estimated that the spongy mass of the lungs contain, altogether, some 600,000,000 alveoli, with oxygen absorption possible over a total surface of at least 600 square feet. Without increasing the total volume of the lungs, then, the surface exposed to absorption has been multiplied 300-fold over the simple sac arrangement. To put it another way, the surface area exposed by the lungs is 25 times the total skin surface of the body.

The lungs, along with the remainder of the respiratory tract, are subject to infectious inflammations. One common lung disease is *lobar pneumonia* ("lung" G). This is often called simply pneumonia, though that term really applies to a whole family of lung inflammations. In an attack of lobar pneumonia, exuded fluid fills the infected section of the lung. Often only a single lobe is involved, whence the name, but when lobes on both lungs are infected, the result is what is popularly known as "double pneumonia."

A second bacterial disease of the lungs is *tuberculosis*. The disease is named for the fact that inflamed nodules called *tubercles* (tyoo'ber-kulz; "little swelling" L) are formed in the infected regions. The alternate name of *consumption* refers to the wasting of tissues that accompanies the disease, which thus gives the impression that the body is being consumed by it. Cancer, which may strike any tissue of the body, is in recent decades finding its way into the lungs with increasing frequency. This rise in lung cancer seems to parallel the large increase in cigarette smoking since World War I and, further, seems to be more common among heavy smokers than among others.

BREATHING

The air within the lungs is not in itself sufficient to maintain life very long. In not very many minutes, its oxygen supply would be gone. It is necessary, then, to renew the air, and this is done by breathing, by forcing old air out and new air in. In the resting adult, the frequency of respiration is 14 to 20 times a minute, depending on the size of the individual. In general, the smaller the person, the faster the normal rate of breathing, so that children breathe more rapidly than adults. (For that matter, a rat breathes 60 times a minute and a canary 108. On the other hand, a horse will breathe only 12 times a minute.)

Even in the short space of time between an inspiration and the following expiration, the composition of the air changes considerably as a result of events in the lungs. The air you breathe in is about 21 per cent oxygen and 0.03 per cent carbon dioxide. The air you breathe out is 14 per cent oxygen and 5.6 per cent carbon dioxide, on the average. (Not quite all the oxygen lost is replaced by carbon dioxide, as you see. Some is bound up as water and this is usually not counted in working out the composition of air. That is generally calculated on a "dry-weight basis" with the water content subtracted.)

The contents of the lungs are not completely renewed in any one inspiration. In fact, under ordinary conditions of peace and quiet, lung expansion and contraction is gentle indeed. With each quiet inspiration, only about 500 cubic centimeters of air is likely to enter the lungs, and with each quiet expiration 500 cubic centimeters of air leaves the lungs. And even this figure gives a somewhat exaggerated picture of affairs. In an ordinary inhalation the first air to enter the lungs themselves is that which was in the bronchi, throat, and nose — air that had just left the lungs in the previous expiration and had not been pushed out as far as the outside world. Then, after an inspiration is complete, some of the fresh air that entered through the nostrils remains in the air passages, where it is useless, and it is expired again before ever it can get to the lungs. The *dead space* represented by the air passages between the nostrils and lungs amounts to 150 cubic centimeters, so that the fresh air actually entering the lungs with each breath may amount to no more than 350 cubic centimeters. This represents only 1/18 of the lungs' total capacity and is called the *tidal volume*.

The partial replacement of the air within the lungs (*alveolar* *air*) by the shallow breathing we normally engage in is sufficient for ordinary purposes. We are quite capable of also taking a deep drag of air as well, forcing far more into the lungs than would ordinarily enter. After 500 cubic centimeters of air have been inhaled in a normal quiet breath, 2500 additional cubic centimeters can be sucked in. On the other hand, one can force 700 cubic centimeters of additional air out of the lungs after an ordinary quiet expiration is completed. By forcing all possible air out of the lungs and then drawing in the deepest possible breath, well over 4000 cubic centimeters of new air can be brought into the lungs in one breath. This is the *vital capacity*.*

Even with the utmost straining, the lungs cannot be completely emptied of air. After the last bubble has been forced out, there remain about 1200 cubic centimeters. This is the *residual volume* and is a measure of the necessary inefficiency of the lungs brought on by the fact that those organs are dead ends. (In this respect, birds are more efficient than mammals, for the former possess air sacs in some of the long bones and among the muscles. During inspiration, alveolar air can be pushed out of the lungs altogether and into these air sacs so that the lungs are thoroughly ventilated. This greater efficiency is important to the birds, for flight through air is more energy-consuming than is motion along the ground.)

Breathing is under both voluntary and involuntary control. You can, if you wish, force your lungs to do your bidding. You can take deep breathing exercises or hold your breath completely for several minutes. This voluntary control is important, making it possible to swim under water or to pass through an area filled with noxious vapors. Less obvious is the fact that we could

---

* It is always nice to give figures, since they make a sharp picture of the situation and this usually pleases the reader. However, there is always the danger that the reader will forget the picture isn't really that sharp. There are all sizes and conditions of human beings and no one set of figures holds for all alike. For instance, a small-lunged sedentary female may have a vital capacity of no more than 3000 cubic centimeters, while a trained athlete may have one as high as 6500 cubic centimeters.

not speak if we did not control the fashion of our breathing. (Try talking without holding your breath and taking quick inspirations between words now and then. It is this breath-holding which forces you to stop to "catch your breath" after you have been talking overrapidly and overlong. And it is one of the necessities of theatrical life that an actor learn to control his breathing in such fashion as to be able to deliver long speeches or sing long arias in a resonant voice without having to stop to catch his breath except at unobtrusive intervals that do not interfere with his performance.)

But it is involuntary control that is chiefly involved in breathing. When we are asleep or when awake but thinking of other things, breathing follows a regular rhythm at a frequency and intensity designed to bring us the oxygen we need at the moment. This involuntary rate of breathing is governed by the concentration of carbon dioxide in the alveoli. If carbon dioxide concentration rises to a value higher than normal, breathing quickens and deepens. If it falls to a value lower than normal, breathing slows and becomes shallow.

When the voluntary control of breathing brings a person to the point of danger, the involuntary control takes over. Thus, if you deliberately breathe shallowly or hold your breath, you grow quickly uncomfortable. Sooner or later you will give up, and since by underventilating your lungs you have allowed carbon dioxide to accumulate in them, you will — willy-nilly — go through a period of deep and rapid breathing that will lower the carbon dioxide concentration to normal. Even if by great determination you hold your breath until you fall unconscious, the involuntary mechanism will then take over. Children who threaten suicide by breath-holding never succeed.

If, on the other hand, you were to stand on a hilltop and be so overcome by the freshness and sweet country smell of the air that you take to deep breathing, you will eventually flush out almost all the alveolar carbon dioxide. You will quickly become dizzy (*oxygen-drunk*), and while you are sitting down to recover you will virtually suspend breathing for a while.

The breathing rate varies involuntarily for reasons other than your own deliberate interference with your lungs. When the rate of the body's chemical activity increases as a result of physical activity, whether through work, sport, flight, or even through anxiety or nervous tension, more carbon dioxide is produced and poured into the lungs. Breathing automatically becomes deep and rapid; you pant.

If, however, you are existing in enforced quiet and under static conditions (that is, where the stimuli assailing your sense organs are few in number or are monotonous in nature) your breathing will become shallow indeed. This in turn seems to trigger the act of falling asleep. Under conditions where falling asleep would be socially unacceptable, it is desirable to ventilate the lungs thoroughly; the type of forced inspiration that then takes place is the yawn. Unfortunately, society recognizes the yawn as a sign of sleepiness and boredom (which it is) rather than as an attempt to break the shallow-breathing rhythm that leads to sleep (which it also is), so the open yawn is as socially unacceptable as falling asleep. Under conditions where you may neither sleep nor yawn the effort to stay awake may become nothing short of torture.

Lung tissue is elastic and in life is in a stretched state, so its normal tendency is to contract. At birth the baby's lungs are, of course, empty of air. As the baby takes its first breath (traditionally stimulated by a sharp slap on the buttocks while it is held upsidedown by the ankles) the lungs fill and expand, pressing against the rib cage. This contact is not direct. The lungs are surrounded by a membrane called the *pleura* (ploor'uh; "rib" G), which adjoins the lungs, then doubles on itself and adjoins the rib cage. There is, in effect then, a double membrane (with fluid between) along which ribs and lungs can slide against each other with very little friction. Sometimes the pleura grows inflamed through infection (a condition known as *pleurisy*), and breathing can then become agonizingly painful.

When the rib cage lifts and the diaphragm presses down, the lungs are forced to expand even against their own contracting tendency. The alternative would be for the two folds of the pleura to separate with a vacuum between, a situation that is unthinkable. (If you own a small suction disk of the kind that is placed at the end of a child's arrow, try pressing it against a moistened tile on the bathroom wall and then pulling it directly off by main force, without sliding or peeling. Your difficulty in doing that is an indication of the force that would be required to separate lungs from ribs under ordinary circumstances.)

During expiration the natural elasticity of lung tissue is helpful, and less muscular effort is required to breathe out than to breathe in. If air does find its way between the ribs and the lungs, the elasticity of lung tissue can become a dangerous thing. A wound in the chest may allow air to enter and break the vacuum so that a lung may at once collapse. If the wound is closed, the lung will slowly expand again as the air between lung and ribs is absorbed by the body.

Surgeons sometimes make use of this effect deliberately. When it is necessary for a lung to recuperate from some disease or from surgery under conditions where it is not being continually irritated by the motions of breathing, air can be introduced between ribs and lung so that one lung (not both, of course) can be collapsed for a period of time. Fortunately, the human body can then proceed to get along quite well with only the remaining lung working.

The motions of respiration are fortunately so simple that they can be imposed from without even when the body's own mechanisms fail entirely. This is done by *artificial respiration,* of which there are a number of methods. In some, the victim's lungs are compressed by main force and allowed to relax, over and over again about 10 or 12 times a minute. Or air can be blown into the lungs in mouth-to-mouth fashion. The latter action can be duplicated mechanically by a Pulmotor when it is necessary to continue the action over long periods of time.

Where infantile paralysis has paralyzed the chest muscles, an "iron lung" is used. This is a steel chamber that completely encloses the patient from the neck down. A flexible collar about the neck keeps the chamber airtight. The air pressure within the chamber is raised and lowered rhythmically. At the high point the patient's chest is compressed and breath is forced out; at the low point the patient's chest is pulled into an expansion and breath is forced in. In this way lung action can be maintained as long as the motor works.

6

OUR HEART AND ARTERIES

THE INNER FLUID

What our respiratory system achieves, with all its intricate design, is merely to get the oxygen molecules across the boundary line that separates the environment from the tissues. Where does the oxygen go from there?

When an organism consists of a single cell, there is no problem. Once the oxygen molecules cross the membrane, they are in the cell, where the substances making up the cell's content pounce upon them; and that's that. Even where more than one cell is involved, matters may sometimes be no more complicated. If each cell is equally exposed to the environment (usually to the ocean, sometimes to fresh water), each obtains its oxygen at once by diffusion. Comparatively large organisms can thus exist, provided each cell has its own "ocean front." This means, however, that such an organism can be no more than two-dimensional. Jellyfish and tapeworms are among the longest animal organisms that exist and still depend on diffusion alone for their oxygen. This is at a price. The jellyfish bell consists of a thin outer layer of cells and has nonliving jelly in the interior, while its long tentacles are so thin that no cell is very far from the ocean. As for tapeworms, they are built like tape, as the name implies: long and wide, but flat.

152

To build up a three-dimensional cellular organization, some cells must be content to be buried in the interior, cut off from the ocean by layer upon layer of other cells. How would the cells in the interior obtain their oxygen? They could not possibly count on diffusion through the hungry cells that lay between their oxygen supply and themselves. The solution was found many hundreds of millions of years ago when some primitive wormlike creatures pinched off a piece of the ocean, in effect, and retained it within the structure of their body. In this way, there is an "internal ocean front," which in time became far more important than the original external one. Eventually, in fact, oxygen absorption from the environment was restricted to a small and specialized portion of the outer body, as I have explained in the previous chapter. The oxygen diffuses through that portion and enters the internal fluid, which is, of course, *blood* (AS).

In relatively small and simple organisms the existence of blood is enough in itself. It can be contained in more or less intricately branched channels so that all cells have a place at or very near the fluid. Oxygen entering the blood will diffuse to all parts of it and, from the blood, into every cell. Diffusion may carry across a relatively long distance but it will not be through layers of oxygen-consuming cells. Every cell will get its fair share.

As an organism becomes larger and more complex, simple diffusion will not do. The length of diffusion is such that parts too distant from the oxygen-absorbing areas might still be starved. It becomes necessary to replace the stagnant pool, so to speak, with a running current that will actively bring oxygen to the cell. It will not be necessary then to rely on the blind, random, and rather slow forces of diffusion. The current is set in motion by a pump in the form of a hollow muscle which, by expanding and contracting, will accept blood and then squirt it powerfully outward. This pump is the *heart* (AS). When blood is forced out of the heart under great pressure, tissues cannot be subjected to the direct blow without damage. The blood leaving the heart must therefore be contained in muscular tubes (*blood vessels*) which absorb the shock and which, by division and subdivision, eventually carry the blood to every part of the body.

In some forms of nonchordate life the blood returns to the heart by filtering its way around the cells. This is slow going, however, and retards the cycle below the point of toleration for large and complex organisms. In chordates (and in some nonchordates) the blood travels by way of blood vessels throughout, both away from the heart and back to it. The blood circulates through a closed system in this way, so that the heart, blood vessels, and blood make up what is called the *circulatory system*. (Actually, the system is not truly closed. There is a type of leakage I shall discuss in the next chapter.)

The structure of the heart is different in the various groups of organisms and, not surprisingly, is more complex in design in the more elaborate creatures. A nonchordate such as the earthworm has a closed circulatory system, and in that system a portion of one of the blood vessels is contractile. A periodic wave of contraction travels down its length, forcing the blood along and driving it forward. This simplest heart, a mere pulsating vessel, is also to be found in a primitive chordate such as amphioxus. Among the vertebrates, however, the pulsating vessel expands into a group of hollow chambers. By enlarging its capacity the pump is capable of squirting blood harder, just as you can blow harder if you take a deep breath first. The enlarged pump naturally develops a muscular wall much thicker and more powerful than that of any blood vessel.

In fish the heart is made up of two main chambers. The anterior chamber is the *atrium* (ay'tree-um; "entrance hall" L, since it serves as one for the more muscular chamber to follow). The atrium contracts and sends the blood into the posterior chamber, which is the *ventricle* ("little belly" L, signifying that it is a small hollow object). The atrium acts as a kind of blood store, collecting it from the incoming blood vessels and then shooting it all at once into the ventricle, which under the stimulus of the sudden muscle-stretching involved in the blood inflow responds by a particularly powerful contraction. When the ventricle contracts, the blood is forced into blood vessels that lead to all the organs of the body. The blood carries oxygen, which is utilized by the cells among which it passes so that by the time the blood returns to the atrium its content of oxygen should be virtually zero. That it is not virtually zero is thanks to the gills. Some blood vessels lead to the gills and there pick up oxygen. The oxygen-rich blood from the gills mixes with the oxygen-poor blood from the remaining organs, and the blood contained in most of the vessels is a combination of the two — an oxygen-fairly-rich blood, so to speak.

This was good enough for fish, but the early forms of land life, having developed lungs, began to separate the lung circulation from the rest. The amphibian heart has two atria. The vessels bringing blood from the lungs (oxygen-rich) enter one atrium and those bringing blood from the rest of the body (oxygen-poor) enter the other. The contracting ventricle then alternates at two jobs, sending oxygen-poor blood to the lungs for more oxygen, then oxygen-rich blood to the rest of the body. Mixing of the two types of blood was cut down but not removed entirely.

In reptiles, the ventricle is well on its way to being separated into two portions, and this final step is brought to completion in the birds and mammals. These last, being warm-blooded, used up oxygen at a fearful rate and efficiency simply had to be boosted. In birds and mammals (including ourselves, of course), the heart is four-chambered and consists of two atria and two ventricles. It is really a double pump, bound into one organ and synchronized very carefully. All the blood passes through each pump in turn. Pump number one sends it to the lungs, where it picks up oxygen. The oxygen-rich blood returns to pump number two. It does not mix with oxygen-poor blood at all, but emerges from pump number two in full richness and carries its large oxygen supply to the remainder of the body. In the process, it loses its oxygen, and upon returning to pump number one is sent out to the lungs again. And so the cycle continues.

But now let us turn to the human being specifically.

THE CIRCULATION

The human heart is a cone-shaped organ, about 5 inches long and 3½ inches broad, or roughly the size of the human fist. It weighs about 10 ounces in the adult male, 8 ounces in the female. It lies in the thoracic cavity, just behind the breastbone and between the lungs. Although it is centrally located, its axis of symmetry is not vertical. The conical point is slanted toward the left. This point thrusts out from behind the breastbone and this is the place where the heartbeat can be most easily felt and heard. It is this which gives rise to the mistaken feeling among the general public that the heart is far on the left side.

The heart is essentially a large muscle that is neither skeletal nor visceral in nature but strikes a compromise between the two; so it is put in a class by itself as *cardiac muscle* ("heart" G). Cardiac muscle must have the strength and force of contraction of the skeletal muscles, so its contractile units occur in sufficient quantity to give it a striated appearance (see Chapter 4). However, unlike ordinary striated muscle, cardiac muscle is under completely involuntary control. In that, it resembles visceral muscle. Cardiac muscle differs from skeletal muscle also in that the cells making it up are not separated but interconnect at various places. Such interconnected cells are called a *syncytium* (sin-sish'ee-um; "cells together" G). The heart is composed of two syncytia, one making up the two ventricles and the other the two atria. The existence of these syncytia makes it the more certain that the heart muscle will react as a unit; and in the heart more than in any other organ perfect synchronization of action is important.

The heart, like the lungs, is surrounded by a multiple membrane. This *pericardium* (per-ee-kahr'dee-um; "around the heart" G) is attached to the breastbone in front and to the diaphragm below, and an inner membrane adheres to the heart. There is fluid between the membranes, and when the heart in the course of its beatings moves against the breastbone and diaphragm, the fluid acts as a lubricant to cut down friction.

Let's begin the description of the human circulation at the right atrium. The human atrium is usually called the *auricle* ("little ear" L) because it seems to drape over the top of the heart like a dog's floppy ear, although anatomists prefer the term atrium. Blood enters the right auricle after having passed through all the body, so it contains virtually no oxygen; the heart's first task is to see that this condition is corrected. An efficient mechanism is therefore set into motion.

Between the right auricle and the right ventricle are three little cusps, or pointed flaps, of tissue. These are connected by ligaments to small *papillary muscles* (pap'i-ler-ee; "pimple" L) fixed to the interior of the ventricle. These flaps fold back on those ligaments and offer no bar to blood flowing from the direction of the auricle. Therefore, as blood enters the auricle it pours past those cusps of tissue into the ventricle also. By the time the auricle is full so is the ventricle.

When the right auricle is full its muscular coat contracts and its contents pour past the cusps, adding to what is already there. The distention of the muscular walls of the ventricle as a result of this influx causes it to contract particularly strongly. When it does this, the first surge of blood back toward the auricle pushes the cusps of tissue against the opening, sealing it tightly.

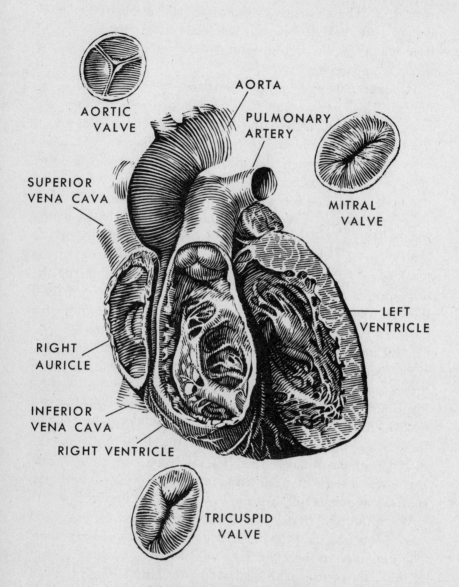

AORTIC
VALVE

AORTA

PULMONARY
ARTERY

MITRAL
VALVE

SUPERIOR
VENA CAVA

LEFT
VENTRICLE

RIGHT
AURICLE

INFERIOR
VENA CAVA

RIGHT VENTRICLE

TRICUSPID
VALVE

SECTION OF HEART
SHOWING CHAMBERS AND VALVES

Nor can the cusps be pushed through, since the ligaments now hold it tightly against the push of blood. In other words, blood can pass from the auricle to the ventricle past those cusps but not vice versa. The cusps form a one-way valve; this one is referred to as the *tricuspid valve*. There are many other valves here and there in the circulatory system, all working on the same principle and all designed to keep the blood flowing in one direction only. Since the blood from the contracting ventricle cannot push back into the auricle, it must emerge through the only other opening the ventricle possesses. Through that opening it pours into a large blood vessel leading it to the lungs.

The wall of the right ventricle is much more muscular than the wall of the right auricle. Whereas the auricle need only squeeze the blood into a neighboring chamber, the ventricle must force it to the lungs. A harder squeeze is required for the latter.

A blood vessel receiving blood from the ventricle and leading it away from the heart and toward other organs is an *artery* ("air duct" G). This name was given the vessels because they are found empty in dead persons and the early anatomists therefore assumed they carried air. The walls of the arteries are themselves muscular and elastic. As blood surges into one, the muscular wall expands to contain the sudden influx. As in the case of the ventricle itself, expansion is followed by a contraction. There are *semilunar valves* at the artery opening (with the flaps, as the name implies, shaped like half-moons). These will allow blood to enter from the ventricle but will not allow it to return. The contracting artery can thus push the blood in only one direction — farther away from the heart.

The impact of the blood striking the artery wall as it surges out of the ventricle is transmitted along the length of the artery and can be felt at those points where an artery lies just under the skin. The most convenient place for measuring the *pulse* ("to beat" L) is at the wrist, below the palm, and that is where it is traditionally taken. The beat of the pulse is, of course, synchronous with the beat of the heart, and in the days when there was little physicians could do but investigate the most obvious workings of the body, the taking of the pulse was an important diagnostic device. Nowadays much more can be deduced from the heart itself by more subtle methods than the sense of touch alone, so that pulse-taking is no longer all-important. (In motion pictures it seems to have retained its popularity. From a quick feel of the pulse and a close look at the whites of the eyes, the movie doctor seems to make the most amazing and presumably accurate diagnoses.)

The particular artery that accepts the blood from the right ventricle and carries it to the lungs is the *pulmonary artery* ("lung" L). The pulmonary artery quickly divides in two, one branch leading to the right lung, the other to the left. The arteries continue dividing and subdividing, forming smaller and smaller vessels with thinner and thinner walls. The smallest arteries are the *arterioles* (ahr-tee′ree-olez) and these finally divide into *capillaries* (kap′i-ler′eez; "hairlike" L, so named because of their fineness, though actually they are much finer than hairs). This change is analogous to that of bronchi becoming bronchioles and then alveoli.

The capillaries have walls consisting of single flattened cells, across which the diffusion of small molecules is easy. The capillaries arising from the arteries are almost as numerous as the alveoli arising from the bronchi and, in fact, along each alveolus there is a section of capillary. Oxygen molecules crossing the alveolar membrane also cross the wall of the capillary and find themselves carried along in the bloodstream. The blood that enters the capillaries of the lung with scarcely any oxygen emerges from those same capillaries with all the oxygen they can hold.

Gradually the capillaries begin to join into slightly larger vessels, then still larger ones. Such larger blood vessels carrying blood back to the heart from the organs are *veins* (from a Latin word of uncertain origin). The smallest of these are *venules* (ven'yoolz). By the time the blood is in the veins, the thrust of the heart pump can be felt no more. It has been completely absorbed by the friction of the blood against the innumerable capillary walls. Within the veins therefore, blood flows much more slowly and more smoothly than in the arteries. Thus, if a vein is cut, blood flows out copiously but smoothly. A cut artery gushes blood in spurts in time to the pumping of the heart. Bleeding from an artery is harder to stop and is far more dangerous than bleeding from a vein.

Since the veins do not have to absorb the shock of heart action, their walls are thinner than those of arteries and are not particularly muscular. This loss of pumping action also means that the blood in the veins is not propelled forward by the direct action of the heart. The motive force is instead the pinching action of neighboring muscles as they contract and thicken in the normal course of their activity. Many of the larger veins have a series of one-way valves set along their lengths (particularly veins that must carry blood toward the heart in opposition to the force of gravity), and these allow blood to pass only in the direction toward the heart.

The particular vein into which the capillaries and venules of the lungs finally unite is the *pulmonary vein.* The pulmonary vein carries the freshly oxygenated blood to the left auricle, which the blood then enters through a one-way valve. The pulmonary artery and pulmonary vein, together with all the smaller vessels between, make up the *pulmonary circulation.*

From the left auricle the oxygenated blood passes into the left ventricle through a valve consisting of two, rather than three flaps of tissue. This is called the *mitral valve* (my'trul) because the two flaps, in coming together, seem to resemble the double peak of a bishop's miter, or ceremonial headdress. The two valves, the tricuspid and the mitral, considered together are the *atrioventricular valves,* or *A-V valves,* lying as they do between the atrium (or auricle) and the ventricle.

It is the function of the left ventricle, through its contraction, to send the blood to all portions of the body (except the lungs, which are taken care of by the right ventricle and the pulmonary circulation). The blood must travel farther, after issuing from the left ventricle, and through many more capillaries than is true of the blood leaving the right ventricle, which need travel only as far as the nearby lungs. For that reason and although both ventricles pump out equal quantities of blood with each contraction, the left ventricle must do so with six times the force of the right. It is not surprising, then, that the muscular wall of the left ventricle is twice the thickness of that of the right (another asymmetry of the heart).

The contraction of the left ventricle forces the blood through a one-way valve into the *aorta* (ay-awr'tuh; "to lift up" G, per-

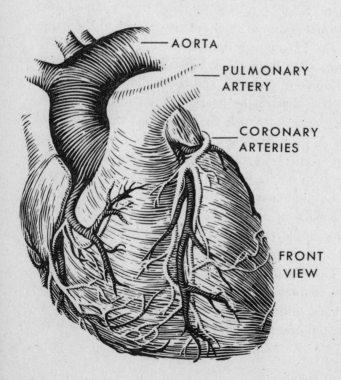

AORTA

PULMONARY ARTERY

CORONARY ARTERIES

FRONT VIEW

haps because the first few inches of the aorta's course leads straight upward). The aorta is the largest single artery in the body, with a diameter of a little over an inch at its beginnings. It moves upward at first (the *ascending aorta*), as I have said, but then arches over dorsally (the *arch of the aorta*) and proceeds to run downward (the *descending aorta*) just in front of the vertebral column. In its downward course, the aorta passes through the diaphragm.

From the ascending aorta, at a point just beyond its junction with the left ventricle, two small branches leave it and conduct blood back to the heart. Because these two arteries encircle the heart like a coronet, they are called the *coronary arteries*. It may seem surprising that the heart does not allow itself to be nourished directly by the blood it contains, but it does not. For one thing, only the left half contains oxygen-rich blood. However, once the blood leaves the heart a portion is at once led

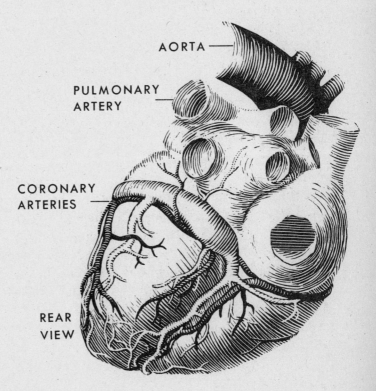

AORTA

PULMONARY
ARTERY

CORONARY
ARTERIES

REAR
VIEW

back so that the heart feeds itself straight from the tap before any other organ or tissue has a chance to get at the blood. Placed in human terms, this may seem selfish of the heart, but if so, it is an enlightened selfishness: its energy requirements are greater than those of any other organ, and upon the heart's smooth and unceasing performance all other organs depend.

From the arch of the aorta, the *brachiocephalic artery* (bray'-kee-oh-see-fal'ik; "arm-head" G) branches off upward. It quickly divides into four chief branches that justify its name. Of these, the two outermost are the *subclavian arteries* (sub-klay'vee-an; "under the clavicle" L, since they travel parallel to that bone to begin with). The subclavian arteries conduct blood to the arms. Between the two subclavian arteries are the two *carotid arteries* (kuh-rot'id; "put to sleep" G), which lead blood up either side of the neck. The name arises from the fact that Greek mountebanks would put goats to sleep by pressing that artery and cutting off the flow of blood to the brain.

The descending aorta gives off numerous branches, narrowing as it does so. In the chest region, there are the *bronchial arteries*. These lead to the lungs, but not, as in the case of the pulmonary arteries, for the purpose of picking up oxygen. They already carry oxygen and they serve to supply those portions of the lung, such as the bronchi, with the oxygen they need but which they cannot pick up directly from the air they carry.

A series of arteries, branching off successively lower portions of the aorta, lead to various portions of the digestive tract (with which I shall deal in a later chapter). These include: the *esophageal arteries* (ee'soh-faj'ee-ul), which receive their name from the fact that they lead to the esophagus, the tube connecting throat and stomach; the *celiac arteries* (see'lee-ak; "belly" G), which lead to the stomach and other nearby organs; and the *mesenteric arteries* (mes-en-ter'ik; "middle intestine" G), which lead to the intestines.

Some others include the *intercostal arteries*, which lead to the intercostal muscles, and the *lumbar arteries*, which lead to the lower vertebrae and the muscles of the abdominal wall. The *phrenic arteries* (fren'ik; "diaphragm" G) lead to the diaphragm and the *renal arteries* (ree'nul; "kidney" G) lead to the kidney, as the names imply. (There are other arteries as well, but I won't try to mention them all.)

In the region of the sacrum, what is left of the descending aorta divides into two *common iliac arteries* (il'ee-ak; "groin" G). Each divides into an *external iliac* and an *internal iliac*. The two external iliac arteries supply the legs and the internal iliacs carry blood to the organs of the pelvis.

All these various arteries divide and subdivide into arterioles and, eventually, into capillaries. The capillaries in turn coalesce into venules and then into veins. Usually these return the blood along routes parallel to those of the respective arteries, and have names like those of the arteries. Thus, the blood carried to the kidneys by the renal artery is returned by the *renal vein;* that taken to the hips and legs by the iliac arteries is returned by the *iliac vein;* and so on.

An interesting exception is that the blood carried up through the neck and into the head by the carotid artery is brought back by the *jugular vein* ("throat" L). The jugular vein lies nearer the surface of the throat than does the carotid artery (veins are generally more exposed than arteries, which makes sense since damage to the veins is the less dangerous), and the jugular has therefore become familiar to the average man as the vein that is severed when the throat is cut.

The blood, returning by way of the veins from the various organs of the body (except the lungs), eventually finds its way into the largest veins of all, the *venae cavae* (vee'nee kay'vee; "hollow veins" L, because they have the largest hollow, or bore). There are two of these. The veins leading from the head, neck, shoulders, and arms coalesce to form the *superior vena cava* and the veins from the lower portions of the torso and from the

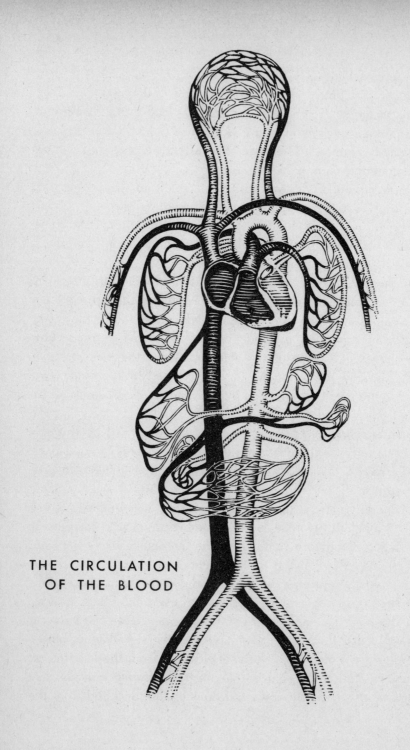

THE CIRCULATION
OF THE BLOOD

hips and legs combine to form the *inferior vena cava*. The two venae cavae empty into the right auricle, their supply of blood depleted of oxygen by the long trip through the various organs. The blood is now back to the point at which I began the description of the circulation, ready to be sent to the lungs once more for a new supply of oxygen. The circulation leading the blood through the aorta to the body generally and back through the venae cavae is referred to as the *systemic circulation*.

THE HEARTBEAT

The human heart beats constantly at a rate of 60 to 80 times a minute, or a trifle faster than one beat per second, throughout a long life that may last over a century. At each beat, the heart ejects about 130 cubic centimeters of blood even under the most restful conditions, so that in one minute, the quietly working heart pumps five liters of blood. In a century of faithful labor, it will beat some four billion times and pump 600,000 tons of blood.

The work done by the heart each minute is equivalent to the lifting of 70 pounds a foot off the ground. This is about twice the energy that can be produced by the powerful muscles of the arms and legs; yet the heart can keep it up indefinitely, whereas the limb muscles, achieving less, nevertheless quickly tire. This unusual ability of cardiac muscle to work so hard and yet so tirelessly makes it of particular interest to physiologists.

The rate of heartbeat depends in part on the size of the organism. The smaller the size, in general, the faster the heartbeat. Thus, women have hearts that beat 6 or 8 times a minute faster than the hearts of men. Children's hearts beat more rapidly still, and rates at birth may be as high as 130 per minute.

This holds true for mammals other than men. The rabbit has a heart that beats at the rate of 200 per minute, and the mouse's tiny heart flutters at 500 beats per minute. Cold-blooded animals that live at a much lower level of internal chemical activity than do birds and mammals get by with a slow beat. The frog, for all its small size, has a heart that beats but 30 times per minute in warm weather, and this beat slows further as the temperature drops. At temperatures near freezing, the rate is down to 6 to 8 per minute.

An animal capable of hibernation shows a remarkable variability of heart rate. A hedgehog has a normal rate of 250 beats per minute, but during the cold weather it survives by going into a cold-blooded suspension of activity during which the heartbeat may drop to 3 per minute. Animals larger than man naturally have slower heartbeats than we do. An ox has a heartbeat of 25 per minute, an elephant has one of 20. The heart rate will also vary in a given creature with his level of activity. During exercise, when the body's requirement for oxygen goes up, the heartbeat is both strengthened and accelerated. The acceleration is brought about also by nervous tension, fear, or joyous expectation and excitement. The "pounding of the heart" under those circumstances is a familiar phenomenon.

Exercise continued over long periods hypertrophies the heart as it would any other muscle. For that reason athletes have a lower rate of heartbeat while resting than sedentary males have. The athletic heart may beat no more than 50 to 60 times a minute. The slower rate is more than made up for by the fact that the heart, enlarged and strengthened through exercise, delivers more blood per beat.

What keeps the heart at its perfect rhythm? The responsibility might be thought to lie with some sort of rhythmic nerve stimulation, but this is not so. Although the heart is indeed outfitted with nerves that can affect its rate, they are not primarily responsible for the beat. This is known from the fact that the heart starts beating in the embryo before it is outfitted with a nerve supply, and it will continue beating in experimental animals even when the nerve supply is cut. The heart muscle will even beat in isolation, provided that it is immersed in an appropriate fluid.

The cells of the heart allow potassium ion to enter but not sodium ion. These ions are electrically charged particles, and by creating a difference in the concentration of such particles within and without the cell an electric potential is set up across the cell membrane. The rise and fall of this electric potential, as ions move across the membrane, sets off a series of contractions (although the details by which this is managed are not yet well understood) and the rhythmicity with which the ions move is reflected in the rhythmicity of the contractions. This means that the working of the heart depends upon the concentration of various ions in the blood, and that these must be controlled within narrow limits. This indeed the body manages; and man himself can imitate this outside the body by using, as I said above, an appropriate fluid.

A heart taken out of the body can be kept alive and beating if it is perfused with a solution containing the proper concentrations of various ions. (By "perfusion" is meant the forcing of liquid through the blood vessels that normally feed an organ.) The first fluid found to be effective for such a purpose was devised by an English physician, Sidney Ringer, and is still known as "Ringer's solution." It is not the intact heart only that beats. A mere portion will beat if properly perfused. It was found, in this way, that different parts of the heart will beat at different rates. That part beating most rapidly, however, forces its rate upon the remainder of an intact heart, for each rise and fall of electric potential moves out along the heart muscle from that most rapidly beating portion and the rest of the heart must follow, having no opportunity to set up potential fluctuations at its own rate. The most rapidly beating part of the heart is therefore referred to as a *pacemaker*.

In the two-chambered heart of the fish, the pacemaker lies

in the *sinus venosus* (sy'nus vee-noh'sus; "hollow of the vein" L). This is a widening at the end of the vein leading into the auricle. The beat begins there and progresses down the auricle and ventricle.

The sinus venosus persists in the embryos of birds and mammals but is gone by time of birth. It fades into the right auricle and its remnants can still be made out there as a bundle of special cells. Because those cells represent the fusion of the sinus venosus and the auricle, they are referred to as the *sino-auricular node,* or, in abbreviated form, the *S-A node.* It is the S-A node that is the pacemaker of the human heart. The wave of electric potential fluctuation that begins at the S-A node spreads out over both auricles (which make up a single fused cell, or syncytium, you may remember), so that both auricles contract simultaneously. There is a momentary pause at the point of division between the auricles and ventricles (the *auriculo-ventricular node,* or A-V node), where one syncytium ends and another begins. The A-V node, however, soon picks up the wave and sends it along the ventricles, which then also contract simultaneously.

If anything goes wrong with the A-V node, then the beat of the S-A node pacemaker cannot be transmitted to the ventricle, and this is called a *heart block.* This does not mean that the ventricles cease beating. They continue to do so, but at their own natural rate, which is only about 35 times per minute. If the A-V node is in working order, the heart can do better than that even if something goes wrong with the S-A node. The A-V node itself then becomes the pacemaker and keeps the heart beating at a rate of 40 to 50 times a minute.

Sometimes the ventricle contracts prematurely, as a result of some unusual stimulation, perhaps that resulting from some chemical agent in the bloodstream. (Heavy smokers seem particularly subject to this.) When this happens, the prematurely contracted ventricle will not be able to contract when the normal impulse reaches the A-V node an instant later. (After every contraction of the heart, or, for that matter, of any muscle, there is a *refractory period,* during which it will not contract again even when stimulated.) The ventricle must then wait for the next beat. This longer-than-usual wait between beats is the sensation, familiar to some of us, of the heart "skipping a beat." It is not dangerous.

Sometimes, despite the existence of the syncytium, the heart muscle does not contract in proper synchronization. Different fibrils may begin to contract on their own and the result is that the walls of the auricles, for instance, can begin to twitch at a rate of up to 10 times per second. This is *auricular fibrillation* (fy′bri-lay′shun). The A-V node cannot accept beats at this rate (fortunately) and, in effect, generally disregards an auricle gone mad in this fashion. It takes over the ventricular contraction at its own rate which is enough to keep the body going. However, enough of the auricular beats do get across the A-V node now and then to make the overall heartbeat disturbingly irregular. The treatment is usually the administration of digitalis, which acts to depress the conductivity of the A-V node. The ventricle is then less affected by the auricle and the heartbeat becomes slower and more regular. More serious by far is *ventricular fibrillation.* Here, it is the ventricle that begins twitching rapidly. No blood can be pumped and death follows quickly.

Since the heartbeat is so dependent upon the rise and fall of an electric potential, it is not surprising that its rhythm can be upset by an externally induced potential. As a matter of fact, what we call electrocution is usually the result of ventricular fibrillation set up by the electric current passing through the body. As it happens, an alternating current of 60 cycles per second, which is the common type used in the household, is particularly effective at setting up the fibrillation. (The moral is by no means that one ought not to use electricity. Rather, it is that one must be very careful in using electricity.)

A great deal can be told about the workings of the heart by using a device to follow the rise and fall of the electric potential and to measure its progress along the heart muscle. This can be done in animals by placing electrodes directly on the surface of the heart. In humans, one cannot be quite that direct. Fortunately, the tissues conduct electricity and the changes in potential that are associated with the heart action can be detected by connecting appropriate parts of the surface of the body to a galvanometer.

Such a device was first perfected by a Dutch physiologist named Willem Einthoven in 1903. He made use of a very fine fiber of quartz that was silvered in order to allow it to conduct a current. Even tiny potential differences caused noticeable deflections of the fiber and the movements could be photographed. The result is an *electrocardiogram* ("writing of heart electricity" G), which is usually abbreviated ECG. The normal ECG shows five waves, labeled P, Q, R, S, and T. There is first a small rise (P) above the base line, and this represents the motion of the potential wave across the auricle. The passage through the A-V node is represented by Q (a tiny dip below the base), R (a sharp, spiky rise above), and S (another dip below the base, a bit deeper than Q). Finally, the T wave is like the P but is higher and broader and represents the spread of the wave across the ventricle. Changes in the shape and duration of the various waves are useful indications of specific disorders in the heart action.

But before the coming of electrical devices there was the ear, and that can still be used to give important information. The heart is a noisy organ, as we all know. If you place your ear against someone's chest, you will hear a series of sounds something like: lub — dub —— lub — dub —— lub — dub —— lub — dub —— These sounds arise from the slamming of valves. When the ventricles contract, the tricuspid and mitral valves close and that is the *lub*. When the ventricles relax again, the semilunar valves in the aorta and in the pulmonary artery close, and that is the *dub*. The *lub — dub*, then, mark the beginning and ending of the period of contraction, or *systole* (sis'tuh-lee; "contraction" G). The lapse of time between one *lub — dub* and the next is the period of relaxation, or *diastole* (dy-as'tuh-lee; "dilation" G).

About 1819 a French physician, René T. H. Laënnec, made use of a short wooden tube, one end of which could be placed over the heart and the other to the ear. This made it possible to listen to the heart sounds of women, especially plump ones, without the embarrassment of trying to place the ear directly against the chest. This was the first *stethoscope* ("to view the chest" G, a misnomer since the examination is by ear and not by eye). It has developed into the modern instrument, without which any self-respecting physician would feel quite naked.

The value of the stethoscope (which is today designed to magnify as well as channel the sound) is in its ability to pick up slight variations in sound that indicate abnormalities in the valves. When the damage to valves leaves them unable to close properly (through the scarring that results from a disease such as rheumatic fever, perhaps), there is a backward leakage of blood, or *regurgitation*. When this happens, the clear sound of a valve closing tightly is replaced by a fuzzier sound called a *murmur*. If it is the *lub* sound that is replaced by a murmur, there is regurgitation at one of the A-V valves, usually the mitral, which as part of the left ventricle receives by far the harder blow. If it is the *dub* that is replaced by a murmur, there is a regurgitation at the semilunar valves, usually those of the aorta, which, again, gets the heavier blow.

It is also possible for the valves to be so thickened by scar tissue that they cannot open properly. Even at their widest separation, the opening is abnormally narrow. This is called *stenosis* (stee-noh'sis; "narrowing" G). The blood flows through the opening more rapidly; since the same volume of blood must pass through a narrowed opening in the usual time, its speed must increase if it is all to get through. The blood, foaming over the rough surface of the scarred tissue, also causes a murmur but at a somewhat different point in the sound pattern. The murmur now comes at the point when the valves are open; that is, before the *lub* or *dub* of valve closure.

Valvular disorders are not necessarily fatal, or even very dangerous. They reduce the efficiency of the heart, but not usually by more than the margin of safety. In addition, the heart can compensate by growing larger.

BLOOD PRESSURE

The powerful contraction of the left ventricle causes the blood to surge into the aorta at a speed of 40 centimeters per second (or, to make better sense to the automobile driver, at 0.9 miles an hour). If the aorta were to narrow, the rate of motion would increase, since the same volume of liquid would have to pass through the narrowed diameter in a given unit of time, and the only way that could be done would be to increase the speed of passage. By the same line of reasoning, the speed would decrease if the aorta were to widen.

If you were to examine the aorta as it passes down the midplane of the body, you would find that it does indeed narrow in diameter, but it is also giving off branches to drain off some of the blood. What counts now is not the width of any one vessel but the sum of the cross-sectional areas of all the different branches. As the aorta divides and subdivides, the individual branches are narrower and narrower but the sum of the areas continually increases. By the time the blood has made its way into the arterioles, the total cross-sectional area of the various vessels through which it is passing is 15 to 30 times that of the aorta and the blood flow is only about 2 centimeters per second.

In the capillaries, which are individually so thin as to be invisible without a microscope, the total cross-sectional area is nevertheless about 750 times that of the aorta, and the blood is creeping along at the rate of but half a millimeter per second. At this slow motion, the blood of the capillaries along the alveoli of the lungs has ample time to pick up oxygen and, in the remaining tissue, has ample time to give off oxygen. Collecting into venules, the total area decreases and the velocity picks up again. The two venae cavae, taken together, have an area four times that of the aorta, so blood re-enters the right auricle at a speed of about 10 centimeters per second.

When blood is forced into the aorta, it exerts a pressure against the walls that is referred to as *blood pressure*. This pressure is measured by a device called a *sphygmomanometer* (sfig'moh-ma-nom'i-ter; "to measure the pressure of the pulse" G), an instrument which, next to the stethoscope, is surely the darling of the general practitioner. The sphygmomanometer consists of a flat rubber bag some 5 inches wide and 8 inches long. This is kept in a cloth bag that can be wrapped snugly about the upper arm, just over the elbow. The interior of the rubber bag is pumped up with air by means of a little rubber bulb fitted with a one-way valve. As the bag is pumped up, the pressure within it increases and that pressure is measured by a small mercury manometer to which the interior of the bag is connected by a second tube.

As the bag is pumped up, the arm is compressed until, at a certain point, the pressure of the bag against the arm equals the blood pressure. At that point, the main artery of the arm is pinched closed and the pulse in the lower arm (where the physician is listening with a stethoscope) ceases.

Now air is allowed to escape from the bag and, as it does so, the level of mercury in the manometer begins to fall and blood begins to make its way through the gradually opening artery. The person measuring the blood pressure can hear the first weak beats and the reading of the manometer at that point is the *systolic pressure,* for those first beats can be heard during systole, when the blood pressure is highest. As the air continues to escape and the mercury level to fall, there comes a characteristic quality of the beat that indicates the *diastolic pressure;* the pressure when the heart is relaxed.

The blood pressure, unlike the rate of heartbeat, is roughly the same in all warm-blooded animals, regardless of size. The systolic pressure is in the range of 110 to 115 millimeters of mercury while the diastolic pressure is about 80 millimeters of mercury. (Atmospheric pressure is 760 millimeters of mercury so that systolic pressure is about 0.15 to 0.20 of an atmosphere, while diastolic pressure is about 0.10 of an atmosphere.)

Blood pressure is not a constant factor in man. For one thing, it varies with age. In a newborn baby, the systolic pressure is no more than 40 millimeters of mercury, though it rises to 80 by the end of the first month. It continues to rise more slowly, reaching 100 millimeters at the start of adolescence and 120 millimeters in the later teens. There is a continued very gradual rise during later adulthood. At the age of 60, a blood pressure of 135 systolic and 90 diastolic would seem quite normal. Exercise and nervous tension also increase the blood pressure, as would seem logical. Where the body generally requires a greater supply of oxygen and the heart, in consequence, beats more rapidly and forcefully, the pressure of the blood on the artery walls will rise. Systolic pressures up to 180 or 200 millimeters of mercury would not be unusual or worrisome as a temporary phenomenon.

The elasticity of the arteries tends to lower the systolic blood pressure, for as they belly out to receive the influx of blood, more room is made for the volume and a smaller push is exerted against the retreating walls. With increasing age, however, arteries lose flexibility, as calcium salts are deposited in their walls, converting them (sometimes) to nearly bone-hard tubes in old age. This is *arteriosclerosis* (ahr-tee'ree-oh-skle-roh'sis; "hardening of the arteries" G). Under these conditions, systolic pressure rises and the slow hardening of the arteries may account for the normal slow rise in systolic pressure in the years after maturity.

Temporary changes in blood pressure can be induced by contraction of the arterioles, the muscular walls of which can close those small vessels altogether. This contractility of the arterioles serves a useful purpose in shifting the distribution of blood to meet the changing needs of the body. Ordinarily, at rest, 25 per cent of the blood is passing through the muscles and another 25 per cent through the kidneys. In addition, 15 per cent is passing through the intestinal regions, with another 10 per cent through the liver. Further, 8 per cent passes through the brain, 4 per cent through the blood vessels feeding the heart, and 13 per cent through lungs and elsewhere.

Under conditions of fright or anger, it is important that the lungs, heart, and muscles be well supplied with blood. The intestinal regions, on the other hand, can temporarily do without; time enough for the slow processes of digestion after the emergency has passed. Through the contraction of appropriate arterioles, the intestines are deprived of some of the blood, which is then distributed through more essential regions.

A more clearly visible display of the variability of blood distribution involves the skin. The skin is well supplied with blood vessels, not merely to supply its cells with needed nourishment, but as a device to carry heat from the interior of the body to the surface, where it may be conducted or radiated into the atmosphere. On warm days, particularly humid ones, or at times when heightened muscular activity produces heat at a greater rate than usual, the vessels in the skin relax. This is *vasodilation* (vas'oh-dy-lay'shun; "vessel dilation" L). There is then room for a greater fraction of the blood in the skin, and loss of heat to the atmosphere is increased. We are visibly flushed as a result on a hot, muggy day or after a strenuous session of work or play. Emotional factors can also produce vasodilation of the skin vessels so that we blush with embarrassment, confusion, shame or, sometimes, pleasure. But on cold days, when it is necessary to cut down the loss of heat to the atmosphere, the blood vessels of the skin will constrict (*vasoconstriction*) and the skin will contain less than its normal content of blood. We can then turn white with cold. Emotion can cause the same color change, this time making us turn pale with fear or shock.

Large veins, particularly of the abdominal region, can also contract so as to contain less blood and thus make more of it available for the capillaries of the muscles and other key organs. Most of all, there is the spleen, a brownish-red organ lying on the left side of the body just behind the stomach. It is about the size of the heart but is not nearly as compact, weighing only 5 or 6 ounces. Its spongy structure serves as a blood reservoir. It can expand to hold a liter of blood and, in case of need, contract to squeeze all but 50 millimeters of its blood supply into the general circulation.

All these devices can be used to change blood volume or blood-vessel volume (or both) and thus change the blood pressure, but under normal conditions a rise in blood pressure is only temporary and is intended only to meet a temporary need. Sometimes, however, blood pressure rises and remains high more or less permanently. The systolic blood pressure may reach 300 millimeters of mercury, the diastolic 150, both values being roughly twice the normal. This is *hypertension* ("stretched beyond" G), or, in direct English, *high blood pressure*. This is dangerous for numerous reasons. It places an unusual strain on the heart and arteries, contributing to degenerative changes in their structure. The smaller arteries, damaged by the constant high pressure on the walls, may undergo unusual hardening and be less able to adjust to the high pressure than ever. They may even rupture.

The rupture of an artery in the brain is a particularly serious phenomenon, since, if a sizable portion of the organ is harmed as a result, paralysis or death follows quickly. The unfortunate

victim is struck down so quickly and so without warning, in
fact, that the condition is termed a *stroke, apoplexy* (ap'oh-plek'-
see; "a striking down" G), or *cerebral hemorrhage.* Naturally,
this is more likely to happen at a time when excitement or
overwork raises the blood pressure beyond even its usual level.

Sometimes hypertension is brought about by a failure of the
machinery by which the kidneys control blood pressure (I shall
discuss this in a later chapter) in which case physicians speak
of *renal hypertension.* Often there is no known cause, and
it is then called *essential hypertension.* One of the meanings of
"essential" in the medical vocabulary is "without known cause."
A synonym for "essential" used in this fashion is "idiopathic"
(id'ee-oh-path'ik; "individual suffering" G), that is, suffering
about which no general statement can be made.*

Arteries do not degenerate with age, only through hardening
as the result of deposition of calcium salts. One change that
can occur in middle age, and one equally disastrous, is the
deposition of certain fatty compounds on the inner lining of the
arteries. The ordinarily smooth lining of the inner walls is roughened by such deposition and takes on an irregular appearance
that seemed to some investigators to be like the grains of cooked
porridge. The disease is therefore called *atherosclerosis* (ath'ur-
roh-skle-roh'sis; "porridge-like hardening" G).

The atherosclerotic artery is dangerous for two reasons. In the
first place, the rough coating can damage small bodies in the
blood whose function it is to initiate clotting. There is therefore
always the chance of clots forming in such an artery. A clot may
break up without damage after being formed, or it may be whirled
along by the bloodstream until it comes to an artery too small to
pass through — in which case it may plug the vessel and stop
that portion of the blood flow. This is *thrombosis* (throm-boh'sis;

---

* The 20th edition of *Stedman's Medical Dictionary,* a very valuable but generally humorless work, unbends far enough to comment as follows upon the term
"idiopathic": "a high-flown term to conceal ignorance."

"clot" G). A thrombosis in an arteriole of the brain is as effective as a vessel rupture in bringing on a stroke. Secondly, the atherosclerotic deposition narrows the bore of the artery, sometimes to an alarming extent, and decreases its flexibility as well. For both reasons, pressure goes up within that artery and blood flow is even so decreased.

Particularly vulnerable to these changes are the coronary arteries. This is not because the coronary arteries are unusually weak, but because the heart's needs are abnormally high, so that there is less margin for safety. Whereas most organs make use of but one fourth of the oxygen supply of the blood pushing through them under ordinary conditions, the heart makes use of four fifths of the available supply. Another organ might make do with a diminished blood supply without too much trouble; the heart cannot.

When the constricted coronary artery cannot carry enough blood, there is a sharp pain in the chest. This may also be felt in areas distant from the actual organ affected ("referred pain"), particularly in the left shoulder and arm. The condition is *angina pectoris* (an-jy'nuh pek'tuh-ris; "a choking in the chest" L). Usually an attack of angina follows a bout of work or a period of emotional tension, when the heartbeat is increased and the heart's demand for blood becomes distinctly greater than the constricted coronaries can supply. Drugs such as amyl nitrate or nitroglycerin are sometimes used in these cases, since they act to bring about a general relaxation of arteries, increasing the blood supply to the heart.

Where a clot blocks one of the divisions of the coronary artery, the result is *coronary thrombosis* (the familiar "heart attack"). This can be quickly fatal, but if the blocked artery is small enough it may result only in the death of that portion of the heart immediately fed by that artery. Scar tissue will form in that spot, and after recovery this need not of itself seriously damage a person's life expectancy — except, of course, that the conditions giving rise to one thrombosis remain, and may in all like-lihood give rise to another and more serious one.

Vessels may sometimes become abnormally dilated through damage to their walls. A hardened aorta may undergo damage in a particular spot which will then heal under the stretched conditions imposed by the pounding of the high-pressure blood. There is then a permanent weakness in the wall, which bellies out with each beat of the heart. This is an *aneurysm* (an'yoo-riz-um; "wide" G). The danger is that the aorta may simply rupture after one heartbeat too many, with death as a consequence.

Veins, too, may become overdilated. There the damaging factor is not the blood pressure, which is comparatively low in the veins, but the force of gravity. Blood returning to the heart from the legs and hips must move against gravity when a person is standing or sitting. This motion against gravity is accomplished by the normal muscular action which pinches the blood of the vessels toward the heart, thanks to the one-way valves in the veins of the legs. If anything happens to damage the valves or make them ineffective, the return of the blood is seriously hampered. Blood collects in the veins, which distend to four or five times their normal diameters and the result is *varicose veins*. The case is naturally aggravated where a person's way of life involves much standing and little activity.

These various disorders of the circulatory system which I have been mentioning in this chapter are of particular importance nowadays. In recent decades, with many infectious diseases that were once deadly scourges of humanity coming under control, the various circulatory disorders have become the major causes of death in the United States. Nearly a million people a year die of some malfunction of the heart or vessels, and this represents about 55 per cent of all deaths in this nation.

7

OUR BLOOD

THE LIQUID TISSUE

The importance of the heart and blood vessels is not so much in themselves as in what they carry, because all their intricate machinery is merely designed to make it certain that each part of the body is properly bathed in a current of blood. The total quantity of blood in a human being is sizable, it being estimated that something like 1/14 of the weight of the body is blood. Men are in this sense bloodier than women: the average man contains about 79 milliliters of blood for each kilogram of body weight, but the corresponding figure for a woman is only 65. A man of average size will therefore contain about 5.5 liters of blood (or about 1½ gallons); an average-sized woman will contain 3.25 liters of blood (or about ⅞ of a gallon).

The most obviously unusual thing about blood is that it is a liquid, whereas other tissues of the body are solid or semisolid. And yet this does not mean that blood is unusually watery. The body as a whole is about 60 per cent water. Considering that life began in the oceans, this is not surprising. On land as in the sea, the chemical reactions in the cells are carried on against a watery background now just as they were when the first living molecule combinations arose in the ocean. If there is to be astonishment, it is that land life has managed to economize on water to the extent of making do with but 60 per cent. Some nonchordate ocean creatures have water contents running up to 99 per cent.

One factor that keeps man's water content as low as it is is that certain relatively inactive tissues can afford to be fairly dry. The fat stores of the body, for instance, are only 20 per cent water, while marrow-free bone is only 25 per cent water. If we consider only the "soft tissues" of the body — the ones in which the chemical business of the body is being actively carried on — the water content runs from 70 to 80 per cent. The liver, for example, is 70 per cent water and the muscles are 75 per cent water.

Blood is 80 per cent water, but this comparatively high value is not the reason for its liquid state, for the kidney, a solid organ, is also 80 per cent water. In fact, the most watery tissue of the body is the gray matter of the brain, which, though certainly not a liquid, is 85 per cent water. The question we should really ask is this: If blood is a liquid, why is its water content lower than that of the gray matter of the brain and almost as low as muscle's? The answer is that although blood may have begun long eons ago as a pinched-off portion of the ocean, its composition is now, as a result of many intricate evolutionary changes, far more complex than the composition of the ocean is, or ever was.

To be sure, there remain important similarities between the blood and the ocean even yet. The blood contains the same ions the ocean does, and in roughly similar proportions. As in the case of the ocean, the most important ions in blood are sodium ion and chloride ion. This gives the blood (and the ocean) its salty taste.

In addition to inorganic ions, however, blood contains organic constituents, complex carbon-containing molecules formed by the body, such as glucose (a kind of sugar), and a large variety of proteins.* What's more, the blood contains objects of cellular

---

* In this book it is not possible to go into any great detail concerning the biochemistry of the blood. If you are curious about the matter, you can find a fairly thorough discussion of the subject in my book *The Living River* (1959).

size. Some of these are actually true cells. Others are not, being smaller than the average cell and lacking nuclei. Nevertheless, these latter objects remain far larger than any molecule, and are marked off from the truly liquid portion of the blood by membranes. These cells and subcells are lumped together as *formed elements.*

It is these formed elements which give blood its viscosity. If the formed elements swelled somewhat and adhered to each other, as cells do in other tissues, blood would be a soft semisolid as brain, kidney, and muscles are. It is because the formed elements do not adhere to each other but float individually in the blood that blood remains fluid. The formed elements are large enough to settle out easily under centrifugal force. Special graduated tubes are filled with blood (to which a small quantity of chemical is added to prevent clotting) and spun at the rate of 50 revolutions per second. Under such conditions, the formed elements are forced away from the center of rotation to the bottom of the tube and compressed there.

In this way, the blood is divided into two parts: a watery portion called the *blood plasma* and the formed elements. Blood itself, consisting of both plasma and formed elements, is sometimes called *whole blood* to emphasize the fact that all its contents are being referred to. The blood plasma is a straw-colored liquid, 92 per cent water. It is the true fluid of the blood, and in it the formed elements float. The plasma makes up roughly 55 per cent of the volume of whole blood under normal conditions. The formed elements make up the remaining 45 per cent, this percentage being the *hematocrit* (hem′uh-toh-krit′; "to separate blood" G).

The blood has numerous functions, among which one of the most important is that of transporting oxygen. When simple organisms first made use of an internal fluid for the purpose of bathing the inner cells of the organism with dissolved oxygen (and other substances), there remained a serious problem.

Water does not really dissolve much oxygen. A liter of ice water will only dissolve 14 milligrams of oxygen out of the air, and this solvent capacity of water actually decreases as the temperature rises. At the temperature of the human blood, a liter of water will dissolve only 7 milligrams of oxygen out of the air. For a simple organism consisting of one cell or a small group of cells, this small solvent capacity of water for oxygen is nevertheless ample, simply because of the huge volume of the ocean. The oxygen supply is virtually unlimited when you think that a cubic mile of ocean water contains up to 60,000 tons of dissolved oxygen and that there are hundreds of millions of cubic miles of water in the oceans.

The situation changes drastically when it is more than a question of individual cells, or even small conglomerations of cells, floating in all those cubic miles, but billions upon billions of cells all depending upon an internal fluid of very limited quantity. If our own blood carried oxygen only by dissolving the gas in its water content, it would at no time carry more than about 30 milligrams of oxygen. This is approximately a 4½-second supply as far as our minimum body needs are concerned, and on such an insignificant margin of safety no complex organism could exist. Some small insects make out with the oxygen dissolved in their water content alone, but certainly we cannot. The mere fact that we can hold our breath for a minute or two without undue trouble is proof enough that our blood carries oxygen through some device more efficient than mere solution.

To get around this problem, we and all other sizable multicellular animals make use of compounds, more or less complex, that are capable of forming loose associations with oxygen molecules. At the gills or lungs, these compounds take up oxygen (and far more oxygen can be held in a given volume of blood in this fashion than through simple solution). At the tissues, the weak hold of the compounds on the oxygen is broken and the oxygen diffuses into the cells. These oxygen-holding compounds are usually colored (although the color has no direct connection with the problem of transporting oxygen) and so they are generally referred to as *respiratory pigments*. These pigments are protein in nature, which means that they consist of large and complex molecules made up of thousands, and sometimes hundreds of thousands, of atoms of carbon, hydrogen, oxygen, and nitrogen. In addition, they almost invariably contain one or more atoms of some metal in each molecule.

The metal involved is most usually iron, but many crustaceans and mollusks make use of a respiratory pigment containing copper. This copper-containing compound is *hemocyanin* (hee'mohsy'uh-nin; "blue blood" G) and because the compound is blue in color, the creatures making use of it have blue blood indeed. Those very primitive chordates the tunicates possess a respiratory pigment containing vanadium and certain mollusks possess one containing manganese, but this is very unusual.

The respiratory pigment of the human being, and indeed of all vertebrates, contains iron and is called *hemoglobin* (hee'mohgloh'bin), for reasons I shall explain later. There are a number of other iron-containing respiratory pigments elsewhere in the animal world but none as efficient as hemoglobin. Nevertheless, the compound is not confined to the vertebrates. As lowly a creature as the earthworm is our cousin in this respect, for it, too, possesses hemoglobin.

The molecule of hemoglobin contains, roughly, 10,000 atoms and has a molecular weight of 67,000. (That is, its molecule weighs 67,000 times as much as a single hydrogen atom, which is the lightest of all atoms.) Most of each molecule of hemoglobin is made up of amino acids, relatively small compounds that go into the structure of all proteins. However, each molecule also contains four groups of atoms not amino acid in nature. These groups contain atoms arranged in a large circle made up of four smaller circles (a very stable arrangement in this particular case) and at the very center is an iron atom.

This iron-containing portion can be isolated from the hemoglobin molecule and is called *heme* (heem), so we can say that there are four heme groups to each hemoglobin molecule. (The Greek word for "blood" is *haima*, which gives rise to numerous terms in connection with blood. The stem derived from *haima* is spelled "hem" in American usage, and "haem" in British usage. I shall follow the American spelling.)

Now in some nonchordate creatures the respiratory pigment is carried in solution in the plasma. This is so in the case of hemocyanin and of some iron-containing pigments. Those creatures possessing hemoglobin, however, always retain the pigment in small containers. This is certainly true of ourselves, and these hemoglobin containers are by far the most numerous of the formed elements I mentioned earlier.

THE ERYTHROCYTE

Hemoglobin in one of its forms is a bright red compound and lends that color to its container, the *erythrocyte* (ee-rith'roh-site; "red cell" G), which thereby receives its name. These particular formed elements are often called, in plain English, *red blood cells*, or simply *red cells*. To be sure, the individual erythrocyte is not red but straw-colored. In quantity, however, the color does deepen to red, and it is this that lends blood as a whole its red color.

There is some question, though, whether the erythrocyte ought to be called a cell, since it contains no nucleus. It is therefore often called a *red blood corpuscle* ("corpuscle" comes from a Latin word meaning, neutrally enough, "little object"). The erythrocyte is smaller than the average cell, having a diameter of 7.2 microns. (A micron is equal to a thousandth of a millimeter, or, if you prefer, 1/25,000 of an inch.) Furthermore, it is disk-shaped, being only 2.2 microns thick. It is narrower in the center, so that it may be described as a biconcave disk. This thinness places the hemoglobin content of the erythrocyte nearer the surface and facilitates the uptake of oxygen.

(When erythrocytes were first studied by microscopes, those early instruments weren't good enough to show the shape precisely. The erythrocytes seemed simply tiny spheres at the limit of vision and were called "globules." Proteins obtained from them were called "globulins" or "globins" in consequence, and it is to that misconception that we owe the word "hemoglobin.")

If the erythrocyte is not a complete cell, it at least begins life as one. It is originally formed in the bone marrow of the skull, ribs, and vertebrae, and, in children, in the marrow at the end of the long bones of the arms and legs as well. The process of erythrocyte formation is *erythropoiesis* (ee-rith'roh-poy-ee'sis; "making of red cells" G). What is later to be an erythrocyte is at first an ordinary, rather large cell, complete with nucleus but containing no hemoglobin. At that early stage it is a *megaloblast* (meg'uh-loh-blast; "large bud" G), since it is the bud, so to speak, out of which the erythrocyte eventually flowers. The megaloblast gains hemoglobin and becomes an *erythroblast* ("red bud" G). Then as it divides and redivides, it shrinks in size and becomes a *normoblast* ("normal bud" G), because it is then the normal size of an erythrocyte. But at that stage it still has a nucleus and is still a true cell.

At the next stage, it loses its nucleus and it then becomes a *reticulocyte* (ree-tik'yoo-loh-site; "network cell" G), because when properly stained its surface can be made to show an intricate network pattern. The reticulocyte is discharged into the bloodstream, and within a few hours it has become a full-fledged erythrocyte. In normal blood, one cell in every two hundred is still in the freshly formed reticulocyte stage. In cases where, for one reason or another, it is desirable to stimulate an increase in the rate of formation of erythrocytes, the earliest sign that the treatment is succeeding is an increase in the proportion of reticulocytes in the blood. This is the *reticulocyte response.*

Erythropoiesis produces an almost incredible quantity of erythrocytes. A single drop of blood contains perhaps 50 cubic millimeters and in each cubic millimeter of male blood there is an average of 5,400,000 erythrocytes. The corresponding figure for female blood is slightly less — 4,800,000.* This means that an average man would possess some 25,000,000,000,000 (that is, 25 trillion) erythrocytes, and the average woman would possess 17 trillion.

Once an erythrocyte has reached the stage where it has lost its nucleus, it can no longer grow and divide. It can only continue in its own person, for as long as it can last. This is not long — its life of bumping along blood vessels and, in particular, squeezing through the capillaries is a strenuous one. The average length of time an erythrocyte endures is 125 days. Signs of disintegrated erythrocytes that have reached the end of their useful and hard-working lives can be seen under the microscope as *hemoconia* (hee'moh-koh'nee-uh; "blood dust" G), or *blood dust* in direct English. This is filtered out in the spleen and absorbed there by large scavenging cells called *macrophages* (mak'roh-fay-jez; "large eaters" G).

On the average, then, we can count upon having 1/125 of our erythrocytes broken up each day, or 2,300,000 each second. Fortunately, the body is perfectly capable of making new erythro-

---

* Although the average woman has less blood for her weight than the average man, and although what blood she does have is less rich in erythrocytes, this does not make her the weaker sex. It is true that up to about a century ago, women had a distinctly lower life expectancy than men, largely because of the deadly danger of childbearing. With the introduction of antiseptic techniques to the childbed, this danger largely passed and women now prove to have a life expectancy anywhere from three to seven years greater than men.

cytes at that rate continuously, throughout life, and at even faster rates, if warranted. One way of stimulating erythropoiesis is to have the blood continuously low in oxygen. This would be the case at high altitudes, where the air is thin. Under those circumstances, more erythrocytes are formed and, among people who live at high elevations, the erythrocyte count can be maintained at an 8,000,000 per cubic millimeter level.

In the larger blood vessels, the erythrocytes tend to stack themselves flat side to flat side. This is called "rouleaux formation" from the French, but we can picture it best, in less esoteric fashion, by thinking of a stack of poker chips. Blood flows through the larger vessels more easily when the erythrocytes neatly stack themselves in this fashion. However, rouleaux formation is not possible in the capillaries, which are in diameter barely, if at all, wider than the erythrocytes themselves. The erythrocytes must crawl along the capillaries singly and slowly, shouldering their way through the narrow openings rather like a man inching through a close-fitting tunnel on hands and knees. This is all for the best, since it gives them ample time to pick up oxygen, or to give it off.

A single erythrocyte contains about 270,000,000 hemoglobin molecules and each molecule possesses four heme groups. Each heme group is capable of attaching one oxygen molecule to itself. Therefore, an erythrocyte that enters the lung capillaries with no oxygen emerges at the other end with a load of something more than a billion oxygen molecules. The same volume of water by simple solution could not carry more than 1/70 the quantity. The existence of hemoglobin thus increases the efficiency of the bloodstream as an oxygen carrier some seventyfold. Instead of having a 4½-second reserve supply of oxygen in our bloodstream, we have a 5-minute supply. This is still not much, and a few minutes' asphyxiation is enough to throttle us, but at least it gives us a sufficient margin of safety to carry on life.

When oxygen diffuses across the triple barrier (the alveolar membrane, the wall of the capillary, and the membrane of the erythrocyte) and attaches itself to the hemoglobin molecule, a new compound — *oxyhemoglobin* — is formed. It is the oxy-hemoglobin that is the bright red we actually think of as the color of blood. The hemoglobin itself, unoxygenated, is a bluish-purple color. As the blood passes through the systemic circulation and loses oxygen, it gradually darkens in color, until in the veins it is quite blue. You can, as a matter of fact, see this blue color in the veins on the back of your hand, on the inside of the wrist, and anywhere else that veins come near the surface of the body, if you are sufficiently fair-skinned. Sometimes the color appears greenish, because you see it through a layer of skin that may contain a small amount of a yellowish pigment. Nevertheless, few of us associate this blue or green color with blood, for the blood we actually see during bleeding is always bright red. Even if we cut a vein and allow the dark blood to gush out-ward, it would absorb oxygen as soon as it touched the air and it would turn bright red.

The bright red oxygenated blood is called *arterial blood*, be-cause it is to be found in the aorta and in the other arteries of the systemic circulation. The dark unoxygenated blood is called *venous blood*, because it is to be found in the veins of the sys-temic circulation. This is not entirely a good set of names, for of course the situation is reversed in the pulmonary circulation. The pulmonary artery leads unoxygenated blood to the lungs and thus carries venous blood despite the fact that it is an artery. As for the pulmonary vein, it carries the freshest arterial blood in the body.

ANEMIA

Any deficiency in erythrocytes or hemoglobin (or both) is, of course, serious for the body economy. Such a condition is called *anemia* ("no blood" G, a slight exaggeration of the condition). In severe anemia the number of erythrocytes may sink to a third of the normal and the quantity of hemoglobin may sink to a tenth. In an anemic the efficiency of oxygen transport is reduced and the amount of energy available for use is correspondingly reduced. Consequently, one of the most prominent symptoms of anemia, aside from paleness, is the ease with which one tires.

The most direct cause of anemia is the loss of blood through a wound, either through accident or disease. Such blood flow is *hemorrhage* ("blood flow" G). In addition to the obvious external flows as a result of cuts, stabs, and scrapes, there is the possibility of *internal hemorrhage* as a result of physical injury or of a disease such as a bleeding ulcer. Nor need the hemorrhage be massive. A small but chronic hemorrhage, such as that involved in tuberculosis lesions of the lungs, can also induce a degree of anemia.

The danger of massive hemorrhages is twofold. First, a quantity of fluid is lost, and second, a proportional quantity of each of the chemical components of that fluid (of which the most important, next to water itself, is hemoglobin) is lost. The body has several devices for making up a reasonable loss of fluid. The arterioles contract, reducing the capacity of the circulatory system, so that the diminished quantity of fluid remaining in the body is nevertheless maintained at as nearly normal a blood pressure as possible. (Normal pressure is more important than normal volume.) The spleen also contracts, adding its reserve supply of blood to the general circulation. Fluid is withdrawn from the tissues outside the circulatory system and is added to the blood; the patient, of course, will also add fluid by drinking.

Where the loss is not too great, water is replaced quickly enough, but a longer time is required to replace some of the substances dissolved in the plasma, particularly the complex protein molecules. The erythrocytes are replaced most slowly, so that there is a definite period of *post-hemorrhagic anemia*. This may last 6 to 8 weeks after the loss of a pint of blood, but it is not serious. The body has its margins of safety and a temporary mild anemia will not interfere with ordinary living. Thus, a person can give a pint of blood to the Red Cross without any subsequent discomfiture to speak of if he is in normal health to begin with.

Larger loss of blood is correspondingly more serious. If more than 40 per cent of the blood is lost, the body's machinery is incapable of bringing about reasonable recovery quickly enough for its needs. It is then advisable to transfer blood directly into the patient's bloodstream. The blood may come from the reserves of a blood bank or from a living donor, and the process is *transfusion* ("pour across" L).

Unfortunately, transfusion cannot involve any two persons taken at random. Human blood falls into four main types, which are categorized as O, A, B, and AB. The erythrocytes of a man with blood type A contain a substance we can call A, while those of a man with blood type B contain one we can call B. A man with blood type AB has erythrocytes containing both A and B, whereas one with blood type O has erythrocytes containing neither A nor B.

These groups are not of equal size. In the United States, out of every 18 people, 8 are of blood type O and 7 are of blood type A. Only 2 are of blood type B and only 1 of blood type AB.

It so happens that blood plasma may contain compounds capable of reacting with A or with B, causing erythrocytes containing the particular substance to clump together, or *agglutinate* ("glue together" L). We can call the substance causing A erythrocytes to agglutinate *anti-A*, and that causing B erythrocytes to agglutinate would be *anti-B*. A person of blood type A, with A in his erythrocytes invariably has anti-B in his plasma. (Naturally, he would not have anti-A for that would cause his own erythrocytes to agglutinate and kill him.)

In the same way, a person of blood type B would be expected to have anti-A in his plasma. A person of blood type AB, with both *A* and *B* in his erythrocytes would have to have neither anti-*A* nor anti-*B* in his plasma; a person of blood type O, with neither *A* nor *B* in his erythrocytes, would have both anti-*A* and anti-*B* in his plasma.

The situation will undoubtedly be made clearer by this brief table:

	Red cell	Plasma
Blood type O	—	anti-*A*, anti-*B*
Blood type A	*A*	anti-*B*
Blood type B	*B*	anti-*A*
Blood type AB	*A, B*	—

Ideally, in making a transfusion, one should have both donor and recipient of the same blood group. Suppose that through accident or ignorance, though, the donor and the recipient are not of the same blood group. Suppose that blood is taken from a B-donor and given to an A-recipient. There are two possibilities of agglutination. First, the B donor has blood containing anti-*A* in the plasma. This anti-*A* agglutinates the erythrocytes of the A-recipient. This, however, is not usually very important. The quantity of anti-*A* in the plasma being transfused is not very much and what is present is quickly diluted by the larger quantity of blood in the recipient's own body. However, the second possibility is more serious. There is anti-*B* in the plasma of the A-recipient. The erythrocytes in the blood of the B-donor are themselves agglutinated by the large quantity of anti-*B* in the patient's blood supply. What the patient receives, then, is not real blood but a helping of clumped erythrocytes that promptly block his blood vessels, with frequently fatal results. The wrong transfusion is worse than none.

The important precaution is to prevent the donation of erythrocytes that will be agglutinated by the recipient's plasma. To illustrate, a patient with blood type A has anti-*B* in his plasma and therefore must not receive erythrocytes containing *B*. That eliminates donors with blood type B or AB. It does not eliminate a donor of either blood type A or blood type O. You can see for yourself, by the same line of reasoning, that a B-patient can receive blood from a donor of blood type B or blood type O, but not from one of blood type A or blood type AB. In fact, it is easy to prepare a table such as the following:

Patient	Possible donor
O	O
A	A, O
B	B, O
AB	AB, A, B, O

As you can see, an O-donor can be used for any patient; he is sometimes referred to as a "universal donor." (Actually, a particular O-donor may have enough anti-A or anti-B in his plasma to cause complications to A, B, or AB patients. It remains safest to use a donor of the patient's own blood group.)

Where large amounts of blood are lost, the fluid loss becomes more dangerous, from a short-term point of view, than the loss of erythrocytes. The fluid loss may be great enough so that despite all the body's compensatory mechanisms what is left is insufficient to maintain normal blood pressure, and this is more immediately perilous than hemorrhagic anemia.

In this case, transfusion must be completed without delay, and if blood is not available transfusion of plasma alone is far, far better than nothing. Blood pressure is maintained and the anemia can be dealt with in more leisurely fashion.

There are even advantages to making use of the plasma alone. Plasma keeps better than whole blood does. In fact, plasma can even be frozen and dried under vacuum to yield a powder that will keep indefinitely and that will be ready for use any time sterile distilled water is added. Secondly, with no red cells present, there is no need to worry about blood types and agglutination.

(There are, of course, blood types in existence other than A, B, O, and AB. In recent years the number of detectable types has increased greatly, but these other blood types are not usually of importance in transfusion.)

Even when there is no loss of blood itself, the body may fail to manufacture some essential component of the oxygen-carrying system. In that case, the body is subjected to the same weariness and disability (if not to the blood-pressure loss) that would result from hemorrhage. The most obvious anemia-producing failure of the body's chemical mechanisms is one where it does not produce hemoglobin, and here the weak point rests with the iron component. Except for the iron atoms, all portions of the hemoglobin molecule can be manufactured from the ordinary and plentiful components of virtually all food. Nothing but serious and long continued undernourishment would interfere with the process of making hemoglobin protein; and this would interfere with protein manufacture generally and not with hemoglobin alone.

The iron atoms (four per molecule) make hemoglobin a special case. Food is not generally rich in available iron. Iron that forms part of an organic molecule, such as heme itself, is not easily absorbed by the body. For this reason meat and eggs, which are rich in iron, nevertheless offer only a marginal supply. Adult men need not be seriously concerned, since the body conserves its iron efficiently and loses virtually none of it, always barring hemorrhage. In the case of children, who grow and whose supply of hemoglobin must increase with the years, the available iron content of the food is a more crucial matter. The iron-enriched cereals constantly fed children these days is helpful in this respect.

Young adult women have a particular problem. Because of menstrual flow they are subjected to periodic losses of 25 milligrams of iron each month. This is not much in an absolute sense (about a thousandth of an ounce) but it must be made up, and young women, often intent on remaining slim at all costs, may not have sufficient iron in their limited diet. In any case, *iron-deficiency anemia* is more common among young women than among other classes of the population.

Fortunately, iron-deficiency anemia is easily treated by the addition of iron to the diet. Iron is most easily absorbed when it is in the form of inorganic salts and "iron pills" are frequently used during pregnancy. Although the menstrual losses come to an end then, the mother's body is depleted of its iron supply in order that the baby might be started with an oversupply. The baby's iron supply, after all, must be more than merely enough to meet its needs at the new-born moment. It must also be enough to allow for new blood manufacture during its first six months of life when milk, very poor in iron, is almost the only item on its diet.

Anemia may exist even when iron is plentiful provided the oxygen-carrying mechanism is disabled in some other fashion. Occasionally, for instance, there is a flaw in body-chemistry which brings about the manufacture of a hemoglobin very slightly different from ordinary hemoglobin. Such an *abnormal hemoglobin* is invariably less efficient as an oxygen-carrier.

The most common form of such an abnormal hemoglobin gives rise to *sickle-cell anemia*. This particular abnormal hemoglobin is less soluble than normal hemoglobin and actually precipitates out of solution within the erythrocyte when the oxygen content of blood is low, as in the veins. The erythrocytes, with the abnormal hemoglobin crystallizing within it, is distorted into bizarre shapes, sometimes into crescents resembling sickles (whence the name of the disease). The distorted erythrocytes are weakened and fragile, breaking up easily to produce an anemia. This is an inherited condition for which there is no treatment. It is found almost exclusively in natives of certain West African regions and in their descendants, including a number of American Negroes.

Striking more arbitrarily is a deficiency in the body's ability to make the material of the erythrocyte itself. This material is the *stroma* ("mattress" G; that is, something on which the cell contents can rest). The erythrocytes that are formed with defective stroma are abnormally weak and have an average life of 40 days rather than 125 days. The erythrocytes decrease steadily in number until a count of less than 2,500,000 per cubic millimeter may be reached. The individual cells are usually larger than normal but that does not compensate for the loss in numbers. This disease, *pernicious anemia* ("pernicious" meaning "deadly"), was so called because until the 1920's, no successful treatment was known and death was inevitable.

In the 1920's it was found that large quantities of liver in the diet would relieve the condition, and by the late 1940's small quantities of a compound called vitamin B_{12} or *cyanocobalamin* (sy'an-oh-koh-bawl'uh-min; thus named because its molecule contains a cyanide group, a cobalt atom and an amine group) were isolated from liver and found to be the curative principle. The vitamin can now be formed cheaply through controlled bacterial fermentation in the laboratory, and, at the cost of taking pills at periodic intervals, people with pernicious anemia can lead normal lives. The anemia is no longer pernicious.

Chemicals accidentally introduced into the body, or toxins from invading microorganisms, can in one way or another damage the oxygen-carrying capacity of the blood. The malarial parasite infests the erythrocyte and breaks it up. This is *hemolysis* (hee-mol'i-sis; "blood destruction" G), and it is during the period of hemolysis when the patient is attacked by the violent chills that accompany malaria. The venom of snakes and other creatures may also hemolyze the blood, or sometimes bring about erythrocyte agglutination. In either case, the results are often fatal.

The gas carbon monoxide represents a danger originating in the inanimate world. Like oxygen, carbon monoxide will combine with the hemoglobin in blood. Unlike oxygen, carbon monoxide is not freely given up again. It remains bound. Even when the air contains but small quantities of carbon monoxide, molecule after molecule of hemoglobin is tied up and rendered unavailable for oxygen transport.

Other gases can behave similarly, but carbon monoxide is most dangerous because it is most common. It can be formed in any poorly ventilated furnace, and it is also to be found in automobile exhaust and in one common form of cooking gas. All three sources of carbon monoxide are commonly implicated in death by asphyxiation, either as accident or suicide.

Too much of a good thing can also be deadly. The manufacture of erythrocytes is stimulated, as I said earlier, by a lower than normal content of oxygen in the blood. Ordinarily, as the number of erythrocytes in the blood is increased, the oxygen content also increases and the rapid formation of new erythrocytes levels off. It is possible, though, that the blood vessels feeding the bone marrow (where the erythrocytes are formed) are thickened, perhaps through atherosclerosis, so that the blood supply to those tissues is cut down. The marrow suffers from an oxygen shortage, which is the result of the narrowed blood vessels and not of any real lack of oxygen in the blood. The manufacture of erythrocytes is accelerated but does not correct the situation, so the manufacture continues without stint. The result is a dangerous crowding of the blood with erythrocytes, a condition called *polycythemia* (pol'ee-sy-thee'mee-uh; "many cells in the blood" G). The blood becomes thick and viscous at levels far beyond normal, circulation breaks down, and the results may be fatal.

LEUKOCYTES AND THROMBOCYTES

In addition to the erythrocytes, the blood contains normal cells, complete with nuclei. These are the *leukocytes* (lyoo'koh-sites;

"white cells" G; since, unlike the erythrocytes, they lack pigment) and, as a matter of fact, they are often called simply *white cells*. They are also frequently termed *white blood corpuscles* by analogy with the red, though the leukocytes are not merely corpuscles but are true cells.

Most of the leukocytes, but not all, are manufactured in the bone marrow along with the erythrocytes. In the initial stages, the cells are first *myeloblasts* (my'uh-loh-blasts; "marrow buds" G) and then *myelocytes* ("marrow cells" G). They are formed in large quantities, but their life is a hard and dangerous one and they do not generally live long. As a result, the number in the blood at any one time is merely 7000 per cubic millimeter, so that erythrocytes outnumber leukocytes some 650 to 1. Nevertheless, over the total blood supply, the number mounts up and the average man possesses some 75 billion leukocytes at any given moment.

The leukocytes exist in a number of varieties, differing among themselves in size and appearance. In general, they can be divided into two classes: those having a granular appearance (*granular leukocytes*) and those which do not (*agranular leukocytes*). The granular leukocytes usually have a nucleus of complicated shape, formed into two or more lobes. They are sometimes called *polymorphonuclear leukocytes* (pol'ee-mor'foh-nyoo'klee-ur; "nucleus of many forms" G) as a result. These ordinarily make up about two thirds of all the leukocytes in the bloodstream. They can in turn be divided into three types, depending on whether they stain with an acid dye such as eosin, a basic dye, or a neutral dye. The types are called, respectively, *eosinophils* (ee'oh-sin'oh-filz; "eosin-loving" G), *basophils*

MYELOBLAST   EOSINOPHIL
                    MYELOCYTE

(bay'soh-filz; "base-loving" G), and *neutrophils* (nyoo'troh-filz; "neutral-loving" G). Of these the neutrophils are by far the most common.

As for the agranular leukocytes, which make up the remaining third of the white cells, they are characterized by large nuclei, simpler in shape than those of the granular leukocytes, without separate lobes and sometimes filling most of the cell. They are also divided into three types, which are, in order of decreasing size, *monocytes* (mon'oh-sites; "single cell" G, referring to the nucleus with its single lobe), *large lymphocytes,* and *small lymphocytes.* The small lymphocytes (I'll explain the name later) are not much larger than erythrocytes in size, and make up about a quarter of all the leukocytes. Next to the neutrophils, the small lymphocytes are the most common of the leukocytes. The agranular leukocytes are not manufactured in the blood marrow — a subject I shall return to later.

It might be helpful to clarify matters by making a table:

	Number per cubic millimeter		
All leukocytes	7000		
Granular leukocytes		4625	
Neutrophils			4500
Eosinophils			100
Basophils			25
Agranular leukocytes		2375	
Small lymphocytes			1700
Monocytes			450
Large lymphocytes			225

BASOPHIL   NEUTROPHIL   MONOCYTE

The neutrophils are remarkable for their ability to progress through amoeboid motion. In fact they, and to a lesser extent other leukocytes, can pinch themselves enough to squeeze between the cells making up the thin walls of a capillary. In this way they can leave the circulatory system altogether and enter other tissues. This process is *diapedesis* (dy'uh-puh-dee'sis; "squeeze through" G).

This ability is extremely important, for the leukocytes are the shock troops of the body, being able to ingest and digest bacteria and other foreign particles. The invasion of bacteria at any point gives rise to a stimulus that brings about diapedesis nearby. Leukocytes carried to the spot by the bloodstream enter the tissue in quantity and devour the bacteria much as an amoeba might ingest some food particle. This process is *phagocytosis* (fag'oh-sy-to'sis; "eating of cells" G), and is one of the chief defenses of the body against infection.

(Another, more subtle, defense rests with certain proteins called *antibodies* in the blood plasma. These are manufactured under the stimulus of the presence of a foreign substance, let us say a bacterial toxin or the carbohydrate in the surface of a bacterial cell. The antibodies that are formed will combine specifically with the particular toxin or the particular bacterial cell surface that stimulated their formation. They will, in one way or another, put the toxin or bacterium out of action. In the course of a lifetime, an individual collects many types of antibodies, which by their mere existence and their continuous readiness to combine with invading substances make him resistant to numerous ills.)

The leukocytes do not find the bacteria harmless. The bacteria contain toxins that can in turn kill the leukocytes. Depending on the nature of the bacteria, a leukocyte may ingest as many as fifty or as few as two before being killed itself. At the site of infection, dead and disintegrating leukocytes collect as *pus* ("corruption" G). We are most commonly made aware of this when an infection of a hair follicle produces a boil. The blood collecting in that spot (bringing leukocytes to the scene of action) reddens and swells the area, while the fluid pressure makes it painful. The tissues between the focal point of infection and the skin are gradually broken down until finally only a thin membrane covers the conglomeration of pus and bacteria. The boil "comes to a head" and finally breaks, discharging the pus.

The number of leukocytes in the blood will rise or fall in response to certain abnormal conditions. A rise is called *leukocytosis* (lyoo'koh-sy-toh'sis; the suffix "osis" being used in medical terminology to signify a pathological increase of something) and a fall is *leukopenia* (lyoo'koh-pee'nee-uh; "poverty of white cells" G). The change is not necessarily uniform among the various types of cells and it is sometimes useful to make a differential count. To do this a smear of blood is stained and studied under the microscope. The changes in proportions of the various types can then be used as an aid in diagnosis. In acute infections, for instance, the neutrophil count goes up (*neutrophilia*).

A particularly serious type of increase in leukocyte number is the result of a cancer of the tissues producing them. Cancer is a disease characterized by unrestrained growth, and in this case the unrestrained growth consists of the manufacture of leukocytes without limit. The leukocyte count may go up to 250,000 per cubic millimeter, a rise of 35-fold, or even more. The white cells, by sheer quantity, invade and involve other organs, impairing their usefulness. The manufacture of erythrocytes is squeezed out by the overflow of the leukocyte-manufacturing mechanism, so an anemia is produced. This disease, invariably fatal, is *leukemia* (lyoo-kee'mee-uh; "white blood" G).

There is a third type of formed element in the blood, smaller and even less of a cell than is the erythrocyte. These are the *platelets*, so called from their platelike flatness. They are only half the diameter of the erythrocytes. Because they are involved in the phenomenon of clotting they are called *thrombocytes* (throm′boh-sites; "clotting cells" G). The thrombocytes are formed in bone marrow, as erythrocytes are. They begin as unusually large cells with a mass of multiple nuclei, called *megakaryocytes* (meg-uh-kar′ee-oh-sites; "giant nucleated cells" G). These are five times the diameter of an ordinary cell, twenty-five times the diameter of the final platelet. A week after formation, a megakaryocyte will develop graininess in its cytoplasm and will then fall apart into small pieces — the thrombocytes. The average lifetime of the thrombocytes once in the blood is only about 8 to 10 days. They are more numerous than leukocytes, but less numerous than erythrocytes; in numbers they come to 250,000 per cubic millimeter.

The thrombocytes come into play whenever, through some sort of wound, blood oozes out past the barrier of the skin. Contact with air breaks the thrombocyte, exposing its contents. These initiate a series of chemical changes which ends by converting *fibrinogen* (fy-brin′oh-jen; "fiber-producing" G), a soluble protein of the blood plasma, into the insoluble fibers of *fibrin* (fy′brin). The fibers of fibrin settle out of the blood as a fine network in which formed elements are trapped. The network plus its trapped cells make up a clot that seals off the wound and stops blood flow. With loss of blood prevented, the wound is repaired, and eventually the hardened clot, or scab, falls off.

Involved in the complicated process of clot formation are a number of *clotting factors,* all of which must respond properly before the final result is satisfactorily achieved. Sometimes one or another of the clotting factors may be missing and clotting fails to take place. This may be brought about deliberately. A sample of blood may be "defibrinated" by rapid stirring while it is being collected. The fibrin that is formed knots about the stirring rod and can be removed. If the formed elements are then centrifuged out, what is left is plasma minus the fibrinogen. This is *blood serum.* It does not offer the problem of clot formation and is so commonly used in laboratory manipulations that "serum" is almost a more familiar word than "plasma" in connection with blood.

Sometimes a chemical such as oxalate or citrate is added to blood as it is collected. This ties up the calcium ion in blood (one of the clotting factors) and clotting cannot take place. Sometimes a compound called *heparin* (hep'uh-rin; "liver" G, because it was first isolated from liver) is added to blood to prevent its clotting, for heparin ties up another of the clotting factors. This is handy during operations, when premature clotting is something a surgeon does not want to happen.

Unfortunately, it sometimes happens that a person is born with an inability to manufacture one of the clotting factors. When this happens, he is a "bleeder"; that is, once bleeding starts, it is extremely difficult to stop it. The condition is *hemophilia* (hee'moh-fil'ee-uh; "love of bleeding" G).

LYMPH

I have already pointed out that the circulatory system is not composed of truly closed tubes, since various leukocytes have no trouble escaping from the capillaries. It is not surprising that if large cells can do so the tiny molecules of water and of some of the substances it holds in solution can also do so. And, actually, under the pressure of the blood pumping through the arteries, fluid *is* squeezed out of the capillaries. This takes place at the arteriole end, where pressure in those tiny vessels is highest.

This exuded fluid, which bathes the cells of the body and acts as a kind of middleman between the blood and the cells, is called *interstitial fluid* (in'ter-stish'ul), because it is to be found in the interstices among the cells. In terms of sheer quantity there is far more interstitial fluid than there is blood plasma, eight liters of the former to only three of the latter in the average human being.

Interstitial fluid is not quite like plasma in composition, for not all the dissolved material in plasma managed to get through the capillary walls. About half the protein remains behind, so interstitial fluid is only 3 to 4 per cent protein, whereas plasma is some 7 per cent protein.

Naturally, the capillaries cannot continue to lose fluid indefinitely and there is a kind of circulation here, too. Some of the interstitial fluid re-enters the capillaries at the venule end, where the blood pressure is considerably less than at the arterial end. In addition, the tissue spaces contain thin-walled capillaries that come to blind ends, and through these capillaries some of the interstitial fluid drains off. Once in the tubes, the interstitial fluid is called *lymph* ("clear water" L); it certainly resembles clear water when compared with the viscous red blood. The vessels themselves are the *lymph capillaries*, or *lymphatics*.

The lymph capillaries join to form larger and still larger lymphatics and eventually join to form the right and left *lymphatic ducts*. These drain into the subclavian veins just behind the collarbone, and in this way lymph is restored to the blood vessels. The left lymphatic duct is the larger of the two, and the largest lymphatic in the body. It is usually called the *thoracic duct* because it passes up through the chest, or thorax, to its point of junction with the subclavian vein.

The lymph flows very slowly through the lymphatics. There is no pumping action and, as in the case of the veins, the chief motive force is the pressure of the muscles during the ordinary activity of the body. Again, as in the case of many of the veins, the lymphatics have one-way valves which see to it that the fluid flows only in the proper direction. Because of the slow flow through the lymphatics, very little of the interstitial fluid is restored to the circulation in that way as compared with the direct return through the venule ends of the capillaries. Nevertheless, the lymphatics act as a useful regulating factor, since flow increases and decreases with the fluid pressure within the tissues, and it acts to keep the pressure at a normal level. The effect of the regulation is most easily noted in its absence. When there is blockage of the lymphatics for any reason, fluid accumulates in tissues, bringing about *edema* (ee-dee′muh; "swelling" G), or *dropsy* ("water" G). The larvae of a tropical worm sometimes invade the body and succeed in blocking the lymphatic system, bringing about so exaggerated a swelling of the legs, for instance, as to give the disease the name of *elephantiasis* (el-e-fan-ty′i-sis).

More localized and temporary edematous conditions occur in the neighborhood of a mosquito bite or bee sting. Edema also accompanies certain allergic reactions, as in *hives*.

Scattered along the lymphatics at various places, particularly at the elbow, knee, armpit, and groin, are little beanlike masses into which several lymphatics enter and from which a larger one emerges. These were originally called *lymph glands* ("acorn" L) because there seemed a resemblance to an acorn. The word "gland" has a peculiar history. Because the lymph glands are small bits of tissue, other small bits of tissue came to be called glands even where there was no resemblance at all to an acorn. Then it was discovered that some of these glands secreted fluids of various sorts, some through a duct leading to the surface of the skin or into the intestines, and some directly into the bloodstream. This is why anatomists came to call any organ that formed a secretion a gland, even when it was quite large and unacornlike. The liver, for instance, a huge organ weighing three to four pounds, is called a gland because it secretes a fluid into the digestive canal.

From this new standpoint, the lymph glands — the original glands — were no longer glands, since they secreted no fluid. For this reason an alternate name, *lymph nodes* ("knot" L, because lymphatics seem to come together at those points to form a knotlike swelling), has gained popularity. It is at the lymph nodes that the agranular leukocytes are formed, and this is why two of the varieties are called *lymphocytes*. Although the lymph contains no erythrocytes or thrombocytes to speak of, it is rich in lymphocytes, and the nodes themselves are crammed with them.

The nodes thus form a second line of defense against infection behind the first line of the neutrophils that go swarming into the tissues immediately affected. Any bacteria or other foreign matter that has evaded or forced its way past the neutrophils and has entered the circulation will be filtered out at the nodes. There bacteria are killed and toxins neutralized (for another function of the nodes is the manufacture of the plasma proteins that form antibodies).

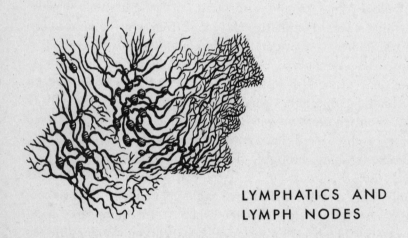

LYMPHATICS AND
LYMPH NODES

In the process, the nodes swell and may become painful; those being particularly affected which are nearer the original site of infection. The presence of "swollen glands" (as they are called by mother and doctor alike, in defiance of the newer terminology) at the angle of the jaw, in the armpit, or in the groin, is an indication of an infection of some sort.

The battle against infection is also carried on by larger bits of tissue similar in nature to the lymph nodes and therefore called *lymphoid tissue*. The spleen, which I mentioned earlier in the chapter, is the largest piece of lymphoid tissue in the body. It too is a filter, removing dying red cells and other debris. The macrophages that consume the debris are a form of monocyte. (This points up another function of the leukocytes, that of scavenging. The large leukocytes are useful since they can take bigger "bites.")

There are also scraps of lymphoid tissue in the throat and nose, standing guard, in a sense, at the points of greatest danger. These may be generally called *tonsils,* but the term is popularly restricted to the two rather large masses (an inch by half an inch) located where the pharynx meets the soft palate. There are also some 35 to 100 tiny scraps of lymphoid tissue at the rear of the tongue. These are the *lingual tonsils*. Where the pharynx meets the nasal passages there are a pair of *pharyngeal tonsils*. All these tonsils act as the lymph nodes do, in filtering out bacteria and combating them by lymphocytes. As in the case of the nodes, they can, when the struggle is hard, become inflamed, swollen, and painful (*tonsillitis*). In extreme cases, their protective function can be drowned out and they can, on the contrary, become a source of infection. It may then be advisable to remove them in a familiar operation referred to as a *tonsillectomy* (the suffix "ectomy," from a Greek word meaning "to cut out," is commonly used in medical terminology to signify the surgical removal of any part of the body. That tells you, for example, what an "appendectomy" is). The swelling of the pharyngeal tonsils may interfere with breathing if extreme enough, and they may be removed also. They are more familiarly known, by the way, as *adenoids* ("glandlike" G).

Certain primitive cells present in lymphoid tissue and in places such as lungs, liver, bone marrow, blood vessels, and connective tissue seem also to serve as scavengers, as do the macrophages in the spleen. They are sometimes lumped together as making up the *reticulo-endothelial system.* The "endothelium" refers to a layer of flat cells lining the interior of lymphatics and "reticulum" means a network. The reticulo-endothelial system is a network of cells that includes those lining the lymphatic vessels, in other words.

8

OUR INTESTINES

FOOD

Oxygen, taken by itself, is not a source of energy. To supply the energy required by the body, oxygen must be combined with carbon and hydrogen atoms making up the molecules to be found in food, forming carbon dioxide and water in the process. The ultimate source of food lies with the green plant. Green plants, at the expense of solar energy, combine carbon dioxide and water to form complex organic molecules formed largely of carbon and hydrogen atoms. These molecules fall mainly into three classes: carbohydrates, lipids (fats), and proteins. Any of these can be combined, through a complicated series of chemical reactions, with oxygen, and in the process the energy needed to support life is liberated.

Animals do not, as plants do, build up the complex molecules of carbohydrates, lipids, and proteins from the simple molecules of carbon dioxide and water and then live on them. Instead, they rifle the stores painfully built up by plants, or they eat animals that have already fed on plants.

The simplest method by which an animal can feed is exemplified in the protozoa. The amoeba, for instance, simply flows about an organism tinier than itself, or about a piece of organic matter, trapping it within itself in a water-filled *food vacuole* (vak′yoo-ole; "empty" L, because it looks like an empty hole in the cell substance, except for the particle of food which it contains). Into the vacuole are discharged specialized proteins called *enzymes* (en′zimez; "in yeast" G, because those found in yeast cells were among the first that were thoroughly studied). The enzymes act to accelerate the breakdown of complex molecules in the trapped food, forming simpler and smaller molecules which the cell can then incorporate into its own substance and build up into complex molecules somewhat different from those of the food and characteristic, instead, of the organism itself.*

This form of feeding requires that the article of food be smaller than the cell involved in the act; and as an organism grows larger, it would clearly be increasingly difficult to live on food particles that were always smaller than the size of its cells. It would be more efficient for one sizable organism to take as its prey another sizable organism, so that the predator could find its food supply in the form of a large and concentrated chunk. Of course, it could not very well engulf this large and concentrated chunk into any of its cells. Instead, it would have to break it down through enzyme action first and then absorb the products.

This would be all but impossible in the open ocean. As food was broken down, water currents would sweep the products away, were the process to take place in the open, and competing eaters would then take their share. The solution was to sequester a small portion of the ocean and in that portion to break down the food in peace and privacy.

The simplest organisms to accomplish this task were those ancestral to modern jellyfish. Essentially such organisms are a double layer of cells built in the shape of a hollow vase. The opening into the "vase" is the primitive *mouth* (AS). In the

---

* For some of the chemical details of the manner in which plants build up complex molecules and animals break them down, I refer you once again to my book *Life and Energy*. The same book considers the nature and workings of enzymes at some length.

case of these animals the mouth is usually fringed by tentacles capable of stinging and stunning the prey, which could then be popped into the interior of the "vase" or *gut* (AS). Into the gut would pour enzymes from the surrounding cells, and the complex organism would be broken down into simpler substances and as much as possible converted into soluble form. This process is *digestion* ("to dissolve" L). The dissolved materials produced by digestion are then absorbed into the various cells forming the lining of the gut, and those portions of the food incapable of being broken down ("indigestible residue") are cast out through the mouth opening. It is because of the development of the gut that the phylum to which the jellyfish belongs is called *Coelenterata* (see-len'tuh-ray'tuh; "hollow gut" L). I mentioned this phylum in Chapter 1 as very probably ancestral to all other multicellular phyla.

Naturally, the larger the animal, the larger the gut, and the larger the individual piece of food that could be handled. Increased size invokes the square-cube law (mentioned in Chapter 5) and increased efficiency becomes also necessary. One obvious bit of room for improvement lies in the fact that the typical coelenterate has only one opening into its gut. Through that opening food must enter and indigestible residue depart. While one function operates, the other cannot.

The next step, then, carried through first by certain worms, was to add a second opening in the rear of the animal, a kind of back door. The original opening would remain for use as a food intake, the second would be reserved for residue ejection. The food would pass through the tube in one direction only and feeding could, in theory, be continuous.

All animals more complex than those worms (and this includes ourselves) retain the fundamental body plan of a tube with two openings running the length of the organism. The tube is called the *alimentary canal* ("food" L), the *digestive canal*, or simply the *food canal*. Substances within the alimentary canal

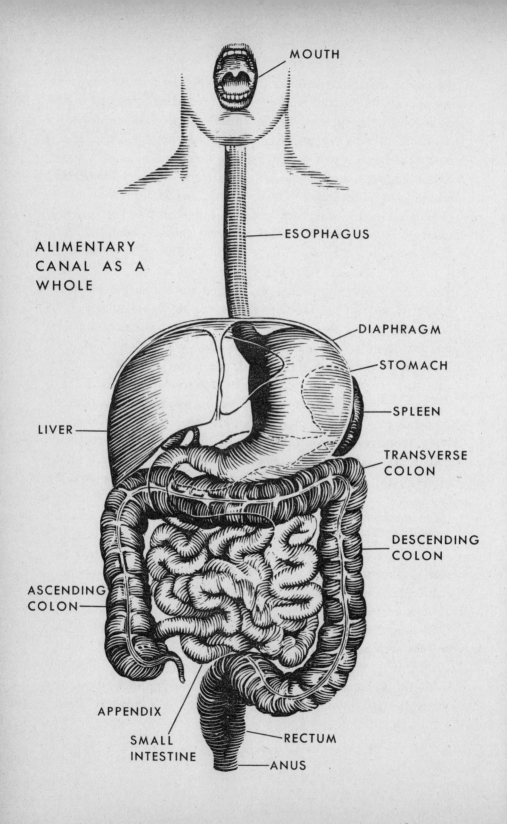

MOUTH

ESOPHAGUS

ALIMENTARY CANAL AS A WHOLE

DIAPHRAGM

STOMACH

SPLEEN

LIVER

TRANSVERSE COLON

DESCENDING COLON

ASCENDING COLON

APPENDIX

SMALL INTESTINE

RECTUM

ANUS

are not truly within the body, therefore; merely inside a tube that is open to the outside world at both ends, like the hole in a doughnut. Actually this fact is not as obvious as it might be, since it's impractical to have the openings to the outer world really open; the canal would then be traversed by wind or current a bit too freely. Instead, both ends are usually pinched off, so that the volume between might be the more thoroughly under the control of the body. In appearance, then, the essential structural similarity between ourselves and a doughnut is obscured.

THE MOUTH

In ourselves, the entrance to the alimentary canal is pinched off by a circular band of muscle that runs around the lips, one that we use when we purse the lips. It is the *orbicularis oris* (awr-bi'kyoo-lay'ris oh'ris; "little circle around the mouth" L).

Such a circular muscle is usually called a *sphincter* (sfink'tur; "to bind tight" G); it ordinarily remains in a state of contraction, drawing an aperture closed as though the drawstrings of a purse had been pulled. In this respect the orbicularis oris is not much of a sphincter, for it is generally partly relaxed and we do not ordinarily go about with pursed lips. Nevertheless, it is sometimes called the *sphincter oris.*

When the lower jaw is pulled downward and the orbicularis oris relaxes, the entrance to the alimentary canal is opened wide and the portion we see is the mouth. The most obvious of its characteristics is that it is red. It is lined, not with skin but with a much thinner mucous membrane. Because it is thinner than skin, the membrane is more transparent and its color is that of the blood in the small blood vessels with which it is liberally supplied.

The mucous membrane folds outward into the face proper, forming a pair of *lips* (AS), a structure which, in its full development, exists in mammals only. The existence of soft and muscular lips in mammals makes sense, for it enables the mammalian infant to form a soft circular seal about its mother's nipple. It can then suck in milk without hurting the nipple and without sucking in unwanted air.

Because the lips are also covered with a thin membrane (not quite as thin, though, as that of the inner portion of the mouth) they are red in color. The lips are not supplied with mucus-producing glands of their own and yet the delicate lining grows uncomfortable when dry so that we periodically, even when not aware of it, moisten the lips with the tongue. In cold dry weather, when there is an increased reluctance to open the mouth, the membrane of the lips grows dry and may split, or "chap."

Although the mouth in the human being is of prime importance in speech (see Chapter 5) it serves, as it does in all other creatures beyond the very simplest, primarily as a food receptor. Where food is not already liquid or at least jelly-like in consistency, it must be made so, and for that purpose the double line of teeth rim the mouth. They are equipped for cutting, tearing, and grinding and their importance is plain enough to those who, through age or disease, have lost their teeth. Although modern dentistry has evolved excellent false teeth, none can quite serve as well as the genuine article.

If food particles are allowed to accumulate between the teeth, they will serve as breeding grounds for bacteria which will not only decay the teeth but will also inflame the fibrous tissues that cover the roots of the teeth. These tissues, covered with mucous membrane as is the rest of the mouth, are the *gums* ("jaw" AS). When inflamed they become uncomfortably tender and prone to bleeding, a condition called *gingivitis* (jin'-ji-vy'tis; "gum inflammation" L). In extreme cases, pockets of decaying debris form between the tooth and the gum border, serving as a source of chronic infection, damaging the root and the neighboring jawbone and, eventually, leading to the loss of teeth. This condition is *pyorrhea* (py'uh-ree'uh; "flow of pus" G), and this has been blamed for most of the loss of teeth in people over thirty-five.

As food is chewed by the teeth, it is moved about by the nimble and muscular tongue, which sees to it that the food does not escape from between the teeth too soon. The lips and cheek stand guard along the outer rim of the teeth. The cheek muscles are especially useful here. The muscle is the *buccinator* (buk'si-nay'ter; "trumpeter" L, since stiff cheeks are essential to blowing a trumpet).

The coordinated movements of all these parts of the mouth are skillful enough to force chewing to completion without any portion of themselves being caught between the line of champing teeth. Once in a very rare while, coordination fails us, to our own great surprise, for the sharp pain of having bitten our own tongue while chewing is always accompanied by an almost involuntary feeling of incredulity.

Among animals the tongue has developed a variety of uses. It may be used to grasp food (as in the giraffe), to lap up liquids (as in cats), to sense the outer environment (as in snakes), to serve as a cooling agent (as in dogs), and even as an organ of attack (as in chameleons and toads) or entrapment (as in anteaters). In man, however, it has the unique function of making speech possible. The medieval punishment of cutting out the tongue did not rule out eating but did put an end to intelligible speech. The importance of the tongue in this respect is recognized in the fact that we will use the phrase "a foreign tongue" when we mean "a foreign language," to say nothing of the fact that "language" itself is derived from the French word for "tongue."

The tongue is covered with a series of small conical projections called *papillae*, which give the top of the tongue a rather velvety feel. (In the cat family they are large enough and hard enough to give the tongue something of the feel of a rasp, and anyone who has been licked by the family cat will know that on the whole it is not a comfortable sensation.) In among the papillae are small groups of cells which react to the chemical nature of the food that touches them and give rise to the sensation of taste. The cell groups are therefore the *taste buds*.

For some reason, not yet understood, deficiencies of various B vitamins produce as one of the prominent symptoms an inflammation of the tongue, or *glossitis* (glo-sy'tis; "tongue-inflammation" G). To give an example, *pellagra* (peh-lay'gruh; "dry skin" Italian) is a disease marked, as the name implies, by a roughened scaly skin. It is caused by a B-vitamin deficiency and is also characterized by a darkening and inflammation of the mucous membranes generally and of the tongue in particular. The same disease in dogs is called *blacktongue* because of that prominent symptom.

In chewing food, we do not merely break it up into smaller portions: we mix it with fluid and turn it into a soft, mushy mixture. The fluid used for the purpose is *saliva* (sa-ly'vuh) which is 97 to 99½ per cent water, but which also contains a mucopolysaccharide (see Chapter 3) called *mucin* (myoo'sin), which even in small quantities suffices to give saliva its stickiness and viscosity.

Saliva also contains an enzyme for which an old name is *ptyalin* (ty'uh-lin; "saliva" G). This acts to bring about the breakdown of starch to the simpler molecules of dextrins and sugars, so that digestion can be said to begin in the mouth. In fact, if you begin with a mouthful of potato, rich in starch and bland in taste, and chew it long enough, you will begin to detect a certain faint sweetness as sugar begins to accumulate. Since the Latin word for starch is *amylum*, the enzyme is nowadays known as *salivary amylase* (am'i-lays).

Saliva is secreted by three pairs of glands: the *sublingual glands* (sub-ling'wool; "beneath the tongue" L), next the *sub-*

maxillary glands (sub-mak'si-leh-ree; "beneath the jaw" L), and finally the *parotid glands* (puh-rot'id; "beside the ear" L). The names in each case are derived from the position of the particular glands. The secretions of these *salivary glands* (the general name for all three pairs) are led into the mouth through narrow ducts.

We become most aware of the salivary glands when they are infected by an all too common virus. The swelling that results, of the parotid glands chiefly, is *mumps* (AS, possibly an old dialectical variation of what we would now call "bumps" in reference to the swollen bumps just beside the jaw). Most children get it at an early age. There are advantages in this, for it is a mild disease and leads to lifelong immunity; those unfortunate enough to escape it as children may catch it as adults, at which time it may be accompanied by unpleasant complications.

A human being will produce from half a liter to a liter of saliva each day, and it is secreted even when we are not engaged in chewing. It serves to keep the mouth moist and clean and lubricates the tongue and cheeks so that friction against the teeth in speaking or chewing does not lead to irritation. The rate of salivary flow increases quickly at the sight, smell, or even thought of food, particularly if one is hungry. The mouth will then "water."

THE STOMACH

Once the food is chewed and moistened and reduced to a semi-liquid state, the tongue rolls it into a ball (a mouthful of food is referred to as a *bolus*, in fact, which is just the Greek version of "ball") and pushes it backward into the pharynx. This is the act of *swallowing* (AS), or *deglutition* (dee-gloo-tish'un; "swallow down" L). At this stage the voluntary portion of the digestive process ceases. After that everything proceeds automatically.

The uvula moves up to close the nasal passages and the epi-

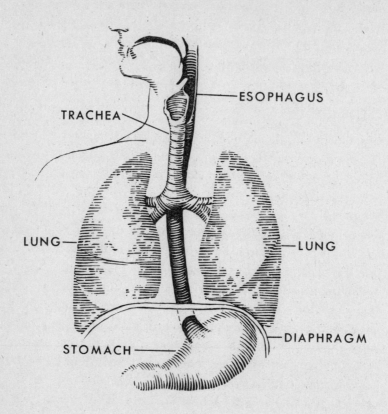

ESOPHAGUS

TRACHEA

LUNG

LUNG

STOMACH

DIAPHRAGM

glottis covers the larynx. The food is debarred from returning by the tongue, and so it can move in only the one remaining direction, into a tube, leading downward, that lies just behind the trachea. This tube is the *gullet* ("throat" L), or *esophagus* (ee-sof'uh-gus; "to carry what is eaten" G). The esophagus is 9 or 10 inches long and is less than an inch wide. In its lower reaches, after traversing the thorax, it passes through the dia-phragm (it and the aorta being the largest structures to do so). The esophagus has a muscular wall, with the muscle fibers arranged both longitudinally and in circles. The muscles in the upper few inches are striated, but they become smooth in the lower portion.

When food enters the esophagus it produces a dilation that stimulates a contraction of the circular muscles just above the area of dilation. This in turn causes a constriction of the ring of muscle just below, then just below that, and so progressively down the esophagus. Each muscle, after contracting, relaxes again and is then ready for another period of contraction when the next bolus comes by. The series of moving constrictions serves to push the food downward along the length of the esophagus. It might be supposed that gravity alone would accomplish this, but the bolus is still semisolid and viscous, and the muscular action, or *peristalsis* (pehr'i-stal'sis; "constriction around" G), serves to hasten matters. It is this peristaltic action that makes it possible to defy gravity and to swallow successfully even while standing on one's head; or, to bring in a matter now topical, under conditions of free fall. (Birds do not generally have this ability, and a bird drinking must throw its head up for each swallow in order to let gravity do its work.)

The esophagus, like the mouth and the alimentary canal generally, is lined with a mucous membrane. The slippery mucus protects the esophagus against the abrasive action of any still intact food particles in the bolus.

At the lower end of the esophagus, just below the diaphragm, the final circular muscle remains, usually, in a state of contraction, so that it serves as a sphincter. This is the *cardiac sphincter,* so named because it is located near the heart and *not* because it is part of the heart or has anything to do with the heart. At the approach of the bolus, the cardiac sphincter relaxes, the opening widens, and the food is shot into the stomach.

The stomach is the widest portion of the alimentary canal and the most muscular. When empty, it is a rather J-shaped tube, with its top pressed against the diaphragm. The upper part of the stomach is usually puffed out a bit with gas, even when the stomach is empty, and it therefore bellies up above the cardiac sphincter. This upper portion is the *fundus.* (Here is an example of a case where the knowledge of Latin is a positive hindrance. The *fundus* in Latin refers to the part of a container farthest from the opening which, in the ordinary course of affairs, is the bottom of the container. "Fundus" therefore has come to mean "bottom." If the stomach were imagined as being held by its entrance and its exit tubes, the fundus would hang down at the bottom, too, but in the living man, standing or sitting, the fundus of the stomach is at the top.)

The lower portion of the stomach is the *pylorus* (py-law'rus; "gatekeeper" G, since it ends with a sphincter that is virtually a gatekeeper for the rest of the canal). The inner wall of the empty stomach exists in longitudinal folds called *rugae* (roo'jee; "wrinkles" L), but as the stomach fills with food, the rugae flatten out and disappear. When full, the stomach becomes pear-shaped, being particularly distended in the fundus. Its capacity in an adult is up to 1.5 liters. The capacity is much less in a youngster, of course, and in a newborn baby it may only be 60 cubic centimeters or so.

The stomach is the nearest thing in man to a storehouse for food in the process of digestion. Not only is its capacity larger than that of any other equivalent section of the alimentary canal, but food usually remains in the stomach three or four hours before passing on. This storage function of the stomach is greatly exaggerated in grazing animals that live on grass and other substances high in cellulose content. Multicellular animals lack the enzymes to break down cellulose into simpler substances that can be absorbed and used; cattle, for instance, are no exception. The steer or cow depends upon the bacteria that infest its alimentary canal to perform this task. The task takes time and it is therefore necessary for the food to remain in the stomach for an extended period, fermenting. The stomach in cattle is for that reason extraordinarily large, holding up to 300 liters, and is divided into four compartments. In the two larger ones, the food is stored and there the bacteria do their work.

Initially cattle swallow grass hurriedly and with little chewing, but after this preliminary storage in the first two chambers of the stomach, they bring up the remains (now called "cud") and chew it thoroughly. When swallowed again, it passes into the final chambers of the stomach.

The lower reaches of our own alimentary canal are likewise filled with bacteria, which usually are not harmful and, at best, perform certain useful functions. Thus, they manufacture a number of vitamins in quantities greater than they themselves can use. We pick up the overflow as a kind of rent for their occupancy. Doubtless if we could store our food in our canal long enough, they would also break down cellulose for us, but we do not and, consequently, they do not. Cellulose passes through our own canal largely unchanged, so we cannot live on grass unless we run it through cattle first, then eat steak and drink milk.

While the food is stored in the stomach its walls undergo peristaltic contractions. With the sphincters at both ends of the stomach closed, the food must remain in the stomach, and the peristaltic action serves merely to mix it thoroughly with the digestive juices produced in that organ. Because of the gas which is usually trapped in the stomach, this churning of the food can produce gurgles sometimes heard as "stomach rumbling."

After the stomach has been empty for a period of time, the peristaltic contractions begin again, and the rumblings may then be louder. The gas, which now occupies the major portion of the volume within the stomach, is compressed in the process and its pressure against the stomach walls produces a feeling of pain, which we refer to as "hunger pangs."

The inner lining of the stomach is a mucous membrane into

which are set numerous (up to 35,000,000) tiny glands that secrete a fluid called *gastric juice* ("stomach" G). This juice is unusual for a body fluid, in that it is strongly acid. It contains up to 0.5 per cent *hydrochloric acid.* This acid was discovered in the Middle Ages along with other strong mineral acids and was long considered a typical product of the inorganic world. Its existence among the delicate tissues of the body was first discovered in 1824 and it came as quite a shock to biologists.

Strong acid in itself accelerates the breakdown of proteins and carbohydrates into smaller substances; during early studies of the gastric juice it was felt that the hydrochloric acid was the digestive agent. Later a protein called *pepsin* ("digestion" G) was discovered and found to be far more effective than acid alone in breaking down proteins. It was one of the first enzymes discovered. A second enzyme, *rennin* ("to curdle" AS), acts upon milk in particular, curdling it as the protein content comes out of solution. The protein is "curds" and the clear liquid is "whey," and this (produced by adding a preparation of calf stomach to milk) is what Little Miss Muffet was eating, to the confusion of generations of youngsters who recite the verse without understanding it.

Thus it is chiefly protein that is broken down by the digestive processes of the stomach. To be sure, gastric juice does indeed contain an enzyme capable of breaking down fat, one called *lipase* (ly'pays; "fat" G). This enzyme, however, is a rather weak one, and even if it weren't, it would be incapable of acting under the acid conditions of the stomach. (Although the mechanism of the human body is marvelous beyond words and can never be sufficiently admired, it is not perfect. The existence of an enzyme under conditions that automatically make it useless is an example of this.)

The acid nature of the stomach contents has been made familiar to all of us by the frenzied activity of the advertising profession. The notion is often left with us that the stomach contents ought not to be acid at all, but of course the acidity of stomach juice is quite natural and beneficial. It is true that on occasion the acidity is higher than usual (*hyperacidity*) and that discomfort can then arise. Under such conditions, gas can accumulate and pressure on the walls of the stomach will increase. This gives rise to pain, as in the case of hunger pangs, but to pain that is more acute — enough, on occasion, to frighten a person into thinking something is wrong with his heart. (The stomach is located higher than most people realize. Ask someone to put his hand on his stomach and chances are he will put it on the navel or just above. The stomach is actually at the level of the lowermost ribs and its upper end is just below the heart.) Relief is usually brought about through the escape of some of the gas through the esophagus and mouth. At times the bubble of gas will carry some of the acid juices up into the esophagus in its struggle to escape. The stomach is insensitive to the acid, but the esophagus is not. The painful sensation in the chest that comes as a result is the familiar "heartburn."

A customary way of combating hyperacidity is to swallow a weak basic substance which will partly neutralize the acidity of the stomach. Sodium bicarbonate is the most familiar remedy. In neutralizing the acid it forms the gaseous carbon dioxide that swirls upward, collecting other droplets of gas with itself. When these escape relief usually follows.

It is not only gas that can escape the stomach. In extreme cases, the stomach can empty itself of its contents generally. This is the act of vomiting. In vomiting, the pyloric portion of the stomach contracts violently while the *pyloric sphincter* between itself and the lower regions of the alimentary canal remains firmly shut. The stomach contents can then only move upward through a suddenly relaxed cardiac sphincter. Vomiting can, of course, be useful, since it serves as a sort of natural stomach pump designed to empty the stomach of contents that may prove harmful if allowed to remain. There are drugs which will activate the vomiting reflex and will accelerate the stomach-emptying process. These are *emetics* ("vomit" G).

Quite extraneous sensations can produce the feeling of nausea that precedes vomiting. A steady rocking motion can do it, and to this some people are more susceptible than others. Those who have experienced "seasickness," the nausea resulting from the slow, relentless sway of a ship, well know the sensation of the utter worthlessness of life that can be produced.* The very word "nausea," by the way, comes from the Greek word for "ship."

Where vomiting is long continued, as in certain infections affecting the digestive system (intestinal flu, for instance, or similar diseases now dismissed by the physician with the awesome, all-inclusive term of "virus"), the condition can be debilitating and even dangerous. It is not merely the loss of food, but rather the loss of body fluid and the mineral ions it contains.

The resistance of the stomach wall itself to the strong acid its glands produce and to the meat-dissolving action of pepsin puzzled biologists for a long time. A piece of the stomach of another creature, used as food, is attacked and digested in the eater's stomach quickly enough. The answer to the paradox, apparently, is that in life the mucus secretions of the stomach (somewhat antacid in nature) coat and protect the wall.

This protection is not always perfect, particularly when the stomach is chronically hyperacidic, and even more so when the individual is particularly prone to tension and anxiety. Under those conditions, a portion of the stomach wall may be irritated and even eroded by the gastric juices to form an *ulcer* ("sore" L). Actually, the term "ulcer" can be applied to any break in the skin or mucous membrane which is accompanied by the destruction of tissue and the discharge of fluid, but in common

---

* There is the story about the seasick passenger who was assured jovially by the ship's steward that no one ever died of seasickness. "Please," muttered the passenger. "It's only the hope of dying that's keeping me alive."

speech the term is confined almost entirely to sores of the lining of the alimentary canal. One that is in the stomach is sometimes specified as a *gastric ulcer*.

There are cases, too, in which the stomach secretions contain virtually no hydrochloric acid. This condition is *achlorhydria* (ay-klawr-hy'dree-uh; "no hydrochloric acid" G). This is not necessarily serious, for though it decreases the efficiency of digestion in the stomach, the body can make out with the remainder of the alimentary canal. People with pernicious anemia, however, are invariably achlorhydric; before the lack of acid is dismissed as unimportant, the possibility of pernicious anemia must be considered.

THE PANCREAS AND LIVER

While food is in the stomach, the pyloric sphincter remains closed as long as any significant portion of the food remains not quite liquid. Gradually, however, the effect of gastric digestion and the addition of the gastric juices reduces the food to an entirely fluid condition. It is then *chyme* (kime; "juice" G). Only then does the pyloric sphincter relax so that the chyme, driven by peristalsis, passes in spurts into the next section of the canal. The chyme is virtually sterile, because stomach acidity has killed any bacteria originally present in the food (but bacteria will reappear and wax numerous in the lower reaches of the canal).

The chyme, on leaving the stomach, enters the *intestines* ("internal" L). These are also sometimes referred to as *bowels* ("sausage" L), because the long, flexible tube, with the periodic contractions produced in it by peristaltic action, bears a resemblance to a string of sausages. The intestines are divided into two portions, a relatively long section called the *small intestine*, which comes first, followed by a relatively short section called the *large intestine*. The "small" and "large" refers to the width, rather than the length. The small intestine is only 1½ to 2 inches in diameter at the point where it leaves the stomach and it narrows somewhat thereafter. The large intestine is up to 2½ inches wide.

The small intestine is 20 feet long or more (in a dead man, anyway; it may be contracted and rather shorter during life). In order to fit into the abdominal cavity, it coils intricately upon itself and, even so, succeeds in filling the major portion of the cavity. This length of intestine is necessary, for it is here that the main task of digestion is accomplished. The small amount of carbohydrate digestion in the mouth and the rather larger amount of protein digestion in the stomach can, in a pinch, be dispensed with. In fact, when for any reason it is necessary to remove part or even all the stomach (*gastrectomy*), it remains possible for the patient to lead a reasonably normal life. Without the storage capacity of the stomach, he must eat smaller and more frequent meals, but this might be a good idea, anyway.

Digestion in the mouth and stomach does not in any case proceed to completion. That is, although some of the foodstuffs are broken down to simpler compounds, the products are still not simple enough to be absorbed. (Small inorganic ions may be absorbed, however. Cyanide ion can even be absorbed in the mouth — with drastic results, since cyanide ion is a deadly poison.) In the small intestine digestion does proceed to completion and it is there, particularly in the lower half, that absorption takes place. This is another reason for the length of the small intestine, since the entire length is needed to make sure that absorption is reasonably complete.

(Herbivorous animals, with a difficult-to-digest food supply, have proportionately longer intestines. The small intestine of a cow may be up to a hundred feet in length. Carnivorous animals have proportionately shorter ones. Man, who will eat anything and everything, is intermediate in this respect.)

The first ten or eleven inches of the small intestine is the *duodenum* (doo'oh-dee'num; "twelve" L). How the name came to be applied to a length of intestine shorter than twelve inches becomes clearer when you understand that the length was originally measured not in inches but in finger widths. In German, in fact, the section is known as *Zwölffingerdarm,* meaning "twelve-finger bowel." The duodenum is the section of the small intestine that receives the initial shock of the highly acid chyme as it pours through the pyloric sphincter, and its role is to neutralize that acid. For this reason, antacid secretions pour into the duodenum from two large glands. Despite this, the lining of the duodenum, like that of the stomach, is in constant danger, and *duodenal ulcers* may result. Since both gastric ulcers and duodenal ulcers are caused by the acid, pepsin-containing stomach secretions, they are sometimes lumped together as *peptic ulcers.*

Of the two glands whose secretions neutralize the acid of the chyme, the smaller is the *pancreas* (pan'kree-is; "all meat" G, because it lacks bones and fat and, as an animal organ, is completely edible without trimming). It is the second largest gland in the body, reddish in color, 5 or 6 inches long and rather carrot-shaped. It weighs about 3 ounces, and lies along the back wall of the abdomen behind the lower portion of the stomach. The wide end of its carrot shape snuggles up against the curve of the duodenum.

The *pancreatic juice* passes through a duct that opens into the duodenum about an inch and a half below the pyloric sphincter and through it about 0.7 liters of fluid are delivered each day. The pancreatic juice contains a large variety of enzymes, with one or more suitable for attacking each different type of foodstuff. There is a starch-splitting enzyme something like that in saliva. It used to be called *amylopsin* (am'i-lop'sin) but is now generally spoken of as *pancreatic amylase.* There is also a fat-splitting enzyme once called *steapsin* (stee-ap'sin; "animal fat" G) but now called *pancreatic lipase.* Of the several

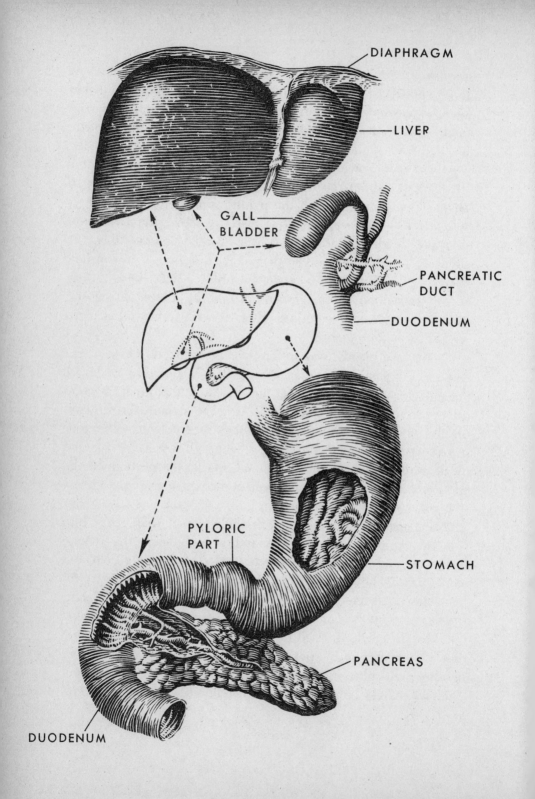

DIAPHRAGM

LIVER

GALL
BLADDER

PANCREATIC
DUCT

DUODENUM

PYLORIC
PART

STOMACH

PANCREAS

DUODENUM

protein-splitting enzymes in pancreatic juice, the first discovered was *trypsin* (trip'sin; "to rub" G, because its initial preparation required the thorough rubbing or grinding of pancreatic tissue with glycerol). Another is *chymotrypsin* (ky'moh-trip'sin, "trypsin in the juice" G). Together trypsin and chymotrypsin carry on the work begun by pepsin in the stomach.

However, neither trypsin nor chymotrypsin can perform their functions in an acid environment. The acidity of the stomach chyme is partly neutralized by the pancreatic juice and partly by the fluid formed by the second gland, the largest in the body. This is the *liver* (AS). The liver is a reddish-brown organ weighing three to four pounds. It lies over the stomach and to its right, just under the diaphragm, and is partly hidden by the lower ribs. It consists of four lobes, of which the one on the extreme right is the largest.

The liver, perhaps because of its size, commanded particular respect among the ancients, who often considered it the particular seat of life. (The similarity between "liver" and "to live" may not be entirely accidental.) As recently as Shakespeare's time, common expressions used the liver as a symbol of the state of the emotions. "Lily-livered," that is, a liver poorly supplied with blood, was a synonym for "coward," to give the most common example.

The secretion formed by the liver is called *gall* ("yellow" AS) because of the yellowish cast of the fresh juice, or *bile*, from a Latin word of uncertain derivation. The Greek term for the juice is "chole" and is used in many medical terms. All three words are used in common expressions, testifying to the old belief in the great importance of the fluid. The Greeks considered it to be two of the four important fluids of the body, for they felt it consisted of two varieties, one colored black and one yellow. (This is not so; there is only one bile, though it may be differently colored, depending on the state of its freshness.) The Greeks felt a person who suffered from an overproduction of black bile was "melancholic," and one suffering an overproduction of yellow bile was "choleric." The supposed connection of the liver and emotion is clear, for we still use those words to indicate dispositions that are given to sadness or anger, respectively. We also speak of "gall" when we mean "impudence" and sometimes use "bilious" as a synonym for "choleric."

The bile is conducted toward the duodenum by means of the *hepatic duct* (hee-pat'ik; "liver" G) and the average output is about 0.5 liters a day. Bile is secreted continuously, but between meals a quantity of it is stored in a special sac called the *gall bladder* (AS; the term "bladder" can be used for any distensible sac). The gall bladder lies just under the right lobe of the liver and is a pear-shaped organ about two or three inches long. It has a capacity of only about 50 milliliters, but water is reabsorbed by the liver from the gall bladder so that the bile stored there is concentrated ten- or twelve-fold. The gall bladder therefore holds the dissolved substances of some 600 milliliters of ordinary bile or, roughly, that of a day's supply. When food arrives in the duodenum, the muscular wall of the gall bladder contracts and its contents are forced through its *cystic duct* (sis'tik; "bladder" G), which joins the hepatic duct to form the *common bile duct*. The common bile duct joins the pancreatic duct just before entrance to the duodenum, which thus receives a mixture of ordinary bile, concentrated bile, and pancreatic juice.

The concentration of the bile in the gall bladder is not without its dangers. The bile is rich in cholesterol (a fatty substance with an ill fame nowadays as the substance characteristically deposited on the inner walls of arteries in atherosclerosis). Cholesterol is rather insoluble, and since the bile is concentrated it may happen that small crystals of cholesterol will precipitate. In some people more than in others (for a reason not as yet known) there is a tendency for these crystals to aggregate into a sizable *gallstone*. If these grow large enough to block the cystic duct and interfere with the flow of bile, they can give rise to considerable pain. Sometimes the solution to the problem is the removal of the gall bladder altogether. This does not appear to interfere seriously with the patient, and it does free him of pain.

The bile does not contain any enzymes, but it is important to digestion anyway. It contains compounds (*bile salts*) possessing a detergent action. This encourages fat to break up into small globules that mix more or less permanently with water; that is, an *emulsion* ("to milk out" L) after the fashion of homogenized milk. This is important, because enzymes are as a class water-soluble and can only act upon substances that are dissolved in water or are, at the very least, well mixed with it. Pancreatic lipase, in its attack upon fat, could at best only perform its work at the edges of fat droplets where in contact with water. If these droplets are large, the fat in the interior would remain unaffected; only with very small, bile-induced droplets does fat digestion become efficient. Without the flow of bile, then, most of the fat in the diet would remain undigested.

Bile contains a number of waste products the body gets rid of via the liver and the alimentary canal. It is in the liver, for instance, that hemoglobin molecules are broken down after the natural disruption of aged erythrocytes. The heme (the portion of the molecule containing the iron and consisting of four circles of atoms set in a larger circle) is broken away from the protein portion of the molecule. The large circle of atoms is then broken and the iron atom is removed. What remains is *bile pigment,* so called because these waste remnants of heme are variously colored red, orange, and green and lend the overall yellow-green color to bile. Through its further course in the intestines the food retains the color of bile pigments, and when finally eliminated from the body it is still reddish brown in color.

A small quantity of bile pigment is absorbed into the blood

and eliminated in the urine. This lends both blood plasma and urine its light straw or amber color. Under certain conditions an abnormally high quantity of bile pigment gets into the blood. Sometimes it is because erythrocytes are being broken down at an unusually high rate, and the formation of bile pigment rises. Or else the bile duct is obstructed so that bile pigment cannot be eliminated in the usual manner and must find its way into the blood instead. Whatever the reason, the yellow-green of the bile pigment then shows up in the skin and mucous membranes, in the whites of the eyes, too, and gives a person a sickly and unpleasant yellowish cast. The condition is known as *jaundice*, from the French word for "yellow."

The liver is the chief chemical factory of the body with a capacity for conducting an amazing array of chemical reactions. Cholesterol and bile pigments are not its only excretory products. Any chemical that gets into the body and cannot be broken down for energy or incorporated into the body structure is likely to end up in the liver for *detoxication* ("unpoisoning" G). The liver usually does this by adding some substance to the chemical which increases its solubility and hastens its elimination by way of the urine. This, of course, renders the liver liable to damage if the supply of foreign chemical is too great to be easily handled. The vapors of carbon tetrachloride, for one (which is used as a nonflammable drycleaner), or of chloroform (sometimes used as an anesthetic) may seriously damage the liver.

When liver tissue is damaged or destroyed, the active liver cells are replaced by fat and connective tissue. This gives the liver a yellowish appearance in place of the original reddish brown. This condition is *cirrhosis* (si-roh'sis; "tawny" G). Such destruction can have a number of reasons but is often associated with overindulgence in alcohol. Presumably, the liver in its continued attempt to deal with the alcohol is slowly and irrevocably ruined.

ABSORPTION

The chyme, with its admixture of pancreatic juice and bile, travels on out of the duodenum and into the small intestine proper, urged on by peristaltic action. The main body of the small intestine is divided, rather arbitrarily, into two sections. The first, making up about two fifths of the length, is the *jejunum* (jee-joo'num; "empty" L, so called because it is usually found empty in cadavers). The final three fifths is the *ileum* (il'ee-um), possibly called this from a Greek word meaning "twisted" because of the coils into which it falls.

Set all along the inner lining of the small intestine are numerous tiny projections something like those of a very fine Turkish towel. These projections are called *villi* (vil'eye; "a tuft of hair" L) and give the inner lining a velvety appearance. Their existence vastly extends the surface area of the intestine and facilitates absorption. In addition, by moving about ceaselessly, so that the liquid in the immediate neighborhood is kept constantly churned up, they further speed absorption. At the base of each villus is a group of cells that secrete still another fluid into the alimentary canal. These are the *intestinal glands,* and the fluid they secrete is *intestinal juice.* The fluid is also called *succus entericus* (suk'us en-ter'i-kus), which is simply "intestinal juice" in Latin.

The intestinal juice possesses a number of enzymes designed to break down the products produced by the digestive processes that have already taken place. Even the enzymes of the pancreatic juice do not complete the task of digestion to the point where the products are simple enough for absorption. But now the job is brought to an end. Thus, intestinal juice contains a number of *peptidases* (pep'tih-day'siz), enzymes designed to break down protein fragments (*peptides*) left behind by pepsin and trypsin. The fragments are broken down to the ultimate protein building blocks, the amino acids.

The carbohydrates are broken down in the mouth and duodenum (by salivary amylase and pancreatic amylase) to a simple
compound called *maltose*. In the intestinal juice is an enzyme,
maltase, which breaks each molecule of maltose into halves,
the still simpler product being *glucose*. Another enzyme, *sucrase*,
breaks molecules of ordinary table sugar (*sucrose*) into halves,
forming glucose and *fructose*, and a third enzyme, *lactase*,
breaks the molecules of the sugar in milk (*lactose*) into glucose
and *galactose*. There is even a weak lipase present in case anything has been left undone by pancreatic lipase, and in this way
fat molecules are broken down to *glycerol* and *fatty acids*.

The overall action of digestion can be summarized in the
following table:

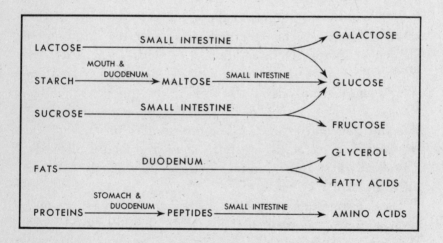

The substances shown on the far right are capable of being
absorbed across the surface of the small intestine, and it is when
this happens that food can finally be said to enter the body.

Within the body these simple molecules serve as building
blocks for larger and far more complicated ones. They can be
built up into carbohydrates, fat, and protein of the human type
(*assimilation*), which means that they are put together into

different combinations and arrangements than had existed in the original organism or organisms from which the food had been derived. (All living creatures on earth, however diverse in appearance, from the minutest virus to the largest whale, are made up of compounds that contain the same building blocks. This means that any one type of organism can serve as food for any other type, directly or indirectly. In the gastronomic sense, all life is definitely and incontrovertibly one.)

The same simple molecules that can be assimilated into tissue structure can also be combined with oxygen to form, eventually, water and carbon dioxide, plus nitrogen-containing wastes. When this happens, energy is released which can be used to power muscular activity and a variety of other energy-consuming tasks of the body (including assimilation, which requires an input of chemical energy).

Absorption through the intestines is similar in design to absorption through the lungs. Within each villus is a network of capillaries into which the end products of protein and carbohydrate digestion are passed. In addition, there is a lymph capillary into which the products of fat digestion move. The droplets of fatty materials turn the clear lymph in those capillaries milky in appearance and because of this these capillaries are termed *lacteals* (lak'tee-ul; "milk" L).

The capillaries of the villi collect into venules, then veins, and finally discharge into the *portal vein* ("to carry" L), a wide, short vein that starts just behind the pancreas and moves to the liver. Its function, as the name implies, is to carry the collected products of carbohydrate and amino-acid digestion to the liver. In the liver, the portal vein breaks up into vessels (*sinusoids*) that are rather wider than capillaries and form a network throughout the liver. Along the walls of the sinusoids are *Kupffer's cells* (named for the German anatomist who discovered them in the mid-19th century). These are members of the reticulo-endothelial system and act as scavengers, filtering out of the blood any debris, particularly any bacteria, that may have made their way across the intestinal wall.

In addition, the cells bordering the sinusoids strip the blood of its excessive supply of glucose and amino acids. The glucose is put together to form large molecules of a kind of starch called *glycogen* (gly'koh-jen; "to give rise to sugar" G, since it can be broken down to sugar again at need). Any fructose or galactose present is converted first to glucose and then to glycogen. The glycogen remains behind in the liver, and the blood emerging from it contains only a small and fixed amount of glucose. The amino acids are taken up by the liver cells and combined into protein molecules and the blood emerging from the liver has the proper content of those, too.

Once past the liver, the blood in the sinusoids is collected again into the *hepatic vein,* which empties into the inferior vena cava and thereby enters the general circulation. As the blood passes through the capillaries of the tissues and as plasma filters across the capillary walls and becomes interstitial fluid, the various cells of the body absorb the glucose fed into the blood by the liver and break it down for energy. They also absorb the proteins, pull them apart, and build up their own special varieties.

Between meals, when the requirements of the cells place a drain upon the glucose supply that is not made up for immediately by new glucose from the intestines, the liver draws upon its reserve supply of glycogen. The glycogen, stored in the lush times just after a meal, is now broken down to glucose and fed, little by little, into the bloodstream.*

The body, within certain limits, can convert one form of foodstuff into another. To give an example: the liver can only store enough glycogen to see an individual through about 18 seden-

---

* All these changes which I describe so quickly and, indeed, negligently, are actually very complicated. My book *Life and Energy* will give you some idea of these complications.

tary hours. If glucose continues to reach the liver, after the liver is completely gorged with glycogen (as for well-nourished individuals it too often is) the glucose must be converted to fat and stored in that form. Fat is a more concentrated form of chemical energy than glycogen is, and it can be stored in indefinite amounts. Contrariwise, when as a result of a day or more of fasting, the liver's glycogen supply is gone, the body can call upon its fat stores as a source of blood glucose.

Fat is stored in the cells of a type of connective tissue. The fat collects as droplets within the cells until these become little more than tiny goblets of fat surrounded by a thin rim of protoplasm. Collections of such cells form *adipose tissue* ("fat" L).

Adipose tissue is a normal component of the body, making up some 15 per cent or even more of the weight of an average, not particularly fat, person. (To be sure, in fat people, the percentage of adipose tissue can easily rise to where it makes up more than half the total weight of the body.) It is only as a result of lengthy starvation that a body is depleted of its fat stores and the victim then takes on an emaciated appearance that departs as far from our normal standards of "good looks" as does the appearance of an obese man.

The normal quantity of adipose tissue in an individual is enough to keep him going for a month without eating, provided he is plentifully supplied with water — and with vitamin and mineral pills. Adipose tissue supplies only calories, and it is quite possible that the body's reserve stores of trace components, such as the vitamins and minerals, is dangerously low regardless of how well supplied it may be with calories alone.

Fat men can have as much as a year's supply of calories tucked here and there about the body, but this does not mean they can fast for a year, even with water and trace components (including mineral protein) supplied. For many reasons, some physical and some psychological, men grow hungry and crave food even when their fat supplies are more than ample. It is for this reason

— at least in part — that loss of weight through dieting is so long and torturing a procedure, and so often a failure.

Adipose tissue serves purposes other than that of a food store. For instance, it is a poor conductor of heat; when stored in the *subcutaneous layer* (sub-kyoo-tay'nee-us; "beneath the skin" L, which exactly describes its location), it acts as an insulating blanket against the cold. Thanks to our lack of any real coating of hair, this is insufficient protection outside the tropic zone and clothing is required in addition. However, a whale, surrounded always by water at near-freezing temperature, and without a hair coating, makes out with a layer of fat ("blubber") up to six inches thick. Other warm-blooded creatures that spend much of their time in the sea are likewise well supplied with subcutaneous fat.

As it happens, there is more subcutaneous fat in the female than in the male and it is more evenly distributed. Women may perhaps feel a trifle annoyed at being told they are fattier (not fatter, but fattier, if you see the difference) than men, but it is this even subcutaneous layer of fat that softens and curves their outline — a consequence which, I have every reason to believe, is quite satisfactory to one and all. What may be the most irritating aspect of this phenomenon, as far as women are concerned, is that additional subcutaneous fat is stored, to a large extent, in the buttocks. This is carried to an amazing extreme among certain groups like the Hottentots of southern Africa. Hottentot women may develop rumps resembling the hump of a camel, with a similar structure and purpose. Such a development, called *steatopygia* (stee'a-toh-py'jee-uh; "fat rump" G), is useful for seeing a woman through a hard winter and is undoubtedly attractive to Hottentot men. Beauty, as we too infrequently remember, is in the eye of the beholder.

Adipose tissue also has a protective function. It serves as a pad that cushions blows, and it is particularly useful as a cushioning support for organs such as the kidneys.

Fat is also stored to an unusual extent in the *omentum* (oh-men'tum, a word of uncertain derivation). This is a membranous sac enclosing the stomach. The *lesser omentum* lines the stomach on the liver side; the *greater omentum* lines the other side of the stomach and drapes down the abdominal wall and over the intestines like an apron. It is in this greater omentum that fat is stored and the excess fat here contributes to the "potbelly" affecting many middle-aged individuals.

The intestines themselves, by the way, are enclosed by a double membranous sac, the *peritoneum* (per'i-toh-nee'um; "stretched around" G). This serves to wall off the viscera from infection, so that the intestines resemble, in a way, the super-market items that are "wrapped in plastic for your better pro-tection." The peritoneum itself can, of course, be infected (*peri-tonitis*), with serious results. In the days before modern sur-gery, any wound or incision in the abdominal regions was almost bound to lead to peritonitis. Modern aseptic procedures have reduced the danger, and the use of modern antibiotics to battle the inflammation, should it arise, has helped further.

THE COLON

It takes food about three hours to pass through the yards of small intestine, and when it does so it finds itself at the entrance-way to the last major portion of the alimentary canal, the large intestine. The large intestine is about five feet long and is often called the *colon* (koh'lon), which is the Greek name for it (and which is why we speak of inflammation of the large intestine as *colitis*, and of the pain caused by gas-distention of the intestine as *colic*). The main portion of the large intestine is divided into three sizable regions, depending upon the direction of the flow of its contents. The small intestine enters the large at the lower right-hand side of the body, near the groin. From that point, the large intestine leads upward to the bottom of the rib cage along the right side, and that portion is called the *ascending colon.* The large intestine then makes a right-angle turn to the left, leading under the liver, stomach, and pancreas, this section being the *transverse colon.* It then leads downward again along the left side to the hipbone, and that part is the *descending colon.*

The point of junction between the small intestine and the large is the *ileocolic sphincter* (il'ee-oh-kol'ik; that is, the sphincter between the ileum and the colon). This is not set at the very bottom of the ascending colon. Rather, it is set about 2½ inches above the bottom, so that the lowermost bit

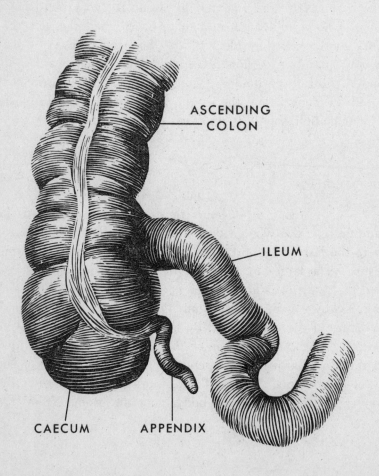

ASCENDING
COLON

ILEUM

CAECUM   APPENDIX

of the ascending colon forms a dead end, or blind alley, and is called the *caecum* (see′kum; "blind" L). In the caecum, through the action of gravity, material can collect. In many herbivorous animals, such as the rabbit, this is exactly what is desired and the caecum is enlarged to the point where it makes up half the total length of the large intestine. It serves as a storehouse in which fermentation can continue to take place.

In man, what is left of the caecum (a vestige perhaps of herbivorous ancestors) is of no particular use and can actually be a source of trouble. To the bottom of the caecum is attached a small appendage, or appendix (the two are essentially the same word), which is a further remnant of a once sizable and usable caecum. This appendage is about 2 to 4 inches long and is shaped very much like a worm. In fact it is called the *vermiform appendix* (vur′mi-form; "worm-shaped" L). An insignificant foreign body, an orange-pit, perhaps, that has survived digestion, can find its way by ill chance into this narrow blind alley set into a wider blind alley. This may set up first an irritation and then a dangerous inflammation (*appendicitis*). It is only in the last century that removing the appendix in such cases (*appendectomy*) has become a simple operation without much danger of peritonitis.

There is no digestion to speak of in the large intestine. Digestion is finished. Absorption goes on, however, particularly the absorption of water. The body has been lavish in its use of water in the various digestive secretions and to lose that water altogether would be very undesirable. As water is subtracted, the contents of the large intestine become increasingly solid. By the time the lower section of the descending colon has been reached, the contents are distinctly solid, although of course still soft.

At the bottom of the descending colon, the large intestine makes an S-shaped curve to get to the center of the hip region and this short portion is the *sigmoid colon* ("S-shaped" G). The final four to five inches of the colon is vertical and this is the *rectum* ("upright" L). The opening of the rectum into the outer world is the *anus* (ay'nus), a word of doubtful origin, although some think it comes from the Latin word for "ring." Under ordinary circumstances, the anus is pinched off by a sphincter, the *anal sphincter,* or *sphincter ani.* (Actually, there are two of these, the inner one being some way up the rectum.)

The solid contents of the final portion of the alimentary canal make up the *feces* (fee'seez; "dregs" L), which consist in part of the indigestible residue of food, of fragments of cellulose and similar substances, of collagen and other constituents of connective tissue, all this being lumped under the name of "roughage" for obvious reasons. The feces also contain many bacteria, which proliferate enormously during the passage through the large intestines. Most of these bacteria are harmless, but some can be definitely dangerous. Diseases such as cholera, typhoid fever, and dysentery can be passed on like wildfire through fecal contamination of water supplies. It is for this reason that modern internal plumbing, efficient sewers, water chlorination, and other measures have done so much to cut down the incidence of epidemics. Finally, feces contain the bile pigments released by the liver, and this gives it its color.

The act of eliminating the feces is *defecation.* This can be taken care of by the natural peristaltic action of the rectum, and can be aided by compression of the diaphragm and of the muscles of the abdominal wall. In infants, the process takes place whenever the rectum is full enough to stimulate peristalsis. It is with some trouble that we "toilet-train" infants and teach them to control the act at least until they can reach the bathroom.

Defecation is usually accompanied or preceded by the escape of intestinal gases. This is *flatus* (flay'tus; "blowing" L). The gas is harmless but contains small quantities of volatile compounds formed by bacterial action in the large intestine and these have an unpleasant fecal odor.

Whenever the interval between defecations is greater than normal for a particular individual, he is suffering from *constipation* ("to press together" L). This happens when the peristaltic action of the large intestine is slower or weaker than usual. The slower passage of food through it allows opportunity for a greater subtraction of water. The feces become harder than usual, are compacted and pressed together, and are eliminated only with great difficulty. Since peristalsis is stimulated by the presence of roughage in the feces, cereals with high content of bran will sometimes counteract constipation. Certain chemicals, found naturally (as in prune juice) or formed synthetically and incorporated into proprietary "laxatives," may also be used. The walls of the large intestine can be lubricated so as to make it easier for the hardened feces to pass along, and it is for this reason that mineral oil and castor oil are effective. Epsom salts brings about an influx of water from the body into the intestines, softening the feces; and, finally, there can be the direct washing action of warm water (an "enema") introduced through the anus.

In reverse, it may also happen that the large intestine pushes food through too quickly, sometimes because of infections that powerfully irritate the intestine. In such a case, little fluid has had a chance to be absorbed and the feces are watery. This is *diarrhea* ("a flow through" G). Diarrhea, like vomiting, can be very debilitating, even quite apart from any infectious disease that may be giving rise to it. It represents a loss of needed water and inorganic ions. In the case of infants, who have a very small water reserve, unchecked diarrhea can easily be fatal.

9

OUR KIDNEYS

CARBON DIOXIDE AND WATER

As I have explained in the past few chapters, oxygen is brought into the blood by the respiratory system and food is brought in by the digestive system. Both are carried to the individual cells of the body by the circulatory system. In the cells, the food and oxygen are combined to produce energy. In the process, however, the substance of the food and oxygen is not destroyed. As far as the body is concerned, the atoms making up the molecules of oxygen and of the various components of food are everlasting. They are merely rearranged into new combinations.

The molecules of carbohydrates and fats are made up of atoms of carbon, hydrogen, and oxygen. When those molecules are combined with additional oxygen atoms (*oxidation*) the products are carbon dioxide (made up of atoms of oxygen and carbon) and water (made up of atoms of oxygen and hydrogen). Protein molecules are far more complicated in structure. They contain not only atoms of carbon, hydrogen, and oxygen, but also numerous nitrogen atoms, plus a scattering of atoms of sulfur, phosphorus, iron and so on. Proteins, therefore, on combination with oxygen give rise not only to carbon dioxide and water but also to nitrogen-containing compounds and to substances containing the other atoms mentioned.

All these products of oxidation may be looked upon as wastes analogous, in a way, to the ashes left behind by a fire that has burned all it can. The process of getting rid of wastes is *excretion* ("to separate out" G) and the organs primarily involved in the excretion of wastes make up the *excretory system* (eks'kreh-toh'ree).

Carbon dioxide is a gas, and in all animals is handled very much as oxygen is, except that it moves in the opposite direction. In animals simple enough to subsist on the direct diffusion of oxygen from the oxygen-rich environment into the oxygen-poor cells, there is a contrary diffusion of carbon dioxide from the interior of the cell, rich in the gas, to the outer environment, poor in it.

More complicated creatures with specialized organs for oxygen absorption and a circulatory system for oxygen transport make use of those same devices for carbon-dioxide excretion. Thus, as cells combine food and oxygen, the carbon dioxide that is produced diffuses out of the cell first into the interstitial fluid and eventually the blood. In a way, the blood can handle carbon dioxide more easily than it can handle oxygen, for carbon dioxide is the more soluble by far. Whereas 100 cubic centimeters of water at body temperature will dissolve only 2.5 cubic centimeters of oxygen, it will dissolve fully 53 cubic centimeters of carbon dioxide. In addition, some of the carbon dioxide can tie loosely onto portions of the hemoglobin molecule that are not involved in oxygen transport.

Partly dissolved in water, partly combined with water to form carbonic acid, partly combined with hemoglobin, the carbon dioxide finds its way at last into the capillaries lining the alveoli of the lungs. There, while oxygen passes from the alveoli into the bloodstream, carbon dioxide passes from the bloodstream into the alveoli. Whereas inspired air is only 0.03 per cent carbon dioxide, expired air is about 5 per cent carbon dioxide.

Water excretion is even less of a problem. In fact, it is no problem at all, since water produced by the oxidation of foods joins the water that already makes up 60 per cent of the human body and is not to be distinguished from it. Actually, water should not even be considered a waste, because it is an absolutely essential component of living tissue, and for any creature living on dry land the problem is not to get rid of it but to conserve it. The body unfortunately cannot help losing water for a variety of reasons. In the first place, the alveoli are permeable to water and are always moist. They must be moist because the diffusion of oxygen and carbon dioxide can only take place after the gases have dissolved in the film of water lining the alveoli. A dry alveolus would not function. Expired air is therefore always saturated with water vapor, and, except on the rare occasions when the local atmosphere itself happens to be saturated with water vapor, this means that our bodies lose water with every breath. In addition, we maintain our constant body temperature, despite changes in the temperature of the environment, very largely through the agency of perspiration. This is an efficient air-conditioning system but it can be prodigal in its use of water, which is then lost to us. In the last place, we need water as a solvent for the wastes arising from protein, so some water is unavoidably lost in the process of getting rid of those wastes.

There are some animals that have developed ways of cutting down these water losses to the point where the water formed by the oxidation of food is sufficient to replace what water is lost. Such animals (usually adapted for desert life) never have to drink but can make out perfectly well on food alone — because, first of all, food is never really dry. Vegetation is often 80 to 90 per cent water, and fresh meat is 70 per cent water. For that matter, bread is at least 30 per cent water if it is fresh, and even something as dry as dried lima beans is more than 10 per cent water. Add to this the water arising from the oxidation of foodstuffs and it is not so surprising that some water-economizing desert animals never have to drink.

The human body, on the contrary, cannot conserve water well enough for food alone to serve as an adequate renewal. The average adult loses up to two liters a day through his lungs and skin and in his urine. (As a result of vomiting or diarrhea, or through excessive perspiration on hot days or during unusually hard work, he can lose considerably more.) For that reason it is necessary that an adult drink some two liters of water (or watery fluids such as fruit juice, beer, etc.) each day. Ordinarily, there is no difficulty about this (provided water is available): when water loss has reached 1 per cent of the body weight the sensation of thirst is experienced, and a thirsty person needs no urging to drink.

The direct stimulus of thirst seems to arise when the pharynx dries and salivation is partially suppressed because of water shortage. However, the deeper cause is the increased concentration of dissolved substances in the blood because of water shortage. Thus, mere wetting of the mouth and throat does not relieve the symptoms of thirst for more than a moment. On the other hand, the introduction of water directly into the stomach does relieve them even though the mouth is not directly wetted.

Thirst is more uncomfortable, more demanding, and less easily withstood than is hunger. This is understandable, since while the average well-nourished man has a considerable food store to draw on in case of emergency, the water store is far smaller. If water is not available, the individual approaches a state of collapse when water loss passes 5 per cent of the body weight and is near death when water loss passes 10 per cent of the body weight. This may seem to compare favorably with the amount of weight of fat lost during starvation, but water loss proceeds far more quickly. The limit of human endurance of thirst is reached in a matter of days, whereas endurance of hunger can proceed for weeks. Water reaches the intestines rapidly once it is swallowed and is there rapidly absorbed, diluting the over-concentrated blood. Thirst therefore vanishes almost with the drinking.

What about the excretion of wastes other than carbon dioxide and water produced by the combination of proteins with oxygen? How does an organism get rid of the waste nitrogen atoms which, next to carbon, hydrogen, and oxygen, are the most common in the protein molecules? It might seem that the logical way would be to allow it to form nitrogen gas and, like carbon dioxide, have it eliminated at the lungs. Alas for logic! The production of gaseous nitrogen is an energy-consuming process of a kind of which no organism above the level of certain bacteria is capable. Then, even if nitrogen were formed, it is even less soluble in water than is oxygen, and its transport, in quantity, by the bloodstream would pose a pretty problem.

An alternative is to produce *ammonia* as a product of the combination of protein with oxygen. Ammonia, like nitrogen, is a gas (with a molecule containing nitrogen and hydrogen atoms) and can be formed by processes that are not energy-consuming. Furthermore, it is extremely soluble in water and its transport by the bloodstream would involve no problem. As a matter of fact, many sea organisms do indeed excrete nitrogen in the form of ammonia.

There is a catch to this as far as we ourselves are concerned, and it is a serious one. Ammonia is extremely toxic to all forms of life. A thousandth of a milligram of ammonia in each liter of blood would be enough to kill a man. The sea creatures that excrete ammonia can get away with it because they have a vast ocean into which to dump the gas as quickly as it is formed. In the ocean, the ammonia forms a solution far less concentrated than even the tiny value that is fatal to life. Nor will the ocean become more concentrated with time, for there exist micro-organisms within it that make use of the ammonia, combining it with other compounds and rebuilding protein out of it.

Land creatures, with a limited supply of body water at their disposal, cannot make use of ammonia as a waste. Many organisms use instead an easily soluble solid substance called *urea* (yoo-ree'uh). The molecule of urea is built up of the fragments of two ammonia molecules and a carbon dioxide molecule. Using it as a nitrogen waste is slightly more inefficient by a couple of per cent than using ammonia would be because, for one thing, urea formation is an energy-consuming process. However, urea is far less toxic than ammonia and that more than makes up for any slight loss in efficiency.

Urea can be allowed to build up to a fair concentration. A hundred milliliters of blood will contain up to 33 milligrams of urea, which is a hundred thousand times and more the quantity of ammonia that would be fatal. Consequently, it would take a hundred thousandth of the quantity of water to excrete the day's supply of urea that would be required to excrete the day's supply of ammonia. Quite a saving of water.

The change is conspicuous in amphibians, which spend their early life as water creatures and their later life as land creatures. The tadpole has gills and tail, then loses both and develops lungs and legs instead. This change is noticeable and startling. Hidden from our eyes is another change just as important, one without which the other changes would be meaningless as far as survival is concerned. For whereas the tadpole excretes ammonia, the adult frog excretes urea.

Reptiles and birds are plagued by an even sharper water shortage than are amphibians. Amphibians lay their eggs in water, but reptiles and birds lay eggs on dry land. The water supply within the egg, at the disposal of the developing young, is particularly limited and even urea will not serve as a means of excreting nitrogen. Although urea is relatively nontoxic, it is not absolutely nontoxic; it will kill if the concentration rises high enough. Reptiles and birds therefore excrete nitrogen in the form of *uric acid*. This is a compound with a relatively complicated molecule built up of fragments of four ammonia and three carbon dioxide molecules (plus several additional atoms). Uric acid is quite insoluble, so that in emergencies, as in the egg, it can be tucked away in odd corners of the organism without tying up any significant amount of water.

For mammals, the water shortage eases up slightly. The developing young, for which, in birds and reptiles, the water shortage was most extreme, remains in mammals amid the watery tissues of the mother. For that reason, urea will do as the excretory form of nitrogen, and the human being, like other mammals, excretes urea.

THE EXCRETORY SYSTEM

Urea cannot remain in the blood, of course. It must somehow be brought to the outside world and there discarded. In many nonchordates and in some primitive chordates too, this is done by means of individual microscopic tubes into which there filters water from the plasma. The wastes accompany the water, are led through the tubes to the surface of the body, and are discharged into the watery environment outside. In the vertebrates the number of these tubes is multiplied enormously and they are brought together into a pair of specialized organs called the *kidneys* (AS).

In man, the kidneys are located against the posterior wall of the abdomen, but higher up than most people suspect. The average man, asked to point to the place where his kidneys are located may very likely indicate the small of his back. Actually, they are just below the diaphragm, in front of the bottom-most ribs and behind the liver and stomach. The right kidney, which is crowded above by the liver, is usually a bit lower than the left. Individually, the human kidney is a liver-colored organ, about 4 to 5 inches long, 2 to 3 inches wide, and 1 to 2 inches thick. It weighs about half a pound and has the familiar lima-bean shape. In fact, there is a bean called the "kidney bean"

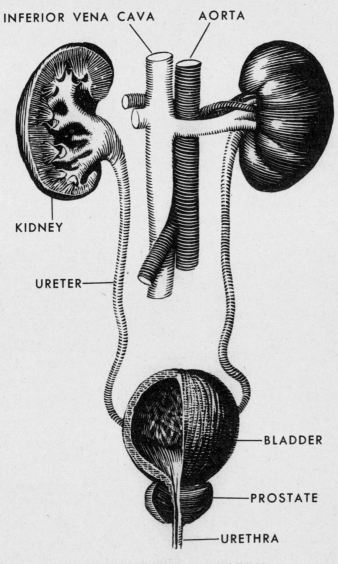

EXCRETORY SYSTEM

because of its shape and color. The kidneys lie outside the peritoneum but are firmly held in place by connective tissue and a cushion of fat. They consist of an outer *cortex* ("bark" L, a word applied by analogy with the bark of a tree to the outer portion of other objects) and an inner *medulla* (me-dul'uh; "marrow" L, applied, by analogy with bone, to the inner portion of other objects).

The kidney consists largely of a huge mass of filter tubes or *nephrons* (nef'ronz; "kidney" G). These are also called *uriniferous tubules* ("urine-carrying" L). There are roughly a million nephrons in each kidney and these represent considerably more than we absolutely need. It is possible for a man to endure the loss of many nephrons through disease, or even the complete removal of one kidney, and still lead a normal life.

Blood is led to the kidneys directly from the aorta by way of the short, thick *renal arteries* (ree'nul; "kidney" L). The importance of the kidney is shown by the fact that at any given moment, as much as one quarter of the blood supply may be passing through them; as much through the single pound of the two kidneys as through the nearly hundred pounds of muscle in the body. The renal artery breaks up into numerous arterioles, each of which, along its path, breaks up further into a mass of coiled and intertwined capillaries shaped in a tiny ball. These combine again into the arteriole, which then passes on to divide into capillaries in the usual manner. (These final capillaries feed the kidney tissue.)

The section of the arteriole before this coiled ball of capillaries is the *afferent arteriole* (af'ur-ent; "carrying toward" L), and the section after it is the *efferent arteriole* (ef'ur-ent; "carrying away" L). The coiled ball of capillaries itself is called the *glomerulus* (gloh-mer'yoo-lus; "small ball of wool" L, which it rather resembles). The blood is brought back from the kidney via the *renal vein* to the inferior vena cava.

The blood passing from the arteriole to the glomerulus suddenly finds the total cross-sectional area of the vessels greatly increased and blood flow is consequently slowed. There is ample time for water, ions, and small dissolved molecules such as urea to diffuse outward from the glomerulus into a section of the nephron which encloses the ball of capillaries like a clutching hand. This enclosing section is called *Bowman's capsule* after Sir William Bowman, the British surgeon who first described it.

It is absolutely essential that the blood be continuously filtered in this fashion; so essential, in fact, that the kidneys have their own special device for maintaining blood flow through themselves at the proper rate. If, for any reason, blood pressure falls so that the blood flow through the kidneys is decreased below the normal range, the kidney is stimulated to produce a substance called *renin* (ree'nin), which it discharges into the blood. This in turn stimulates the contraction of arterioles, reducing the volume of the circulatory system and increasing the blood pressure to a safe level. Where the blood flow through the kidneys is interfered with for reasons other than low blood pressure — as by an abnormal thickening of the walls of the renal artery — the kidneys will produce a more or less permanent hypertension to make up for it. (However, most cases of hypertension are not caused by the kidneys, but are of unknown cause.)

The hard-working kidney is sometimes subjected to inflammation through bacterial infection, or, occasionally, for other reasons. This is called *nephritis* (nef-ry'tis; "kidney inflammation" G). Where kidney tissue undergoes degeneration or destruction without inflammation, the disease is *nephrosis* (nef-roh'sis). In view of the importance of the kidney, both diseases can be extremely serious. Both are sometimes lumped under the name of *Bright's disease,* after the British pathologist Richard Bright, who first described their symptoms systematically.

The fluid that diffuses from the glomerulus into Bowman's capsule has left the body at that point, and is carried through a series of tubes eventually eliminating it into the outer environment altogether. The kidney's work is not done, however; in fact, the truly important portion has not yet begun. What gets into Bowman's capsule is an almost indiscriminate filtrate of the plasma. It contains everything except some of the protein molecules that are just too large to get through. It contains not only urea, which it is desirable to discard, but also a great deal of water, plus useful ions, plus glucose, plus numerous other substances that it is not desirable to discard.

Bowman's capsule leads into a *convoluted tubule* (that is, a coiled little tube) where the desirable material is reabsorbed. By the time the fluid has passed through this tubule it has become a relatively concentrated solution, carrying wastes only. In a creature dwelling in fresh water and therefore having no fear of water shortage, as in the case of the frog, the convoluted tubule is comparatively short, and reabsorption of water is only

**TUBULE STRUCTURE
OF KIDNEY**

moderate. The fluid eliminated is very dilute. In a land animal such as man, reabsorption must be more extensive, since water cannot be wasted. In man, therefore, the convoluted tubule is divided into two parts: the part leading from Bowman's capsule is the *proximal convoluted tubule* and the more distant portion is the *distal convoluted tubule*. Between the two parts and connecting them is a long, straight, and particularly narrow section that is bent upon itself like a hairpin. This is *Henle's loop* (hen'liz), named for Friedrich Henle, the German anatomist who first described it.

This additional length of the tubule increases the efficiency of reabsorption, and makes its extent adjustable. In man, about 80 per cent of the water and ions that pass out of Bowman's capsule are reabsorbed in the proximal convoluted tubule. This represents a minimal reabsorption, and if a person has been drinking water copiously, little more is absorbed in Henle's loop. The fluid finally excreted is fairly dilute. Under ordinary circumstances, however, considerably more is absorbed in Henle's loop. The greater the dehydration of the individual, the more (up to a certain maximum) is reabsorbed.

On the whole, 120 cubic centimeters of fluid filters out of the glomerulus every minute. This amounts to 50 gallons a day, but 99 per cent of this is reabsorbed through the convoluted tubule and Henle's loop. This ability to reabsorb water is regulated by a hormone formed by the *pituitary gland* (pi-tyoo'i-ter'ee), a small organ at the base of the brain. In some individuals the supply of this hormone dwindles, and reabsorptive ability likewise dwindles. The fluid produced by the kidney (*urine*) is therefore both copious and dilute.

A disease characterized by an abnormal quantity of urine, or *polyuria* (pol-ee-yoo'ree-uh; "much urine" G), is called *diabetes* (dy-uh-bee'teez; "siphon" G), because water seems to pour through the body, in at one end, out the other, as through a siphon. This particular variety of the disease is *diabetes insipidus* (in-sip'i-dus; "tasteless" L), since the very dilute and watery urine is virtually tasteless as compared with another form of diabetes where it is sweetish. A person with diabetes insipidus must necessarily replace the lost water and is therefore plagued by incessant thirst.

The kidney may also fail in its ability to reabsorb water through Bright's disease. This alone may be compensated for by frequent drinking, as in diabetes insipidus. Eventually, however, failure of kidney function can progress to the point where urea is not efficiently filtered out of the bloodstream in the first place. The urea concentration in blood rises, a condition called *uremia* (yoo-ree'mee-uh; "urine in the blood" G), and death ensues.

But to return to the tubules. Finally, having passed through the two sections of the convoluted tubule and Henle's loop between, the fluid enters a *collecting tubule*, which is, indeed, just a duct for waste matter and receives the influx of numerous convoluted tubules. The fluid is now properly to be considered urine (from a Greek word of uncertain derivation). The compounds urea and uric acid were so named because they were first discovered in urine. The individual tubules of the kidney are microscopic but not short, for if they were straightened out they would be an inch long or more. All the tubules in both kidneys would come to a length of about 40 miles. And although each collecting tubule receives the merest trifle of urine — it would take two years for an individual nephron to deliver a single cubic centimeter of urine — all of them, working together, deliver something like a cubic centimeter of urine each minute.

The tubules collect into larger ducts until finally all merge into the *renal pelvis*, a space that fills most of the interior of the concave side of the kidney. The renal pelvis narrows into a tube called the *ureter* (yoo-ree'ter; "urinate" G), which leads down along the rear wall of the abdomen some 10 to 12 inches. Just in front of the lower reaches of the intestines, the two ureters, one from each kidney, open into a muscular-walled sac, the *urinary bladder*. (This is often referred to simply as the "bladder," but there are other bladders in the body — notably the gall bladder.) The bladder serves as a storage place for urine, so that although the kidneys constantly form the fluid we need not constantly eliminate it, but can do so at intervals, according to convenience. The muscles of the bladder slowly relax as urine enters until it has expanded upward into a sphere bulging into the abdomen. At maximum expansion it can hold more than a pint of urine.

The ureters enter the bladder at points near the bottom. At the very bottom of the bladder is a thicker tube, the *urethra* (yoo-ree'thruh), a word which is but another form of "ureter." Through the urethra the urine is finally carried to the outer world. The urethra is considerably different in length in the two sexes. In women it is not more than 1 to 1½ inches long. In men, however, it is some 8 inches long, passing through the length of the penis. About the male urethra is the prostate gland which I shall talk about later in the book.

The exit way from the bladder to the urethra is closed off by a pair of sphincters; because of these, under ordinary circumstances, the urine does not leave the bladder. As the bladder fills up, however, there comes a point where the muscular wall begins to contract rhythmically, setting up an increased fluid pressure against the base of the urethra which makes itself felt by the individual as a desire to urinate. This continues with increasing urgency until urination takes place.

In infants this rhythmic contraction actuates a reflex that relaxes the urethral sphincter and leads to urination at once. As the child grows older, he usually learns (with the more or less forceful encouragement of the parents) to control the reflex. This is most difficult to do during sleep, of course, and bedwetting may continue for months after a child is otherwise toilet-trained. In some cases, bed-wetting may continue onward into adolescence and even adulthood.

The bladder may be inflamed through bacterial infection, a condition called *cystitis* (sis-ty'tis; "bladder inflammation" G). This is sometimes in association with kidney inflammation, but it is the bladder inflammation that is the more likely to force itself upon the victim's attention, since its most noticeable symptom is a painful urination.

URINE

About one to one and a half liters of urine are formed and discharged per day. It is an amber-colored liquid with a distinct odor not too annoying when fresh. It is free of bacteria to begin with (unless there is an infection of the kidneys or bladder), but if it is allowed to stand in the open, bacteria will infest it and the consequent putrefaction will produce an unpleasant stench.

Thanks to reabsorption of fluid in the tubules, the urine is comparatively concentrated, but at best it is still some 95 per cent water. It is impossible for the human excretory system to reduce the water content any further; and since wastes must be disposed of if life is to continue at all, the urine continues to drain the body's water supply even when a person is in the extremity of thirst. It is for this reason that a human being adrift in a lifeboat cannot help himself by drinking ocean water. The salt content of the ocean must be excreted, and that takes more water than was in the ocean water consumed. The result is a net loss of water and a quicker death. (Sea water contains about 3.5 per cent of salt and other inorganic constituents. Urine contains about 1 per cent of these, so for every milliliter of sea water a human being must pay with three milliliters of urine — a losing proposition.)

The chief solid carried in solution in the urine is, of course, not inorganic, but is the organic compound urea; and it is urea that builds up the concentration of urine to the 5 per cent mark.

The actual amount of urea eliminated per day depends on the quantity of protein in the diet for it is from protein that urea is derived. On a good protein-rich diet, over 40 grams of urea can be eliminated each day.

Small amounts of other nitrogen-containing compounds are also eliminated. There is uric acid, for example. We, unlike birds and reptiles, do not form it from proteins. Nevertheless, we do form it from some of the building blocks of the nucleic acids (essential compounds found in all cells). There is also *creatine* (kree'uh-teen; "muscle" G) and *creatinine* (kree-at'i-neen), formed to a small extent from the breakdown of proteins; particularly, as the names imply, from the protein of the muscles. There is even a bit of ammonia formed in the process of urine manufacture. In addition, there are various inorganic ions, the breakdown products of hormones, products formed by liver out of foreign molecules, and so on.

The urine serves not only as a reservoir for wastes but also as a device by which to regulate the concentration of many body components. Any substance, ordinarily useful, which is present in excess, is very likely to find its way out of the body by way of the urine. When that same substance is in short supply, however, urinary loss is cut down, in some cases nearly to zero. The most dramatic example of this arises in those cases where the body's normal supply of a hormone called *insulin** (in'syoo-lin) dwindles. This hormone is necessary for the proper break-down of glucose by the body. With insulin in short supply, abnormal breakdown products called *ketone bodies* accumulate, and so does glucose itself.

The ketone bodies are quite dangerous, for in more than a certain minimal concentration they increase the acidity of the blood to the point where the patient goes into a coma and dies. If the disease remains untreated this eventuality is inevitable,

* This hormone is produced in the pancreas, and it will be considered in greater detail in the companion volume to this book.

but the kidneys postpone the evil day by eliminating all the ketone bodies they can. For the purpose, the volume of urine is increased beyond the normal range, so that the disease is a form of diabetes (but the polyuria is not as extensive in this case as in diabetes insipidus). The individual with an advanced and untreated case of this disease is naturally excessively thirsty and also excessively hungry, because although he eats his body is not using the food efficiently. Even though he may be eating well, he will be losing weight.

The inefficient way in which such a person makes use of his food is most dramatically shown in the fate of his body glucose. The fluid passing out of the glomerulus always contains glucose, of course, but in the course of its passage through the tubule, all the glucose is reabsorbed so that normal urine is glucose-free. In this form of diabetes, however, the concentration of glucose in the blood rises to abnormally high levels and it becomes harder and harder for the tubules to reabsorb it all. Finally a point is reached where reabsorption remains incomplete. Glucose concentration is then said to have risen above the *renal threshold* and it makes its appearance in the urine. The presence of a form of sugar in the urine of some people appears to have been discovered in ancient times, when it was noticed that such urine attracted flies. Cautious tasting must have revealed the presence of sweetness, and this particular disease is therefore *diabetes mellitus* (meh-ly'tus; "honey" L). Diabetes mellitus is both more serious and more common than diabetes insipidus. It is the former disease that is usually meant when the word "diabetes" is used by itself.

The inefficiency involved in urinating away good food is not entirely without its compensations. If the glucose concentration in the blood were allowed to increase without check, the viscosity of the blood would increase to the point where circulation would be fatally interfered with. Excretion of glucose is wasteful but it prolongs life.

From the diagnostic standpoint, the value of urinary glucose is that its presence can be easily tested and is a sure indication of well-advanced diabetes. The disease can now be easily treated by injections of insulin obtained from domestic animals slaughtered for food, and it pays to diagnose diabetes at the earliest possible moment, *before* glucose appears in the urine. This is done by tests involving the blood itself.

The presence of other abnormal constituents in the urine may also be indicative of disorders in body chemistry; disorders, fortunately, which are not usually as serious as diabetes. Sometimes amino acids, the building blocks of proteins, appear in the urine in more than normal quantity; sometimes certain breakdown products appear. There is, for instance, a compound called *homogentisic acid* (hoh'moh-jen-ti'sik) that appears in the urine of some people who from birth are lacking in the ability to break down an amino acid called *tyrosine* (ty'roh-seen) in the proper manner. The urine containing homogentisic acid will, under the proper conditions, turn black upon standing, but despite this startling fact, the disease is not in the least serious.

The principle of kidney action rests, of course, upon the fact that all the wastes to be eliminated can be flushed out of the body by a current of water. One might assume then that those wastes are soluble in water. Unfortunately this is not exactly so. Some of the substances eliminated by way of the kidneys are not at all soluble in water. As an example, there is uric acid. Although the human being eliminates this in small quantities in the urine, it is quite insoluble. Other mammals break up the uric acid into a more soluble compound, but primates, including man, lack the ability to do this. Again, some of the inorganic ions ordinarily present in urine can combine to form insoluble substances such as calcium phosphate and calcium oxalate.

The question then is this: How are these insoluble materials disposed of? The answer is that even solids can be carried along by a current of water, if present in small enough pieces. Urine often contains microscopic crystals of solid matter that are carried along without particular difficulty. These crystals do not have much of a tendency to aggregate under ordinary circumstances. The reasons for this are not entirely established, but one reasonable guess is that the individual tiny crystal is coated with a thin layer of some protective substance, such as protein or mucopolysaccharide, that keeps them from aggregating even when they make contact. In some individuals, this protective device fails and there is then a tendency for the crystals to merge into *kidney stones*, or *urinary calculi* (kal'-kyoo-leye; "small stones" L). These may easily become too large to pass through the ureters. In some cases, calcium phosphate stones (which grow quickly) may virtually fill the renal pelvis. Calcium oxalate stones, which grow more slowly, are jagged and irregular and cause intense pain (like a hugely magnified and unending stomach ache) when trapped in the ureter. The pain of kidney stones is sometimes called *renal colic* because of this resemblance to intestinal pains, though it has nothing to do with the colon.

Organic substances will also, though more rarely, form stones. The amino acid *cystine* (sis'teen) is a normal component of proteins and is the least soluble of the amino acids. It is sometimes excreted in small quantities in the urine and can collect to form a stone in the bladder. In fact, cystine was first isolated from such a *bladder stone*, and its name comes from the Greek word for "bladder."

Uric acid will also form stones, and here a new area of danger arises. Sometimes uric acid is deposited in the joints of the extremities, particularly of the big toe, to give rise to the extraordinarily painful disease *gout*. (This word arises from a Latin word meaning "drop" because in the Middle Ages there arose the misconception that gout was caused by the gathering of some fluid in the joints, "drop by drop.") Gout seems to have been more prevalent in previous centuries than now, partly because conditions which were once diagnosed as "gout" are now diagnosed as some form of arthritis.

10

OUR SKIN

SCALES AND EPIDERMIS

In primitive animals, both unicellular and multicellular, the outer surface makes contact with the surrounding environment, and it is at the outer surface that most of the interactions with the environment take place. As animals grew complex, however, more and more of these interactions were performed on interior surfaces. The food canal was brought into being and placed in the interior. The respiratory and excretory systems evolved interiorly. Only very small portions of the outer surface came to be involved with the intake of food and air and with the outlet of wastes. The outer surface, except for these minor regions, could therefore be preserved for the passive task of protection.

Many phyla of animals developed shells of one sort or another to serve as such protection. These, nonetheless, added weight and reduced the sensitivity and responsiveness of the creature to stimuli from the outer world, and their mobility as well. The chordates, with their internal bracing, could afford to be unshelled and the risk that was therein involved was more than made up for by the improvement in efficiency. Even so, the victory of the unshelled was not a quick one. Among the nonvertebrate chordates the tunicates, at least, developed a tunic serving the function of a shell. As for the vertebrates, the first two classes backed up their internal skeleton with an external skeleton as well. In fact, as I explained in Chapter 1, bone was first developed not as an internal skeleton (which remained cartilage for millions of years) but as external armor. Even in man the collarbone and the bones of the skull are inherited remnants of this external armor, drawn inward now beneath the skin.

The armored vertebrates of the sea lost out to the more efficient sharks and bony fish, which abandoned shells and relied instead on the speed and maneuverability made possible by the reduction in mass. (Nevertheless, even in classes developed later there continued the tendency to fall back upon the defensive safety of armor. Among creatures now living, the turtles among the reptiles and the armadillos among the mammals are examples. It never proved a spectacularly successful maneuver, and yet turtles and armadillos still survive, so we can't toss it aside as altogether unsuccessful, either.)

The loss of a bony armor did not mean that fish were entirely naked and unprotected. In the place of bone they developed light, cleverly overlapping scales — tough and flexible. Among the land vertebrates, scales of a somewhat different variety developed, a more superficial type, easily capable of being shed and replaced from below. These are best developed among the reptiles and the ability of the snake to shed its scaly cover periodically is well known. The reptilian scale persisted in specialized fashion among the warm-blooded descendants of the reptiles, the birds and the mammals. They are to be found, for instance, on birds' legs (look at a chicken leg next time you have a chance) and on rats' tails. Even in a human being, fingernails and toenails are a version of the reptilian scale.

However, birds and mammals are warm-blooded and, in order to be effectively so, insulation is required against the excessive loss of heat to the outer world. Scales are not sufficiently insulating unless they can be made loose in order that they might trap a layer of unmoving air next to the body. (Unmoving air is an excellent insulator.) In birds such loosened scales developed into feathers, and in mammals they developed into hair.

Feathers are the more efficient of the two as insulators. They have other essential uses as well. The large feathers of the wings make flight possible and the large feathers of the tails serve as balancing devices. The connection between feathers and flight seems to result in the fact that no flying bird is without a full complement of feathers even in warm environments (with a few minor exceptions, such as the unfeathered heads of vultures). Even flightless birds keep their feathers, although these can become pretty ragged in some cases, with little left beside the central shaft. Hair, on the other hand, has no essential purpose other than that of insulating against heat loss (though some animals have developed specialized uses), so hair-poor animals are not uncommon in the tropics. Such creatures as the elephant and hippopotamus possess few hairs. Whales, who use blubber as insulation, are completely hairless, although a few bristles make their appearance in the embryo. Beneath the scales, feathers, or hair is the soft and sensitive skin of the vertebrate which still serves as protection. Through its unbroken surface, microorganisms and foreign bodies cannot enter; and it can withstand the buffeting of rain, wind, heat, and cold as internal organs could not.

The characteristic protein of skin and skin appendages is *keratin* (ker'uh-tin; "horn" G, because it occurs in horns). Keratin is an extraordinarily tough protein, insoluble, indigestible, and relatively immune to damage by shifting environment. The toughness of the protein component is reflected in the skin itself.

Skin is divided into two main regions. Inside, under the part we actually see, is the *dermis* ("skin" G). This is a living tissue, rich in nerve endings, blood vessels, and various glands. Beneath it is a layer of connective tissue containing the subcutaneous fat I mentioned in Chapter 8. Above the dermis is the portion of the skin we actually see, the portion that fronts the outside world. This is the *epidermis* ("upon the skin" G) and it is dead. The cells at the base of the epidermis are alive, and are constantly growing and multiplying so that cell after cell is pushed upward and away from the blood supply of the dermis. Without a blood supply, the cell dies and much of it, aside from the inert keratin, atrophies. The vicissitudes of existence are constantly rubbing away some of this dead material from the surface of our body, but this is constantly being replaced from below, and we retain our epidermis ever fresh.

This process takes place rather quickly, too. It has been shown that the epidermis of a rat's foot undergoes complete replacement in three weeks and those regions of man's epidermis most exposed to friction may be equally renewable. The fact that epidermis is constantly growing means that it is a region we can reconstruct, or *regenerate*, if a section of it is destroyed. The dermis itself is not so easily reconstructed after destruction. The breach is indeed healed over, but only by a bridge of connective tissue. The specialized structure of that section of the dermis is lost and the featureless section of connective tissue replacement forms a *scar* ("fireplace" G, because burns are a common cause of scarring).

Reptilian scales, avian feathers, mammalian hair are all epidermal in origin, and like the epidermis itself are constantly being shed and replaced. The scales of fish are of dermal origin and their loss is a more serious matter.

The surface of the dermis is ridged and possesses tonguelike processes. The epidermis, for the most part, fills in the spaces between the processes and covers it all smoothly. On the palms of the hands and the soles of the feet, however, the epidermis rises and falls with the processes, so small parallel lines extending in gentle curves are to be found there. On the balls of the most distal joints of the digits the lines fall into whorls and loops. The purpose of these tiny ridges is to supply a surface of greater friction in order that feet grip the ground better in walking and hands grip anything better in grasping. They serve the purpose that tire treads do. The exact pattern of the ridges upon the palms and soles are highly individual; if two "fingerprints" are found to be identical in every respect, it is quite safe to assume that the same person made them both. (The prints are outlined by tiny beadlets of sweat and oil produced by glands in which the palms are particularly rich. The film of moisture produced in this way further improves the gripping capability of the hands and feet.)

The soft sensitivity of the skin is not to be attributed to the epidermis, which is itself dead and insensitive. The epidermis is thin enough so that the nerve endings in the dermis are sufficiently close to the surface to supply the sensitivity. Where areas of the skin are chronically subjected to friction, in response the epidermis thickens, to accentuate the protection it offers. A *callus* ("hard skin" L) is formed. Thus the soles of the feet are commonly callused among those who habitually walk barefoot, and the palms of the hands are callused in laborers. (In the days when most labor was manual labor, soft hands were the sign of aristocracy, and one of the feats of Sherlock Holmes was the ability to discern the specialized occupation of someone from the type of calluses he possessed. It was because the bluish veins were visible through the soft, uncallused, and un-weather-beaten skin of the hands and arms of those who did not labor, that aristocrats were said to be "blue-blooded.")

The deadness of the epidermis is quite apparent on callused spots, for there the skin is notably hard and inflexible, as well as relatively insensitive. It is as though the living and sensitive dermis has exchanged its ordinary thin latex gloves for a pair made of leather. Sometimes an area of excessive irritation or pressure, such as that caused by ill-fitting shoes, may produce an area of abnormal epidermal thickening on a toe. This is a *corn*, and it can become quite painful.

A word derived from the same root as "corn" is *horn,* and indeed the two are quite similar in chemical structure. The horns and antlers of various animals are keratinized and hardened modifications of the epidermis. So are the hoofs of various grazing animals and the claws of the various carnivores. We ourselves have such horny outgrowths in our fingernails and toenails, which are analogous to claws and hoofs. Our fingernails are no longer very useful to us as weapons of offense or defense (although women have been known to use them with fearful effect). Nevertheless, they stiffen the tips of the fingers and, if allowed to grow, offer thin, hard surfaces which can be used for such delicate tasks as picking up pins or prying into narrow crevices.

Skin protects not only against the mechanical shocks, the blows and scrapes, of the environment; it protects also against the impingement of various forms of energy. Before mankind's technology had developed to the point where it could create concentrations of types of energy with which the body was not designed to cope, the chief form of concentrated energy encountered was sunlight. Most animals are protected from sunlight by a thickness of water (if they are sea creatures) or by an intervening layer of dead matter (if they are land creatures). Scales, hair, and feathers effectively absorb the energetic rays of the sun without harm to themselves, and even the frog, with none of these skin appendages, has at least a thick coating of mucus.

Man is unusual in that his dry naked skin is exposed to the sun with only the relatively thin layer of epidermis as protection. To the ultraviolet rays of the sun, the epidermis of those men with fair skins is quite transparent and might as well not be there.

Ultraviolet light is energetic enough to bring about chemical changes within the cell. Some of these are beneficial. For instance, the dermis contains a type of *sterol* (stee'role; "solid alcohol" G, which is an adequate description of its chemical nature) that in itself is of little value to the body; but under the influence of ultraviolet light it undergoes a slight change that converts it into a form of vitamin D. (This is why vitamin D is called the "sunshine vitamin" by advertising men. It is not in sunshine, but it can be produced in the skin by sunshine.)

Vitamin D is essential to the proper formation of bone (see Chapter 3), and since it is present in very few articles of diet, there was, before the 20th century, constant danger of improper bone formation among children born at the start of the northern winter. The sun was almost the only agency by which the vitamin could be obtained. Considering that man originally evolved as a tropical animal, you can see that this reliance on the sun was safe, to begin with.

When man migrated to the north, however, he reached regions where the sun was in the heavens for but a few hours a day for much of the year (and low in the heavens at that, so most of its ultraviolet was absorbed by the atmosphere). The vitamin was not formed in sufficient quantity, and rickets was the result. When vitamins were discovered and the cause of rickets worked out, fish-liver oils (particularly cod-liver oil), which were rich in vitamin D, became a favored beverage for the young. Modern vitamin preparations are just as effective, and fortunately far less fishy in aroma. In addition, food such as milk and bread can be irradiated (that is, exposed to ultraviolet light) so that some of the sterols they contain may be changed to compounds with vitamin D activity.

However, this example of vitamin D formation as a beneficent result of exposure to ultraviolet is rather the exception. Other chemical reactions brought on by the energetic action of ultraviolet light are harmful and the skin can respond by an inflammation called *sunburn*. The condition is in every respect a burn and, as those who have suffered it know, it can be uncomfortable and painful.

More serious still is the fact that the ultraviolet in the sun, like energetic radiation generally, can induce cancer. The ultraviolet light is by no means as dangerous as the still more energetic radiations of the X-ray machine and of radioactive substances, but constant exposure to sunlight does increase somewhat the chances of contracting skin cancer. As protection against the irritating effects of ultraviolet light, human skin is equipped with the capacity to form a dark brown pigment called *melanin* (mel'uh-nin; "black" G). This can absorb ultraviolet light without harm to itself and thus acts as a protective umbrella over the regions beneath. It is in tropical areas, where the sun is strongest, that the possession of considerable melanin in the skin is most valuable and it is there that evolutionary processes have slowly increased the quantity of pigment from generation to generation. It is melanin in quantity that is responsible, then, for the dark rich color of tropical peoples such as the Negro of Africa, the Dravidian of India, the Aborigines of Australia, the Papuans of Melanesia, and the Indians of tropical America. Even among Europeans there is a tendency for increasing swarthiness of skin as one proceeds southward.

The pale skins to be found in northern Europe may, on the other hand, also be brought about by evolutionary pressures. Where the sunlight is weak, the presence of melanin is unimportant. Instead, it is better to keep the epidermis transparent so that as much of the weak sunlight as possible reaches the dermis and produces the necessary vitamin D. Under conditions of low melanin content the skin is pale or "white" but permits the redness of the blood in the blood vessels of the dermis to show dimly through so that the actual color is what we call "flesh color."

The formation of melanin is stimulated by exposure to sunlight. This is most apparent among people who are intermediate in melanin content, those who possess little enough to be distinctly "white" in color but possess enough to be "brunet" in complexion. Exposure to the sun darkens the skin to produce a "tan."

When people are very fair they may lack not only melanin but even the capacity to form much. Since hair and eyes also owe their color to melanin, such particularly fair people are likely to have blond hair and blue eyes, and it is these who most often have the characteristic of burning rather than tanning. Some light-skinned individuals produce melanin in localized spots when exposed to sunlight. This is particularly true among those whose light hair contains a reddish pigment that would ordinarily be drowned out if much melanin were also present. It is these "redheads" that form the localized spots of tan we call *freckles* (AS).

Even the lightest normal individuals can form enough melanin to tint their eyes blue. However, individuals are occasionally born who, through a particular flaw in their chemical makeup, are incapable of forming any melanin at all. Skin and hair are white and the eyes are red, because in the absence of pigment the tiny blood vessels are clearly visible in the iris of the eye (the colored part). Such a person is an *albino* (al-by'noh; "white" L). Albinos can occur among any group of human beings; therefore albino Negroes can be found.

Other species of animals may also develop albinism. The white rat and the white rabbit are familiar examples. The white elephant, so venerated in Thailand, is an albino, and one can even have that apparent contradiction in terms, a "white blackbird."

Melanin is not the only skin pigment. A yellow pigment, called *carotene* (kar'oh-teen') also occurs in the skin. It is a common substance in the plant and animal world (in fact, the name is derived from carrots, which are rich in it) and it is related to vitamin A. Ordinarily it is drowned out by the more deeply colored melanin, but there are groups of people, particularly in eastern Asia, with skins rich in carotene and yet

not overrich in melanin, and the result is a definite yellowish
tinge in the skin color.

PERSPIRATION

Since the skin is adjacent to the outside world it is important as
the means of regulating body heat by offering a radiating surface. The chief source of body heat is not the skin itself, of
course, but the internal organs, particularly those engaged in
intense chemical activity, such as the liver, kidneys, and heart.
The heat produced by those organs is carried off by the blood,
which in the course of its circulation distributes the heat evenly.
Some of the heat is carried to the dermis and from there part
is radiated away. The ease with which this radiation takes
place depends on the difference in temperature between the
body and its surroundings. When the difference is low, radiation is slow; when the difference is high, radiation is rapid.

In warm weather, when the atmosphere is only a little cooler
than the body and the rate of heat loss by radiation is low, the
arterioles of the dermis relax, so an unusually large fraction of
the blood is in the skin. The slowness of radiation is thus made
up for, at least in part, by increasing the supply of heat to be
radiated. On the other hand, in cold weather the arterioles of
the dermis contract so that the overrapidity of radiation is made
up for, at least in part, by reducing the availability of heat for
such radiation.

Control by simple radiation is not efficient enough, however,
particularly in warm weather when heat must be got rid of
quickly. Use is therefore made not merely of simple radiation but
of the evaporation of liquid. The conversion of any liquid into
its vapor form is an energy-consuming process, and in the case
of water the quantity of energy consumed per weight vaporized
is higher than for almost any other liquid. The energy for the
vaporization is withdrawn from the most convenient place; that

is, from whatever the liquid is in contact with. Wet your finger and blow upon it or step directly from a shower into a breeze and the sensation of coolness as vaporization withdraws heat from the skin is unmistakable.

An obvious way of increasing the rate at which water is evaporated from the body is to breathe rapidly and carry quantities of air across the moist surfaces of the mouth, throat, and lungs. We ourselves cannot do this in comfort, but it is the chief method of cooling available to the dog, for instance, which in warm weather will sit with mouth open, quivering tongue extended, and pant.

We don't do this because we have a better device, one the dog lacks. We are equipped with tiny glands distributed all over our skin, about two million of them altogether, the purpose of which is to bring water to the surface of the skin. On the surface this water is vaporized and heat is in this manner withdrawn from the body. The glands are *sweat glands* and the liquid produced is *sweat* (AS), or *perspiration* ("breathe through" L, a reminder of the misconception that the skin breathes through these glands). A sweat gland consists of a tiny coiled tube, the main body of which is situated deep in the dermis. The tube straightens out finally and extends up through the epidermis. The tiny opening on the surface is a *pore* ("passage" G) and is just barely visible to the naked eye.

Sweat is constantly being produced, usually in proportion to the temperature of the environment and, therefore, the need to lose heat by means more effective than simple radiation. In cool, dry weather the amount of sweat produced is relatively small and the rate of evaporation can keep up with it. The skin remains dry to the touch, and you are not aware of sweating. This is *insensible perspiration,* and, for all that you are not aware of it, it can involve the loss of a liter of water per day.

When you are working or playing hard, and heat production of the body is increased, the sweat glands accelerate their production of perspiration. This is also true when the temperature is unusually high. The rate of production may then outstrip the rate of evaporation, particularly if humidity is high, since the rate of evaporation declines with the rise in humidity. Perspiration will then collect on the body in visible drops and we are conscious of sweating. The liquid alone does us little good as far as cooling is concerned; we must wait upon the evaporation. Consequently, when we are visibly sweating we are usually hot and uncomfortable as well, and go around saying, "It's not the heat, it's the humidity" — which is true enough.

On the other hand, when the humidity is quite low, so that the rate of evaporation is high, even hot summer weather does not feel particularly uncomfortable. It is then possible for the temperature of the air to be higher than that of the body, and if radiation alone were involved the body would gain heat; yet, thanks to perspiration and evaporation, the body still feels comfortable. Even when the air is fairly dry, that portion of the air adjacent to our bodies will take up water vapor from our perspiration and will become humid. It is for this reason that it is important there be some sort of ventilation, even if only a small breeze, to replace the humid air adjacent to ourselves with drier air from a distance.

Sweating can be stimulated by emotion or tension as well as heat. This brings on a "cold perspiration," because at lower temperatures the cooling induced by copious perspiration can result in a rather unpleasantly cold sensation. Whereas under the influence of heat the sweat glands of the forehead and neck are most active, under the influence of emotion those of the palms are; and so it is that the palms grow clammy.

Sweat is almost pure water, with dissolved material making up only about half of 1 per cent of the total. Most of that small quantity of dissolved material is sodium chloride, or salt. This loss of salt is ordinarily insignificant, but where perspiration is particularly copious, as much as a liter or a liter and a half of sweat can be lost per hour and then the drain on the body's salt supplies can become appreciable. Loss of water through perspiration naturally stimulates the thirst sensation, and when water is available a copiously sweating person need not be urged to drink. However, such drinking replaces only the water and not the salt. Salt loss, if extreme, can bring about painful cramps, and even where matters are not carried to this point, salt loss will bring on an uncomfortable consciousness of heat. It has become customary, then, for people subjected to intense heat or intense work to take salt tablets with their water.

People adapted to hot, humid climates (Negroes as compared to Europeans, for instance) have more sweat glands and secrete perspiration with a smaller concentration of salt.

As a result of the workings of our sweat-gland air-conditioning system, the temperature of the body is held with amazing constancy between 98 degrees F. and 100 degrees F. The usual "normal temperature" is given as 98.6 degrees F., but this is just an average, and the exact value varies slightly from time to time and from individual to individual. A rise in temperature above the 100-degree F. mark, usually in response to infection, is a *fever* ("I am warm" L). Even where the fever involves a rise of only one or two degrees, the result is great discomfort and a feeling of lassitude. So well does our thermostat work, that a fever is a sure sign of trouble, and a clinical thermometer is every mother's most prized piece of diagnostic machinery.

Perspiration has its unpleasant side too, for odor is associated with it. The ordinary sweat glands of the body generally are not at fault in this respect. There is a special variety of sweat gland, somewhat larger than the ordinary kind, which is concentrated in relatively few areas of the body, notably in the armpits and about the genital organs. These also secrete an odorless sweat but one containing small quantities of organic substances easily broken down by bacteria on the skin. The breakdown products are responsible for the characteristic human "body odor." Since these sweat glands become active only in puberty, children are relatively free of such body odor (although they can, of course, smell for a variety of other reasons).

Undoubtedly body odor must have been of use in primitive tribal days. It may have helped keep the tribe together in wooded areas or at night, where sight would not entirely serve. It may also have been a means of distinguishing a fellow tribesman from a stranger, since there would be slight variations in odor which the better developed sense of smell of early man might have picked up easily. It may even have served as a sexual stimulant.

In our own crowded society of today, however, in which each of us is placed in contact with hundreds or even thousands of strangers daily, and where odor is required neither for togetherness nor for counterespionage (though the matter of sex remains moot), odor has become a source of discomfort. Hence our modern emphasis on frequent bathing and on the use of soaps, perfumes, and chemical deodorants in an unending war against a natural phenomenon.

An important type of modified sweat gland is the milk-producing *mammary gland* ("breast" G). This would make milk a modification of sweat, which seems odd and even repellent, but this is no stranger than considering the larynx a modified gill-bar or a leg a modified fin. The mammary glands are present only in mammals, and the very name of this class of chordates is derived from that fact. In general, they develop along two *mammary lines* down the ventral surface of the body. A number of the glands come together here and there along those lines to form a series of protuberances called *nipples* (AS). (The most primitive of living mammals, the duckbill platypus, lacks nipples, and milk that oozes out of the mammary glands must be lapped up by the young. In all other mammals the existence of a nipple makes it possible for sucking to take place, and this is a more efficient method for collecting the milk.)

In animals that produce a number of young at a birth, a number of nipples are retained along each mammary line. This can be easily observed among cats, dogs, and pigs. The cow, which usually brings forth one young at a time, retains but two pairs of nipples at the abdominal end of the mammary lines, and combines all four into one large baglike *udder* (AS). In the human being, which also brings forth but one young at a time ordinarily, only one pair of nipples is retained, toward the thoracic end of the mammary line, and these retain their separate structures.

In children and in adult males, the nipples remain small and without function; that is, they are *rudimentary* ("a beginning" L). About the time of puberty, however, the mammary glands of girls begin to change. The nipples enlarge, and the individual glands (of which there may be 15 to 20 on either side, each possessing an individual duct through the nipple) are surrounded and bound together by connective tissue and fat to produce a pair of soft, rounded *breasts* (AS). The individual female breast extends from the second to the sixth rib and from the breastbone to the armpit. The nipple is situated a little below the center of the breast, is pink in color to begin with, and is surrounded by a light pink area called the *areola* (a-ree'oh-luh; "small area" L). The nipple and areola are usually darker in brunettes than in blondes. After the first pregnancy, melanin is, for some reason, deposited in the nipple and areola, which consequently are more or less permanently darkened.

Milk is produced only after the birth of a child, and then only for as long as it is periodically withdrawn from the breast. Through evolutionary pressures, each species of mammal produces milk particularly adapted to the needs of its young. Human milk is 1.5 per cent protein, 7.2 per cent lactose, 3.6 per cent fat, and 0.2 per cent minerals. The rest is water.

Among animals generally, milk is a food of infancy only, to be abandoned forever after weaning (unless the adult animal is supplied with some by a human being). Even in prehistoric times man recognized it as a valuable food for adults, and kept cows, goats, sheep, even horses in order that these might be milked at such times as they were lactating.

Milk itself was difficult to keep fresh in the days before refrigeration became commonplace, and it was found best to direct its fermentation into pleasant channels to produce yogurt, or soured cream, or hundreds of varieties of cheeses. Milk fat was isolated as butter. Nowadays, of course, we use milk itself, kept uncontaminated by disease-producing bacteria through a preliminary process of gentle heating. This is called *pasteurization*, after Louis Pasteur, who introduced the process (in connection with wine, by the way, rather than milk).

Cow's milk, which is the variety drunk almost exclusively in the United States, does not have quite the same composition as human milk. It is only half as rich in lactose and is twice as rich in protein. (Calves grow at a faster rate than babies do and need more protein in their food.) Adults can tolerate this difference with ease, but infants cannot. For that reason, when human mothers are unable to (or choose not to) feed their infants at the breast, the cow's milk they use instead must be suitably modified. It must be diluted to keep the proteins from being too concentrated, and then because the carbohydrate content is brought even lower as a result, additional sugar must be added. The sugar added is usually in the form of dextrins (breakdown products of starch), which have the energy content of sugar but, like lactose, are relatively tasteless.

HAIR

The regulation of heat is aided in most mammals, as I have said earlier in the chapter, by a coat of hair. In addition to this primary use as a heat insulator, hair can be put to specialized uses. Crinkly hair with a pattern of overlapping scales that cause each to catch on its neighbor forms a mat or felt that is commonly called *wool*. Sheep are especially bred for this variety of hair.

Short, stiff, unusually thick hairs, like those on the back of swine, are *bristles*. The bristles in the walrus mustache may be up to a quarter of an inch in diameter. The spines of the hedgehog and the quills of the porcupine are hairs stiffened, pointed, and even barbed to serve as weapons of defense and offense. A still more extreme organ of defense born of the hair is the hornlike projection on the snout of the rhinoceros, which is formed by the fusion of a large number of hairs. Then, too, long, rather stiff hairs, richly supplied with nerve endings at the root, can be used as delicate organs of touch. Examples are the long hairs forming the cat's mustache.

Such specializations are absent in man and, indeed, our coat of hair is a poor one altogether. In part this is a general primate characteristic, for the primates as a group are less hairy than are most nonprimates. This need not be surprising, for primates are tropical animals, among whom hair is not particularly important as an insulator. Then, too, the larger the animal the smaller the surface in relation to volume, by the square-cube law (see Chapter 5). For this reason it is easier for a large animal to stay warm because there is a large volume to produce heat and a comparatively small surface to radiate it away. It is for this reason that polar animals (such as the polar bear, the muskox, the walrus) tend to run to large size. Tropical animals when large in size must do something to improve the ability of the skin to radiate heat, and the easiest solution is to cut down on the hair cover or lose it entirely. The elephant, hippopotamus, and rhinoceros are all virtually hairless for example (though during the glacial ages woolly species of both elephant and rhinoceros roamed the north). The elephant, particularly the African species, has also developed large ears, which serve as heat radiators.

There is a similar tendency to lose hair among the larger primates. The gorilla, to take an example, has a hairless face and chest. In man the tendency has progressed the farthest, although he is smaller than the gorilla. This has not been in the direction of a true loss of hair. There are only restricted areas of the human body, such as the palms of the hands and the soles of the feet, that are truly hairless. As for the rest of the skin, hairs are numerous — as numerous per unit area as in other primates. In man, however, most of the hairs remain small and fine and do not grow thick enough or long enough to form a continuous cover or to trap an insulating layer of quiet air next to the skin.

Nevertheless we possess one ability that is reminiscent of ages past when our ancestors did possess a shaggy pelt of hair. Animals, under the stimulus of cold, can erect their hair, causing the coat to extend farther from the skin. In this way a thicker layer of air is trapped and insulation against heat loss is improved. We still possess small bundles of smooth muscle, *arrectores pilorum* (ar'ek-toh'reez py-loh'rum; "hair-erectors" L), which can tighten the skin and lift the hair. All we can do, however, is to erect a tiny useless hair while the skin at its base puckers and rises in "gooseflesh." Hair also stands erect in response to the stimulus of fright, as can be seen spectacularly when a cat comes unexpectedly face to face with a dog. The thicker coat of hair apparently serves to increase the dimensions of the animal and make it seem more formidable. We respond similarly to fright and develop gooseflesh.

Man has retained a true coat of hair, or at least patches of hair, in those areas where it will serve a protective function. The area where this is most marked is the top of the head. Here the purpose served is one of insulation, not so much against the loss of body heat as against the heat of the sun. There are brain proteins that are unusually unstable under even relatively mild degrees of heat, and the direct heat of the sun upon the exposed skull can, under severe conditions, produce unconsciousness and prostration, an effect called *sunstroke*. The coating of hair reduces the likelihood of this and the crisp even coating of frizzy, wool-like hair among many African Negroes is particularly efficient in this respect. Even with a coating of hair in full bloom, it is perhaps advisable for those not acclimated to the tropic sun to wear a head covering for further protection.

The various orifices leading into the body are usually protected by hairs. In addition to the hairs of the nostrils, mentioned in Chapter 5, there is usually a growth of hair about the ear canal and about the anus. The eye is fringed with eyelashes and, farther above, with an eyebrow. The former protect the eye against foreign particles, the latter against the glare of the sun.

The social custom among us which compels men and boys to cut the hair of their head short gives the illusion that female hair is longer than male hair. (In fact, it is my experience that American children of preschool age uniformly distinguish the sexes by the length of hair.) Actually this is not so, and in eras when it was permissible for males to let their hair grow they did as well at it as women did.

Hairiness increases with age. In some ways this increase is uniform among the sexes. At puberty, for instance, both males and females begin to grow hair in the armpits and about the genitals. The former is *axillary hair* (ak'si-ler'ee; "armpit" L); the latter *pubic hair* ("adult" L). Since the hair appears at the same time that the specialized odor-producing sweat glands do, it is natural to suppose that the function of the hair is to encourage odor-formation by serving as collectors for the bacteria producing it. This presents problems to our own odor-conscious society.

In other ways, the increase of hairiness with age is a particularly male phenomenon. In the later teens hair sprouts along the cheeks, chin, and upper lip to produce the beard and mustache. This cannot have any truly vital use (though it might serve to protect the mouth), since the female gets on very well without it. It might therefore be classified as a secondary sexual characteristic; one developed because it serves to advertise the sexual maturity of the male and to act as a stimulant to female susceptibility — like the mane of the male lion or the beautiful colors of most male birds. In addition, men develop more prominent and longer hairs on the shoulders and chest. This varies radically from group to group, so that men of European descent are considerably hairier, by and large, than other groups are. It also varies from individual to individual, so that some men are virtually bald-chested and others of similar descent are almost shaggy.

There is an opposing tendency that also varies radically from individual to individual: that of losing the hair on the head (though not elsewhere) in middle life and beyond. In some cases, signs of loss appear even in the twenties. A tendency to such *baldness* (AS), or *alopecia* (al'oh-pee'shee-uh; "baldness" G), is apparently inherited and is, in a small way, a sign of masculinity, since the tendency does not manifest itself, even though inherited, unless there is more than a certain critical concentration of male sex hormone in the blood. As a result, women rarely go bald, and men who are castrated before adolescence apparently never do.

With age there is also an increasing tendency for a loss of pigment in the hair. As the years pass, hair becomes more and more markedly gray, the process often beginning at the temples. Eventually it can turn completely white. As in the case of baldness, the process may start at quite an early age in particular individuals; and the tendency to premature graying is also an inherited one.

Hair is a product of the epidermis, which buckles deep into the dermis at the point where a hair grows. This deep dip of a thin layer of epidermis is the *hair follicle* ("little bag" L). Each follicle holds a single hair. Within a bulge at the bottom of the follicle is the *hair root*. This is alive. As hair is formed by the root, it pushes upward as a shaft covered with tiny, regularly placed scales and reaches the surface of the skin. The hair above the root is a nonliving structure consisting mainly of keratin.

Human hair grows at the rate of about 0.3 millimeters a day, which is equivalent to about an inch in ten weeks. Periodically a hair will fall out and a new hair will grow in its place. The frequency with which this happens will control the maximum length of hair. In certain animals, there are definite times of "shedding." This sometimes heralds a seasonal change, so that there is a growth of longer, thicker hair for the winter season. The new hair may even show a change in color: an animal may turn white for the winter — a condition that improves its chances of survival, since it is less easily seen against the snow.

In man, however, each hair has its own individual life cycle independent of its neighbor's. There are always some hairs falling out and being replaced and the thickness and texture of the hair (barring the advent of baldness) and the color (except for graying) remains constant.

Hair may be straight, wavy, or frizzy, but the exact reasons for this difference are not known. Since American fashion decrees that women ought to have wavy hair, the prevalence of straight hair among them is a source of dismay to the woman and of income to beauty parlors. The keratin molecules of hair are bound together by atom-chains that can be broken by damp heat and the action of certain chemicals. If the hair is then curled and left so for a period of time, new atom chains form in the new position. The hair will be held in a permanently curled position then — a "permanent wave," in fact — as long as it remains in the head. The new hair formed at the root will be straight, and after it falls out an artificially curled hair will be replaced by a straight one. A permanent wave is therefore only temporarily permanent.

Associated with virtually every hair is a small *sebaceous gland* (see-bay'shus; "tallow" L), which produces *sebum* (see'-bum), a waxy secretion. A duct leads this to the hair follicle. The hair and surrounding skin is constantly coated with sebum, unless it is painstakingly soap-and-watered away. Sebum contributes to the glossiness of hair and acts as a protective and waterproofing agent to both hair and skin. Hair so protected sheds water. It has been pointed out that the natural direction

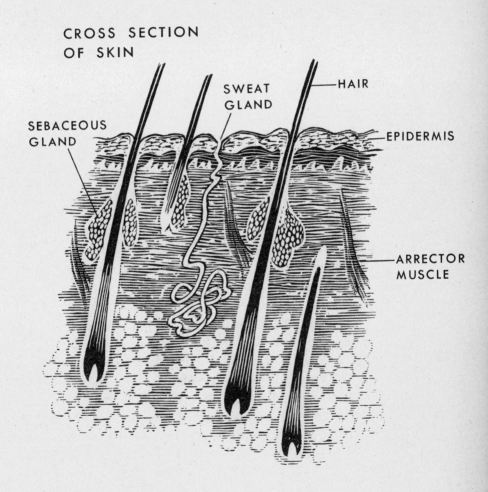

CROSS SECTION
OF SKIN

SWEAT GLAND

HAIR

SEBACEOUS GLAND

EPIDERMIS

ARRECTOR MUSCLE

in which hair lies on the human body is such that if a man squatted with knees pulled up to his chin and with his hands behind his neck, elbows pointing downward (a position a primitive man might well take up in a miserable attempt to reduce exposure to a pelting rain), all the body hairs would point downward, shedding rain.

A woman's nose is particularly well supplied with sebaceous glands. It is sebum that produces the "shiny nose" against which women, armed with powder puffs, wage constant war. It is collected sebum that forms earwax and the matter that accumulates in the corners of the eyes after sleep. It is also sebum, rather than perspiration, that makes a person's hair and skin markedly greasy after a period without washing.

On the other hand, washing, if carried to an extreme, can unnecessarily deprive hair and skin of a useful protective agent. It should be pointed out that lanolin, which is widely touted by advertisers as a component of various preparations designed to help the hair and skin by replacing the sebum lost through over-application of various other preparations as widely touted by the same advertisers, is itself a product of sheep sebum.

Despite all natural protective devices the skin, particularly if allowed to become overly dirty, is exposed to infection. The openings represented by pores and hair follicles are the weak points in this respect. Unwashed skin tends to pick up dirt, which, trapped in the sebum and dried perspiration, will fill pores to form unsightly "blackheads." The richer concentrations of bacteria on dirty skin are likely to start an infection at the site of the blackhead or in a hair follicle to produce the inflamed areas we call pimples and boils.

The activity of some microorganisms is apt to elicit a protective response in the form of an exaggerated secretion of sebum, or *seborrhea* (seb'oh-ree'uh; "sebum-flow" L). This in turn causes or is accompanied by skin inflammation (*dermatitis*) and itching. The sebum collects and produces a greasy scale that is most noticeable when trapped by and accumulated in hair. We know this condition as *dandruff* (AS), which is unsightly, uncomfortably itchy, and, in extreme cases, can bring about loss of hair.

Seborrhea seems to increase the likelihood of the development of chronic pimple-formation, or *acne* (ak'nee). There seem to be hormonal imbalances involved here, because the condition appears most often at puberty, when the body's hormonal pattern is shifting radically, and among girls is most marked during the menstrual period, when the same is true. (In fact one theory as to the derivation of the word "acne" is that it was originally a misprint of "acme," and that it was meant to indicate that the condition struck at the height of youth, the acme of life.) Probably no other disease of so mild a character has such serious psychological effects, for the young man or woman is usually disfigured at just that time of life when he or she has discovered the opposite sex and is most insecure and self-conscious about the whole matter. Furthermore, although acne is usually a passing phase and tends to vanish with the teens, it leaves scars behind on the face as well as the personality.

The skin is also subject to fungus infections, of which the best known is "athlete's foot," and subject to itchy, scaly disorders that don't always have a recognized cause or a secure treatment — such as *eczema* (ek'zi-muh; "eruption" G), *psoriasis* (so-ry'uh-sis; "itch" G), and *impetigo* (im'peh-ty'goh; "to attack" L). Rashes and pustule formation are common in many diseases like measles and chicken pox. Next to the clinical thermometer, the mother's best diagnostic aid is the eye with which she scans her child's body for any telltale rash.

Chicken pox may result in scarring, but the real villain in this respect is the now happily conquered smallpox. The real terror of smallpox in the days before vaccination was not so much the possibility of death — which, after all, accompanied almost any other disease in those medically ignorant days — as the possibility of continuing life with so scarred a face that every vestige of good looks, and almost of humanity, was gone.

The skin may contain local heterogeneities. If these are pigmented and darker than the surrounding skin, they are *moles* (AS). Sometimes the disfigurement is caused by a small knot of dilated blood vessels in the skin and from its color and appearance it is then called a "strawberry mark." When moles are present at birth, particularly if they have an irregular shape, they are called "birthmarks." Most people have small moles and are generally sufficiently accustomed to them to be unaware of them. Moles, however, can occasionally become cancerous, and although this does not happen often, the possibility makes it advisable for individuals to note any changes in the appearance of a mole and to consult a doctor promptly in this connection. Warts are not merely large moles, but are apparently the result of a virus infection. Although disfiguring they are not dangerous.

Still, though the catalog of skin disorders is long and although man is more aware of them than of disorders in other organs, simply because it is the skin that is exposed to view, it should be emphasized that on the whole skin is an extremely effective shield. It performs its guardian duties well and the wonder is not that it occasionally gives way somewhat to the buffets of the environment but that it gives way so infrequently and has such a remarkable talent for recovery.

11

OUR GENITALS

REPRODUCTION

Despite the beautiful and awesome adaptation of the human body to its functions, it is at best but a temporary structure. Even if the body were — by luck, by care, by innate health — to avoid the infectious diseases and maladjustments I have mentioned here and there in this book, it cannot go on forever. There are inevitable changes that come with age, a hardening and loss of resilience of the connective tissue and of the artery walls; a slow deterioration and loss among the nerve cells; tiny losses of essentials and tiny accumulations of wastes here and there. We are not certain what the exact nature of the fundamental changes with time may be, but, taken together, they make up the aging process.

The result is "old age." This is not a strictly chronological matter, for some human beings retain alertness and a measure of vigor into the nineties and others begin to dodder in their sixties. Medical science has not yet learned how to prevent, or even slow, the fundamental aging process; and although the conquest of many infectious diseases and the successful treatment of some metabolic disorders have raised the life expectancy over recent centuries from 30 to 70, the maximum age which may be reached remains at a little over a hundred. And in the end, inevitably and universally, comes death.

The human body as I have described it in previous chapters must yet contain some organs I have not described, for if human life is to continue while individual bodies die, provision must be made for the formation of new bodies at a rate at least equal to that at which old bodies die. This process of *reproduction* is fundamental to all living things.

A one-celled creature can reproduce itself simply by dividing in two;* that is, by *binary fission*. Among the simpler multicellular organisms, binary fission is sometimes retained as a method of reproduction. Some coelenterates can divide along a longitudinal plane (from head to foot) and form two of themselves. Some simple worms can divide along a transverse plane (from side to side) and form two of themselves; or may fragment (*multiple fission*), each piece that results giving rise to a separate organism.

Such fission, binary or multiple, requires that each fragment be able to regenerate the rest of the organism. This can be done when the organism is a single cell or when it is made up of relatively few and unspecialized cells. However, it seems a rule that the more specialized a tissue the less regenerative it becomes. In the human being, tissues as specialized as nerve and muscle can regenerate little, if at all. It is reasonable, then, to expect that as the cells of a given organism grow more numerous and specialized, reproduction by binary fission becomes more and more impractical. Fission must therefore give way to more sophisticated methods of reproduction, or a quick limit

---

* The use of the word "simply" is misleading — there is nothing simple about the process. The chemical functioning of the cell is guided by structures in the nucleus (called chromosomes) which are made up of a series of molecules of deoxyribonucleic acid, a name usually abbreviated as DNA. When a one-celled creature divides, the various DNA molecules form replicas of themselves in order that, after cell division, each "daughter cell" possess an identical set of its own. The process by which this is accomplished is only becoming understood in the years since 1950, and this is described in considerable detail in my book *The Wellsprings of Life*.

is placed on the permissible complexity of multicellular life.*

One way out is to restrict the reproductive process to a small region of the organism which remains relatively unspecialized, and is therefore capable of regenerating all the rest of the organism. The beginnings of such a process can be traced back to one-celled forms of life, for yeast cells do not multiply by dividing evenly in two, but form small outgrowths of protoplasm at restricted regions of the cell boundary. These outgrowths grow larger and finally break away as full cells. This is *budding*. In the yeast cell there seems scarcely any way to distinguish this from binary fission, but in multicellular animals, the analogous process represents a clear specialization. The fresh-water hydra, a coelenterate, will grow a small group of cells at one point on its surface and these will multiply and form a new hydra that will eventually break off. Only some cells, rather than all, are involved.

The end toward which this specialization aims seems inevitable. The logical result is for an organism to produce a single cell, supremely specialized through its very lack of ordinary specialization, designed for the sole purpose of regenerating an entire organism like the one that produced it in the first place. Such a cell is an *egg cell*, or *ovum* ("egg" L).

So far, reproduction as I have described it seems to be the function of a single organism, but it is only in the simplest forms of life that this is true. Among the organisms most familiar to us, each species is divided into two groups or *sexes* ("to divide" L) and it is as a result of the combined activity of one of each sex that new individual organisms are produced. Reproduction on the basis of the activity of two separate individuals is therefore

* Nevertheless, the ability to reproduce by binary fission is never entirely lost, no matter how complicated an organism grows. The individual cells of all organisms, including ourselves, if they are capable of multiplying at all, multiply by binary fission. Therefore, although man does not reproduce by fission, he grows by fission.

sexual reproduction, whereas fission and budding are examples of *asexual reproduction.*

Sexual reproduction can be traced back to the more complex one-celled creatures. Among these a period of reproduction through binary fission seems slowly to reduce the vigor of the individual. When this happens, two of the tiny creatures not closely related (that is, they have not formed from a single ancestral cell of a relatively small number of generations before) meet. The cell membrane between them breaks down over a limited area, and the two interchange portions of their nuclei. This is *conjugation* ("yoke together" L), and the process restores cellular vigor.

Why this should be is not certainly known, but one can speculate that, after a period of asexual reproduction, tiny errors accumulate in the replication of the chromosome material and that this may slowly lessen the efficiency of the chemical machinery of the cell. Through conjugation, each individual receives part of the DNA of the other, and this dilutes out the changes for the worse. One individual is likely not to suffer the particular evils of the other, and the strengths of each negate the weaknesses of the other. Furthermore, any accidental change in the chromosome material that may be for the better is spread by means of conjugation from one group of individuals to the remainder.

In general, this would seem to exemplify the purpose of sexual reproduction. Through this process there is a mixing of the mechanism of inheritance of two individuals, allowing new combinations to develop in each generation and spreading changes developed by one to all the others of a species. This apparently hastens the evolutionary machinery and in the end seems to work for the good of the species.

The ultimate proof of this lies in the changes we observe in the course of evolution. Only the simplest organisms reproduce by asexual mechanisms only. The more specialized one-celled organisms reproduce by asexual mechanisms, with an occasional sexual step (conjugation) introduced. In many of the simpler multicellular animals there is an alternation of generations. That is, there is first an asexual reproduction, producing individuals capable of sexual reproduction; these in turn produce, by sexual mechanisms, individuals that reproduce only asexually. In the more complex multicellular animals, including ourselves, however, asexual reproduction is dropped entirely and sexual reproduction becomes the norm.

Once an organism reaches the stage where it can produce an egg cell, it is almost invariably involved in sexual reproduction. It is possible, to be sure, for an egg cell by itself and without interference of any other cell, to form an organism. This is called *parthenogenesis* (pahr'theh-noh-jen'eh-sis; "virgin birth" G), and it can take place among numerous invertebrates. Among the bees it takes place routinely, for example. Taking life as a whole, though, this is unusual, and among vertebrates it never occurs.

In general, an egg cell will not produce an organism until it is fused with another type of cell called a *sperm cell* ("seed" G), or *spermatozoon* (spur'muh-toh-zoh'on; "animal seed" G). This

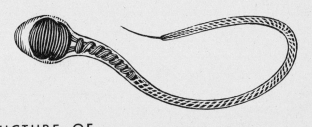

STRUCTURE OF
SPERMATAZOON

process of fusion of egg and sperm is *fertilization,* and the combined cell, now capable of forming a complete organism, is a *fertilized ovum.* In a number of simple animal forms, the same individual can produce both egg cells and sperm cells. Theoretically, it is then possible for a sperm cell to fertilize the egg cell of the same individual. This defeats the entire purpose of sexual reproduction, however, and such an animal is usually so designed that this form of self-fertilization cannot take place. Thus, an earthworm produces both egg cells and sperm cells. But reproduction comes about only when two earthworms make contact in such a fashion that the sperm-producing region of each is next to the egg-producing region of the other. Each earthworm fertilizes the other and not itself.

The natural step that would outlaw all possibility of self-fertilization and make certain that the purpose of sex is not thwarted is to arrange for individuals to produce only egg cells or only sperm cells, never both. The egg-producing individual is the female and the sperm-producing one the male. All vertebrates, including man of course, are divided in this way into a male sex and a female sex.

THE EGG

When a one-celled animal divides, each daughter cell is already large enough and complicated enough to continue independent life on its own. It is virtually born an adult. The fertilized ovum of an even fairly simple multicellular creature must, however, undergo a number of cell divisions before it becomes large enough and specialized enough to be able to assume an independent existence. During this period of development, the cell mass requires energy and, since it cannot eat, it must have a pre-existing food supply. The egg cell therefore contains food material or *yolk* (yoke; "yellow" AS, which describes its usual color) in sufficient quantity to bridge the gap between fertilized ovum and an organism complicated enough to feed independently. The presence of the yolk makes the egg cell larger than ordinary cells and all the more immobile by virtue of that fact.

If a fertilizing union between sperm cell and egg cell is to take place, then, the full responsibility of the meeting of the two must lie with the sperm cell. The sperm cell must therefore be capable of motion. To attain this end, the sperm cell is made light by being supplied with virtually no food. It need only live long enough to travel from its point of release to the point where the egg cell lies. If it doesn't succeed in that one task its reason for existence is gone and there is no point in feeding it further. Nor need it carry any cytoplasm; the egg cell will have enough for both.

In short, the sperm cell need carry nothing but the nuclear material within which lies the inheritance machinery. For that reason the sperm cell is much smaller than the average cell, and a veritable pygmy in comparison with the yolk-bloated egg cell. Nevertheless, the two cells, the tiny sperm and the giant egg, contain equal amounts of the nuclear material and both contribute equally to the inheritance of the new organism.

To move the tiny sperm cell a flagellum is all that is needed. By use of it, the sperm cell, looking for all the world like a microscopic tadpole, lashes its way through the water to the egg

FERTILIZATION
OF OVUM

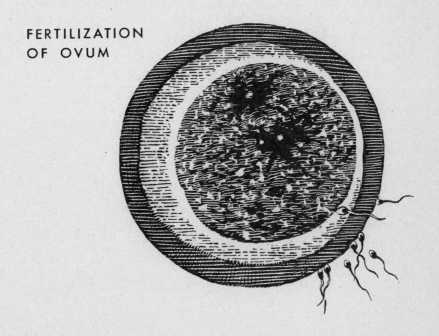

cell — provided, of course, it finds itself in a watery medium.

Fertilization for sea animals, immersed as they are in a watery medium, can, therefore, be simple enough. A female of the species will deposit a mass of eggs in some secluded spot, and when she has finished a waiting male will swim over the eggs, emitting a stream of sperm cells. The sperm cells move in the direction of the egg cells and the two parents swim away, their work done.

Among land creatures matters are more complicated, since sperm cells cannot swim through air or along the ground. It is therefore necessary that the male deposit the sperm cells, plus fluid, within the duct through which the eggs will eventually emerge. The sperm cells will reach the egg cells within the body of the female and when the eggs are later laid, they will be already fertilized. This process of fertilization within the body is called *copulation* ("to couple" L), and for the purpose the male has developed a copulatory organ which can be inserted into the female.*

The helplessness of an egg during the time in which it is developing into an organism makes it desirable from the standpoint of survival that it reach the independent organism stage as quickly as possible. Yet the more complex the phylum, the longer it takes for development to full complexity to take place. In many cases a compromise is struck; the egg is rushed to the stage of independent organism before full complexity is reached. Such a simplified but independent organism is a larva. The larva feeds and grows until it is ready to undergo a kind of new birth and become an adult. (Sometimes the larval stage grows more and more important and actually eliminates the adult form, as I explained in Chapter 1.)

We are most familiar with this phenomenon in the case of certain insects, for we all know the caterpillar which at a certain

* Human beings, like other land animals, must engage in copulation if reproduction is to take place. However, because there is a certain shamefacedness about discussing the process which, in our culture, is kept very private, it is referred to by the rather prissy term *sexual intercourse*.

stage of its life cycle makes what is almost a second egg for itself, in the form of a cocoon, and emerges as the adult butterfly. Among the vertebrates the frog is the best-known example, for it hatches as the larval tadpole and later gradually becomes a frog, without, however, immobilizing itself in a cocoon stage in the process.

Even so, there is a tremendous mortality among larvae, which are too small and simple to be as successfully self-defensive as the adult of the species. To ensure survival of the species, the most common device is therefore to lay eggs by the millions, in the hope that out of all those millions at least one or two will survive to adulthood by sheer good fortune. This actually happens; otherwise most species of fish would be extinct by now.

The alternative is to adopt some form of protection for the eggs and larvae till they can fend more successfully for themselves. Thus, some fish build nests or keep the eggs in pouches or in their mouths until development has well progressed. There are even cases where fertilized eggs remain within the body cavities of the female until the larval stage is reached. These alternates are poorly developed among sea creatures, however.

Among land vertebrates the care of eggs becomes more important for several reasons. In the first place, the larval stage must be eliminated on land. The land, as an environment for life, is unbelievably hard and cruel as compared with the kindly sea, within which life was first developed. The force of gravity is uncanceled by buoyancy on land and it must be combated by fully developed muscles; the atmosphere must be breathed by fully developed lungs; and water conserved by a fully developed kidney. The young reptile therefore must emerge from the egg, smaller than the adult perhaps, and weaker, but not essentially simpler in structure. It is always recognizably of the adult form and is capable of independent life in the fashion of its parents.

To eliminate the larval stage means a lengthening of development within the egg, which in turn means that the egg must contain a large quantity of yolk. Consequently, each egg represents a tremendous investment, and because of its size there is a sharp limit to the number that can be laid. Where fish and frogs can lay vast numbers of eggs and trust to luck that some will survive, reptiles and birds must lay small numbers and take some care of them in consequence. Reptiles may bury their eggs in sand or even remain in the vicinity until hatching time, but birds are the classic examples of creatures that care for their eggs.

The care of eggs is made all the more necessary in that birds are warm-blooded. This is something of great advantage to survival, for it means that the birds' body mechanisms proceed at the same rapid rate under all conditions of outward temperature. Birds are as busily energetic in the chilly morning as in the hot afternoon and need not, like the reptiles, wait until the sun warms their sluggish cold-immobilized muscles. Birds can even survive the cold of the winter without trouble as long as they can find food.

But warm-bloodedness has a disadvantage in that it must be maintained. Bird tissues can no longer endure the chilling that reptilian tissues can. This temperature-maintenance can be handled by the bird while it is an adult, as long as it is alive at all, but what about the developing bird within the egg? It is too small to produce heat at a rate great enough to match the radiation of heat from the egg surface. Left to themselves, bird eggs would not hatch. This is why the parent birds (usually the mother, but sometimes the father as well) must incubate the eggs with the warmth of the adult body. It is a tedious job, but it ensures the survival of all or almost all the eggs. Even after the birth, the parent birds often undergo a long and patient ordeal during which they must feed the perpetually yawning beaks of the still helpless young.

An alternative to the complex care of egg and young as displayed by the birds arises through tendencies already present among the reptiles and even among the sharks. Sometimes the fertilized egg is retained within the ducts that would ordinarily lead them to the outer world and kept there until they hatch. It is then the living young that are "laid" rather than the egg. Whereas an egg-laying creature is said to be *oviparous* (oh-vip'uh-rus; "to bring forth eggs" L), those which retain eggs and allow the living young to issue are *ovoviviparous* (oh'voh-vy-vip'uh-rus; "to bring forth eggs alive" L). The eggs of an ovoviviparous animal are sure of survival as long as the mother survives, and this is itself important. Even more important for us is the fact that it gained a subsidiary use. When a particular group of reptiles developed warm blood and became the first primitive mammal, the retention of eggs within the ducts served not only as protection but also as a means of keeping them warm. Ovoviviparity became a kind of internal incubation.

THE PLACENTA

The earliest mammals did not completely develop the ovoviviparous mechanism. We know that because some of them have survived to this day, although only in Australia and New Guinea. These lands had split away from Asia before higher and more efficient forms of mammals had developed. Secure from competition with the latecomers, early mammals survived in this out-of-the-way continent. Elsewhere on the earth they did not. When early explorers of Australia returned with reports of animals with hair (and therefore mammals) that nevertheless laid eggs, they were scoffed at, but they turned out to be telling the truth. These egg-laying mammals are placed in a separate subclass by themselves, the *Prototheria* (proh'toh-thee'ree-uh; "first beasts" G). Their eggs have not quite finished developing at the time they issue from the body and so they must be incubated during the final stages of development.

The Prototherians show other primitive characteristics too. They are imperfectly warm-blooded; and although they produce milk, one of the species of these beasts, the platypus, lacks nipples. Furthermore, the urethra, rectum, and birth canal of the Prototherians all empty into a final common channel with one opening to the outside world. This single channel is the *cloaca* (kloh-ay′kuh; "sewer" L). The cloaca exists among the other vertebrate classes generally, but it is unusual for a mammal to have one. All mammals except the Prototherians have more than one opening from the pelvis to the outer world. The various living members of Prototheria are therefore classified in the single order of *Monotremata* (mon′oh-tree′muh-tuh; "one hole" G).

A second subclass of mammals are the *Metatheria* (met′uh-thee′ree-uh; "middle beasts" G), and these are ovoviviparous. The egg is reduced in size and the time of the development within the egg is consequently shortened. The young hatch out before the egg is laid, so living creatures issue from the birth canal. The difficulty here, though, is that the shortening of the time of development leads to the birth of young too undeveloped to be capable of leading an independent existence. They have just the strength to work their way through the maternal hair to an abdominal pouch and to climb within. There they fasten on to a nipple and remain affixed while they complete their development. What the egg left unfinished the pouch finishes, and it is almost a return to the larval system. Because of the presence of the pouch, all species of this subclass are lumped into the single order *Marsupialia* (mahr-syoo′pee-ay′lee-uh; "pouch" L).

Though the marsupials were more successful than the monotremes and survive today in a larger number of species, the device of the pouch is inferior to what was to come, so that almost all the marsupials (the kangaroo is the most familiar example) are, like the monotremes, confined to Australia and to nearby islands. The only marsupials outside that area are the opossums of the Americas, and they survive only through sheer fecundity.

In fact, although mammals first developed comparatively early in the Age of the Reptiles, they remained quite unremarkable little creatures for tens of millions of years, during which time reptiles dominated everywhere. The scurrying mammals gave no signs of being the future lords of the planets, and one of the reasons for it perhaps was that they were all members of either Prototheria or Metatheria, or of a third undistinguished and primitive group which is now extinct.

It wasn't until after the climatic changes heralded the end of the Mesozoic that a final group of mammals, the only one which in the long run proved truly successful, was developed. These were of the subclass *Eutheria* (yoo-thee'ree-uh; "true beasts" G). Among the Eutherians, the Metatherian advance was carried on to its ultimate end. The egg was made still smaller until, indeed, it was down to pinhead size, smaller even than most fish eggs. It was impossible for any creature as complex as a mammal to develop out of such an egg with enough life in it even to get to a pouch. The solution was therefore to leave it within the body and feed it there. In other words, the developing Eutherian egg attached itself to the wall of the birth canal, which developed an extensible pouch, or *womb* (AS), designed to hold the developing egg or eggs and to grow the developing young.

The membranes that surround all amniote eggs were modified among the Eutherians into an organ that hugs the inner surface of the womb. This is the *placenta* (pluh-sen'tuh; "cake" G, because it is flat and broad, like a pancake). The marsupials, some reptiles and sharks, and even a few nonvertebrates, develop organs with placenta-like functions in the course of the development of the eggs, but only among the Eutherians does it reach full development; and we ourselves, of course, are included among the Eutherians. The placenta is well infiltrated with blood vessels developed by the embryo,* while the wall of the birth canal is equally well supplied with blood vessels developed by the mother. There is no direct connection, to be sure. No actual blood flows from mother to embryo or vice versa. However, glucose, oxygen, amino acids — all the necessities of life — diffuse from the mother's blood vessels into those of the embryo. On the other hand, carbon dioxide, urea, and all the wastes formed by the embryo diffuse across into the mother's bloodstream.

Two arteries lead from the embryo through a narrow *umbilical cord* (um-bil'i-kul; "navel" L) to the placenta, where it breaks up into numerous capillaries. These collect again into a vein that leads the blood back through the umbilical cord. Naturally, it is the vein that, in this case, carries arterial blood, made so with oxygen taken from the maternal blood supply. The arteries of

---

* *Embryo* ("to swell within" G) is the common term for developing young before it has reached the stage of independent existence. Among vertebrates, it is used to designate the earlier stages only, the later stages being designated by the term *fetus* ("fruitful" L). In the case of the human, the developing egg is an embryo for the first three months and a fetus thereafter.

UMBILICAL CORD AND SECTION OF PLACENTA

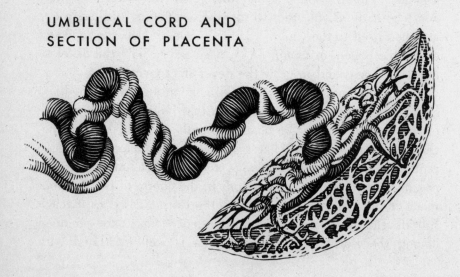

the umbilical cord carry venous blood. (This is analogous to the situation involving the pulmonary artery and veins in the free-living human being [see Chapter 6], and logically so, since in the embryo the placenta serves the same function that the lungs serve in the free-living human.)

The developing young has a form of hemoglobin somewhat different from the ordinary. This different form is *hemoglobin F* (F for "fetus") while ordinary hemoglobin is *hemoglobin A* (A for "adult"). Hemoglobin F forms a tighter union with oxygen than hemoglobin A does, so that oxygen is, so to speak, torn from the mother's hemoglobin A by the fetus's hemoglobin F and diffuses readily across the membranes from mother to fetus, but not vice versa. Hemoglobin F begins to be replaced by hemoglobin A even before birth, and the process is completed by four months after birth.

When the young issue from the womb, the placenta and other membranes emerge also, as the "afterbirth." The umbilical cord is severed but the place to which it was once attached is clearly visible in the human being as the *umbilicus* or *navel*.

The placenta-equipped Eutherians are sometimes called the *placental mammals*. Sometimes, also, the Eutherians and the Metatherians are combined into a single subclass, *Theria* (thee'ree-uh; "beasts" G), and are considered separate groups within that subclass, but with such refinements of classifications we need not concern ourselves.

THE HUMAN FEMALE

The organs involved in the process of reproduction may be lumped together as the *genitals*, or *genitalia* (jen'i-tay'lee-uh; "to give birth" G). Of these the most important are those which form the egg cells in the female or the sperm cells in the male. These are the *gonads* (gon'adz; "generator" G); in addition to the sex cells they produce hormones which govern the changes that take place in the human body at adolescence and maintain the reproductive system at working efficiency.

The female gonads, in which the ova are formed, are, very naturally, termed the *ovaries*. In the adult human female the ovaries are a pair of small organs, about the shape of a large but flattened olive, being 1½ inches long by 1 inch wide and ½ inch thick. They are formed in the kidney region, to begin with, but during the course of fetal development they descend to the pelvis, where they remain somewhat more ventral than the rectum but more dorsal than the bladder.

The ovary contains up to 400,000 potential egg cells, each located in a *primitive Graafian follicle* (named for a 17th-century Dutch anatomist, Regnier de Graaf). At the beginning of adolescence, when important hormonal changes begin sweeping over the female, a follicle-stimulating hormone is produced by the pituitary gland. This hormone brings about the maturing of the ova within the ovary, but usually one at a time and ordinarily at four-week intervals. This continues for something over thirty years, and in that interval perhaps 400 mature ova are formed, one for every thousand potential ova. (A number of follicles will develop simultaneously, but usually only one will carry through to completion, the others degenerating after their false start.)

The potential ovum, also called an *oocyte* (oh'oh-site; "egg cell" G), together with its follicle, grows and develops through a series of complex stages until it is larger than any other cell in the human body. After all, even though the embryo is to be nourished by its mother through the placenta, it must be supplied with enough of a yolk to carry it through the very early stages of development, during which it attaches itself to the wall of the womb and develops a placenta. Yet the ovum, though the largest human cell, is not really very large in an absolute sense. It is about 1/120 of an inch in diameter, which makes it just visible to the naked eye as the barest speck. About ten days after the beginning of the development of the oocyte, the follicle, which has become large enough to be sticking out of the ovary like a tiny blister, breaks open and the ovary is discharged into the body cavity. This is *ovulation*. The ruptured follicle fills first with blood and then with a yellow fatlike material. It is then called the *corpus luteum* (kawr'pus lyoo'tee-um; "yellow body" L).

Near each ovary is a duct, about 5½ inches long, called the *Fallopian tube* (named for the 16th-century Italian anatomist Gabriello Fallopio). It flares out near the ovary into a wide fringed opening (called *fimbria* from a Latin word for "fringe"). The ovum as it bursts out of its follicle is caught in this opening. Slowly the ovum makes its way down the tube. The tube is lined with cilia that through their motion sweep the ovum along.

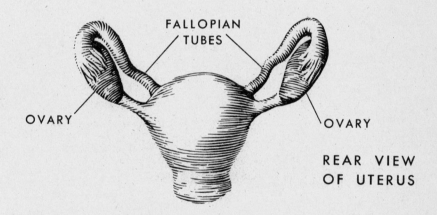

FALLOPIAN
TUBES

OVARY

OVARY

REAR VIEW
OF UTERUS

During its stay in the Fallopian tube, the ovum goes through the final stages of its development. It is also in the Fallopian tube where it meets the sperm cells if any are around. They will be there, of course, only if copulation has taken place at the time of ovulation. If copulation has not taken place, the ovum remains unfertilized and, after a day or two of waiting, dies. Since a

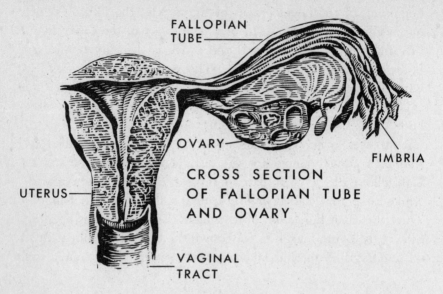

FALLOPIAN
TUBE

OVARY

FIMBRIA

UTERUS

CROSS SECTION
OF FALLOPIAN TUBE
AND OVARY

VAGINAL
TRACT

woman usually ovulates only once in four weeks, this means she is only fertile a couple of days a month.

This waiting of fertilization on the chance of copulation is more marked among human beings than among most mammals. In many mammals, ovulation takes place only at certain times of the year, and during those times the female invites copulation. The male of the species is himself brought to eagerness through hormonal changes and the copulation that then takes place leads almost inevitably to fertilization. Such a restricted time of sexual activity is called a "rutting season" and during this season animals are said to be "in heat."

A woman may be in heat in the sense that she is somewhat readier for sexual activity at the time of ovulation than at other times, but there is no true rutting season for *Homo sapiens*. The individual human being is capricious enough to be willing to engage in sexual activity at some times and not at other times, but this has no particular relation to the calendar. Under the proper circumstances, both man and woman can engage in sexual intercourse at any time. This reduces the efficiency of copulation as a means of fertilization, and sexual activity often goes for naught as far as the production of young are concerned. However, this inefficiency is clearly not serious, in view of the human birthrate and the manner in which the human population is increasing.

The Fallopian tubes, one on either side, lead into a hollow pear-shaped organ in the midplane of the body, just above the bladder. This is the womb, or *uterus* (yoo'tuh-rus; "womb" L). The uterus has strong muscular walls and a mucous membrane as an inner lining, one that is well equipped with blood vessels. This inner lining is the *endometrium* (en'doh-mee'tree-um; "inner womb" G). As the ovum makes its way down the Fallopian tube, the corpus luteum it has left behind produces a hormone that prepares the endometrium for the oncoming ovum. The endometrium becomes soft, moist, and even better supplied with blood vessels. When the ovum enters the uterus it will, if it is fertilized, adhere to the endometrium and begin to develop a placenta. It will remain in the uterus through the full term of embryonic and fetal development and during that time the uterus

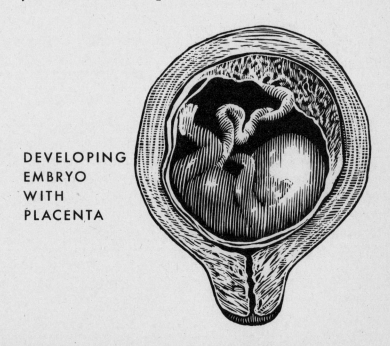

DEVELOPING
EMBRYO
WITH
PLACENTA

will grow along with the developing child. The increase in size becomes very noticeable in the latter half of pregnancy, as we all know.

On rare occasions more than one ovum ripens at one time, and if sperm cells are waiting each is fertilized by a separate sperm cell. In this way, if two ova are fertilized, *twins* develop and are born; *triplets* if there are three, and so on. Two children born simultaneously of separate ova fertilized by separate sperm cells are *fraternal twins*. They have each their own pattern of inheritance and resemble each other no more closely than do ordinary brothers and sisters born at separate times. Fraternal twins need not even be of the same sex. It may also happen that a single fertilized ovum in the course of its development will break up into two halves, each of which may proceed to develop and form complete organisms. (This is a form of asexual reproduction that can take place even in man.) Since these two individuals stem from a single ovum fertilized by a single sperm cell, they share the same pattern of inheritance. They are *identical twins,* always of the same sex and always very similar in form and feature. There may also be identical triplets, quadruplets, or even quintuplets.

It has been estimated that fraternal twins outnumber identical twins three to one. It has also been estimated that one out of 85 births are twins, one out of 7500 are triplets, one out of 650,000 are quadruplets, and one out of 57,000,000 are quintuplets. The greater the number of children at a birth the smaller each must be, on the average, and the less advanced in development. The chances of survival are less as the number at a birth increases, therefore. This accounts for the world excitement back in 1934 when Mrs. Oliva Dionne gave birth to girl quintuplets (identical), all of whom lived. It was the first such case in recorded history.

If, on the other hand, the ovum is not fertilized when it enters the uterus, it will quickly degenerate, as I have said earlier. The corpus luteum fades out also, leaving a scar on the ovary. (With age and repeated ovulations, the ovary loses its original smooth exterior and becomes pitted and uneven through scar formation.)

With the corpus luteum gone, its hormone is also gone, and the endometrium begins to break up. Eventually it sloughs off and, together with a quantity of blood, is discharged from the body over a period of several days. It leaves through the opening at the narrow lower end of the pear-shaped uterus. This narrow end is the *cervix* ("neck" L). The cervical opening leads into a 3-inch-long tube, the *vagina* (vuh-jy'nuh; "sheath" L, for, during intercourse, it serves as a sheath for the penis). The vagina opens to the outside world just behind the much narrower urethra and somewhat before the anus. The sensitive area about these three openings is the *perineum* (per'i-nee'um; "around the wastes," in reference to the excretory openings).

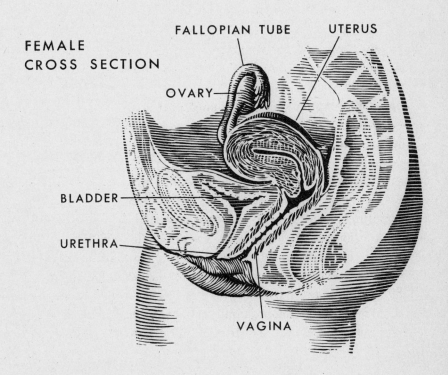

FEMALE
CROSS SECTION

FALLOPIAN TUBE   UTERUS

OVARY

BLADDER

URETHRA

VAGINA

The vaginal and urethral openings are enclosed, when the thighs are in the ordinary position, by two folds of tissue, the inner being the *labia minora* (lay'bee-uh mi-naw'ruh; "smaller lips" L) and the outer the *labia majora* (muh-jaw'ruh; "larger lips" L). The vaginal opening and the labia enclosing it are sometimes spoken of as the *vulva* (vul'vuh), from another Latin term for "womb." At the anterior end of the vulva, between the two labia minora, is a small organ about an inch long, richly supplied with nerve endings and very sensitive. It is the *clitoris* (kly'tuh-ris or klit'uh-ris; "to enclose" G, perhaps because it is enclosed by the labia).

It is through the vagina that the contents of the uterus are discharged. Where successful fertilization has taken place, it is a living child that ultimately comes forth. Where fertilization has not taken place, it is the degenerating endometrium that must do so in a slow bloody discharge that lasts for some days and is referred to as the *menses* (men'seez; "month" L) or the *menstrual flow*. When that is completed the cycle begins again, and a new ovum begins to mature.

The cycle and its accompanying menstrual flow begins at about the thirteenth year, the first appearance of the menses being the *menarche* (meh-nahr'kee; "beginning of the monthly" G). It continues at monthly intervals, except where interrupted by pregnancy, until the age of 45 or 50, at which time it becomes increasingly irregular and ceases. The period during which it ceases is the *menopause* ("ending of the monthly" G). The whole process can be an uncomfortable one for the female. The menses are sometimes painful and may be preceded by a period of nervous tension and depression. It is occasionally difficult, during the time of menstruation, to engage in the ordinary business of life without precautions that are sometimes uncomfortable and usually troublesome, particularly since social custom demands that the whole matter remain unmentioned and ignored. The menarche itself often comes as a frightening experience to a young

girl who may not be sufficiently prepared for it; and the menopause may involve months and even years of unpleasant symptoms while the body adjusts itself to the interruption of a long
continued hormonal cycle.

The supposed greater emotional instability of the female as
compared with the male may arise, in part, from the difficulties
brought on by this cycle and the physical and temperamental
upsets involved. It is a condition that is all the more frustrating
to women in that its existence is either unsympathetically dismissed by men or completely ignored.

Nevertheless, the Greeks sensed the connection between a
woman's emotionality and her genitals. The Greek word for
"uterus" is *hystera*, a term we still use when we speak of the
surgical excision of the uterus as a *hysterectomy*. It is because
of the Greek realization of some connection between the uterus
and the emotions that we still refer to an uncontrolled emotional
outburst as *hysteria*. However, as we all know, men can be
hysterical too, and without woman's uterus to excuse it.

THE HUMAN MALE

The male gonads consist of a pair of *testes* (tes'teez), or *testicles*,
the latter term being merely the diminutive form of the former.
The word is derived from a Latin term meaning "witness."
There are several explanations for this, but the most logical
seems to be that the testicles, when present on a man, were wit-
nesses to his virility.

This made more sense in ancient times than it does now because it was then a fairly common practice to cut off the testicles
of young slaves, a process called *castration*. This did not interfere with growth or life, but since the testes produce the hormones that in the man bring about the changes associated with
puberty, a castrated boy never develops a beard, or a deep voice,
and of course lacks sexual urges and is incapable of intercourse.

A castrated male is a *eunuch* (yoo'nook; "guardian of the bed-chamber" G), so called because he could be used as a guardian with whom a harem of women could be left in safety. An ordinary man, of normal sexual abilities, would obviously be unsuitable for the post. Fortunately the brutal and degrading practice of castration has fallen into desuetude in the civilized world.

The testes are somewhat like the ovaries in size and shape, and, like the ovaries, are originally formed in the kidney region and descend during embryonic development. In nonmammalian vertebrates they remain within the pelvis as the ovaries do. In mammals, however, they descend further. In man, about a month before birth, they leave the pelvis altogether, pushing the peritoneum ahead of them. In doing so the testes enter a pouch of skin called the *scrotum*, a Latin word of uncertain origin.

The scrotum, dangling as it does between the thighs, exposes the testicles to a temperature a few degrees lower than they would be exposed to if they were enclosed within the body. This apparently is essential for the proper development of sperm cells. Occasionally, a child is born with testicles that have not completed their descent and remain within the pelvis. This condition is *cryptorchidism* (krip-tawr'ki-diz-um; "hidden testicles" G)* and a cryptorchidist is invariably sterile, apparently through the inability of the sperm to develop at body temperature.

The interior of the testicle is one large mass of very narrow tubules that follow twisted and meandering paths. These are the *convoluted seminiferous tubules* (sem'i-nif'uh-rus; "seed-bearing" L). The inner lining of these tubules is composed of numerous cells that are continually dividing and redividing, forming the tiny sperm cells. The head of a human sperm cell, which con-

---

* The Greek word for "testicle" is *orchis*, and the "orchid" is so named because of the testicular shape of the tuber from which it grows. Undoubtedly few women who wear an orchid corsage know the semantic inappropriateness of doing so.

tains the nuclear material, is only 0.004 millimeters long. This represents a tiny cell indeed, since it is only a third of the volume of an erythrocyte, itself an unusually small cell. Attached to the head of the sperm cell is a tail that may be up to 0.15 millimeters long, but the full length of the sperm, tail and all, is considerably less than the bloated diameter of the human ovum. The sperm cell in volume is less than 1/100,000 the size of the ovum.

Each convoluted seminiferous tubule if straightened out would be one to two feet in length. Since there are about 800 of them in each testicle, this means that each man has about half a mile of sperm-producing tubule altogether. It is not surprising, then, that the extremely tiny sperm cells are constantly being produced in vast numbers. In contrast to the case in the female, there seems no upper limit to the number of sperm cells that can be produced, and males may continue their production to quite an advanced age.

As they are formed, the sperm cells move through the tubules,

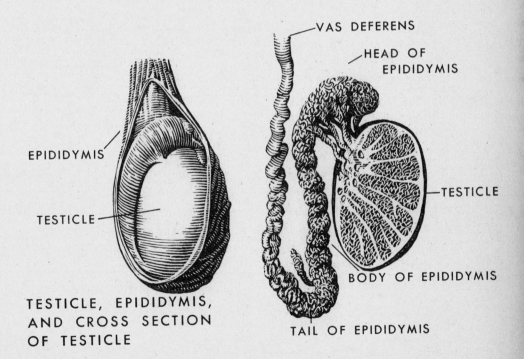

VAS DEFERENS

HEAD OF EPIDIDYMIS

EPIDIDYMIS

TESTICLE

TESTICLE

BODY OF EPIDIDYMIS

TESTICLE, EPIDIDYMIS, AND CROSS SECTION OF TESTICLE

TAIL OF EPIDIDYMIS

are collected in ducts which combine, and finally enter a large convoluted tube that opens at the upperpart of each testis. This is the *epididymis* (ep'i-did'mis; "upon the twins" G, the "twins" being a coy reference to the testicles, of course). The epididymis runs down the length of the testicle, slowly narrowing and straightening out, then turns upward again, as a relatively narrow and straight tube, the *vas deferens* (vas def'eh-rens; "duct carrying down" L). The vas deferens is about two feet long and carries the sperm cells up into the pelvis, around the bladder, and down toward the urethra.

At the base of the bladder are a pair of *seminal vesicles* (ves'i-kulz; "small bladder" L) which produce a fluid that is carried through a small duct into the vas deferens. From this point of junction the final section of the duct, now called the *ejaculatory duct* (ee-jak'yoo-luh-toh'ree), leads both sperm and fluid into the urethra. The genital opening thus combines with the urethral, so that the male has two openings out of the pelvis, rather than three as in the female.

In the neighborhood of the region where the ejaculatory duct enters the urethra and almost encircling the upper end of the urethra, is a chestnut-shaped organ, the *prostate gland* (pros'-tayt; "to stand before" G, the reason for the name being uncertain). The prostate gland secretes a thickish fluid into the urethra which, apparently, serves to improve the motility of the sperm and to provide a more suitable environment for it. The final fluid in which the sperm is immersed is the *semen* (see'men). (The prostate is the source of considerable trouble in later life, since there is a tendency for it to become enlarged, thus interfering with urination by its too close embrace of the urethra. It also has a distressingly large chance of developing cancer.)

The male urethra passes through the *penis* (pee'nis), which is composed of three masses of erectile tissue held together by connective tissue. The erectile tissue is a spongy mass of blood vessels for the most part. Under the proper stimulus, the arteries leading blood to the penis are enlarged and the veins leading blood away are constricted. Blood can enter the organ but not leave. The penis, engorged with blood, becomes hard and stiff.

The lowermost of the three erectile tissue masses (the one through which the urethra runs) expands at the end to form a soft, smooth, hairless, and sensitive tip to the organ. This tip is the *glans penis* (*glans* is the Latin word for "acorn," the name being obviously derived from the shape).

In the ordinary penis the glans is covered by a fold of skin called the *foreskin*, or *prepuce* (pree′pyoos; "before the penis" L). Among the Jews and Mohammedans, as well as among others, a religious ritual is built around the removal of the foreskin, a process called *circumcision* ("to cut around" L). When this is done, the glans penis is left visible at all times. Circumcision is becoming more common among the population generally, quite apart from religion, since it has a sanitary value. The circumcised penis is more easily kept clean. It seems quite

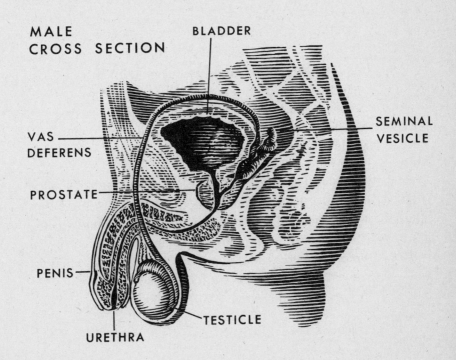

MALE CROSS SECTION

BLADDER

VAS DEFERENS

SEMINAL VESICLE

PROSTATE

PENIS

TESTICLE

URETHRA

well established that circumcision in no way interferes with sexual activity.

The penis when flaccid is about four inches long. When erect it is about six inches long. The length is remarkably constant from man to man, having little relation to the overall size of the body. The erect penis in sexual intercourse is placed within the female vagina. At the height of the activity that follows, the genital organs of both sexes are involved in a series of spasmodic muscular contractions that make up the *orgasm* (awr'gaz-um; "to boil" G). A peristalsis begins in the testes and moves along the epididymis and ducts, driving sperm cells and semen forward and shooting them out of the urethral opening and into the vagina. This process is *ejaculation* ("to throw out" L).

About three to four milliliters of semen are ejected at an ejaculation, and this may contain up to half a billion (!) sperm cells. The female genital organs also begin peristaltic motions, the direction of movement being inward rather than outward, so that sperm cells are drawn into the Fallopian tubes. Only one sperm cell can enter an egg cell, but the hundreds of millions of others have their uses, too. This is shown by the fact that when the number of sperm cells in a single ejaculate falls below about 150 million, fertilization does not generally take place. Though only one sperm cell may be needed for penetration, many others seem to be needed to produce enzymes in sufficient quantity to break down the protective encasement of the egg cell so that that one sperm cell might enter.

With the egg cell fertilized, the process starts which in nine months will convert it into a human body of the intricate design described in this book. From that one cell will eventually come a structure with every bone and muscle in place, every nerve and blood vessel properly laid down, every organ ready to play its part. And, eventually, the body so formed is mature enough to take part in the production of still another body.

And so on, we hope, for the indefinite future.

POSTSCRIPT

OUR LONGEVITY

TOWARD the end of 1961 America's well-known painter of primitives, Grandma Moses, died. She had begun her career of painting rather late in life, when she was almost 80. Nevertheless, she enjoyed many years in this profession, for she died at the matriarchal age of 101. I mention this because in this book on the intricacies of the human body I have laid some emphasis on the numerous ailments and disorders that can afflict it. Perhaps I ought to emphasize the reverse for a moment.

The automobile, despite its being one of mankind's most polished machines, is ancient if it lasts ten years. The human body, far more fragile, far less amenable to repair (a car's engine can be replaced; a human heart cannot), incapable of being shut down for an overhaul, and subject to far greater and more continuous difficulties, can last a hundred.

Nor need we compare the human body to inanimate objects only. How many living things that greeted the day and responded to the changing environment at the moment of Grandma Moses' birth in 1860, were still doing so on the day of her death in 1961? The list is tiny. Some trees can live centuries, and even millennia. Some giant tortoises can live up to 200 years or so. No other creatures aside from man, however, are known to top the century mark. (To be sure, there are popular stories concerning the long life span of such creatures as swans and parrots, but none of them have actually been observed to live long enough even to approach the century mark.) When Grandma Moses died, then, the world of life of 1860 had as its representative a few trees, a very few tortoises — and a few ancient men and women.

Now consider that trees live slowly, remain rooted, and stolidly stand against the buffeting of the environment. They buy longevity at the price of passivity. The giant tortoise moves — but just barely. He too buys longevity at a price: that of cold-blooded slow motion. Man is warm-blooded, however, and is as fast-moving and as deft as any creature alive. He races through life and yet manages to outlive all organisms that, like him, race, and almost all organisms that, unlike him, crawl or are motionless.

Let us restrict ourselves to the land representatives of the order to which man belongs, Mammalia. Here we can best make comparisons, for all its members are warm-blooded and all are built about the same body plan, differing only in rather minor variations.

Here it turns out that longevity is strongly correlated with size: the larger the mammal, the longer-lived. Thus, the smallest mammal, the shrew, may live $1\frac{1}{2}$ years and a rat may live 4 or 5 years. A rabbit may live up to 15 years, a dog up to 18, a pig up to 20, a horse up to 40, and an elephant up to 70. To be sure, the smaller the animal the more rapidly it lives — the faster its heartbeat and breathing rate, the quicker its motions relative to its size, the more it must eat, the higher its metabolism per unit mass. For that reason, longevity becomes a more constant thing when it is measured by heartbeat rather than by year. A shrew with a heartbeat of 1000 per minute can be matched against an elephant with a heartbeat of 20 per minute and it would seem that a day in the life of a shrew sees as many heartbeats as seven weeks in the life of the elephant. In fact, mammals in general seem to live, at best, as long as it takes their hearts to beat about one billion times.

The rule is not absolute. There are exceptions, and the most astonishing exception is man. Man is considerably smaller than a horse and far smaller than an elephant, yet he lives (or can live) to be more than 100. Nor is this the effect of modern medicine; even in days when medicine was a collection of witch doctor's superstitions, an occasional human being attained great age. On the other hand, animals, receiving the best of domestic care and medicine, wear out much more quickly than man.

Nor is this longevity the result of a metabolism that is unusually slow for a mammal. Man's heartbeat of about 72 per minute is just what is to be expected of a mammal of his size. It is faster than that of a horse and slower than that of a dog. In 70 years, which is the average life expectancy of man in the technologically advanced areas of the world, the human heart beats 2½ billion times. As for Grandma Moses' heart, that beat over 3½ billion times before she died. Considering that trees have no hearts and that tortoises (and cold-blooded creatures generally) have only very slowly beating ones, it is safe to say that the human heart outperforms all others. Certainly it outperforms other mammalian hearts by a ratio of 2½ or even 3½ to 1.

Nor can man's closest relatives, evolutionarily speaking, match him. The chimpanzee, somewhat smaller than a man, is a dotard in the late thirties. The gorilla, considerably larger than a man, is a dotard in the late forties. In terms of heartbeat they fit much more closely into the mammalian scheme than does man.

The human body, therefore, in all modesty, and from a completely objective viewpoint, is the most marvelous structure we know of. It may not have the grace of a cat or the sleek power of a horse or the tremendous strength of an elephant. It may not have the swimming ability of the seal, or the racing ability of the cheetah, or the flying ability of the bat, but it is put together for endurance and it outlives and outproduces them all.

Why should this be? Actually, no one *really* knows, and yet one can speculate —

The human being, like other mammals and, indeed, like all other living creatures above the level of the microorganism, is made up of a number of specialized cells. However, the cells of different organisms are much more alike than are the organisms themselves. The cells of any organism are made of roughly the same constituents and engage in chemical reactions of roughly the same nature. Nor are the cells very different in size. The cells of a shrew are not markedly smaller than the cells of a man; nor are the cells of an elephant markedly larger. The difference in size of the organism is due to the difference in the number of the cells, not in their individual size.

The average human body consists of about 50,000,000,000,000 (50 trillion) cells, whereas a large elephant may consist of as many as 6,500,000,000,000,000 (6½ quadrillion) cells. A small shrew, on the other hand, may possess as few as 7,000,000,000 (7 billion cells).

Now although the life of an organism is fundamentally based on the cell, it is more than merely the sum of the individual lives of the constituent cells of the organism. If a human being were divided into its separate cells and if those separate cells were somehow to remain alive, they would nevertheless not reconstitute a human being if merely piled together again in a random heap. The life of a multicellular organism depends not only upon the life of its constituent cells, then, but also upon the effective organization of those cells into a smoothly working whole.

Death can easily be the result of the failure of the organization. A man who suddenly dies of a heart attack or of a stroke dies with almost all his cells alive and healthily functioning. Only relatively few cells have died, but those few, by their death, disrupted the organization. An analogy can be made here between an organism and a city. New York is made up of more than seven and a half million human beings and yet they alone do not make up the city. Let a heavy snowstorm bury the city streets, or let all electric power suddenly fail, or let the city transportation workers go out on strike — and the city is in serious trouble. No one person may be directly damaged; the city's population is intact; but its organization is put out of order and that is enough to create chaos.

Let us return to the organism. It seems fair enough to suppose that the greater the number of cells composing it the more intricate is the intercellular organization necessary to keep the organism going. Yet the larger the organism the more elaborately constructed can be those organs that are primarily concerned with such organization. The two effects seem to meet in a standoff among Mammalia. The large mammals, requiring and possessing a more intricate organization, manage to maintain the function of their greater number of cells for as long as the smaller mammals do in terms of heartbeat, and far longer in terms of absolute chronology.

It might be maintained that the shrew packs as much living in its 1½ years as does the elephant in its 70, so that piling together a million times as many cells (as the elephant does, compared to the shrew) and building up a correspondingly more intricate organization achieves nothing. This, however, is not entirely so. Increased size carries with it more strength and power, a lessened fear of predators, a heightened independence of the minor vagaries of the weather. In short, a large animal is less the sport of the universe, in many ways, than a small animal is.

Again an analogy with a city is possible. A large city requires a much more elaborate organization than a small one does. Its traffic problems are much huger; its subjection to dirt and noise is much greater; its endangerment by fires, earthquakes, or other natural disasters more intense. The tremendously complicated organization enforced by its size keeps the large city viable, yet there is room to argue that it is as comfortable (or even more comfortable) to live in a small town than in a metropolis. Still, sheer size is not entirely wasted; it is the large cities of a nation that are the center of its intellectual life, of its art and culture, and even of its wealth and comfort. There is something about a Paris or a New York, that an Abbeville or a Wichita (with all due love and respect) simply cannot offer.

But surely, again returning to the organism, about man there is no question, for he is long-lived in terms of heartbeat as well as in absolute chronology. This cannot be accounted for in the cell itself, since the human cell is not markedly different from that which is to be found in other organisms. What is left, then, but to consider our intercellular organization? It seems to me that our long life is based on the fact that our intercellular organization is far more highly developed than is to be expected from our size alone. It can therefore take more buffeting and stress before breaking down than can the intercellular organization of any other living creature. It must be for this reason that we take longer to age and live longer before dying.

Then, too, we take longer to mature. We are thirteen before we are mature enough to reproduce and eighteen before we reach our full size and strength. No other land mammal takes nearly as long. Surely the stretched-out length of our maturation is enforced by the fact that it takes longer for the superior human intercellular organization to develop its full powers.

Nor need the intercellular organization be considered as something too abstract to be reduced to material terms. That portion of the body most nearly concerned with organization is the nervous system (a portion of the body I did not take up in this book). The key organ of the nervous system is the brain, and if there is one human organ that is particularly unusual it is the brain. The human brain is nothing short of monstrous in size. No other land creature the size of man approaches him in brain size. The elephant has a somewhat larger brain, but that brain must exert a control over a *much* larger body than man's must.

We can conclude, then, that there are two aspects of the human body that are far, far out of line of the general mammalian pattern. One is his giant brain and the other is his long life. It would be odd indeed if there were no connection between the two.

This book has concerned itself with the parts of the human body, the separate organs composing it. It would seem that what is left — the nervous system and other organs controlling intercellular organization — makes up the better half and, in fact, makes up that which is most peculiarly and particularly *human*. It is to the intercellular organization that I shall, therefore, turn in this book's companion piece, *The Human Brain*.

Part II

THE HUMAN BRAIN

Its Capacities and Functions

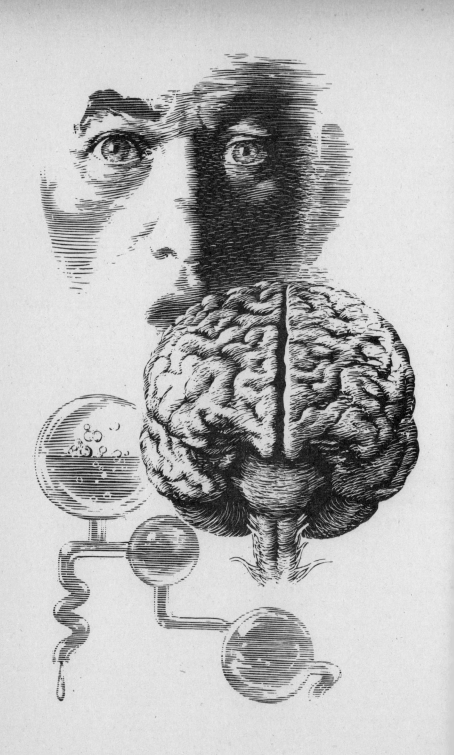

ACKNOWLEDGMENTS

To Professors John D. Ifft and Herbert H. Wotiz for their reading of the manuscript and their many helpful suggestions, I would like to express my appreciation and gratitude.

I.A.

INTRODUCTION

In 1704, a Scottish sailor named Alexander Selkirk was a member of the crew of a ship sailing the South Seas. He quarreled with the captain of the ship and asked to be marooned on an island named Más a Tierra, which is one of the Juan Fernández Islands in the South Pacific, about 400 miles west of central Chile.

He remained on the island from October 1704 to February 1709, a period of almost four and one-half years, before being taken off by a ship that passed by. He survived the period well and went back to sea, attaining the position of first mate by the time of his death. The story of his years of isolation was written up in an English periodical in 1713, and it proved to be a fascinating story.

The tale intrigued the English author Daniel Defoe, among others, who proceeded to write a fictional treatment of such a marooning, and improved it in some ways. His sailor was marooned in the Caribbean (perhaps on the island of Tobago) and he lived there for twenty-eight (!) years.

The name of the sailor and of the novel was Robinson Crusoe, and it has remained a classic for two and a half centuries and will undoubtedly continue to remain so for an indefinite time in the future. Part of the interest in the book arises out of Defoe's masterly way of handling details and of making the account sound real. But most of the interest, I think, arises out of being able to witness one man alone against the universe.

Crusoe is an ordinary human being, with fears and anxieties and weaknesses, who nevertheless by hard labor, great ingenuity, and much patience builds a reasonable and even a comfortable life for himself in the wilderness. In doing so, he conquers one of man's greatest fears, solitude. (In cultures where direct physical torture is frowned upon, hardened criminals are placed "in solitary" as the ultimate punishment.)

If Robinson Crusoe fascinates us, surely it is the fascination of horror. Which of us would be willing to take his place in isolation, regardless of what physical comforts we might be able to take with us? What it amounts to is that a society consisting of a single human being is conceivable (for one generation at least) but in the highest degree undesirable. In fact, to make a society viable, it is a case, up to a certain point at least, of "the more the merrier." Nor is it entirely a matter of company, or even of sexual satisfaction, that makes it well for a society to consist of a good number of individuals. It is the rare human being who could himself fulfill every variety of need involved in the efficient conduct of a society. One person may have the muscular development required to chop down trees and another the ingenuity to direct the construction of a house and a third the patience and delicacy required in good cooking.

Even if one presupposes a quite primitive society, a number of specializations would be in order, including, for instance, someone who understood some rule-of-thumb medicine, someone who could manage animals, someone with a green thumb who could keep a garden under control, and so on. And yet if such a many-person society has its obvious advantages over Robinson Crusoe alone, it also has some disadvantages. One person may be lonely, but at least he is single-minded. Two people may quarrel, in fact probably will; and large numbers of people left to themselves will certainly be reduced to factionalism, and energy that should be expended against the environment will be wasted in an internal struggle. In other words, in the list of specialties we must not forget the most important of all, the tribal chieftain.

He may do no work himself, but in organizing the work of the others, he makes the society practical. He directs the order of business, decides what must be done and when, and, for that matter, what must cease to be done. He settles quarrels and, if necessary, enforces the peace. As societies grow more complex, the task of the organizer grows more difficult, at a more rapid pace than does the task of any other specialist. In place of a chieftain, one finds a hierarchy of command, a ruling class, an executive department, a horde of bureaucrats.

All this has a bearing on the biological level.

There are organisms that consist of a single cell, and these may be compared to human societies of a single individual (except that a single cell can reproduce itself and persist into the indefinite future, whereas a single human being can survive for only one lifetime). Such single-cell organisms live and flourish today in competition with multicellular organisms and may even in the long run survive when the more complicated creatures have met their final doom. Analogously, there are hermits living in caves even today in a world in which cities like New York and Tokyo exist. We can leave to philosophers the question as to which situation is truly superior, but most of us take it for granted it is better to be a man than an amoeba, and better to live in New York than in a cave.

The advance from unicellularity to multicellularity must have begun when cells divided and then remained clinging together. This does indeed happen now. The one-celled plants called algae often divide and cling together; and the seaweeds are huge colonies of such cells. The mere act of clinging together, as in seaweeds, involves no true multicellularity, however. Each cell in the group works independently and is associated with its neighbor only by being pushed against it.

True multicellularity requires the establishment of a "cellular society" with needs that overbalance those of the individual cell. In multicellular organisms, the individual cells specialize in order to concentrate on the performance of some particular function even to the point where other quite vital functions are allowed to fade or even to lapse completely. The cell, then, loses the ability to live independently, and survives as part of the organism only because its inabilities are made up for by other cells in the organism that specialize in different fashion. One might almost regard the individual cell of a multicellular organism as the parasite of the organism as a whole.

(It is not too farfetched to make the analogy that the human citizens of a large modern city have become so specialized themselves as to be helpless if thrown on their own resources. A man who could live comfortably and well in a large city, performing his own specialized function, and depending on the vast network of services offered by the metropolis — and controlled by other equally but differently specialized citizens — would, if isolated on Robinson Crusoe's island, quickly be reduced to animal misery. He would not survive long.)

But if cells by the trillions are specialized, and if their various functions are organized for the overall good of the organism, there must, in analogy to what I have said about human societies, be cells that specialize as "organizers." The job is a perfectly immense one; far more terrifyingly complex on the cellular level of even a fairly simple creature than any conceivable job of analogous sort could be in the most complex human society.

In *The Human Body** I discussed in some detail the structure and operation of the various organs of the body. The operation is obviously complexly interrelated. The various portions of the alimentary canal performed their separate roles in smooth order. The heart beats as a well-integrated combination of parts. The bloodstream connects the various portions of the body, performing a hundred tasks without falling over its own capillaries. The lungs and kidneys form complicated but efficient meeting grounds of the body and the outer environment.

Organization is clearly there, but throughout *The Human Body*

---

* *The Human Body* was published in 1963, and the book you are reading now may be considered a companion piece.

I glossed over the fact. In this book, however, I shall gloss over it no longer. In fact, this book is devoted entirely and single-mindedly to the organization that makes multicellular life possible and, in particular, to the organization that makes the human body a dynamic living thing and not merely a collection of cells. The brain is not the only organ involved in such organization, but it is by far the most important. For that reason I call the book *The Human Brain,* although I shall deal with more than the brain. The whole is generally greater than the sum of its parts, despite Euclid, and if in *The Human Body* I considered the parts, in *The Human Brain* I shall try to consider the whole.

1

OUR HORMONES

Even primitive man felt the need for finding some unifying and organizing principle about his body. *Something* moved the arms and legs, which of themselves were clearly blind tools and nothing more. A natural first tendency would be to look for something whose presence was essential to life. An arm or leg could be removed without necessarily ending life; or even diminishing its essence, however it might hobble a man physically. The breath was another matter. A man just dead possessed the limbs and all the parts of a living man but no longer had breath. What is more, to stop the breath forcibly for five minutes brought on death though no other damage might be done. And, to top matters off, the breath was invisible and intangible, and had the mystery one would expect of so ethereal a substance as life. It is not strange, then, that the word for "breath" in various languages came to mean the essence of life, or what we might call the "soul." The Hebrew words *nephesh* and *ruakh*, the Greek *pneuma*, the Latin *spiritus* and *anima* all refer to both breath and the essence of life.

Another moving part of the body which is essential to life is the blood; a peculiarly living liquid as breath is a peculiarly living gas. Loss of blood brings on loss of life, and a dead man does not bleed. The Bible, in its prescription of sacrificial rites, clearly indicates the primitive Israelite notion (undoubtedly shared with neighboring peoples) that blood is the essence of life. Thus, meat must not be eaten until its blood content has been removed, since blood represents life, and it is forbidden to eat living matter. Genesis 9:4 puts it quite clearly: "But flesh with the life thereof, which is the blood thereof, shall ye not eat."

It is but a step to pass from the blood to the heart. The heart does not beat in a dead man, and that is enough to equate the heart with life. This concept still lingers today in our common feeling that all emotion centers in the heart. We are "broken-hearted," "stouthearted," "heavyhearted," and "lighthearted."

Breath, blood, and heart are all moving objects that become motionless with death. It may be an advance in sophistication to look beyond such obvious matters. Even in the earliest days of civilization, the liver was looked upon as an extremely important organ (which it is, though not for the reasons then thought). Diviners sought for omens and clues to the future in the shape and characteristics of the liver of sacrificed animals.

Perhaps because of its importance in divining, or because of its sheer size — it is the largest organ of the viscera — or because it is blood-filled, or for some combination of these reasons, it began to be thought by many to be the seat of life. It is probably no coincidence that "liver" differs from "live" by one letter. In earlier centuries, the liver was accepted as the organ in charge of emotion; and the best-known survival of that in our language today is the expression "lily-livered" applied to a coward. The spleen, another blood-choked organ, leaves a similar mark. "Spleen" still serves as a synonym for a variety of emotions; most commonly anger or spite.

It may seem odd to us today that, by and large, the brain was ignored as the seat of life; or as the organizing organ of the body. After all, it alone of all internal organs is disproportionately large in man as compared with other animals. However, the brain is not a moving organ like the heart; it is not blood-filled like the liver or spleen. Above all, it is out of the way and hidden behind a close concealment of bone. When animals, sacrificed for religious or divining purposes, were eviscerated, the various abdominal organs were clearly seen. The brain was not.

Aristotle, the most renowned of the ancient thinkers, believed that the brain was designed to cool the heated blood that passed through it. The organ was thus reduced to an air-conditioning device. The modern idea of the brain as the seat of thought and, through the nerves, the receiver of sensation and the initiator of motion was not definitely established until the 18th century.

By the end of the 19th century, the nervous system had come into its own, and actually into more than its own. It was recognized as the organizational network of the body. This was the easier to grasp since by then mankind had grown used to the complicated circuits of electrical machinery. The nerves of the body seemed much like the wires of an electrical circuit. Cutting the nerve leading from the eye meant blindness for that eye; cutting the nerves leading to the biceps meant paralysis for that muscle. This was quite analogous to the manner in which breaking a wire blanked out a portion of an electrical mechanism. It seemed natural, then, to suppose that *only* the nerve network controlled the body. For instance, when food leaves the stomach and enters the small intestine the pancreas is suddenly galvanized into activity and pours its digestive secretion into the duodenum. The food entering the intestine is bathed in the digestive juice and digestion proceeds.

Here is an example of excellent organization. If the pancreas secreted its juices continuously that would represent a great waste, for most of the time the juices would be expended to no purpose. On the other hand, if the pancreas secreted its juices intermittently (as it does), the secretions would have to synchronize perfectly with the food entering the intestine, or else not only would the secretions be wasted but food would remain imperfectly digested.

By 19th-century ways of thinking, the passage of food from the stomach into the small intestine activated a nerve which then carried a message to the brain (or spinal cord). This, in response, sent a message down to the pancreas by way of another nerve, and as a result of this second message the pancreas secreted its juices. It was not until the beginning of the 20th century that, rather unexpectedly, the body was found to possess organization outside the nervous system.

SECRETIN

In 1902 two English physiologists, William Maddock Bayliss and Ernest Henry Starling, were studying the manner in which the nervous system controlled the behavior of the intestines and of the processes of digestion. They made the logical move of cutting all the nerves leading to the pancreas of their experimental animals. It seemed quite likely that the pancreas would fail to secrete digestive juices at all, once the nerves were cut, whether food passed into the small intestine or not.

That was *not* what happened, to the surprise of Bayliss and Starling. Instead, the denervated pancreas behaved promptly on cue. As soon as food touched the intestinal lining, the pancreas began pouring forth its juice. The two physiologists knew that the stomach contents were acid because of the presence of considerable hydrochloric acid in the stomach's digestive secretions. They therefore introduced a small quantity of hydrochloric acid into the small intestine, without food, and the denervated pancreas produced juice. The pancreas, then, required neither nerve messages nor food, but only acid; and the acid needed to make no direct contact with the pancreas itself but only with the intestinal lining.

The next step was to obtain a section of intestine from a newly killed animal and soak it in hydrochloric acid. A small quantity of the acid extract was placed within the bloodstream of a living animal by means of a hypodermic needle. The animal's pancreas reacted at once and secreted juice, although the animal was fasting. The conclusion was clear. The intestinal lining reacted to the trigger action of acidity by producing a chemical

that was poured into the bloodstream. The bloodstream carried the chemical throughout the body to every organ, including the pancreas. When the chemical reached the pancreas it somehow stimulated that organ into secreting its juice.

Bayliss and Starling named the substance produced by the intestinal lining *secretin* (see-kree′tin; "separate" L),* since it stimulated a secretion. This was the first clear example of a case in which efficient organization was found to be produced by means of chemical messages carried by the bloodstream rather than electrical messages of the nerves. Substances such as secretin are in fact sometimes referred to rather informally as "chemical messengers."

The more formal name was proposed in 1905, during the course of a lecture by Bayliss. He suggested the name *hormone* ("to arouse" G). The hormone secreted by one organ, you see, was something that aroused another organ to activity. The name was adopted, and ever since it has been quite clear that the organization of the body is built on two levels: the electrical system of brain, spinal cord, nerves, and sense organs; and the chemical system of the various hormones and hormone-elaborating organs.

Although the electrical organization of the body was recognized before the chemical organization was, in this book I shall reverse the order of time and consider the chemical organization first, since this is the less specialized and the older of the two. Plants and one-celled animals, after all, without a trace of anything we would recognize as a nervous system nevertheless react to chemical stimuli.

---

* In this book I shall follow the practice initiated in *The Human Body* of giving the pronunciation of possibly unfamiliar words. I shall also include the meaning of the key word from which it is derived with the initial — L, indicating the derivation to be from the Latin and G indicating it to be from the Greek. In this case, the derivation from "separate" refers to the fact that a cell forms a particular substance and separates that substance, so to speak, from itself, discharging it into the bloodstream, into the intestines, or upon the outer surface of the body. A secretion is thought of as being designed to serve a useful purpose, as, for instance, is true of the pancreatic juice. Where the separated material is merely being disposed of, it is an *excretion* ("separate outside" L); thus urine is an excretion.

In line with this mode of progression, let us begin by looking at secretin more closely; from its behavior and properties we shall be able to reach conclusions that will apply to other and far more glamorous hormones. For example, a question may arise as to what terminates hormone action. The gastric contents arrive in the small intestine. The acidity of those contents stimulates the production of secretin. The secretin enters the bloodstream and stimulates the production of pancreatic secretion. So far, so good; but there comes a time when the pancreas has produced all the juices it need produce. What now stops it?

For one thing, the pancreatic secretion is somewhat alkaline (an alkaline solution is one with properties the reverse of those of an acid solution; one will neutralize the other, and produce a mixture neither acid nor alkaline). As the pancreatic secretion mixes with the food, the acid qualities the latter inherited from the stomach diminish. As the acidity decreases, the spark that stimulates the formation of secretin dies down.

In other words, the action of secretin brings about a series of events that causes the formation of secretin to come to a halt. The formation of secretin is thus a self-limiting process. It is like the action of a thermostat which controls the oil furnace in the basement. When the house is cold, the thermostat turns on the furnace and that very action causes the temperature to rise to the point where the thermostat turns off the furnace. This is called "feedback," a general term for a process by which the results brought about by some control are fed back into the information at the disposal of the control, which then regulates itself according to the nature of the result it produces. In electrical circuits we speak of input and output; but in biological systems we speak of *stimulus* and *response*. In this case, the successful response is sufficient in itself to reduce the stimulus.

This sort of feedback is surely not enough. Even though secretin is no longer formed, what of the secretin that has already been formed and which, one might expect, remains in the bloodstream and continues to prod the pancreas? This, however, is taken care of. The body contains enzymes* specifically designed to catalyze the destruction of hormones. An enzyme has been located in blood which has the capacity of hastening the breakup of the secretin molecule, rendering the hormone inactive. Enzymes are very often named for the substance upon which they act, with the addition of the suffix "ase," so this enzyme to which I have referred is *secretinase* (see-kree'tih-nays).

There is consequently a race between the production of secretin by the intestinal linings and the destruction of secretin by secretinase. While the intestinal linings are working at full speed, the concentration of secretin in the blood is built up to stimulating level. When the intestinal linings cease working, not only is no further secretin formed but any secretin already present in the blood is quickly done away with. And in this fashion, the pancreas is turned on and off with a sure and automatic touch that works perfectly without your ever being aware of it.

AMINO ACIDS

Another legitimate question could be: What is secretin? Is its nature known or is it merely a name given to an unknown substance? The answer is that its nature is known but not in full detail.

Secretin is a protein, and proteins are made up of large molecules, each of which consists of hundreds, sometimes thousands, sometimes even millions of atoms. Compare this with a water molecule (H_2O), which contains 3 atoms, 2 hydrogens and 1 oxygen; or with a molecule of sulfuric acid (H_2SO_4), which contains 7 atoms, 2 hydrogens, 1 sulfur, and 4 oxygens.

It is understandable, therefore, that the chemist, desiring to know the exact structure of a protein molecule, finds himself faced with an all but insuperable task. Fortunately, matters are eased

---

* Enzymes are proteins that behave as catalysts — they hasten particular reactions when present in small quantities. That is all we need to know for our present purposes. If you are interested in the nature and the method of operation of enzymes, I refer you to my book *Life and Energy* (1962).

somewhat by the fact that the atoms within the protein molecule are arranged in subgroupings called *amino acids* (the first
word is pronounced either "a-mee'noh" or "a'mih-noh"; you may
take your pick — I prefer the first).

By gentle treatment with acids or with alkali or with certain
enzymes, it is possible to break up the protein molecule into its
subgroup amino acids instead of its separate atoms. The amino
acids are themselves rather small molecules made up of only 10
to 30 atoms and they are comparatively simple to study.

It has been found, for example, that all the amino acids isolated
from protein molecules belong to a single family of compounds,
which can be written as the following formula:

$$NH_2-\overset{\displaystyle R}{\underset{\displaystyle H}{\vert\ \ \ \vert}}-COOH$$

$$\begin{array}{c} R \\ | \\ NH_2-C-COOH \\ | \\ H \end{array}$$

The C at the center of the formula represents a carbon atom
(C for carbon, of course). Attached to its right, in the formula
as shown, is the four-atom combination COOH, which represents
a carbon atom, two oxygen atoms, and a hydrogen atom. Such a
combination gives acid properties to a molecule and it is called a
carboxylic acid group (carbon plus oxygen plus acid). Attached
to the left is a three-atom combination, NH_2, which represents
a nitrogen atom and two hydrogen atoms. This is the *amine group*,
because it is chemically related to the substance known as "ammonia." Since the formula contains both an amine group and an
acid group this type of compound is called an amino acid.

In addition, attached to the central carbon is an H, which
simply represents a hydrogen atom, and an R, which represents
a *side-chain*. It is this R, or side-chain, that is different in each
amino acid. Sometimes the side-chain is very simple in structure;
it may even be nothing more than a hydrogen atom in the very
simplest case. In some amino acids the side-chain can be quite

complicated and may be made up of as many as 18 atoms. For our own purposes, we don't have to know the details of the structure of the side-chains for each amino acid. It is enough to know that each structure is distinctive.

Amino acids combine to form a protein by having the amino group of one amino acid connected to the carboxylic acid group of its neighbor. This is repeated from amino acid to amino acid so that a long "backbone" is formed. From each amino acid unit in the chain a side-chain sticks out, and it is the unique pattern of side-chains that makes each type of protein molecule different from all others.

There are more than two dozen amino acids to be found in various protein molecules, but of these only 21 can be considered as being really common. To give ourselves a vocabulary we can use, I shall name these:

1. *Glycine* ("sweet" G, because of its sweet taste),
2. *Alanine* (a name selected for euphony alone, apparently),
3. *Valine* (from a compound called valeric acid, to which it is chemically related),
4. *Leucine* ("white" G, because it was first isolated as white crystals),
5. *Isoleucine* (an isomer of leucine; isomers are pairs of substances with molecules containing the same number of the same type of atoms, but differing in the arrangement of the atoms within the molecules),
6. *Proline* (a shortened version of "pyrrolidine," which is the name given to the particular atom arrangement in proline's side-chain),
7. *Phenylalanine* (a molecule of alanine to which an atom combination called the phenyl group is added),
8. *Tyrosine* ("cheese" G, from which it was first isolated),
9. *Tryptophan* ("trypsin-appearing" G, because it appeared, when first discovered, in the fragments of a protein molecule that had been broken up by the action of an enzyme named trypsin),
10. *Serine* ("silk" L, from which it was first isolated),

11. *Threonine* (because its chemical structure is related to that of a sugar called threose),

12. *Asparagine* (first found in asparagus),

13. *Aspartic acid* (because it resembles asparagine; although aspartic acid possesses an acid group, COOH, in the side-chain and asparagine possesses a similar group, $CONH_2$, with no acid properties),

14. *Glutamine* (first found in wheat gluten),

15. *Glutamic acid* (which differs from glutamine as aspartic acid differs from asparagine),

16. *Lysine* ("a breaking up" G, because it was first isolated from protein molecules that had been broken up into their sub-groupings),

17. *Histidine* ("tissue" G, because it was first isolated from tissue protein),

18. *Arginine* ("silver" L, because it was first isolated in combination with silver atoms),

19. *Methionine* (because the side-chain contains an atom grouping called the "methyl group," which is in turn attached to a sulfur atom, called *theion* in Greek),

20. *Cystine* (sis'teen; "bladder" G, because it was first isolated in a bladderstone),

21. *Cysteine* (sis'tih-een; because it is chemically related to cystine).

I shall have to use these names fairly frequently. To save space, let me give you the commonly used abbreviations for each of them, a system first proposed and used in the 1930's by a German-American biochemist named Erwin Brand. Since most of the abbreviations consist of the first three letters of the name, they are not difficult to memorize:

glycine	gly	asparagine	asp·NH_2
alanine	ala	aspartic acid	asp
valine	val	glutamine	glu·NH_2
leucine	leu	glutamic acid	glu

isoleucine	ileu	lysine	lys
proline	pro	histidine	his
phenylalanine	phe	arginine	arg
tyrosine	tyr	methionine	met
tryptophan	try	cystine	cy-S-
serine	ser	cysteine	cy-SH
threonine	thr		

Of the abbreviations that are more than the first three letters of the names, ileu, asp·NH$_2$, and glu·NH$_2$ should be clear. The abbreviations for cystine and cysteine are more cryptic and deserve some explanation, for they will be important later on.

Cystine is a double amino acid, so to speak. Imagine *two* central carbon atoms, each with a carboxylic acid group and an amine group attached. The side-chain attached to one of these central carbon atoms runs into and coalesces with the side-chain attached to the other. Where the side-chains meet are two sulfur atoms. We might therefore symbolize cystine as cy-S-S-cy, the two S's being the sulfur atoms that hold the two amino acid portions together.

Each amino acid portion of cystine can make up part of a separate chain of amino acids. You can get the picture if you imagine a pair of Siamese twins, each one holding hands with individuals in a different chain. The two chains are now held together and prevented from separating by the band of tissue that holds the Siamese twins together.

Similarly, the two amino acid chains, each holding half a cystine molecule, are held together by the S-S combination of the cystine. Since chemists are often interested in the makeup of a single amino acid chain, they can concentrate on the half of the cystine molecule that is present there. It is the "half-cystine" they usually deal with in considering protein structure and it is this that is symbolized by cy-S-.

One way of breaking the S-S combination and separating the two amino acid chains is to add two hydrogen atoms. One hydrogen atom attaches to each of the sulfur atoms and the combination is broken. From -S-S-, you go to -S-H plus H-S-. In this way, one cystine molecule becomes two cysteine molecules (there's the relationship that has resulted in two such similar names, hard to distinguish in speaking except by exaggeratedly and tiresomely pronouncing the middle syllable in cysteine). To show this, cysteine is symbolized cy-SH.

STRUCTURE AND ACTION

Now if I return to secretin and describe it as a protein molecule, we know something of its structure at once. What's more, it is a small protein molecule, with a molecular weight of 5000. (By this is meant that a molecule of secretin weighs 5000 times as much as a hydrogen atom, which is the lightest of all atoms.)

A molecular weight of 5000 is high if we are discussing most types of molecules. Thus, the molecular weight of water is 18, of sulfuric acid 98, of table sugar 342. However, considering that the molecular weight of even average-sized proteins is from 40,000 to 60,000, that a molecular weight of 250,000 is not rare and that proteins are known with molecular weights of several millions, you can see that a protein with a molecular weight of merely 5000 is really small.

This is true of protein hormones generally. The hormone molecule must be transferred from within the cell, where it is manufactured, to the bloodstream. It must in the process get through, or *diffuse* through, the cell membrane and the thin walls of tiny blood vessels. It is rather surprising that molecules as large as those with a molecular weight of 5000 can do so; but to expect still larger molecules to do so would certainly be expecting too much. In fact the molecules of most protein hormones are so small, for proteins, that the very name is sometimes denied them.

When the amino acid chain of a protein molecule is broken up into smaller chains of amino acids by the action of the enzymes in the digestive juices, the chain fragments are called *peptides* ("digest" G). It has become customary to express the size of such small chains by using a Greek number prefix to indicate the number of amino acids in it: a *dipeptide* ("two-peptide" G) is a combination of two amino acids, a *tripeptide* ("three-peptide" G) of three, a *tetrapeptide* ("four-peptide" G) of four, and so on.

Where the number is more than a dozen or so but less than a hundred, the chain is a *polypeptide* ("many-peptide" G). Secretin and other hormones of similar nature are built up of amino acid chains containing more than a dozen and less than a hundred amino acids and are therefore sometimes called *polypeptide hormones* rather than protein hormones.

Having said that secretin is a polypeptide hormone, the next step, logically, would be to decide which amino acids are to be found in its molecule and how many of each. This, unfortunately, is not an easy thing to determine. Secretin is not manufactured in large quantities, and in isolating it from duodenal tissue a variety of other protein molecules are also obtained. The presence of such impurities naturally complicates analysis.

In 1939, however, secretin was produced in crystalline form (and only quite pure proteins can be crystallized). These crystals were analyzed and it was reported that within each secretin molecule there existed 3 lysines, 2 arginines, 2 prolines, 1 histidine, 1 glutamic acid, 1 aspartic acid. and 1 methionine. This is a total of 11 amino acids in a molecule which, from the data available, seems to contain 36 amino acids altogether. Using the Brand abbreviations, the formula for secretin, as now known, would be:

$$\text{lys}_3\text{arg}_2\text{pro}_2\text{his}_1\text{glu}_1\text{asp}_1\text{met}_1\text{X}_{25}$$

X standing for those amino acids still unknown.

Even if with further progress all the amino acids in the secretin molecule were determined, that would not give us all we need to determine the exact structure of the secretin molecule. There would still remain the necessity of discovering the exact order of the various amino acids within the chain. If you knew that a certain four-digit number was made up of two 6's, a 4, and a 2, you would still be uncertain as to the exact number being referred to. It might be 6642, 2646, 4662 or any of several other possibilities.

There are fixed methods for calculating the number of possible patterns that can be built up of different sets of units and the results are startling. Suppose that the 36 amino acids of the secretin molecule consisted of two of each of 18 different amino acids. The total number of possible arrangements would be somewhat in excess of 1,400,000,000,000,000,000,000,000,000,000,000,000. This may sound incredible but it is quite true. This, mind you, is for a small protein molecule. The situation for even an average-sized one is far, far more complicated, and this helps account for the difficulties biochemists have in attempting to work out protein structure.

It also speaks amazingly well for the fact that biochemists, since World War II, have actually developed ingenious techniques that have made it possible for them to work out the exact order of the amino acids (out of trillions upon uncounted trillions of possible orders) in particular protein molecules.

Emphasizing the complexity of structure of a protein molecule, as I have just done, gives rise to the natural wonder that cells can elaborate such complex molecules correctly, choosing one particular arrangement of amino acids out of all the possible ones. This, as a matter of fact, is perhaps the key chemical process in living tissue, and in the last ten years much has been discovered about its details. Unfortunately, this book is not the place to consider this vital point, but if you are interested, you will find it in some detail in my book *The Genetic Code*.

Even if we grant that the cell can elaborate the *correct* protein molecule, can it do it so quickly from a cold start that the spur of the acid stimulation of the stomach contents suffices to produce an instant flood of secretin into the bloodstream? This would perhaps be too much to expect, and, as a matter of fact, the start is not a cold one.

The secretin-forming cells of the intestinal lining prepare a molecule called *prosecretin* ("ahead of secretin") at their leisure.

This they store and therefore always have a ready supply of it. The prosecretin molecule requires, apparently, one small chemical change to become actual secretin. The stimulus of acid is not, therefore, expected to bring about a complete formation of a polypeptide molecule, but only one small chemical reaction. It is logical to suppose that prosecretin is a comparatively large molecule, too large to get through the cell membrane and therefore safely immured within the cell. The influx of acid from the stomach suffices to break the prosecretin molecule into smaller fragments, and these fragments — secretin — diffuse out into the bloodstream. The prosecretin might be thought of as resembling a perforated block of stamps. It is only when the stamps are torn off at the perforations and used singly that they bring about the delivery of ordinary letters; but the blocks can be bought and kept in reserve for use when and as needed.

Another question that may well arise is this: How do hormones (and secretin in particular, since I am discussing that hormone) act to bring about a response? Oddly enough, despite more than a half century of study, and despite amazing advances made by biochemists in every direction, the answer to that question remains a complete mystery. It is a mystery not only with respect to secretin but with respect to all other hormones. The mechanism of action of not a single hormone is indisputably established. At first, when secretin and similar hormones were discovered and found to be small protein molecules that were effective in very small concentration,* they were assumed to act as enzymes. Enzymes are also proteins that are effective in very small concentration. Enzymes have the ability to hasten specific reactions to a great degree and it seemed very likely that hormones might do the same.

When secretin reached the pancreas, it might hasten a key reaction that, in the absence of secretin, would proceed very slowly. This key reaction might set in motion a whole series of reactions

* As little as 0.005 milligrams of secretin (that is, less than one five-millionth of an ounce) is sufficient to elicit a response from a dog's pancreas.

ending with the formation and secretion of quantities of pancreatic juice. A small stimulus could in this way easily produce a large response. It would be like the small action of pulling a lever in a firebox, which would send a signal to a distant firehouse, arouse the firemen, who would swarm upon their fire engines, and send them screaming down the road. A large response for pulling a lever. Unfortunately, this theory does not hold up. Ordinary enzymes will perform their hastening activity in the test tube as well as in the body and, in fact, enzymes are routinely studied through their ability to act under controlled test-tube conditions.

In the case of hormones, however, this cannot be done. Few hormones have ever displayed the ability of hastening a specific chemical reaction in the test tube. In addition, a number of hormones turned out to be nonprotein in structure and, as far as we know, all enzymes are proteins. It seems, then, that the only conclusion to be drawn is that hormones are not catalysts. A subsidiary theory is that hormones, although not themselves enzymes, collaborate with enzymes — some enzyme, that is, which is designed to hasten a certain reaction and will not do so unless a particular hormone is present. Or perhaps there is a whole enzyme system that sets up a chain of reactions intended to counteract some effect. The hormone by its presence prevents one of the enzymes in the reaction chain from being active. It *inhibits* ("to hold in" L) the enzyme. This stops the entire counteraction, and the effect, which is ordinarily prevented, is permitted to take place. Thus, the pancreas might always be producing secretions but for some key reaction that prevents it. By blocking that key reaction, secretin may allow the pancreatic juice to be formed. This seems like a backward way of doing things, but such a procedure is not unknown in man-made mechanisms. A burglar alarm may be so designed that an electric current, constantly in being, prevents it from ringing. Break the electric current, by forcing a door or a window, and the alarm, no longer held back, begins to ring.

Unfortunately, here too the cooperation between a particular hormone and a particular enzyme is very difficult to demonstrate. Even where some cooperation, either to accelerate or to inhibit the action of an enzyme, is reported for some hormone, the evidence remains in dispute.

Still another theory is that the hormone affects the cell membrane in such a way as to alter the pattern of materials that can enter the cell from the bloodstream. To put this in human terms, one might suppose that the workers constructing a large skyscraper one day were presented with loads of aluminum siding. They would on that day undoubtedly work on the face of the building as far as they could. If, instead, large loads of wiring arrived but no aluminum siding, work would have to switch to the electrical components of the building.

In similar fashion, the hormone action might determine cellular action by permitting one substance to enter the cell and prohibiting another from doing so. It may be that only when secretin acts upon the cell membranes of the pancreas is the pancreas supplied with some key material needed to manufacture its digestive juice.

But this theory, too, is unproved. The whole question of the mechanism of hormone action remains open, very open.

MORE POLYPEPTIDE HORMONES

I have been concentrating on secretin, so far, to a much greater extent than is strictly necessary for its own sake, because secretin is a minor hormone, as hormones go. Nevertheless, it has the historical interest of being the first hormone to be recognized as such and, in addition, much of what I have said in this chapter applies to other hormones as well.

But it is important to stress the fact that there *are* other hormones. There are even other hormones that deal with pancreatic secretion. If secretin is purified and added to the bloodstream, the pancreatic juice that is produced is copious enough and alkaline enough, but it is low in enzyme content, and it is the enzymes that do the actual work of digestion. A preparation of secretin that is less intensively purified brings about the formation of pancreatic juice adequately rich in enzymes.

Evidently a second hormone, present in the impure preparation but discarded in the pure, stimulates enzyme production. Extracts containing this second hormone have been prepared and have been found to produce the appropriate enzyme-enriching response. This hormone is *pancreozymin* (pan'kree-oh-zy'min; which is a shortened form of "pancreatic enzymes").

Secretin seems to have a stimulating effect on the liver too, causing it to produce a more copious flow of its own secretion, which is called *bile*. The bile produced in response to secretin is low in material (ordinarily present) called *bile salt* and *bile pigment*. The gallbladder, a small sac attached to the liver, contains a concentrated supply of liver secretion, with ample content of bile salt and bile pigment. This supply is not called upon by secretin, but still another hormone produced by the intestinal lining will stimulate the contraction of the muscular wall of the gallbladder and will cause its concentrated content to be squirted into the intestine. This hormone is *cholecystokinin* (kol'eh-sis-toh-ky'nin; "to move the gallbladder" G).

The secretion of cholecystokinin is stimulated by the presence of fat in the stomach contents as they enter the intestine. This makes sense, since bile is particularly useful in emulsifying fat and making it easier to digest. A fatty meal will stimulate the production of unusually high quantities of cholecystokinin, which will stimulate the gallbladder strongly, which will squirt a greater-than-usual supply of bile salt (the emulsifying ingredient) into the intestine, which will emulsify the fat that started the whole procedure and bring about its digestion.

I have mentioned that one of the effects of secretin is to neutralize the acidity of the stomach contents by stimulating the production of the alkaline pancreatic juice. This is necessary because the enzymes in pancreatic juice will only work in a slightly alkaline medium and if the food emerging from the stomach were to remain acid, digestion would slow to a crawl. Part of this desirable alkalizing effect would be negated if the stomach were to continue to produce its own acid secretions at a great rate after the food had left it. However necessary those secretions might be while the stomach was full of food, they could only be harmful if produced in an empty stomach and allowed to trickle into the intestine. It is not surprising, then, that yet another function of the versatile secretin has been reported to be the inhibition of stomach secretions.

This is more efficiently done, however, by a second hormone designed just for the purpose. Several of the different substances in food serve to stimulate the intestines to produce a substance called *enterogastrone* (en'ter-oh-gas'trohn; "intestine-stomach" G, that is, produced by the intestine and with its effect on the stomach). Enterogastrone, unlike most hormones, inhibits a function rather than stimulates one. It has been suggested that substances which are like hormones in every respect except that they inhibit instead of arousing be called *chalones* (kal'ohnz; "to slacken" G). Nevertheless, the name has not become popular, and the word "hormone" is used indiscriminately, whether the result is arousal (as "hormone" implies) or the opposite.

But if food in the upper intestine releases a hormone inhibiting stomach secretion of digestive juices, then food in the stomach itself ought to bring about the release of a hormone stimulating that secretion. After all, when the stomach is full, those juices are wanted. Such a hormone has indeed been detected. It is produced by the cells of the stomach lining and it is named *gastrin* ("stomach" G).

Other hormones that affect the flow of a particular digestive secretion one way or another have been reported as being produced by the stomach or small intestine. None of them have been as well studied as secretin, but all are believed to be polypeptide in nature. The only real dispute here is over the structure of gastrin. There are some who believe that the gastrin molecule is made up of a single modified amino acid. All these hormones collaborate to keep the digestive secretions of the stomach and intestines working with smooth organization, and they are all lumped together as the *gastrointestinal hormones*.

If polypeptide hormones bring about the production of digestive juices, the compliment is, in a way, returned. There are digestive juices that produce polypeptide hormones in the blood. This was discovered in 1937, when a group of German physiologists found that blood serum and an extract of the salivary gland mixed were capable of bringing about the contraction of an isolated segment of the wall of the large intestine. Neither the serum nor the salivary extract could accomplish this feat singly. What happens, apparently, is that an enzyme extracted from the saliva has the ability to break small fragments off one of the large protein molecules in the blood (like tearing individual stamps off a large block of them). The small fragments are polypeptide hormones capable of stimulating the contraction of smooth muscle under some conditions and its relaxation under other conditions.

The enzyme was named *kallikrein* (kal-ik'ree-in) and it, or very similar enzymes, have been located in a number of other tissues. The hormone produced by kallikrein was named *kallidin* (kal'ih-din). It exists in at least two separate and very similar varieties, called *kallidin I* and *kallidin II*. The actual function of kallidin in the body is as yet uncertain. It lowers blood pressure, for one thing, by stretching the small blood vessels and making them roomier. This causes the vessels to become a bit leakier, a condition that in turn may allow fluid to collect in damaged areas, forming blisters, while also allowing white blood corpuscles to get out of the blood vessels more easily and collect at these sites.

A substance similar to kallidin is produced in blood by the action of certain snake venoms. The net effect on tissues is similar in various ways to that produced by a compound called histamine but is somewhat slower in establishing itself (30 seconds against

5 seconds). The kallidin-like substance produced by the venom was therefore named *bradykinin* (brad'ih-ky'nin; "slow-moving" G). Eventually, bradykinin, kallidin, and all similar hormones were grouped under the name *kinins*. There are kinins, ready made, in the venom of the wasp. These are injected into the bloodstream when the wasp stings and are probably responsible, at least in part, for the pain and the swelling that comes with the accumulation of fluid as the small blood vessels grow leaky.

The molecules of the kinins are simpler than are those of the gastrointestinal hormones. Being made up of no more than 9 or 10 amino acids, they are scarcely even respectable polypeptides. The comparative simplicity of their structure has made it possible for biochemists to work out the exact order of the amino acids. Bradykinin, for instance, turned out to be identical with kallidin I and to have a molecule made up of 9 amino acids. These, in order, and using the Brand abbreviations, are:

arg·pro·pro·gly·phe·ser·pro·phe·arg

Kalladin II has a tenth amino acid, lysine (lys), which occurs at the extreme left of the bradykinin chain.

And yet, knowing the exact structure, however satisfying that may be in principle to biochemists, doesn't help in one very important respect. Even with the structure in hand, they can't tell exactly how the kinins bring about the effects they do.

2

OUR PANCREAS

DUCTLESS GLANDS

The word "gland" comes from the Latin word for acorn, and originally it was applied to small scraps of tissue in the body which seemed acornlike in shape or size. Eventually the vicissitudes of terminology led to the word being applied to any organ that had the prime function of producing a fluid secretion.

The most noticeable glands are large organs such as the liver and pancreas. Each of these produces quantities of fluid which are discharged into the upper reaches of the small intestine through special ducts. Other smaller glands also discharge their secretions into various sections of the alimentary canal. The six salivary glands discharge saliva into the mouth by way of ducts. There are myriads of tiny glands in the lining of the stomach and the small intestine, producing gastric juice in the first case and intestinal juice in the second. Each tiny gland is equipped with a tiny duct.

In addition, there are glands in the skin, sweat glands and sebaceous glands, that discharge fluid to the surface of the skin by way of tiny ducts. (The milk-producing mammary glands are modified sweat glands, and milk reaches the skin surface by way of ducts.)

But there arose the realization that there were organs producing secretions that were not discharged through ducts either to the skin or to the alimentary canal. Instead, their secretions were discharged directly into the bloodstream, not by means of a duct but by diffusion through cell membranes. A controversy arose as to whether organs producing such secretions ought to be considered glands; as to whether it was the secretion or the duct that was crucial to the definition. The final decision was in favor of the secretion, and so two types of glands are now recognized: ordinary glands and *ductless glands*. (The simple term "gland" can be used for both.)

The nature of the secretion is differentiated by name as well. Secretions that left the gland (or were separated from it, in a manner of speaking) and were led to the skin or alimentary canal are *exocrine secretions* (ek'soh-krin; "separate outside" G). Secretions that left the gland but remained in the bloodstream so as to circulate within the body, are *endocrine secretions* (en'doh-krin; "separate within" G). The former term is rarely used but the latter is common to the point where the phrase *endocrine glands* is almost more frequently used than "ductless glands." The systematic study of the ductless glands and their secretions is, for this reason, called *endocrinology*.

The gastrointestinal hormones, discussed in Chapter 1, are produced by cells of the intestinal lining which are not marked off in any very noticeable way, making it difficult to define actual glands in that case. It is better to say, simply, that the intestinal lining has glandular functions. This is an exception. In the case of virtually all other hormones definite glands are involved. Often these glands constitute separate organs. Sometimes they are groups of cells marked off, more or less clearly, within organs dedicated principally to other functions. An interesting example of the latter is that of a group of endocrine glands inextricably intermingled with an exocrine gland, and a very prominent one, too. I refer to the pancreas.

Since the 17th century at least, the pancreas has been known to discharge a secretion into the intestines, and in the early 19th century, the digestive function of that secretion was studied.

The pancreas has a prominent duct and produces a secretion that contains so many different digestive enzymes that it is actually the most important single digestive juice in the body. There seemed no particular reason to think that the pancreas had any secretory function other than this one.

However, the cellular makeup of the pancreas showed curious irregularities. A German anatomist, Paul Langerhans, reported in 1869 that amid the ordinary cells of the pancreas were numerous tiny clumps of cells that seemed marked off from the surrounding tissue. The number of these cell clumps is tremendous, varying from perhaps as few as a quarter million in some human beings to as many as two and a half million in others. Still, the individual clump is so small that all of them put together make up only 1 or 2 per cent of the volume and mass of the pancreas. Since the human pancreas weighs about 85 grams (3 ounces) the total mass of these clumps of cells in man would be in the neighborhood of one gram. The clumps have received the romantic-sounding name of *islets of Langerhans* in honor of their discoverer.

The islets, whatever their function, can have nothing to do with the ordinary secretion of the pancreas. This is shown by the fact that when the pancreatic duct is tied off in an animal, the ordinary cells of the pancreas wither and atrophy (as muscles do when because of paralysis they are not put to use). The cells of the islets, nevertheless, remain vigorous. Their function is not interfered with by the tying off of the duct so that if they have glandular function, it is ductless in nature.

Furthermore, if the pancreas is removed from the body of an experimental animal, one would fully expect that digestion would be interfered with; but there seemed no reason at first to suspect that anything else would happen. It was certainly not expected that the removal would be fatal; and if predigested food were fed the animal, it seemed reasonable to suppose the animal would not even be seriously discommoded.

Nevertheless, when two German physiologists removed the

pancreas of a dog, in 1889, they found that a serious and eventually fatal disease was produced that seemed to have nothing to do with digestion at all but which, instead, strongly resembled a human disease known as *diabetes mellitus* (dy'uh-bee'teez mehly'tus). Grafting the pancreas under the skin kept the dog alive, although in the new position its duct was clearly useless. Whatever the pancreas did to prevent diabetes mellitus, then, had nothing to do with the ordinary pancreatic juice which in normal life was discharged through that duct.

When, a little over a decade later, Bayliss and Starling worked out the concept of a hormone, it seemed very likely that the islets of Langerhans were ductless glands producing a hormone and that lack of this hormone brought on diabetes mellitus.

Diabetes mellitus is a disease that has been recognized among human beings since ancient times. It is one of a small group of diseases characterized by the production of abnormally high quantities of urine, so that water seemed simply to pass through the body in a hurry. This gave rise to the name "diabetes," from a Greek word meaning "to pass through." The most serious variety of the disease is characterized by an abnormally sweet urine. (This was first attested to by the fact that flies swarmed about the urine of such a diabetic, but eventually some curious ancient physician must have confirmed the fact by means of the taste buds.) The word "mellitus" is from the Greek word for honey. Diabetes mellitus may therefore, in popular terminology, be called "sugar diabetes" and often is referred to simply as "diabetes" without any modifier.

Diabetes mellitus is a common disease since between 1 and 2 per cent of the population in Western countries develop it at some time during their life. There are well over a million diabetics in the United States alone. Its incidence increases in middle age, is more common among overweight people than in those of normal weight, and is one of the few diseases that is more common among women than among men. It tends to run in families, so that relatives of diabetics are more apt to develop the disease than are

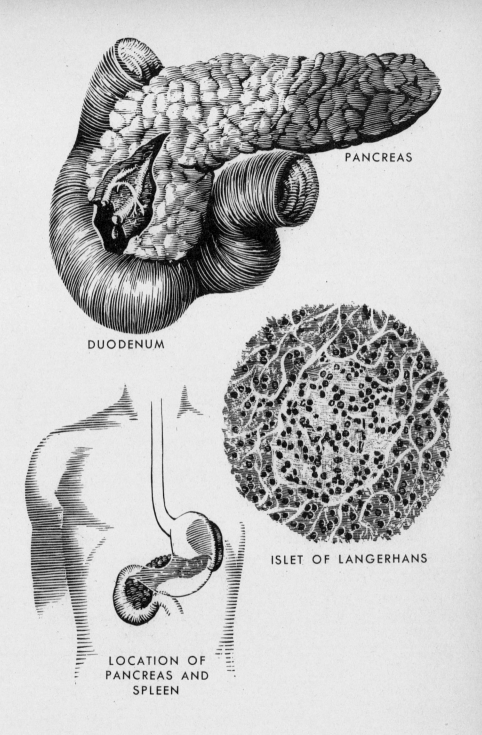

PANCREAS

DUODENUM

ISLET OF LANGERHANS

LOCATION OF
PANCREAS AND
SPLEEN

people with no history of diabetes in their family. The symptoms include excessive hunger and thirst and yet, even by eating and drinking more than normally, the untreated diabetic cannot keep up with the inefficiency of his body in handling foodstuffs. Urination is excessive and there is a gradual loss of weight and strength. Eventually, the diabetic goes into a coma and dies.

The disease is incurable in the sense that a diabetic can never be treated in such a way as to become a nondiabetic and require no further treatment. However, he can submit to a lifelong treatment that will enable him to live out a reasonably normal existence (thanks to the developments of this century), and this is by no means to be scorned.

INSULIN

For a generation, attempts were made to isolate the hormone of the islets of Langerhans.

Success finally came to a thirty-year-old Canadian physician, Frederick Grant Banting, who in the summer of 1921 spent time at the University of Toronto in an effort to solve the problem. He was assisted by a twenty-two-year-old physician, Charles Herbert Best. Banting and Best took the crucial step of tying off the pancreatic duct in a living animal and waiting seven weeks before killing the animal and trying to extract the hormone from its pancreas.

Previous attempts had failed because the hormone is a protein and the enzymes within the ordinary cells of the pancreas, some of which are particularly designed for protein digestion, broke up the hormone even while efforts were being made to mash up the pancreas. By tying off the duct, Banting and Best caused the pancreas to atrophy and its ordinary cells to lose their function. The hormone could now be isolated from the still-vigorous islets and no protein-destroying enzymes were present to break up the hormone. Once methods for producing the hormone were worked out, patients with diabetes mellitus could be treated successfully. For his feat, Banting received the Nobel Prize in Medicine and Physiology in 1923.

Banting suggested the name of "isletin" for the hormone, since it was produced in the islets of Langerhans. However, before the hormone had actually been isolated, the name *insulin* ("island" L) had been advanced, and it was the Latinized form of the name that was adopted. Insulin is one of a group of hormones that acts to coordinate the thousands of different chemical reactions that are constantly proceeding within living tissue. All these thousands of reactions are intermeshed in an exceedingly complicated fashion, and any substantial change in the rate at which any one of these reactions proceeds will affect other reactions that make use of substances produced by the first reaction. The reactions that are thus secondarily affected will in turn affect still other reactions, and so on.*

This interconnectedness, this mutual dependence, is such, that a drastic slowdown of a few key reactions, or even in only one, may be fatal, and sometimes quickly so. There are some poisons that in tiny quantities act quickly and put a sudden end to life by virtue of their ability to stop key reactions. It is rather like an intricate display of canned goods, or an elaborate house of blocks, in which the removal of one can or one block can lead to a quick and complete shattering of order.

But if the general pattern of metabolism is so intricate as to be vulnerable to the intrusion of a bit of alien poison, it might also be vulnerable to the general wear-and-tear of normal events. In our analogy, even if no one came up to a display and deliberately removed a can from the bottom row, there would still be the chance that the vibration of traffic outside, the thud of footsteps within the store, the accidental touch of a toe, might push a can out of place. Presumably, store employees passing such a display would notice if a can were dangerously off-center and push it back into position. It would be even more convenient if the dis-

---

* It is to this vast complex of chemical reactions within living tissue that we refer when we speak of *metabolism* ("to throw into a different position" G).

play were somehow so organized that a can out of position would automatically trip a circuit that would set up a magnetic field to pull it back into place.

Our metabolism, better organized than the displays in a store, has just such self-regulating features. Let's take an example. After a meal, the carbohydrate content of the food is broken down to simple sugars, mostly one called *glucose* ("sweet" G). This diffuses across the intestinal wall and into the bloodstream.

If the bloodstream accepted the glucose in full flood and if matters ended there, the blood would quickly grow thick and syrupy with the glucose it carried, and the heart, no matter how strongly it might work, would have to give up. But this does not happen. A short vein called the *portal vein* carries the glucose-laden blood to the liver, and in that organ the sugar is filtered out of the blood and stored within the liver cells as an insoluble, starch-like material called *glycogen* (gly′koh-jen; "sugar producer" G).

The blood emerging from the liver immediately after a meal will usually have a glucose content of no more than 130 milligrams per cent* as a result of the storage work of the liver. This quickly drops further to somewhere between 60 and 90 milligrams per cent. This range is called the "fasting blood glucose."

Glucose is the immediate fuel of the cells. Each cell absorbs all the glucose it needs from the blood, then breaks it down, through a complicated series of reactions, to carbon dioxide and water, liberating energy in the process. With each cell drawing upon the glucose, the total glucose supply in the blood might be expected to last only a matter of minutes. The glucose is not used up, however, because the liver is perfectly capable of breaking down its stored glycogen to glucose and delivering that into the bloodstream at a rate just calculated to replace the amount being abstracted by cells.

And so the liver is involved in maintaining the glucose level in the blood in two different ways, one opposed to the other, and

---

* A milligram (mg.) per cent is one milligram per hundred milliliters of blood.

both involving a number of intricately related reactions. When the glucose supply is temporarily greater than needed, as after a meal, glucose is stored in the liver as glycogen. When the glucose supply is temporarily smaller than needed, as during fasting intervals, glycogen is broken down to glucose. The net result is that the level of glucose in the blood is (in health) maintained within narrow limits; with a concentration never so high as to make the blood dangerously viscous; nor ever so low as to starve the cells.

But what keeps the balance? Meals can be large or small, frequent or infrequent. Fasting intervals may be long. Work or exercise may be greater at one period than at another so that the body's demands for energy will fluctuate. In view of all these unpredictable variations, what keeps the liver maintaining the balance with smooth efficiency?

In part, at least, the answer is insulin.

The presence of insulin in the bloodstream acts somehow to lower the blood glucose level. If for any reason, then, the glucose level should rise unexpectedly above the normal range, that high level in the blood passing through the pancreas stimulates the secretion of a correspondingly high quantity of insulin and the blood glucose level is pushed down to the normal range again. As the blood glucose level drops the stimulus that produces the insulin flow falls off, and so does the insulin. When the blood glucose level reaches the proper point, it falls no lower. Naturally, there is an enzyme in the blood designed to destroy insulin. This *insulinase* sees to it that no insulin remains to push the blood glucose level too low.

Again the condition is one of feedback. The condition to be corrected stimulates, of itself, the correcting phenomenon. And the response, as it corrects the condition, removes the very stimulus that calls it forth.

In the diabetic the capacity of the islets of Langerhans to respond to the stimulus of high glucose concentration fails. (Why this should be is not known, but the tendency for such failure is inherited.) As a result, the rise in glucose concentration after a meal is counteracted with increasing sluggishness as the extent of islets' failure increases. In fact, clinicians can detect the onset of diabetes at an early stage by deliberately flooding the blood with glucose. This is done by having the suspected person drink a quantity of glucose solution after a period of fasting. Samples of blood are then withdrawn before the meal and periodically afterward, and the glucose content is measured. If, in such a *glucose-tolerance test,* the rise in glucose concentration is steeper than is usually the case and if the return to normal is slower, then the patient is probably in the early stages of diabetes.

If the disease is not detected and is allowed to progress, the islets of Langerhans continue to fail to an increasing extent. The insulin supply goes lower and the glucose concentration becomes permanently high and, then, higher. When the concentration reaches a level of 200 mg. per cent or so (rather more than twice normal) the *glucose threshold* is passed and some glucose is lost through the kidneys. This is a waste of good food, but it is the best thing to be done under the unfortunate circumstances. If the glucose were allowed to continue to pile up, the blood would become dangerously, even fatally, viscous.

Ordinarily, the urine contains only traces of glucose, perhaps as little as 1 mg. per cent. In untreated diabetics, the concentration rises a thousandfold and is easily detected. By the time sugar is detected in the urine, however, the disease has progressed uncomfortably far.

The islets of Langerhans, having once failed, cannot have their function restored by any treatment known to man. The patient can, nevertheless, be supplied with insulin from an outside source. The insulin taken from the pancreas of a slaughtered steer is as effective in reducing the blood glucose concentration as is the insulin supplied by the patient's own pancreas. One or two milligrams of insulin per day will do the job.

The difficulty is that, whereas the patient's own pancreas in its days of health and vigor supplied insulin in the precise quantity needed and in a continuous but varying flow, insulin from the outside must be supplied in set quantities that can be made to match the need only approximately. The adjustment of the body's metabolism must therefore proceed by jerks, with the glucose concentration being driven too low at the first flood of insulin and being allowed to drift too high before the next installment. It is as though you placed the thermostat of your furnace under manual control, pushing it up and down by hand and trying to attain a continuously equable temperature.

It is for this reason that a diabetic, even under insulin treatment, must watch his diet carefully, so that he places as little strain as possible upon the blood glucose level. (You could control the thermostat manually with somewhat greater success if there were no sudden cold snaps to catch you by surprise.) The use of externally produced insulin has the disadvantage also of requiring hypodermic injection. Insulin cannot be taken by mouth, for it is a protein that is promptly digested in the stomach and broken into inactive fragments.

A possible way out lies in an opposite-tack approach. The insulin-destroying enzyme insulinase can be put out of action by certain drugs. Such drugs, which can be taken by mouth, would therefore allow a diabetic's limited supply of insulin to last longer and could, at least in some cases, replace the hypodermic needle.

INSULIN STRUCTURE

It is easy to observe that insulin lowers the blood glucose level. This level, however, is the result of a complex interplay of many chemical reactions. How does insulin affect those reactions in order to bring about a lowering of the level? Does it affect just one reaction? More than one? All of them?

In the search for answers to these questions, suspicion fell most strongly on a reaction catalyzed by an enzyme called *hexokinase* (hek'soh-ky'nays). This was chiefly the result of work by the husband-and-wife team of Czech-American biochemists, Carl Ferdinand Cori and Gerty Theresa Cori, who had worked out much of the detail of the various reactions involved in glucose breakdown and had, for that reason, shared in the Nobel Prize in Medicine and Physiology for 1947. The Coris maintained that the hexokinase reaction was under continual inhibition under ordinary circumstances and that the action of insulin was to counteract this inhibition and to allow the reaction to proceed. They were able to demonstrate how the effect on that one reaction would account for the lowering of blood glucose concentration.

However, this seems to have been too simple an explanation. The metabolism of the diabetic is disordered in various ways. Although it is possible to account for a variety of disorders through the effect of the upsetting of a single reaction (so interconnected is the metabolic web), to account for all the disorders in diabetes mellitus out of the one hexokinase reaction required a great deal of complicated reasoning that grew the less convincing as it grew more complicated. The most recent experiments seem to indicate instead that insulin exerts its effect on the cell membranes. The rate at which cells absorb glucose depends partly on the difference in concentration of glucose within and without the cell; and also on the nature of the cell membrane through which the glucose must pass.

To make an analogy: if men are entering a building from the street, the rate at which they will enter will depend partly on the number of men trying to get in. It will also depend on the width of the door or on the number of open doors. After a certain point of crowding is reached, only a certain number of men can enter the building each second, no matter how many men are in the street pushing to get in. An attendant, however, who quickly opens two more doors at once triples the rate of entry.

Apparently insulin molecules attach themselves to the membranes of muscle cells and of other types of cells as well and act to increase the permeability of those membranes to glucose. (In effect, opening additional doors.) So, when glucose floods the bloodstream after a meal, insulin is produced. This opens the "membrane doors" and the glucose concentration in blood is rapidly reduced, since it vanishes within the cells, where it is either utilized or stored. In the diabetic, glucose knocks at the various cell membranes, but in the absence of insulin it knocks to a certain extent in vain. It cannot enter with sufficient speed and it therefore accumulates in the blood. Obviously, anything else that will facilitate entry of glucose into the cells will, at least partially, fill the role of insulin. Exercise is one thing that will, and regular exercise is usually prescribed for the diabetic.

We must inevitably ask: What is it that insulin does to the cell membrane to increase the facility with which glucose enters? It is partly in the hope of answering this question (and partly out of sheer curiosity) that biochemists attempted to determine the exact structure of the insulin molecule.

The molecule of insulin is a polypeptide, as are those of the gastrointestinal hormones, but it is more complicated. While the secretin molecule is made up of 36 amino acid units, the insulin molecule is made up of about 50. Since the problem of secretin's exact structure has not been solved, one might reasonably suppose that insulin's exact structure would also be still unknown; but the drive for a solution to the problem in the case of insulin, which is involved in mankind's most serious "metabolic disease," is far greater than the drive to solve the problem of the structure of the gastrointestinal hormones, which have little clinical importance. In addition, far greater quantities of pure insulin are available for analysis.

By the late 1940's it had been discovered that insulin had a molecular weight of a trifle under 6000. (Its molecules have a tendency to double up and to join in even larger groups so that molecular weights of 12,000 and even 36,000 had been reported at first.) The molecule was then found to consist of two chains of amino acids held together by cystine molecules after the fashion explained on page 12. When the chains were pulled apart, one (chain A) turned out to consist of 21 amino acids, while the other (chain B) consisted of 30.

The individual amino acids in each chain were easily determined by breaking down the chains separately and then analyzing for the different amino acids.* But, as I explained in the previous chapter, knowing the individual amino acids is only the beginning. One must also know the exact order in which they are arranged. The 21 amino acids of chain A can be arranged in any of about 2,800,000,000,000,000 ways. The 30 amino acids of chain B offer more leeway, obviously, and can be arranged in any of about 510,000,000,000,000,000,000,000,000,000 different ways.

The problem of determining the exact arrangements in the actual molecule of insulin obtained from the ox pancreas, out of all the possibilities that could exist, was tackled by a group headed by the British biochemist Frederick Sanger. The method used was to break down the amino acid chains only partway by the use of acid or of various enzymes. The breakdown products were not individual amino acids but small chains containing two, three, or four amino acids. These small chains were isolated and studied and the exact order of the amino acids determined. (Two amino acids can only be placed in two different orders, A-B and B-A. Three amino acids can be placed in six different orders: A-B-C, A-C-B, B-C-A, B-A-C, C-A-B, and C-B-A. Even four amino acids can only be placed in 24 different orders. The possible arrangements in the case of the small fragments can be checked and the correct one chosen without insuperable difficulty. At the most, a couple of dozen possibilities are involved and not a couple of quintillion.)

Once all the small chains are worked out, it becomes possible to fit them together. Suppose that chain A has only one molecule of a particular amino acid that we shall call q, and suppose that two short chains of three amino acids each have been located,

* The method of doing this involves a procedure called *paper chromatography* that was first developed in 1944 and has succeeded in revolutionizing biochemistry. If you are interested in this, you will find the procedure described in some detail in the chapter "Victory on Paper" in my book *Only a Trillion* (1957).

one being *r-s-q* and the other *q-p-o*. Since only one *q* is present, there must be a five amino acid sequence in the original molecule that goes *r-s-q-p-o*. You will then get either *r-s-q* or *q-p-o*, depending on which side of the *q* the chain breaks.

It took eight years for Sanger and his group to work out the complete jigsaw puzzle. By 1955 they had put the fragments together and determined the structure of the intact molecule. It was the first time the structure of any naturally occurring protein molecule had ever been determined in full, and for this Sanger was awarded the Nobel Prize in Chemistry for 1958.

The formula of the molecule of ox insulin, in Brand abbreviations, is as follows:

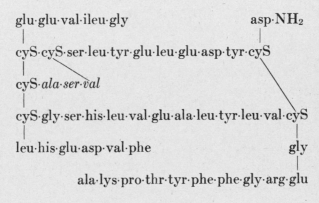

OX INSULIN

Unfortunately, nothing in the structure of the molecule gives biochemists any clue as to why insulin affects the cell membrane as it does.

It might be possible to tackle the matter by comparing the structures of insulin produced by different species. Swine insulin is just as effective for the diabetic as ox insulin is. If the two insulins differ in molecular structure, then only that which they possess in common need perhaps be considered necessary to their functioning, and attention could be focused to a finer point. When swine insulin was analyzed, it was found to differ from ox insulin only in the three amino acids italicized in the formula given above, the three that are pinched off in a corner, so to speak, between the two cystine groups.

Whereas in ox insulin the three amino acids are ala-ser-val, in swine insulin they are thr-ser-ileu. These same three amino acids and *only* these three also vary in the insulin molecules of other species. In sheep it is ala-gly-cal, in horses it is thr-gly-ileu, and in whales it is thr-ser-ileu. Of these three the one at the left can be either alanine or threonine, the one in the middle can be either serine or glycine, and the one at the right can be either valine or isoleucine.

While many other species remain to be tested, it does not seem likely that startling differences will be found. Furthermore, any change imposed on the insulin molecule by chemical reaction from without, unless the change is a rather trifling one that does not seriously affect the complexity of the molecule, produces loss of activity. Whatever it is that insulin does to the cell membrane, all, or virtually all, of the molecule is involved, and that is about as much as can be said. At least so far.

GLUCAGON

Where a hormone exerts its push in a single direction, as insulin does in the direction of lowered glucose concentration in the blood, it would be reasonable to suspect that another hormone might exist which exerts an opposing effect. This would not result in a cancellation of effect, but rather in an equilibrium that can be shifted this way and that more delicately and accurately through the use of two opposing effects than through either alone. You can see this best perhaps when you consider that a tottering ladder is most easily steadied by being held with both hands, the two pressing gently in opposing directions.

There does exist such an "opposition hormone" for insulin, one also produced in the islets of Langerhans. This second hormone is far less well known than insulin because there is no clinical disorder that is clearly associated with it; nothing, that is, corresponding to diabetes mellitus.

The islets of Langerhans contain two varieties of cells, named *alpha cells* and *beta cells*. (Scientists very often, perhaps too often, follow the line of least resistance in distinguishing a series of similar objects by use of the first few letters of the Greek alphabet.) The alpha cells are the larger of the two types and are situated at the outer regions of the islets, making up about 25 per cent of their total volume. At the centers of each islet are the smaller beta cells. It is the beta cells that produce the insulin, and the alpha cells produce the hormone with the opposing effect.

This second hormone was discovered when, soon after Banting's discovery of a method of insulin preparation, some samples were found to induce an initial rise in blood glucose concentration before imposing the more usual lowering. Something that exerted an effect opposed to that of insulin was therefore searched for and located. The new hormone was found to bring about an acceleration of the breakdown of the glycogen stored in the liver. The glycogen was broken down to glucose, which poured into the bloodstream. In this fashion the blood glucose level was raised.

When the presence of a hormone is only suspected by the effects it brings about, it is named after those effects in many cases; this new hormone was therefore named *hyperglycemic-glycogenolytic factor* (hy'per-gly-see'mik gly'koh-jen'oh-lih'tik; "high-glucose, glycogen-dissolving" G) in order to mark the manner in which it raised the blood glucose level and lowered the quantity of glycogen in the liver. Since biochemists don't really like long names any more than do the rest of us, this was quickly abbreviated to *HGF*. In recent years an acceptable name, shorter than the first, has become popular — *glucagon* (gloo'kuh-gon).

By 1953 glucagon had been prepared in pure crystalline form and was easily shown to be a polypeptide with a molecule made up of a single chain containing 29 amino acids. At first thought it might have seemed that perhaps glucagon was a fragmented insulin molecule, but a closer look disproved that. By 1958 the order of the amino acids had been worked out, by use of the methods introduced by Sanger. Here it is:

his·ser·glu·NH₂·gly·thr·phe·thr·ser·asp·tyr·ser·-
lys·tyr·leu·asp·ser·arg·arg·ala·glu·NH₂·asp·phe·-
val·glu·NH₂·try·leu·met·asp·NH₂·thr

GLUCAGON

There is, as you see, no similarity in this chain to either of the chains in insulin. As a matter of fact, some of the amino acids present in glucagon (methionine, say) are not present in insulin at all, while others (as, for example, isoleucine) which are present in insulin are not present in glucagon. There is no question but that insulin and glucagon are two completely different hormones.

EPINEPHRINE

Insulin and glucagon are by no means the only hormones that affect the metabolism of carbohydrates in a manner that shows up in the level of glucose concentration in the blood. Another hormone with such an effect is produced by two small yellowish organs, roughly pyramidlike in shape, about one or two inches in length in the adult and weighing about 10 grams (⅓ ounce) each. They lie in contact with the upper portion of either kidney and are the first organs I have had occasion to mention that are completely endocrinological in functioning.

Because of their location, the organs are called the *adrenal glands* (ad-ree′nul; "near the kidneys" L), or *suprarenal glands* (syoo′pruh-ree′nul; "above the kidneys" L); see illustration, page 411.

The adrenal glands are made up of two sections, an outer and an inner, and these are different in cellular makeup, in function, and in origin. In the more primitive fish, the material corresponding to the two sections of the adrenal glands exists separately. What is in us the outer portion is an elongated structure in these fish, about as long as the kidneys. Our inner portion forms two lines of small collections of cells, running nearly twice the length of the kidney. In amphibians, reptiles, and birds, the glandular material is more compact and the two sets of cells become intermingled. Among the mammals compactness reaches the extreme, and one set of cells entirely encloses the other.

The outer portion of the adrenal glands, which makes up about nine tenths of the mass of the organs is the *adrenal cortex* (kawr'-teks; "bark" L, because it encloses the inner portion as the bark encloses a tree). The inner portion is the *adrenal medulla* (mehdul'uh; "marrow" L, because it is within the outer portion as marrow is within a bone). The hormone to be discussed now is formed in the medulla.

As long ago as 1895 it was known that extracts of the adrenal glands had a powerful action in raising the blood pressure. In 1901 a pure substance was obtained from the glands by the Japanese biochemist Jokichi Takamine and this markedly raised the blood pressure even in very tiny quantities. The name by which this compound is best known is *Adrenalin* (ad-ren'uh-lin), which, however, is only one of many trade names for the material. The proper chemical name for the compound is *epinephrine* (ep'ih-nef'rin; "on the kidney" G).

The year after Takamine's feat, Bayliss and Starling demonstrated the possibility of chemical coordination in the absence of nerve action. Once that was clearly understood, it was recognized that epinephrine was a hormone. It was the first hormone to be isolated in pure form, and the first hormone to have its structure determined. This is less remarkable than it might otherwise appear: of all known hormones, epinephrine has the simplest structure.

Where secretin, insulin, and glucagon are all made up of chains of several-dozen amino acids, epinephrine is, in its essentials, a modified version of a single amino acid, tyrosine. This is most clearly shown by comparing the chemical formulas. Even if you are not familiar with such formulas and don't understand the details of what is represented, the resemblance between the two substances will still be clear:

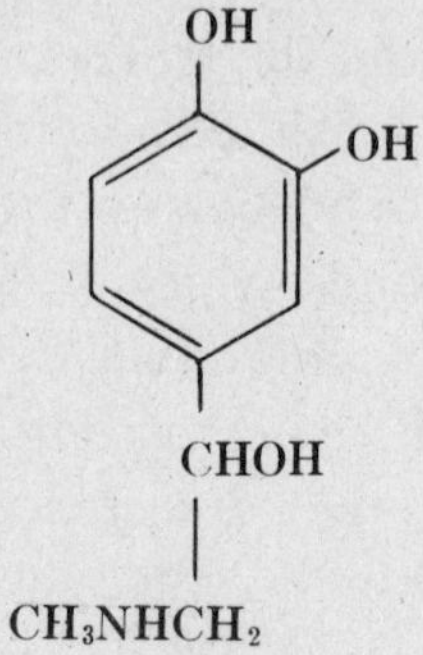

OH
OH

CHOH
|
CH_3NHCH_2

EPINEPHRINE

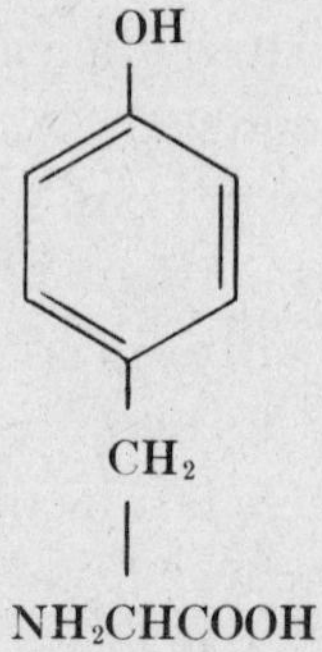

OH

CH_2
|
$NH_2CHCOOH$

TYROSINE

Chemists have had little difficulty in showing that the adrenal medulla manufactures its epinephrine out of tyrosine.

As far as its effect on carbohydrate metabolism is concerned, epinephrine resembles glucagon in hastening the breakdown of glycogen to glucose so that the blood level of glucose rises. The difference is this: glucagon works under normal conditions; epinephrine works in emergencies. To state it differently, glucagon maintains a more or less steady effect designed to help keep the glucose level constant (in cooperation with the opposite action of insulin) under the ordinary fluctuations of glucose supply and glucose consumption. Epinephrine, in contrast, is called into play under conditions of anger or fear, when a massive supply of glucose is quickly needed to supply the energy requirements of a body about to engage in either fight or flight.

Then, too, where glucagon mobilizes only the glycogen supplies of the liver (supplies that are for the general use of the body), epinephrine brings about the breakdown of the glycogen in muscle as well. The muscle glycogen is for use by the muscles only, and by stimulating its breakdown epinephrine makes possible the drawing on private energy supply by the muscles (which will be primarily concerned in the fight-or-flight situation).

Epinephrine has other effects on the body beside the mobilization of its glucose reserves. For one thing, there is the effect on blood pressure, by which its existence was first recognized, and its ability to speed the heartbeat and the breathing rate. These last effects are brought about via the interplay of epinephrine and the nervous system, something I shall discuss in more detail in Chapter 9. I might pause to mention, though, that the two levels of organization, the chemical (hormones) and the electrical (nerves) are by no means independent, but are interrelated.

The situation, incidentally, whereby a single modified amino acid functions as a hormone (and is classified as one) is represented by more than one case. There is *histamine*, for another example, a compound very similar in structure to the amino acid histidine, as the following formulas show:

| HISTIDINE | HISTAMINE |

In small concentrations histamine stimulates the secretion of hydrochloric acid by the glands in the stomach lining. There are biochemists who suspect that gastrin (one of the gastrointestinal hormones pointed out in the previous chapter, see p. 356) is really histamine. This is by no means certain yet.

As in the case of epinephrine, histamine affects blood pressure and other facets of the body mechanism. (The kinins, described on page 358, have some effect similar to histamine.) Histamine is believed responsible for some of the unpleasant accompaniments of allergies (runny nose, swelling of the mucous membrane of nose and throat, constriction of the bronchioles, and the like). Apparently the foreign protein, or other substance, which sparks the allergic reaction does so by stimulating the production of histamine. Drugs that counteract the effect of histamine (anti-histamines) relieve these symptoms.

3

OUR THYROID

IODINE

There is still another hormone that is a modified amino acid, one a bit more complicated in structure than either epinephrine or histamine is. To discuss it properly, I shall begin by introducing a new organ. The prominent cartilage in the neck, commonly called the "Adam's apple," is more correctly termed the *thyroid cartilage*. The word "thyroid" is from a Greek term meaning "shieldlike," in reference to the large oblong shields carried by Homeric and pre-Homeric warriors which had a notch on top for the chin to rest upon. You can feel the notch on top of the thyroid cartilage if you put your finger to your neck.

Now at the bottom of the thyroid cartilage is a soft mass of yellowish-red glandular tissue about two inches high, a bit more than two inches wide, and weighing an ounce or a little less. It exists in two lobes, one on either side of the windpipe, with a narrow connecting band running in front of the windpipe just at the bottom boundary of the thyroid cartilage. Seen from the front, the gland resembles a letter H. The gland, for some centuries, has borrowed its name from the cartilage it hugs and is therefore known as the *thyroid gland* even though there is nothing shieldlike about it.

Before the end of the 19th century, the function of the thyroid gland was not known. It is somewhat more prominent in women

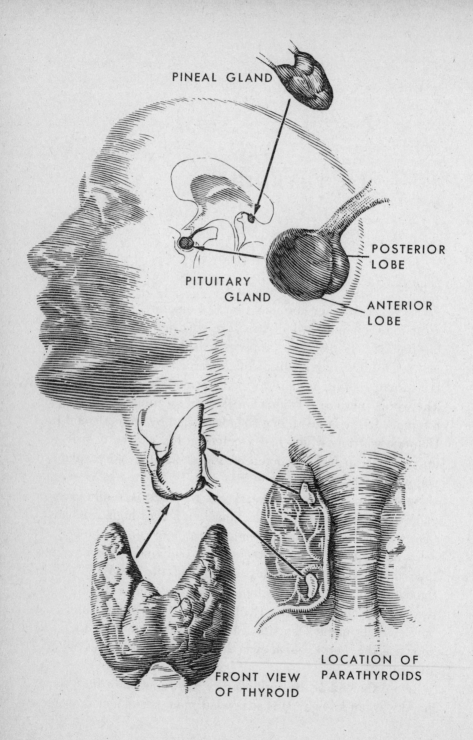

PINEAL GLAND

PITUITARY
GLAND

POSTERIOR
LOBE

ANTERIOR
LOBE

FRONT VIEW
OF THYROID

LOCATION OF
PARATHYROIDS

than in men, and for that reason the opinion was variously maintained that the thyroid was nothing more than padding designed to fill out the neck (of women especially) and make it plumply attractive. There were regions of Europe where the thyroid (again, particularly in women) was enlarged beyond the normal size, and this, which meant a somewhat swollen neck, was accepted as an enhancement of beauty rather than otherwise. An enlarged thyroid gland is referred to as a *goiter* ("throat" L).

The cosmetic value of a goiter was rather deflated when it came to be recognized about 1800 or so that the condition could be associated with a variety of undesirable symptoms. Confusingly enough, goitrous individuals were apt to have either of two opposing sets of symptoms. Some were dull, listless, and apathetic, with soft, puffy tissues, cool, dry skin, and slow heartbeat. In contrast, some were nervous, tense, unstable, with flushed, moist skin and fast heartbeat. And finally, as you might guess, there were people with goiters who showed neither set of symptoms and were reasonably normal.

That this connection of the goiter and at least one set of symptoms was no coincidence was clearly demonstrated in 1883, when several Swiss surgeons completely removed goitrous thyroids from 46 patients. (Switzerland is one of the regions where goiter was common.) The thyroids had enlarged to the point where they were interfering with surrounding tissue, and there seemed no logical argument against removal. Unfortunately, in those patients the symptoms of the dull, listless variety appeared and intensified. To remove the entire thyroid appeared *not* to be safe.

Then in 1896 a German chemist, E. Baumann, located iodine in the thyroid gland. Not much was present, to be sure, for the best modern analyses show that the human thyroid at most contains 8 milligrams (or about 1/2000 ounce) of iodine. About four times the amount is distributed throughout the rest of the body. The rest of the body, however, is so much more massive than the thyroid that the iodine content there is spread thin indeed. The iodine concentration in that one organ, the thyroid gland, is more than 60,000 times as high as is the concentration anywhere else in the body.

Certainly this sounds significant now, but it didn't seem so in 1896. Iodine had never been located in any chemical component of the human body, and it seemed reasonable to suppose that it was an accidental contaminant. The fact that it was present in such small quantities made this seem all the more probable, for it was not yet understood in 1896 that such things as "essential trace elements" existed; elements that formed parts of hormones or enzymes and were therefore necessary to proper functioning of the body and even to life itself, without having to be present in more than tiny quantities.

It was a decade later, in 1905, that David Marine, an American physician just out of medical school, took Baumann's discovery seriously. Coming to the American Midwest from the East, he wondered if the relative frequency of goiter in the Midwest had anything to do with the relative poverty of the soil in iodine.° Perhaps the iodine was not merely an accidental contaminant, but formed an integral part of the thyroid; and perhaps in the absence of iodine the thyroid suffered a disorder that evidenced itself as a goiter.

Marine experimented upon animals with diets low in iodine; they developed goiter, showing the dull, listless set of symptoms. He added small quantities of iodine to the diet and cured the condition. By 1916 he felt confident enough to experiment on girls and was able to show that traces of iodine in the food cut down the incidence of goiter in humans. It then took another ten years to argue people into allowing small quantities of iodine compounds to be added to city water reservoirs and to table salt. The furious opposition to such procedures was something like

° Iodine is actually a rare element; the sea is richer in iodine than the land is. Seaweed is a major source of iodine because plant cells actively concentrate the iodine of the sea. The iodine in soil is often there only because storms spray the coastline with droplets of ocean water that evaporate, leaving the tiny bits of salt content to be blown far inland. The salts contain iodine, and as a matter of course land near the sea would, all things being equal, be richer in iodine than areas far inland.

the similar opposition to fluoridation today. Nevertheless, iodination won out; iodized salt is now a commonplace; and goiter, in the United States at least, is a rarity.

The symptoms that accompany goiter depend on whether the goiter forms in response to an iodine deficiency or not. The thyroid gland consists of millions of tiny hormone-producing follicles, each filled with a colloidal (that is, jellylike) substance called, simply enough, *colloid* ("gluelike" G). The colloid contains the iodine and so does the hormone it produces.

If the iodine supply in the diet is adequate, and if for any reason the thyroid increases in size, the number of active follicles may be multiplied as much as ten or twenty times and the hormone is produced in greater-than-normal quantities. The nervous, tense set of symptoms are produced, and this is *hyperthyroidism*. If, on the contrary, there is a deficiency of iodine, the thyroid may enlarge in an effort to compensate. The effort inevitably must be unsuccessful. No matter how many follicles form and how much colloid is produced, the thyroid hormone cannot be manufactured without iodine. In that case, despite the goiter, the hormone is produced in less-than-normal quantities and the dull, listless set of symptoms results. This is *hypothyroidism.*

The two forms of goiter can be distinguished by name. The form of goiter associated with hypothyroidism is simply *iodine-deficiency goiter*, a self-explanatory name. The form of goiter associated with hyperthyroidism is *exophthalmic goiter* (ek'sof-thal'mik; "eyes out" G) because the most prominent symptoms are bulging eyeballs. The latter form is also called *Graves' disease*, because it was well described by an Irish physician, Robert James Graves, in 1835. In hypothyroidism, the puffy flabbiness of the tissues seems to be brought about by an infiltration of mucuslike

* "Hyper" is from a Greek word meaning "over" and "above," and "hypo" is from the Greek for "under" or "below." The former prefix is commonly used to indicate any condition involving overactivity of an organ or the production or occurrence of some substance in greater-than-normal quantities. The latter prefix is used to indicate the opposite. It is a pity that opposites should sound so alike and offer such chance of confusions, but it is too late to correct the Greek language now.

materials, and the condition is therefore called *myxedema* (mik'suh-dee'muh; "mucus-swelling" G).

The symptoms in either direction, that of hyperthyroidism or hypothyroidism, can be of varying intensity. A reasonable measure of the intensity was first developed in 1895 by a German physician, Adolf Magnus-Levy, and that was partly a result of accident. At the time, physiologists had developed methods for measuring the uptake of oxygen by human beings and deducing the rate at which the metabolic processes of the body were operating. Naturally, this rate increased with exercise and decreased during rest. By arranging to have a fasting person lie down in a comfortably warm room and under completely relaxed conditions it was possible to obtain a minimum waking value for the rate of metabolism. This was the *basal metabolic rate,* usually abbreviated *BMR,* and it represented the "idling speed" of the human body.

Magnus-Levy was briskly and eagerly applying BMR measurements to the various patients in the hospital at which he worked in order to see whether the BMR varied in particular fashion with particular diseases. Obviously if it did, BMR determinations could become a valuable diagnostic tool and could help in following the course of a disease. Unfortunately, most diseases did not affect the BMR. There was one important exception. Hyperthyroid individuals showed a markedly high BMR and hypothyroid individuals a markedly low one. The more serious the condition the higher (or lower) the BMR was.

In this way the overall function of the thyroid hormone was established. It controlled the basal metabolic rate, the idling speed. A hyperthyroid individual had, to use an automotive metaphor, a racing engine; a hypothyroid individual had a sluggish one. This lent sense to the two sets of symptoms. With the chemical reactions within a body perpetually hastening, a person would be expected to be keyed-up, tense, nervous, overactive. And with those same reactions slowed down, he would be dull, listless, apathetic.

THYROXINE

The search for the actual thyroid hormone started as soon as the importance of iodine in the thyroid gland was recognized. In 1899 an iodine-containing protein was isolated from the gland. This had the properties associated with a group of proteins called "globulins" and was therefore named *thyroglobulin* (thy'roh-glob'-yoo-lin). It could relieve hypothyroid symptoms as well as mashed-up thyroid could, and do it in smaller quantities; so it might be considered at least a form of the thyroid hormone.

However, thyroglobulin is a large protein molecule, possessing a molecular weight, we now know, of up to 700,000. It is far too large to get out of the cell that formed it and into the bloodstream in intact form. For this reason it quickly seemed clear that thyroglobulin was at best merely the stored form of the hormone, and that what passed into the bloodstream were small fragments of the thyroglobulin molecule.

Iodine assumed increasing significance as biochemists labored in this direction. The thyroid gland, rich in iodine though it might be compared with the rest of the body, is still only about 0.03 per cent iodine. Preparations of thyroglobulin itself were 30 times or so as rich in iodine as was the intact thyroid gland and contained up to almost 1 per cent iodine. Furthermore, when the thyroglobulin molecule was broken down, the most active fragments had iodine contents as high as 14 per cent. Iodine was clearly the key. It was even possible to add iodine to quite ordinary proteins, such as casein (the chief protein of milk), and to produce an artificial *iodinated protein* containing some degree of thyroid hormone activity.

Finally, in 1915 the American chemist Edward Calvin Kendall isolated a small molecule that had all the properties of the thyroid hormone in concentrated form and yet seemed to be a single amino acid. Since it was found in the thyroid and since it controlled the rate of oxygen utilization in the body, the molecule was named *thyroxine* (thy-rok'sin).

An additional decade was required to determine the exact molecular structure of this amino acid. It turned out to be related to tyrosine, differing in its possession of a sort of doubled side-chain. You can see this clearly in the formulas below:

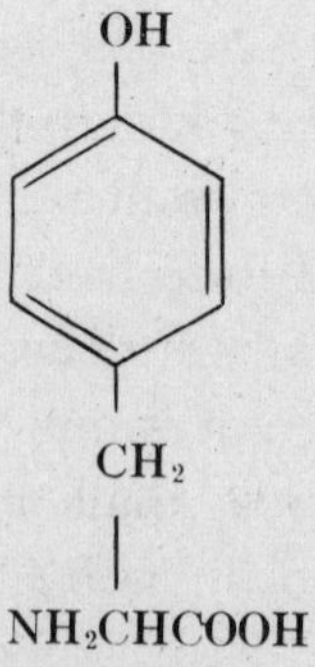

OH

I ⟨benzene ring⟩ I

O

I ⟨benzene ring⟩ I

OH

⟨benzene ring⟩

CH₂
|
NH₂CHCOOH

TYROSINE

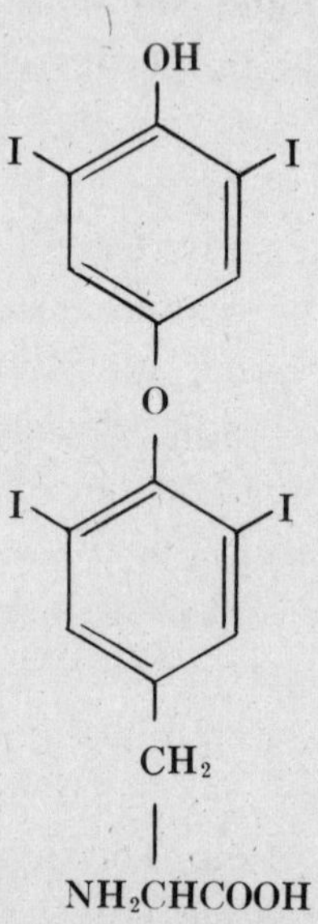

CH₂
|
NH₂CHCOOH

THYROXINE

The most unusual point about the structure of the thyroxine molecule is the fact that it contains four iodine atoms, symbolized in the formula above by I. (If the four iodine atoms were removed, what would be left of the molecule would be named *thyronine*.)

The four iodine atoms are quite heavy, much heavier than all 31 carbon, hydrogen, nitrogen, and oxygen atoms making up the rest of the molecule.* For that reason, iodine makes up about 63 per cent of the weight of the thyroxine molecule.

Apparently the thyroid gland traps the small traces of iodine

* Of all the atoms that are essential to life, iodine is by far the heaviest. The four most common atoms in the body are all quite light. Thus, if the weight of the hydrogen atom is considered 1, then carbon has an atomic weight of 12, nitrogen of 14, and oxygen of 16. Compare this with iodine, which has an atomic weight of 127.

present in food, adds them to the tyrosine molecule, doubles the side-chain, and adds more iodine to form thyroxine. (This can be done artificially, to a certain extent, by adding iodine to casein, as I mentioned above.) The thyroxine molecules are then united with other, more common amino acids and stored as the large thyroglobulin molecule. At need, the thyroxine content of the thyroglobulin is stripped off and sent out into the bloodstream.

For some thirty-five years after the discovery of thyroxine, it was considered *the* thyroid hormone. In 1951 the British biochemist Rosalind Pitt-Rivers and her co-workers isolated a very similar compound, one in which one of the iodine atoms was absent from the molecule, leaving only three in place. The new compound, with its three iodine atoms, is *tri-iodothyronine*, and is rather more active than thyroxine. For this reason I shall refer hereafter to "thyroid hormone" rather than to any one particular compound.

Now where thyroid hormone is severely deficient, the BMR may drop to half its normal value; where it is quite excessive, the BMR may rise to twice or even two and a half times its normal value. The thyroid control can therefore push the rate of metabolism through a fivefold range.

Yet what is it that thyroxine, tri-iodothyronine, and possible related compounds do to bring about such changes? What particular reaction or reactions do they stimulate in order to lift the entire level of metabolism? And how does iodine play a role? This is perhaps the most fascinating aspect of the problem, because no compound without iodine has any thyroid hormone activity whatever. Furthermore, there is no iodine in any compound present in our body except for the various forms of thyroid hormone.

By now you should not be surprised at learning that there is no answer as yet to these questions. The answer, when it comes, will have to explain more than a simple raising or lowering of the BMR, since that is by no means the only effect of the thyroid hormone. It plays a role in growth, in mental development, and in sexual development.

It sometimes happens that children are born with little or no thyroid tissue. Such children live but one can scarcely say more than that. If the condition is not corrected by the administration of hormone, the deficient creatures never grow to be larger than the normal seven- or eight-year-old. They do not mature sexually and are usually severely retarded mentally. They are often deaf-mutes. (These symptoms can be duplicated in animals if the thyroid is removed while they are young; actually it was in this fashion that the symptoms just described were first associated with the thyroid gland.)

Such virtually thyroidless unfortunates are called *cretins* (kree'tinz). The word is from a southern French dialect and means "Christians." The use of this word is not intended as a slur on religion but is, rather, an expression of pity, as we might say "poor soul." It could also be a hangover from an earlier day, reflecting the widespread belief among many primitive peoples that any form of mental aberration is a sign that the sufferer is touched by a god. (And do we not sometimes say of a madman that he is "touched in the head"?)

This inability of a thyroidless child to develop into an adult is also evidenced among the lower vertebrates; most startlingly among the amphibians. In amphibians the change from the young to the adult forms involves such dramatic overhauls of body structure as the replacement of a tail by legs, and of gills by lungs. Such changes cannot be carried through partway without killing the creature. The change is either completed or it is not begun.

If thyroid tissue is removed from a tadpole, the change is never begun. The creature may grow, yet it remains a tadpole; but if thyroid extract is added to the water in which the tadpole is swimming, it makes the change and becomes a frog. In fact, if thyroid extract is added to the water in which small tadpoles are swimming (tadpoles too small to produce their own hormone and change to frogs in the course of nature) the change nevertheless takes place. Tiny frogs are produced, much smaller than those produced under normal conditions.

There are creatures called axolotls, which are amphibians that remain tadpoles, so to speak, throughout life. They remain water creatures with gills and tail, but differ from ordinary tadpoles in that they can develop sexual maturity and reproduce themselves. They evidently are naturally hypothyroid, but through evolutionary processes have managed to survive and adjust to their lot. Now if the axolotl is supplied thyroid extract, it undergoes the change that in nature it does not. Legs replace the tail, lungs replace gills, and it climbs out upon land, a creature forever cut off from the rest of its species.

The sensitivity of amphibians to thyroid hormone is such that tadpoles have been used to test the potency of samples of thyroid extracts.

THYROID-STIMULATING HORMONE

One would expect the thyroid hormone to be produced in amounts matching the needs of the body. Where the rate of metabolism is high, as during exercise or physical labor, the hormone is consumed at a greater-than-normal rate and the thyroid gland must produce a correspondingly greater amount. The reverse is true when the body's needs are low, as when it is resting or asleep.

In the case of insulin, the blood glucose level can act as a feedback control. No such opportunity seems to be offered the thyroid gland. At least no blood component is, as far as we know, clearly affected by the quantity of thyroid hormone produced, and so there is no shifting level of concentration of some component to act as a thyroid control.

The concentration of thyroid hormone in the blood must itself vary. If body metabolism rises, so that the hormone is more quickly consumed, its blood level must show a tendency to drop. If body metabolism is low, the blood level of the hormone must show a tendency to rise. It might seem, then, that the thyroid could respond to the level of its own hormone in the blood passing through itself. This is clearly dangerous. Since the thyroid produces the hormone, the blood concentration in its own vicinity would always be higher than in the remainder of the body, and it would receive a blurred and distorted picture of what is going on. (It would be something like an executive judging the worth of his ideas by the opinions of his yes-men.)

The solution is to put a second gland to work; a gland in a different region of the body. The second gland turns out to be, in this case, a small organ at the base of the brain. This is the *pituitary gland* (pih-tyoo′ih-tehr′ee; "phlegm" L). The name arises from the fact that, since the gland is located at the base of the brain just above the nasal passages, some of the ancients thought its function was to supply the nose with its mucous secretions. The idea held force till about 1600.

This, of course, is not so; the only secretions produced by the pituitary are discharged directly into the bloodstream. Nevertheless, the name persists, although there is the alternative of *hypophysis cerebri* (hy-pof′ih-sis cehr′uh-bree; "undergrowth of the brain" G), or simply *hypophysis*. This term, which came into use about half a century ago, is at least accurately descriptive.

In man the pituitary gland is a small egg-shaped structure about half an inch long, or about the size of the final joint of the little finger; see illustration, page 382. It weighs less than a gram, or only about 1/40 of an ounce, but don't let that fool you. In some respects it is the most important gland in the body. The location alone would seem to indicate that — just about at the midpoint of the head, as though carefully hidden in the safest and most inaccessible part. The gland is connected by a thin stalk to the base of the brain, and rests in a small depression in the bone that rims the base.

The pituitary is divided into two parts, which (as in the case of the adrenal glands) have no connection with each other functionally. They do not even originate in the same way. The rear portion, or *posterior lobe*, originates in the embryo as an outgrowth of the base of the brain, and it is the posterior lobe that remains attached to the brain by the thin stalk. The forward portion, or *anterior lobe,* originates in the embryo as a pinched-off portion of the mouth. The anterior lobe loses all connection with the mouth and eventually finds itself hugging the posterior lobe. The two are lumped together as a single gland only by this accident of meeting midway and ending in the same place. (In some animals, there is an *intermediate lobe* as well, but in man this is virtually absent.) Both lobes produce polypeptide hormones. The anterior lobe produces six hormones that have been definitely isolated as pure, or nearly pure, substances, and these may be spoken of, generally, as the *anterior pituitary hormones.* (The existence of several other hormones is suspected.)

Of the six anterior pituitary hormones, one has the function of stimulating the secretion of the thyroid gland. This is easily shown, since removal of the pituitary in experimental animals causes atrophy of the thyroid gland, among other unpleasant effects. This also takes place in cases of *hypopituitarism,* where the secretions of the pituitary gland fall below the minimum required for health. The symptoms of this disease (which are quite distressing since they tend to show up in young women and to induce premature aging, among other things) were described by a German physician named Morris Simmonds, so the condition is often called *Simmonds' disease.*

On the positive side, the administration of preparations of pituitary extracts to animals can cause the thyroid gland to increase in weight and become more active. It is reasonable, therefore, to suppose that at least one of the anterior pituitary hormones is concerned with thyroid function. The hormone has been isolated and has been labeled the *thyroid-stimulating hormone,* a name usually abbreviated as *TSH.* It may also be called the *thyrotrophic hormone* (thy'roh-troh'fic; "thyroid-nourishing" G).*

* There is a tendency to use the suffix "tropic" in place of "trophic" in the case of TSH and certain other hormones. The suffix "tropic" is from a Greek word meaning "to turn" and makes no sense in this connection. Unfortunately, the difference lies in but one letter and few biochemists seem to be terribly concerned over the proper meaning of a Greek suffix, so "thyrotropic" is a fairly common term and may become even more common.

With two hormones at work, a mutual feedback can take place. A lowering of the thyroid hormone concentration in the blood stimulates a rise in TSH production; and a rise in thyroid hormone concentration inhibits TSH production. Conversely, a rise in TSH concentration in the blood stimulates a rise in thyroid hormone production; and a fall in TSH concentration inhibits thyroid hormone production.

Now suppose that, as a result of racing metabolism, inroads are made on the thyroid hormone supply, causing the blood level to drop. As the blood passes through the anterior pituitary, the lower-than-normal level of thyroid hormone stimulates the secretion of additional TSH, and the blood level of TSH rises. When the blood passes through the thyroid carrying its extra load of TSH, the secretion of thyroid hormone is stimulated and the demands of the high metabolic rate are met.

If the thyroid hormone should now be greater than the body's requirements, its blood level will rise. This rising thyroid hormone level will cut off TSH production, which will in turn cut off thyroid hormone production. By the action of the two glands in smooth cooperation, the thyroid hormone level will be maintained at an appropriate blood level despite continual shifts in the body's requirements for the hormone.

The working of the "thyroid-pituitary axis" can, understandably, be imperfect. The mere fact that a second gland is called into action means there is another link in the chain, another link that may go wrong. It is likely, for instance, that hyperthyroidism arises not from anything wrong with the thyroid itself but from a flaw in the anterior pituitary. The secretion of TSH can, as a result, be abnormally high and the thyroid kept needlessly, and even harmfully, overactive. (The anterior pituitary serves as regulating gland, after this fashion, for several other glands in the body. It is this that makes it seem to be the "master gland" of the body.)

TSH is not one of the anterior pituitary hormones that have been prepared in completely pure form, and so information about its chemical structure is as yet a bit fuzzy. Its molecular weight, as it is formed, may be about 10,000; this would mean that its polypeptide chain could contain nearly a hundred amino acids. However, there seem to be signs that the chain can be broken up into smaller portions without loss of activity. This ability to confine the area of activity to a relatively small region of the whole molecule is true of some other hormones as well (though it does not seem to be true of insulin).

PARATHYROID HORMONE

Behind the thyroid gland are four flattened scraps of pinkish or reddish tisue, each about a third of an inch long. Two are on either side of the windpipe, one of each pair being near the top of the thyroid, and one near the bottom. These are the *parathyroid glands* ("alongside the thyroid" G); see illustration, page 382.

The parathyroids were first detected (in the rhinoceros, of all animals) in the middle 19th century, and little attention was paid them for some decades. If physicians or anatomists thought of them at all, it was to consider them as parts of the thyroid. There were cases when, in removing part or all of the thyroid, these scraps of tissue were casually removed as well. This proved to have unexpectedly drastic consequences. The removal of the thyroid might result in severe myxedema, but the patient at least remains alive. In contrast, with the removal of the parathyroids, death follows fairly quickly and is preceded by severe muscular spasms. Experiments on animals, which proved more sensitive to loss of the parathyroids than men were, showed that muscles tightened convulsively, a situation called *tetany* (tet'uh-nee; "stretch" G). This resembled the situation brought on by abnormally low concentration of calcium ion* in the blood and it was found that

* Some atoms or groups of atoms have a tendency to lose one or more of the tiny electrons that form component parts of themselves. Or they may gain one or more electrons from outside. Since electrons carry a negative electric charge, atoms that lose them possess a positive charge, and those that gain them possess a negative one. Atoms charged either way can be made to move through a fluid in response to an electric field, and are therefore called *ions* (eye'onz; "wander" G).

calcium ion levels in the blood were indeed abnormally low in animals that had been deprived of the parathyroids. As tetany progressed and worsened, the animal died, either out of sheer exhaustion or because the muscles that closed its larynx did so in a tight death grip so that, in effect, the animal throttled itself and died of asphyxiation. By the 1920's, surgeons grew definitely cautious about slicing away at the thyroid and supremely careful about touching the parathyroids.

As is now understood, the parathyroid hormone is to the calcium level in the blood as glucagon is to the glucose level. Just as glucagon mobilizes the glycogen reservoir in the liver, bringing about its breakdown to glucose, which pours into the blood, so the parathyroid hormone mobilizes the calcium stores in bone, bringing about its breakdown to calcium ions in solution, which pours into the blood.

The blood contains from 9 to 11 mg. per cent of calcium ion,[*] so the total quantity of calcium ion in the blood of an average human being is something like 250 milligrams (less than 1/100 ounce), whereas there is something like 3 kilograms (or about 6½ pounds) of calcium ion in the skeleton of the body. This means there is 12,000 times as much calcium in the skeleton as in the blood, so bone is a really effective reservoir. A small amount of calcium withdrawn from bone — not enough to affect perceptibly the strength and toughness of the skeleton — would suffice to keep the blood content steady for a long time.

The properties of an ion are quite different from those of an uncharged atom. Thus, calcium atoms make up an active metal that would be quite poisonous to living tissue, but calcium ions are much blander and are necessary components of living tissue. Nor are calcium ions metallic; instead they make up parts of substances classified by chemists as "salts." The difference between ordinary atoms and ions is expressed in symbols. The calcium atom is symbolized as Ca. The calcium ion, which has lost two electrons and carries a double positive charge, is Ca^{++}.

[*] Calcium ion is essential to blood coagulation, and to the proper working of nerve and muscle. To do its work properly, calcium ion must remain within a narrow range of concentration. If it rises too high or drops too low, the entire ion balance of the blood is upset; neither nerves nor muscles can do their work; and the body, through a failure in organization, dies. It is the proper functioning of the parathyroid gland which keeps this from happening.

Under the influence of the parathyroid hormone, those cells whose function it is to dissolve bone are stimulated. Bone is eroded at a greater-than-normal rate and the calcium ion thus liberated pours into the bloodstream. As this happens, phosphate ion also enters the bloodstream, for calcium ion and phosphate ion are knit together in bone and one cannot be liberated without the other. The phosphate ion does not remain in the blood but is excreted through the urine. It is possible that parathyroid hormone has as another function the stimulation of the excretion of phosphate ion in the urine.

It is the calcium ion level in the blood that controls the rate of secretion of parathyroid hormone (just as the blood glucose level controls that of insulin). If the diet is consistently low in calcium, so that there is a chronic danger of subnormal levels in the blood, the parathyroids are kept active and bone continues to be eroded away. If the diet is adequate in calcium, the raised level in blood acts to inhibit the activity of the parathyroid and the bone erosion subsides. It was reported in 1963 that the parathyroid produces a second hormone, *calcitonin,* acting in opposition to the parathyroid hormone, as insulin acts in opposition to glucagon. Calcitonin acts to reduce the calcium ion level of the blood. In addition, other processes (in which vitamin D is somehow involved — but that is another story) act to bring about buildup of bone, and any bone previously lost is replaced. Any excess calcium beyond what is needed is excreted through the urine.

It is possible for the parathyroids to remain overactive even when the blood level is adequately high. This can take place when a parathyroid tumor greatly increases the number of hormone-producing cells and the condition is *hyperparathyroidism.* In such a case, bone erosion continues unchecked, while the body survives by continually dumping excess calcium ion into the urine. Eventually bones may be weakened by calcium loss to the point where they will break under ordinary stresses, and such apparently reasonless breakage may be the first noticeable symptom of the disease.

The parathyroid hormone was isolated in pure form in 1960. It is a small protein molecule with a molecular weight of 9500 and a structure consisting of a chain of 83 amino acids. The molecule can be broken into smaller units, and a chain of 33 amino acids is found to exert the full effect of the parathyroid hormone. Why the other 50, then? The best guess seems to be that the additional 50 are needed to increase the stability of the molecule as a whole. (To use an analogy, only the blade of a knife cuts, and yet the wooden handle, though contributing nothing to the actual cutting, makes the knife easier to hold and therefore more useful generally.)

The exact order in which amino acids occur in the parathyroid hormone has not yet been worked out.

POSTERIOR PITUITARY HORMONES

Now that we have examples of how hormones like insulin and glucagon can maintain the level of concentration of an organic substance such as glucose, and of how hormones like those of the parathyroid gland can maintain the level of concentration of an inorganic substance such as calcium ion, it would round out matters to produce a hormone that controls the level of concentration of the water in which both inorganic and organic substances are dissolved. Water enters and leaves the body in a variety of ways. We take in water with the food we eat and with the fluids (particularly water itself) we drink. We lose water through perspiration, through the expired breath, through the feces, and, most of all, through the urine. Water loss can be increased or decreased with circumstances. The most common way in which we are subjected to unusually great water loss is through perspiration caused by unusual heat or by strenuous physical activity. We make up for that by drinking more water than usual at such times.

This is the "coarse control." There is a "fine control" too, which enables the body to adjust continuously (within limits) to minor changes and fluctuations in the rate of water loss, so we are not as slavishly tied to the water tap as we would otherwise be. In the fine control, the kidneys are involved. The blood, in passing through the kidneys, is filtered. Wastes pass out of the blood vessels and into the renal tubules. The phrase "pass out" is actually too weak a term. The wastes are flushed out by the lavish use of water; more water than we could ordinarily afford to lose. However, as the blood filtrate passes down the tubules, water is reabsorbed. What eventually enters the ureter and travels down to the bladder is a urine in which the waste materials are dissolved in comparatively little water. If the body is short of water, reabsorption takes place to the maximum of which the body is capable, and the urine is concentrated, scanty, and dark in color. (Desert mammals can conserve water to the point where the urine is so scanty as to be almost nonexistent; we do not have that talent.) If, on the contrary, we drink considerable water or other fluids, so that the body finds itself with more than it needs, the reabsorption of water in the tubules is repressed by the necessary amount and the urine is dilute, copious, and very light in color.

In the early 1940's, it was discovered that this ability of the body to control reabsorption of water in the tubules in order to help keep the body's water contents at a desirable level was mediated by a hormone. Extracts from the posterior lobe of the pituitary gland seemed to have a powerful effect on the manner in which water was reabsorbed. These extracts, usually called *pituitrin,* encouraged the reabsorption of water and therefore diminished the volume of urine. Now any factor which increases urine volume is said to be *diuretic* (dy'yoo-ret'ik; "to urinate" G). The posterior pituitary extract had an opposite effect and was therefore felt to contain an *antidiuretic hormone,* usually referred to by the abbreviation *ADH.*

In addition, as it turned out, pituitrin possesses two more important abilities. It tends to increase blood pressure through a contraction of blood vessels. This is referred to as vasopressor (vas'oh-pres'or; "vessel-compressing" L) activity. It also induces

contractions of the muscles of the pregnant uterus at the time it
becomes necessary to force the fully developed fetus out into the
world. This is called the oxytocic (ok'see-toh'sik; "quick birth"
G) effect. And, as a matter of fact, the preparation can be used
to encourage a quick birth by forcing a uterus into action at some
convenient moment.

The American biochemist Vincent du Vigneaud and his asso-
ciates obtained two pure substances from the posterior pituitary
extracts, of which one possessed the blood-pressure-raising effect
and was named *vasopressin* and the other possessed the uterus-
stimulating effect and was named *oxytocin*. There was no need to
search for a third hormone with the antidiuretic effect: vasopressin possessed it in full. By the mid-1950's, therefore, the
phrase "antidiuretic hormone" vanished from the medical vocabulary. ADH was vasopressin and the latter term was sufficient.

Du Vigneaud found oxytocin and vasopressin to be unusually
small peptides, with molecular weights just above 1000. Analysis
of these peptides by the methods worked out by Sanger was not
difficult. Du Vigneaud found both to possess molecules made up
of no more than 8 amino acids. He worked out the order in which
they appeared:

$$\overbrace{cyS-Scy}$$
$$tyr \cdot ileu \cdot gluNH_2 \cdot aspNH_2 \cdot pro \cdot leu \cdot glyNH_2$$

OXYTOCIN

$$\overbrace{cyS-Scy}$$
$$tyr \cdot phe \cdot gluNH_2 \cdot aspNH_2 \cdot pro \cdot arg \cdot glyNH_2$$

VASOPRESSIN

As you see, the two molecules are very much alike, with only
two amino acids of the eight different. That is enough, nevertheless, to make their properties completely different and shows
what a minor alteration in the nature of the side-chains can do.
(On the other hand, vasopressin obtained from hog pituitaries

contains a lysine in place of the arginine in the above formula —
which is for vasopressin taken from cattle — and that change
makes no significant difference.)

Du Vigneaud, having determined the structure of these two
hormones, went a step further. He built up an amino acid chain,
placing the amino acids in the order analysis had told him was
correct. In 1955 he prepared synthetic molecules that showed
all the oxytocic, vasopressor and antidiuretic functions of the
natural molecules. Thereby he was the first to synthesize a natural active protein (albeit a very small one), and for that feat
was, that very year, awarded the Nobel Prize in Chemistry.

It happens occasionally that vasopressin may fail to be produced in adequate quantities in a particular individual. When
this happens, water is not properly reabsorbed in the kidney tubules and urination becomes abnormally copious. In bad cases,
where water is not reabsorbed at all, the daily volume of urine
may reach twenty or thirty quarts, and water must then be drunk
in equally voluminous quantities. Such a disease, with water
"passing through" so readily, rightly deserves to be considered
a form of diabetes.

Since the ordinary wastes present in urine are not increased
in this condition but are merely spread thin through the large
quantity of water produced, the urine becomes very little removed from tap water. It lacks the odor and amber color of
ordinary urine. In particular, when compared with the sugar-
filled urine of the sufferer of diabetes mellitus, it lacks a taste.
The condition is therefore *diabetes insipidus* (in-sip'ih-dus;
"tasteless" L).

4

OUR ADRENAL CORTEX

CHOLESTEROL

So far, all the hormones I have discussed are based on the amino acid. Some, such as thyroxine, epinephrine, and histamine have molecules that are modifications of single amino acids; tyrosine in the first two cases, histidine in the last. Other hormones are chains of amino acids, made up of as few as eight members or as many as a hundred. There are, however, certain hormones that are completely unrelated in structure to the amino acid, and their story begins with that usually painful and certainly unromantic phenomenon we know as gallstones.

In 1814 a white substance with a fatty consistency was obtained from gallstones and was named *cholesterin* (koh-les′ter-in; "solid bile" G). The name was reasonable enough since gallstones precipitated out of the bile and could therefore be looked upon as a kind of solidified bile. Investigations into the molecular structure of the substance met with frustrating lack of success for over a century, but one fact that eventually turned up after some decades was that the molecule possessed one oxygen-hydrogen combination (-OH) as part of its structure. This is a group occurring, characteristically, in alcohols, and, toward the end of the 19th century, it became conventional to give the alcohols names ending with the suffix "ol." For this reason, cholesterin came to be called *cholesterol,* and the family of compounds of which it was a member came to be called the *sterols.*

As time went on, it was discovered that many compounds clearly related to cholesterol did not possess the -OH group and were therefore not entitled to names with the "ol" suffix. In the 1930's a more general term was proposed to include the entire class of compounds, both with and without the -OH group. The name proposed was *steroid* ("sterol-like" G).

And by then the molecular structure of cholesterol was finally worked out. The molecule is made up, it turned out, of 27 carbon atoms, 46 hydrogen atoms, and just 1 oxygen atom. Seventeen of the carbon atoms are arranged in a four-ring combination, which can be schematically presented as follows:

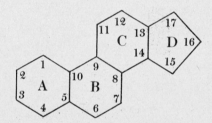

STEROID NUCLEUS IN CHOLESTEROL

The carbon atoms are arranged, you see, in three hexagons and one pentagon, joined together as shown. At every angle of these rings you can imagine a carbon atom as existing. The lines connecting the angles are the "bonds" connecting the carbon atoms. The rings are lettered from A to D and the angles (or carbon atoms) are numbered from 1 to 17, according to the conventional system shown above, which is accepted by all chemists. This particular four-ring combination of carbon atoms is called the *steroid nucleus*.

Each carbon atom has at its disposal four bonds by which connections may be made with other atoms. The carbon atom at position 2, for example, is making use of two of its bonds already, one for attachment to carbon-1 and another for attachment to carbon-3. This means that two bonds still remain and each of these can be attached to a hydrogen atom.* (A hydrogen atom

* It is conventional in such schematic formulas as I am using in this chapter to

has only one bond at its disposal.) As for the carbon at position 10, that is making use of three of its bonds, one leading to carbon-1, one to carbon-5, and one to carbon-9. It has only one bond left over.

Sometimes a carbon atom is held to the neighboring carbon atom by two bonds; this is referred to as a *double bond*. Suppose such a double bond exists between positions 5 and 6. In that case, carbon-5 is connected by two bonds to carbon-6, by a third bond to carbon-10 and by a fourth bond to carbon-4. All its bonds are used up.

Now let's return to cholesterol. Of its 27 carbon atoms, 17 are accounted for by the steroid nucleus. There remain 10. Of these, 1 is attached to the lone remaining bond of carbon-10 and 1 to the lone remaining bond of carbon-13. The final 8 form a chain (with a detailed structure that need not concern us) attached to carbon-17, with finally, a double bond between carbons 5 and 6.

What of the lone oxygen atom? This is attached to carbon-3. The oxygen atom has the capacity to form two bonds. One of these is taken up by the carbon-3 attachment, but the other is joined to a hydrogen atom, forming the -OH combination that is characteristic of alcohols. This gives us all the information we need to present a schematic formula for the cholesterol molecule:

CHOLESTEROL

leave out the hydrogen atoms that are connected to carbon atoms, for simplicity's sake. Therefore wherever there are bonds left unaccounted for in a formula, as is true of those two extra bonds of carbon-2, you may safely assume that hydrogen atoms are attached.

I have gone into detail on the cholesterol molecule for two reasons: first, it is an important molecule in itself and, second, it is the parent substance of other molecules at least as important. The importance of cholesterol is attested by the mere fact that there is so much of it in the body. The average 70-kilogram (154-pound) man contains some 230 grams, or just about half a pound, of the substance. A good deal of it is to be found in the nervous system (which is reason enough to stress the compound in this book). About 3 per cent of the weight of the brain is cholesterol. Considering that 80 per cent of the brain is water, you can see that cholesterol makes up some 15 per cent, nearly a sixth, of the dry weight of the brain.

It is present elsewhere, too. The bile secreted by the liver contains 2½ to 3 per cent of dissolved matter, and of this about 1/20 is cholesterol. The bile in the gallbladder is stored in concentrated form, and the cholesterol content there is correspondingly enriched. The cholesterol in the bile may not really seem like a large quantity (about 1/10 of a per cent all told) but it is enough to cause trouble at times. The quantity of cholesterol in the bile within the gallbladder is just about all that the liquid can hold, since cholesterol is not particularly soluble in body fluids. It is not uncommon to have crystals of cholesterol precipitate out of the bile. On occasion such crystals conglomerate to form sizable gallstones that may block the cystic duct through which bile ordinarily passes into the small intestine. It is this blockage that produces the severe abdominal pains with which sufferers from gallstones are all too familiar.

Of the dissolved material in blood, about 0.65 per cent is cholesterol. This, too, is sufficient to make trouble on occasion. There is a tendency for cholesterol to precipitate out of blood and onto the inner lining of arteries, narrowing the bore, and roughening the smoothness. This condition, *atherosclerosis*, is currently the prime killer of mankind in the United States. (Mankind, literally, since men are affected more often than women.)

Cholesterol, although only very slightly soluble in water, is freely soluble in fat and is therefore to be found in the fatty portions of foods. Animal fats are far richer in cholesterol than plant fats are. In addition, there is some evidence to the effect that the body can handle cholesterol more efficiently if the diet contains a sizable quantity of fat molecules marked by several double bonds between carbon atoms. These are called *polyunsaturated fats* and are of considerably more common occurrence in plant fats than in animal fats. For this reason, the last few years have seen a swing in American dietary habits away from animal fat and toward plant fat.

Nevertheless, increasing consciousness of the dangers of atherosclerosis must not cause us to think of cholesterol as merely a danger to life. It is, in fact, vital to life. It is a universal component of living tissue and no cell is entirely without it. It is rather frustrating, as a consequence, to be forced to confess that biochemists have only the haziest notion of what it actually does in living tissue.

OTHER STEROIDS

There are other steroids in the body, which may be formed out of cholesterol or which are, perhaps, formed simultaneously with cholesterol by similar chemical processes. The bile, for instance, contains steroids called *bile acids* in concentrations seven or eight times that of cholesterol itself. (The bile acids create no troubles, though, because unlike cholesterol they are fairly soluble and do not come out of solution to form stones.)

The molecules of the bile acids differ from that of cholesterol chiefly in that the eight-carbon chain attached to carbon-17 (in cholesterol) is chopped off at the fifth carbon. That fifth carbon forms part of a carboxyl group (-COOH), and it is the acid property of this carboxyl group that gives the bile acids their name.

There are several varieties of bile acids. One has a single hydroxyl group attached to carbon-3, as in the case of cholesterol. Another has a second hydroxyl group attached to carbon-12, and still another has a third hydroxyl group attached to carbon-7. Each of these bile acids can be combined at the carboxyl group to a molecule of the amino acid, glycine, or to a sulfur-containing compound called "taurine." These combinations make up the group of compounds called bile salts. The bile salts have an interesting property. Most of the molecule is soluble in fat, whereas the carboxyl group and its attached compound is soluble in water. The bile-salt molecule therefore tends to crowd into any interface that may exist between fat and water, with the fat-soluble portion sticking into the fat and the water-soluble portion sticking into the water.

Ordinarily the interface represents a greater concentration of energy than does the body of either liquid, so the amount of interface is kept to a minimum. If oil and water are both poured into a beaker, the interface is a flat plane between the two. If the mixture is shaken violently bubbles of oil are formed in water, and bubbles of water are formed in oil. The energy of shaking is converted into the energy of the additional interface formed; but when the shaking ceases, the bubbles break and the interface settles back into the minimum area of the flat plane.

The presence of bile salts in the interface, however, lowers its energy content. This means that the interface can be easily extended so that the churning of the food within the small intestine easily breaks up fatty material into bubbles and then smaller bubbles. (The smaller the bubbles, the larger the area of interface for a given weight of fat.) Furthermore, the bubbles that are formed have little tendency to break up again, as bile salt crowds into every new interface formed. The microscopic fat globules eventually formed are much easier to break up through the digestive action of enzymes than large masses of fat would be, because enzymes are not soluble in fat and can only exert their effects on the edges of the bubbles.

A rather drastic change of sterol structure often occurs when one is exposed to ultraviolet light. The bond between carbon-9 and carbon-10 breaks and ring B opens up. The resulting structure is no longer, strictly speaking, a steroid, since the steroid nucleus is no longer intact. However, the molecule remains so clearly related to the steroids that it is usually discussed as though it were part of the group.

Many of these "broken steroid" molecules possess vitamin D activity; that is, they somehow encourage the normal deposition of bone. That deposition cannot take place in the absence of vitamin D. The broken steroid developed from cholesterol itself does not have vitamin D properties. Nevertheless, cholesterol is almost invariably accompanied everywhere in the body by small quantities of a very similar sterol that differs from cholesterol itself only in that it has a second double bond located between carbon-7 and carbon-8. This second compound, when broken by ultraviolet light *does* have vitamin D properties. There is cholesterol and its double-bonded partner in the fat layers in the skin. The ultraviolet of sunlight can reach it, forming the vitamin when it does so. For this reason vitamin D is called the "sunshine vitamin," and not because it, or any vitamin — or any material substance whatever for that matter — is in sunshine itself.

If vitamin D were formed by the body, particularly if it were secreted by some organ of the body, it would certainly be very tempting to consider it a hormone. It might even be considered a hormone that like the recently discovered calcitonin (see p. 397) opposed the action of the parathyroid hormone (depositing bone, whereas parathyroid hormone erodes it) as glucagon opposes the action of insulin. Since the body does not form vitamin D directly but must have it formed by the action of sunlight or, failing that, by absorbing such trace quantities as may be present in the food, it is called a vitamin.

A number of classes of steroids not formed in the human body are nevertheless found in the living tissue of other species. Almost invariably these have profound effects when administered to human beings even in small quantities. There are such steroids in the seeds and leaves of the purple foxglove. The drooping purple flowers look like thimbles, and the Latin name of the genus is *Digitalis* (dih-jih-tal'is; "of the finger" L, which is what thimbles certainly are). The steroids in digitalis are something like the bile acids in structure except that the carboxyl group on the side-chain combines with another portion of the chain to form a fifth ring that is not part of the four-ring steroid nucleus. This five-ring steroid combines with certain sugarlike molecules to form *glycosides* (gly'koh-sidez; "sweet" G, in reference to the sugar). Such compounds are used in the treatment of specific heart disorders and are therefore called the *cardiac glycosides* (kahr'dee-ak; "heart" G).

The cardiac glycosides are helpful and even life-saving in the proper doses, but in improper doses can, of course, kill. Steroids similar to those in the cardiac glycosides are found in the secretions of the salivary glands of toads, and these are called *toad poisons*. Another group of steroids, found in certain plants are called *saponins* (sap'oh-ninz; "soap" L, because they form a soapy solution). They are poisonous, too.

But why do steroids have such profound physiological effects in small quantities? For one thing, many of them, like the bile salts, tend to crowd into interfaces. Many physiological effects are dependent on the behavior of substances at interfaces. By changing the nature of those interfaces, steroids succeed in changing the behavior of substances generally and of the physiological effects dependent on that behavior.

For living tissue the most important interface of all is that between the cell and the outside world. The boundary of a cell is its *membrane,* which is an extremely thin structure. It is so thin that only in the 1950's, with the aid of the best electron microscopes available, could it really be studied. It appears to consist of a double layer of phosphorus-containing fatlike molecules (*phospholipid*), coated on each side with a single thickness of protein molecule. It is through this thin membrane that substances enter and leave the cell. Entry or exit may be by way of tiny pores existing in the membrane, or that are formed, but such entry or exit, whatever the mechanism, cannot be a purely passive thing. Some atoms and molecules can pass through more easily and rapidly than can other atoms and molecules of similar size. The fact that the cell membrane is made up of both phospholipid and protein may be significant here. The phospholipid is largely fat-soluble and the protein is largely water-soluble. It may be that the manner in which a particular substance can (or cannot) get through the cell membrane depends on the manner of its relative solubility in fat and in water.

In Chapter 1, I mentioned the theory that hormones achieved their effects by altering the manner in which the cell membranes allowed the entry and exit of particular substances. One can imagine a peptide molecule layering itself over the cell membrane and substituting for the original pattern of side-chains a new pattern that might, for instance, encourage the entry of glucose at greater-than-normal rates, thus lowering the glucose-concentration in blood. (This, as you may remember, is the effect of insulin.)

Now it would seem reasonable that, if a protein molecule could accomplish this by altering the pattern of the protein portion of the membrane, a fat-soluble molecule such as a steroid might also do so by altering the pattern of the phospholipid portion of the membrane. It may be in this fashion that vitamin D encourages the growth of bones, by altering the membrane of bone cells to permit the entry of calcium ions at a greater-than-normal rate. It may also explain the workings of other steroids that not only have hormone functions, as vitamin D does, but are elaborated by special glands and therefore carry the name of hormones, too.

In fact, all hormones fall into two, and only two, chemical groups. They are either (1) protein or amino acid in nature, and presumably affect the water-soluble portion of the cell membrane, or (2) steroid in nature, presumably affecting the fat-soluble portion.

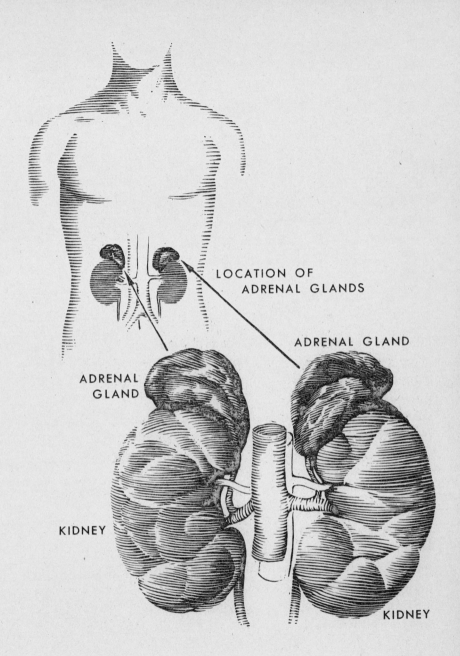

LOCATION OF
ADRENAL GLANDS

ADRENAL GLAND

ADRENAL
GLAND

KIDNEY

KIDNEY

CORTICOIDS

One of the glands that produces steroid hormones is the adrenal cortex. (I referred to it in passing on page $_{377}$ when I talked about epinephrine, which is formed by the adrenal medulla.)

The importance of the adrenal cortex was first made clear in 1855, when an English physician named Thomas Addison described in detail the clinical symptoms that accompanied deterioration of this organ (a deterioration sometimes brought on by the ravages of tuberculosis). The most prominent symptom was a discoloration of the skin, a kind of mottled-bronze or grayish effect produced by the overproduction of the skin pigment melanin. Anemia, muscle weakness, and gastrointestinal symptoms were also found. Modern methods of analysis have added to these marked abnormalities in water distribution and in the concentrations of glucose and of various inorganic ions ("minerals") in the blood. Thus, sodium ion concentration in the blood falls because too much is excreted in the urine and potassium ion concentration rises because too much escapes into the blood from the cells, where it is usually firmly retained. The disease grows progressively worse and death generally follows two to three years after its onset, if untreated. Because Addison was the first to describe the symptoms of the disease arising from adrenal cortical insufficiency with such care, it has been called *Addison's disease* ever since.

If there was any doubt that the adrenal cortex is essential to life, this was banished as a result of animal experimentation. Animals in which the adrenal cortex was removed rapidly developed all the symptoms of Addison's disease in exaggerated form and died within two weeks.

By 1929 methods were developed that enabled biochemists to prepare extracts of the adrenal cortex which served to lengthen the life of adrenalectomized animals (those from which the adrenal glands had been removed). By that time biochemists had sufficient experience with hormones to be quite certain that the extract, called *cortin*, had to contain at least one hormone. A number of different groups of researchers set about the task of locating it.

Throughout the 1930's two groups particularly, an American group headed by Edward Kendall (the discoverer of thyroxine) and a Swiss group headed by the Polish-born Tadeus Reichstein, followed hot on the trail. The success that stemmed from their researches led to both Kendall and Reichstein sharing in the Nobel Prize in Medicine and Physiology for 1950.

By 1940 more than two dozen different crystalline compounds had been prepared from the adrenal cortex. This was no mean task, for out of a ton of adrenals, obtained from hecatombs of slaughtered cattle, about half an ounce of a particular compound might be obtained. At first there was no notion of what the structure of these compounds might be. Kendall called them simply "compound A," "compound B," and so on, whereas Reichstein referred to them as substances rather than compounds. With investigation, however, it developed that these compounds were one and all steroid in character. They were therefore lumped under the heading of *adrenocortical steroids*, or, by telescoping the phrase, as *corticoids*.

The steroid nature of the various cortical substances solved one problem at once. The adrenal cortex is rich in cholesterol, richer than any other organ but the brain. Earlier this had been puzzling, but now it seemed clear that cholesterol was the store upon which the cortex drew in its manufacture of the various corticoids.

All the important corticoids have the same carbon skeleton, one differing from that of cholesterol chiefly in that the carbon chain attached to carbon-17 is reduced to 2 carbon atoms only, in place of cholesterol's 8. Therefore the corticoids have 21 carbon atoms altogether instead of cholesterol's 27.

The formula of one steroid produced by the adrenal cortex is presented schematically on page 414, with each of the 21 carbon atoms marked off by number.

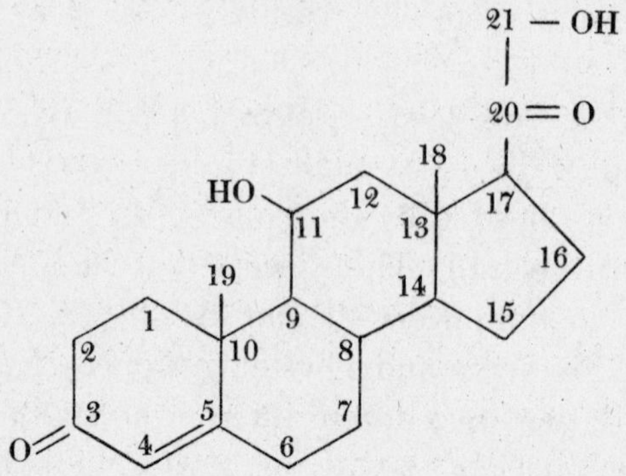

CORTICOSTERONE

Notice that it has four oxygen atoms instead of just one, as is the case of cholesterol. Two of the oxygens form part of the -OH alcohol group. The other two, however, are bound to a carbon atom by both bonds. This C=O group was first found to exist in a simple organic compound called "acetone." For this reason compounds possessing such groups are often given names with a "one" suffix. Since all the important corticoids possess a C=O group attached to carbon-3 (in place of the -OH group of cholesterol), all have this suffix. The particular compound shown above (which Kendall called "compound B" and Reichstein called "substance H" in the days before its structure was determined) is now called *corticosterone* (kawr'tih-kos'ter-ohn).

One effect of this hormone is to promote the storage of glycogen in the liver. This is similar to the action of insulin and opposed to the action of glucagon, so that it represents another item in the complex hormonal balance controlling the glucose level in the blood.

There are other corticoids with effects similar to corticosterone, and of these the best-known is one which Kendall called "compound E" and Reichstein "substance Fa." It differs from corticosterone in possessing a fifth oxygen atom, attached to carbon-17 in the form of an -OH group. In addition, the oxygen atom attached to carbon-11 is not an -OH group, as in corticosterone, but is a C=O group. To a chemist these differences are perfectly well described in the official name of the compound which is 17-*hydroxy*-11-*dehydrocorticosterone*. When this compound gained clinical importance, however, for a reason I shall shortly describe, a shorter name was absolutely necessary, and, by leaving out most of the letters, the word *cortisone* was arrived at.

In a couple of corticoids there is no oxygen attached to carbon-11. One of them, which Reichstein isolated from cattle, has a molecule with exactly the corticosterone structure, except for that missing oxygen. It is called, reasonably enough, *deoxycorticosterone*, a name usually abbreviated to *DOC*. DOC is not particularly concerned with glycogen storage, but instead with the maintenance of the proper balance of water and of mineral ions. It promotes increased reabsorption of salt in the kidney tubules, keeps potassium ions from leaving the cells to an undue extent, and maintains the proper volume of water outside the cells.

The corticoids have been divided into two groups: those which, like corticosterone and cortisone, possess an oxygen attached to carbon-11 are the *glycocorticoids* and are concerned with glycogen storage; those which, like DOC, do not possess an oxygen attached to carbon-11 are the *mineralocorticoids* and are concerned with the mineral balance.

The mineralocorticoids seem to be more immediately vital to life than are the glycocorticoids, for adrenalectomized rats are kept alive longer by the administration of DOC than by use of corticosterone.

In 1953, more than a decade after the discovery of four important glycocorticoids and two important mineralocorticoids, there came the rather surprising isolation of another mineralocorticoid. This was produced by the cortex in far smaller quantities than those previously discovered — which accounts for its late detection. However, it was also terrifically potent. Weight for weight, its efficiency in promoting the survival of an adrenalectomized rat was twenty-five times as great as was that of DOC.

This new mineralocorticoid had an unusual structure, too. In all other steroids, without exception, carbon-18 is attached to three hydrogen atoms, forming a *methyl group* (CH_3). In this new steroid, it was discovered, the carbon-18 is attached to a hydrogen and an oxygen. The resulting atom combination, -CHO, is called an *aldehyde group*, for reasons we need not go into. In consequence the new mineralocorticoid was named *aldosterone* (al-dos'ter-ohn).

Aldosterone is also unusual, for a mineralocorticoid, in possessing an oxygen at carbon-11. This, it would seem, should make it a glycocorticoid; but the aldehyde group making up carbon-18 has the ability to combine with the -OH group on carbon-11, a combination that neutralizes it, in effect. That, perhaps, is the particular importance of the unusual aldehyde group at carbon-18.

It might seem odd to put an oxygen at carbon-11 and then design the molecule in such a way as to neutralize it. Why not leave the oxygen off carbon-11 in the first place? Why this should be we cannot yet tell, but this point of putting the oxygen on, then neutralizing it, results in a mineralocorticoid that is much more powerful than any of those in which the oxygen is absent in the first place.

The various corticoids, singly and together, could be used in cases of adrenal cortical failure much as insulin is used in diabetes. This, nonetheless, would not suffice to make them nearly as important as insulin, for cortical troubles are by no means as common as diabetes.

However, after the isolation of the corticoids, their effects on various diseases of metabolism were inevitably studied. Hormones sometimes have such a wide variety of effects that one can never tell when one of them might not indirectly bring about at least a relief of symptoms, if not an actual cure. Nothing very startling was noted until 1948, when cortisone first became available in reasonable quantity. The American physician Philip Showalter Hench, working in Kendall's group, tried it on patients with rheumatoid arthritis. Surprisingly, it produced great relief.

This was something to crow about. Arthritis is a crippling disease and an extremely painful one. It can strike anyone, and there is no true cure. Anything that can relieve the pain and make it more possible to use the joints is to be hailed in glory even if it is not a cure. Hench shared the 1950 Nobel Prize in Medicine and Physiology with Kendall and Reichstein, in consequence.

Cortisone is also used to promote healing of skin lesions, in the treatment of gout, and as an anti-inflammatory drug. Despite all this, it has not attained the status of insulin as a savior of man. Cortisone, like the other corticoids, has a particularly complex effect on the body, and there is always the danger of undesirable side effects. Physicians must use it with caution; the more conservative ones prefer not to use it at all, if that use can be avoided.

Because the steroid molecule is a relatively simple one compared with molecules of even the smaller proteins, it has been possible to experiment a good deal with synthetic steroids, produced in the laboratory and not found in nature. To cite one case, a steroid that differs from the natural corticoids in possessing a fluorine atom attached to carbon-9 is an unusually active glycocorticoid, ten times as active as the natural ones. Unfortunately, its activity in bringing about undesirable side effects is also enhanced.

ACTH

The production of corticoids is not controlled by direct feedback as insulin is by the blood glucose level it controls, or parathyroid hormone by the blood calcium level it controls. Instead, as in the case of the thyroid hormone, a second gland must be called into the balance, and again it is the anterior pituitary.

In 1930 it was noticed that in animals from which the pituitary was removed, the adrenal cortex shriveled. Yet it has been found that when extracts from the anterior pituitary are injected into an animal the cholesterol concentration in the adrenal cortex drops precipitously, presumably because cholesterol is being used up in the manufacture of corticoids.

The connection is also made clear by the relationship of the pituitary to stress; that is, to sudden adverse changes in the environment of the body. Exposure to severe cold or to mechanical injury, to hemorrhage or to bacterial infection are all examples of stress. The body must shift balance radically to meet such changes and survive, and the burden of directing such changes seems to fall upon the corticoids. At least under stress the cholesterol content of the adrenal cortex falls, signifying that corticoids are being manufactured rapidly to meet the situation.

In an animal from which the anterior pituitary has been removed there is no such reaction to stress. Even if the adrenal cortex is still in working condition, nothing happens. Apparently, then, something among the anterior pituitary hormones stimulates the cortex.

The hormone that does so is named, very reasonably, the *adrenocorticotrophic hormone* (ad-ree′noh-kawr′tih-koh-troh′fic; "adrenal-nourishing" G) and is abbreviated, equally reasonably, as *ACTH*. In the late 1940's, when cortisone was found to be effective in combatting the painful symptoms of rheumatoid arthritis, ACTH was found to be likewise effective; not so much in itself as because it stimulated the adrenal cortex to form larger quantities of cortisone and other such hormones for itself. ACTH, like cortisone itself, made newspaper headlines and was on everybody's lips as a "wonder drug," particularly since in abbreviated form its name was so easy to rattle off.

Research into its molecular structure was carried on ardently, therefore, and by the early 1950's its molecular weight had been determined as 20,000. This is fairly large for a polypeptide hormone, and it was quickly found that if the isolated protein were subject to breakdown by acid or by enzyme it was possible to isolate molecular fragments which possessed full activity. These fragments are called *corticotropins*. One of them was found to contain 39 amino acids in the following sequence:

ser·tyr·ser·met·glu·his·phe·arg·try·gly·lys·pro·val·gly·lys·-
lys·arg·arg·pro·val·lys·val·tyr·pro·asp·gly·ala·glu·asp·-
gluNH₂·leu·ala·glu·ala·phe·pro·leu·glu·phe

CORTICOTROPIN

This corticotropin, obtained from the adrenals of swine, is still larger than it need be. A fragment consisting of the first 24 amino acids only is still fully active. In 1963 a 17-amino acid fragment was reported which had only 1/10 the corticoid-stimulating effect of natural ACTH but which still possessed certain other properties in full. Yet, if the serine group at the extreme left is removed, the loss of that one amino acid wipes out all activity.

The relationship between ACTH and the corticoids is analogous to that between TSH and the thyroid hormones. A fall in the corticoid levels of the blood below that required by the body stimulates the production of ACTH, which in turn raises corticoid production. Too high a corticoid level inhibits ACTH production, which in turn allows the corticoid level to drop.

Stress stimulates ACTH production, which in turn stimulates the production of corticoids. Stress does not affect the adrenal cortex directly. The stimulation of ACTH production by stress is mediated, it would seem, at least partly through the action of epinephrine (see pp. 376 ff.), which is secreted in response to some stressful situations. (This is another example of the complex way in which hormones mesh their labors.)

Where the pituitary (perhaps because of a tumorous overgrowth) produces a consistently too great quantity of ACTH, there is chronic overproduction of the corticoids and the condition that results has some symptoms similar to those of diabetes mellitus. The stimulation of glycocorticoid production produces a high blood-glucose level. The too great supply of glucose in the blood tends to be stored as fat, so sufferers from this disease tend to grow grotesquely obese. The first to describe the disease in detail was the American brain surgeon Harvey Cushing, and it has been called *Cushing's disease* ever since.

Similar symptoms can be produced where the tissue of the adrenal cortex is multiplied by a tumor of its own and begins to overproduce corticoids even without any encouragement from the pituitary. For reasons I shall explain on page 106, such adrenal tumors may bring on sexual precocity in children, or a marked increase in masculine characteristics in women, the latter condition being known as *virilism* ("man" L).

ACTH has the ability of influencing the skin pigmentation of animals, and even man is affected. As corticoid production falls with destruction of the adrenal cortex in Addison's disease, ACTH rises to considerable (but useless) heights. The pigmentation effect then produces the skin-darkening described on page 76.

Among the lower animals, particularly the amphibians, it was known that a special hormone existed which had its effect on pigment-producing cells and made it possible for such animals to darken many shades in a matter of minutes. The hormone is produced by the portion of the posterior lobe nearest the anterior lobe. Since this region is sometimes called the intermediate lobe, the hormone is named *intermedin*. For some years it was assumed that nothing like intermedin existed in mammals, but in 1955 biochemists at the University of Oregon were able to isolate from the mammalian pituitary a hormone that stimulated the activity of the *melanocytes* (mel'uh-noh-sites), which are the cells that produce the skin pigment melanin. The hormone was named *melanocyte-stimulating hormone*, in perfectly straightforward fashion, a name usually abbreviated as *MSH*. The molecule of the hormone, as obtained from swine pituitary, was found to consist of 18 amino acids in the following order:

asp·glu·gly·pro·tyr·lys·met·glu·his·phe·arg·try·gly·ser·-
pro·pro·lys·asp

MSH

If you compare the molecule of MSH with that of ACTH given on page 419, you will see that there is a seven-amino-acid sequence that the two hold in common: met·glu·his·phe·arg·try·gly.

The possession of this sequence in common may account for a certain overlapping of properties, as evidenced by the pigment-stimulating effect of ACTH. The production of MSH by the pituitary is, like the production of ACTH, stimulated by low corticoid levels. In Addison's disease both pituitary hormones are produced in higher than normal quantities and the MSH contributes even more to the skin-darkening than does the ACTH.

While we are on the subject of pigmentation, we can mention another small glandular organ that has several points of glamor and mystery about it. It is a conical reddish-gray body attached, like the pituitary, to the base of the brain. Because it vaguely resembles a pinecone in shape it is called the *pineal gland* (pin'ee-ul). It is smaller than the pituitary and is located on the other side of that portion of the brain which, extending downward, merges with the spinal cord. The pituitary lies to the front of this extension and the pineal to the rear; see illustration, page 382.

The pineal entered one period of glory in the early 17th century, when the influential French mathematician and philosopher René Descartes, under the impression that the pineal gland was found only in humans and never in the lower animals, maintained that this small scrap of tissue was the seat of the human soul. It was not long before this notion was put to rest, because the pineal occurs in all vertebrates, and is far more prominent in some than it is in man.

Much more exciting to the modern zoologist is the fact that the pineal was not always hidden deep in the skull as it is in human beings and in most modern-day vertebrates. There was a time, apparently, when the pineal was raised on a stalk and reached the top of the skull, there performing the function of a third eye, of all things. A primitive reptile on some small islands in the New Zealand area exists even today with such a "pineal eye" almost functional.

But turning to man, what is the function of the pineal? It seems glandular in structure, and when the hormones were being isolated and studied it was taken more or less for granted that there was a pineal hormone, too. However, as intense research failed to locate one doubts multiplied. Perhaps the pineal was merely a vestigial remnant of a onetime eye and has no function at all now; perhaps it is on its way out, like the vermiform appendix. The habit grew of denying it the very name "gland" and of speaking of it as the "pineal body."

The discoverers of MSH, having succeeded in one direction, took to investigating the pineal anew in the late 1950's. They worked with 200,000 beef pineals obtained from slaughterhouses and finally isolated a tiny quantity of substance that, on injection, lightened the skin of a tadpole. The substance, clearly a hormone and therefore worthy of restoring the name "gland" to the pineal, was named *melatonin*. Notwithstanding, the hormone does not appear to have any effect on human melanocytes.

5

OUR GONADS
AND GROWTH

The hormones I have thus far discussed (with the exception of the gastrointestinal hormones) have as their function the holding of the body's mechanism in one place, or, at the most, of allowing it to vary over a very restricted range. Insulin, glucagon, epinephrine, and the glycocorticoids all combine their efforts to keep glucose concentration in the blood within a narrow range of values designed to best meet the needs of the body. The parathyroid hormone calcitonin and vitamin D do the same for the calcium ion concentration in the blood. The mineralocorticoids do the same for mineral ions generally. Thyroid hormone does the same for the overall rate of metabolism. Vasopressin does the same for the body's water content.

And yet the human body is not entirely an equilibrium structure, shifting this way and that merely to keep its balance and remain in the same place. For at least part of our life we go through a long period of imbalance, in which the general trend is not cyclic but progressive; not back and forth, but onward and upward.

In short, a child must grow; and in that simple phrase there is a wealth of complexity of fact.

The growth of a single cell, although complex enough chemically, has its rather simple physical aspects. As more and more food is turned into cellular components of one sort or another, the volume of the cell increases, and the membrane swells outward. Eventually the difficulty of absorbing sufficient oxygen through the slowly expanding area of the membrane to maintain the rapidly expanding bulk of the cell interior sparks cell division.

In multicellular animals, however, there is an added dimension to growth. The individual cells making up the body do indeed grow and divide, but there must also be coordination involved. No group of cells must be allowed to outgrow the limits set down for it, and all growth must be neatly balanced between one set of cells and another, so that at all times each group of cells can perform its functions efficiently, without undue interference from the rest.

In the human being, for example, some cells, such as those of the nervous system, do not multiply at all after birth. Other cells grow and multiply only in response to some out-of-the-ordinary need, as when bone cells will spring into action to heal a broken clavicle or when liver cells will suddenly resume rapid multiplication to replace a portion of a liver cut away by the surgeon's knife. (This is called *regeneration.*) Then, too, there are cells that continue to grow and multiply unceasingly throughout life, however extended that life might be. The best examples are the cells of the skin, which continue throughout life to reproduce and multiply in order to form the dead but protective epidermis — forever sloughed away and forever renewed.

This process of coordinated growth requires the most delicate and subtle adjustment of chemical mechanisms. One measure of the subtlety of these mechanisms is the fact that biochemists have not yet discovered the essential chemical steps initiating growth and keeping it under control. If this is ruled out as too subjective a measure, another form of evidence of the delicate complexity of the process is the unfortunate ease with which it can go out of order, allowing one batch of cells or another to involve itself suddenly in uncontrolled growth.

Uncontrolled growth is not necessarily rapid or wild; the danger lies in the mere fact of its being uncontrolled — in that the mechanisms ordinarily calling it to a halt are no longer in action. The cells growing in uncontrolled fashion do so indefinitely, burdening the body with their unnecessary weight, drowning out neighboring tissues, and gradually preventing them from carrying out their normal functions, in consequence outgrowing their own blood supply and sickening. The wild cells may break off sometimes and be carried by the bloodstream to another part of the body where they may take root and carry on their anarchic activity.

Any abnormal growth, anywhere in the body, is referred to as a *tumor* ("swelling" L). Sometimes the abnormal growth is restricted, forming warts or wens which may be unsightly and inconvenient but are not generally dangerous to life. Such tumors are *benign tumors* (bih-nine'; "good" L). Where the abnormal growth is not restricted but continues indefinitely, and in particular where it invades normal tissues, it is said to be *malignant* ("evil" L). Galen, a physician of Roman times, described a malignant tumor of the breast which distended nearby veins until the whole figure looked like a crab with its legs jutting out in all directions. Since that time, malignant tumors have been referred to as *cancers* ("crab" L).

Cancer has become far more common in our times than ever in the past, for three reasons. First, methods of diagnosis have improved, so that when a person dies of cancer, we know it and don't put the death down to some other reason. Second, the incidence of many other disorders, particularly infectious diseases, has been lowered drastically in the past century. Therefore, a number of people who in times past would have died of diphtheria, typhoid fever, cholera, or the like now live long enough to fall prey to cancer. Third, there are environmental conditions newly inflicted upon us by our advancing technology which are known to induce cancer, or are suspected of doing so. Among these are the radiations of X-rays and radioactive substances, various synthetic

chemicals, atmospheric pollution through coal smoke and automobile exhaust, and even inhaled tobacco smoke.

However, let us return to normal growth —

In view of the fact that hormones so delicately control the chemical processes within the body, it would be very strange if one or
more did not control this all-important phenomenon of growth.
It is another aspect of the universal nature of growth that it is here,
more than anywhere else, where we are conscious of hormones
even in the plant kingdom.

Growth in plants is far less bound within limits than is growth in
animals. The limbs of an animal grow in fixed numbers and in
fixed shape and size. The limbs of a tree, in contrast, grow in comparatively wide variety, neither fixed in numbers nor shape nor
size. And yet, even among plants controls are necessary.

Substances capable of accelerating plant growth when present
in solution in very small concentration were first isolated in pure
form in 1935. They were named *auxins* ("to increase" G). The
best-known of these auxins is a compound called *indolyl-3-acetic
acid*, commonly abbreviated *IAA*. It is another of the hormones
that are actually modified amino acids in structure. In this case,
the amino acid involved (and from which the plant cells manufacture IAA) is tryptophan:

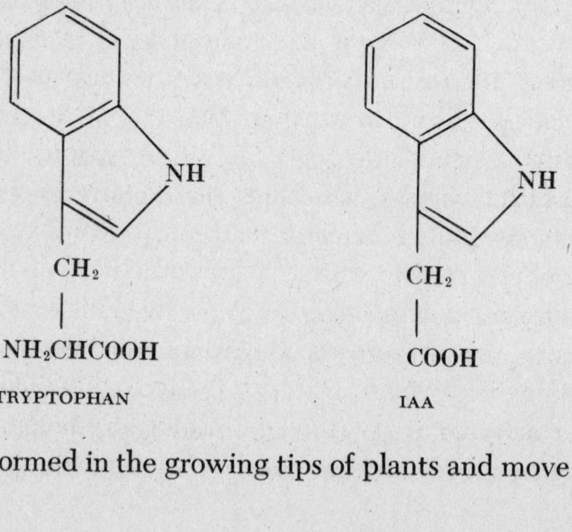

$$CH_2$$
$$|$$
$$NH_2CHCOOH$$
TRYPTOPHAN

$$CH_2$$
$$|$$
$$COOH$$
IAA

Auxins are formed in the growing tips of plants and move downward. They bring about an elongation of cells rather than actual cell division. Many of the movements of plants are governed by the distribution of these auxins. For instance, they are present in higher concentration on the side of the stem away from the sun. This side of the stem will elongate and the stem will therefore bend in the direction of the sun. In the same way, auxins will concentrate on the lower side of a stem held horizontally, curving the tip upward.

Plant hormones, like hormones generally, can cause disorders when present in excess. One of the most powerful of the auxins was discovered through studies of a plant disease. Japanese farmers cultivating rice plants had often observed that certain shoots would for no clear reason suddenly extend themselves high in the air, becoming weakened and useless. The Japanese referred to this as *bakanae,* which in English means (rather charmingly) "foolish seedling." In 1926 a Japanese plant pathologist noticed that such lengthened shoots were fungus-infested. A dozen years of work finally resulted in the isolation in 1938 of growth-stimulating compounds from the fungus. The particular fungus at fault belongs to the genus *Gibberella,* so the compound was named *gibberellin* (jib'ur-el'in).

The structure of the gibberellins (for there are a number of closely related varieties), worked out in 1956, is quite complicated, the molecule being made up of five rings of atoms. Gibberellins have been isolated from certain types of beans; this shows that they occur naturally in at least some plants and may therefore qualify as auxins. They (and plant hormones generally) can be used to hasten the process of germination, of flowering and fruiting. In short, they can race plants through life — to our advantage, of course.

Auxinlike compounds can also race plants through life to death — again to our advantage. There is a synthetic molecule, called *2,4-dichlorophenoxyacetic acid,* usually abbreviated as *2,4-D,* that has auxinlike properties. Sprayed upon plants, it encourages a too rapid and too disorganized growth, killing them through what practically amounts to an induced cancer. Plants with broad leaves absorb more of such a spray than those with narrow leaves, and the former are therefore killed by a concentration of 2,4-D that leaves the latter unaffected. It often happens that the plants man wishes to cultivate, such as the various grasses and grains, are narrow-leaved, whereas the intruding and unwanted plants ("weeds"), which compete for sun and water with our pets, are broad-leaved. For this reason, 2,4-D has gained fame in recent years as an effective weed killer.

There are also plant hormones that accelerate actual cell division in otherwise mature and nondividing cells. This is useful whenever new tissue growth is necessary to cover externally caused damage. Compounds bringing about such repair-growth are called, dramatically, *wound hormones*. One example of these, a compound with a molecule composed of a chain of 12 carbon atoms, with a carboxyl group (-COOH) at each end and a double bond between carbon-2 and carbon-3, is called *traumatic acid* (troh-mat'ik; "wound" G).

GROWTH HORMONE

As for animals — and of course for the human being in particular — it is difficult to pin a complex phenomenon such as growth down to a single hormone. The misfunctioning of any hormone insofar as it upsets the body's chemical mechanisms is going to interfere with growth to some extent. The most extreme example I have mentioned is that of the thyroid hormone, the absence of which in children produces the dwarfish cretin.

Naturally, then, one would expect the pituitary, which works in conjunction with several glands (the thyroid and adrenal cortex have already been pointed out) to have an effect on growth. As a matter of fact, it was noted as long ago as 1912 that an animal from which the pituitary had been removed ceased growing. What is more, this pituitary effect is not entirely due to the atrophy of other glands brought about by the loss of certain hormones of the anterior lobe. In the 1920's and 1930's, pituitary extracts were prepared which, when injected into growing rats and dogs, caused growth to continue past normal and produced giant animals. Furthermore, these extracts could be purified to the point where such components as ACTH and TSH were definitely missing and where, indeed, no other glands were affected. The pituitary was doing it all on its own.

Apparently the anterior pituitary produces a hormone that does not act upon other glands (the only pituitary hormone not to do so) but upon the body's tissues directly, accelerating growth. The name for this substance in plain English is *growth hormone*. It may also be called, with a more scholarly tang, *somatotrophic hormone* (soh'muh-toh-troh'fik; "body-nourishing" G), which is in turn abbreviated, usually, *STH*.

The structure of the growth hormone is less well known than that of some of the other pituitary hormones. The hormone obtained from cattle is rather large for a protein hormone and has a molecular weight of 45,000. The molecule seems to be made up of some 370 amino acids arranged in two chains. Ordinarily, protein hormones obtained from different species of vertebrates may differ in minor ways and yet remain functional across the species lines. Thus insulin from cattle is slightly different from that of swine and yet both will substitute for human insulin with equal efficiency. Growth hormone obtained from cattle or swine, however, is without effect on man. Man is affected only (as far as is known) by growth hormone obtained from man himself and from monkeys. The molecules of such primate growth hormones have molecular weights of only 25,000 or so. It seems probable that the molecules of any growth hormone so far obtained could be broken down substantially without loss of biological activity.

Growth hormone has several overall effects on metabolism (though, of course, the exact details of its chemical effects are unknown). One of these is to accelerate the conversion of amino acids to protein, a natural accompaniment of any process that is to bring about growth. In addition, an oversupply of growth hormone administered to experimental animals increases glucose concentration in the blood and diminishes insulin. This may be because the wildly growing animal places so many demands on the energy mechanisms of the body that the insulin-producing cells wear out and die, leaving a more or less permanent diabetes behind.

Growth hormone encourages the enlargement of bones in all dimensions. Usually the secretion of growth hormone is high during childhood and youth, when the body (and skeleton in particular) is growing, and tapers off in late adolescence, when growth itself tapers off in consequence. If the secretion of growth hormone by the pituitary is less than normal during youth the bones cease growth prematurely, and the result is a midget. Such midgets (sometimes reaching heights of only 3 feet or even less), produced by underproduction of growth hormone, retain their proper proportions and, although retaining a childlike cast of features, are not deformed, grotesque, or mentally retarded. In some cases they even attain sexual maturity and become miniature but fully adult human beings. The most famous midget of this sort was Charles Sherwood Stratton, who was made famous by P. T. Barnum as "Tom Thumb." He was about 3 feet tall, but perfectly proportioned. He died in 1883 at the age of 45.

An oversupply of growth hormone during youth, or a supply that does not taper off appropriately with age, results in overgrowth and giantism. A recent example, which made the newspapers regularly, was that of Robert Wadlow, born in Alton, Illinois, in 1918. He grew with remarkable speed. There are pictures of him as a boy showing him head and shoulders taller than his normally sized father but with boyish features and proportions. He finally attained a height of 8 feet 9½ inches before dying at the age of 22.

It sometimes happens that the pituitary of an adult, who has achieved his full measurements and has ceased growing long since, begins to produce an oversupply of growth hormone. The bones have ossified and can no longer grow in proper proportions. Despite this, the ends of some of the bones at the body extremities still possess the capacity for growth, and these respond. The hands and feet enlarge, therefore, as do the bones of the face, particularly of the lower jaw. The result of this condition, which is called *acromegaly* (ak'roh-meg'uh-lee; "large extremities" G), is a rather grotesque distortion of features.

METAMORPHOSIS

Growth is not merely a process in which each organ lengthens and widens and thickens in proportion. In the course of the life of most creatures there come periods where qualitative changes take place as well as quantitative ones. Where such sudden qualitative changes are very marked, amounting to a radical alteration in the overall shape and structure of the creature, the process is referred to as a *metamorphosis* ("transform" G). It would be natural to expect a metamorphosis to take place under the control of one or more hormones. Among the vertebrates the most common example of metamorphosis is that by which a tadpole turns into a frog; and, as a matter of fact, I pointed out in Chapter 3 that this is mediated by thyroid hormone.

Metamorphosis also takes place among a number of invertebrate groups, notably among the insects, where the caterpillar-butterfly conversion is at least as spectacular and well known as the tadpole-frog conversion. In insects in the larval stage (as in caterpillars), growth takes place, so to speak, in jumps. The external skeleton prevents the smooth enlargement that is so characteristic of the growth of the soft-surfaced vertebrates. Instead, every once in a while the horny outer coat of the insect splits and then a new and larger coat is formed, one large enough to allow a spurt of growth. This business of exchanging an old shell for a new and larger one is commonly called *molting* ("change" L). A less common word for the process is *ecdysis* (ek'dih-sis; "get out" G).

Insect molting is controlled by a hormone produced by a gland located in the forward portion of the thorax and therefore called the *prothoracic gland*. This gland apparently produces a hormone named *ecdysone* (ek'dih-sohn), which is stored in a small organ near the heart. The action of a group of cells in the brain causes the organ to release some of the stored ecdysone periodically and this stimulates a molt. Ecdysone therefore is sometimes called *molting hormone*.

After a number of such molts, the young of many insect species enter a quiescent stage during which metamorphosis takes place. As a result of radical changes, an adult, sexually mature insect is formed. The caterpillar, encircling itself with a cocoon and becoming a butterfly, is, as I said before, the most familiar case.

But after which particular molt in the larval stage does the metamorphosis take place? One might think that this would be determined by a hormone that is secreted at the proper time, neutralizing ecdysone, ending the molts, and initiating metamorphosis. Instead, it is the reverse that takes place. A hormone is continuously secreted by a pair of glands in the head. This *prevents* metamorphosis and keeps the larva molting and growing. Once the formation of this hormone decreases and its concentration falls below a certain point, the next molt is then followed by metamorphosis.

Since this metamorphosis-preventing hormone keeps the insect in the larval form, it is called the *larval hormone*, or even the *juvenile hormone*. (There is something fascinating about the term "juvenile hormone" that brings to mind vague glimmers of thought concerning the fountain of youth; needless to say, these insect hormones are without effect on the human being.) So far, chemists have not worked out the structure of any of the insect hormones.

Human beings do not undergo metamorphosis in the sense that tadpoles and caterpillars do, and yet there are marked changes that do appear in adolescence as a boy becomes a man and a girl becomes a woman. They may not be as drastic as the change from water-breathing to air-breathing, or from crawling to flying, but it is not altogether unspectacular when the smooth cheeks of a boy begin to sprout a beard and when the flat chest of a girl begins to bulge with paired breasts.

These changes, associated with sexual maturity but not directly involved in the processes of reproduction, are referred to as the development of the *secondary sexual characteristics*. Such development represents a very mild human metamorphosis. It is to be expected that it is under the control of a hormone or hormones.

Occasionally in the past there were speculations as to the effect on adolescence, and the changes that took place at this time, of the *thymus gland* (from a Greek word of uncertain derivation). The thymus gland lies in the upper chest, in front of the lungs and above the heart, extending upward into the neck. In children, it is soft and pink, with many lobes, and is fairly large. When the age of 12 is attained it may reach a weight of 40 grams (or about 1½ ounces). With puberty, however, as the signs of adulthood begin to appear, the thymus begins to shrink. In the adult it is represented by no more than a small patch of fat and fiber.

One is tempted to think that the thymus might produce some secretion which, like the juvenile hormone of insects, keeps a child from maturing. It would then be the disappearance of the hormone (as the gland shrivels) that would bring about the onset of puberty. However, even the most intense investigation has brought to light no such hormone. The removal of the thymus in experimental animals does not bring on sudden maturity, and the injection of thymus extracts in young animals does not delay maturity. Consequently, that theory has been abandoned.

A second possibility arises from the fact that the thymus is composed of lymphoid tissue, very like that of the spleen, the tonsils, and the lymph nodes. It has seemed possible, therefore, that the thymus shared the functions of such lymphoid tissue and, one way or another, combatted bacterial infection. It might produce antibodies (protein molecules specifically designed to neutralize bacteria, bacterial toxins, or viruses), and if so, that is very important, for these antibodies are of prime importance in the body's mechanisms of immunity to disease.

This theory received strong support in 1962. Jacques F. A. P. Miller at the Chester Beatty Research Institute in London has shown that not only does the thymus produce antibodies but it is the first organ to do so. With time, the cells of the thymus migrate to other sites such as the lymph nodes. The thymus degenerates at puberty, then, not because its function is gone but because it has, in a sense, spread itself through the body.

In support of this notion is the fact that mice from which the thymus was removed very soon after birth died after several months, the various tissues engaged in immunological mechanisms being undeveloped. Where the thymus was removed only after the animals were three weeks old, there were no bad effects. By that time enough of the thymus had migrated to ensure the capacity of the animal to protect itself against germ invasion. Evidently this spreading out of the thymus is accelerated by the same hormones that bring about puberty, which is why the thymus shrinks rapidly after the age of 12 or 13.

Removal of the thymus in very young mice also makes it possible for the creature to accept skin grafts from other animals. These would ordinarily be rejected through the development of antibodies against the "foreign protein" of the skin graft. If thymus glands from other animals are inserted into such mice, they regain the antibody-manufacturing (and graft-resisting) ability. If the thymus inserts are from another strain of mice, skin grafts from that other strain will still be accepted. There is a distant hope here that someday techniques involving thymus grafts may make it easier to graft tissues and organs on human patients.

ANDROGENS

The organs directly connected with the appearance of secondary sexual characteristics are those which produce the cells essential to reproduction — the sperm-producing organs (testicles) in the male and the egg-producing organs (ovaries) in the female. These are grouped under the name of *gonads* (gon′adz; "that which generates" G). A more common name for them is *sex glands*. The connection between the gonads and the changes associated with puberty would seem a logical one, and might be accepted even without evidence. However, logic-minus-evidence has proved insidiously deceiving many times in the history of science. Fortunately there is ample evidence on the side of logic in this connection, evidence dating from prehistoric times.

Sometime before the dawn of history, the early herdsmen discovered, perhaps through accident at first, that a male animal from which the testicles were removed in youth (*castration*) developed quite differently from one that retained its testicles. The castrated animal was not fertile and, indeed, showed no interest in sexual activity. Furthermore, it tended to put on fat, so its meat was both tenderer and tastier than that of the uncastrated male. Additionally, it developed a placid, stolid disposition, which made the animal much easier to handle and easier to put to work than the uncastrated male would be. Through castration the savage bull becomes the slow-moving ox, the fierce stallion becomes the patient gelding, and the stringy rooster becomes the fat capon.

It would be naïve, alas, to expect that such a procedure should not be applied by man to his fellowman. A castrated man is a *eunuch* (yoo′nook; "to guard the bed" G), so called because his chief function was to serve as guard in the harem of rich men who needed wardens incapable of taking undue advantage of their ordinarily enviable position.

Where castration is performed in childhood, before the development of the male secondary sexual characteristics, those characteristics do not develop. The eunuch does not grow a beard and remains generally unhairy, although he retains the hair of his head and virtually never grows bald. (Baldness in males is in part a secondary sexual characteristic and bears a relationship to the male sex hormone concentration in the blood — although it is possible, and even very common, to be amply virile without being bald.)

The eunuch also retains the small larynx of the child, so his voice remains high and womanish. In Christian times, when polygamy and harems were frowned upon, eunuchs were still valued for their soprano voices, and such singers (called castratos) were renowned in the early days of opera. They were also used in choirs. It was not until 1878 that Pope Leo XIII abolished the inhuman custom of manufacturing eunuchs for use in the papal choir.

The eunuch puts on fat in feminine distribution, lacks a sexual drive, and develops (perhaps through association with women in the harem) the personality traits we ordinarily associate with women. His intelligence is not affected, however. The sly and intriguing court eunuch is a staple of historical fiction, and at least one eunuch, the Byzantine general Narses, was an able administrator and general, capable in his seventies of defeating the Goths and Franks in Italy.

With the close of the 19th century and the beginning of the 20th, chemists began to work with extracts of the testicles and found that changes occurring after castration (in experimental animals) could be prevented by injection of such extracts. Capons, in this way, could be made to grow the lordly comb of the intact rooster.

As knowledge of hormones developed, it became quite clear that the testicles, in addition to producing sperm cells, produced hormones capable of initiating the formation of secondary sexual characteristics. These were called *androgens* (an'droh-jenz; "male-producing" G) and may also be called the *testicular hormones* or the *male sex hormones*.

In the early 1930's, compounds with androgenic properties were isolated and proved to be steroids. This was accomplished chiefly through the labors of the German chemist Adolf Butenandt, who, as a result, shared the Nobel Prize in Chemistry for

1939 with the Yugoslav-born Swiss chemist Leopold Ruzicka, another worker in the field. (Butenandt was forbidden by the Nazi government to accept the Nobel Prize and was unable to do so until 1949, after a war which he survived and the Nazi government did not.) Two well-known androgens are *andros-terone* (an-dros'tur-ohn) and *testosterone* (tes-tos'tur-ohn). The formulas are given below:

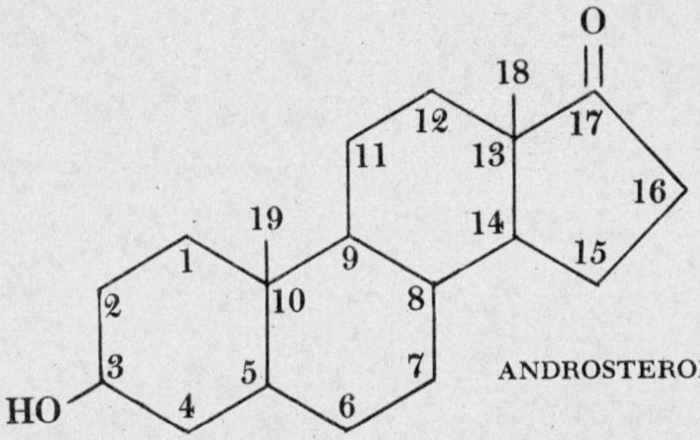

ANDROSTERONE

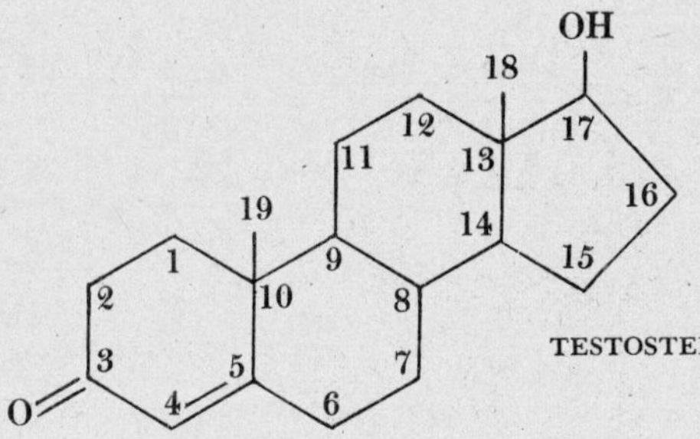

TESTOSTERONE

The androgens differ from the other steroids I have discussed in this book chiefly in lacking altogether the carbon-chain attachment at carbon-17. (You may remember that cholesterol has an eight-carbon chain attached at that site, bile acids a five-carbon chain, and corticoids a two-carbon chain.)

The androgens have an effect similar to growth hormone in that they somehow encourage the formation of protein from amino acids. However, growth hormone does this generally throughout the body, whereas the androgens do so, for the most

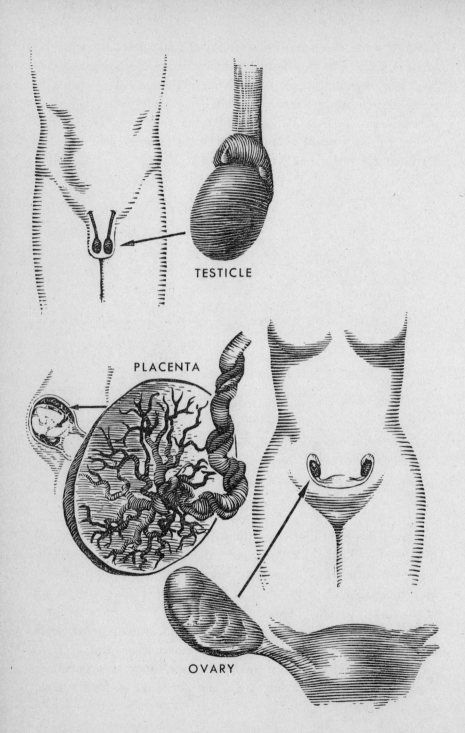

TESTICLE

PLACENTA

OVARY

part, locally and selectively, so those organs associated with reproduction or with the secondary sexual characteristics are chiefly involved. A general effect is not altogether absent. Until puberty boys and girls are not very different in size and weight, but after puberty, with androgens pouring into the blood, the male grows larger and more muscular than the female.

Testosterone is about ten times as active as androsterone; that is, it will produce equivalent effects in one-tenth the dose. An androgen more potent than testosterone does not occur naturally, but has been prepared in the laboratory. It is *methyltestosterone*, which differs from testosterone in that a one-carbon methyl group ($-CH_3$) is attached to carbon-17 in addition to the hydroxyl group already present.

It is also possible to prepare synthetic androgens that retain the general protein-forming property and not the specialized masculinizing one. An example is 19-*nortestosterone*, which differs from ordinary testosterone in that carbon-19 is missing.

ESTROGENS

At about the same time that the hormones produced by the testicles were being studied, those produced by the ovaries in females were isolated. Since ovaries are located well within the pelvic region and are not conveniently exposed as the testicles are, early man had far less experience with ovariectomy (removal of the ovaries) than with castration. Nowadays, however, ovariectomies conducted on young experimental animals result in the suppression of female secondary sexual characteristics and there is no doubt that there are *female sex hormones* (or *ovarian hormones*) analogous to the male androgens.

Extracts containing these hormones caused female rats to become eager to accept the sexual attentions of the male of the species. Ordinarily this took place only at periodic intervals when the female rat was "in heat," or, to use the more classical term, in *estrus* ("frenzy" G). The female sex hormones were therefore named *estrogens* (es'troh-jenz; "estrus-producing" G) and most of the individual hormones contain the letter-combination "estr" in their names. (The androgens and estrogens together may be referred to simply as *sex hormones.*)

The estrogens differ from the androgens chiefly in that ring A (the one at the lower left of the steroid nucleus) possesses three double bonds. This makes it a "benzene ring," in chemical language. Carbon-10, as you will see in the formula below, has all four of its bonds in use. Two lead to carbon-5, one to carbon-1, and one to carbon-9. No bond is available for the usual attachment of carbon-19 at that point and so that carbon is missing. (The compound, 19-nortestosterone, defined above, also has carbon-19 missing but it is not an estrogen. It lacks the necessary three double bonds in ring A.)

One of the best-known of the estrogens is *estrone* (es'trohn), which possesses the following formula:

ESTRONE

Two others are *estradiol* (es'truh-dy'ole), in which both oxygen atoms form part of -OH groups, and *estriol* (es'tree-ole), in which a third -OH group is attached to carbon-16.

As in the case of the androgens, the most powerful estrogens are synthetic. Thus, there is 17-*ethynylestradiol*, in which a two-carbon chain is attached to carbon-17 in addition to the hydroxyl group. This two-carbon chain possesses a triple bond and is called an *ethynyl group* (eth'in-il), which accounts for the name of the compound. Taken orally, 17-ethynylestradiol will produce the effects of the natural estrogens in one-tenth the dose.

Another synthetic estrogen is *stilbestrol* (stil-bes'trole), so called because it is related to an organic chemical called "stilbene"). It is not quite as powerful as 17-ethynylestradiol, but it is three to five times as powerful as the natural hormones. Stilbestrol is unusual in that it is not a steroid. This is useful, too, since its molecule is far easier to synthesize than the molecule of a steroid would be. Hence stilbestrol is cheaper and more easily available than either the natural or synthetic steroid estrogens.

The estrogens and androgens are quite similar in chemical structure. The molecule of estrone, for instance, differs from that of androsterone only in the presence of three double bonds and in the absence of carbon-19. Such a similarity in structure might seem by "common-sense" reasoning to imply a similarity in function. Nevertheless, it frequently happens in biochemical reactions that a particular compound will inhibit (that is, slow down or even stop) the working of a very similar compound by competing with it for union with a particular enzyme. The enzyme cannot, in effect, distinguish between the proper compound and the very similar inhibitor. The extent to which the enzyme will work and therefore possibly the entire course of metabolism will depend on slight changes in the relative concentrations of the two similar compounds. This is called *competitive inhibition.*

The two groups of sex hormones, so similar in structure, may very likely compete for the same spot on the cell membranes. The course of metabolism would then shift drastically in one direction or the other, depending on which group of hormones is predominant and wins the competition.

The effects of estrogens and androgens are opposed, and adding one is much like subtracting the other. To illustrate: the injection of estrogens will caponize a rooster just as castration (removal of androgens) will. And, predictably, the injection of androgens will have much the same effect on a female animal as an ovariectomy would. This is useful in the treatment of certain diseases involving the tissues most affected by these hormones. Estrogens have in this way been used to treat cancer of the prostate. Androgens stimulate the growth of the prostate and estrogens inhibit that growth even, sometimes, when the growth is cancerous.

The androgens and estrogens are so closely related chemically that it is perhaps unreasonable to expect that an organ capable of producing one should not be also capable of producing the other. Indeed, both testicles and ovaries produce hormones of each variety. A male is male not because he produces only androgens but only because he produces mostly androgens. The same, in reverse, is true of the female. Masculinity can be accentuated not merely by increasing the quantity of androgens produced but by getting rid, with increased efficiency, of any estrogens that are produced. Thus, a rich source of estrogen is the urine of the stallion.

One gland besides the gonads produces steroid hormones. That gland, the adrenal cortex, also produces sex hormones, and especially androgens. It is for this reason that a tumor of the cortex, leading to the overproduction of its steroids, does have a strongly masculinizing effect on women.

The business of being a female is in many ways more complicated than that of being a male. Once a male has attained sexual maturity, he continues on an even keel, producing sperm cells in regular fashion. The adult female, in contrast, undergoes a complicated sexual cycle in which an egg cell is produced every four weeks or so. The changes involved in this process are brought about by the action of a particular hormone. It seems reasonable that the very structure that produces the egg cell also produces the hormone.

The egg cell is produced by a follicle in the ovary, which, after it has reached pinhead size and ruptured (thus allowing the egg cell to escape into the Fallopian tubes, which lead to the uterus), turns reddish yellow. It becomes the *corpus luteum* ("orange-yellow body" L), and it is this which produces the hormone.

The first action of the hormone of the corpus luteum is to stimulate the growth of the inner lining of the uterus, preparing it for the reception of the fertilized egg. Since it thus paves the way for pregnancy, the hormone was first named *progestin* (prohjes'tin; "before pregnancy" L). When the hormone was shown to be a steroid, its name was altered to *progesterone*.

Progesterone resembles the corticoids more than it does the estrogens. Like the corticoids it has a 2-carbon chain attached to carbon-17, and it lacks the benzene ring of the estrogens. The chief difference between progesterone and the corticoids is that the latter have a hydroxyl group on carbon-21, whereas progesterone does not. As a matter of fact, except for that missing hydroxyl group, progesterone has precisely the formula of deoxycorticosterone (DOC); see page 415. But the one missing oxygen atom makes all the difference as far as function is concerned.

If the egg cell is not fertilized, the corpus luteum withers away and progesterone ceases to be formed. The lining of the uterus, with its blood supply, is sloughed off, and the menstrual period is the result. Some two weeks later there is another ovulation and the uterus is prepared for another egg cell and another try. If the egg cell is fertilized, then it embeds itself in the lining of the uterus, which is maintained by the continuing existence of the corpus luteum and the hormone it produces. Progesterone not only maintains the lining but also stimulates the formation of the placenta, the organ through which the developing embryo is fed. The role of progesterone in this respect has been made clear through work with experimental animals. If the ovaries of a rabbit are removed shortly after it has become pregnant, the embryo is not retained and there is an abortion. If extracts from the corpus luteum are injected into such ovariectomized animals, however, pregnancy can be made to continue normally to its natural conclusion.

Yet once the placenta (see p. 438) is formed, it too produces progesterone, supplementing that of the corpus luteum, which continues to flourish and to increase in size until the later months

of pregnancy. In late pregnancy, with the placenta well established and its progesterone supply ample, the removal of the
ovaries will no longer affect pregnancy.

Obviously, during the period of pregnancy, the ordinary cycle
of egg cell production must be interrupted. It is part of the effect
of progesterone to put a stop to the steady production of eggs
at the rate of one every four weeks, at least for the duration of
the pregnancy.

This has suggested a method for the development of oral contraceptives. Compounds having the effect of progesterone but
capable of easy synthesis in the laboratory might render a woman
infertile. If it could be shown that there were no undesirable
side effects and if the conscientious objections of various religious
groups could be overcome, this could become the most practical
method for controlling the present-day overrapid expansion of
population. Actually, such progesterone analogs have been manufactured and have passed many tests successfully.

GONADOTROPHINS

As with the corticoids and with thyroxine, there is an interplay
between the various sex hormones and the pituitary. This can
easily be shown to be so, because if the pituitary is removed from
an experimental animal the sex glands atrophy and pregnancy
will not take place, or will end in abortion if already under way.
Then, too, lactation, if under way, will cease.

There turned out, not surprisingly, to be several different hormones produced by the anterior pituitary gland which affected
sexual development. Each had its specialized function, but they
are lumped together (along with substances of similar effect produced by other organs) as *gonadotrophins* (gon'uh-doh-troh'finz;
"gonad-nourishing" G). One of these gonadotrophins has as a
noticeable effect the stimulation of the growth of the follicles of
the ovary, preparing them for the production of egg cells. It is
therefore called the *follicle-stimulating hormone*, usually abbrevi-

ated *FSH*. Don't suppose, though, that this hormone has a function only in the female. In the male it stimulates the epithelium of the portions of the testicles that produce sperm cells.

A second hormone takes over where FSH leaves off. In the female it stimulates the final ripening of the follicles, their rupture to release the egg, and the conversion of the ruptured follicle into the corpus luteum. It is therefore called *luteinizing hormone*, usually abbreviated as *LH*. In the male this hormone stimulates those cells which form testosterone. Such cells (as well as analogous cells in the ovary, also stimulated by the hormone) are called "interstitial cells." For that reason a second name for the luteinizing hormone is *interstitial cell-stimulating hormone*, or *ICSH*.

This second name, although longer, would seem more reasonable. Otherwise there would be confusion with the third of the pituitary gonadotrophins, which carries on the work of the second, acting to maintain the corpus luteum, once formed, and to stimulate the production of progesterone. This third hormone is therefore the *luteotrophic hormone*. It has functions for the period following the completion of pregnancy, since it cooperates with the estrogens in stimulating the growth of the breast and the production of milk. This function was discovered before the effect of the hormone on the corpus luteum was worked out. Older names for it are *lactogenic hormone* (lak'toh-jen'ik; "milk-producing," a word of mixed Greek and Latin origin) and *prolactin* ("prior to milk" L).

Prolactin stimulated other post-pregnancy activities. Young female rats injected with the hormone would busy themselves with nest-building even though they had not given birth. On the other hand, mice whose pituitaries had been removed shortly before giving birth to young exhibited little interest in the baby mice. The newspapers at once termed prolactin the "mother-love hormone."

The interplay between the estrogens (or androgens) and the various pituitary gonadotrophins is exceedingly complex; the network of effect and countereffect has not yet been entirely worked out. In general, the gonadotrophin production is stimulated by a low concentration of sex hormones in the blood and inhibited by a high one.

A more direct influence, on prolactin at least, is the stimulating effect of suckling. This increases prolactin production and, therefore, milk secretion. Undoubtedly the occasional news reports of increased milk production by dairy cattle when soft music is played in the stalls is due to the stimulation of prolactin secretion by any environmental factor that brings on a sensation of well-being and freedom from insecurity.

Because of this interrelationship between the pituitary and the gonads, the failure of the pituitary to hold up its end is as surely asexualizing as castration or ovariectomy would be. Such pituitary failure in young produces dwarfism, a tendency to gross obesity, and arrested sexual development. The symptoms were described in 1901 by an Austrian neurologist named Alfred Fröhlich, and the condition has been called *Fröhlich's syndrome* ever since. (Syndrome, from Greek words meaning "to run with," is a term applied to a collection of symptoms of widely different character which occur together in a particular disorder — which run with each other, so to speak.)

Of the three gonadotrophins of the pituitary, lactogenic hormone is the only one to have been isolated in reasonably pure form. All are proteins, of course, (the pituitary gland produces only proteins) with molecular weights running from 20,000 to 100,000. Such preparations of FSH and ICSH as have been studied seem to contain sugars as part of the molecule, but whether these sugars are essential to the action is not yet certain.

The placenta produces a gonadotrophin of its own that is not quite like those of the pituitary. It is called *human chorionic gonadotrophin,* usually abbreviated *HCG.* ("Chorion" [kaw'ree-on] is the name, from the Greek, for the membranes surrounding the embryo.) As early as two to four weeks after the beginning of pregnancy, HCG is already produced in large enough quantities to give rise to the problem of its removal. At least some of it is excreted in the urine. The urinary content of HCG rises to a peak during the second month of pregnancy.

HCG can produce changes in experimental animals that would ordinarily be expected of the pituitary gonadotrophins. If the injection of extracts of a woman's urine into mice, frogs, or rabbits produces such effects, it is a clear sign that HCG is present and that the woman is therefore in the early stages of pregnancy. This forms the basis for the various now routine pregnancy tests that can give a reasonably certain decision weeks before the doctor could otherwise tell by less subtle examinations.

6

OUR NERVES

Throughout the first five chapters of this book I have described the manner in which the complex activities of the body are coordinated by means of the production and destruction of certain complex molecules, sometimes working in coordination and sometimes in balanced opposition, and achieving their effects (probably, though not certainly) by their addition to and alteration of the cell membrane. This form of coordination, present from the very beginning of life, is useful and practical but it is slow. Hormone action must wait on the chemical construction of molecules, on the piling together of atom upon atom. The product must then be secreted into the bloodstream and carried by that fluid to every point in the body, even though it may only be useful at one particular point. Then, its mission done, the hormone must be pulled apart and inactivated (usually in the liver) and its remnants must be filtered out of the body by the kidneys.

There is, however, an entirely different form of coordination that represents an advance in subtlety, efficiency, and speed. It is not complex molecules, but single atoms and particles far smaller than atoms. These atoms and other particles are not carried by the bloodstream; they move along special channels at velocities considerably greater than those at which the viscous blood can be forced through small vessels. These channels, fur-

448

thermore, lead from (or to) specific organs so that this form of coordination, electric in nature, will stimulate a certain organ and do so exclusively, without the fuzzy broadcasting of side effects that often accompany hormone action.

The difference in the seeming intensity of life between plants and animals is due mainly to the fact that animals have this electrical form of coordination in addition to the chemical, whereas plants have only the chemical. But let's start at the beginning —

When the animal body is dissected, thin white cords are to be found here and there. They look like strings. The word *nerve* now applied to them is from the Latin *nervus*, which is traced back to the Sanskrit *snavara*, meaning a string or cord. Indeed, the term was originally applied to any stringlike object in the body; to tendons, for one. It was the tendons, the stringlike connections between muscles and bones, that were the original "nerves."

The Greeks of Alexandria in Julius Caesar's time recognized that the tendons themselves were tough connective fibers, whereas other strings were comparatively fragile and fatty rather than connective. The latter were connected to muscle at one end as the tendons were, but not connected to bones at the other. Galen, the Roman physician who lived A.D. 200, finally completed the semantic switch by applying the term "nerve" only to the nontendons, and this is what we still do today.

Nevertheless, traces of the pre-Galenic situation persist in the language. We say, when we make a supreme effort, that we are "straining every nerve," whereas we obviously mean that we are straining every tendon because of the fierce contraction of our muscles. Again, the unabridged dictionary gives "sinewy" as its first definition of "nervous." To speak of a hand as nervous, which today would imply weakness and trembling, would have meant precisely the opposite in older times — that it was strong and capable of firm action.

Throughout ancient and medieval times the nerves were felt to be hollow, as the blood vessels were, and (again like the blood vessels) to function as carriers of a fluid. Rather complicated theories were developed by Galen and others that involved three different fluids carried by the veins, the arteries, and the nerves respectively. The fluid of the nerves, usually referred to as "animal spirits," was considered the most subtle and rarefied of the three.

Such theories of nerve action, lacking a firm observational basis on which to anchor, went drifting off into obscurity and mysticism, and the structure so reared had to be torn down entirely and thrown away. And yet, as it turned out, the ancients had not entirely missed the target. A kind of fluid actually does travel along the nerves; a fluid far more ethereal than the visible fluid that fills the blood vessels, or even than the lighter and invisible fluid that fills the lungs and penetrates into the arteries. The effects of this fluid had been observed for centuries before the time even of Galen. As long ago as 600 B.C., the Greek philosopher Thales had noted that amber if rubbed gained the ability to attract light objects. Scholars turned to the phenomenon (now called "electricity" from the Greek word for amber) occasionally over the centuries, unable to understand it yet interested.

In the 18th century, methods were discovered for concentrating electricity in what was called a Leyden jar. (It was particularly studied at the University of Leyden in the Netherlands.) When a Leyden jar was fully charged, it could be made to discharge if a metal-pointed object were brought near the knob on top. The electricity jumped from the knob to the metal point and produced a visible spark like a tiny lightning bolt. Accompanying it was a sharp crackle like a minute bit of thunder. People began to think of electricity as a subtle fluid that could be poured into a Leyden jar and be made to burst forth again.

The American scientist Benjamin Franklin first popularized the notion of electricity as a single fluid that could produce electric charges of two different types, depending on whether an excess of the fluid were present (positive charge) or a deficiency (negative charge). More than that, Franklin, in 1752, was able to show that the spark and crackle of the discharging Leyden jar did not merely resemble thunder and lightning but were identical with those natural phenomena in nature. By flying a kite in a thunderstorm, he drew electricity out of the clouds and charged a Leyden jar with it.

The discovery excited the world of science, and experiments involving electricity became all the rage. The Italian anatomist Luigi Galvani was one of those drawn into the electrical orbit in the 1780's. He found, as others had, that an electric shock from a Leyden jar could cause a muscle dissected out of a dead frog to contract spasmodically, but he went further and (partly by accident) found more. He found that a frog muscle would contract if a metal instrument were touching it at a time when an electric spark was given off by a Leyden jar not in direct contact with the muscle. Then he discovered that the muscle would contract if it made simultaneous contact with two different metals even where no Leyden jar was in the vicinity.

Galvani thought the muscle itself was the source of a fluid similar to the electricity with which scientists were experimenting. He called this new fluid he thought he had discovered "animal electricity." Galvani was quickly shown to be wrong in his theory even if he was tremendously right in his observation. Galvani's compatriot Alessandro Volta was able to show, in 1800, that the electricity did not originate in the muscle but in the two metals. He combined metals in appropriate fashion — but in the complete absence of animal tissue of any sort — and obtained a flow of electricity. He had constructed the first electric battery and obtained the first electric current.

The electric current was in turn set to stimulating tissues, and it was quickly discovered that although muscles did contract under direct stimulation they were contracted more efficiently if the nerve leading to the muscle were stimulated. The concept grew firmer, throughout the 19th century, that nerves conducted stimulations and that the conduction was in the form of an electric current.

The source of the electricity in the lightning, in Volta's battery, and in the nerves was not truly understood until the inner structure of the atom began to be revealed about 1900. As the 20th century wore on it was discovered that the atom was composed of much smaller, *subatomic particles,* most of which carried an electric charge. In particular, the outer regions of various atoms consisted of circling *electrons,* tiny particles each of which carried a charge of the type that Franklin had arbitrarily described as negative. At the center of the atom, there was an *atomic nucleus* which carried a positive charge that balanced the negative charges of the circling electrons. If the atom were considered by itself, the two types of electric charges would balance and the atom as a whole would be neutral.

However, atoms interact with each other, and there is a tendency for some to gain electrons at the expense of others. In either case, whether electrons are gained or lost, the electrical neutrality is upset and the atom gains an overall charge and becomes an ion (see footnote, pp. 395-396). The electrons flowing from one set of atoms to another is like Franklin's fluid, except that Franklin had the flow in the wrong direction. (Nevertheless, we needn't worry about that.)

The atoms of the metals sodium and potassium have a strong tendency to lose a single electron each. What results are *sodium ion* and *potassium ion,* each carrying a single positive charge. On the other hand, the atom of the element chlorine has a strong tendency to pick up a single electron and become a negatively charged *chloride ion.* *

The body is rich in sodium, potassium, and chlorine but the atoms of these elements invariably occur within the body in the form of ions.** It also contains many other ions. Calcium and

* It is "chloride ion" and not "chlorine ion" for reasons buried deep in the history of chemistry; it would be tedious to try to root them out. This is not a misprint.

** As a matter of fact, they occur in inanimate nature only in the form of ions. The neutral atoms of sodium and potassium make up active metals that can be isolated in the laboratory after expending considerable effort. And unless special precautions are taken, they will revert back to ionic form at once. Similarly, the neutral atoms of chlorine combine in pairs to form the poisonous chlorine gas that does not exist on earth except where it is manufactured through the manipulations of chemists.

magnesium each occur as doubly charged ions. Iron occurs in the form of ions carrying either two or three positive charges each. Sulfur and phosphorus combine with oxygen and hydrogen atoms to form groups that carry an overall negative charge. The groups of atoms making up the amino acid side-chains in protein molecules have in some cases a strong tendency to pick up an electron and in others to give one off (and in other cases neither), with the result that a protein molecule may have hundreds of positive and negative electric charges scattered over its surface.

Positively charged particles repel other positively charged particles and negatively charged particles repel other negatively charged particles. Positively and negatively charged particles, on the contrary, attract each other. These attractions and repulsions result in charges tending to exist in an even mixture. In any volume of reasonable size (say, large enough to be seen under the microscope) there is electrical neutrality therefore, as positives and negatives get as close as possible, each neutralizing the effect of the other. It takes considerable energy to maintain even a small separation of charge, and when this is done there is a tendency for the charges to mix once again. This can be done catastrophically in the form of a lightning bolt, or on a much smaller scale in the form of a Leyden jar discharge. In a chemical battery there is a small separation of charge that is continually set up in the metals; the electric current is the perpetual attempt of the electrons to flow from one metal to the other in an effort to restore neutrality.

If there is any form of electrical flow in the nerves, there must be a separation of charge first, and the answer to such a separation lies in the cell membranes.

THE CELL MEMBRANE

The cell is surrounded by a *semipermeable membrane*. It is semipermeable because some substances can penetrate it freely, whereas others cannot. The first generalization we can make is that small molecules, such as those of water and of oxygen, can pass through it freely; large molecules, such as those of starch and proteins, cannot. The simplest explanation of the method by which the membrane works would then seem to be that it contains submicroscopic holes so small that only small molecules can pass through.

Suppose this were so and that a particular small molecule bombarded the cell membrane from without. By sheer chance, a certain molecule would every once in a while strike one of the submicroscopic holes sufficiently dead-center to move right through into the cell interior. Such a molecule would be entering the cell by *diffusion* ("pour out" L). The rate at which molecules would enter the cell by diffusion would depend on the number of molecules hitting the tiny holes per unit of time. That would in turn depend on the total number of molecules striking the membrane altogether. And that would depend on the concentration of those molecules outside the cell. The greater the concentration, the larger the number of molecules striking the membrane and the larger would be the group finding their way through the holes. To sum up, the rate of diffusion into the cell depends on the concentration outside the cell.

If the particular molecule we are discussing existed also inside the cell, it would be bombarding the inner surface of the membrane as well. And occasionally a molecule inside would strike a hole and pass through out of the cell. Here also, the rate of diffusion out of the cell would depend on the concentration inside the cell.

If the concentration were higher outside the cell than inside, the rate of diffusion inward would be greater than that outward. The net movement of molecules would be toward the inside. The greater the concentration difference (or *concentration gradient*, as it is called), the faster this net movement. If the concentration were higher inside the cell than outside, the net movement of molecules would be outward. In either case, the net movement of molecules is from the region of higher concentration to that of lower concentration, in the direction of the slope of the concentration gradient, like an automobile coasting downhill. As the molecules move, the side with the low concentration builds up and that with the high concentration settles down. The concentration gradient becomes more gentle, the net movement slows, until at last, when the concentrations are equal on both sides of the membrane, no concentration gradient is left and there is no net movement at all.* It is like a coasting automobile reaching level ground and coming to a halt.

All this is to be expected of simple passive diffusion and, in fact, is found to be true of many types of molecules. In some cases, the cell acts as though it cannot wait upon the process of diffusion but must hurry it up. A substance such as glucose will enter the cell at a rate considerably faster than can be accounted for by diffusion alone (like an automobile moving downhill with its motor working and in gear). Such a situation is called *active transport* and consequently takes energy (the equivalent of the automobile's working motor). The exact mechanism by which this is accomplished is not yet known.

But let us apply this to ions. The cell membrane is freely permeable both to sodium ion and to potassium ion, which consist of single atoms and are not very much different in size from the water molecule. It might be expected, then, that if there were any difference in concentration of sodium ions and potassium ions inside and outside a cell the process of diffusion would equalize matters, and that, in the end, the concentration of these ions would be the same within and without. This, as a matter of fact, is true of dead cells. But not of living cells!

In living tissue, sodium ion is to be found almost entirely outside the cells in the *extracellular fluid*. The concentration of sodium ion is ten times as high outside the cell as it is inside. Potassium ion, in contrast, is found almost entirely within the cells in the *intracellular fluid*. The concentration of potassium ion

---

* With concentrations equal on both sides of the membrane, molecules are still moving, some going into the cell and some leaving. However, they go and leave at equal rates, so there is no net shift. Such a balance in the face of rapid movement in both directions is called a *dynamic equilibrium*.

is thirty times as high inside the cell as outside. What is more, under ordinary circumstances there seems no tendency to equalize this imbalance.

Such an unequal distribution of ions in the face of a concentration gradient can only be maintained through a continual expenditure of energy on the part of the cell. It is as though you were pulling apart one of those spring devices that gymnasiums use to develop the arm muscles. The natural state of the spring is one of contraction; but you can expand it through an expenditure of energy, and to keep it expanded requires a continuous expenditure of energy. If for any reason you were unable to maintain the energy expenditure, through weariness perhaps, or as a result of having some funny fellow poke you in the short ribs without warning, the spring contracts suddenly. When the cell dies and no longer expends energy, the ion concentrations on either side of the membrane equalize quickly.

The cell maintains the unequal distribution of ions by extruding the sodium ion — by kicking it out of the cell, in effect — as quickly as it drifts into the cell by diffusion; or, possibly, by turning it back before it even penetrates the membrane all the way. The sodium ion is thus forced to move against the concentration gradient like an automobile moving uphill. (Such an automobile cannot be conceived of as coasting; it *must* be expending energy; and so, likewise, must the cell.) To move sodium ion against a concentration gradient in this fashion is, to use still another simile, like pumping water uphill; the mechanism by which this sodium movement is accomplished is called the *sodium pump*. As yet no one knows precisely how the sodium pump works.

As the positively charged sodium ions are forced out of the cell, the interior of the cell builds up a negative charge, and the outside of the cell builds up a positive one. The positively charged potassium ions outside the cell are strongly repelled by the excess of positive charge in their neighborhood and are attracted by the negatively charged interior of the cell. They are thus both pushed and pulled into the cell. There is no "potassium pump" to undo this movement and the potassium ions remain inside the cell once there. Nor do they diffuse outward minus pump activity (as they would ordinarily, in order to equalize concentrations on both sides of the membrane), because the distribution of electric charge holds them in place. The inflowing potassium ions do not entirely neutralize the negative charge of the cell's interior. Instead, when all is done, a small negative charge still remains within the cell and a small positive charge remains outside.

The energy expended by the cell in running the sodium pump does three things. First, it maintains the sodium ion concentration unequal on the two sides of the membrane against a natural tendency toward equalization. Second, it maintains the potassium ion concentration unequal as well. Third, it maintains a separation of electric charge against the natural tendency of opposite charges to attract each other.

POLARIZATION AND DEPOLARIZATION

When there is a separation of charge, so that positive charge is concentrated in one place and negative charge in another, physicists speak of a *polarization of charge*. They do so because the situation resembles the manner in which opposite types of magnetic force are concentrated in the two ends, or poles,* of a bar magnet. Since, in the case we are discussing, there is a concentration of positive charge on one side of a membrane and a concentration of negative charge on the other, we can speak of a *polarized membrane*.

But whenever there is a separation of charge, an *electric potential* is set up. This measures the force tending to drive the separated charge together and wipe out the polarization. The electric potential is therefore also termed the *electromotive force* (the force tending to "move the electric charge"), which is usually abbreviated *EMF*.

* The magnetic poles derive their name, originally, from the fact that when allowed freedom of movement they pointed in the general directions of the earth's geographic poles.

The electric potential is spoken of as "potential" because it does not necessarily involve a motion of electricity, since the separation of charge can be maintained against the force driving the charges together if the proper energy is expended for the purpose (and in the cell, it is). The force is therefore only potential — one that will move the charge if the energy supply flags. Electric potential is measured in units named *volts*, after Volta, the man who built the first battery.

Physicists have been able to measure the electric potential that exists between the two sides of the living cell membrane. It comes to about 0.07 volts. Another way of putting it is to say it is equal to about 70 millivolts, a millivolt being equal to one thousandth of a volt. This is not much of a potential if it is compared with the 120 volts (or 120,000 millivolts) that exist in our household power lines, or with the many thousands of volts that can be built up for transmission of electric power over long distances. Notwithstanding, it is quite an amazing potential to be built up by a tiny cell with the materials it has at its disposal.

Anything that interrupts the activity of the sodium pump will bring about an abrupt equalization of the concentrations of the sodium ions and potassium ions on either side of the membrane. This will in turn automatically bring about an equalization of charge. The membrane will then be *depolarized*. Of course, this is what happens when the cell membrane is damaged or if the cell itself is killed. There are, nevertheless, three types of stimuli that will bring about depolarization without injuring the cell (if the stimuli are sufficiently gentle). These are mechanical, chemical, and electrical.

Pressure is an example of mechanical stimulation. Pressure upon a point in the membrane will stretch that portion of the membrane and (for reasons as yet unknown) bring about a depolarization. High temperature will expand the membrane and cold temperature contract it, and the mechanical change brought about in this fashion may also result in a depolarization.

A variety of chemicals will effect the same result, and so will a small electric current. (The last is the most obvious case. After all, why should not the electrical phenomena of a polarized membrane be upset by the imposition of an electric potential from without?)

When depolarization takes place at one point in a membrane, it acts as a stimulation for depolarization elsewhere. The sodium ion that floods into the cell at the point where the sodium pump has ceased to operate forces potassium ion out. The sodium ions, however, which are the smaller and nimbler of the two types, enter just a trifle more quickly than the potassium ions can leave. The result is that the depolarization overshoots the mark, and for a moment the interior of the cell takes on a small positive charge, thanks to the surplus of positively charged sodium ions that have entered, and a small negative charge is left outside the cell. The membrane is not merely depolarized, it is actually very slightly polarized in the opposite direction.

This opposed polarization may act as an electrical stimulus itself, one that stops the sodium pump in the regions immediately adjacent to the point of original stimulus. Those adjacent areas depolarize and then polarize slightly in the opposite direction, so as to stimulate depolarization in areas beyond. In this way a wave of depolarization travels along the entire membrane. At the initial point of stimulus the opposed polarization cannot be maintained for long. The potassium ions continue moving out of the cell and eventually catch up with the faster sodium ions; the small positive charge within the cell consequently is wiped out. This somehow reactivates the sodium pump at that point in the membrane, and sodium ions are pushed out once more and potassium ions drawn in. That portion of the membrane is *repolarized*. Since this happens at every point where the membrane is depolarized, there is a wave of repolarization following behind the wave of depolarization.

Between the moment of depolarization and the moment of complete repolarization the membrane will not respond to the usual stimuli. This is the *refractory period;* it lasts only a very short portion of a second. The wave of depolarization that follows a stimulus at any point on a membrane makes certain the cell's response to that stimulus as a unit. Exactly how the tiny electrical changes involved in a depolarization bring about a particular response is not known, but the fact of response is clear, and so is the fact that the response is unified. If a muscle is stimulated at one point by a gentle electric shock, it contracts, because this is the natural muscular response to a stimulus. But it is not just the stimulated point that contracts. It is an entire muscle fiber. The wave of depolarization travels through a muscle fiber at a rate of anywhere from 0.5 to 3 meters per second, depending on the size of the fiber, and this is fast enough to make it seem to contract as a unit.

These polarization-depolarization-repolarization phenomena are common to all cells, but are far more pronounced in some than in others. Cells have developed that take special advantage of the phenomena. These specializations can take place in one of two directions. First, and rather uncommonly, organs can be developed in which the electric potential is built up to high values. On stimulus the resultant depolarization is not translated into muscular contraction or any of the other common responses but makes itself evident, instead, as a flow of electricity. This does not represent a waste: if the stimulus arises from the activity of an enemy, the electrical response can hurt or kill that enemy.

There are seven families of fish (some in the bony fish group, some among the sharks) that have specialized in this fashion. The most spectacular example is the fish popularly called the "electric eel," which has the very significant formal name of *Electrophorus electricus*. The electric eel occurs in the fresh waters of northern South America: the Orinoco River, the Amazon River and its tributaries. It is not related to the common eels, but receives its name because of its elongated eel-like body, which reaches lengths of some 6 to 9 feet. This elongation is almost entirely due to tail — some four fifths of the creature is tail. All the ordinary organs are crowded into the forward 12 to 18 inches of the body.

More than half of the long tail is filled with a series of modified muscles that make up the "electric organ." The individual muscles produce no more potential than any ordinary muscle would, but there are thousands upon thousands of them arranged in such a fashion that all the potentials are added. A fully rested electric eel can develop a potential of up to 600 or 700 volts, and it can discharge as often as 300 times per second when first stimulated. Eventually this fades off to perhaps 50 discharges per second, but that rate can be maintained for a long time. The electric shock so produced is large enough to kill quickly any smaller animal it might use for food and hurt badly any large animal that might have the misguided intention of eating the eels.

The electric organ is an excellent weapon in itself. Perhaps more creatures would have specialized in this fashion if the organ were not so space-consuming. Imagine how few animals would have developed powerful fangs and claws if, in order to do so, more than half of the mass of the body would have had to be devoted to them.

The second type of specialization involving the electrical phenomena of cell membranes lies not in the direction of intensifying the potential but in that of hastening the speed of transmission of depolarization. Cells with thin elongated processes are developed, and these processes are, after all, virtually all membrane. They have as their chief function the very rapid transmission of the effects of a stimulus at one part of the body to another part. It is such cells that make up the nerve — which brings us back to the subject of concern at the beginning of this chapter.

THE NEURON

The nerves that are easily visible to the unaided eye are not single cells. Rather, they are bundles of *nerve fibers,* sometimes a good many of them, each of which is itself a portion of a cell. The fibers are all traveling in the same direction and are bound

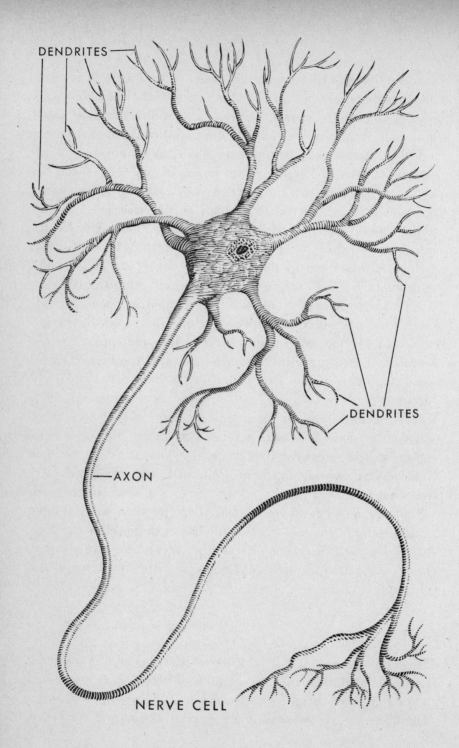

DENDRITES

DENDRITES

AXON

NERVE CELL

together for the sake of convenience, though the individual fibers of the bundle may have widely differing functions. The principle is the same as that in which a number of conducting wires, insulated from each other and each fulfilling its own function, are bound together for convenience's sake into an electric cable.

The nerve fiber itself is part of a *nerve cell*, which is also known as a *neuron* (nyoo'ron). This is the Greek equivalent of the Latin-derived "nerve" and was applied by the Greeks of the Hippocratic age to the nerves themselves and to tendons. Now the word is applied exclusively to the individual nerve cell. The main portion of the neuron, the *cell body*, is not too different from other cells. It contains a nucleus and cytoplasm. Where it is most distinct from cells of other types is that out of the cell body, long, threadlike projections emerge. Over most of the cell there are numerous projections that branch out into still finer extensions. These branching threads resemble the branchings of a tree and are called *dendrites* ("tree" G).

At one point of the cell, however, there is a particularly long extension that usually does not branch throughout most of its sometimes enormous length. This is the *axon* (so named for reasons to be given later). It is the axon that is the nerve fiber in the typical nerve, and such a fiber, although microscopically thin, is sometimes several feet long, which is unusual, considering that it is part of a single cell.

Depolarization setting in at some point of these cell projections are rapidly propagated onward. The wave of depolarization traveling along these nerve-cell processes is referred to as the *nerve impulse*. The impulse can travel in either direction along the processes; and if the fiber is stimulated in the middle the impulse will travel out in both directions from this point. However, in the living system it happens that the nerve impulse in the dendrites virtually always travels toward the cell body, whereas in the axon it travels away from the cell body.

The speed of the nerve impulse was first measured in 1852 by the German scientist Hermann von Helmholtz. He did this by stimulating a nerve at different points and noting the time it took for the muscle, to which it was attached, to respond. If an additional length of nerve was involved there was a small delay and that represented the time it took for the nerve impulse to cross that additional length. Interestingly enough, this demonstration took place just six years after the famous German physiologist Johannes Müller, in a fit of conservatism such as occasionally afflicts scientists in their later years, had stated categorically that no man would ever succeed in measuring the speed of the nerve impulse.

The impulse does not move at the same rate in all nerves. For one thing, the rate at which a nerve impulse travels along an axon varies roughly with the width of the axon. The wider the axon, the more rapid the rate of propagation. In very fine nerve fibers the impulse moves quite slowly, at a rate of two meters per second or less; no faster, in other words, than the motion of the wave of depolarization in muscle. Obviously, where an organism must react quickly to some stimulus, faster and faster rates of nerve-impulse propagations are desirable. One way of arranging this is to make use of thicker and thicker fibers. In the human body, where the smallest fibers are 0.5 microns in diameter (a micron being 1/1000 of a millimeter), the largest are 20 microns in diameter. The largest are thus 40 times as wide as the smallest and possess 1600 times the cross-sectional area.

One might think that since the vertebrates had a better-developed nervous system than do any other group of creatures, they would naturally have the fastest-moving nerve impulses and therefore the thickest nerve fibers. This is not so. The lowly cockroach has some axons thicker than any in man. The extreme, as far as sheer size is concerned, is reached in the largest and most advanced mollusks, the squids. The large squids probably represent the most advanced and highly organized of all the invertebrates. Combining that with their physical size, we find it not surprising that they require the fastest nerve-impulse rates and the thickest axons. Those leading to the squid's muscles are commonly referred to as "giant axons" and are up to a millimeter in diameter. These are 50 times the diameter of the thickest mammalian axons and possess 2500 times the cross-sectional area. The giant axons of the squid have proved a godsend to neurologists, who were able to perform experiments on them easily (such as measuring directly the electrical potential across the axon membrane) that could be performed only with great difficulty upon the tenuous fibers present in vertebrates.

And yet why should invertebrates outpace vertebrates in axon thickness when the vertebrates have the more highly developed nervous system? The answer is that vertebrates do not depend on thickness alone. They have developed another and more subtle method for increasing the rate of propagation of the nerve impulse.

In vertebrates, the nerve fiber is surrounded during its process of formation in very early life with "satellite cells." Some of these are referred to as Schwann's cells (shvahnz) after the German zoologist Theodor Schwann, who was one of the founders of the cell theory of life. The Schwann's cells fold themselves about the axon, wrapping in a tighter and tighter spiral, coating the fiber with a fatty layer called the *myelin sheath* (my'uh-lin; "marrow" G, the reason for the name being uncertain). The Schwann's cells finally form a thin membrane called the *neurilemma* (nyoo'rih-lem'uh; "nerve-skin" G), which still contains the nuclei of the original Schwann's cells. (It was Schwann who first described the neurilemma in 1839, so that it is sometimes called the "sheath of Schwann." As a result a rather unmusical and unpleasant memorial to the zoologist lies in the fact that a tumor of the neurilemma is sometimes called a "schwannoma.")

A particular Schwann's cell wraps itself about only a limited section of the axon. As a result, an axon has a myelin sheath that exists in sections. In the intervals between the original Schwann's cells are narrow regions where the myelin sheath does not exist, so that the axon rather resembles a string of sausages. These constricted unmyelinated regions are called *nodes of Ranvier* (rahn-vee-ay), after the French histologist Louis Antoine

Ranvier, who described them in 1878. The axon is like a thin line running down the axis of the interrupted cylinder formed by the myelin sheath. The word "axon" comes from "axis," in fact, with the "on" suffix substituted because of the presence of that suffix in the word "neuron."

The functions of the myelin sheath are not entirely clear to us. The simplest suggestion is that they insulate the nerve fiber, allowing a smaller loss of electric potential to the surroundings. Such a loss increases as a nerve fiber grows thinner, so that the presence of insulation allows a fiber to remain thin without undue loss of efficiency. Evidence in favor of this rests in the fact that the myelin sheath is composed largely of fatty material, which is indeed a good electrical insulator. (It is this fatty material that gives nerves their white appearance. The cell body of the nerve is grayish.)

If the myelin sheath served only as an insulator and nothing else, very simple fat molecules would do for the purpose. Instead, the chemical composition of the sheath is most complex. About two out of every five molecules within it are cholesterol. Two more are phosphatides (a type of phosphorus-containing fat molecule), and a fifth is a cerebroside (a complex sugar-containing fatlike molecule). Small quantities of other unusual substances are present, too. The existence of sheath properties other than mere insulation would therefore seem very likely.

It has also been suggested that the myelin sheath serves somehow to maintain the integrity of the axon. The axon stretches so far from the cell body that it seems quite reasonable to assume it can no longer maintain active communication throughout its length with the cell nucleus — and the nucleus is vital to cellular activity and integrity. Perhaps the sheath cells, which retain their nuclei, act as nursemaids, in a manner of speaking, for successive sections of the axon. Even nerves without myelin sheaths have axons that are surrounded by layers of small Schwann's cells with, of course, nuclei.

Finally, the sheath must somehow accelerate the speed of

propagation of the nerve impulse. A fiber with a sheath conducts the impulse much more rapidly than a fiber of the same diameter without a sheath. That is why vertebrates have been able to retain thin fibers and yet vastly increase the speed of impulse.

In the mammalian myelinated nerve, the impulse travels at a velocity of about 100 meters per second, or, if you prefer, 225 miles an hour. This is quite fast enough. The greatest stretch of mammalian tissue that has ever existed in a single organism is the hundred feet separating the nose end of a blue whale from its tail end; the nerve impulse along a myelinated axon could negotiate that distance in 3/10 of a second. The distance from head to toe in a man six feet tall could be covered in 1/50 of a second. The superiority of the nerve impulse, in terms of speed, over hormone coordination is, as you see, tremendous.

The process of myelination is not quite complete at birth, and various functions do not develop until the corresponding nerves are myelinated. Thus, the baby does not see at first; this must await the myelinization of the optic nerve, which, to be sure, is not long delayed. Also, the nerves connecting to the muscles of the legs are not fully myelinated until the baby is more than a year old, and the complex interplay of muscles involved in walking are delayed that long.

Occasionally an adult will suffer from a "demyelinating disease" in which sections of myelin sheathing degenerates, with consequent loss of function of the nerve fiber. The best known of these diseases is *multiple sclerosis* ("hard" G). This receives its name because demyelination occurs in many patches, spread out over the body, the soft myelin being replaced by a scar of harder fibrous tissue. Such demyelination may come about through the effect on the myelin of a protein in the patient's blood. The protein seems to be an "antibody," one of the class of substances that usually react only with foreign proteins, and often produce symptoms with which we are familiar as "allergies." In essence, the sufferer from multiple sclerosis may be allergic to himself and multiple sclerosis may be an example of an auto-allergic disease.

Since those nerves that receive sensations are most likely to be attacked, double vision, loss of the ability to feel, and other abnormal sensations are common symptoms. Multiple sclerosis most often attacks people in the 20-to-40 age group. It may be progressive — that is, more and more nerves may become involved, so that death eventually follows. The progress of the disease can be slow, however, death sometimes not following for ten or more years after its onset.

ACETYLCHOLINE

Any neuron does not exist in isolation. It usually makes contact with another neuron. This happens through an intermingling of the axon of one neuron (the axon branches at its extreme tip) with at least some of the dendrites of another. At no point do the processes of one cell actually join the processes of another. Instead there is a microscopic, but definite, gap between the ends of the processes of two neighboring neurons. The gap is called a *synapse* (sih-naps'; "union" G, although a union in the true sense is exactly what it is not).

This raises a problem. The nerve impulse does indeed travel from one neuron to the next, but how does it travel across the synaptic gap? One thought is that it "sparks" across, just as an electric current leaps across an ordinarily insulating gap of air from one conducting medium to another when the electric potential is high enough. However, the electric potentials involved in nerve impulses (with the exception of certain reported instances in the crayfish) are not high enough to force currents across the insulating gap. Some other solution must be sought, and if electricity will not help we must turn to chemistry.

A very early effect of a stimulus on a nerve is that of bringing about a reaction between acetic acid and choline, two compounds commonly present in cells. The substance formed is *acetylcholine* (as'ih-til-koh'leen). It is this acetylcholine which alters the working of the sodium pump so that depolarization takes place and the nerve impulse is initiated.

It is easy to visualize the acetylcholine as coating the membrane and altering its properties. This is the picture some people draw of hormone action in general, and for this reason acetylcholine is sometimes considered an example of a *neurohormone* — that is, a hormone acting on the nerves. The resemblance, however, is not perfect. Acetylcholine is not secreted into and transported by the bloodstream, as is true in the case of all hormones I described in the first part of this book. Instead, acetylcholine is secreted at the nerve-cell membrane and acts upon the spot. This difference has caused some people to prefer to speak of acetylcholine as a *neurohumor,* "humor" being an old-fashioned medical term for a biological fluid (from a Latin word for "moisture").

The acetylcholine formed by the nerve cannot be allowed to remain in being for long, because there would be no repolarization while it is present. Fortunately, nerves contain an enzyme called *cholinesterase* (koh′lin-es′tur-ays) which brings about the breakup of acetylcholine to acetic acid and choline once more. Following that breakup the cell membrane is altered again and repolarization can take place. Both formation and breakup of acetylcholine is brought about with exceeding rapidity, and the chemical changes keep up quite handily with the measured rates of depolarization and repolarization taking place along the course of a nerve fiber.

The evidence for the acetylcholine/cholinesterase accompaniment to the nerve impulse is largely indirect, but it is convincing. All nerve cells contain the enzymes that form acetylcholine and break it down. This means that the substance is found in all multicellular animals except the very simplest: the sponges and jellyfish. In particular, cholinesterase is found in rich concentration in the electric organs of the electric eel, and the electric potential generated by the eel is at all times proportional to the concentration of enzyme present. Furthermore, any substance that blocks the action of cholinesterase puts a stop to the nerve impulse.

And so the picture arises of a nerve impulse that is a coordinated chemical and electrical effect, the two traveling together down the length of an axon. This is a more useful view than that of the nerve impulse as electrical in nature only, for when we arrive at the synapse and find that the electrical effect cannot cross we are no longer helpless: the chemical effect can cross easily. The acetylcholine liberated at the axon endings of one nerve will affect the dendrites, or even the cell body itself, across the synapse and initiate a new nerve impulse there. The electrical effect and chemical effect will then travel down the second neuron together until the chemical effect takes over alone at the next synapse, and so on. (The impulse moves from axon to dendrites and not in the other direction. It is this which forces nerve messages to travel along a one-way route despite the ability of nerve processes to carry the impulse either way.)

The axon of a neuron may make a junction not only with another neuron but also with some organ to which it carries its impulse, usually a muscle. The tip of the axon makes intimate contact with the *sarcolemma* (sahr'koh-lem'uh; "skin of the flesh" G), which is the membrane enclosing the muscle fiber. There, in the intimate neighborhood of the muscle, it divides into numerous branches, each ending in a separate muscle fiber. Again there is no direct fusion between the axon and the muscle fibers. Instead, a distinct — if microscopic — gap exists. This synapse-like connection between nerve and muscle is called the *neuromuscular junction* (or *myoneural junction*).

At the neuromuscular junction, the chemical and electrical aspects of the nerve impulse arrive. Once more the electrical effect stops, but the chemical effect bridges the gap. The secretion of acetylcholine alters the properties of the muscle cell membrane, brings about the influx of sodium ion, and, in short, initiates a wave of depolarization just like that which takes place in a nerve cell. The muscle fibers, fed this wave by the nerve endings, respond by contracting. All the muscle fibers to which the various branches of a single nerve are connected contract as a unit, and such a group of fibers is referred to, consequently, as a *motor unit*.

Any substance that will inhibit the action of cholinesterase and put an end to the cycle of acetylcholine buildup and breakdown thus will not only put an end to the nerve impulse but will also put an end to the stimulation and contraction of muscles. This will mean paralysis of the voluntary muscles of the limbs and chest and of the heart muscle as well. Death will consequently follow such inhibition quickly, in from two to ten minutes.

During the 1940's German chemists, in the course of research with insecticides, developed a number of substances that turned out to be powerful cholinesterase inhibitors. These are deadly indeed. As liquids they penetrate the skin without damage or sensation, and, once they reach the bloodstream, kill quickly. They are much more subtle and deadly than were the comparatively crude poison gases of World War I. Germany did not make use of them in World War II, but under the name "nerve gases" mention is sometimes made of their possible use in World War III (assuming anything is left to be done after the first nuclear stroke and counterstroke).

Nature need not in this case take a back seat to human ingenuity. There are certain alkaloids that are excellent cholinesterase inhibitors and, therefore, excellent killers. There is *curare* (kyoo-rah'ree), which was used as an arrow poison by South American Indians. (When news of it penetrated the outside world, this gave rise to legends of "mysterious untraceable South American toxins" that filled a generation of mystery thrillers.) Another example of natural cholinesterase inhibitors is the toxins of certain toadstools, including one that is very appropriately entitled "the angel of death."

Even nerve gases have their good side, nevertheless. It sometimes happens that a person possesses neuromuscular junctions across which the nerve impulse travels with difficulty. This condition is *myasthenia gravis* (my-as-thee'nee-uh gra'vis; "serious muscle weakness" G) and is marked by a progressive weakening of muscles, particularly of the face. Here the most likely fault is that the acetylcholine formation at the neuromuscular junction is insufficient, or perhaps that it is formed in normal amounts but is too quickly broken down by cholinesterase. The therapeutic use of a cholinesterase-inhibitor conserves the acetylcholine and can, at least temporarily, improve muscle action.

Although muscle tissue can be stimulated directly and made to contract — by means of an electric current, for illustration — muscle is, under normal conditions, stimulated only by impulses arriving along the nerve fibers. For that reason, any damage to the fibers, either through mechanical injury or as a result of a disease such as poliomyelitis, can result in paralysis. An axon which has degenerated through injury or disease can sometimes be regenerated, provided its neurilemma has remained intact. Where the neurilemma has been destroyed or where the axon is one lacking a neurilemma (as many are) regeneration is impossible. Further, if the cell body of any nerve is destroyed, it cannot be replaced. (Nevertheless, all is not necessarily lost. In 1963 human nerves were transplanted successfully from one person to another for the first time. There is a reasonable possibility that the time will come when "nerve banks" will exist and when paralysis through loss of nerve function can be successfully treated.)

A particular nerve fiber shows no gradations in its impulse. That is, one does not find that a weak stimulus sets up a weak impulse, while a stronger stimulus sets up a stronger impulse. The neuron is constructed to react completely or not at all. An impulse too weak to initiate the nerve impulse does nothing effective; it is "subthreshold." To be sure, some minor changes in the membrane potential may be noted and there may be the equivalent of a momentary flow of current, but that dies out quickly. (If, however, a second subthreshold stimulus follows before that momentary flow dies out, the two together may be strong enough to initiate the impulse.)

It would seem that a small current of electricity won't last long in the nerve — its resistance is too high. On the other hand, a stimulus just strong enough to initiate the impulse ("threshold stimulus") results in an electrical and chemical effect which is regenerated all along the nerve fiber and does not fade out. (How the regeneration takes place is uncertain, though there is a strong suspicion that the nodes of Ranvier are involved.) The threshold stimulus produces the fiber's maximum response. A stronger stimulus can produce no stronger impulse. This is the "all-or-none law" and may be simply stated: a nerve fiber either propagates an impulse of maximum strength or propagates no impulse at all.

The all-or-none law extends to the organ stimulated by the nerve. A muscle fiber receiving a stimulus from a nerve fiber responds with a contraction of constant amount. This seems to go against common knowledge. If a nerve fiber always conducts the same impulse, if it conducts any at all, and if a muscle fiber always contracts with the same force, if it contracts at all, then how is it we can contract our biceps to any desired degree from the barest twitch to a full and forceful contraction?

The answer is that we cannot consider nerve and muscle isolated either in space or time. An organ is not necessarily fed by a single nerve fiber, but may be fed by dozens of them. Each nerve fiber has its own threshold level, depending on its diameter, for one thing. The larger fibers tend to have a lower threshold for stimulation. A weak stimulus, then, may be enough to set off some of the fibers and not the others. (A stimulus so weak that it suffices to set off only one nerve fiber is the *minimal stimulus*.) A muscle would merely twitch if a single motor unit would contract under the minimal stimulus. As the stimulus rises, more and more nerve fibers would fire; more and more motor units would contract. Eventually, when the stimulus was strong enough to set off all the nerve fibers (*maximal stimulus*), the muscle would contract completely. A stimulus stronger than this will do no more.

There is also the matter of time. If a nerve fiber carries an impulse, the motor unit to which it is connected contracts and then relaxes. The relaxation takes time. If a second impulse follows before relaxation is complete, the muscle contracts again, but from a headstart, so that it contracts further the second time. A third impulse adds a further total contraction, and so on. The faster one impulse follows another the greater the contraction of the muscle. The number of impulses per second that can be delivered by a nerve fiber is very high and depends upon the length of the refractory period. Small fibers have refractory periods of as long as 1/250 of a second, which, even so, means that as many as 250 impulses per second can be delivered. Ten times as many can be delivered by the large myelinated nerve fibers.

In actual fact, a muscle is usually stimulated by some portion of the nerve fibers that feed into it, each fiber firing a certain number of times a second. The result of these two variable effects is that, without violating the all-or-none law, a muscle can be made to contract in extremely fine gradations of intensity.

7

OUR NERVOUS SYSTEM

CEPHALIZATION

For nerve cells to perform their function of organizing and coordinating the activity of the many organs that make up a multicellular creature, they must themselves be organized into a nervous system. It is the quality and complexity of this nervous system that more than anything else dictates the quality and complexity of the organism. Man considers himself to be at the peak of the evolutionary ladder, and although self-judgment is always suspect there is at least one good objective argument in favor of this. The nervous system of man is more complex, for his size, than is that of any other creature in existence (with the possible exception of some cetaceans). Since our nervous system is the clearest mark of our superiority as a species, I think it is important to see how it came to develop to its present state.

The simplest creatures that possess specialized nerve cells are the *coelenterates* (sih-len'tur-ayts), which include such organisms as the freshwater hydra and the jellyfish. Here already there is a nervous system of sorts. The neurons are scattered more or less regularly over the surface of the body, each being connected by synapses to those nearest to it. In this fashion, a stimulus applied to any part of the creature is conducted to all parts. Such a nervous system in a sense is merely an elaboration on a larger scale of what already existed in unicellular creatures. Among them, the cell membrane is itself excitable and conducts the equivalent of a nerve impulse to all parts of itself. The nerve network of the coelenterate does the same thing, acting as a supermembrane of a supercell. The results of such an arrangement, however, represent no great advance. Any stimulus anywhere on the coelenterate body alerts the entire organism indiscriminately and results in a response of the whole, which proceeds to contract, sway, or undulate. Fine control is not to be expected. Furthermore, since there are so many synapses to be passed (each a bottleneck), conduction of the nerve impulse is in general slow.

The next more complicated group of animals are the flatworms, which, although still simple, show certain developments that foreshadow the structure of all other, more complicated, animals. They are the first to have the equivalent of muscle tissue and to make effective use of muscles; the efficiency of the neuron network hence must be improved. Such improvements do indeed take place in at least some flatworms. The nerve cells in these creatures are concentrated in a pair of *nerve cords* running the length of the body. At periodic intervals along the length of the cords, there emerge nerves that receive stimuli from or deliver impulses to various specific body regions. The nerve cords represent the first beginnings of what is called the *central nervous system*, and the nerves make up the *peripheral nervous system*. This division of the nervous system into two chief portions holds true for all animals more advanced than the flatworm, up to and including man.

In any creature with a central nervous system, a stimulus will no longer induce a response from the whole body generally. Instead, a stimulus at some given part of the body sets off a nerve impulse that is not distributed to all other neurons but is carried directly to the nerve cord. It passes quickly along the nerve cord to a particular nerve, which will activate a specific organ, or organs, and bring about a response appropriate to the original stimulus.

The coelenterate system would correspond to a telephone network in which all subscribers are on a single party line, so that any call from one to another rouses every one of the subscribers, who are then free to listen and probably do. The flatworm system resembles a telephone network in which an operator connects the caller directly with the desired party. We can see at once that the operator-run telephone network is more efficient than the one-big-party line.

Early in the evolutionary process, however, the nerve cords became more than simple cords. The nerve cord had to specialize, even in the flatworms, and this specialization arose, in all probability because of the shape of the flatworm. The flatworm is the simplest living multicellular animal to have *bilateral symmetry*, and its primeval ancestors must have been the first to develop this. (By bilateral symmetry, we mean that if a plane is imagined drawn through the body it can be drawn in such a way as to divide the creature into a right and left half, each of which is the mirror-image of the other.) All animals more complicated than the flatworms are bilaterally symmetrical; ourselves most definitely included. One seeming exception is the starfish and their relatives, for these possess *radial symmetry*. (In radial symmetry, similar organs or structures project outward from a center, like so many radiuses in a circle.) The seeming exception is only a seeming one, for the radial symmetry of the starfish is a secondary development in the adult. The young forms (larvae) exhibit bilateral symmetry; the radial symmetry develops later as a kind of regression to an older day.

Animals simpler than the flatworms, such as the coelenterates, sponges, and single-celled creatures, generally have either radial symmetry or no marked symmetry at all. The same is true of plants: the daisy's petals are a perfect example of radial symmetry and the branches of a tree extend unsymmetrically in all directions from the trunk. This grand division of living creatures into those with bilateral symmetry and those without is of vital importance. An animal with no marked symmetry or with radial symmetry need have no preferred direction of movement. There is no reason why one particular leg of a starfish should take the lead in movement over any other.

A creature with bilateral symmetry is usually longest in the direction of the plane of symmetry and tends to progress along that plane. Other directions of movement are possible, but one direction is preferred. If a bilaterally symmetric creature, by reason of its very shape and structure, adopts one preferred direction of movement, then one end of its body is generally breaking new ground as it moves. It is constantly entering a new portion of the environment. It is that end of the body which is the head.

Obviously, it is important that the organism have ways of testing the environment in order that appropriate responses be made, responses of a nature to protect its existence. It must be able to check the chemical nature of the environment, avoiding poison and approaching food. It must detect temperature changes, vibrations, certain types of radiation, and the like. Organs designed to receive such sensations are most reasonably located in the head, since that is the ground-breaking portion of the body. It meets the new section of the environment first. The mouth also is most reasonably located in the head, since the head is the first portion of the body to reach the food. The end opposite the head (that is, the tail) is comparatively featureless.

In consequence, the two ends of the bilaterally symmetric creature are in general different, and living creatures of this type have distinct heads and tails. The differentiation of a head region marked by sense organs and a mouth is referred to as *cephalization* ("head" G). The process of cephalization has its internal effects on the nervous system. If a bilaterally symmetric creature were equal-ended, the nerve cords would, understandably enough, be expected to be equal-ended as well. But with a distinct head region containing specialized sense organs, it would be reasonable to suppose that the nerve cords in that head region would be rather more complex than elsewhere. The nerve endings in the specialized sense organs would be more numerous than elsewhere in the body, and the receiving cell bodies (most logically placed at the head end of the cord, since this is the portion nearest the sense organs) would likewise have to be more numerous.

Even in flatworms there is an enlargement and enrichment of the nerve cord at the head end, therefore. Such an enlargement might be called the first and most primitive *brain*.* Not surprisingly, the brain grows more complex as the organism itself grows more complex. It reaches the pinnacle of its development in the Phylum** *Chordata*, the one to which we ourselves belong.

The special position of Chordata with respect to the nervous system is shown in the very nature of the nerve cord. The double nerve cord of the flatworms persists in most phyla. It remains a solid tube in structure and is ventrally located; that is, it runs along the abdominal surface of the body. Only in Chordata is this general scheme radically altered. In place of a solid double nerve cord, there is a single cord in the form of a hollow cylinder. Instead of being ventrally located, it is dorsally located — it lies along the back surface of the body. This single, hollow, dorsal nerve cord is possessed by all chordates (members of the Phylum Chordata), and by chordates only; and, if we judge by results, it is much preferable to the older form that had been first elaborated by the distant ancestors of the flatworms.

THE CHORDATES

The Phylum Chordata is divided into four subphyla, of which three are represented today by primitive creatures that are not very successful in the scheme of life. In these three, the nerve cord receives no special protection any more than it does in the phyla other than Chordata.

* The word "brain" is from the Anglo-Saxon but it may be related to a Greek word referring to the top of the head. A less common synonym for brain is *encephalon* (en-sef'uh-lon; "in the head" G). This name is most familiar to the general public in connection with a disease characterized by the inflammation of brain tissue, since this disease is known as *encephalitis*.

** The animal kingdom is divided into *phyla* (fy'luh; "tribe" G, singular, *phylum*), each representing a group with one general type of body plan. A discussion of the various phyla and of the development of Chordata is to be found in Chapter 1 of *The Human Body*.

In the fourth and most advanced subphylum of Chordata, on the contrary, the nerve cord receives special protection in the form of enclosure by a series of hard structures of either cartilage or bone. These structures are the vertebrae, and for this reason the subphylum is called *Vertebrata* (vur'tih-bray'tuh) and its members commonly referred to as the vertebrates.

And it is only among the vertebrate subphylum that the brain becomes prominent. Of the other three subphyla, the most advanced (or, at least, the one that most resembles the vertebrates) is the one that contains a small fishlike creature called the amphioxus. The similarity to fish (resting chiefly on the fact that it has a cigar-shaped body) vanishes upon closer inspection. For one thing, the amphioxus turns out to have not much of a head. One end of it has a fringed suckerlike mouth and the other a finny fringe, and that is about all the difference. The two ends come to roughly similar points. In fact, the very name amphioxus is from Greek words meaning "both-pointed," with reference to the two ends. This lack of advanced cephalization is reflected internally; the nerve cord runs forward into the head region with scarcely any sign of specialization. The amphioxus is virtually a brainless creature.

Among the vertebrates, however, the situation changes. Even in the most primitive living class of vertebrates (a class containing such creatures as the lamprey, an organism that has not yet developed the jaws and limbs characteristic of all the other and more complex vertebrate classes) the forward end of the nerve cord has already swelled into a clear brain. Nor is it a simple swelling. It is, rather, a series of three — a kind of triple brain — the swellings being named (from the front end backward) the *forebrain, midbrain,* and *hindbrain.* These three basic divisions remain in all higher vertebrates, although they have been much modified and have been overlaid with added structures.

When the vertebrates first developed, some half-billion years ago, the early primitive specimens developed armor covering their head and foreparts generally. Such armor has the disad-

vantage of adding deadweight to the creature and cutting down speed and maneuverability; among vertebrates generally, the development of armor has never been a pathway to success.*
And yet the brain had to be protected. A compromise was struck whereby the armor was drawn in beneath the skin and confined to the brain alone. In this way the skull was developed.

The vertebrates rely not on the passive defense of a shell but on speed, maneuverability, and the weapons of attack. The central nervous system — the brain and nerve cord — was excepted; for in all vertebrates it is carefully enclosed in cartilage or bone, a shelled organ within an unshelled organism. Certainly this seems a rather clear indication of the special importance of the brain and nerve cord in vertebrates.

The three sections of the brain show further specializations, even in primitive vertebrates. From the lower portion of the most forward portion of the forebrain are a pair of outgrowths which received the nerves from the nostrils and are therefore concerned with the sense of smell. These outgrowths are the *olfactory lobes* ("smell" L); see illustration, page 532. Behind the olfactory lobes are a pair of swellings on the upper portion of the forebrain, and these make up the *cerebrum* (sehr'uh-brum; "brain" L). The portion of the forebrain that lies behind the cerebrum is the *thalamus* (thal'uh-mus).** The midbrain bears swellings that are particularly concerned with the sense of sight and are therefore termed the *optic lobes* ("sight" G).

The hindbrain develops a swelling in the upper portion of the region adjoining the midbrain. This swelling is the *cerebellum* (sehr'uh-bel'um; "little brain" L). The region behind the cerebellum narrows smoothly to the point where it joins the long section of unspecialized nerve cord behind the head. This final region is the *medulla oblongata* (meh-dul'uh ob'long-gay'tuh;

* Examples of modern armored vertebrates are the turtles, armadillos, and pangolins, all relatively unsuccessful.
** This word is from the Greek and refers to a type of room. The name arose among the Romans who felt this section of the brain was hollow and therefore resembled a room.

"rather long marrow" L). It is "marrow" in the sense that it is a soft organ set within hard bone, and, unlike other portions of the human brain, is elongated rather than bulgy.

This is the essence of the brain throughout all the classes of Vertebrata. There are shifts in emphasis, though, depending on whether smell or sight is the more important sense. In fish and amphibians smell is the chief sense, so the olfactory lobes are well developed. In birds, smell is comparatively unimportant and sight is the chief sense. In the bird brain, therefore, the olfactory lobes are small and unimpressive, whereas the optic lobes are large and well developed.

The development of the brain into something more than a sight-and-smell machine involved the cerebrum primarily. The outer coating of the cerebrum, containing numerous cell bodies that lend the surface a grayish appearance, is the *cerebral cortex* ("cortex" being the Latin word for outer rind, or bark), or the *pallium* ("cloak" L). It can also be termed, more colloquially, the "gray matter." This, in fish or amphibians, is chiefly concerned with sorting out the smell sensations and directing responses that would increase the creature's chance to obtain food or escape an enemy.

In the reptiles the cerebrum usually is distinctly larger and more specialized than in fish or amphibians. One explanation for this may well be that the dry-land habitat of the reptile is much more hostile to life than the ocean and fresh water in which the older classes of Vertebrata developed. On land, the medium of air is so much less viscous than that of water that faster movement is possible, which in itself requires more rapid coordination of muscular action. In addition, the full force of gravity, unneutralized by buoyancy, presents greater dangers and again places a premium on efficient muscle action.

Therefore, although the reptilian cerebrum is still mainly concerned with the analysis of smell and taste sensations, it is larger, and in the part of the cerebral cortex nearest the front end there is the development of something new. This new portion of the cortex is the *neopallium* (nee'oh-pal'ee-um; "new cloak" L). It consists of tracts of nerve cell bodies involved with the receipt of sensations other than smell. In the neopallium a greater variety of information is received and more complicated coordinations can be set up. The reptile can now move surefootedly, despite the upsetting pull of gravity. The neopallium was developed further in that group of reptiles which, about 100 million years ago or so, underwent some remarkable changes — changing scales into hair, developing warm-bloodedness, and, in general, becoming mammals, the most complex and successful class of Vertebrata.

In primitive mammals the cerebrum is even larger than in reptiles, although remaining just as specialized for reception of smell sensations. At least the pallium remains so. However, there is a large expansion in the size of the neopallium, which spreads out to cover the top half of the cerebral cortex.

The larger the neopallium, which is the center of a great variety of coordinations among stimuli and responses, the more complex the potentialities of behavior. A simple brain may have room for only one response to a particular stimulus; a more complex brain will have room to set up neuron combinations that can distinguish different gradations of a stimulus and take into account the different circumstances surrounding the stimulus, so that a variety of responses, each appropriate to the particular case, becomes possible. It is the presence of an increased variety of response that we accept as a sign of what we call "intelligence." It is the enlarged neopallium, then, which makes mammals in general more intelligent than any other group of vertebrates and, indeed, more intelligent than any group of invertebrates.

During the course of mammalian evolution, there was a general tendency toward an increase in body size. This usually implies an increase in the size of the brain and, as a result, in the cerebrum and neopallium. With increase in size, it is at least possible, therefore, that an increase in intelligence would follow. This is not necessarily so, since, normally, the larger the animal the more complex is the coordination required, even when there is no advance in intelligence. Sensations arrive from larger portions of the environment and are therefore more complicated. The larger, heavier, and more numerous muscles require more careful handling. If an animal increases in size without increasing its brain in proportion, and even more than in proportion, it is likely to become more stupid rather than more intelligent.

An extreme example of this was in the giant reptiles of the Mesozoic Era. Some grew larger than any land mammal ever has, but very little of that increase went into the brain. In fact, one of the most startling things about the monsters is the pin-head brain they carried atop their mountains of flesh. There seems no doubt but that they must have been abysmally stupid creatures. In the worst cases, the creatures lacked enough brain to take care of the minimal requirements of muscular coordination. The stegosaur, to name one, which weighed some ten tons or more (larger than any elephant), had a brain no larger than that of a kitten. It was forced to develop a large collection of nerve cells near the base of the spinal cord which could coordinate the muscles of the rear half of the body, leaving only the front half to the puny brain. This "spinal brain" was actually larger than the brain in the skull. The phenomenon of large size associated with decreased intelligence exists in mammals, too, though in not nearly as marked a fashion. The large cow is a rather stupid mammal, not nearly so bright as the comparatively small dog.

Some mammals, as they increased in size, enlarged the area of the neopallium *more* than in proportion, so they increased in intelligence as well. To enlarge the neopallium at that rate, however, meant that it would outgrow the skull. With the larger and more recently developed mammals, therefore, the cerebral cortex, which by then had become all neopallium, must wrinkle. In place of the smooth cerebral surface found in all other creatures, even among the smaller and more primitive mammals, the cerebral surface of the larger and higher mammals rather resembles a large walnut. The surface has folded into *convolutions* ("roll together" L). The gray matter, following the ins and outs of the wrinkles, increased in area.

In terms of sheer bulk, brain growth reaches an extreme in the very largest mammals, the elephants and whales. These have the largest brains that have ever existed. What is more, the cerebral surface is quite convoluted; the brains of some of the whale family are the most convoluted known. It is not surprising that both elephants and whales are unusually intelligent animals. Yet they are not the most intelligent. Much of their large brain — too much — is the slave of the coordination requirements of their muscles. Less is left for the mysterious functions of reason and abstract thought.

To look for a record intelligence, then, we must find a group of animals that had developed large brains without neutralizing this by developing excessively huge bodies. What we want, in other words, is a large value for the brain/body mass ratio.

THE PRIMATES

For such an increase in brain-body mass ratio, we must turn to that Order of mammals called *Primates* (pry-may'teez), usually referred to, in Anglicized pronunciation, as the primates (pry'mits). The term is from the Latin word for "first," a piece of human self-praise, since included in the Order is man himself.

About 70 million years ago, the primates first developed out of the Order *Insectivora* (in-sek-tiv'oh-ruh; "insect-eating" L). The living examples of the insectivores are small and rather unremarkable creatures such as the shrews, moles, and hedgehogs, and the earliest primates could not have been much different from these. As a matter of fact, the most primitive living primates are small animals, native to Southeast Asia, called *tree-shrews*. They are indeed much like shrews in their habits, but are larger (the shrews themselves are the smallest mammals). They are large enough to remind people of diminutive squirrels, so they are sometimes called "squirrel-shrews" and are placed in the Family *Tupaiidae* (tyoo-pay'ih-dee; from a Malay word for "squirrel"). Their brains are somewhat more advanced than those of ordinary insectivores and they possess various anatomical characteristics which to a zoologist spell "early primate" rather than "late insectivore."

An important difference between the tree-shrew and the shrew lies in just that word "tree." The primates began as arboreal (tree-living) creatures, and all but some of the larger specimens still are. The arboreal environment is the land environment exacerbated still further, to almost prohibitive difficulty. The hard land is at least steady and firm, but the branches of trees do not offer a continuous surface and sway under weight or in the wind. The dangers of gravity are multiplied, too. In case of a misstep, an organism does not merely fall the height of its legs; it falls from the much greater height of the branch.

There are a number of ways in which mammals can adapt to the difficult arboreal life. Reliance can be placed on smallness, nimbleness, and lightness. For a squirrel, the thin branches are negotiable and the danger of a fall is minimized. (The smaller a creature, the less likely it is to be hurt by a fall.) With the development of a gliding surface of skin, as in the "flying" squirrel, the fall is actually converted into a means of locomotion. An alternative is to trade nimbleness for caution, to move very slowly and test each step as it is taken. This is a solution adopted by the sloths, which have attained considerable size at the cost of virtually converting themselves into mammalian turtles.

The early primates took the path of the squirrel. These include not only the tree-shrews but also the *lemurs* (lee'merz; "ghost" L, because of their quiet and almost ghostly movements through the night — they being nocturnal creatures). Together, the tree-shrews and the lemurs are placed in the Suborder *Prosimii* (prohsim'ee-eye; "pre-monkeys" L).

The whole Suborder is still marked by its insectivorous beginnings. The members have pronounced muzzles, with eyes on either side of the head; the cerebral cortex is still smooth and is still mainly concerned with smell. Notwithstanding, a crucial change was taking place. Slowly, more and more, the early primates tackled the difficulties of arboreal life head on. They did not follow a course of evasions. They did not merely patter along the branch but developed a grasping paw — that is, a hand — with which to seize the branch firmly.

Nor did they escape the dangers of gravity by developing a gliding membrane.* Rather, they relied on an improvement of the coordination of eye and muscle. In judging the exact position of a swaying branch, no sense is as convenient as that of sight, and even among the tree-shrews a larger proportion of the brain is devoted to sight and a lesser amount to smell than is true of the insectivores. This tendency continues among the lemurs.

The most specialized of the lemurs is the *tarsier* (tahr'see-ur; so called because the bones of its tarsus, or ankle, are much elongated). Here the importance of sight as opposed to sound makes itself evident in a new way. The eyes are located in front rather than on either side of its face. Both can be brought to bear simultaneously on the same object and this makes stereoscopic, or three-dimensional, vision possible. Only under such conditions can the distance of a swaying branch be estimated with real efficiency. (The tarsier's eyes are so large for its tiny face that its silent, staring appearance at night has given it the name "spectral tarsier.") With the development of grasping hands capable of holding food and bringing it to the mouth, the importance of the muzzle declines; the tarsier in reality lacks one, and is flat-faced like a man. The decline of the muzzle, together with the ascendancy of the eye, allows the sense of smell to become less important.

---

* There is an animal called a flying lemur, which has developed such a membrane, but it is an insectivore and not a primate.

The suborder including all the remaining primates is *Anthropoidea* (an'throh-poi'dee-uh; "manlike" G), and within this grouping are the monkeys, apes, and man himself. Among all of these, the traits in the tarsier are accentuated. All are primarily eye-and-hand-centered, with stereoscopic vision and with the sense of smell receding into the background.

Of all the senses, sight delivers information to the brain at the highest rate of speed and in the most complex fashion. The use of a hand with the numerous delicate motions required to grasp, finger, and pluck requires complex muscle coordination beyond that necessary in almost any other situation. For an eye-and-hand animal to be really efficient there must be a sharp rise in brain mass. If such a rise had not come about the primates would have remained a small, inconspicuous, and unsuccessful group with eyes and hands incapable of developing their full potentiality. But there *was* a sharp rise in brain mass. No other animal the size of a monkey has anywhere near the mass of brain a monkey possesses. (For their body size, the smaller monkeys have larger brains than we do.) Nor has any other animal its size a brain as convoluted as that of a monkey.

The higher primates are divided into two large groups, the *Platyrrhina* (plat'ih-ry'nuh; "flat-nosed" G) and *Catarrhina* (kat'uh-ry'nuh; "down-nosed" G). In the former, the noses are flat, almost flush against the face, with the nostrils well separated and opening straight forward. In the latter, the nose is a prominent jutting feature of the face, and within it the two nostrils are brought close together, with the openings facing downward, as in our own case.

The platyrrhines are to be found exclusively on the American continents and are therefore usually referred to as "New World monkeys." They frequently possess a prehensile tail; one able to curl about a branch and bear the weight of the body even without the supporting help of any of the legs. These prehensile-tailed monkeys are a great favorite at the zoos because of their breathtaking agility. Their four limbs are long and are all equipped for grasping.* The tail acts as a fifth limb. Often the tail and all the limbs are long and light, with a small body at the center. One common group of platyrrhines is commonly known as "spider monkeys" because of their slight, leggy build.

This is all very well as far as adaptation to arboreal life is concerned, but long arms that can stretch from branch to branch reduce the importance of the eye. A tail that can act almost literally as a crutch does the same. The adaptation to arboreal life is wonderful, but in effect some of the pressure is off the brain. The platyrrhines are the least intelligent of the higher primates.

The catarrhines are confined to the Eastern Hemisphere and are therefore ordinarily termed the "Old World monkeys." No catarrhine has a prehensile tail, which means one crutch less. The catarrhines are stockier in build and lack some of the advantageous agility of the platyrrhines. They are forced to make up for it by greater intelligence. The catarrhines are divided into three families. Of these the first is *Cercopithecidae* (sir′koh-pih-thee′sih-dee; "tailed-monkey" G). This family, as the name implies, possesses tails, though not prehensile ones. The most formidable of the family are the various baboons, which are stocky enough to have abandoned the trees for the ground but have not abandoned the tree-developed eye-and-hand organization, or the intelligence that developed along with it. In addition to their intelligence, they travel in packs and have redeveloped muzzles that are well equipped with teeth.

And yet even the baboons with their short tails must take a backseat in intelligence with respect to the remaining two families of the catarrhines. In the remaining two families there are no tails at all, and the hind legs become increasingly specialized for support rather than for grasping. It is as though intelligence

---

* Indeed, an old-fashioned name for monkeys is *Quadrumana* (kwod-roo′muh-nuh; "four handed" L), and this came to be applied to all higher primates except man. The term has fallen into disuse because this grand division between man on the one hand and all other higher primates on the other is zoologically unsound, however soothing it may be to our pride.

is forced to increase as the number of grasping appendages sinks from five to four, and then from four to two.

APES AND MEN

The second catarrhine family is *Pongidae* (pon'jih-dee), which includes the animals known as "apes." The name of the family is from a Congolese word for ape. The apes are the largest of the primates and therefore possess the largest brains in absolute terms. This, too, is a factor in making them the most intelligent of all the "lower animals."

There are four types of creatures among the apes. These are, in order of increasing size, the gibbon, the chimpanzee, the orangutan, and the gorilla. The gibbons (of which there are several species) are, on the average, less than three feet high and weigh between 20 and 30 pounds. Furthermore, they have gone nearly the way of the spider monkey. Although without tails, their forearms have lengthened almost grotesquely and they can make their way through the trees, hand-over-hand, with an uncanny accuracy that makes them a fascination in zoos. Between a small size and an overdependence on long limbs, it is not surprising that the gibbon is the least intelligent of the apes.

The remaining three pongids, approaching or even exceeding man in size, are lumped together as the "great apes." The weight of the brain of an orangutan has been measured at about 340 grams (12 ounces), that of a chimpanzee at 380 grams (13½ ounces), and that of a gorilla at 540 grams (19 ounces, or just under 1¼ pounds). Of these, the most intelligent appears to be the chimpanzee, since the greater mass of the gorilla's brain seems to be neutralized to an extent by the much greater mass of its body.

The similarities between the apes (particularly the chimpanzee) and man are unmistakable and sufficiently apparent to cause the Pongidae to be referred to frequently as the *anthropoid apes* ("manlike" G). And yet there are distinctions of considerable importance between apes and man, enough difference so that, quite fairly and without too much self-love on our own part, man may be put into a third catarrhine family all by himself, *Hominidae* (hoh-min'ih-dee; "man" L). Some millions of years ago the creatures ancestral to man branched off from the line of evolution leading to the modern apes. It was from this branch of the family that the first hominids developed. The hominids stood upright, finally and definitely. The hind legs became fully specialized for standing only and it is solely as a kind of stunt that a modern man, for instance, can pick up anything with his small, hardly maneuverable toes. The hominids became definitely two-handed, and the arms did not, as in the gibbon's case, unduly specialize themselves for a single function. The one specialization, that of the opposable thumb, rather served to accentuate the Jack-of-all-trades ability.

The loss of equipment again placed the accent on the brain. The hominids advanced in size, to be sure, outstripping the gibbon, and equaling or even slightly surpassing the chimpanzee. The hominids never attained the weight of the orangutan or the gorilla, and yet the hominid brain developed almost grotesquely; the expanding cranium came to overshadow the shrinking face.

The skull of the oldest creature we can definitely consider a hominid was discovered in Tanganyika in 1959. It has been given the name *Zinjanthropus* (zin-jan'throh-pus; "East Africa man"), from the native term for East Africa, the region in which it was discovered. The Zinjanthropus skull is much more primitive than any living human skull but also it is much more advanced than any living ape skull. Associated with the fossil, in the strata in which it was found, were tools. Therefore Zinjanthropus was a tool-making creature and deserves the name "hominid" in the cultural as well as the zoological sense. In 1961 the age of the strata in which Zinjanthropus was found was determined by measuring the radioactive decay of the potassium within it. The fossil, it would seem, is 1,750,000 years old. This is quite startling, because until the moment of the time measurement it had

been felt that tool-making hominids had been inhabiting the
planet only for half a million years or so. However, the finding
is somewhat controversial, and perhaps the last word has not
been said.

Zinjanthropus is an example of a small-brained hominid and
there are other varieties, too, such as those popularly known as
Java man and Peking man from the sites at which the first skeletal remains were discovered. The reference "small-brained" is
only relative. Brought to life, such hominids would indeed look
pinheaded to us, but their brains approached the 1000-gram (2¼
pounds) mark and were nearly twice the size of that of any
living ape.

Nevertheless, as the hominid group continued to evolve, the
accent continued to be on the brain. What we might call the
"large-brained hominid" developed, and it was these only which
survived to inherit the earth. Today (and since well before the
dawn of history) only one species of hominid remains. This is
Homo sapiens (hoh'moh say'pee-enz; "man, the wise" L), to
whom we can refer as "modern man."

The specimens of modern man existing today are not actually
the largest-brained hominids. An early variety of modern man,
called the Cro-Magnons (kroh-man'yon; from the region in
France where their skeletal remains were first discovered), seems
to have the record in this respect. Even Neanderthal man (nay-
ahn'der-tahl; so called from the region in Germany where their
skeletal remains were first discovered), who seems distinctly
more primitive than modern man in skull formation and in jaws,
had a brain that was slightly larger than our own. However, between the Neanderthals and ourselves there seemed to be an
improvement not so much in size of the brain as in internal organization. In other words, those portions of the brain believed to
be most important for abstract thought seem better developed
and larger in modern man than in Neanderthal man.

(Nevertheless, there are some who fear that the human brain
may have reached its peak and may be on the point of begin-

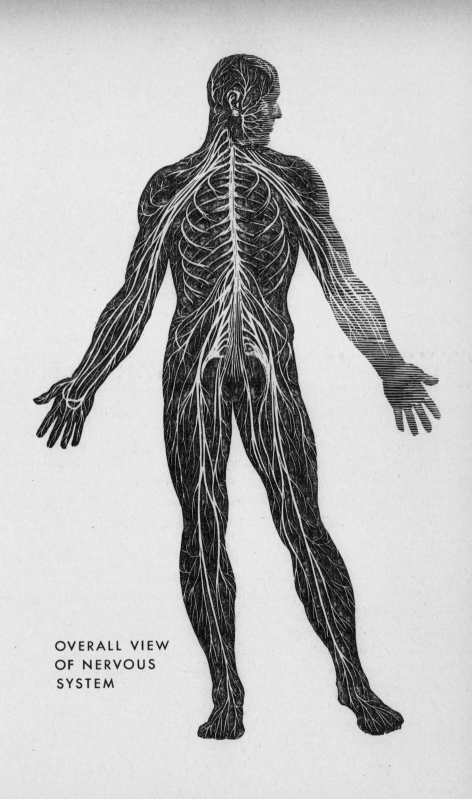

OVERALL VIEW
OF NERVOUS
SYSTEM

ning a downhill slide. They point out that individual intelligence is no longer of key importance, since all members of a society, intelligent or not, benefit from the accomplishments of the intelligent few, while those few are forced to pay the penalty of nonconformity by leading a less comfortable life. Evolutionary pressures would therefore now favor declining intelligence. This, however, may be an overly pessimistic view. I hope so, certainly.)

In modern man the brain at birth is about 350 grams (12 ounces) in weight and is already as large as that of a full-grown orangutan. In maturity, the average weight of a man's brain is 1450 grams (3¼ pounds). The average weight of a woman's brain is about 10 per cent less on the average, but her body is smaller too and there is no reason for thinking that either sex is inherently the more intelligent. Among normal human beings, in fact, there can be marked differences in weight of brain without any clear correlation in intelligence. The Russian novelist Ivan Turgenev had a brain that was just over the 2000-gram mark in weight, but Anatole France, also a skilled writer, had one that was just under the 1200-gram mark.

This represents the extremes. Any brain that weighs as little as 1000 grams is apparently below the minimum weight consistent with normal intelligence and is sure to be that of a mental defective. On the other hand, there have been mental defectives with brains of normal or more than normal size. Weight of brain alone, although a guide to intelligence, is by no means the entire answer.

If we consider the average weight of a man as 150 pounds and the average weight of his brain as 3¼ pounds, then the brain-body ratio is about 1:50. Each pound of brain is in charge (so to speak) of 50 pounds of body. This is a most unusual situation. Compare it with the apes, for example — man's nearest competitors. A pound of chimpanzee brain is in charge of 150 pounds of chimpanzee body (differently expressed, the brain/body ratio is 1:150), whereas in the gorilla the ratio may be as low as 1:500. To be sure, some of the smaller monkeys and also some of the hummingbirds have a larger brain/body ratio. In some monkeys the ratio is as great as 1:17½. If such a monkey were as large as a man and its brain increased in proportion, that brain would weigh 8½ pounds. The brain of such a monkey is in actual fact very small; so small that it simply lacks the necessary mass of cortical material to represent much intelligence despite the small amount of body it must coordinate.

Two types of creatures have brains considerably larger in terms of absolute mass than the brain of man. The largest elephants can have brains as massive as 6000 grams (about 13 pounds) and the largest whales can have brains that reach a mark of 9000 grams (or nearly 19 pounds). The size of the bodies such brains have to coordinate is far, far larger still. The biggest elephant brain may be 4 times the size of the human brain, but the weight of its body is perhaps 100 times that of the human body. Where each pound of our own brain must handle 50 pounds of our body, each pound of such an elephant's brain must handle nearly half a ton of its body. The largest whales are even worse off: each pound of their brain must handle some five tons of body.

Man strikes a happy medium, then. Any creature with a brain much larger than man's has a body so huge that intelligence comparable to ours is impossible. Contrarily, any creature with a brain/body ratio much larger than ours has a brain so small in absolute size that intelligence comparable to ours is impossible.

In intelligence, we stand alone! Or almost. There is one possible exception to all this. In considering the intelligence of whales, it is perhaps not fair to deal with the largest specimens. One might as well try to gauge the intelligence of primates by considering the largest member, the gorilla, and ignoring a smaller primate, man. What of the dolphins and porpoises, which are pygmy relatives of the gigantic whales? Some of these are no larger than man and yet have brains that are larger than man's (with weights up to 1700 grams, or 3¾ pounds), and more extensively convoluted.

It is not safe to say from this alone that the dolphin is more intelligent than man, because there is the question of the internal organization of the brain. The dolphin's brain (like that of Neanderthal man) may be oriented more in the direction of what we might consider "lower functions."

The only safe way to tell is to attempt to gauge the intelligence of the dolphin by actual experiment. Some investigators, notably John C. Lilly, seem convinced that dolphin intelligence is indeed comparable to our own, that dolphins and porpoises have a speech pattern as complicated as ours, and that a form of interspecies communication possibly may yet be established. If so, it would surely be one of the most exciting developments in human history. So far, the matter remains controversial, and we must wait and see.

8

OUR CEREBRUM

Now that I have discussed the nerve cells (the mode of action of which is identical, as far as we can tell, in all animals) and have briefly taken up the manner in which their organization into a nervous system has grown more intricate through the course of evolution, reaching a climax in ourselves, it is time to take up the human nervous system in particular. The central nervous system (the brain plus the spinal cord) is clearly the best protected part of the body. The vertebrae of the spinal column are essentially a series of bony rings cemented together by cartilage, and through the center of those protecting rings runs the spinal cord. At the upper end of the neck, the spinal cord passes through a large opening in the base of the skull and becomes the brain. The brain is surrounded snugly by the strong, dense bone of the skull.

The protection of the bone alone is rather a harsh one, however. One would not like to entrust the soft tissue of the brain to the immediate embrace of bone. Such an immediate embrace fortunately does not exist, since the brain and spinal cord are surrounded by a series of membranes called the *meninges* (mehnin'jeez; "membranes" G). The outermost of these is the *dura mater* (dyoo'ruh may'ter; "hard mother"* L), and indeed it is

* The use of the word "mother" dates back to a theory of the medieval Arabs, who felt that out of these membranes all the other body membranes were formed.

hard. It is a tough fibrous structure that lines the inner surface of the vertebral rings of bone and the inner surface of the skull, smoothing and somewhat cushioning the bare bony outlines. Sheets of dura mater extend into some of the major dividing lines within the central nervous system. One portion extends downward into the deep fissure separating the cerebrum into a right and left half; another extends into the fissure dividing the cerebrum and the cerebellum. On the whole, though, the dura mater is a bone lining.

The innermost of the meninges is the *pia mater* (py'uh may'ter; "tender mother" L). This is a soft and tender membrane that closely lines the brain and the spinal cord, insinuating itself into all the unevennesses and fissures. It is the direct covering of the central nervous system. Between the dura mater and the pia mater is the *arachnoid membrane* (a-rak'noid; "cobweblike" G, so called because of the delicate thinness of its structure). Inflammation of the membranes, usually through bacterial or viral infection, is *meningitis*. Bacterially caused meningitis, in particular, was a very dangerous disease before the modern age of antibiotics. Even the membranes, taken by themselves, are not sufficient protection for the brain: between the arachnoid membrane and the pia mater (the *subarachnoid space*) is the final touch, the *cerebrospinal fluid*. One way in which the cerebrospinal fluid protects the brain is by helping to counter the effects of gravity. The brain is a soft tissue; as a matter of fact, its outermost portions are 85 per cent water, making this the most watery of all the solid tissues of the body. It is even more watery than whole blood. Hence it is not to be expected that the brain can be very hard or rigid — it isn't. It is so soft that if it were to rest unsupported on a hard surface the pull of gravity alone would be sufficient to distort it. The cerebrospinal fluid supplies a buoyancy that almost entirely neutralizes gravitational pull within the skull. In a manner of speaking, the brain floats in fluid.

The fluid also counters the effect of inertia. The bony framework of the skull protects the brain against the direct impact of a blow (even a light tap would suffice to damage the unprotected tissue of the brain). This protection in itself would scarcely be of much use if the sudden movement of the head, in response to a blow, smashed the brain against the hard internal surface of the skull, or even against the fibrous dura mater. It is of little moment whether it is the enemy club that delivers the blow or your own bone. For that matter, even the mere sudden lifting or turning of the head would be enough to press the brain with dangerous force against the skull in the direction opposite the movement. The cerebrospinal fluid acts as a cushion in all these cases, damping the relative motions of brain and skull. The protection isn't unlimited, of course. A strong enough blow or a strong enough acceleration can be too much for the delicate brain structure, even if the disturbance is not sufficient to produce visible damage. Even if the brain is not directly bruised, sudden twisting of the skull (as is produced in boxing through a hard blow to the side of the chin) may stretch and damage nerves and veins as the brain, through inertia, lags behind the turning head. Unconsciousness can result and even death. This is spoken of as *concussion* ("shake violently" L).

The cerebrospinal fluid is also to be found in the hollows within the brain and spinal cord, and this brings us to another point. Despite all the specialization and elaboration of the human brain, the central nervous system still retains the general plan of structure of a hollow tube, a plan that was originally laid down in the first primitive chordates. Within the spinal cord this hollowness is almost vestigial, taking the form of a tiny *central canal*, which may vanish in adults. This central canal, like the spinal cord itself, broadens out within the skull. As the spinal cord merges with the brain, the central canal becomes a series of specialized hollows called *ventricles*.* There are four of these,

---

* "Ventricle," from a Latin word meaning "little belly," can be used for any hollow within an organ. The most familiar ventricles to the average man are those within the heart.

numbered from the top of the brain downward. Thus, the central canal opens up at the base of the brain into the lowermost of these, the *fourth ventricle*. This connects through a narrow aperture with the *third ventricle,* which is rather long and thin.

Above the third ventricle there is a connection, through another narrow aperture, with the two foremost ventricles, which lie within the cerebrum, one on either side of the fissure that divides the cerebrum into a right and left portion. Because of the fact that they lie on either side of the midline they are referred to as the *lateral ventricles.* The lateral ventricles are far larger than the third and fourth and have a rather complicated shape. They run the length of the cerebrum in a kind of outward curve, beginning near each other at the forehead end, and separating increasingly as the back of the skull is approached. A projection of each lateral ventricle extends downward and still outward into the lower portion of the cerebrum.

These hollows — the central canal and the various ventricles — are filled with cerebrospinal fluid. The cerebrospinal fluid is very similar in composition to the blood plasma (the liquid part of the blood), and in reality is little more than filtered blood. In the membranes surrounding the ventricles there are intricate networks of fine blood vessels called *chorioid plexuses* (koh'ree-oid plek'sus-ez; "membrane networks" L). These blood vessels leak, and are the source of the cerebrospinal fluid. The cells and subcellular objects within the blood, such as the white cells, the red corpuscles, and the platelets, do not pass through, of course; the leak isn't that bad. Nor do most of the protein molecules. Virtually all else in the blood does leak out, nevertheless, and pass into the ventricles.

The cerebrospinal fluid circulates through the various ventricles, and in the fourth ventricle escapes through tiny openings into the subarachnoid space outside the pia mater. Where the subarachnoid space is greater than usual, the fluid collects in *cisternae* (sis'tur-nee; "reservoirs" L). The largest of these is to be found at the base of the brain, just above the nape of the neck; it is the *cisterna magna* ("large reservoir" L). The total volume

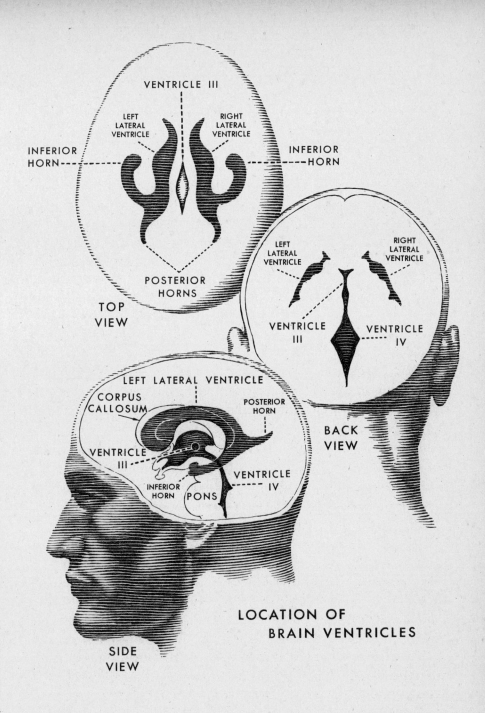

TOP
VIEW

BACK
VIEW

SIDE
VIEW

LOCATION OF
BRAIN VENTRICLES

of cerebrospinal fluid amounts to only a few drops in the new-born child but increases to 100 or 150 milliliters (about 4½ fluid ounces) in the adult.

Since cerebrospinal fluid is continually seeping into the ventricles, it must be allowed to escape somewhere. In the arachnoid membrane are small areas called *arachnoid villi* (vil'eye; "tufts of hair" L, so named because they have the appearance of tiny tufts). These are richly supplied with blood vessels, and into these the cerebrospinal fluid is absorbed. There is a resultant active circulation of the fluid from the chorioid plexuses, where it leaks out of the blood, through the ventricles, out into the subarachnoid space, and through the arachnoid villi, where it is absorbed back into the blood.

It is possible for the circulation of the cerebrospinal fluid to be interfered with. There may be blockage at some point, perhaps through the growth of a brain tumor, which closes off one of the narrow connections between the ventricles. In that case, fluid will continue to be formed and will collect in the pinched-off ventricles, the pressure rising to the point where the brain tissue may be damaged. Inflammation of the brain membranes (meningitis) can also interfere with the reabsorption of the fluid and lead to the same results. At such times, the condition is *hydrocephalus* (hy'droh-sef'ah-lus; "water-brain" G), or as it is commonly referred to, in direct translation, "water on the brain." This condition is most dramatic when it takes place in early infancy, before the bones of the skull have joined firmly together. They give with the increased internal pressure so that the skull becomes grotesquely enlarged.

Cerebrospinal fluid can be removed most easily by means of a *lumbar puncture;* that is, by the introduction of a needle between the fourth and fifth lumbar vertebrae in the small of the back. The spinal cord itself does not extend that far down the column, therefore the needle may be inserted without fear of damaging spinal tissue. The collection of nerves with which the canal is filled in that region make easy way for the needle. Fluid may be obtained, with greater difficulty, from the cisterna magna, or even from the ventricles themselves if conditions are grave enough to warrant drilling a hole through the skull. From the fluid pressure and from its chemical makeup it is possible to draw useful conclusions as to the existence or nonexistence of a brain tumor or abscess, of meningitis or other infection, and so on.

The cerebrospinal fluid offers more than mechanical protection: it is also part of a rather complex system of chemical protection for the brain. The brain, you see, has a composition quite different in some respects from that of the rest of the body. It contains a high percentage of fatty material, including a number of unique components. Perhaps for this reason brain tissue cannot draw upon the material in the blood as freely as other tissues can. It is far more selective, almost as though it had a finicky taste of its own. As a result, when chemicals are injected into the bloodstream it is often true that these chemicals may be quickly found in all the cells of the body except for those of the nervous system. There is a *blood-cerebrospinal barrier* that seems to prevent many substances from entering the fluid. There is also a direct *blood-brain barrier* that prevents them from passing from the blood directly into the brain tissue.

The blood-brain barrier may be the result of an extra layer of small cells surrounding the blood capillaries that feed the brain. These cells make up part of the *neuroglia* (nyoo-rog'lee-uh; "nerve-glue" G) that surrounds and supports the nerve cells themselves. These neuroglial cells, or simply *glia cells*, outnumber the nerve cells by 10 to 1. There are some 10 billion nerve cells in the cerebrum but 100 billion glia, and these latter make up about half the mass of the brain. A coating of these about the capillaries would serve to deaden the process of diffusion between blood and brain and so erect a selective barrier. (It has usually been assumed that these glia cells serve only a supporting and subsidiary function in the brain. Some recent research, however, would make it appear they are more intimately concerned with some brain functions such as memory.)

The brain is highly demanding in another fashion. It uses up a great deal of oxygen in the course of its labors; in fact, in the resting body, ¼ of the oxygen being consumed by the tissues is used up in the brain, although that organ makes up only 1/50 of the mass of the body. The consumption of oxygen involves the oxidation of the simple sugar (glucose) brought to the brain by the bloodstream. The brain is sensitive to any shortage of either oxygen or glucose and will be damaged by that shortage sooner than any other tissue. (It is the brain that fails first in death by asphyxiation; and it is the brain that fails in the baby if its first breath is unduly delayed.) The flow of blood through the brain is therefore carefully controlled by the body and is less subject to fluctuation than is the blood flow through any other organ. What is more, although it is easy to cause the blood vessels in the brain to dilate by use of drugs, it is impossible to make them constrict and thus cut down the blood supply.

The existence of a tumor can destroy the blood-brain barrier in the region of the tumor. This has its fortunate aspect. A drug labeled with a radioactive iodine atom and injected into the bloodstream will pass into the brain only at the site of the tumor and collect there. This makes it possible to locate the tumor by detecting the radioactive region.

THE CEREBRAL CORTEX

Since we stand upright, our nervous system, like all the rest of us, is tipped on end. Where in other vertebrates the spinal cord runs horizontally, with the brain at the forward end, in ourselves the cord runs vertically, with the vastly enlarged brain on top. During the course of the development of the nervous system, new — and what we might call "higher" — functions (involving the more complex types of coordination and the ability to reason and indulge in abstract thought) were added to the forward end of the cord through the process of cephalization. Since in the human being the forward end is on top, it follows that when we speak of

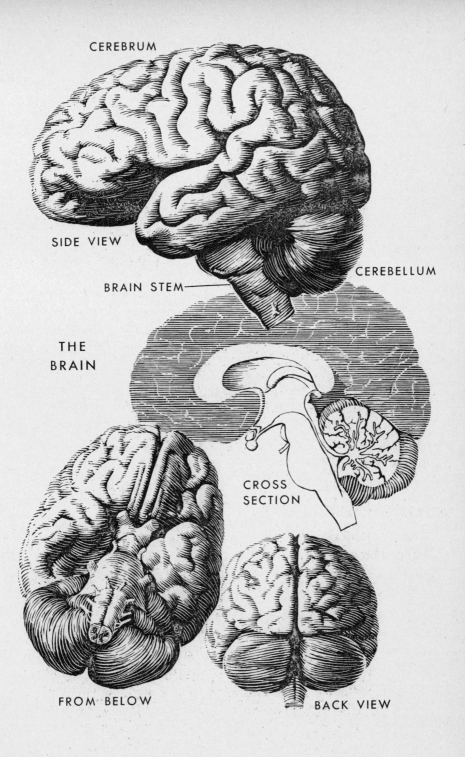

CEREBRUM

SIDE VIEW

BRAIN STEM

CEREBELLUM

THE
BRAIN

CROSS
SECTION

FROM BELOW

BACK VIEW

higher and lower levels of the central nervous system we mean this both literally and in some ways figuratively.

Furthermore, in the human being the higher levels have come to predominate not only in terms of our own estimate of importance but in that of actual mass. The central nervous system in the average man weighs about 1480 grams, or just over 3 pounds. Of this, the spinal cord — the lowest and most primitive level — weighing about an ounce, makes up only 2 per cent of the total. And of the brain, the cerebrum — which stands at the highest level and is the most recently developed — makes up 5/6 of the total mass.

In describing the central nervous system in detail, then, let us begin with the cerebrum, which is almost divided, longitudinally, into right and left halves, each of which is called a *cerebral hemisphere*. The outermost layer of the cerebrum consists of cell bodies which, grayish in color, make up most of the *gray matter* of the brain. This outermost layer of gray matter is the cerebral cortex (where "cortex" has the same meaning it has in the case of the adrenal cortex mentioned on page 377). Below the cortex are the nerve fibers leading from the cell bodies to other parts of the brain and to the spinal cord. There are also fibers leading from one part of the cortex to another. The fatty myelin sheath of these fibers lend the interior of the cerebrum a whitish appearance, and this is the *white matter* of the brain.

The cortex is intricately wrinkled into convolutions, as I mentioned in the previous chapter. The lines that mark off the convolutions are called *sulci* (sul'sy; "furrows" L), the singular form being *sulcus* (sul'kus). Particularly deep sulci are termed *fissures*. The ridges of cerebral tissue between the sulci, which look like softly rolled matter that has been flattened out slightly by the pressure of the skull, are called *gyri* (jy'ry; "rolls" L), the singular form being *gyrus* (jy'rus). The convoluted form of the cerebrum triples the surface area of the gray matter of the brain. There is twice as much gray matter, that is, lining the various sulci and fissures as there is on the flattish surface of the gyri.

The sulci and gyri are fairly standardized from brain to brain, and the more prominent ones are named and mapped. Two particularly prominent sulci are the *central sulcus* and *lateral sulcus*, which occur, of course, in each of the cerebral hemispheres. (The cerebral hemispheres are mirror images as far as the details of structure are concerned.) The central sulcus begins at the top of the cerebrum, just about in the center, and runs curvingly downward and forward. It is sometimes called the *fissure of Rolando*, after an 18th-century Italian anatomist, Luigi Rolando, who was the first to describe it carefully. The lateral sulcus starts at the bottom of the hemisphere about one third of the way back from the forward end and runs diagonally upward on a line parallel to the base of the cerebrum. It comes to an end after having traversed a little over half the way to the rear of the cerebrum. It is the most prominent of all the sulci, and is sometimes called the *fissure of Sylvius*, after the professional pseudonym of a 17th-century French anatomist who first described it. (See the illustration on page 508.)

These two fissures are used as convenient reference points by which to mark off each cerebral hemisphere into regions called *lobes*. The portion of the cerebral hemisphere lying to the front of the central sulcus and before the point at which the lateral sulcus begins is the *frontal lobe*. Behind the central sulcus and above the lateral sulcus is the *parietal lobe* (puh-ry'ih-tal). Below the lateral sulcus is the *temporal lobe*. In the rear of the brain, behind the point where the lateral sulcus comes to an end, is the *occipital lobe* (ok-sip'ih-tal). The name of each lobe is that of the bone of the skull which is approximately adjacent to it.

It seems natural to think that different parts of the cortex might control different parts of the body, and that through careful investigation the body might be mapped out on the cortex. One of the early speculators in this direction was an 18th-19th century Viennese physician named Franz Joseph Gall. He believed the brain was specialized even to the extent that different sections controlled different talents or temperamental attri-

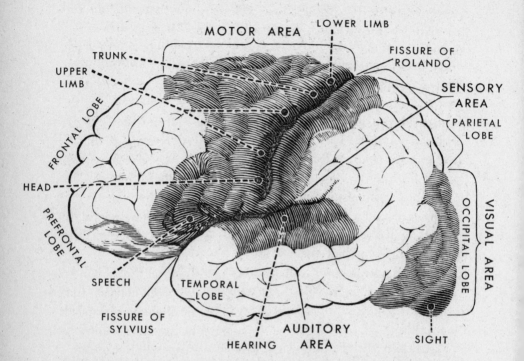

MOTOR AREA
LOWER LIMB
TRUNK
FISSURE OF ROLANDO
UPPER LIMB
SENSORY AREA
FRONTAL LOBE
PARIETAL LOBE
HEAD
OCCIPITAL LOBE
VISUAL AREA
PREFRONTAL LOBE
SPEECH
TEMPORAL LOBE
FISSURE OF SYLVIUS
AUDITORY AREA
SIGHT
HEARING

LOCATION OF IMPORTANT AREAS OF CEREBRUM

butes. Hence, if a portion of the brain seemed more than normally well developed, the talent or attribute should be correspondingly noticeable. His students and followers went further than he did. They conceived the notion that a well-developed portion of the brain would be marked by a corresponding bump on the skull, the bump being required in order to leave room for the overdevelopment of gray matter in that region. It followed that by taking careful note of the fine detail of the shape of the skull, so went the theory, one could tell a great deal about the owner of that skull. So began the foolish pseudoscience *phrenology* ("study of the mind" G).

But if Gall, and especially his followers, went off on a wrong turning, there was nevertheless something in their notion. In 1861 a French surgeon named Pierre Paul Broca, by assiduous

postmortem study of brains, was able to show that patients with
an inability to speak or to understand speech — a disorder called
aphasia ("no speech" G) — possessed physical damage to a particular area of the brain. The area involved was found to be the
third left frontal gyrus, which is often called *Broca's convolution*
as a result.

Following that, in 1870, two Germans, Gustav Fritsch and
Eduard Hitzig, began a line of research in which they stimulated
different portions of the cerebral cortex of a dog in order to take
note of what muscular activity, if any, resulted. (It was also
possible to destroy a patch of the cortex and to take note of
what paralysis might or might not result.) In consequence, the
skeletal muscles of the body were to a certain extent mapped
out on the cortex.

It was discovered by such lines of investigation that a band of
the cortex lying in the frontal lobe just before the central sulcus
was particularly involved in the stimulation of the various skeletal muscles into movement. This band is therefore called the
motor area. It seems to bear a generally inverted relationship to
the body: the uppermost portions of the motor area, toward the
top of the cerebrum, stimulate the lowermost portions of the leg;
as one progresses downward in the motor area, the muscles
higher in the leg are stimulated, then the muscles of the torso,
then those of the arm and hand, and finally of the neck and head.

The cerebral cortex in the motor area, as elsewhere, is composed of a number of layers of cells which are carefully distinguished by anatomists. One of these layers contains, in each
hemisphere, some 30,000 unusually large cells. These are called
pyramidal cells (from their shape), or *Betz cells* (after the Russian
anatomist Vladimir Betz, who first described them in 1874). The
fibers from these cells stimulate muscular contractions, each
pyramidal cell controlling a particular portion of a particular
muscle. Fibers from the smaller cells in the layers above the
pyramidal cell layer do not by themselves stimulate muscle contraction, but instead seem to sensitize the muscle fibers so that

they will more easily and readily respond to pyramidal stimulation.

The fibers from the motor area form into a bundle called the *pyramidal tract,* or *pyramidal system.* This leads downward through the various portions of the brain below the cerebrum and into the spinal cord. Because the tract connects the cortex and the spinal cord it is also called the *corticospinal tract.* The two portions of the tract, one from each cerebral hemisphere, happen to cross each other in the lower regions of the brain and in the uppermost portion of the spinal cord. The result is that stimulation of the motor area of the left cerebral hemisphere results in an effect in the right side of the body, and vice versa.

The existence of the pyramidal system is an indication of the way in which the nervous system is bound into a functional unit. That is, there may be separate anatomical parts, the cerebrum, the cerebellum, and others (which I shall discuss in some detail) but it is not to be supposed that each has a distinct and separate function. Rather, the pyramidal system in its control of motion draws on all parts of the central nervous system, from cortex to spinal column. There are also nerve fibers involved in the control of motion which do not stem from the pyramidal cells, and these, the *extra-pyramidal system,* likewise connect with all parts of the central nervous system. While the nervous system may be sliced up anatomically in a horizontal fashion, it is much better to slice it in a vertical fashion, functionally.

At each step of the descent from the motor area of the cortex, down through the lower regions of the pyramidal and extra-pyramidal systems to the muscle fibers themselves, there is a multiplication of effect. The fiber from a single pyramidal cell will exert an effect on a number of cells in the spinal cord. Each of these spinal cells will control a number of neurons in the peripheral nervous system (the portion outside the brain and spinal cord) and each neuron will control a number of muscle fibers. All in all, a single pyramidal cell may end up in indirect charge of possibly 150,000 muscle fibers. This helps in the coordination of muscular activity.

By controlling the amount of this "divergence," the body can be subjected to varying degrees of "fine control" as required. In this way the motion of the torso can be controlled adequately by relatively few pyramidal cells, since the necessary variety of motion is quite limited. Divergence is great here, and one pyramidal cell controls many thousands of fibers. A special situation exists with the fingers, which must be capable of delicately controlled motions of many varieties. Here there is considerably less divergence, and pyramidal cells are in control of definitely fewer muscle fibers.

But the cortex is not involved in merely controlling responses. To make the responses useful ones, it must also receive sensations. In the parietal lobe, therefore, just behind the central sulcus, is a band which is called the *sensory area* (see illustration, p. 508, for location of this and areas described below).

Despite this name, it does not receive *all* sensations. The sensations arising from the nerve endings in the skin and in the interior of the body are led through bundles of fibers up the spinal cord and into the brain. Some are sidetracked by the spinal cord itself, others by the lower portions of the brain. Most, however, finally reach the cortex. Those reaching the sensory area are primarily the sensations of touch and temperature, together with impulses from the muscles which give rise to knowledge concerning body position and equilibrium. These are the generalized body senses not requiring any specialized sensory organs.*
The sensory area is therefore sometimes referred to in more limited fashion as the *somesthetic area* (soh′mes-thet′ik; "body sensation" G). Even this is overgenerous, since one important somesthetic sense, that of pain, is not represented here; it is received in lower portions of the brain. The fact that the sensations are received at various horizontal levels of the nervous system shows that here, too, there is a longitudinal unification of function. There is a *reticular activating system* which coordinates the various levels in their task of receiving sensations.

---

* I shall discuss these senses and the others, too, in some detail in Chapters 10, 11, and 12.

As in the case of the motor area, the regions of the sensory area in the cerebral cortex are divided into sections that seem to bear an inverse relation to the body. Sensations from the foot are at the top of the area, followed successively as we go downward with sensations from the leg, hip, trunk, neck, arm, hand, fingers. Below the area that receives finger sensations are the areas receiving sensations from the head. Lowest of all are the sensations from the tongue; here one specialized sense is involved, because it is in the lowest portion of the sensory area that taste is received. (The other chemical sense, that of smell, is received in a region at the floor of the frontal lobe — the remnant in man of the extensive olfactory lobes in most other vertebrates.)

The sections of the sensory area devoted to the lips, tongue, and hand are (as one might expect) larger in proportion to the actual size of those organs than are the sections devoted to other parts of the body. In fact, distorted little men are sometimes drawn along diagrams of sections of the brain in an attempt to match up graphically the cortex and the body. Both in the motor area and the sensory area, the result is a tiny torso to which a small leg with a large foot is attached in the direction leading to the top of the cranium, and a large arm with a still larger hand is attached in the other direction. Beneath is a large head that seems all mouth and tongue.

This is reasonable enough. As far as movements are concerned, the manipulations of the mouth and tongue that make speech possible and the manipulation of the hand that makes tool-wielding possible are what have been the main factors in making man. As for the senses, one must expect that the flexible manipulation of a hand could not be fully efficient if we did not know, at every moment and in great detail, what it was feeling. The senses related to the mouth are less distinctively human, but while food remains important (and it does, even to intellectual *Homo sapiens*) sensations from the mouth area will require great attention.

Each of the two important specialized senses, sight and hearing, has a separate lobe reserved to itself. That portion of the temporal lobe just beneath the sensory area is reserved for the reception of sound and is therefore the *auditory area* ("hear" L), or the *acoustic area* ("hear" G). The occipital lobe carries the *visual area*, which receives and interprets the sensation of sight. This is located at the extreme rear of each cerebral hemisphere.

ELECTROENCEPHALOGRAPHY

There are some 10 billion nerve cells in the cerebral cortex, as I have said, and all are capable of undergoing the chemical and electrical changes that accompany the nerve impulse. (If they didn't, they would be dead.) A specific cell would conduct an impulse only when stimulated, and it is only then, at perhaps rare intervals, when it would be undergoing variations in electrical potential. However, at any given moment a sizable fraction of the 10 billion cells would be firing, so the brain as a whole is constantly active.

Under ordinary conditions, sensations are constantly being funneled into the cerebrum and motor impulses are constantly being sprayed outward. Even if many sensations were cut off, if you were surrounded by complete darkness and silence, if there were nothing to smell or taste, if you were floating weightless in space and could feel nothing, there would still be sensations arising from your own muscles and joints to tell you the relative position of your limbs and torso. And even if you were lying in complete relaxation, moving no muscle consciously, your heart must still pump, the muscles of your chest still keep you breathing, and so on.

It is not surprising that at all times, awake or asleep, the brain of any living creature, and not of man only, must be the source of varying electric potentials. These were first detected in 1875 by an English physiologist, Richard Caton. He applied electrodes directly to the living brain of a dog on which he had operated for the purpose and could just barely detect the tiny currents.

During the half century after his time, the techniques of detecting and amplifying tiny changes in electric potential improved vastly. By the 1920's it was possible to detect the currents even through the thickness of skin and bone covering the brain.

In 1924 an Austrian psychiatrist named Hans Berger placed electrodes against the human scalp and found that by using a very delicate galvanometer he could just detect electric potentials. He waited until 1929 before publishing his work. Since then, the use of more sophisticated technology has made the measurements of these currents a routine affair. The process is called *electroencephalography* (ee-lek'troh-en-sef'uh-log'ruh-fee; "electric brain-writing" G). The instrument used is an *electroencephalograph*, and the recording of the fluctuating potentials is an *electroencephalogram*. The abbreviation *EEG* is commonly used to represent all three words.

The electric potential of the brain waves (as these fluctuations in potential are commonly referred to) are in the millivolt (a thousandth of a volt) and microvolt (a millionth of a volt) ranges. At the very beginning of the history of EEG, Berger noticed that the potentials fluctuated in rhythmic fashion, though the rhythm was not a simple one, but made up of several types of contributory waves.

Berger gave the most pronounced rhythm the name of *alpha wave*. In the alpha wave the potential varies by about 20 microvolts in a cycle of roughly 10 times a second. The alpha wave is clearest and most obvious when the subject is resting with his eyes closed. At first Berger's suggestion that the brain as a whole gives rise to this rhythm seemed acceptable. Since his time increasingly refined investigation has altered things. More and more electrodes have been applied to the skull in various places (the positions kept symmetrical about the midplane of of the skull) and now as many as twenty-four places may be tapped and the potential differences across a number of these can be recorded simultaneously. In this way it has been discovered that the alpha wave is strongest in the occipital region of the skull, or, to say it differently, in the area where the visual center is located.

When the eyes are opened, but are viewing featureless illumination, the alpha wave persists. If, however, the ordinary variegated environment is in view, the alpha wave vanishes, or is drowned by other, more prominent rhythms. After a while, if nothing visually new is presented, the alpha wave reappears. It is possible that the alpha wave represents the state of readiness in which the visual area holds itself when it is being only minimally stimulated. (It would be almost like a person shifting from foot to foot or drumming his fingers on the table as he waits for some word that will rouse him to activity.) Since sight is our chief sense and provides us with more information than any other sense does, and is therefore the chief single factor in keeping the brain busy, it is not surprising that the alpha wave dominates the resting EEG. When the eyes actually begin reporting information and the nerve cells of the cortex go to work on it, the "waiting" rhythm vanishes. If the visual pattern remains unchanged so that the brain eventually exhausts its meaning, the "waiting" rhythm returns. The brain cannot "wait" indefinitely, however. If human beings are kept for long periods without sensory stimulation, they undergo difficulties in trying to think or concentrate and may even begin to suffer from hallucinations (as though the brain in default of real information begins to make up its own). Experiments reported in 1963 indicated that men kept in environments lacking sensory stimulation for two weeks showed progressively smaller alpha waves appearing in the EEG.

In addition to alpha waves, there are also *beta waves*, representing a faster cycle, from 14 to 50 per second, and a smaller fluctuation in potential. Then, too, there are slow, large *delta waves* and rather uncommon *theta waves*.

The EEG presents physiologists with reams of fascinating data, most of which they are as yet helpless to interpret. For instance, there are differences with age. Brain waves can be detected in the fetus, though they are then of very low voltage and very slow.

They change progressively but do not become fully adult in characteristics till the age of 17. There are also changes in brain waves characteristic of the various stages of falling asleep and waking up, including changes when, presumably, the subject is dreaming. (Delta waves accompanied by rapid movements of the eyes are prominent during these dream intervals.) In contrast to all this variegation, the EEG of the various animals tested are quite similar in general characteristics among themselves and when compared with those of man. The brain, of whatever species, seems to have but one basic fashion of operation.

As far as analyzing the EEG is concerned, we might make an analogy with a situation whereby all the people on earth are listened to from a point out in space. It might be possible to detect human noise as a large buzz with periodic tiny irregularities (representing the passage of rush-hour traffic, evening hilarity, nighttime sleep, and so on) progressing around the world. To try to get information from the EEG as to the fine details of behavior within the cortex would be something like trying to analyze the overall buzz of the world's people in order to make out particular conversations.

Specially designed computers are now being called into battle. If a particular small environmental change is applied to a subject, it is to be presumed that there will be some response in the brain that will reflect itself in a small alteration in the EEG pattern at the moment when the change is introduced. The brain will be engaged in many other activities, however, and the small alteration in EEG will not be noticeable against the many complicated wave formations. Notwithstanding, if the process is repeated over and over again, a computer can be programed to average out the EEG pattern and compare the situation at the moment of environmental change against that average. In the long run there would be, it is presumed, a consistent difference.

Yet there are times when the EEG has diagnostic value in medicine even without the refined work of the latest computers. Naturally, this is so only when the EEG is radically abnormal and therefore when the brain is suffering from some serious mal-function. (Thus, the hypothetical listener to the overall buzz of the world's people might be able to detect a war, and even locate its center of action, by the unusual sound of artillery rising above the ordinary melange of sound.)

One case in which EEG is useful is in the detection of brain tumors. The tissue making up the tumor itself is not functional and delivers no brain waves. The areas of the cortex immediately adjacent to the tumor deliver distorted brain waves. If enough EEG records are taken over enough areas of the brain and if these are subjected to careful enough analysis, it is possible some-times not only to detect the existence of a tumor but even to locate its position on the cortex. However, it will not detect a tumor in any part of the brain but the cerebral cortex.

The EEG is also useful in connection with *epilepsy* ("seizure" G), so called for reasons explained below. Epilepsy is a condi-tion in which brain cells fire off at unpredictable moments and without the normal stimulus. This may be due to damage to the brain during prenatal life or during infancy. Often it has no known cause. The most dramatic form of such a disease is one where the motor area is affected. With the motor nerves stimu-lating muscles randomly, the epileptic may cry out as the mus-cles of the chest and throat contract, fall as the muscular coordi-nation controlling balance is disrupted, and writhe convulsively. The fit doesn't last long, usually only a few minutes, but the patient can do serious damage to himself in that interval. Such fits, at unpredictable intervals, are referred to as *grand mal* (grahn mal; "great sickness," French). A more direct English name is "falling sickness."

In another version of epilepsy, it is the sensory area that is primarily affected. Here the epileptic may suffer momentary hallucinations and have brief lapses of unconsciousness. This is *petit mal* (puh-tee mal; "small sickness" French). Both areas may be mildly affected, so that a patient may have illusions followed by disorganized movements. These are *psychomotor attacks*.

Epilepsy is not very uncommon, since about 1 in 200 suffer from it, though not necessarily in its extreme form. It has a fascinating history. Attacks of grand mal are frightening and impressive, particularly in primitive societies (and some not so primitive) that do not understand what is taking place. During the attack, the epileptic's muscles are clearly not under his own control and it is easy to conclude that his body has been momentarily seized by some supernatural being. (Hence, the fit is considered a "seizure" and thus the name "epilepsy" arises.) Some famous people, including Julius Caesar and Dostoyevsky, have been epileptics.

The supernatural being may be conceived of as an evil demon, and the existence of epileptic seizures are partly to blame for the belief, even down to modern times, in demonic possession. The epileptic may be felt to have gained supernatural insights into the future as a result of his intimate relationship with the supernatural. A Delphic prophetess was always more impressive if she experienced (or counterfeited) an epileptic fit before delivering her prophecy. Modern mediums, during spiritualistic séances, are careful to writhe convulsively. To the Greeks epilepsy was "the sacred disease." Hippocrates, the "father of medicine" (or possibly some disciple), was the first to maintain that epilepsy was a disease like other diseases, caused by some organic failing, and potentially curable without recourse to magic.

The EEG is characteristic for each variety of epilepsy. Grand mal shows a pattern of high-voltage fast waves; petit mal, fast waves with every other one a sharp spike; psychomotor attacks, slow waves interspersed by spikes. The brain-wave pattern can be used to detect subclinical attacks that are too minor to be noticed otherwise. It can also be used to follow the reaction of patients to treatment by noticing the frequency and extent of these abnormal patterns.

Other uses of EEG are in the process of being developed. Thus, the brain, because of its critical need for oxygen and glucose, is the first organ to lose function in a dying patient. With modern techniques of resuscitation, it is not impossible that patients may be revived while the heart is still beating but after the higher centers of the brain are irretrievably gone. Life under those conditions is scarcely to be called life, and it has been suggested that loss of EEG rhythms be considered as marking death even though the heart is still struggling to beat.

EEG may be useful in diagnosing and even in learning to understand various psychotic states, which is something I shall come back to in Chapter 14.

THE BASAL GANGLIA

The portion of the cerebrum below the cortex is, as mentioned earlier in the chapter, largely white matter, made up of myelin-sheathed nerve fibers. Just above the various ventricles making up the hollow within the brain, for example, is a tough bridge of white matter, the *corpus callosum* (kawr'pus ka-loh'sum; "hard body" L), which binds the two cerebral hemispheres together (see illustration, p. 501). Nerve fibers cross the corpus callosum and keep the cerebrum acting as a unit, but in some ways the hemispheres are, at least potentially, independent.

The situation is somewhat analogous to that of our eyes. We have two eyes which ordinarily act as a unit. Nevertheless, if we cover one eye we can see well enough with the remaining eye; a one-eyed man is not blind in any sense of the word. Similarly, the removal of one of the cerebral hemispheres does not make an experimental animal brainless. The remaining hemisphere learns to carry on. Ordinarily each hemisphere is largely responsible for a particular side of the body. If both hemispheres are left in place and the corpus callosum is cut, coordination is lost and the two body halves come under more or less independent control. A literal case of "twin brains" is set up. Monkeys can be so treated (with further operation upon the optic nerve in order to make sure that each eye is connected to only one hemisphere), and when this is done each eye can be separately trained to do particular tasks. A monkey can be trained to select a cross over a circle as marking, let us say, the presence of food. If only the left eye is kept uncovered during the training period, only the left eye will be useful in this respect. If the right eye is uncovered and the left eye covered, the monkey will have no right-eye memory of his training. He will have to hunt for his food by trial and error. If the two eyes are trained to contradictory tasks and if both are then uncovered, the monkey alternates activities, as the hemispheres politely take their turns.

Naturally, in any such two-in-charge situation, there is always the danger of conflict and confusion. To avoid that, one cerebral hemisphere (almost always the left one in human beings) is dominant. Broca's convolution, see page 509, which controls speech, is in the left cerebral hemisphere, not the right. Again, the left cerebral hemisphere controls the motor activity of the right-hand side of the body, which may account for the fact that most people are right-handed (though even left-handed people usually have a dominant left cerebral hemisphere). Ambidextrous people, who may have cerebral hemispheres without clear-cut dominance, sometimes have speech difficulties in early life.

The subcortical portions of the cerebrum are not all white matter. There are collections of gray matter, too, below the cortex. These are called the *basal ganglia*.* The piece of gray matter that lies highest in the cerebral interior is the *caudate nucleus* ("tailed" L, because of its shape). The gray matter of the caudate nucleus bends upon itself, and its other end is the *amygdaloid nucleus* ("almond-shaped," again because of its shape). To one side of the caudate nucleus is the *lentiform nucleus* ("lens-shaped") and between the two is the white matter of the internal capsule. The nuclei are not uniformly gray but contain white matter with fibers of gray matter running through it and giving

* The word *ganglion* (gang'lee-on) is Greek for "knot" and was originally used by Hippocrates and his school for knotlike tumors beneath the skin. Galen, the Roman physician who flourished about A.D. 200, began to use the word for collections of nerve cells which stood out like knots against the ordinarily string-like nerves, and it is still so used.

the region a striated appearance. The region including the two nuclei is therefore called the *corpus striatum*.

Within the curve of the caudate-nucleus, corpus-striatum, and lentiform-nucleus complex lies a mass of gray matter that represents the thalamus. (The reason for the name is given on page 481.) The thalamus is usually not included among the basal ganglia, though it is right there physically.

The basal ganglia are difficult to study, obscured as they are by the cerebral cortex. Yet there are indications of importance both in the passive and active sense. The white matter of the corpus striatum is a bottleneck. All motor nerve fibers descending from the cortex and all sensory fibers ascending up toward it must pass through it. Consequently, any damage to that region can have the most widespread effects. Such damage can, for instance, lead to loss of sensation and capacity for motion in a whole side of the body; the side opposite to that of the cerebral hemisphere within which the damage took place. Such one-sided loss is called *hemiplegia* (hem-ee-plee'jee-uh; "half stroke" G).°

It has been suggested that one of the functions of the basal ganglia is to exert a control over the motor area of the cortex (by way of the extra-pyramidal system of which it forms a part) and to prevent the motor area from kicking off too readily. When this function of the basal ganglia is interfered with, sections of the motor area may indeed fire off too readily, and then there are rapid involuntary muscle contractions. The muscles usually affected in this way are those controlling the head and the hands and fingers. As a result, the head and hand shake continuously and gently. This shaking is most marked when the patient is at rest and smooths out when a purposeful motion is superimposed; in other words, when the motor area goes into real action instead of leaking slightly.

° The loss of the capacity for motion is referred to as *paralysis* from a Greek word meaning "to loosen." The muscles fall loose, so to speak. Conditions that bring on sudden paralysis, as the rupture of a blood vessel in the brain, is referred to as a "stroke" both in plain English and in the Greek, because the person is felled as though struck by a blunt instrument.

Other muscles become abnormally immobile in such cases, although there is no true paralysis. The facial expression becomes comparatively unchanging and masklike; walking becomes stiff, and the arms remain motionless instead of swinging naturally with the stride. This combination of too little movement in arms and face and too much movement in head and hands receives the self-contradictory name of *paralysis agitans* (aj'ih-tans; "to move" L). The self-contradictoriness is maintained in the English name of "shaking palsy." (The word "palsy" is a shortened and distorted form, descended through medieval French, of "paralysis.") Paralysis agitans was first clinically described in 1817 by an English physician named James Parkinson; it is also commonly known as *Parkinson's disease*.

Relief from some of the symptoms has been achieved by deliberately damaging the basal ganglia, which seems to be a case of "a hair of the dog." One technique is to locate the abnormal region by noting at which point a touch of a thin probe wipes out, or at least decreases, the tremor and rigidity, and then cooling the area to $-50°$ C. with liquid nitrogen. This can be repeated if the symptoms recur. Apparently, nonfunctioning ganglia are preferable to misfunctioning ones.

Sometimes damage to the basal ganglia may result in more spasmodic and extensive involuntary muscular movements; almost as though a person were dancing in a clumsy and jerky manner. Such movements are referred to as *chorea* (koh-ree'ah; "dance" G). This may strike children as an aftermath of rheumatic fever, where the infection has managed to involve the brain. An English physician named Thomas Sydenham first described this form of the disease in 1686, so that it is usually called *Sydenham's chorea*.

During the Middle Ages there were instances of "dancing manias" that swept over large areas. These probably were not true chorea epidemics, but had roots in abnormal psychology. It is possible, however, that specific cases of mania may have been set off by a true case of chorea. Someone else might have fallen into line in hysterical imitation, others followed, and a mania was under way. It was felt at one time that to be cured of the dancing mania one ought to make a pilgrimage to the shrine of St. Vitus. It is for this reason that Sydenham's chorea has the common name of "St. Vitus's dance."

There is also *hereditary chorea,* often referred to as *Huntington's chorea,* from the American physician George Sumner Huntington, who described it in 1872. It is much more serious than the St. Vitus's dance, from which, after all, one recovers. Huntington's chorea does not appear until adult life (between 30 and 50). Mental disorders accompany it; it grows steadily worse, and is eventually fatal. It is an inherited condition, as one of its names implies. Two brothers afflicted with the disease migrated to the United States from England, and all modern American patients are supposed to be descended from them.

The thalamus acts as a reception center for the somesthetic sensations — touch, pain, heat, cold, and the muscle senses. It is indeed an important portion of the reticular activating system which accepts and sifts incoming sensory data. The more violent of these, such as pain, extreme heat or cold, rough touch, are filtered out. The milder sensations from the muscles, the gentle touches, the moderate temperatures are passed on to the sensory area of the cortex. It is as though mild sensations can be trusted to the cerebral cortex, where they can be considered judiciously and where reaction can come after a more or less prolonged interval of consideration. The rough sensations, however, which must be dealt with quickly and for which there is no time for consideration, are handled more or less automatically in the thalamus.

There is a tendency, therefore, to differentiate between the cortex as the cold center of reason and the thalamus as the hot focus of emotion. And, as a matter of fact, the thalamus controls the movement of facial muscles under conditions of emotional stress, so that even when cortical control of those same muscles is destroyed and the expression is masklike in calm states, the face can still twist and distort in response to strong emotion. In addition, animals in which the cortex is removed fall easily into all the movements associated with extreme rage. Despite the foregoing, this sharp distinction between cortex and thalamus would seem to be an oversimplification. Emotions do not arise from any one small part of the brain, it would appear. Rather, many parts, including the frontal and temporal lobes of the cortex, are involved — in a complex interplay. Removing the temporal lobes of animals may reduce their emotional displays to a minimum even though the thalamus is not affected.

In recent years, attention has been focused on certain portions of the cerebrum — old portions, evolutionarily speaking, related to ancient olfactory regions — which are particularly associated with emotion and with emotion-provoking stimuli such as hunger and sex. This region seems to coordinate sensory data with bodily needs, with the requirements of the viscera, in other words. It is therefore referred to as the *visceral brain*. The convolutions associated with the visceral brain were named the *limbic lobe* ("border" L) by Broca because they surrounded and bordered on the corpus callosum. For this reason, the visceral brain is sometimes called the *limbic system*.

THE HYPOTHALAMUS

Underneath the third ventricle and, consequently, underneath the thalamus, is the *hypothalamus* ("beneath the thalamus" G), which has a variety of devices for controlling the body. Among the most recently discovered is a region within it which on stimulation gives rise to a strongly pleasurable sensation. An electrode affixed to the "pleasure center" of a rat, so arranged that it can be stimulated by the animal itself, will be stimulated for hours or days at a time, to the exclusion of food, sex, and sleep. Evidently all the desirable things in life are desirable only insofar as they stimulate the pleasure center. To stimulate it directly makes all else unnecessary. (The possibilities that arise in connection with a kind of addiction to end all addictions are distressing to contemplate.)

Because of the several ways in which the hypothalamus sets up automatic controls of bodily functions, one can look upon it as having functions not very different from those of sets of hormones acting in cooperating antagonism (such as insulin and glucagon, for instance). There is, in reality, a physical connection between the hypothalamus and the world of hormones as well as a vague functional one. It is to the hypothalamus that the pituitary gland is attached, and the posterior lobe of the pituitary actually arises from the hypothalamus in the course of its development.

It is not surprising, then, that the hypothalamus is involved in the control of water metabolism in the body. I have already described how the posterior pituitary controls the water concentration in the body by regulating reabsorption of water in the kidney tubules. Well, it would seem that one can go a step beyond the posterior pituitary to the hypothalamus. Changes in the water concentration in the blood stimulates a particular hypothalamic center first, and it is the hypothalamus that then sets off the posterior pituitary. If the stalk connecting the hypothalamus to the posterior pituitary is cut, diabetes insipidus results, even though the gland itself remains unharmed.

The hypothalamus also contains a group of cells that acts as a very efficient thermostat. We are conscious of temperature changes, of course, and will attempt to rectify extremes by adding or subtracting clothing and by the use of furnaces and air-conditioners. The hypothalamus reacts analogously, but much more delicately and with built-in devices.

Within the hypothalamus appropriate cells are affected by the temperature of the bloodstream, and small variations from the norm bring quick responses. The body's furnace is represented by a constant gentle vibration of the muscles of from 7 to 13 times a second. (This was detected and reported in 1962.) The heat liberated by such muscular action replaces that lost to a cold environment. The rate of these vibrations increases as the temperature drops and, if it grows cold enough, the amplitude becomes marked enough to be noticeable and we shiver. The body's air-conditioner is represented by perspiration, since the evaporation of water absorbs heat, and the heat absorbed is withdrawn from the body. The hypothalamus, by controlling the rate of muscle vibration and of perspiration, keeps the body's internal temperature within a Fahrenheit degree of normal (98.6° F. is usually given as the normal) despite the alteration (within reason) of outside temperatures.

There are conditions where the setting of the hypothalamus thermostat can be raised. Most frequently, this is the result of the liberations of foreign proteins, or *toxins* ("poison" G), in the body by invading germs. Even small quantities of these toxins may result in raising the temperature of the body by several degrees to produce a *fever*. In reaching the higher-than-normal temperatures of fever, all of the body's devices for raising temperature are called into play. Perspiration is cut down, and the body feels dry and the muscles are set to shivering. This is customarily the reaction to cold; the patient, whose teeth may be chattering, complains of "chills"; hence the common expression "chills and fever." When the invasion of bacteria is brought under control so that body temperature can drop to normal, the body's cooling reactions become evident. In particular, the rate of perspiration is greatly increased. This sudden onset of perspiration is the crisis, and its appearance is, in many infectious diseases, a good sign that the patient will recover.

The raising of temperature hastens the destruction of protein molecules to a much greater extent than it hastens other types of reactions. Since there are numerous proteins in the body that are essential to life, a body temperature of 108° F., only 10 Fahrenheit degrees above normal, is sufficient to place a man in serious danger of death. (Such a raised temperature also endangers the functioning of the proteins of the alien bacteria; the ideal situation is to find a temperature high enough to kill the bacteria without being high enough to affect the human cells too adversely.)

The body is much less sensitive to temperatures lower than

normal, that is, to *hypothermia* ("below-heat" G). Human beings, trapped in snowdrifts, have been snatched from slow freezing and brought back to complete recovery from temperatures as low as 60° F. The lowering of temperature decreases the rate at which chemical reactions take place in the body (lowers the "metabolic rate"), and at 60° F. the metabolic rate is only 15 per cent normal.

As a matter of fact, many normally warm-blooded animals, such as bears and dormice, react to the cold season by dropping the thermostat of the hypothalamus precipitously. Everything slows down. The heartbeat falls to a feeble few per minute and breathing is shallow. The fat supply is then sufficient to last all winter. Man lacks this ability to hibernate, and if his temperature is forced below 60° F. death follows, apparently because the coordination of the heart muscle is destroyed. Nevertheless, there are times when hypothermia is useful; especially when operations on the heart itself are in progress. Through the sufficient lowering of rate of metabolism (but not too much for safety), heart action is slowed and the heart can be tampered with for longer intervals without harm.

The human body temperature can be lowered by brute force — by packing the anesthetized body in ice water, or in a blanket cooled by refrigerant circling within. Less drastic measures are required if the hypothalamus is tackled. This can be done by withdrawing the blood from an artery, sending it through refrigerated tubes, and restoring it to the body. If the blood is taken from the carotid artery in the neck and restored there, the brain is most directly cooled. The hypothalamus is frozen out of action, and after that the body temperature can be lowered more easily. Furthermore, the brain can be brought to an especially low temperature, lower than that of the rest of the body. This decreases the metabolic rate within the brain especially and drastically cuts down its need for oxygen. It is the brain's needs that limit the time for any operation which shuts off the blood flow for a while. Under these conditions, a heart operation has lasted for as long as 14 minutes without harm to the body.

A section of the central region of the hypothalamus controls the appetite of the body just as the thermostat area controls the heat. By analogy, this appetite-controlling region can be called the *appestat*. Its existence was discovered when animals began to eat voraciously and became grotesquely obese after the appropriate area of the hypothalamus was destroyed. It appears that as the thermostat tests the blood passing through for temperature so the appestat tests it for glucose content. When, after a period of fasting, the glucose content drops below a certain key level, the appetite is turned on, one might say, and the person will eventually eat if food is available. With the glucose level restored, the appetite is turned off. In this way the average human being, eating when hungry and not eating when not hungry, can maintain a reasonable weight with reasonable constancy — and without thinking about it too much.

There are people (all too many) who maintain their weight at levels considerably higher than is optimum for health. The simplest explanation is that such people are "gluttons"; and the most romantic explanation is that there is some psychiatric reason making it necessary for them to overeat. Between the two is the ordinary physiological suggestion that the appestat is for some reason set too high, so that they become hungry sooner and stay hungry longer. A recent suggestion is that there are two appetite-controlling centers: one to turn it on (a "feeding center") and one to turn it off (a "satiety center"), and that it is the latter which is often malfunctioning in the somewhat overweight person. It is not, perhaps, that he is actively hungry as that he is constantly ready to nibble; whereas the normal person would find such eating unnecessary and even distasteful.

Finally, the hypothalamus contains an area that has to do with the wake-sleep cycle. The human being has a twenty-four-hour cycle that must have originated in response to the alternation of light and dark as the earth rotates. (Modern air travel, which puts the human cycle out of phase with the earthly cycle, can disrupt a man's regular habits of eating, sleeping, and excreting.) During the periods of sleep, a man goes through a kind of very mild hibernation. His metabolic rate drops 10 to 15 per cent below the lowest wakeful values, his heartbeat slows, his blood pressure drops, and his muscle tone slackens.

The amount of sleep required varies from person to person but decreases generally with age. For a period after birth the baby sleeps whenever it is not eating. Children, in general, sleep from ten to twelve hours a day, and adults from six to nine hours.

The purpose of sleep, one would almost naturally assume, is to make up the wear and tear of the working day; but there are many organs that work constantly day and night, without much in the way of wear and tear. When wakefulness is enforced, no bodily functions go seriously awry except those of the brain. Apparently, extended wakefulness affects the coordination of various parts of the nervous system, and there is the onset of hallucinations and other symptoms of mental disturbance. This is quite enough, however. Lack of sleep will kill more quickly than lack of food.

The onset of sleep may be mediated by a section of the hypothalamus, since damage to parts of it induces a sleeplike state in animals. The exact mechanism by which the hypothalamus performs its function is uncertain. One theory is that it sends signals to the cortex, which sends signals back in response, in mutually stimulating fashion. With continuing wakefulness, the coordination of the two fails, the oscillations begin to fail, and one becomes sleepy. When the coordination is restored, arousal takes place, even if violent stimuli (a loud noise, a persistent shake of the shoulder) does not intervene.

The reticular activating system, which filters out sensory data, is also involved in the arousal mechanism, since by refusing to pass stimuli along, it encourages sleep, and by passing them it helps bring about waking, and, what's more, maintains consciousness during the waking interval. It is therefore referred to as an "activating system." The reason for the "reticular" portion of the name will be made clear later.

The working of the reticular activating system and the mutual stimulation of hypothalamus and cortex may be insufficient to maintain wakefulness in the absence of a normal amount of varying stimuli entering the cortex. Drabness or dullness of the surroundings may send one to sleep, and deliberate concentration on a repetitive stimulus (a swinging, glittering object, say) may induce the trance well known to all of us who have watched hypnotic demonstrations. And, of course, we commonly put babies to sleep by slow, rhythmic rocking. On the other hand, if the cortex is unusually stimulated, the failure of the hypothalamic signals may be insufficient to induce sleep. The unusual stimulation may be from without (a gay party, perhaps) or from within, when the cortex is absorbed in matters arising out of anxiety, worry, or anger. In the latter case especially, sleep may not come even when all the external factors (darkness, quiet, a soft bed) usually associated with it are present. Such *insomnia* ("no sleep" L) can be exasperating indeed.

There are diseases that inflame the brain tissue (encephalitis) and can produce continuous sleep. One variety, *encephalitis lethargica* (le-thahr'jih-kuh; "forgetfulness" G), commonly called *sleeping sickness,* can produce long periods of *coma* ("put to sleep" G). In extreme cases a patient can remain in such a coma for years, provided he is properly cared for and all his needs are met by attendants.

In Africa there is an endemic disease caused by a kind of protozoon called a *trypanosome* (trip'uh-noh-sohm'; "augur-body" G, from its shape). The disease, properly called *trypanosomiasis* (trip'uh-noh-soh-my'uh-sis), is commonly called "African sleeping sickness." It is spread from person to person by the bite of the tsetse fly, which carries the protozoon and is famous for that reason. Trypanosomiasis induces a coma that usually deepens into death. Large areas of Africa are deadly to men and cattle, as a result.

9

OUR BRAIN STEM
AND SPINAL CORD

THE CEREBELLUM

All the structure of the brain from the cerebral cortex down to the hypothalamus is developed from the forebrain of the original fishy ancestor of the vertebrates. All this may therefore be referred to as the *prosencephalon* (pros'en-sef'uh-lon; "forebrain" G). This may be divided into two parts. The cerebral hemispheres themselves are the *telencephalon* ("end-brain" G), because this is the end of the central nervous system if you work from the bottom up, whereas the basal ganglia, thalamus, and hypothalamus are the *diencephalon* ("between-brain" G).

Although the forebrain has grown to be so overwhelmingly prominent a feature of the human nervous system, it does not follow that the brain is all forebrain. Below that there remain the midbrain and the hindbrain. The midbrain in the human being is comparatively small and lies about the narrow passage connecting the third and fourth ventricle. It appears as a pair of stout columns that extend vertically downward from the thalamic regions. Below it is the *pons* ("bridge" L), so named because it is a bridge connecting the midbrain with the chief portion of the hindbrain; and below that is the medulla oblongata (defined on p. 481).

The midbrain, pons, and medulla taken together form a stalk-like affair leading downward and slightly backward from the

531

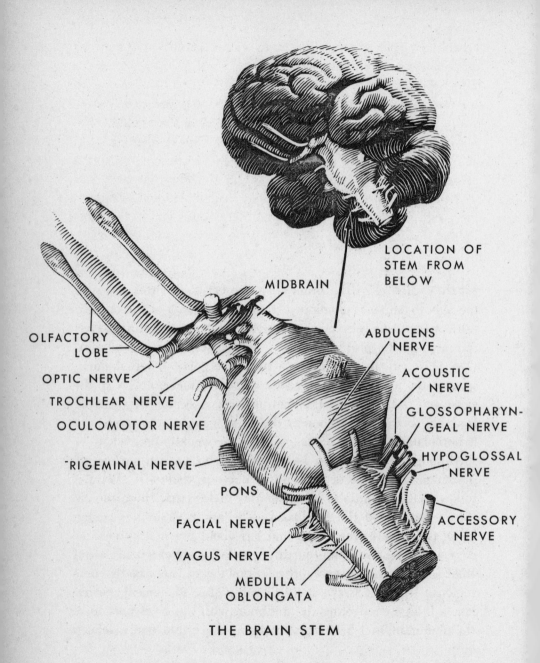

LOCATION OF STEM FROM BELOW

MIDBRAIN

OLFACTORY LOBE

OPTIC NERVE

TROCHLEAR NERVE

OCULOMOTOR NERVE

TRIGEMINAL NERVE

PONS

FACIAL NERVE

VAGUS NERVE

MEDULLA OBLONGATA

ABDUCENS NERVE

ACOUSTIC NERVE

GLOSSOPHARYN-GEAL NERVE

HYPOGLOSSAL NERVE

ACCESSORY NERVE

THE BRAIN STEM

cerebrum. The cerebrum seems to rest on these lower portions as though it were a piece of fruit balanced upon its stem. The lower structure is commonly referred to as the *brain stem* for that reason. The brain stem narrows as it proceeds downward, until it passes out through an opening in the cranium, the *foramen magnum* (foh-ray'men mag'num; "great opening" L), at the base of the skull and enters the neural canal of the spinal column. There the brain stem merges with the spinal cord.

Attached to the brain stem, behind and above, and lying immediately below the rear overhang of the cerebrum is the cerebellum (see p. 481). This originated in the primitive vertebrates as a portion of the hindbrain. Like the cerebrum, the cerebellum is divided into two portions by a longitudinal fissure, these portions being the *cerebellar hemispheres*. There is a connecting structure between the hemispheres which, seen on edge from behind, seems thin, segmented, and elongated and is consequently called the *vermis* (vur'mis; "worm" L). Like the cerebrum, the cerebellum contains white matter within and the gray matter of the cell bodies occupies the surface, which is the *cerebellar cortex*. The cerebellar cortex is more tightly wrinkled than the cerebral cortex, and its fissures lie in parallel lines.

Each cerebellar hemisphere is connected to the brain stem by three *peduncles* (peh-dung'kulz; "little feet" L) made up of nerve fibers. The uppermost connects it with the midbrain, the next with the pons, and the lowermost with the medulla oblongata. There are also connections by way of the peduncles with the cerebrum above and the spinal cord below.

The brain stem has much to do with the more automatic types of muscle activity. For example, in standing we are actively using muscles to keep our back and legs stiff against the pull of gravity. We are not ordinarily aware of this activity, but if we have been standing a long time a feeling of weariness makes itself unpleasantly evident, and if we lose consciousness while standing we at once relax the muscles that counteract gravity, and crumple to the ground.

If we were forced to keep our muscles in completely conscious play in order to stand without falling, standing would become an activity that would occupy our minds greatly and prevent us from doing much of anything else. This is not so, fortunately. The muscular effort of standing is taken care of without much of a conscious effort. As a result, we can allow our minds to be completely occupied with other matters and, if circumstances so dictate, stand easily while lost in a brown study. No one falls simply because his mind is distracted. This automatic control of the standing muscles is centered in the brain stem, particularly in a portion of it characterized by a mixture of gray and white matter so interspersed as to give it a netlike appearance. This is the *reticular area* ("little net" L). It is here, too, that the sensory filter is located, which we have been referring to as the reticular activating system (see p. 529).

Assuredly we do not wish to stand all the time. In order to sit down, the standing muscles must relax. This is done in response to impulses from the basal ganglia above the brain stem. These impulses allow the body to fall down, one might say, in a controlled fashion and to assume the sitting position. If an animal's brain is cut between the cerebrum and the brain stem, these relaxing impulses from the basal ganglia can no longer reach the muscles. As a result the animal becomes rigid all over and remains so. Its war against gravity becomes permanent and uncompromising.

Standing is not a static matter, though it may seem so. The human body is in a relatively unstable position while standing, because it has a high center of gravity and is balanced on two supports placed close together. (Most other vertebrates are quadrupeds, with a relatively lower center of gravity, and balance on four supports, generously spaced, at the vertexes of a rectangle.) Consequently, if a man tries to stand absolutely rigid without moving a muscle under any circumstances, he can be easily toppled by a brisk push against the shoulder. In an actual situation of that sort, the man would automatically shift his muscular effort to counteract the force, spread his legs wider apart, and push back. If in the end he fell, it would only be after a struggle.

The forces tending to upset equilibrium are constant. If no kindly friend is testing you by a push, you still may be altering the position of your center of gravity by the natural motions of the body — by reaching, lifting, stooping. You may be withstanding the erratic pressure of the wind. In short, you are constantly tending to fall in one direction or another, and the muscles of your trunk and legs must constantly adjust their tensions in order to counteract and neutralize these falling tendencies.

Here there is an intimate connection, again, between the brain stem and the basal ganglia. The overall position of the body with respect to the pull of gravity is revealed by structures in the inner ear which I shall discuss later in the book. Nerve messages from the inner ear are received by the brain stem and the basal ganglia. In addition, sensations from muscles and joints continually arrive at the reticular activating system in the brain stem. In cooperation, basal ganglia and brain stem act so that appropriate muscles are stiffened or relaxed, so that equilibrium is constantly maintained.

Far from being troublesome, this constant necessity of altering muscular tension to produce equilibrium is useful. If we were to imagine a human being in perfect balance, we would see that the muscles would be forced to maintain a constant and unchanging tension and would grow weary more rapidly. By constant adjustment of equilibrium, different muscles bear the brunt at different times and each has a certain chance to rest. Actually, when we are forced to stand a long time we exaggerate these varying tensions on the muscles by altering the position of the center of gravity. We do this by shifting restlessly from foot to foot, or by shifting weight in other parts of the body.

Walking consists of throwing ourselves off balance by leaning forward and then catching ourselves before we fall by moving a foot ahead into a new position. It is a difficult feat for a child to learn, and during his early attempts it takes up all his concentration. If his mind wanders, he plops down.

However, walking involves rhythmic motion; the same muscles tense and relax in a fixed pattern that is repeated over and over again. With time, the control of these rhythmic muscular movements can be shifted to the brain stem, which can then keep the arms and legs swinging along without any need for much conscious effort on our part. We can even walk with reasonable efficiency while engaged in an absorbing conversation or with our head buried in a book.

This perpetual loss and regaining of equilibrium during standing and walking involves constant feedback. Thus, if the body is out of equilibrium and if the basal ganglia begin a change in the tension of particular muscles in order to restore equilibrium, sensory impulses must be received at each instant to indicate the departure from equilibrium at that moment, in order for the tension of the muscles to be constantly adjusted (feedback). This means the body must look ahead.

The reason for this may perhaps be more easily understood if we consider a mechanical analogy. If you are turning a corner while driving an automobile, you must begin to turn your wheel before you reach the corner, turning it more and more as you proceed, until you have reached maximum turn midway around the corner. Otherwise, if you reach the corner while your wheels are still perfectly straight, you will have to turn too sharply. Again, you must begin to straighten your wheel long before you complete the turn. You must begin to straighten it, in fact, as soon as you have reached midway around the corner, and adjust the straightening process in such a way that the wheels are perfectly straight, at last, just as you complete the turn. Otherwise, if your wheels are still turned when you are finally heading in the right direction, you will find yourself turning into the curb and forced to right yourself by a quick curve in the opposite direction.

So, you see, a proper turn requires you to look ahead, to be aware of not only your position at the moment but of your future position a few moments later. This is not easy for a beginner.

When first learning to drive a car, a man is forced to take corners very slowly in order to avoid turning erratically first this way and that. As experience grows, he begins to handle the wheel without conscious thought and to make smooth and perfect turns every time — well, nearly every time.

A situation exactly analogous to this takes place in the controlling centers of the nervous system when equilibrium must be maintained or when a specific motion of any sort is necessary. Suppose that you move your arm forward to pick up a pencil. Your hand moves forward rapidly but must begin to slow up before it quite reaches the pencil. The fingers must begin to close before the pencil is touched. If the hand looks as though it might go to one side, its position is adjusted correspondingly; if it looks as though it will overshoot the mark, it must be slowed further; or hastened, if it will fall short. All this continuous correction of motion is unconscious, and we might feel ready to swear that it does not take place. Nevertheless, it is why we look at the pencil we are to pick up, or the jaw we are to punch, or the shoe-lace we are to tie. It is the continual message sent to the brain by the eye which enables us to adjust the controls constantly. If you reach for a pencil without looking, even if you know where it is, you are very apt to have to grope a bit.

To be sure, looking is not always required. If you are told to touch your nose with your finger, you can do it quite accurately even in the dark. You are normally aware of the position of various parts of your body at all times through the somesthetic senses. Likewise, you might be able to type or knit without looking, but your fingers are making very short-range motions where, through long practice, there is scarcely room to go astray.

It is a chief role of the cerebellum, evidently, to take care of this adjustment of motion by feedback. It looks ahead, and predicts the position of the arm a few instants ahead, organizing motion accordingly. When the system fails, the results can be dramatic. A hand reaching for a pencil will overshoot the mark, come back, overshoot the mark in the reverse direction, go forward, and continue to do this over and over. There are wild oscillations that may resemble those of a novice driver trying to round a corner at too great a speed. In mechanical devices such oscillations are referred to as "hunting." Damage to the cerebellum induces such hunting, and anything that requires the coordination of several muscles becomes difficult or even impossible. An attempt to run leads to an instant fall. Motions become pathetically jerky, and even the attempt to touch the finger to the nose can result in a ludicrous miss of the target. This condition is called *ataxia* (a-tak'see-uh; "disordered" G). *Cerebral palsy* refers to any disturbance in muscle use resulting from brain damage taking place during fetal development or during the birth process. About 4 per cent of such cases show ataxia.

The brain stem also controls specific functions and motions of the digestive tract. For instance, the rate of salivary secretion is controlled by certain cells in the upper medulla and the lower pons. The sight and smell of food, or even the thought of food, will trigger those cells to stimulate salivary secretion so that the mouth "waters." On the contrary, fear or tension may inhibit their action so that the mouth grows dry. The process of swallowing brings about a number of automatic movements in the throat, and a subsequent wave of constriction in the esophagus that pushes the food ahead of it into the stomach. These, too, are under the control of cells in the brain stem.

Then, too, a region in the brain stem controls the respiratory rate. This is to a certain extent under voluntary control and hence amenable to impulses from the cerebrum. We can force ourselves to breathe quickly or slowly; we can even hold our breath. All these voluntary interferences with rate of respiration quickly grow difficult and wearisome and the automatic control of the brain stem takes over.

Below the brain stem, beyond the foramen magnum, is the lowermost portion of the central nervous system, the *spinal cord*. This is what is left of the undifferentiated nerve cord of the original chordates. The spinal cord is roughly elliptical in cross sec-

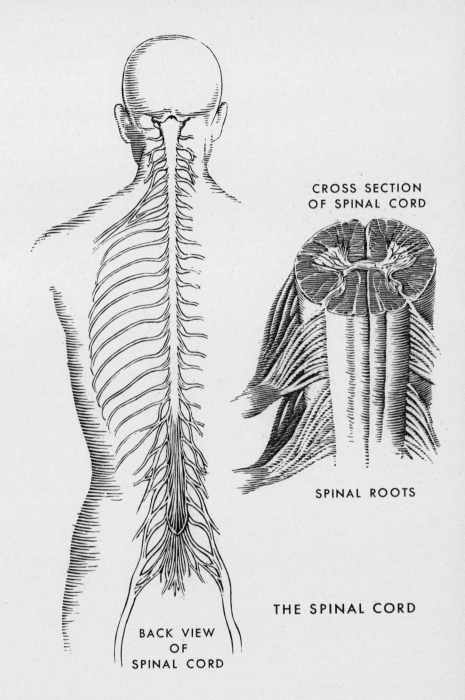

CROSS SECTION
OF SPINAL CORD

SPINAL ROOTS

BACK VIEW
OF
SPINAL CORD

THE SPINAL CORD

tion, being wider from right to left than from front to back. There is a furrow running down the back of the cord and a somewhat wider but shallower depression running down in front. Together these almost, but not quite, divide the cord into a right and left half that are mirror images. Running down the axis of the cord is the small central canal (which sometimes vanishes in adults), all that is left of the hollow in the original chordate nerve cord.

The inner portion of the cord is filled with a mass of nerve cell bodies, so the spinal cord has its gray matter as the brain has. Only, whereas the gray matter of the brain is on the outside cortex, that of the spinal cord lies within. When the spinal cord is viewed in cross section, the gray matter forms a more or less vertical line in both right and left halves. The two lines are connected by gray matter reaching across the central canal region. As a result, the gray matter in cross section looks like a rather straggly *H*. As shown in the illustration (p. 539), the lower bars of the letter H are those which extend dorsally — toward the back. They are relatively long and reach almost to the surface of the spinal cord. These are the *posterior horns,* or *dorsal horns.* The upper bars of the H, extending ventrally — toward the abdomen — are shorter and stubbier. These are the *anterior horns,* or *ventral horns.* Surrounding the H-shaped gray matter and filling out the elliptical cross section are the massed nerve fibers, which, because of their myelin sheathing, make up the white matter. In the spinal cord the white matter is on the surface, and not, as in the brain, in the interior.

The spinal cord does not run the full length of the spinal column in man. It ends at about the first or second lumbar vertebra, just in the small of the back. The spinal cord, therefore, is only about 18 inches long. It is about ½ inch wide and in the adult weighs about 1 ounce.

THE CRANIAL NERVES

Outside the brain and spinal cord, which make up the central nervous system, is the peripheral nervous system (see p. 140).

This consists of the various nerves that connect particular parts of the central nervous system with particular organs. The nerves in turn consist of bundles of hundreds, sometimes thousands, of individual nerve fibers. Some nerve fibers conduct impulses from the different organs to the central nervous system and are therefore *afferent fibers* (af'ur-ent; "carry toward" L). Because the impulses carried toward the brain and spinal cord are interpreted by the central nervous system as sensations of various sorts, the afferent fibers have the alternate name of *sensory fibers*. There are also nerve fibers that conduct impulses from the central nervous system to the various organs. These are *efferent fibers* (ef'ur-ent; "carry outward" L). They induce responses in the organs to which they are connected, and since the most noticeable of the responses are the motions induced in muscles, the efferent fibers are also called *motor fibers*.

There are a few *sensory nerves*, containing only sensory fibers, and *motor nerves*, containing only motor fibers. Most are, nonetheless, *mixed nerves* and contain both sensory and motor fibers. Nerves contain not only nerve fibers but sometimes, in addition, collections of the cell bodies to which these fibers are attached. These cell body collections are ganglia, a word I discussed on page 520.

In man 43 pairs of nerves, all told, lead into the central nervous system. Of these, 12 pairs are connected to the brain; they are the *cranial nerves* (see illustration, p. 532). The remaining 31 pairs join the spinal cord. The cranial nerves can simply be numbered one to twelve in Roman numerals (as they often are) according to the point of junction with the brain, beginning at the cerebrum and ending at the bottom of the medulla oblongata. Each has its own proper name, too, and these are as follows:

I. *Olfactory Nerve.* Each consists of a number of closely associated nerves (about twenty) that originate in the mucous membrane of the upper part of the nose. They extend upward, passing through small holes in the bones that make up the base of the cranium and ending in the olfactory lobes, which are small projections of the cerebrum, lying immediately above the floor of the cranium. As the name implies, these nerves are involved in the sense of smell.

The olfactory nerve is the only nerve to connect to the cerebrum; it reminds us that the cerebrum was originally primarily a smell organ until the mammals made something more of it. The remaining eleven cranial nerves are all attached to various portions of the brain stem.

II. *Optic Nerve.* This has to do with sight, as the name implies, and originates in the retina of the eye. The optic nerves from the two eyes extend backward and join at the midbrain. In this joined structure some of the fibers from each eye cross over to the opposite side, some remain on the original side. The fibers thus form an X shape; and the structure is the *optic chiasma* (ky-az'muh), because the Greek letter "chi" looks like our X (see illustration, p. 610). The optic nerve is not a true nerve, but is actually an extension of the brain structure.

III. *Oculomotor Nerve* (ok'yoo-loh-moh'tor; "eye movement" L). It extends from the midbrain to all but two of the muscles involved in the movement of the eyeball. Obviously, it controls eye movements.

IV. *Trochlear Nerve* (trok'lee-er). It is the smallest of the cranial nerves and extends from the midbrain to a muscle that helps to move the eyeball — one of the muscles not innervated by the oculomotor nerve. The word "trochlear" is from a Greek expression for a sheaf of pulleys. The muscle innervated passes through a ring of connective tissue so that it resembles a small pulley, whence the name.

V. *Trigeminal Nerve* (try-jem'ih-nul; "triplet" L). It is the largest of the cranial nerves. Whereas the olfactory and optic nerves are sensory and the oculomotor and trochlear nerves are motor; the trigeminal nerve is a mixed nerve, containing both sensory and motor fibers, each attached to the pons by a separate structure. The sensory fibers are in three groups (hence the name of the nerve as a whole) and are connected to different

regions of the face. The *ophthalmic nerve* (of-thal′mik; "eye" G)
supplies the skin of the forward half of the scalp, of the forehead,
upper eyelid, and nose. The *maxillary nerve* (mak′sih-lehr′ee;
"jaw" L) supplies the skin of the lower eyelid, part of the cheek,
and the upper lip. The *mandibular nerve* (man-dib′yoo-ler;
"chew" L) supplies the skin of the lower jaw and the regions of
the cheeks behind those supplied by the maxillary nerve. The
ophthalmic and maxillary nerves are sensory nerves, but the
mandibular nerve is mixed. Its motor fibers control the movement
of those muscles involved in chewing.

A *neuralgia* ("nerve pain" G) associated with the trigeminal
nerve can be very painful. When it is spasmodic, it is associated
with a twitching of the facial muscles. Such a twitch is usually
known as a *tic* (a word arising from the same root that "twitch"
does, perhaps). The painful muscular spasms associated with
trigeminal neuralgia are sometimes referred to as *tic douloureux*
(tik doo-loo-ruh′; "painful twitch" French).

VI. *Abducens Nerve* (ab-dyoo′senz; "lead away" L). It
arises from the pons a little before its junction with the medulla
and leads to the external rectus muscle of the eyeball. This
muscle pulls the eyeball in such a way that the pupil moves away
from the midline of the body, and it is from this that the name
of the nerve arises. It is a motor nerve. (It may seem rather
surprising that three of the twelve cranial nerves are concerned
with motions of the eyeball, the abducens and trochlear nerves
supplying one muscle each, the oculomotor nerve supplying the
rest. In view of the importance of vision, it is perhaps not so
surprising at that.)

VII. *Facial Nerve*. It arises from the pons just above its
junction with the medulla. Like the trigeminal nerve, the facial
nerve is a mixed nerve. Its sensory fibers arise from the forward
two thirds of the tongue and it is through these that the sensation of taste reaches the brain. They also innervate the salivary
glands and the tear-producing glands of the eye. The motor fibers
lead to the various muscles of the face, which by their interplay

give rise to the facial expressions that are so familiar to all of us.

VIII. *Stato-acoustic Nerve*. This sensory nerve is attached at the junction of the pons and the medulla. It innervates the inner ear and is concerned with the sense of hearing. For that reason it is frequently called the *acoustic nerve* ("hear" G), or *auditory nerve* ("hear" L). Since it also receives the sensations enabling the body to judge and control the equilibrium position while standing, the prefix "stato" ("stand" G) is added.

IX. *Glossopharyngeal Nerve* (glos′oh-fa-rin′jee-ul; "tongue-throat" G). This mixed nerve arises in the medulla, near its junction with the pons, and innervates the mucous membrane of the rear of the tongue and of the throat. These are sensory fibers. A motor fiber runs to a muscle in the throat.

X. *Vagus Nerve* (vay′gus; "wandering" L). Here is another mixed nerve. It receives this name because its course carries it over a far larger part of the body than is true of the remaining cranial nerves. The vagus nerve arises in the medulla as a series of rootlets that pass through the base of the cranium and join into a single nerve. Some of the motor fibers supply muscles in the larynx and the throat, and some reach downward to the muscles of the bronchi, to the heart muscle, and to the muscles of most of the digestive tract. It also innervates the pancreas and helps control that organ's rate of secretion of digestive juice (though the main job of regulating pancreatic secretion, as I explained in Chapter 1, rests with secretin).

XI. *Accessory Nerve*. This motor nerve supplies muscles of the throat and some of those in the arms and shoulder. A few of its fibers join the vagus nerve. It also receives some of its fibers from a spinal root. The name of the nerve arises from this fact, since spinal fibers are accessories to the nerve, as it is itself an accessory to the vagus nerve.

And, finally, there is —

XII. *Hypoglossal Nerve* (hy′poh-glos′ul; "below the tongue" G). This, another motor nerve, arises from the medulla and supplies the muscles controlling the movement of the tongue.

THE SPINAL NERVES

The spinal nerves differ from the cranial nerves in several respects. First, they are more regularly placed. The cranial nerves are attached to the brain at irregular intervals, many of them crowded into the region where the pons and the medulla oblongata meet. The spinal nerves, on the contrary, emerge from the cord at regular intervals in a manner that makes sense if we consider chordate history. The chordates are one of three segmented phyla — segmentation involving a division of the body structure into similar sections, as a train is divided into separate coaches. (The other two segmented phyla are the arthropods, which include insects, spiders, centipedes, and crustaceans, and the annelids, which include the earthworm.)

Chordates have specialized to the point where segmentation is not clearly marked. The clearest evidence of segmentation in the adult human is the repeated vertebrae of the spinal cord (one to each segment) and the repeating line of ribs attached to twelve of them. The nervous system also shows the existence of segmentation, and does so most clearly in the repeated and regular emergence of pairs of spinal nerves from between vertebrae all down the spinal column.

Whereas the cranial nerves are sometimes motor, sometimes sensory, and sometimes mixed, as has been shown, the spinal nerves are all mixed. At each segment of the cord a pair of nerves emerge; one from the left half and one from the right half of the H of gray matter. Each nerve, moreover, is connected both to the ventral horn and the dorsal horn of its side of the H. Each nerve thus has a *ventral root* (or *anterior root*) and a *dorsal root* (or *posterior root*). From the ventral root emerge motor fibers and from the dorsal root sensory fibers. These two sets of fibers join a short distance from the cord to form a single mixed nerve. The cell bodies to which the motor fibers are attached are found within the gray matter of the spinal cord itself. In contradistinction to this, the sensory fibers have their cell bodies lying just outside the spinal cord proper. These cell bodies are referred to as *ganglia of the posterior root.*

Each pair of spinal nerves, formed of the fusion of anterior and posterior roots, makes its way out between adjacent vertebrae. The first pair makes its way out between the skull and the first vertebra, the second pair between the first and second vertebrae, the third pair between the second and the third vertebrae, and so on. The first seven vertebrae are the cervical vertebrae of the neck region.° Consequently, the first eight pairs of spinal nerves, from the first which passes above the first vertebra, to the eighth, which passes below the seventh, are the *cervical nerves.*

Beneath the cervical vertebrae are twelve thoracic vertebrae of the chest region, and under each of these passes a pair of spinal nerves, so that there are twelve pairs of *thoracic nerves.* And since there are five lumbar vertebrae in the region of the small of the back, there are five pairs of *lumbar nerves.* Beneath the lumbar vertebrae is the sacrum. In the adult it seems to be a single bone, but in the embryo it consists of five separate vertebrae. These fuse into a solid piece during the course of our independent life in order to supply a strong base for our two-legged posture. However, the organization of the spinal nerves antedates the time when man rose to his hind legs, so there are still five pairs of *sacral nerves.* Finally, at the bottom of the spine are four buttonlike remnants of vertebrae that once formed part of a tail (when the animals ancestral to man had tails). These are the coccygeal vertebrae, and there is one final pair of *coccygeal nerves.*

To summarize: 8 cervical nerves, 12 thoracic nerves, 5 lumbar nerves, 5 sacral nerves, and 1 coccygeal nerve make up a total of 31 pairs of spinal nerves.

If the spinal column and the spinal cord it contained were of the same length, then one would expect the segments of the cord to run even with the vertebrae, and each successive nerve would just run straight out, horizontally. This is not so,

° For a detailed discussion of the various vertebrae, see *The Human Body.*

the spinal column is some ten inches longer than the cord, and the segments of the cord, therefore, are considerably smaller than the individual vertebrae.

As one progresses down the cord, then, the individual nerves must run vertically downward in order to emerge from underneath the proper vertebrae. The farther one progresses, the longer is the necessary vertical extension. Below the end of the cord there is a conglomeration of ten (to begin with) pairs of nerve running down the neural canal and being drained off, one could say, pair by pair at each vertebra. The lowermost portion of the neural canal thus seems filled with a mass of coarse parallel threads that seem to resemble the tail of a horse. And, indeed, the nerve mass is called *cauda equina* (kaw′duh ee-kwy′nuh; "tail of a horse" L). When anesthesia of the lower sections of the body is desired, the injection of anesthetic is made between the lumbar vertebrae, and never higher. At higher levels the cord can be injured. In the lumbar regions, the needle moves between adjacent nerves and does no mechanical damage. The technique is called *caudal anesthesia* (kaw′dul; "tail" L) because of the region of the body punctured.

After the spinal nerves leave the column they divide into two branches, or *rami* (ray′my; "branches" L), the singular form of the word being *ramus*. The *dorsal ramus* of each nerve supplies the muscle and skin of the back; the *ventral ramus* supplies the remainder of the body.

In general, the original chordate body plan had each pair of spinal nerves innervate the organs of its segment. Even in the human body the first four cervical nerves connect to the skin and muscles of the neck, whereas the next four connect to the skin and muscles of the arm and shoulder. In the same way, nerves from the lowermost segments of the cord supply the hips and legs. It is down here that the longest and largest nerve of the human body is to be found, passing out of the pelvis and down the back of the thigh and leg. It is the *sciatic nerve* (sy-at′ik; a word arising from a distortion of the Latin word *ischiadicus* meaning "pertaining to pains in the hipbone"). Inflammation of the sciatic nerve can be very painful. It is one form of neuralgia that has earned a special name for itself — *sciatica*.

The human body cannot be separated into clear segments, each handled by a special spinal nerve, however, because there are complications. For one thing, the segments are somewhat distorted as a result of evolutionary changes since the days of the first simple chordates. To illustrate: the diaphragm is a flat muscle separating the chest from the abdomen and lying in an area where one would expect it to be innervated by thoracic nerves; but in the embryo it develops, at least in part, in the neck region and is therefore innervated (as one might expect) by cervical nerves; when in the course of development the diaphragm moves downward to its position in the fully formed infant, it carries its cervical nerve supply with it.

Also, many muscles and other organs are formed in regions where nerves from two adjoining segments can be connected to them. This overlapping is quite usual, and there are few muscles that don't have a nerve supply reaching it from two different spinal nerves. This allows a margin of safety, by the way, since severing one nerve may then weaken muscles but is not likely to bring about complete paralysis of any region.

Lastly, the nerves themselves do not maintain a neat isolation after leaving the spinal column. Several adjacent nerves tend to meet in a complicated interlacing pattern called a *plexus* (see p. 500). They don't lose their identity there, apparently, but the intermixing is sufficiently tortuous to make it impractical to trace the course of the individual nerves. To give examples, the first four cervical nerves form the *cervical plexus* and the remaining four, plus the first thoracic nerve, form the *brachial plexus* (bray'kee-ul; "arm" L). The latter is so named because it is at the level of the upper arm. The other thoracic nerves remain individual, but the lumbar nerves join to form the *lumbar plexus*, and the sacral nerves form the *sacral plexus*.

In general, then, when the spinal cord is severed, through disease or through injury, that part of the body lying below the severed segment is disconnected, so to speak. It loses sensation and is paralyzed. If the cord is severed above the fourth nerve death follows, because the chest is paralyzed, and with it the action of the lungs. It is this which makes a "broken neck" fatal, and hanging a feasible form of quick execution. It is the severed cord, rather than a possible broken vertebra, that is fatal.

The various spinal nerves are not independent but are coordinated among themselves and with the brain. The white matter of the spinal cord is made up of bundles of nerve fibers that run up and down the cord. Those that conduct impulses downward from the brain are the *descending tracts* and those that conduct them upward to the brain are the *ascending tracts*.

I have already mentioned, on page 510, the pyramidal system, which is one of the descending tracts. It arises in the motor area of the cortex, passes down through the basal ganglia and the brain stem, then down the spinal cord on either side, right and left, forming synaptic connections with the various spinal nerves. In this way the muscles of the limbs and trunk, which are innervated by spinal nerves, are subject to voluntary movement and are under cortical control. Other descending tracts such as the extra-pyramidal system pass through the various levels of the nervous system. The muscles of the trunk and limbs, connected in this fashion to the brain stem via the spinal nerves, can be controlled by the cerebellum, for instance, so that equilibrium is maintained.

The ascending tracts collect the various sensations picked up by the spinal cord and carry them upward, through the reticular activating system. It is by use of this information that the various portions of the brain can evolve the appropriate responses.

THE AUTONOMIC NERVOUS SYSTEM

Nerve fibers can be divided into two classes, depending on whether the organs they deal with are under the control of the will or not. The organs we most commonly think of as being under the control of the will are the skeletal muscles. It is by the contraction of these that we move the hinged bones of the skeleton and move certain nonskeletal portions of the body as well. The movements of the limbs, the flexings of the torso, the motion of the lower jaw, and the various movements of the tongue and face are all under voluntary control.

The skeletal muscles sheathe the body and flesh out the limbs so that we can move virtually all parts of the body surface at will. To the casual eye, it seems that we can move the body itself, without need for qualification. For this reason nerve fibers leading to and from skeletal muscles are called *somatic fibers* (soh-mat′ik; "body" G).

Within the body, hidden from the casual eye, are organs not under voluntary control in the full sense of the word. You can force your lungs to pump air more slowly or more quickly, but it is an effort to do so, and as soon as you relax (or fall unconscious, if you are too persistent in your interference) breathing proceeds at an automatically regulated pace. And too, you cannot force your heart to beat more slowly or more quickly (although, if you are highly imaginative you can make it pound by indirect action, as by talking yourself into a state of terror). Other organs change without your being especially aware of it. The pupils of your eyes dilate or contract, the various blood vessels of the body may expand their bore or narrow it, various glands may secrete more fluid or less, and the like.

The internal organs not subject to the will can — most of them — be grouped under the heading *viscera* (vis′ur-uh). This term may arise from the same Latin root that gives us "viscous," implying that the organs are soft and sticky. Nerve fibers supplying the viscera are called *visceral fibers*. One would expect that nerve fibers which control organs in response to the conscious will would not follow the same paths as would those which control organs without regard to the will. The latter, in a manner of speaking, have to short-circuit our consciousness, and to do so something new must be involved.

Thus, sensory fibers, whether somatic or visceral, lead from the various organs directly to the central nervous system. Motor fibers that are somatic, and therefore govern voluntary responses, likewise lead directly from the central nervous system to the organs they innervate. Motor fibers that are visceral, and therefore govern involuntary responses, do not lead directly to the organs they innervate. That is the "something new" I referred to above. Instead, they make their trips in two stages. The first set of fibers leads from the central nervous system to ganglia (which are, you may remember, collections of nerve cell bodies) that lie outside the central nervous system. This first set of fibers are the *preganglionic fibers*. At the ganglia the fibers form synaptic junctions with the dendrites of as many as twenty different cell bodies. The axons of these cell bodies form a second set of fibers, the *postganglionic fibers*. It is these postganglionic fibers that lead to the visceral organs, usually by way of one spinal nerve or another, since the spinal nerves are "cables" including all varieties of nerve fibers.

These two sets of visceral fibers, the preganglionic and the postganglionic, taken together with the ganglia themselves, make up that portion of the nervous system which is autonomous — or, not under the control of the will. It is for this reason called the *autonomic nervous system*. The chief ganglia involved in the autonomic nervous system form two lines running down either side of the spinal column. They are outside the bony vertebrae, and not inside as is the gray matter of the spinal cord and the ganglia of the posterior root.

These two lines of ganglia outside the column resemble a pair of long beaded cords, the beads consisting of a succession of 22 or 23 swellings produced by massed nerve cell bodies. At the lower end, the two cords join and finish in a single central stretch. These lines of ganglia are sometimes called the *sympathetic trunks.** Not all ganglia of the autonomic nervous system are located in the sympathetic trunks. Some are not; and it is possible for a preganglionic fiber to go right through the sympathetic trunks, making no synaptic junction there at all, joining instead with ganglia located in front of the vertebrae. These ganglia are called *prevertebral ganglia,* or *collateral ganglia.*

The *splanchnic nerves* (splank'nik; "viscera" G), which originate from some of the thoracic nerves, have their preganglionic fibers ending in a mass of ganglia (a "plexus") lying just behind the stomach. This is the *celiac plexus* (see'lee-ak; "belly" G), and it represents the largest mass of nerve cells that is not within the central nervous system. In fact it is sometimes called the "abdominal brain." A more common name for it, and one known to everyone interested in boxing, is the *solar plexus.* The word "solar" refers to the sun, of course, possibly because nerves radiate outward, like the sun's rays. Another theory is that a sharp blow to the solar plexus (to the pit of the stomach just under the diaphragm) can stun a person in agonizing fashion, so that for him darkness falls and the sun seems to set, at least temporarily.

In some cases, the ganglia separating the preganglionic fibers from the postganglionic fibers are actually located within the organ the nerve is servicing. In that case, the preganglionic fiber runs almost the full length of the total track, whereas the postganglionic fiber is at most just a few millimeters long.

Those fibers of the autonomic nervous system that originate from the first thoracic nerve down to the second or third lumbar nerve (in general, the central stretches of the spinal cord) make

* The word "sympathetic" was in the past used to describe the autonomic nervous system, because of ancient theories of the control of organs through sympathy. "Sympathy" comes from Greek words meaning "with suffering." One's own actions may be dictated not through outside force but through an inner impulse of sorrow over another's suffering. In the same way, an organ might act not through being forced to do so by the will but through a kind of sympathy with the needs of the body. Nowadays, as I shall shortly explain, the term sympathetic is applied only to part of the autonomic nervous system.

up the *sympathetic division.* Because of the origin of the fibers involved, it is also called the *thoracicolumbar division.* The fibers starting from the region above and below the sympathetic division form another division. Some fibers start from the cranial nerves above the spinal cord. Others originate from the sacral nerves at the bottom of the spinal cord. These make up the *parasympathetic division* ("beyond the sympathetic"), or the *craniosacral division.*

The difference between the two divisions is more than a mere matter of origin. For instance, the divisions differ in structure. The preganglionic fibers of the sympathetic division end at the sympathetic trunks or at the prevertebral ganglia, so these fibers are quite short. The postganglionic fibers, which must travel the remaining way to the organs they are concerned with, are relatively long. The parasympathetic nerve fibers, on the contrary, travel to ganglia within the organ they are aiming at; as a result, the preganglionic fibers are quite long and the postganglionic fibers very short.

Also, the functions of the two divisions are in opposition to each other. The sympathetic division has the wider distribution to all parts of the viscera, but many of the visceral organs are innervated by fibers of both divisions. When this happens, what one does the other undoes. Thus, the sympathetic nerve fibers act to accelerate the heartbeat, dilate the pupil of the eye and the bronchi of the lungs, and inhibit the activity of the smooth muscles of the alimentary canal. The parasympathetic nerve fibers, on the other hand, act to slow the heartbeat, contract the pupil of the eye and the bronchi of the lungs and stimulate the activity of the alimentary canal muscles. The sympathetic nerve fibers act to constrict the blood vessels in some places (as in the skin and viscera) and to dilate them in others (as in the heart and skeletal muscles). Oppositely, the parasympathetic fibers, where present, dilate the first set of blood vessels and constrict the second.

The two divisions of the autonomic nervous system show an

interesting chemical difference, too. The nerve endings of all
fibers outside the autonomic nervous system secrete acetylcholine
when an impulse passes down them (see p. 470). This is true
also of all the preganglionic nerve endings in the autonomic
nervous system, but there is a deviation from this norm in connection with the postganglionic nerve endings. The postganglionic nerve endings of the parasympathetic division secrete
acetylcholine, but the postganglionic nerve endings of the sympathetic division do not. They secrete a substance which, in
the days before its molecular structure was known, was called
sympathin. Eventually sympathin was found to be a molecule
named *norepinephrine* (also called *noradrenalin*), which is very
similar in structure to epinephrine (or adrenalin), discussed
toward the end of Chapter 2 (see pp. 376–379). As a result, those
nerve fibers which secrete acetylcholine are referred to as
cholinergic nerves and those which secrete norepinephrine are
adrenergic nerves.

The secretion of norepinephrine seems to make sense, since
the effect of the sympathetic division is to put the body on an
emergency basis in just the same way that the hormone epinephrine does. The sympathetic division speeds up the heart and
dilates the blood vessels to the muscles and the heart so that
muscle can expend energy at a greater rate. It dilates the bronchi
so that more oxygen can be sucked into the lungs. It cuts down
on the action of the muscles of the alimentary canal and on the
blood vessels feeding the digestive apparatus and the skin because
digestion can wait and the blood is needed elsewhere. It also
suspends kidney action, hastens the release of glucose by the
liver, and even stimulates mental activity. It does the things
epinephrine does, as one might expect of a chemical compound
that is virtually the twin of epinephrine.

As a matter of fact, we can see once again that the chemical
and electrical controls of the body are not entirely independent,
for the adrenal medulla itself is stimulated by sympathetic fibers
and releases epinephrine in response, so its effect is added to that

of the norepinephrine, which helps to conduct impulses along the sympathetic nerve fibers. The sympathetic system also stimulates the secretion of ACTH by the pituitary gland, which in turn stimulates the secretion of corticoids by the adrenal cortex, and these (see p. 419) are needed in greater-than-normal concentration in periods of stress. The parasympathetic division, in contrast, acts to bring the body back from its emergency posture when the need is passed.

The sympathetic system, and the adrenal medulla, too, are not necessary for life, except insofar as failure to react properly to an emergency may be fatal. The adrenal medulla can be removed and sympathetic nerves can be cut without fatal results. Indeed, if the organism can be guaranteed a placid and nonstressful life, it is not even seriously inconvenienced.

10

OUR SENSES

TOUCH

Now that I have described the structure of the nervous system, let us consider how it works. To begin with, it is easy to see that in order for the nervous system to control the body usefully it must be constantly apprised of the details of the surrounding environment. It is useless to duck the head suddenly unless there is some collision to be avoided by the action. It is, on the other hand, dangerous not to duck the head if a collision is to be avoided.

To be aware of the environment, one must sense or perceive it.* The body senses the environment by the interaction of specialized nerve endings with some aspect or another of the environment. This interaction is interpreted by the central nervous system in a way that is different for each type of nerve ending. Each form of interaction and interpretation may be distinguished as a separate kind of *sense perception.*

In common speech, five different senses are usually recognized: *sight, hearing, taste, smell,* and *touch.* Of these, the first four reach us through special organs which are alone involved in a particular sense. Sight reaches us through the eye, hearing through the ear, taste through the tongue, and smell through the

---

* The word "sense" is from a Latin word meaning "to feel" or "to perceive," whereas "perceive" itself is from Latin words meaning "to take in through"; that is, to receive an impression of the outside world through some portion of the body.

nose. These are therefore grouped under the heading of *special senses* — senses, in other words, that involve a special organ.

Touch involves no special organ. The nerve endings that give rise to the sensation of touch are scattered everywhere on the surface of the body. Touch is an example of a *general sense*.

We are apparently less aware of senses when specific organs are not involved, and so we speak of touch as though that were the only sense present in the skin generally. We say that something is "hot to the touch," yet heat and touch arise from different nerve endings. Cold stimulates still another type of nerve ending, and pressure and pain each have their own nerve endings also. All of these — touch, pressure, heat, cold, and pain — are examples of *cutaneous senses* ("skin" L), and are so designated because they are located in the skin. They also represent *exteroceptive sensations* ("received from outside" L). The "outside" of course exists within us as well — within the digestive tract, which opens to the outside world at the mouth and anus. Sensations received there are sometimes considered to be additional examples of exteroceptive sensations, but are frequently differentiated as *interoceptive sensations* ("received from inside" L), or *visceral sensations*.

Lastly, there are sensations arising from organs within the body proper — from muscles, tendons, ligaments, joints, and the like. These are the *proprioceptive sensations* ("received from one's self" L). It is the proprioceptive sensations with which we are least familiar but take most for granted. These arise in specific nerve endings in various organs. In the muscles, to illustrate, there are such nerve endings attached to specialized muscle fibers. The stretching or contraction of these fibers sets up impulses in the nerve endings, which travel to the spinal cord and through ascending tracts to the brain stem. The greater the degree of stretching or contraction, the greater the number of impulses per unit time. Other nerve endings respond to the degree of pressure on the soles of the feet or on the muscles of the buttocks. Still others respond to the stretching of ligaments, the angular positions of bones hinged at an individual joint, and so on.

The lower portions of the brain utilize these sensations from all over the body in order to coordinate and organize muscular movements to maintain equilibrium, shift from uncomfortable positions, and adjust similarly. However, although the routine work is done at the lower levels and we are not consciously aware of what is going on in our busy body while we sit, stand, walk, or run, certain sensations do eventually reach the cerebrum, and through them we remain consciously aware at all times of the relative positions of the parts of our body. We are quite aware, without looking, of the exact position of an elbow or a big toe and can point to it with our eyes closed if asked to do so. If one of our limbs is bent into a new position by someone else, we know what the new position is without looking. To do all this, we interpret the nerve impulses arising from the miscellaneous stretchings and bendings of muscles, ligaments, and tendons.

The various proprioceptive sensations are sometimes lumped together as the *position sense* for this reason. It is also sometimes called the *kinesthetic sense* (kin′es-thet′ik; "movement-feeling" G). How far this sense is dependent on gravitational force in the long run is uncertain. This question has become an important one to biologists, now that astronauts are put into orbit for extended periods and are in "free fall," unaware of the usual effects of gravity.

As for the exteroceptive sensations — touch, pressure, heat, cold, and pain — each originates from a definite type of nerve ending. For all but pain, the nerve endings that receive these sensations are elaborated into specialized structures named in each case for the man who first described them in detail.

Thus, the touch-receptors (and a "receptor" is, of course, any nerve ending capable of receiving a particular sensation) often end in *Meissner's corpuscle,* described by the German anatomist Georg Meissner in 1853. The cold-receptors end in *Krause's end bulb,* named for the German anatomist Wilhelm Krause, who described them in 1860. The heat-receptors end in *Ruffini's end organ,* after the Italian anatomist Angelo Ruffini, who described them in 1898. The pressure-receptors end in a *Pacinian corpuscle*, described in 1830 by the Italian anatomist Filippo Pacini. Each of these specialized nerve-ending structures is easily distinguishable from the rest. (The pain-receptors are, however, nerves with bare endings, lacking any specialized end structure.)

Each type of specialized nerve ending is adapted to react to one kind of sensation: a light touch in the neighborhood of a touch-receptor will cause that nerve ending to initiate an impulse; it will have no effect on the other receptors. In the same way contact with a warm object will fire off a heat-receptor but not the others. The nerve impulse itself is identical in every case (actually, it is identical, as far as we can tell, for all nerves), but the interpretation in the central nervous system varies according to the nerve. A nerve impulse from a heat-receptor is interpreted as warmth whatever the nature of the stimulus. Each of the other receptors similarly gives rise to its own characteristic interpretation whatever the stimulus.

(This is true of the special senses as well. The most familiar case is that of the optic nerve, which is ordinarily stimulated by light. A sudden pressure will also stimulate it, and the stimulus will be interpreted not as pressure but as light. This is why a punch in the eye causes us to "see stars." Similarly, the stimulation of the tongue by a weak electric current will result in the sensation of taste.)

The various cutaneous receptors do not exist everywhere in the skin, and where one is another is not. The skin can actually be mapped out for its senses. If we use a thin hair we can touch various points on the skin and find that in some places a touch will be felt and in others it will not. With a little more effort, we can also map the skin for heat-receptors and cold-receptors. The gaps between them are not very large, however, and in the ordinary business of life we are not apt to come in contact with a stimulus that will not affect some of the appropriate receptors. Altogether, the skin possesses some 200,000 nerve endings for temperature, half a million for touch or pressure, and three million for pain.

As is to be expected, the touch-receptors are found most thickly strewn on the tongue and fingertips, which are the parts of the body most likely to be used in exploration. The tongue and fingertips are hairless, but elsewhere on the body the touch-receptors are associated with hairs. Hairs themselves are dead structures and have no sensations; yet the lightest touch upon a hair is felt, as we all know. The apparent paradox is explained when we realize that when the hair is touched it bends and exerts a leverlike pressure on the skin near its root. The touch-receptors near the root are stimulated by this.

This is a useful arrangement, because it enables the environment to be sensed without actual contact. At night, inanimate objects (which cannot be seen, heard, or smelled) can make themselves impinge upon our consciousness, just short of actual contact, by touching the hairs on our body. (There is also the possibility of echolocation, something I discuss on pages 598 ff.)

Some nocturnal animals carry sensations-through-hair to an extreme. The most familiar examples belong to the cat family, including the domestic cat itself. Its "whiskers" are properly called *vibrissae* (vy-bris′ee; "vibrate" L, because the ends are so easily moved). These are long hairs that will be touched by objects at comparatively great distances from the body. They are stiff so that the touch is transmitted to the skin with minimal loss. They are located in the mouth region where the touch-receptors are thickly strewn. In this way, dead structures, unfeeling themselves, become extraordinarily delicate sense organs.

If a touch becomes stronger, it eventually activates the Pacinian corpuscle of a pressure-receptor. Unlike the other cutaneous senses, the pressure-receptors are located in the subcutaneous tissues. There is a greater thickness between themselves and the outside world, and the sensation activating them must be correspondingly stronger to penetrate the deadening pad of skin.

On the other hand, if a touch is continued without change, the touch-receptor becomes less sensitive to it and ends by being unresponsive. You are conscious of a touch when it is first experienced, but if the touch is maintained without change, you become unaware of it. This is reasonable, since otherwise we would be constantly aware of the touch of our clothing and of a myriad other continuing sensations of no import which would be crowding our brain with useless information. The temperature-receptors behave similarly in this regard. The water of a hot bath may seem unpleasantly hot when we first step in but becomes merely relaxingly warm when we are "used to it." In the same way, the cold lake water becomes mild and bearable once we have undergone the shock of plunging in. The reticular activating system, by blocking sensations that no longer carry useful or novel information, keeps our cerebrum open for important business.

In order for the sensation of touch to be continuous, it must be applied in a continually changing fashion, so that new receptors are constantly being stimulated. In this way a touch becomes a tickle or a caress. The thalamus can to a certain extent localize the place at which a sensation is received, but for fine discrimination the cerebral cortex must be called in. It is in the sensory area that this distinction is made, so that if a mosquito lands on any part of the body, a slap can be accurately directed at once even without looking. The fineness with which a distinction can be made concerning the localization of a sensation varies from place to place. As is to be expected, the mouth parts and fingertips, which are the most important areas for feeling generally, can be interpreted most delicately. Two touches on the tip of the tongue which are 1.1 millimeters (about 1/25 inch) apart can be felt as two touches. At the fingertip the two touches must be separated by 2.3 millimeters (about 1/10 inch) before being felt separately. The lips and nose tip are somewhat less sensitive in this respect. The nose requires a separation of 6.6 millimeters (about ¼ inch) before it can detect a double touch. Compare this, though, with the middle of the back, where two touches must be separated by 67 millimeters (nearly 3 inches) before being felt as two touches rather than one.

In interpreting sensation, the central nervous system does not merely differentiate one type of sense from another and one location from another. It also estimates the intensity of the sensation. To give an example — we can easily tell which is the heavier of two objects (even though they may be similar in bulk and appearance) by placing one in each hand. The heavier object exerts a greater pressure on the hand and more strongly activates the pressure-receptors, causing a more rapid series of impulses. Or we can "heft" them; that is, make repeated lifting motions. The heavier object requires a greater muscular force for a given rate of lift and our proprioceptive senses will tell us which arm is exerting the greater force. (This is true of other senses, too. We can tell differences in degrees of warmth or of cold, in intensity of pain, in brightness of light, loudness of sound, and sharpness of smell or taste.)

Obviously there is a limit to the fineness of the distinction that can be made. If one object weighs 9 ounces and another 18 ounces, it would be easy to tell, with eyes closed and by merely feeling the pressure of each upon the hand, which is the heavier. If one object weighs 9 ounces and the other 10 ounces, considerable hesitation and repeated "heftings" might be required, but finally the correct answer would be offered. However, if one object weighs 9 ounces and the other 9½ ounces, it is likely that a distinction could no longer be clearly made. A person would be guessing, and his answer would be wrong as often as right. The ability to distinguish between two intensities of a stimulus lies not in the absolute difference but in the percentage difference. In distinguishing 9 ounces from 10, it is the 10-per-cent difference that counts, not the 1-ounce difference. We could not distinguish a 90-ounce weight from a 91-ounce weight, although here the difference is 1 ounce again, and would barely distinguish the difference between a 90-ounce weight and a 100-ounce weight. Yet it would be quite easy to distinguish a 1-ounce weight from a 1¼-ounce weight, even though here the difference is considerably less than an ounce.

Another way of saying this is that the body detects differences in the intensity of any sensory stimulus according to a logarithmic scale. This is called the *Weber-Fechner Law* after the two Germans, Ernst Heinrich Weber and Gustav Theodor Fechner, who worked it out. By functioning in this manner, a sense organ can work over far greater ranges of stimulus intensity than would otherwise be possible. Suppose, for instance, that a particular nerve ending could record twenty times as intensely at maximum as at minimum. (Above the maximum it would be physically damaged and below the minimum it would not respond at all.) If it reacted on a linear scale, the twenty-fold range would mean that the strongest stimulus would only be 20 times as intense as the weakest. On a logarithmic scale — even a gentle one using 2 as a base — the nerve would record at maximum only when there was a stimulus 2^{20} times as strong as that capable of arousing a minimum response. And 2^{20} is equal, roughly, to 1,000,000.

It is because of the manner in which the body obeys the Weber-Fechner Law that we can with the same sense organ hear a crash of thunder and a rustling leaf, or see the sun and a single star.

PAIN

Pain is the sensation we feel when some aspect of the environment becomes actively dangerous to some portion of the body. The event need not be extreme to elicit pain — a scratch or a pinprick will do it — but, of course, as the event becomes more extreme the pain becomes greater. A sensation that ordinarily does not cause pain will become painful if made so intense as to threaten damage. A pressure too great, contact with temperature too high or low, or, for that matter, a sound too loud or a light too bright will cause pain.

Of the cutaneous senses, pain is the least likely to adapt. It is difficult to get used to pain. As anyone who has experienced a toothache knows, pain can continue and continue and continue. This state of affairs makes sense, too, since pain signals a situation in a way that is more than merely informative; it cries for an immediate remedy, if a remedy exists. If pain vanished in time as the sensation of a continuous touch does, the condition giving rise to the pain would inevitably be ignored, with the consequence of serious illness, or even death, rather probable.

And yet when the situation giving rise to pain cannot be remedied, it is surely human to search for methods of alleviating it, if only that a sufferer might die in something less than total anguish. Or, if pain actually accompanies attempts to remedy harm to the body, as it would in a tooth extraction or in a surgical operation, the pain is a positive hindrance and should be removed if possible.

Primitive tribes have in their time discovered that various plant extracts (opium and hashish, to cite two) would deaden pain. These have a *narcotic* ("to benumb" G), or *analgesic* ("no pain" G), effect and are not scorned even in modern medical practice. The most commonly used analgesic still is *morphine*, an opium derivative that manages to hold its own in this respect, despite the possibility of the development of an addiction and despite the development of synthetic analgesics. A mild analgesic in common use is acetylsalicylic acid, better known by what was originally a trade-name, aspirin.

In 1884 an Austro-American ophthalmologist, Carl Koller, introduced the use of *cocaine* as a compound to deaden limited areas, and for operations. (The compound was first investigated by an Austrian neurologist, Sigmund Freud, who went on to gain fame in other directions.) Cocaine is an extract from the leaves of the coca tree, leaves that South American natives chewed to relieve pain, fatigue, and even hunger. (Such relief obviously is illusory, removing only the sensations and not the conditions that give rise to them.) Chemists went on to synthesize compounds not found in nature which showed properties equal or superior to cocaine and yet possessing fewer undesirable side-effects. The best-known of these is procaine, or to use its most common trade-name, Novocain.

In order to make major surgery humane, something was needed

that would induce general insensibility. The first step in this direction came in 1799, when the English chemist Humphry Davy discovered the gas nitrous oxide, and found that upon inhalation it made a person insensible to pain. He suggested that operations might be conducted while a patient was under its influence. Eventually it did come to be used in the dentist's office, where it was better known under its colloquial name of "laughing gas." It was not until the 1840's, however, that operations under conditions of insensibility were first performed, and then not with nitrous oxide but with the vapors of ether and chloroform. Of the two, ether is far the safer and it serves even now as the most common substance in use for this purpose.

A number of men contributed to this development, but chief credit is usually given to an American dentist, William G. T. Morton, who first used ether successfully in September 1846 and arranged a month later for a public demonstration of its use in a surgical operation at the Massachusetts General Hospital in Boston. The American physician Oliver Wendell Holmes (better known as a poet and essayist) suggested the name *anesthesia* ("no feeling" G) for the process.

The method by which anesthetics produce their effects is not certain. The most acceptable theory seems to be that (since they are always fat-soluble compounds) they concentrate in the fatty sections of the body. This would include the myelin sheaths of nerve fibers, and there the anesthetic acts somehow to inhibit the initiation of the nerve impulse. As the concentration of anesthetic is increased, more and more of the nervous system is put out of action. The sensory area of the cortex is most easily affected, whereas the medulla oblongata is most resistant. This is a stroke of fortune, since heart and lung action are controlled from the medulla and these activities must on no account be suspended. Surgery without anesthesia (except under emergency conditions where anesthetics are simply not available) is now practically unheard of.

And yet pain is amenable to modification from within, too. It is subject, though to a lesser extent than the other cutaneous sensations, to thalamic modification. Each sense is channeled into a different portion of the thalamus, which by this means distinguishes among them. A region in the very center of the thalamus called the *medial nuclei* also makes the sort of distinction that is interpreted by us as "pleasant" or "unpleasant." A cool shower may be interpreted as either pleasant or unpleasant on the basis of the temperature and humidity of the surroundings, and not directly on the temperature of the water. A caress may be pleasant under one set of conditions and unpleasant under another, although the same touch sensations may be affected in the same way. Usually, pleasant sensations are soothing and unpleasant ones are upsetting.

Even pain can be modified by the thalamus in this fashion. It may never, under ordinary and normal conditions, be actually pleasant, but the degree of unpleasantness can be sharply reduced. This is most noticeable perhaps in the manner in which, under the pressure of conflict or the stress of strong emotion, injuries are suffered without conscious pain. It is as though there are situations in which the body cannot afford to be distracted by pain; in which it seems to discount possible injury as unimportant in the light of the greater purposes at hand. On the other hand, the fear of pain, and apprehension as to its effects, will heighten the intensity of its sensation. (Folk wisdom marks this phenomenon with the well-known phrase to the effect that the coward dies a thousand deaths and the brave man dies but once.)

There is a social effect on the experience of pain, too. A child brought up in a culture that considers the stoic endurance of pain a sign of manliness will go through barbarous initiation rites with a fortitude incredible to those of us who are brought up to regard pain as an evil to be avoided whenever possible. The modification of pain can on occasion be made a matter of the conscious will through determination and practice; and Hindu fakirs, having nothing better to do, can pierce their cheeks with pins or rest on beds of nails with utter callousness.

Ordinary men and women, who do not make a profession out of the suppression of pain, can nevertheless be induced to suppress it by suggestion from outside, provided their own conscious will has more or less been put out of action. This undoubtedly has been known to individuals throughout history, and many men have earned reputations as miracle workers by their ability to place others in trancelike states and then to substitute their own will, so to speak, for the suspended will of the subject in the trance. The most famous example of such a man was the Austrian physician Friedrich Anton Mesmer, who in the 1770's was the rage of Paris. The phrase "to mesmerize" is still used to mean "to put into a trance."

Mesmer's work was riddled with mysticism and was generally discredited. In the 1840's a Scottish physician, James Braid, re-opened the subject, studied it carefully and objectively, renamed it "neurohypnotism," and brought it, minus its mysticism, into the purview of recognized medicine. It is now known by the abbreviated name, *hypnotism* ("sleep" G).

Hypnotism is by no means a device for making men do the impossible through some mystic or supernatural means. Rather, it is a method for inducing a subject to exert a form of conscious control that he can exert under some conditions but ordinarily does not. Thus, a man can be persuaded to suppress pain under hypnotic influence, but he could do that without hypnotism if, for instance, he were fighting for his life or making an agonized effort to save his child from a fire. But hypnotism, no matter how proficient, could never enable him to rise upward one inch in defiance of gravity.

The interoceptive, or visceral, sensations are almost always pain. You may drink hot coffee or iced coffee and be conscious enough of the difference while the liquid is in your mouth. Once it is swallowed, the temperature sensation (except in extreme cases) vanishes. Nor is one ordinarily conscious of touch as food makes its way through the alimentary canal, or of simple pressure. Internal pain is felt, however, under appropriate conditions, but not necessarily as a result of stimuli that would cause pain on the skin. Cutting the internal organs, even the brain itself, causes little or no pain. The walls of the intestinal tract are, nevertheless, strongly affected by stretching, as through the distention produced by trapped gas, which gives rise to the pains of colic or indigestion. In similar fashion, the distention of blood vessels in the cranium give rise to the all-too-familiar headache. The pressure of blocked fluid can likewise give rise to pain, such as that produced by gallstones and kidney stones. Inflamed tissues can be a source of pain, as in appendicitis and arthritis. Pain can also be induced by muscle spasm, which gives rise to the well-known "cramp."

One distinction between visceral pain and cutaneous pain is that the former is much less subject to localization. A pain in the abdomen is usually quite diffuse and it isn't easy to point to an area and say "It hurts here" as is possible if one has barked one's shin.

In fact, it is quite likely that when pain can be localized, it may appear at a spot more or less removed from the actual site of the sensation. This is then called *referred pain*. The pain of an inflamed appendix (the appendix being located in the lower right quadrant of the abdomen) often makes itself felt in the region just below the breastbone. Also, the pain of angina pectoris, which originates through a reduction in the blood flow to the heart muscle, is generally felt in the left shoulder and arm. Headache can be a referred pain, as when it arises from strains of the eye muscles. So characteristic are these wrong locations, actually, that they can be used in diagnosing the actual area of trouble.

At this point, I wish to pause. Before passing on to the special senses, it is only fair to ask whether we have really exhausted the list of the general senses. Probably not; there may well be senses so taken for granted as to be ignored in the main, even today. For example, it seems quite likely that we possess a "time sense" enabling us to judge the passage of time with considerable accuracy. Many of us can rouse ourselves out of a reasonably sound sleep at some desired time morning after morning, and do so often, with surprising precision. In addition, it has often been tempting to suppose that senses exist — perhaps in other living organisms — of which we ourselves are completely ignorant. It may be possible somehow to detect radio waves, radioactive emanations, magnetic fields, and the like. One can only answer, "Well, perhaps."

It is even suggested that human beings (or just a few gifted individuals) have such extraordinary senses, or, better yet, are capable of perceiving the environment through means that are independent of any sense. The last is called *extrasensory perception*, a phrase customarily abbreviated as *ESP*. Examples of extrasensory perception are: *telepathy* ("feeling at a distance" G), where one can detect another's thoughts or emotions directly; *clairvoyance* ("see clearly" French), which involves the ability to perceive events that are taking place at a distance, and out of reach of the senses; and *precognition* ("know in advance" L), the ability to perceive events that have not yet taken place.

All these, plus other abilities of the sort, are very attractive matters. People would like to believe that it is possible to know more than it seems possible to know; and that "magical" powers exist which perhaps they themselves might learn to use. Extrasensory perception of one sort or another has been the stock in trade of mystics, witch doctors, and self-deluded individuals throughout history. It has also been the stock in trade of a large number of deliberate rascals and knaves. The alleged extrasensory powers of so many individuals have been shown to be fraudulent (even where many sober and trustworthy individuals were ready to swear to their legitimacy) that men of science are reluctant to accept the reality of any such cases at all, whatever the circumstances.

In recent years, the work of the American psychologist Joseph Banks Rhine has given the study of ESP a kind of quasi-respect-

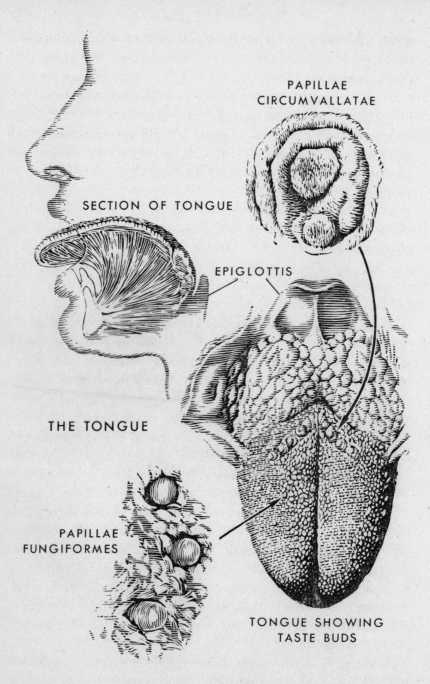

PAPILLAE
CIRCUMVALLATAE

SECTION OF TONGUE

EPIGLOTTIS

THE TONGUE

PAPILLAE
FUNGIFORMES

TONGUE SHOWING
TASTE BUDS

ability. Phenomena not easily explainable except by supposing the existence of some form of ESP have been reported. However, these phenomena depend so heavily on statistical analyses that are at least arguable, on individual subjects whose supposed abilities are strangely erratic, and on controls that many scientists feel to be inadequate that most people will not accept the work as significant. Moreover, the loudest proponents of ESP and like phenomena are not those who seriously study it (and who are generally most moderate in their suggestions), but are precisely those mystics whose antipathy toward the recognized procedures of scientific analysis make them the spiritual descendants of the grand fakers of the past.

TASTE

The general senses, by and large, respond to physical factors in the environment — to mechanical forces and to temperature differences. Of the special senses, two, hearing and sight (which will be discussed in the succeeding chapters), likewise respond to physical factors: sound waves in the first case and light waves in the second.

Differing from all of these are the senses of smell and taste. They respond to the chemical structure of molecules. In other words, of two substances resting on the tongue with equal pressure and at equal temperature, one will stimulate numerous nerve impulses and the other will not. The only difference between the objects seems to be their chemical structure. The same is true of two vapors breathed into the nose. For this reason, smell and taste are grouped together as the *chemical senses*.

The tongue is the organ primarily involved in taste. It is covered with small projections called *papillae* (pa-pil'ee; "nipple" L). The papillae at the edges and tip of the tongue are small and conical in shape, resembling the cap of a mushroom (*fungus* in Latin) when seen under magnification. These are the *papillae fungiformes*, and they give the tongue its velvety feel. Toward the rear of the tongue, the papillae are larger and give the tongue a certain roughness to the touch. These larger papillae are surrounded by a little groove, like a castle surrounded by a moat. They are the *papillae circumvallatae* ("wall around" L).

The actual taste-receptors consist of *taste buds* distributed over the surface of the papillae and, to some extent, in adjacent areas of the mouth. These are tiny bundles of cells that make up an ovoid structure with a pore at the top. Four different types of taste buds have been described. Each is usually considered to respond to a particular variety of substance and its nerve impulse is interpreted in the central nervous system as a particular variety of taste.

It is customary to classify tastes into four categories: sweet, salt, sour, and bitter. Each of these is elicited by an important group of substances. Sweetness is elicited by sugars, saltiness by a number of inorganic ions, sourness by acids, and bitterness by alkaloids. The usefulness of such a categorization seems clear. Sugar is an important component of foods. It is easily absorbed and quickly utilized by the body for energy. Any natural food that is sweet to the taste is usually worth eating, and sweetness is interpreted by the thalamus as a pleasant sensation.

In contrast, the most likely origin of a sensation of sourness in foods as they are found in nature is in unripe fruits, which have not yet developed their full sugar content and are therefore not as edible as they will soon be. Sourness is ordinarily interpreted as unpleasant. The same is even truer of the sensation of bitterness, since the presence of alkaloids in plants is usually a sign of poison and, indeed, it is the alkaloids themselves that are often both intensely bitter and intensely poisonous. Bitterness is therefore intensely unpleasant, and a bitter morsel of food is likely to be discarded at once; even the initial bite is not swallowed.

Saltiness is a rough measure of the mineral content of food. Sodium ion and chloride ion, the components of ordinary table salt, from which the taste takes its name, are by far the most common inorganic ions in food. Whether saltiness is pleasant or unpleasant would depend on the concentration of salt in the bloodstream. Where the salt level is low, either through mineral deficiency in the diet or through excessive loss of salt through perspiration, saltiness becomes a pleasanter sensation than otherwise.

The different kinds of taste buds are not evenly distributed over the tongue. The tip of the tongue is the portion most sensitive to sweetness, and the back of the tongue is most sensitive to bitterness. The sensations of saltiness and sourness are most easily detected along the rim of the tongue. Nor is the tongue equally sensitive to each variety of taste. It is least sensitive to sweetness; table sugar must be present in solution to at least 1 part in 200 before it can be tasted. This is reasonable, since such a comparatively dull sense makes it certain that anything that does taste sweet contains a large amount of sugar and is worth eating.

Saltiness is less uniformly desirable than sweetness; salt can be detected in a solution of 1 part in 400. Sourness, which is distinctly undesirable, can be detected (in the form of hydrochloric acid) in a solution of 1 part in 130,000. Last of all, bitterness, which is the most dangerous, is, usefully enough, the most delicately sensed. One part of quinine in 2,000,000 parts of water will yield a solution that is detectably bitter. Notice that I speak of solutions. In order for anything to be tasted, it must be dissolved in water (or in the watery saliva). A perfectly dry piece of sugar on a dry tongue will not be tasted. Starch, which is related to sugar chemically but differs in being insoluble, is tasteless.

The manner in which a particular substance gives rise to a characteristic taste is not known. The fact that some of the tastes are stimulated by a veritable grab bag of substances does not make the problem of finding out any easier. Sourness is the most orderly of the taste sensations. All acids liberate hydrogen ions in solution, and the taste of sourness is stimulated by these hydrogen ions. The intensity of the taste of sourness varies with the concentration of hydrogen ion, and this seems understandable enough.

Saltiness is stimulated by many inorganic ions other than the hydrogen ion, of course. Yet some inorganic compounds, especially those of the heavy metals, are bitter. To be sure, this is useful, since these compounds of the heavy metals are generally poisonous. Why should it be, though, that salts of lead and beryllium are liable to be sweet? Lead acetate is called "sugar of lead," and an alternate name of beryllium is "glucinum," which comes from the Greek word for "sweet." This would certainly seem to be unfortunate, because salts of both lead and beryllium are quite poisonous. However, both are rare elements that are not likely to be consumed in the ordinary course of nature.

Sweetness also offers puzzles. This sensation is stimulated by the presence of hydroxyl groups (a combination of an oxygen atom with a hydrogen atom) in a water-soluble molecule. Nevertheless, the various sugars, which resemble each other very closely in molecular structure — down to the possession of equal numbers of hydroxyl groups, sometimes — can be quite different in sweetness. A substance such as glycine (this name too comes from the Greek word for "sweet"), which is not related to the sugars and does not possess an ordinary hydroxyl group, is sweet to the taste.

Oddly enough, there are synthetic organic compounds, also not related to the sugars in any way, which are not only sweet but intensely sweet, and can be detected by the tongue in much smaller concentrations than ordinary sugar can. The sweet taste of the best-known of these synthetics, *saccharin* ("sugar" L), can be detected in a concentration 550 times more dilute than that required before sugar itself can be tasted. This means that one teaspoon of saccharin will sweeten 550 cups of coffee to the same extent that one teaspoon of sugar will sweeten one cup of coffee. And there are substances even sweeter than saccharin.

Nor is taste entirely uniform from individual to individual. This is most noticeable in the case of certain synthetic organic compounds that give rise to widely varying subjective opinion. There is a compound called phenylthiocarbamide (usually abbreviated as PTC) which some 70 per cent of those people who are asked to taste it report as having a pronounced bitterness. The remaining 30 per cent find it completely tasteless. Such "taste-blindness" might seem to be a purely academic matter, since it concerns a compound not found in nature. Notwithstanding, there is speculation as to whether other compounds among the many that do occur in nature may not taste differently to different people, and whether this may not account for at least some of the personal idiosyncrasies in diet.

What we popularly consider the taste of food does not, of course, arise solely from the sensations produced by the taste buds. There are general sense-receptors in the tongue and mouth which also play a role. Pepper, mustard, and ginger all stimulate heat-receptors as well, and menthol stimulates the cold-receptors. The feel or texture of food stimulates touch-receptors, so these too play their role in the palatability of the dish. A smooth jelly-like dessert will seem to taste better than a lumpy one of the same sort, and an oily dish may seem repulsive even though the oil itself has no taste.

However, by far the greatest contribution of nontaste to the general taste of food is that of the sense of smell, which it is now time to consider.

SMELL

Smell differs from taste in the matter of range. Whereas taste requires actual physical contact between a substance and the tongue, smell will operate over long distances. A female moth will attract male moths for distances of half a mile or more by virtue of the odor of a chemical she secretes.* Smell is there-fore a "long-distance sense."

* Although smell does not require the actual contact of a solid or liquid sub-stance with the body, it does sense the molecules of vapors. These molecules make contact with the body, so the sense does involve physical contact after a fashion. However, since we are not usually aware of vapors as we are of solids and liquids, and since vapors travel long distances as a result of diffusion through the air and actual transport by wind, it is still fair enough to think of smell as operating over a great range.

The other senses too may be differentiated in this way. Touch, pressure, and pain all require direct contact, usually. To a lesser extent so do the temperature senses, although these can also be detected at a distance. You can detect the heat radiated by a hot stove from the other end of a room and you can detect the heat radiated by the sun from a distance of about 93,000,000 miles. However, the detection of heat (or, to a lesser extent, cold) at a distance requires a stimulus of considerable intensity, and in order to detect the mild temperatures we ordinarily encounter, we must make physical contact.*

Hearing and sight, the two remaining senses, are like smell — long-distance senses — but for most forms of mammalian life smell is *the* important long-distance sense. Smell has its advantages: sight is (in a state of nature) dependent on the sun and is to a great extent useless at night, but smell is on day-and-night duty. Also, hearing is dependent on the production of sound, and if animal A is trying to locate animal B, animal B may succeed in refraining from making a sound. Odor, on the contrary, is beyond conscious control A hidden animal may be quiet as the grave but it cannot help being odorous.

Carnivores, then, commonly detect their prey by the sense of smell, and herbivores detect their enemies by means of it. Furthermore, the sense of smell can make the most amazing distinctions. It is the grand recognition signal whereby a bee will know others of its hive, distinguishing its own hive smell from all others, and a seal mother will easily recognize her offspring from among thousands (which to us all seem identical) on the beach. In the same way, a bloodhound will follow the scent of one man (even an old scent) crosscountry with unerring accuracy.

---

* Cold is not a phenomenon independent of heat; it is merely lack of heat. You detect heat by sensing the flow of heat from an outside object into your skin and you detect cold by sensing the flow of heat from your skin into an outside object. The temperature of the skin rises in the first case and falls in the second. Fires are at least 600 Centigrade degrees warmer than our skins but we rarely meet objects at temperatures of more than 100 Centigrade degrees cooler than our skins. That is why we are easily aware of feeling heat at a distance but not so aware of feeling cold.

Among primates generally, and humans especially, the sense of smell has been displaced for long-distance purposes by the sense of sight. This is the result not only of a sharpening of sight but of a deadening of smell. Our sense of smell is far less delicate than that of a dog; this shows up in the physical fact that the area of smell reception in our noses is much less, and so is the area of the brain given over to the reception and analysis of olfactory sensation.

Even so, the sense of smell is not as rudimentary or meaningless among human beings as we might think it to be as a result of too strenuous a comparison of ourselves with dogs. We may not be able to distinguish individual body odors as readily as a bloodhound, but the truth is, we never try. In intimate relationships odors become individual enough. And there is nothing like a chance odor to evoke a memory, even across many years, of people and situations otherwise forgotten.

The smell-receptors are located in a pair of patches of mucous membrane in the upper reaches of the nasal cavity. Each is about 2½ square centimeters in area and colored with a yellow pigment. Ordinarily, vapors make their way into the upper reaches through diffusion, but this process can be hastened by a stronger-than-usual inspiration, so that when we are anxious to detect the suspected presence of an odor, we sniff sharply.

Since the nasal cavity opens into the throat, any vapors or tiny droplets arising from the food we place in our mouths finds its way without trouble to the smell-receptors. Therefore what we consider taste is smell as well, and, in fact, smell is the major portion of what we consider taste and adds all the richness, delicacy, and complexity to the sense. When a cold in the nose swells the mucous membrane of the upper nasal cavities and deadens the smell-receptors under a layer of mucus and fluid, the sense of smell may blank out temporarily through the sheer physical inability of vapors to make contact with the sensory area. This does not affect the ability of the tongue to taste sweet, sour, salt and bitter, but how primitive and unsatisfying is pure taste alone.

So unsatisfying is it that in the absence of smell the cold-sufferer considers himself to have lost his sense of taste as well, ignoring the fact that his tongue is performing its functions faithfully.

The sense of smell, even in the blunted case of man, is far more delicate than is that of taste. The ability to taste quinine in a concentration of 1 part in 2,000,000 shrinks in comparison with the ability to smell mercaptans (the type of substance produced by skunks when those animals are seized with a fit of petulance) in concentrations of 1 part in 30,000,000,000.

Furthermore, the sense of smell is far more complex than the sense of taste. It has proved quite impossible to set up a table of individual smells to serve as a standard for comparison of smell mixtures. There have been attempts to classify smells under headings such as ethereal, aromatic, fragrant, ambrosial, garlic, burning, goaty, and fetid, but these attempts are rather crude and unsatisfying.

The mechanism by which a particular chemical activates a certain receptor — that is, why one chemical smells thus and another smells so — is as yet unknown. Recently, there have been suggestions that chemicals smelled as they did because of the over-all shape of their molecules, or because they punctured the membranes of the smell-receptors, or because parts of the molecules vibrated in some ways. Substances with the same molecular shape, or the same manner of puncturing, or the same fashion of vibrating would all smell the same. However, all such theories are as yet only at the stage of conjecture.

Whatever the mechanism of smell, the sense itself is most remarkable. Although some human senses can be outdone by mechanical devices, smell cannot. The living nose is not likely to be replaced by any nonliving contrivance in the foreseeable future. That is why, in an age of superlative mechanization, the master chef, the tea-taster, and the perfume-compounder are likely to remain immune to the possibility of technological unemployment.

11

OUR EARS

The two senses we are most conscious of are those of sight and hearing. The eye and the ear are our most complicated sense organs and our most vulnerable ones. They are vulnerable enough, at any rate, to give us the only common words for sense-deprivation, blindness and deafness, and neither affliction is uncommon.

Both sight and hearing are long-distance senses, gathering information from afar. To ourselves, as human beings, sight seems perhaps the more important of the two, and blindness a more disabling affliction than deafness. That, however, is a human-centered point of view. For most animals, the reverse would be true, since hearing has certain important advantages over sight. For one thing, sound waves have the property of bending about objects of moderate size, whereas light waves travel in straight lines. This means that we can see something only by looking directly at it, but can hear something no matter what our position may be with reference to it. Any creature on guard against the approach of an enemy can, as a consequence, much more safely rely on its hearing than its sight, especially if it must be engaged in ordinary business of life even while it is on guard. We have all seen animals prick up their ears and come to quivering attention long before they could possibly have seen anything.

To repeat, far and away the most important source of light, as far as any creature other than man is concerned, is the sun. This means that within an area shielded from the sun, as in forest recesses or, better yet, in a cave, the value of sight is reduced or even wiped out. Animals living permanently in the darkness of caves usually possess only rudimentary eyes, as though the vital energies of the organism were not to be wasted on a useless organ.

And, of course, for half the time the sun is below the horizon and sight is almost useless for most creatures. (To be sure, the night is not totally dark, particularly when the moon's reflected sunlight is available. Animals such as the cat or the owl, with eyes designed to detect glimmerings of light with great efficiency, are at an advantage over prey that lack this ability. They go hunting by night for this reason.) And in the ocean below the thin topmost layer, sunlight does not penetrate, so the sense of sight is largely useless. Yet hearing works as well by night as by day. (Better, perhaps, because background noise diminishes as the tempo of life subsides, and there is less distraction from the suspended sense of sight.) Hearing works as well in caves as in the open, and as well in the ocean depths as on its surface.

With comparatively few exceptions, light cannot be produced by living creatures. Even when it can be, as by glowworms or by luminescent fish, so little variation in the nature of the lighting can be deliberately produced that it is used for only the most rudimentary of signals, to attract the opposite sex or to lure prey.

In contrast to this, many creatures, including quite simple ones, can make sounds, and can vary the sounds sufficiently to make use of them for a variety of signaling purposes. (Even the sea is a noisy place, as was found out during World War II, when the growing importance of detecting submarine engines made it necessary to study the background noises produced by booming fish and clacking shrimp.)

The more complex the creature, the more capable it is of varying the nature of the sound to suit the occasion. Obviously not all communication is by sound. A bee's dance can locate a new patch of clover for the benefit of the rest of the hive. A dog's wagging tail communicates one thing and the drawing back of his lips quite another. However, this is not to be compared with the more common communication by sound — with the roaring, whining, chattering, yowling, purring, and all the remainder of the pandemonium of the animal kingdom.

And yet this increasing variability of sound with complexity of creature reaches a sudden discontinuity at the level of man. Here is no smooth advance of variability but a precipitous leap upward. Between man on the one hand and all other species of land animals on the other, there is a vast gulf in connection with sound-making. Even the chimpanzee cannot begin to bridge that gulf. Only man can make at will sounds so complex, so varying, and so precisely and reproducibly modulated as to serve as a vehicle for the communication of abstract ideas.*

Man's unique ability in this respect is twofold. In the first place, only man's brain is complex enough to store all the associations, memories, and deductions that are required to give him something to talk about. An animal can communicate pain, fear, warning, sexual drive, and a number of other uncomplicated emotions and desires. For these, a modest armory of different sounds is ample. An animal cannot, it would seem, experience a wonder about the nature of life, nor can it speculate on the causes and significance of death, or possess a philosophic concept of brotherhood, or even compare the beauties of a present sunset with those of a particular starlit night seen last year. And with none of this, where is the need for speech after the human fashion?**

And even if such attractions could somehow hover dimly in the nonhuman mind, the nonhuman brain would still be insufficiently complex to be able to control muscles in such a way as

* I distinguish between man and "land animals" because the dolphins of the sea may represent another species capable of speech (see p. 496).
** This is not to say that all human beings spend much time in pondering abstractions or to ignore the fact that a surprisingly high percentage of our fellows make out with a total vocabulary of 1000 words or so.

to produce the delicate variations in sound that would be required to communicate those abstractions. Nor can one short-circuit matters by supposing communication to consist of something other than sound. Whatever the nature of the signal — sound, gestures, bubbles in water, even thought waves — they must attain a certain level of complexity to make abstract communication possible, and only the human brain (the dolphin's brain possibly added) is complex enough.

In fact, it is possible to make a plausible case for the belief that it was the development of the ability to speak which made the early hominids "human." It was only then, after all, that individual knowledge and experience could be pooled among the members of a tribe and passed on across the generations. No one man, however brilliant, can of himself create a culture out of nothing; but a combined body of men spread through space and time can.

The sense of hearing, complex enough in man to be capable of analyzing the sounds of speech and therefore essential to our humanness, depends upon the conversion of sound waves into nerve impulses. Sound waves are set up by mechanical vibrations and consist of a periodic displacement of atoms or molecules.

Imagine the prong of a tuning fork vibrating rapidly and alternately from left to right. As it bends leftward, it forces the neighboring air molecules together on the left, creating a small area of high pressure. The elasticity of air forces those molecules to move apart again, and as they do so they compress the molecules of the neighboring region of air. Those molecules in turn move apart, compressing still another region. The net result is that a wave of high pressure radiates out from the vibrating prong.

While this is happening, though, the prong of the tuning fork has bent rightward. The result is that in the place where previously an area of high pressure had been formed, the molecules are now pulled apart into the room made for it by the prong bending away. An area of rarefaction, of low pressure, is formed. Molecules from the neighboring region of air rush in to fill the gap, creating a new area of low pressure, which thus radiates outward.

Since the vibrating prong moves first left, then right in regular rhythm, the result is a radiation of successive areas of high pressure and low pressure. The molecules of air scarcely move themselves; they only slide back and forth a short distance. It is the areas of compression and rarefaction that move, and it is the periodic nature of these areas that give them the name "waves." Since they are detected in the form of sound, they are *sound waves*.

The rate at which these waves travel (the "speed of sound") depends on the elasticity of the medium through which they travel; the rate at which a given atom or molecule will restore itself to its position if displaced. In air, the rate at the freezing point is 1090 feet per second, or 745 miles an hour. In other media, such as water or steel, with elasticities greater than air, the speed of sound is correspondingly higher. Through a vacuum, where there are no atoms or molecules to displace, sound cannot be transmitted.

The distance between successive points of maximum pressure (or, which is the same thing, between successive points of minimum pressure) is the *wavelength*. The number of waves emitted in one second is the *frequency*. To illustrate: a tuning fork that sounds a tone corresponding to middle C on the piano is vibrating 264 times a second. Each second, 264 areas of high pressure followed by areas of low pressure are produced. The frequency is therefore 264 cycles per second. During that second, sound has traveled 1090 feet (if the temperature is at the freezing point). If 264 high-pressure areas fit into that distance, then the distance between neighboring high-pressure areas is 1090 divided by 264, or about 4.13 feet. That is the wavelength of the sound wave that gives rise to the sound we recognize as middle C.

THE EXTERNAL AND MIDDLE EAR

We can see that there is nothing mysterious about the conversion of sound waves to nerve impulses. From one point of view, hearing is a development and refinement of the pressure sense. Sound waves exert a periodic pressure on anything they come in contact with. The pressure is extremely gentle under ordinary circumstances, and a single high-pressure area associated with sound would not affect the ear, let alone any other part of the body. It is the periodic nature of the sound wave, the constant tapping, so to speak — not the tiny pressure itself, but the unwearying reiteration of the pressure according to a fixed pattern — that sparks the nerve impulse. A fish hears by means of sensory cells equipped to detect such a pressure pattern. These sound-receptor cells are located in a line running along the mid-region of either side and are referred to as the *lateral lines*.

The emergence of vertebrates onto land created new problems in connection with hearing. Air is a much more rarefied medium than water is, and the rapid periodic changes in pressure that represent the sound waves in air contain far less energy than the corresponding pressure changes of sound waves in water do. For this reason, land vertebrates had to develop sound-receptors more delicate than the fish's lateral line.

The organ that underwent the necessary development is located in a cavity of the skull on either side of the head, this small cavity being the *vestibule*. In the primitive vertebrates, the vestibule contained a pair of liquid-filled sacs connected by a narrow duct. One is the *saccule* (sak'yool; "little sack" L), the other the *utricle* (yoo'trih-kul; "little bottle" L). For all vertebrates, from the fish upward, these little organs in the vestibule represented a sense organ governing orientation in space, something which may be referred to as the *vestibular sense*. The utricle and its outgrowths remain concerned with the vestibular sense in all higher vertebrates, too, including man, and I shall describe this later in the chapter.

From the saccule, however, a specialized outgrowth developed in land vertebrates. This was adapted as a sound-receptor, one that was much more sensitive for the purpose than the lateral-line cells of the fish. It remained, then, to transmit the sound waves from air to the new sensing organ within the vestibule. For this purpose, the parsimony of nature made use of the hard structure of some of the gills, which, after all, were no longer needed as gills in the newly emerging land vertebrates. The first gill bar, for instance, was altered into a thin diaphragm that could be set to vibrating very easily, even by pressure alterations as weak as those of sound waves in air. Another gill bar became a small bone between the diaphragm and the sound-receptor, and acted as a sound transmitter.

With the development of mammals, a further refinement was added. The mammalian jaw is much simpler in structure (and more efficiently designed) than is the ancestral reptilian jaw. The mammalian jaw is constructed of a single bone rather than a number of them. The reptilian jawbones that were no longer needed did not entirely disappear. Some were added to the nearby sound-sensing mechanism (check for yourself and see that your jawbone extends backward to the very neighborhood of the ear). As a result, there are three bones connecting diaphragm and sense-receptors in mammals instead of the one of the other land vertebrates such as the birds and reptiles. The three-bone arrangement allows for a greater concentration and magnification of sound-wave energies than the one-bone does.

Let me emphasize at this point that the hearing organ is not what we commonly think of as the ear. What we call the ear is only the external, clearly visible, and least important part of the complex system of structures enabling us to hear. Anatomically, the visible ear is the *auricle* ("little ear" L), or *pinna** (see illustration, p. 589).

---

* The word "pinna" is from a Latin expression for "feather" and can be used for any projection from the body. "Fin," for example, is derived from the same root as pinna. The application to the ear is fanciful, but reasonable.

The auricle is another uniquely mammalian feature. In many mammals it is trumpet-shaped and acts precisely as an old-fashioned earphone does; an effect carried to an extreme in such animals as donkeys, hares, and bats. The ear trumpet collects the wave-front of a sound wave over a comparatively broad area and conducts it inward toward the sound-receptors, the sound wave intensifying as the passage narrows (much as the tide grows higher when it pours into a narrowing bay like the Bay of Fundy). By use of such a trumpet, which, moreover, is movable so that sounds can be picked up from specific directions, the hearing organ of mammals is made still more sensitive. By all odds, then, the mammals have the keenest sense of hearing in the realm of life.

In man, and in primates generally, there is a recession from the extreme of sensitivity. The trumpet shape is lost, and the auricle is but a wrinkled appendage on either side of the head. The outermost edge of the auricle, curving in a rough semicircle and folding inward, sometimes yet bears the traces of a point that seems to hark back to an ancestry in which the ear was trumpet-shaped. Charles Darwin used this as one of the examples of a vestigial remnant in man that marked lower-animal ancestry. The ability to move the ear is also lost by primates, but in man three muscles still attach each auricle to the skull. Although these are clearly intended for moving the ear, in most human beings they are inactive. A few people can manage to work those muscles slightly, and by doing so can "wiggle their ears," another clear harking back to lower-animal ancestry.

This shriveling of the ear trumpet in man is usually considered an indication of the growing predominance of the sense of sight. Whereas some vertebrates grew to depend upon their ears to detect the slightest sound, perhaps to warn of an enemy, the developing order of primates threw more and more weight on their unusually efficient eyes. With alert eyes flashing this way and that, it became unnecessary to waste effort, one might say, in moving the ear, or in bearing the inconvenience of long auricles for the purpose of unnecessarily magnifying extremely faint sounds. Nevertheless, though we do miss a faint sound that might cause a dog to prick up its ears, our shriveled auricle does not really indicate any essential loss of hearing. Within the skull, our hearing apparatus can be matched with that of any other mammal on an all-round basis.

In the center of the human auricle is the opening of a tube which is about an inch deep, a quarter of inch in diameter, reasonably straight, and more or less circular in cross section. This is the *auditory canal*, or the *auditory meatus* (mee-ay'tus, "passage" L). Together the auricle and the auditory canal make up the *external ear*. Sound collected by the auricle is conducted through the auditory canal toward the vestibule. The canal is lined with some of the hardest portions of the cranium, and the functioning parts of the ear — the actual sound-receptors — are thus kept away from the surface and are well protected indeed. Birds and reptiles, which lack auricles, do have short auditory canals and so do not lack external ears altogether.

The inner end of the auditory canal is blocked off by a fibrous membrane, somewhat oval in shape and 1/10 of a millimeter (about 1/250 inch) thick. This is the *tympanum* (tim'puh-num; "drum" L), or *tympanic membrane*.° The tympanum is fixed only at the rim, and the flexible central portion is pushed inward when the air pressure in the auditory canal rises and outward when it falls. Since sound waves consist of a pattern of alternate rises and falls in pressure, the tympanum moves inward and outward in time to that pattern. The result is that the sound-wave pattern (whether produced by a tuning fork, a violin, human vocal cords, or a truck passing over a loose manhole cover) is exactly reproduced in the tympanum. As the name implies, the tympanum vibrates just as the membrane stretched across a drum would, and its common name is, in fact, the *eardrum*.

Along the edges of the tympanum are glands which secrete a

° This is the diaphragm I described on page 585 as having been developed out of the first gill bar of our fishy ancestors.

soft, waxy material called *cerumen* (see-roo′men; "wax" L), though *earwax* is its common name. This serves to preserve the flexibility of the tympanum and may also act as a protective device. Its odor and taste may repel small insects, which might otherwise find their way into the canal. The secretion of cerumen is increased in response to irritation and the wax may accumulate to the point where it will cover the tympanum and bring about considerable loss of hearing until such time as the ear is washed out.

On the other side of the tympanum is a small air-filled space called the *tympanic cavity*. Within that cavity are three small bones to conduct the vibrations of the tympanum still farther inward toward the vestibule. Collectively the three bones are the *ossicles* ("little bones" L). The outermost of the three ossicles is attached to the tympanum and moves with it. Because in doing so it strikes again and again on the second bone, this first ossicle is called the *malleus* (mal′ee-us; "hammer" L). The second ossicle which receives the hammer blows is the *incus* ("anvil" L).

The incus moves with the malleus and passes on the vibrations to the third bone, which is shaped like a tiny stirrup (with an opening not much larger than the eye of a needle) and therefore called the *stapes* (stay′peez; "stirrup" L).* The inner end of the stapes just fits over a small opening, the *oval window*, which leads into the next section of the ear. The whole structure from the tympanum to this small opening, including the tympanic cavity and the ossicles, is called the *middle ear*.

The function of the ossicles is more than that of transmitting the vibration pattern of the tympanum. The ossicles also control intensity of vibration. They magnify gentle sounds, because the oval window is only 1/20 the area of the tympanum and sound waves are once more narrowed down and in that way

* The malleus and the incus are the remnants of bones that in our reptilian ancestors were to be found in the jaw, as I explained earlier. They are found in the mammalian ear only. The stapes originated from one of the gill bars of the ancestral fishes, and is found in the ears of birds and reptiles as well as in those of mammals.

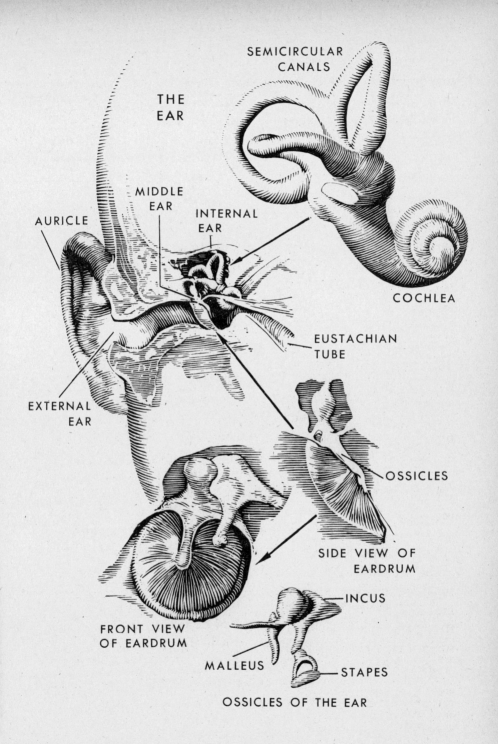

SEMICIRCULAR
CANALS

THE
EAR

MIDDLE
EAR

INTERNAL
EAR

AURICLE

COCHLEA

EUSTACHIAN
TUBE

EXTERNAL
EAR

OSSICLES

SIDE VIEW OF
EARDRUM

INCUS

FRONT VIEW
OF EARDRUM

MALLEUS

STAPES

OSSICLES OF THE EAR

intensified. In addition, the lever action of the ossicles is such that sound-wave energy is concentrated. The net result is that in passing from the tympanum to the oval window sound is amplified as much as fiftyfold.

The ossicles also damp out loud sounds. Tiny muscles that extend from the malleus to the skull place tension on the tympanum and prevent it from vibrating too strenuously; an even tinier muscle attached to the incus keeps the stapes from pressing too vigorously against the oval window. This action of magnification-and-damping extends the range of loudness we can hear. The loudest sounds we can hear without damage to the ears result from sound waves containing about 100 trillion times the energy of the softest sounds we can just barely make out. These softest sounds, by the way, result from movements of the eardrum of a two-billionth of an inch, and this represents far less energy than that in the faintest glimmer of light we can see. From the standpoint of energy conversion, then, the ear is far more sensitive than the eye.

Sound waves are conducted through the bones of the skull, but the ossicles do not respond to these with nearly the sensitivity with which they respond to tympanic movements, and this is also most helpful. Were they sensitive to bone vibration we would have to live with the constant rushing sound of blood through the blood vessels near the ear. As it is, we can hear the blood-noise as a constant hum if there is a reasonable silence and we listen carefully. This sound can be magnified by a cupped hand, or, traditionally, by a seashell; children are told that it is the distant roaring of the sea.

This filtering out of bone-conducted sound also means that we are not deafened by the sound of our voice, for we do not hear it through bone conduction chiefly, but through the sound waves carried by the air from mouth to ear. Nevertheless, bone conduction is a minor factor and adds a resonance and body to our voice we do not hear in others. When we hear a recording of our own voice, we are almost invariably appalled at its seeming inferior quality. Even the assurance of bystanders that the recording is a precise reproduction of our voice leaves us somehow incredulous.

The ossicles can sometimes be imperfect in their functioning. If the tiny muscles attached to them are damaged, or if the nerves leading to those muscles are, the ossicle movements become somewhat erratic. There may be needless vibration (something like the frame of an automobile plagued with a loose bolt). In that case, there is a continuous sound in the ears (*tinnitis;* "jingle" L), which can be endlessly irritating.

From the middle ear a narrow tube leads to the throat. This tube is called the *Eustachian tube** (yoo-stay'kee-an) after the Italian anatomist Bartolommeo Eustachio, who described the structure in 1563; see illustration, page 589. The middle ear is thus not truly within the body, but is connected to the outer world by way of the throat. This is important, because the tympanum will move most sensitively if the air pressure is the same on both sides. If the air pressure were even slightly higher on one side than on the other, the tympanum would belly inward or outward. In either case it would be under a certain tension and would then move with lesser amplitude in response to the small pressure changes set up by sound waves.

The pressure of our atmosphere changes constantly through a range of 5 per cent or so, and if the middle ear were closed, the pressure within it would rarely match the changing air pressure in the auditory canal. As it is, however, air flows in and out through the Eustachian tube, keeping the pressure within the tympanic cavity continually equal to that in the auditory canal. When external air pressure changes too rapidly, the narrow bore of the Eustachian tube is insufficient to keep the inner pressure in step. The pressure difference then causes a pressure on the tympanum which is uncomfortable and can even be painful. Everyone who has traveled up or down in a rapid elevator knows the sensation. Swallowing or yawning forces air through the

---

* The Eustachian tube evolved from the first gill slit of the ancestral fish.

Eustachian tube in one direction or the other and relieves the condition.

When the Eustachian tube is closed through inflammation during a cold, the resulting discomfort is less easily relieved, and is one more addition to the annoying symptoms of this most common of infectious diseases. The Eustachian tube offers a route, too, whereby bacteria can penetrate the recesses of the skull and find there a perfect haven. Such middle ear infections are more common in children than in adults. They are painful and hard to treat (though the coming of antibiotics has helped), and can be dangerous.

THE INTERNAL EAR

On the other side of the oval window covered by the stapes is the vestibule referred to on page 584. Both the vestibule and the structures within it are filled with a thin fluid much like the cerebrospinal fluid. Here the sound waves are finally converted from vibrations in air to vibrations in liquid. It is to the latter that the hearing sense was originally adapted in the first vertebrates, and the whole elaborate structure of the outer and middle ear is designed, in a way, to convert air vibrations to liquid vibrations with maximum efficiency.

There are two organs in the vestibule. Lying above and forward are the utricle and the structures developed from it, and lying below and behind are the saccule and the structures developed from it. All the contents of the vestibule are lumped together as the *internal ear*, but only the saccule portion is concerned with hearing. The utricle and attendant structures are concerned with the vestibular sense, and I leave them to one side for now.

The tube that in land vertebrates developed from the saccule is the *cochlea* (kok'lee-uh; "snail-shell" L), which is a spiral structure that does indeed have a close resemblance to a snail shell, except that its width does not narrow as it approaches its central apex, but remains constant (see illustration, p. 589).

The acoustic nerve leads from the cochlea. It is the cochlea that contains the sense-receptors making it possible for us to hear. The cochlea is not a single coiled tube but, rather, is a triple one, all coiling in unison. The upper part of the cochlea, which leads from the stapes and the oval window, consists of two tubes, the *vestibular canal* and the *cochlear canal*, separated by a very thin membrane. This membrane is too thin to block sound waves, and so, for hearing purposes, the two tubes may be considered one. The lower half of the cochlea is the *tympanic canal*. Between this and the double tube above is a thick *basilar membrane* (bas'ih-ler; "at the base" L). The basilar membrane is not easily traversed by sound waves.

Resting on the basilar membrane is a line of cells which contain the sound-receptors. This line of cells was described in 1851 by the Italian histologist Marchese Alfonso Corti, and so it is often called the organ of Corti. Among the cells of the organ of Corti are *hair cells* which are the actual sound-receptors. The hair cells are so named because they possess numerous hairlike processes extending upward. The human organ of Corti is far richer in such hairs than is that of any other species of animal examined. Each cochlea has some 15,000 hairs altogether. This seems reasonable in view of the complexity of the speech sounds human beings must listen to and distinguish. Delicate nerve fibers are located at the base of the hair cells. These respond to the stimulation of the hair cells by the sound waves and carry their impulses to the auditory nerve, which in turn transmits its message, via various portions of the brain stem, to the auditory center in the temporal lobe of the cerebrum.

An interesting question, though, is how the cochlea enables us to distinguish differences in pitch. A sound wave with a relatively long wavelength, and therefore a low frequency, is heard by us as a deep sound. One with a relatively short wavelength and high frequency is heard by us as a shrill sound. As we go up the keyboard of a piano from left to right we are producing sounds of progressively shorter wavelength and higher frequency, and though the progression is in small steps we have no difficulty in distinguishing between the tones. We could even distinguish tones that were more closely spaced — represented on the keyboard by the cracks between the piano keys, one might say.

To solve the problem of pitch perception, the cochlea must be considered in detail. The sound waves entering the cochlea by way of the oval window travel through the fluid above the basilar membrane. At some point they cross the basilar membrane into the fluid below and travel back to a point just beneath the oval window. Here there is an elastic membrane called, from its shape, the *round window*. Its presence is necessary, for liquid cannot be compressed, as air can. If the fluid were in a container without "give," then sound waves would be damped out because the water molecules would have no room to push this way or that. As it is, though, when the sound waves cause the stapes to push into the cochlea, the round window bulges outward, making room for the fluid to be pushed. When the stapes pulls outward, the round window bulges inward.

One theory of pitch perception suggests that the crux lies in the point at which the sound waves are transmitted from the upper portion of the fluid across the basilar membrane into the lower portion. The basilar membrane is made up of some 24,000 parallel fibers stretching across its width. These grow wider as one progresses away from the stapes and the oval window. In the immediate neighborhood of the oval window the fibers are about 0.1 millimeters wide, but by the time the far end of the cochlea is reached they are some 0.4 millimeters wide. A fiber has its own natural frequency of vibration. Any frequency may, of course, be imposed upon it by force, but if it is allowed freedom, it will respond much more vigorously to a period of vibration equal to its natural period than to any other. This selective response to its natural period of vibration is called *resonance*. Of two objects of similar shape, the larger will have a lower natural frequency. Consequently, as one travels along the basilar membrane its resonance will respond, little by little, to lower and lower frequencies.

It was tempting to think that each type of sound wave crossed the basilar membrane at the point where the resonance frequency corresponded to its own. High-pitched sounds with short wavelengths and high frequencies crossed it near the oval window. Deeper sounds crossed it at a greater distance from the oval window; still deeper sounds crossed it at a still greater distance, and so on. The hair cells at the point of crossing would be stimulated and the brain could then interpret pitch in accordance with which fibers carried the message.

This theory would seem almost too beautifully simple to give up, but evidently it has to be abandoned. The Hungarian physicist Georg von Bekesy has conducted careful experiments with an artificial system designed to possess all the essentials of the cochlea and has found that sound waves passing through the fluid in the cochlea set up wavelike displacements in the basilar membrane itself.

The position of maximum displacement of the basilar membrane — the peak of the wave — depends on the frequency of the sound wave. The lower the frequency, the more distant the peak displacement is from the oval window, and it is at the point at which this peak is located that the hair cells are stimulated. The alteration of the form of displacement of the basilar membrane with pitch does not seem to be great. However, the nerve network can, apparently, respond to the peak of the wave without regard to lesser stimulations near by and can record slight changes in the position of that peak with remarkable fidelity. (In a way, this is similar to our ability to "listen," that is, to hear one sound to which we are paying attention, while damping out the surrounding background noise. We can carry on a conversation in a crowd in which many are talking simultaneously, or amid the roar of city traffic.)

Naturally, any given sound is going to be made up of a variety of sound waves of different frequencies, and the form of the displacement pattern taken up by the basilar membrane will be complex indeed. Hair cells at different points among the basilar membrane will be stimulated and each to a different extent. The combination of all the stimulations will be interpreted by the brain as a variety of pitches which, taken all together, will make up the "quality" of a sound. Thus, a piano and a violin sounding the same tone will produce effects that are clearly different. Each will set up a number of sets of vibrations at varying frequencies, even though the dominant frequency will be that of the tone being sounded. Because a violin and piano have radically different shapes, each will resonate in different fashion to these varying frequencies, so one may reinforce frequency A more than frequency B and the other may reverse matters.

In musical sounds, the differing frequencies of the sound waves set up bear simple numerical relationships among themselves. In nonmusical sounds, the various frequencies are more randomly distributed. The basilar membrane of the cochlea can undergo displacements in response to any sound, musical or not. However, we interpret the simple numerical relationships among simultaneous frequencies as "chords" and "harmonies" and find them pleasant, whereas the frequencies not in simple numerical relationships are "discords" or "noise" and are often found unpleasant.

The delicacy with which we can distinguish pitch and the total range of pitch we can hear depend on the number of hair cells the cochlea can hold and therefore on the length of the organ of Corti. It is clearly advantageous, then, to have the cochlea as long as possible; the human cochlea is one and a half inches long. Or at least it would be that length if it were straight; by being coiled into a spiral (forming two and a half turns), it takes up less room without sacrifice of length.

The human ear can detect sound from frequencies as low as 16 cycles per second (with a wavelength of about 70 feet) to frequencies as high as 25,000 cycles per second (wavelength, about half an inch). In music each doubling of frequency is considered an *octave* ("eight" L, because in the diatonic scale each octave is divided into seven different tones, the eighth tone starting a new octave) and, therefore, the ear has a range of a little over ten octaves. The width of this range may be emphasized by the reminder that the full stretch of notes on the piano extends over only 7½ octaves.

The ear is not equally sensitive to all pitches. It is most sensitive to the range from about 1000 to 4000 cycles per second. This range corresponds to the stretch from the note C two octaves above middle C to the note C that is two octaves higher still. With age, the range of pitch shrinks, particularly at the shrill end; children can easily hear high-pitched sounds that to an adult are simply silence. It is estimated that after the age of forty, the upper limit of the range decreases by about 13 cycles per month.

There are sound waves of frequencies outside the range we can hear, of course. Those with frequencies too high to hear are *ultrasonic waves* ("beyond sound" L), and those with frequencies too low are *subsonic waves* ("below sound" L).* In general, larger animals, with larger sound-producing and sound-sensing organs, can produce and hear deeper sounds than can smaller animals. The smaller animals, in turn, can produce and hear shriller sounds. The trumpet of an elephant and the squeak of a mouse represent reasonable extremes.

While few animals are sensitive to the wide range of pitch we are sensitive to, we are comparatively large creatures. It is easy to find among smaller creatures examples of animals that can readily hear sounds in the ultrasonic reaches. The songs of many birds have their ultrasonic components, and we miss much of the beauty for not hearing these. The squeaking of mice and bats is also rich in ultrasonics, and in the latter case, at least, these have an important function which I shall describe below. Cats and dogs can hear shrill sounds we cannot. The cat will

---

* These days the adjective "supersonic" ("above sound" L) is much used. This does not refer to a range of sound frequencies, but to a velocity that is greater than the speed of sound.

detect a mouse's high-pitched squeak which to us may be a faint sound or nothing at all, and dogs can detect easily the ultrasonic vibrations of the silent "dog-whistles" that are silent only to ourselves.

ECHOLOCATION

In hearing we not only detect a sound but to a certain extent we also determine the direction from which it comes. That we can do so is largely thanks to the fact that we have two ears, the existence of which is not a matter of symmetrical esthetics alone. A sound coming from one side reaches the ear on that side a little sooner than it does the ear on the other. Furthermore, the head itself forms a barrier that sound must pass before reaching the more distant ear; the wave may be slightly weakened by the time it gets there. The brain is capable of analyzing such minute differences in timing and intensity (and the experience of living and of years of trying to locate sounds in this manner and observing our own success sharpens its ability to do so) and judging from that the direction of the sound.

Our ability to judge the direction of sound is not equal throughout the range of pitch we can hear. Any wave-form reacts differently toward obstacles according to whether these are larger or smaller than its own wavelength. Objects larger than a wavelength of the wave-form striking them tend to reflect the wave-form. Objects that are smaller do not; instead the wave-form tends to go around it. The smaller the object in comparison to the wavelength, the less of an obstacle it is and the more easily it is "gone around."

The wavelengths of the ordinary sounds about us is in the neighborhood of a yard, which means that sound can travel around corners and about the average household obstacle. (It will, however, be reflected by large walls and, notoriously, by mountainsides, to produce echoes.) The deeper the sound the more easily does it move around the head without trouble and the less is it weakened before reaching the far ear. One method of locating a sound is therefore denied us. The effect is to be seen in the way the majestic swell of the organ in its lower registers seems to "come from all about us," and thereby to be the more impressive. On the other hand, a particularly shrill note with a wavelength of an inch or so finds the head too much of a barrier, and possibly the far ear does not get enough of the sound to make a judgment. Certainly it is difficult to locate a cricket in a room from the sound of its shrill chirp.

The use of both ears, *binaural hearing* (bin-aw'rul; "two ears" L), does not merely help in locating a sound but also aids sensitivity. The two ears seem to add their responses, so that a sound heard by both seems louder than when heard by only one. Differences in pitch are also more easily distinguished with both ears open than with one covered.

Echoes themselves can be used for location of the presence of a barrier. Thus, when driving along a line of irregularly parked cars, we can, if we listen, easily tell the difference in the engine sound of our own car as we pass parked cars and the engine sound as we pass empty parking places. In the former case the engine sound has its echo added, and there would be no difficulty in locating, through the contrast, an unoccupied parking place with our eyes closed. Unfortunately, we could not tell whether that unoccupied parking place contained a fireplug or not. An automobile is large enough to reflect the wavelengths of some of our engine noises but a fireplug is not. To detect objects smaller than a car would require sound waves of shorter wavelength and higher frequency. The shorter the wavelength and the higher the frequency, the smaller the object we can detect by the echoes to which it gives rise. Obviously, ultrasonic sound would be more efficient in this respect than ordinary sound.

Bats, for example, have long puzzled biologists by their ability to avoid obstacles in flight and to catch insects on the wing at night, even after having been blinded. Deafening bats destroys this ability, and this was puzzling indeed at first. (Can a bat see with its ears? The answer is yes, in a way it can.) It is now known that a flying bat emits a continuous series of ultrasonic squeaks, with frequencies of 40,000 to 80,000 cycles per second (and with resulting wavelengths of from 1/3 of an inch down to 1/6 of an inch). A twig or an insect will tend to reflect such short wavelengths, and the bat, whose squeaks are of excessively short duration, will catch the faint echo between squeaks. From the time lapse between squeak and echo, from the direction of the echo and the extent of the echo's weakening, it can apparently tell whether an object is a twig or an insect and exactly where the object is. It can then guide its flight either with an intention of avoiding or intersecting, as the case may be. This is called *echolocation,* and we should not be surprised that bats have such large ears in relation to their overall size.

Dolphins apparently have a highly developed sense of echolocation, too, though they make use of generally lower sounds, since they require reflection from generally larger objects. (Dolphins eat fish and not insects.) It is by echolocation that dolphins can detect the presence of food and move toward it unerringly even in murky water and at night, when the sense of sight is inadequate.

Man has more of this power of echolocation than he usually suspects. I have already mentioned the ability to locate an empty parking spot, which you may try for yourself. That we do not depend on such devices more than we do is simply because our reliance on sight is such that we ordinarily ignore the help of the ear in the precise location of objects, at least consciously.

Nevertheless, a blindfolded man walking along a corridor can learn to stop before he reaches a blocking screen, as a result of hearing the change in the echoes of his footsteps. He can do this even when he is not quite aware of what it is he is sensing. He may then interpret matters as "I just had a feeling —" Blind men, forced into a greater reliance on hearing, develop abilities in this respect which seem amazing but are merely the result of exploiting powers that have been there all the time.

Mechanically, man has learned to use ultrasonic waves for echolocation (in the precise manner of bats) in a device called *sonar*, which is an abbreviation for "sound navigation and ranging." Sonar is used for detecting objects such as submarines, schools of fish, and bottom features in the ocean. In the open air men now make use of microwaves (a form of light waves with wavelengths in the range of those of ultrasonic sound) for the same purpose. Echolocation by microwave is generally referred to as *radar*, an abbreviation for "radio detection and ranging." (Microwaves are sometimes considered very short radio waves, you see.)

THE VESTIBULAR SENSE

The acoustic nerve, which leads from the cochlea, has a branch leading to the other half of the contents of the internal ear, the utricle and its outgrowths, introduced on page 584. It is time to consider in detail their function. In its simplest form, the utricle may be viewed as a hollow sphere filled with fluid and lined along its inner surface with hair cells. (The structure is similar to the saccule and its outgrowths.) Within the sphere is a bit of calcium carbonate which, thanks to gravity, remains at the bottom of the sphere and stimulates the hair cells there.

Imagine a fish swimming at perfect right angles to the pull of gravity — in a perfectly horizontal line, and leaning neither to one side nor the other. The bit of calcium continues to remain at the bottom of the sphere, and it is the stimulation of those particular hair cells which is interpreted by the nervous system as signifying "normal posture." If the fish's direction of swimming tilts upward, the sphere changes position and the bit of calcium carbonate settles to the new bottom under the pull of gravity, stimulating hair cells that are farther back than the normal-posture ones. If the direction of swim tilts downward, hair cells in front of the normal-posture ones are stimulated. Again there is a shift to the right with a rightward tilt and to the left with a leftward tilt. When the fish is upside-down, the calcium carbonate is stimulating hair cells that are removed by 180 degrees from the normal-posture ones.

In all these cases, the fish can automatically right itself by moving in such a way as to bring the bit of calcium carbonate back to the normal-posture hair cells. The function of the utricle, we observe, is to maintain the normal posture. To us that would be an upright standing position, so a utricle used for this purpose may be called a *statocyst* ("standing-pouch" G) and the bit of calcium carbonate is the *statolith* ("standing-stone" G).

This function can be shown dramatically in crustaceans. The statocysts in such creatures open to the outside world through narrow apertures, and the statoliths are not bits of calcium carbonate but are, rather, sand particles the creature actually places within the statocysts. When the crustacean molts, those bits of sand are lost and must be replaced. One experimenter removed all sand from a tank and substituted iron filings. The shrimp with which he was experimenting innocently introduced iron filings into the statocyst. Once this was done, a magnet held above the shrimp lifted the filings against the pull of gravity and caused them to stimulate the uppermost hair cells instead of the lowermost. In response the animal promptly stood on its head, so that the lowermost hair cells might be stimulated by the "up-ward-falling" filings.

Because the statocyst is located in the internal ear, it is more commonly, though less appropriately, called the *otocyst* (oh'toh-sist; "ear pouch" G). The material within, if present in relatively large particles, is called *otoliths* ("earstone" G), and if present in fine particles is called *otoconia* (oh'toh-koh'nee-uh; "ear-dust" G). Otoconia persist in the utricle of the land vertebrates. The vestibular sense made possible by the utricle is somewhat reminiscent of the proprioceptive senses (see p. 557). However, where the proprioceptive senses tell us the position of one part of the body with relation to another, the vestibular sense tells us the position of the body as a whole with respect to its environment, especially with regard to the direction of the pull of gravity.

A cat can right itself when falling and land on its feet, even though it was dropped feet up. It does this by automatically altering the position of its head into the upright, being guided by the position of its otoconia. This in turn brings about movements in the rest of its body designed to bring it into line with the new position of the head. Down it comes, feetfirst every time. Nor are we ourselves deprived. We have no difficulty in telling whether we are standing upright, upside-down, or tilted in any possible direction, even with our eyes closed and even when floating in water. A swimmer who dives into the water can come up headfirst without trouble and without having to figure out his position consciously.

But the utricle is not all there is to the vestibular sense. Attached to the utricle are three tubes that start and end there, each bending in a semicircle so they are called *semicircular canals*. Each semicircular canal is filled with fluid and is set in an appropriate tunnel within the bone of the skull but is separated from the bone by a thin layer of the fluid. The individual semicircular canals are arranged as follows. Two are located in a vertical plane (if viewed in a standing man) but at right angles to each other, one directed forward and outward, the other backward and outward. The third semicircular canal lies in a horizontal plane. The net result is that each semicircular canal lies in a plane at right angles to those of the other two. You can see the arrangement if you look at a corner of the room where two walls meet the floor. Imagine the curve of one canal following the plane of one wall, that of a second canal following the plane of the other wall, and that of the third canal following the plane of the floor. One end of each canal, where it joins the utricle, swells out to form an *ampulla* (am-pul'uh; "little vase" G, because of its shape). Within each ampulla is a small elevated region called a *crista* ("crest" L), which contains the sensitive hair cells.

The semicircular canals do not react to the body's position with respect to gravity; they react to a change in the body's position. If you should turn your head right or left or tilt it up or down, or in any combination of these movements, the fluid within one or more of the semicircular canals moves because of inertia. There is thus a flow in the direction opposite to the head's motion. (If your car makes a right turn you are pressed against the left, and vice versa.) By receiving impulses from the various stimulated hair cells as a result of this inertial flow of liquid and by noting which were stimulated and by how much, the mind can judge the nature of the motion of the head.°

The semicircular canals judge not motion itself, then, but change of motion. It is acceleration or deceleration that makes fluid move inertially. (In a car at steady speed, you sit comfortably in your seat. But when the car speeds up, you are pressed backward, and when the car slows down, you are pressed forward.) This means that stopping motion is as effective as starting motion in stimulating the semicircular canals. This becomes very noticeable if we spin about as rapidly as we can and continue it long enough to allow the fluid within the semicircular canals to overcome inertia and to turn with us. Now if we stop suddenly, the fluid, thanks to its inertia, keeps on moving and stimulates the hair cells strongly. We interpret this as signifying that there is relative motion between ourselves and our surroundings. Since we know we are standing still, the only conclusion is that the surroundings are moving. The room seems to spin about us, we are dizzy, and in many cases can do nothing but fall to the ground and hold desperately to the floor until the fluid in our semicircular canals settles down and the world steadies itself.

The steady rocking motion of a ship also stimulates the semicircular canals, and to those who are not used to this overstimulation the result often is seasickness, which is an extremely unpleasant, though not really fatal affliction.

° The lampreys, among the most primitive living vertebrates, have only two semicircular canals. Their prefish ancestors were bottom-dwellers who had to contend with motions left and right, forward and backward, but not up and down. They lived a two-dimensional life. The fish developed the third canal for the up-down dimension as well, and all vertebrates since — including ourselves, of course — have had a three-dimensional vestibular sense.

12

OUR EYES

The earth is bathed in light from the sun and one could scarcely think of a more important single fact than that. The radiation of the sun (of which light itself is an important but not the only component) keeps the surface of the earth at a temperature that makes life as we know it possible. The energy of sunlight, in the early dawn of the earth, may have brought about the specific chemical reactions in the ocean that led to the formation of life. And, in a sense, sunlight daily creates life even now. It is the energy source used by green plants to convert atmospheric carbon dioxide into carbohydrates and other tissue components. Since all the animal kingdom, including ourselves, feeds directly or indirectly on green plants, sunlight supports us all. Again, the animal kingdom, and man in particular, has grown adapted to the detection of light. That detection has become so essential to us as a means of sensing and interpreting our environment that blindness is a major affliction, and even fuzzy vision is a serious handicap.

Light has also had a profound influence on the development of science. For the last three centuries the question of the nature of light and the significance of its properties has remained a crucial matter of dispute among physicists. The two chief views concerning the nature of light were first propounded in some detail by 17th-century physicists. The Englishman Isaac Newton believed that light consisted of speeding particles; the Dutchman Christian Huygens believed that it was a wave-form. Central to the dispute was the fact that light traveled in straight lines and cast sharp shadows. Speeding particles (if unaffected by gravity) would naturally move in straight lines, whereas all man's experience with water waves and sound waves showed that wave-forms would not, but would bend about obstacles. For a century and a half, then, the particle theory held fast.

In 1801 the English scientist Thomas Young demonstrated that light showed the property of interference. That is to say, two rays of light could be projected in such a way that when they fell upon a screen together areas of darkness were formed. Particles could not account for this, but waves could — because the wave of one ray might be moving upward while the wave of the other was moving downward, and the two effects would cancel.

The wave theory was quickly made consistent with the straight-line travel of light, since Young also worked out the wavelength of light. As I have said in the previous chapter, the shorter the wavelength the less a wave-form is capable of moving about obstacles, and the more it must move in a straight line and cast shadows. The very shortest wavelengths of audible sound are in the neighborhood of half an inch, and they already show considerable powers of straight-line travel. Imagine, then, what light must be able to do in this respect when we consider that a typical light wave has a wavelength of about a fifty-thousandth of an inch. Light is much more efficient than even the most ultrasonic of life-produced sound in echolocation. We may be able to detect the position of an object by the sound it makes, but we do so only fairly well. When we see an object, on the contrary, we are quite certain that we know exactly where it is. "Seeing is believing," we say, and the height of skepticism is "to doubt the evidence of one's own eyes."

Light waves contain far more energy than do the sound waves we ordinarily encounter; enough energy, as a matter of fact, to bring about chemical changes in many substances. It is quite feasible for living organisms to detect the presence of light by the presence or absence of such chemical changes and to respond accordingly. For the purpose it is not even necessary to develop an elaborate light-detecting organ. Plants, for instance, climb toward the light, or bend toward it, without any trace of such an organ. A response to light is clearly useful. All green plants must grow toward the light if they are to make use of its energy. Water animals can find the surface layers of the sea by moving toward the light. On land, light means warmth and animals may seek it or avoid it depending on the season of the year, the time of day, and other factors.

Detecting light by its chemical effect can, however, be dangerous as well as useful. In living tissue, with its delicate balance of complex and fragile interacting compounds, random changes induced by light can be ruinous. It proved evolutionarily useful to concentrate a chemical particularly sensitive to light in one spot. Because of its individual sensitivity, such a chemical would react to a low intensity of light, one that would not damage tissue generally. Furthermore, its location in a certain spot would enable the remainder of the organism's surface to be shielded from light altogether.

(In order for any substance to be affected by light to the point of chemical change, it must first absorb the light. Generally it will absorb some wavelengths of light to a greater extent than others, and the light it reflects or transmits will then be weighted in favor of the wavelengths it does not absorb. But we sense different wavelengths, as I shall explain later in the chapter, as different colors, so when we see the light-sensitive substance by the light it transmits or reflects we see it as colored. For this reason the light-sensitive compounds in organisms are commonly referred to as pigments, a word reserved for colored substances, and specifically as *visual pigments*.)

Even one-celled animals may have light-sensitive areas, but the true elaboration of course comes in multicellular animals, in which discrete organs — eyes — are devoted to *photoreception*. (The prefix "photo" is from the Greek word for "light.")

The simplest photoreceptors can do no more than detect light or not detect it. Nevertheless, even when an organism is limited to this detection it has a useful tool. It can move either toward or away from the light sensed. Furthermore, if the level of stimulation suddenly falls, the obvious interpretation is that something has passed between the photoreceptor and the light. Flight could be a logical response, since the "something," after all, might very well be an enemy.

The more sensitive a photoreceptor can be made the better, and one method of increasing the sensitivity is to increase the amount of light falling upon the visual pigment. A way of doing this depends upon the fact that light does not necessarily travel in a straight line under all conditions. Whenever light passes obliquely from one medium to another it is bent or *refracted* ("bent back" L). If the surface between media is flat, all the light entering it bends as a unit.* If the surface is curved, things are rather more complicated. Should light pass from air into water across a surface that is more or less spherical, the rays tend to bend in the direction of the center of the sphere, no matter where they strike. All the light rays converge therefore and are eventually gathered together into a *focus* ("fireplace" L, since that is where light is gathered together, so to speak, in a household).

To concentrate light, organisms use not water itself but a transparent object that is largely water. In land animals it is shaped like a lentil seed, which in Latin is called *lens* and which lent its name to the shape. A lens is a kind of flattened sphere that does the work but economizes on room. The lens acts to concentrate light; all the light that falls on its relatively broad width is brought into the compass of a narrow spot. A child can use a lens to set paper on fire, whereas unconcentrated sunlight would be helpless to do so. In the same way a particular photo-

---

* This is strictly so only if all the light is of the same wavelength. Where it is not there is another important effect (see p. 630).

receptor could respond to feeble light which, in the absence of lens-concentration, would leave it unaffected.

Since light, left to itself, travels primarily in straight lines, a photoreceptor — whether equipped with a lens or not — will sense light only from the direction it faces. To sense light in other directions a creature must turn, or else it must be supplied with photoreceptors pointed in a number of directions. The latter alternative has much to recommend it since it saves the time required to turn, and even a fraction of a second may be important in the eternal battle to obtain food and avoid enemies.

The development of multiple photoreceptors reaches its climax in insects. The eyes of a fly are not single organs. Each is a *compound eye* made up of thousands of photoreceptors, each of which is set at a slightly different angle. A fly without moving can be conscious of changes in light intensity at almost any angle, which is why it is so difficult to catch one by surprise while bringing it the gift of a flyswatter. Each photoreceptor of the compound eye registers only "light" or "dark" but their numbers enable something more to be done. If an object lies between the compound eye and the light, the insect can obtain a rough estimate of the object's size and shape by the number and distribution of those photoreceptors that register "dark." A kind of rough mosaic picture is built up of the object. Furthermore, if the object moves, individual photoreceptors go dark progressively in the direction of its motion, and others light up progressively as it leaves. In this way, the insect can obtain an idea of the direction and velocity of a movement.

The vertebrates have adopted a different system. Use is made of large individual eyes that concentrate light on an area of photosensitive cells. Each cell is individually capable of registering light or dark. The individual photoreceptors are cell-sized and microscopic; and not, as in insects, large enough to be seen by the naked eye. The vertebrate mosaic of sight is fine indeed.

Suppose that you try to draw a picture of a man's face on a sheet of paper using black dots after the fashion of a newspaper

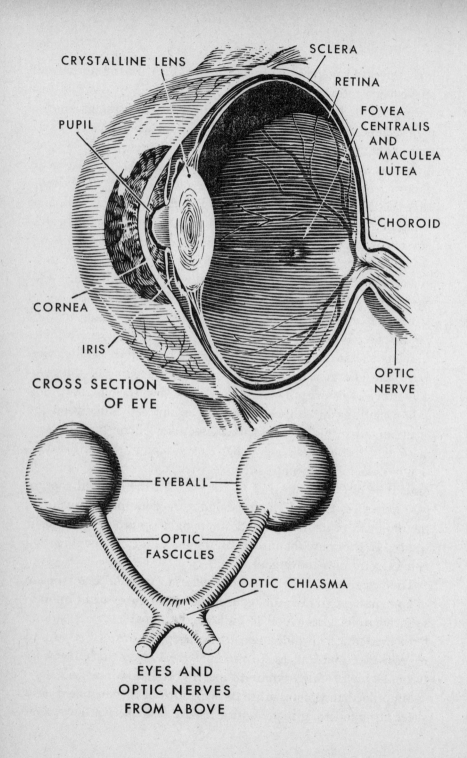

CRYSTALLINE LENS

SCLERA

RETINA

FOVEA CENTRALIS AND MACULEA LUTEA

PUPIL

CHOROID

CORNEA

IRIS

OPTIC NERVE

CROSS SECTION OF EYE

EYEBALL

OPTIC FASCICLES

OPTIC CHIASMA

EYES AND OPTIC NERVES FROM ABOVE

photograph (look at one under a magnifying glass and you will see what I mean). If you use large dots for the purpose, you can't get much detail into the picture. If you use smaller dots (for a picture of the same size) you can make out more detail; still smaller dots, still greater detail.

The "dots" used by insects are the size of the individual facets of their compound eyes; the dots used by ourselves are the size of cells. We can therefore see much more detail than an insect can; our vision is much more acute. In the space which a honeybee might cover with one dot, either light or dark — and that is all the information it would have — we could squeeze in some 10,000 dots in a possibly intricate pattern of light and dark that could yield a great deal of information.

The use of an eye with cell-sized photoreceptors offers such advantages that it has actually been devised by a number of quite unrelated groups of animals. In particular, certain groups of mollusks developed an eye quite independently of the development going on in vertebrates, and ended almost in the same place. The eye of the squid, though possessing a completely different history than ours does, resembles ours closely, part for part.

THE EYEBALL

The human eye, which is just about an inch in diameter, is very nearly a sphere in shape, so the expression *eyeball* for the eye as a physical structure is quite apt. About five sixths of the eyeball is enclosed by a strong, fibrous outermost layer called the *sclera* (sklee'ruh; "hard" G). It is white, and portions of it are visible in that part of the eye to be seen between the eyelids. This is referred to as "the white of the eye."

In the front of the eye, facing the outside world directly, is a section about half an inch in diameter which is transparent. It is the *cornea*. (This word is from the same root as the word "horn," and since thin layers of horn are semitransparent, and since horn and cornea are both modified skin, the name is not as farfetched as it might seem.) The cornea does not really complete the sphere of the eyeball smoothly. Its curvature is sharper than is that of the sclera and it bulges outward from the eye's smooth curve, like a portion of a small sphere set into the side of a larger one. If you close your eyes lightly, place your finger upon the eyelid, and move your eye, you will definitely feel the bulge of the cornea.

A layer of dark tissue, lining the inner surface of the sclera, continues the smooth curve of the eyeball and extends out into the cavity formed by the cornea's bulge, almost closing the transparent gap. This is the *choroid* (koh'roid; "membrane" G) and it is well supplied with blood vessels, some of which occasionally show through the white of the sclera. The portion of the choroid visible under the cornea contains the dark pigment, melanin, which is responsible for the brown or black color of hair, and for the swarthiness of skin. In most human beings, there is enough melanin in this portion of the choroid to give it a brown color. Among fair-skinned individuals with less-than-average capacity for forming melanin, the color is lighter. If the spots of pigment are sparse enough, they do not absorb light so much as scatter it. Light of short wavelength (as, for example, blue) is more easily scattered than light of long wavelength (such as red), so that the visible choroid usually appears blue or blue-green under these conditions, viewed as it is by the light it scatters. At birth, babies' eyes are always blue but as pigment is formed in increasing quantities during the time of infancy, most sets of eyes gradually turn brown. Among albinos, incapable of forming melanin altogether, the choroid contains no pigment and the blood vessels are clearly seen, giving the choroid a distinctly reddish appearance.

The different colors found among individuals in this portion of the eye give it the name *iris* ("rainbow" G). We are particularly conscious of this color, and when we speak of "brown eyes" or "blue eyes" we are referring to the color of the iris and not of the whole eye, of course. The function of the iris is to screen the light entering the interior of the eyeball. Naturally, the more pigmented the iris, the more efficiently it performs this function. The evolutionary development of blue eyes took place in northern countries, where sunlight is characteristically weak and where imperfect shading could even be useful in increasing the eye's sensitivity. An albino's eyes are unusually sensitive to light because of the lack of shading, and he must avoid bright lights.

To allow for changes in the intensity of outside illumination the iris is equipped to extend or contract the area it covers by means of the tiny muscle fibers it contains. In bright light, the fibers relax and the iris covers almost the entire area under the cornea. A tiny round opening is left through which light can enter the eyeball, and this opening is the *pupil* ("doll" L, because of the tiny image of oneself one can see reflected there). In dim light, the fibers tighten and the iris draws back, so that the pupil enlarges and allows more light to enter the eyeball.

The pupil is the opening through which we actually see, and this is evident even to folk-wisdom, which refers to it as "the apple of the eye" and uses it as a synonym for something carefully loved and guarded. It is partly through the variation in its size that we adapt to a specific level of light. Entering a darkened movie theater from the outer sunlight leaves us blind at first. If we wait a few minutes, the pupil expands and our vision improves greatly as more light pours in. Conversely, if we stumble into the bathroom at night and turn on the light we find ourselves momentarily pained by the brilliance. After a few moments of peering through narrowed eyelids, the pupil decreases in size and we are comfortable again. At its smallest the pupil has a diameter of about 1.5 millimeters (about 1/16 inch), at its widest about 8 or 9 millimeters (over 1/3 inch). The diameter increases sixfold, and since the light-gathering power depends on the area — which varies as the square of the diameter — the pupil at maximum opening admits nearly forty times as much light as at minimum opening. (Our pupil retains a circular shape as it grows larger and smaller. This is not true of some other animals. In the cat, to cite the most familiar case, the pupil is round in the dark, but with increasing light it narrows from side to side only, becoming nothing more than a vertical slit in bright light.)

The eye is carefully protected from mechanical irritation as well as from the effects of too much light. It is equipped with eyelids which close rapidly at the slightest hint of danger to the eyes. So rapid is this movement that "quick as a wink" is a common phrase to signify speed, and the German word for "an instant" is *ein Augenblick* ("an eyewink"). Nor is the movement of the eyelid itself a source of irritation. For one thing, there is a delicate membrane covering the exposed portion of the eyeball and the inner surface of the eyelid. This is the *conjunctiva* (kon'-junk-ty'vuh; "connective" L, because it connects the eyeball and the eyelids). The conjunctiva is kept moist by the secretions ("tears") of the *tear glands,* a name that is Latinized to *lacrimal glands* ("tear" L). These are located just under the bone forming the upper and outer part of the eye socket.

When the eyelid closes, conjunctiva slides along conjunctiva with a thin, lubricating layer of fluid between. In order to keep the eye's surface moist and flexible, the eyelid closes periodically, moving fluid over the exposed portion of the eye, despite the fact that danger may not be present. We are so used to this periodic blinking, even when not consciously aware of it, that we are made uneasy by an unwinking stare. The fact that snakes do not have eyelids and therefore have just such an unwinking stare is one factor in their appearance of malevolence.

Some animals have a third eyelid in the form of a transparent membrane that can be quickly drawn across the eye, usually in a horizontal sweep from the inner corner of the eye (the *inner canthus*) near the nose. This is the *nictitating membrane* ("wink" L) and cleans the eye without introducing a dangerous, even if short, period of complete blindness. Man does not possess a functional nictitating membrane, but a remnant of it is to be found in the inner canthus.

Tears also serve the purpose of washing out foreign matter that gets onto the eye's surface. The eye is protected against such foreign matter not only by the eyelid itself but by the eyelashes that rim the lids and permit sight while maintaining a protective (but discontinuous) barrier across the opening. Thus, we automatically squint our eyes when the wind stirs up dust. There also are the eyebrows, which protect the overhang of the forehead, entangling raindrops and insects.

Still, foreign matter will invade the eye occasionally. Sometimes an eyelash will get in so that the protective device itself can be a source of trouble. In response to such invasion (which can be exquisitely uncomfortable), the lacrimal glands secrete their tears at an increased rate and the eyes "water." Eyes will also water in response to the irritation of smoke, chemicals (as in the case of the well-known "tear gas"), strong wind, or even strong light. Ordinarily tears are carried off by the thin *lacrimal ducts* placed at the inner canthus. The fluid is then discharged into the nasal cavity. Usually not enough of it is disposed of in this fashion to be noticed. When the lacrimal ducts grow inflamed during infection, tear outflow is cut down, and we notice the lack of the duct action easily enough since watering eyes make up one of the unpleasant symptoms of a cold.

In response to strong emotions the lacrimal glands are particularly active, and secrete tears past the capacity of the lacrimal ducts, even at their best, to dispose of them. In such cases, the tears will collect and overflow the lower lids so that we weep with rage, with joy, with frustration, or with grief, as the case may be. The escape of tears into the nasal cavity does become noticeable under these conditions, too, and it is common to find one must blow one's nose after weeping.) Tears are salt, as are all body fluids, and also contain a protein called *lysozyme,* which has the ability to kill bacteria and thus lend tears a disinfecting quality.

Despite all the protection offered them, the eyes, of necessity, are unusually open to irritation and infection, and the inflammation of the conjunctiva that results is *conjunctivitis.* The engorged blood vessels, unusually visible through the sclera, give the eye a "bloodshot" appearance. Newborn babies are liable to develop conjunctivitis because of infections gained during their passage through the genital canal. This, however, is controlled and prevented from bringing about serious trouble by the routine treatment of their eyes with antibiotics or with dilute silver nitrate solution.

A serious form of conjunctivitis, caused by a virus, is *trachoma* (tra-koh'muh; "rough" G), so called because the scars formed on the eyeball give it a roughened appearance. The scars on the cornea can be bad enough to blind a sufferer of the disease. Since trachoma is particularly common in the Middle East, this may possibly account for the number of blind beggars featured in the stories of the Arabian Nights.

The fact that we have two eyes is part of our bilateral symmetry, as is the fact that we have two ears, two arms, and two legs. The existence of two eyes is useful in that the loss of vision in one eye does not prevent an individual from leading a reasonably normal-sighted life. However, the second eye is more than a spare.

In most animals, the two eyes have separate fields of vision and nothing, or almost nothing, that one of them sees can be seen by the other. This is useful if a creature must be continually on the outlook for enemies and must seemingly look in all directions at once. Among the primates, though, the two eyes are brought forward to the front of the head, so that the fields of vision overlap almost entirely. What we see with one eye is just about what we see with the other. By so narrowing the field of vision, we look at one thing and see it clearly. Moreover, we gain importantly in depth perception.

We can judge the comparative distances of objects we see in a number of ways, some of which depend upon experience. Knowing the true size of something, say, we can judge its distance from its apparent size. If we don't know its true size we may compare it with nearby objects of known size. We can judge by the quantity of haze that obscures it, by the convergence of parallel lines reaching out toward it, and so on. All this will work for one eye as well as for two, so that depth perception with one eye is possible.* Nevertheless, we have but to close one eye to see that, in comparison with two-eyed vision, one-eyed vision tends to be flat.

With two eyes, you see, the phenomenon of parallax is introduced. We see a tree with the left eye against a certain spot on the far horizon. We see the same tree at the same time with the right eye against a different spot on the far horizon. (Try holding a pencil a foot before your eyes and view it while closing first one eye then the other without moving your head. You will see it shift positions against the background.) The closer an object to the eye, the greater its shift in position with change from one view to the other. The field of vision of the left eye therefore differs from that of the right in the relative positions of the various objects the field contains. The fusion of the two fields enables us to judge comparative distance by noting (quite automatically and without conscious effort) the degrees of difference. This form of depth perception is *stereoscopic vision* ("solid-seeing" G), because it makes possible the perceiving of a solid as a solid, in depth as well as in height and breadth and not merely as a flat projection.**

The fixing of the eyes upon a single field of vision does not obviate the necessity of seeing in all directions. One way of making up for the loss of area of the field of vision is to be able to turn the neck with agility. The owl, whose stereoscopic eyes are fixed in position, can turn its neck in either direction through almost 180 degrees so that it can look almost directly backward.

---

* By cleverly altering backgrounds to take advantage of the assumptions we are continually making, we can be tricked into coming to false conclusions as to shapes, sizes, and distances, and this is the explanation of many of the "optical illusions" with which we all amuse ourselves at one time or another.

** In the days before movies a popular evening pastime was to look at stereoscope slides. These consisted of pairs of pictures of the same scene taken from slightly different angles, representing the view as it would be seen by a left eye alone and also by a right eye. Looking at these through a device that enables the eyes to fuse the pictures into one scene caused the view to spring into a pseudo-three-dimensional reality. In the 3-D craze that hit the movies in the 1950's, two pictures were taken in this same left-eye-right-eye manner and the two were viewed separately by either eye when special spectacles of oppositely polarized film were put on.

Our own less flexible neck will not permit a turn of more than 90 degrees, but, on the other hand, we can turn our eyeballs through a considerable angle. The human eyeball is outfitted with three pairs of muscles for this purpose. One pair turns it right or left; one pair up or down; and one pair rotates it somewhat. As a result, a reasonable extension of the field of vision is made possible by a flicker of movement taking less time and effort than moving the entire head.

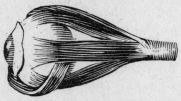

EYE MUSCLES

The restriction of field of vision makes it possible for a man to be surprised from behind ("Do I have eyes in the back of my head?" is the plaintive cry), but to the developing primates in the trees, stereoscopic vision, which made it possible to judge the distance of branches with new precision, was well worth the risk of blindness toward the rear. In nonstereoscopic vision there is no reason why the motion of the eyes might not be independent of each other. This is so in the chameleon, to cite one case, and the separate movements of its eyes are amusing to watch. In stereoscopic eyes such as our own, however, the two eyeballs must move in unison if we are to keep a single field in view.

Occasionally a person is to be found who has an eyeball under defective muscular control, so that when one eye is fixed on an object, the other is pointed too far toward the nose ("cross-eyes") or too far away from it ("wall-eyes"). The two conditions are lumped as "squint-eyes," or *strabismus* (stra-biz'mus; "squint" G). This ruins stereoscopic vision and causes the person to favor one eye over the other, ignoring what is seen with the unfavored eye and causing the latter's visual ability to decline.

To be sure, the eyes do not, under normal conditions, point in exactly parallel fashion. If both are to orient their pupils in the direction of the same object, they must converge slightly. Usually this convergence is too small to notice, but it becomes more marked for closer objects. If you bring a pencil toward a person's nose, you will see his eyes begin to "cross." The extent of the effort involved in such convergence offers another means by which a person can judge distance.

WITHIN THE EYE

Immediately behind the pupil is the lens, sometimes called the *crystalline lens*, not because it contains crystals, but because, in the older sense of the word "crystalline," it is transparent (see illustration, p. 610). The lens is lens-shaped (of course) and is about a third of an inch in diameter. All around its rim is a ringlike *suspensory ligament*, which joins it to a portion of the choroid layer immediately behind the iris. That portion of the choroid layer is the *ciliary body*, and this contains the *ciliary muscle*.

The lens and the suspensory ligament divide the eyes into two chambers, of which the forward is only one fifth the size of the portion lying behind the lens. The smaller forward chamber contains a watery fluid called the *aqueous humor* ("watery fluid" L), which is much like cerebrospinal fluid in composition and circulates in the same way that cerebrospinal fluid does. The aqueous humor leaks into the anterior chamber from nets of capillaries in the ciliary body and out again through a small duct near the point where the iris meets the cornea. This duct is called the *canal of Schlemm* after the German anatomist Friedrich Schlemm, who described it in 1830.

The portion behind the lens is filled with a clear, jellylike substance, the *vitreous humor* ("glassy fluid" L), or, since it is not really a fluid, the *vitreous body*. It is permanent and does not circulate. For all its gelatinous nature, the vitreous body is ordinarily as clear as water. However, small objects finding their way into it are trapped in its jellylike network and can then make themselves visible to us as tiny dots or filaments if we stare at some featureless background. They usually cannot be focused upon but drift away if we try to look at them directly, and so are called "floaters." The Latin medical name *muscae volitantes* (mus'see vol-ih-tan'teez) sounds formidable but is rather colorful, really, since it means "flying flies." Almost everyone possesses them, and the brain learns to ignore them if the situation is not too extreme. Recent research would make it seem that the floaters are red blood corpuscles that occasionally escape from the tiny capillaries in the retina.

The eye is under an internal fluid pressure designed to keep its spherical shape fairly rigid. This internal pressure is some 177 millimeters of mercury higher than the external air pressure, and this pressure is maintained by the neat balance of aqueous humor inflow-and-outflow. If the canal of Schlemm is for any reason narrowed or plugged — through fibrous ingrowths or inflammation, infection, or the gathering of debris — the aqueous humor cannot escape rapidly enough and the internal pressure begins to rise. This condition is referred to as *glaucoma* (gloh-koh'muh), for reasons to be described later. If pressure rises high enough, as it only too often does in glaucoma, permanent damage will be done to the optic nerve and blindness will result.

Coating the inner surface of the eyeball is the *retina* ("net" L, for obscure reasons), and it is the retina that contains the photoreceptors (see illustration, p. 610). Light entering the eye passes through the cornea and aqueous humor, through the opening of the pupil, then through the lens and vitreous humor to the retina. In the process, the rays of light originally falling upon the cornea are refracted, gathered together, and focused at a small point on the retina. The sharper the focus, the clearer and more sensitive the vision, naturally.

The lens, despite what one might ordinarily assume, is not the chief agent of refraction. Light rays are bent twice as much by the cornea as by the lens. However, whereas the refractive powers of the cornea are fixed, those of the lens are variable. Thus, the lens is normally rather flat and refracts light comparatively little. The light rays reaching the cornea from a distant object diverge infinitesimally in the process and may be considered to be reaching the cornea as virtually parallel rays. The refractive powers of the cornea and the flat lens are sufficient to focus this light upon the retina. As the distance of the point being viewed lessens, the light rays reaching the cornea become increasingly divergent. For distances under twenty feet, the divergence is sufficient to prevent focusing upon the retina without an adjustment somewhere. When that happens, the ciliary muscles contract, and this lessens the tension on the suspensory ligaments. The elasticity of the lens causes it to approach the spherical as far as the ligaments permit, and when the latter relax the lens at once bulges outward. This thickening of the lens curves its surface more sharply and increases its powers of refraction, so that the image of the point being viewed is still cast upon the retina. The closer a point under view, the more the lens is allowed to bulge in order to keep the focus upon the retina. This change of lens curvature is *accommodation*.

There is a limit, of course, to the degree to which a lens can accommodate. As an object comes nearer and nearer, there comes a point (the *near point*) where the lens simply cannot bulge any further and where refraction cannot be made sufficient. Vision becomes fuzzy and one must withdraw one's head, or the object, in order to see it. The lens loses elasticity with age and becomes increasingly reluctant to accommodate at all. This means that with the years the near point recedes. An individual finds he must retreat from the telephone book bit by bit in order to read a number and, eventually, may have to retreat so far that he can't read it once he finally has it in focus, because it is too small. A young child with normal vision may be able to focus on objects 4 inches from the eye; a young adult on objects 10 inches away; whereas an aging man may not be able to manage anything closer than 16 inches. This recession of the near point with age is called *presbyopia* (prez'bee-oh'pee-uh; "old man's vision" G).

Ideally, the light passing through the cornea and lens should focus right on the retina. It often happens, though, that the eyeball is a bit too deep for this. Light focuses at the proper distance, but the retina is not there. By the time light reaches the retina, it has diverged again somewhat. The eye, in an effort to compensate, allows the lens to remain unaccommodated in order that light may be refracted as little as possible and the focus therefore cast as far back as possible. For distant vision, however, where refraction must be less than for close vision, the lens is helpless. It cannot accommodate less than the "no-accommodation-at-all" that suffices for near vision. An individual with deep eyeballs is therefore *nearsighted;* he sees close objects clearly and distant objects fuzzily. The condition is more formally referred to as *myopia* (my-oh'pee-uh; "shut-vision" G). The name arises out of the fact that in an effort to reduce the fuzziness of distant objects, the myopic individual brings his eyelids together, converting his eyes into a sort of pinhole camera that requires no focusing. However, the amount of light entering the eye is decreased, so it is difficult to see (to say nothing of eyelash interference) and the strain on the eyelid muscles will in the long run bring on headaches.

The opposite condition results when an eyeball is too shallow and consequently the light falls on the retina before it is quite focused. In this case the lens, by accommodating, can introduce an additional bit of light refraction that will force light from a distant source into focus on the retina. Light from a near source, requiring still more refraction, cannot be managed. Such an individual has an unusually far-distant near point. He is *farsighted*, seeing distant objects with normal clarity and near ones fuzzily. This is *hyperopia* (hy'per-oh'pee-uh; "beyond-vision" G).

For light passing through the cornea and lens to focus precisely, the cornea and lens must each be smoothly curved. The degree of curvature along any meridian (vertical, horizontal, diagonal) must be equal. In actual fact this ideal is never quite met; there are always unevennesses, and, as a result, light does not focus in a point but in a short line. If the line is short enough this is not serious; but if it is long, there is considerable fuzziness of vision in both near and far objects. This is *astigmatism* ("no point" G). Fortunately such defects in refraction are easily corrected by introducing refraction from without by means of glass lenses. (The use of spectacles was one of the few medical advances made during the Middle Ages.) For myopia, lenses are used to diverge light minimally and push the focus backward; and for hyperopia, lenses are used to converge light minimally and push the focus forward. In astigmatism, lenses of uneven curvature are used to cancel out the uneven curvature of the eye.

The transparency of the cornea and lens is not due to any unusual factor in the composition, despite the fact that they are the only truly transparent solid tissues of the body. They are composed of protein and water and their transparency depends, evidently, on an unusual regularity of molecular structure. They are living parts of the body. The cornea can heal itself, for instance, if it is scratched. The level of life, however, must remain low, since neither tissue may be directly infiltrated by blood vessels — that would ruin their all-important transparency. Yet it is only with blood immediately available that a tissue can go about the business of life in an intensive fashion.

This has its advantages. A cornea can, if properly preserved, maintain its integrity after the death of an organism more easily than it would if it had been accustomed, as tissues generally are, to an elaborate blood supply. A cornea will also "take" if transplanted to another individual, whereas a more actively living tissue would not. This means that a person whose cornea has clouded over as a result of injury or infection but whose eyes are completely functional otherwise may regain his sight through a corneal transplantation.

Transparency is not easy to maintain. Any loss of regularity of structure will give rise to opaque regions, and the lens, especially, is subject to the development of opacities. This condition can spread so that the entire lens becomes opaque and useless and vision is lost. The possibility of lens opacity increases with age, and it is the greatest single cause of blindness, accounting for about a quarter of the cases of blindness in the United States. Luckily it is possible to remove the lens and make up for the lost refractive powers by properly designed glasses. Since aged lenses have lost accommodative powers anyway, little is sacrificed beyond the inconvenience of the operation and of having to wear glasses, and such inconvenience is certainly preferable to blindness.

The opacity within a lens is called a *cataract*. The ordinary meaning of the word is that of "waterfall," but it is derived from Greek terms meaning "to dash downward" and that need not refer to water only. The lens opacity is like a curtain being drawn downward to obscure the window of the eye. Because the presence of the cataract causes the ordinarily black pupil to become clouded over in a grayish or silvery fashion, the word "glaucoma" ("silvery gray" G) was applied to it in ancient times. When "cataract" came into favor, "glaucoma" was pushed away from the lens condition and came to be applied to another optical disorder (described earlier in the chapter), one to which the word does not truly apply etymologically.

THE RETINA

The retinal coating is about the size and thickness of a postage stamp pasted over the internal surface of the eyeball and covering about four fifths of it. (It sometimes gets detached, bringing about blindness, but techniques now exist for binding it back into position.) The retina consists of a number of layers, and of these the ones farthest toward the light are composed largely of nerve cells and their fibers. Underneath these are the actual photoreceptors, which in the human eye are of two types, the *rods* and the *cones,* obviously named from their shapes. Under the rods and cones and immediately adjacent to the choroid is a film of pigmented cells that send out projections to insinuate themselves between the rods and the cones. These pigmented cells serve to absorb light and cut down reflection that would otherwise blur the retinal reaction to the light falling on it directly.

In animals adapted to vision in dim light, however, the reverse is desired. In them the retina contains a reflecting layer, the *tapetum* (ta-pee′tum; "carpet" L), which sends light back and gives the retina a second chance at it. Clarity of vision is sacrificed to sensitivity of detection. Some light, even so, escapes the retina after reflection has allowed that tissue a second chance, and this escaping light emerges from the widespread pupils. It is why cats' eyes (tapetum-equipped) gleam eerily in the dark. They would not do so if it were truly dark, because they do not manufacture light. The human eye, needless to say, does not have a tapetum. It sacrifices sensitivity to clarity.

The arrangement of layers in the retina is such that approaching light must in general first strike the layers of nerve cells and pass through them in order to reach the rods and cones. This seems inefficient, but things are not quite that bad in the human eye. At the point of the retina lying directly behind the lens and upon which the light focuses, there is a yellow spot (yellow because of the presence of a pigment) called the *macula lutea* (mak′yoo-luh lyoo′tee-uh; "yellow spot" L); see illustration, page 610 . In it the photoreceptors are very closely packed, and vision is most acute there.

In order for us to see two separate objects actually as two and not have them blur together into one object (and this is what is meant by visual acuity), the light from the two objects would have to fall upon two separate photoreceptors with at least one unstimulated photoreceptor in between. It follows that the more closely packed the photoreceptors, the closer two objects may be and yet have this happen. In the macula lutea the photoreceptors are crowded together so compactly that at ordinary reading distance a person with normal vision could see two dots as two dots when separated by only a tenth of a millimeter.

Furthermore, in the very center of the macula lutea there is a small depression called the *fovea centralis* (foh'vee-uh sen-tray'lis; "central pit" L) which is right where light focuses. The reason the spot is depressed is that the nerve layers above the photo-receptors are thinned out to almost nothing so that light hits the photoreceptors directly. This situation is most highly developed in the primates. This is one of the reasons why the primate Order, including ourselves, has to such a large extent sacrificed smell and even hearing to the sense of sight. The very excellence of the sense of sight that we have evolved has made it tempting to do so.

Naturally, the retina outside the fovea is not left unused. Light strikes it and the brain responds to that. When we are looking at an object we are also conscious of other objects about it (*peripheral vision*). We cannot make out small details in peripheral vision, but we can make out shapes and colors. In particular, we can detect motion, and it is important even for humans to see "out of the corner of the eye." In this age of auto-mobiles, many a life has been saved by the detection of motion to one side; license examiners routinely test one's ability to do so by waving pencils to one side while having the applicant stare straight ahead. The loss of peripheral vision (popularly called *tunnel vision* because one can then only see directly forward) would make one a dangerous person behind the wheel.

The fibers of the nerve cells of the retina gather into the optic nerve (which, along with the retina itself, is actually a part of the brain, from a structural point of view; see illustration, p. 532). The optic nerve leaves the eyeball just to one side of the fovea and its point of exit is the one place in the retina where photo-receptors are completely absent. It therefore represents the *blind spot*. We are unaware of the existence of a blind spot ordinarily because, for one thing, the light of an object which falls on the blind spot of one eye does not fall on the blind spot of the other. One eye always makes it out. With one eye closed, it is easy however to show the existence of the blind spot. If one looks at a black rectangle containing a white dot and a white cross and focuses, let us say, on the dot, he will be able to locate a certain distance at which the cross disappears. Its light has fallen on the blind spot. At distances closer and farther, it reappears.

The photoreceptors when stimulated by light initiate impulses in the nearby nerve cells, and the message, conducted to the brain by the optic nerve and eventually reaching the optic area in the occipital lobe, is interpreted as light. The photoreceptors can also be stimulated by pressure, and that stimulation too is interpreted as light so that we "see stars" as the result of a blow near the eye. Such pressure-induced flashes of light can appear if we simply close our eyelids tightly and concentrate. What we see are *phosphenes* (fos'feenz; "to show light" G).

The two types of photoreceptors, rods and cones, are each adapted to a special type of vision. The cones are stimulated only by rather high levels of light and are used in daylight or *photopic* (foh-top'ik; "light-vision" G) vision. The rods, on the other hand, can be stimulated by much lower levels of light than the cones can and are therefore involved in *scotopic* (skoh-top'ik; "darkness-vision" G) vision — that is, in vision in dim light.

Nocturnal animals often possess retinas containing only rods. The human eye goes to the other extreme in one respect. To be sure, the rods greatly outnumber the cones in our retinas, since the human retina contains 125 million rods and only 7 million cones. However, the macula lutea, which carries the burden of seeing, contains cones only and virtually no rods. Each cone, moreover, generally has its own optic nerve fiber, which helps maximize acuity. (Yet as many as ten or even a hundred rods may be connected to the same nerve fiber; in dim light only sensitivity is sought and acuity is sacrificed on its altar.)

Man's acuity is thus centered on photopic vision, as seems right since he is a creature of the daylight. This means, though, that at night acuity of vision does not exist for dim light. If one looks directly at a faint star at night, it seems to vanish altogether, because its light strikes only cones, which it is too weak to stimulate. Look to one side, nevertheless, and the star jumps into view as its light strikes rods. (Contrarily, it is because the cones become progressively less numerous away from the macula lutea that we have so little acuity in peripheral vision in daylight.)

The two forms of vision differ in another important respect, in that of color. As I shall explain shortly, specific colors involve only a portion of the range of wavelengths of light to which the eye is sensitive. The cones, reacting to high levels of light, can afford to react to this portion or that and therefore to detect color. The rods, reacting to very low levels, must detect all the light available to achieve maximum sensitivity and therefore do not distinguish colors. Scotopic vision, in other words, is in black and white, with, of course, intermediate shades of gray; a fact well expressed by the common proverb that "at night all cats are gray."

The rods contain a rose-colored visual pigment and it is that which actually undergoes the chemical change with light. It is commonly called *visual purple* (though it is not purple), but its more formal and more accurate name is *rhodopsin* (roh-dop'sin; "rose eye" G). The molecule of rhodopsin is made up of two parts: a protein, *opsin,* and a nonprotein portion, very similar in structure to vitamin A, which is *retinene.* Retinene can exist in two forms, different in molecular shape, called *cis-retinene* and *trans-retinene.* The shape of cis-retinene is such that it can combine with opsin to form rhodopsin, whereas trans-retinene cannot. In the presence of light, cis-retinene is converted to transretinene and, if it already makes up part of the rhodopsin molecule, it falls off, leaving the largely colorless opsin behind. (Rhodopsin may therefore be said to be bleached by light.) In the dark, trans-retinene changes into cis-retinene and joins opsin once more to form the rhodopsin.

There is thus a cycle, rhodopsin being bleached in the light and formed again in the dark. It is the bleaching that stimulates the nerve cell. In ordinary daylight the rhodopsin of the eyes is largely in the bleached state and is useless for vision. This does not ordinarily matter, since rhodopsin is involved in scotopic vision only and is not used in bright light. As one passes into a darkened interior, however, vision is at first almost nil because of this. It improves, as noted earlier in the chapter, by the expansion of the pupil to permit more light. It also improves because rhodopsin is gradually re-formed in the darkness and becomes available for use in dim light. This period of improving vision in dim light is called *dark adaptation*. The bleaching of rhodopsin and the narrowing of the pupil on re-emergence into full light is *light adaptation*.

Retinene, under ideal circumstances, is not used up in the breakdown and re-formation of rhodopsin; but the circumstances, unfortunately, are not quite ideal. Retinene is an unstable compound and, when separated from the rhodopsin molecule, has a tendency to undergo chemical change and lose its identity. Vitamin A, which is more stable, is, however, easily converted into retinene, so that the vitamin A stores of the body can be called upon to replace the constant dribbling loss of this visual pigment. The body cannot make its own vitamin A, alas, but must find it in the diet. If the diet is deficient in vitamin A, the body's stores eventually give out and retinene is not replaced as it is lost. Rhodopsin cannot then be formed, and rod vision fails. The result is that although a person may see perfectly normally in daylight, he is virtually without vision in dim light. This is *night blindness*, or *nyctalopia* (nik'tuh-loh'pee-uh; "night-blind-eye" G). Carrots are a good source of vitamin A and can help relieve this condition if added to the diet, and it is in this sense that the popular tradition that "carrots are good for the eyes" is correct.

COLOR VISION

The wavelength of light is usually measured in *Angstrom units*, named for a 19th-century Swedish astronomer, Anders J. Ångstrom. An Angstrom unit (abbreviated A) is a very small unit of length, equal to 1/100,000,000 of a centimeter, or 1/250,000,000 of an inch. The human eye can detect light with wavelengths as short as 3800 A and as long as 7600 A. Since the wavelength just doubles at this interval, we can say that the eye can detect light over a range of one octave.

Just as there are sound waves beyond the limits of human detection, so there are light waves beyond the limits of detection, too. At wavelengths shorter than 3800 A there are, progressing down the scale, ultraviolet rays, X-rays, and gamma rays. At wavelengths above 7600 A there are, progressing up the scale, infrared rays, microwaves, and radio waves. All told, at least 60 octaves can be detected in one way or another, and of these, as aforesaid, only one octave can be detected by the eye.

We are not as deprived as this makes us seem. The type of radiation emitted by any hot body depends on its temperature, and at the temperature of the sun's surface, the major portion of the radiation is put out in the octave to which we are sensitive. In other words, throughout the eons, our eyes and the eyes of other living things have been adapted to the type of light waves actually present, in predominant measure, in our environment.

The entire range of wavelengths is commonly referred to as *electromagnetic radiation* because they originate in accelerating electric charges with which both electric and magnetic fields are associated.* The word "light" is usually applied to the one octave of electromagnetic radiation we can sense optically. If there is a chance of confusion, the phrase *visible light* can be used.

Even the one octave of visible light is not featureless, at least not to normal individuals and not in photopic vision. Just as the

* In the case of light, the accelerating electric charge is associated with the electron within the atom.

brain interprets different wavelengths of sound as possessing different pitch, so it interprets different wavelengths of light as possessing different color. Ordinary sunlight is a mixture of all the wavelengths of visible light; this mixture appears to us as white and its total absence appears to us as black. If such white light is passed through a triangular block of glass (a "prism"), refraction is not uniform. The different wavelengths are refracted by characteristic amounts, the shortest wavelengths exhibiting the highest refraction, and longer and longer wavelengths refracting progressively less and less. For this reason, the band of wavelengths are spread out in a *spectrum* which seems to us to be made up of the full range of colors we can see. (The spectrum reminds us irresistibly of a rainbow, because the rainbow is a natural spectrum occurring when sunlight passes through tiny water droplets left in the air after a rain has just concluded.)

The number of shades of color we see as we look along the spectrum is very large, but it is traditional to group them into six distinct colors. At 4000 A we see violet; at 4800 A, blue; at 5200 A, green; at 5700 A, yellow; at 6100 A, orange; and at 7000 A, red. At wavelengths in between, the colors exhibit various grades of intermediateness.*

If the different wavelengths of light thus spread out into a spectrum are recombined by a second prism (placed in a position reversed with respect to the first), white light is formed again. But it is not necessary to combine all the wavelengths to do that. The 19th-century scientists Thomas Young and Hermann von Helmholtz showed that green light, blue light, and red light if combined would produce white light. Indeed, any color of the spectrum could be produced if green, blue, and red were combined in the proper proportions.

* Comparatively few animals possess a capacity for color vision, and those that do are not, apparently, quite as good at it as are the primates, including man, of course. There are interesting cases, though, where other animals may outdo us in some detail. Bees, for instance, do not respond to wavelengths in the uppermost section of the human range. They do, however, respond to wavelengths shorter than those of violet light, wavelengths to which our eyes are insensitive. In other words, bees do not see red but do see ultraviolet.

(Nowadays, color photography and color television make use of this. Three films, each sensitive to one of these three colors, will combine to give a photograph — or a motion picture — with a full color range; and three kinds of receiving spots on the TV screen, each sensitive to one of these three colors, will give a TV picture with a full color range.)

It seems reasonable to suppose that this is a reflection of the manner in which the human retina works. It, like the color film or the color TV screen, must have three types of photoreceptors, one sensitive to light in the red wavelengths, one to light in the blue wavelengths, and one to light in the green wavelengths. If all three are equally stimulated, the sensation is interpreted as "white" by the brain. The myriads of tints and shades the eye can differentiate are each an interpretation of the stimulation of the three photoreceptors in some particular proportion.*

Color vision is, to repeat, confined to the cones, which are not present in the far peripheral areas of the retina. They are present in increasing concentration as one approaches the macula lutea, where only cones are present. The cones themselves evidently are not identical; that is, they do not each possess all three pigments in equal proportion. Instead, there seem to be three different types of cones, each with a preponderance of its own characteristic pigment. The three types are distributed unequally over the retina. Thus, blue can be detected farther out into the retinal periphery than red can; and red, in turn, can be detected farther out than green can. At the macula lutea and in the immediately surrounding region all three are present, of course.

It sometimes happens that a person is deficient in one or more of the photoreceptors. He then suffers from *color-blindness*, a disorder of which there are a number of varieties and a number of gradations of each variety. One out of twelve American males shows some sort of color-vision deficiency, but very few women

---

* This theory does not explain all the facts in color vision, and there are several competing theories, some involving as many as six or seven different photoreceptors. However, the three-photoreceptor theory seems to retain most popularity among physiologists.

are affected.* The lack, most commonly, is in the red-receptor or in the green-receptor. In either case, the person suffering the lack has difficulty in distinguishing between colors ranging from green to red. Very occasionally a person lacks all color-receptors and is completely color-blind, a condition called *achromatism* (ay-kroh′muh-tiz-um; "no color" G). To such a person, the world is visible only in black, white, and shades of gray.

* Color-blindness is a "sex-linked characteristic." The gene controlling it is located on the X-chromosome, of which women have two and men only one. Women have a spare, so that if one gene fails the other takes over. Men do not.

13

OUR REFLEXES

RESPONSE

Any organism must be able to combine sensation with appropriate action. Some factor in the environment is sensed and some action follows. It is assumed through general experience that the action is brought about by the sensation and would not take place in its absence. If we observe someone make as though to strike us, we duck; we would not have ducked had we not experienced the sensation.

The sensation is a *stimulus* ("goad" L, since it goads us into the action). The action itself, which is an answer to the stimulus, is a *response*. This action of stimulus-and-response is characteristic of life. If we were to come across an object that did not respond to any stimulus we could think of, we would come to the conclusion that it was inanimate; or, if once alive, was now dead. On the other hand, if there was a response, we would tend to conclude instantly that the object was alive. And yet it is not a response alone that is required. If we strike a wooden plank a blow with an ax, it will respond to the stimulus of the blow by splitting; if we set a match to a mixture of hydrogen and oxygen, that will respond to the stimulus of heat by exploding. Yet this does not fool any of us into suspecting the wood or the gas mixture to be alive.

What is required of living objects is a response that maintains the integrity of the object; one that avoids damage or increases well-being. This is an *adaptive response.*

We are best acquainted with our own responses, of course. In ours there exists something we call "purpose"; we know in advance the end we are aiming at. If we are in a fight, we intend to avoid blows because we know, before the blow is received, that we shall suffer pain if we don't. What is more, we intend to strike a blow because we know in advance of the blow being struck that it will help end the fight and enforce our own desires.

Because this alliance of purpose and response is so well known to us, we tend to read purpose into the action of other creatures; even into the actions of creatures that cannot possibly have modes of thought akin to ours. For example, in observing that a green plant will turn toward the light, and knowing that light is essential to the plant's metabolism (so that receiving light contributes to its "well-being"), we are tempted to conclude that the plant turns to the light because it wants to, or because it likes the sensation, or because it is "hungry." Actually this is not at all so. The plant (as nearly as we can tell) has no awareness of its action in any sense that can be considered even remotely human. Its action is developed through the same blind and slow evolutionary forces that molded its structure.

Since light is essential to the plant's metabolism, individual seedlings (all things else being equal) which happen to possess the ability to get more than their share of sunlight will best survive. The ability may rest in a superior rate of growth enabling them to rise above the shade of neighboring plants; or, conversely, in the possession of broad leaves that grow quickly and shade the struggling neighbors, absorbing the light that would otherwise be theirs. It may be a chemical mechanism that more efficiently uses the light received, or one that enables the leaves to turn toward the light so that a "broadside blow" rather than a glancing one may be received.

Whatever the mechanism for snatching at light, the successful snatchers among plants flourish and leave more numerous descendants than their less aggressive competitors. With each generation, those responses that develop, through sheer chance, and happen to be adaptive, increasingly prevail and in the end are all but universal. If, in the course of this slow development, plant individuals arise which, through chance, tend to turn away from the light or manipulate light with lesser efficiency, such strains as they manage to establish will be quickly beaten and will drop out of the game. The same evolutionary development through chance mutation and natural selection holds for all forms of behavior, the complex varieties exhibited by man as well as the simple varieties exhibited by plants.

A nervous system is not necessary for the development of a meaningful stimulus-and-response. As I have just explained, plants, without a nervous system, will nevertheless turn portions of themselves toward the light. Such a turning in response to a stimulus is called a *tropism* (troh'pizm; "turning" G). Where the specific stimulus is light, the phenomenon is *phototropism* ("light-turning" G). The mechanism where this is accomplished is differential growth, which is in turn (see p. 426) sparked by the greater activity of auxin on the shaded side of the growing tip of the stem. When the stem receives equal stimulation from both sides, turning action ceases. (This is analogous to the manner in which we turn toward the origin of the sound, turning in the direction of that ear which gets the greater stimulus and ceasing to turn when both ears receive equal stimuli. The mechanism in ourselves is, of course, completely different from that of plants.)

Once plant life invaded the land it was subject to the action of gravity, and *geotropism* ("earth-turning" G), involving an automatic and adaptive response to gravity, was developed. To take an illustration: if a seed falls into the ground "upside-down," the stem may begin its growth downward, but in the grip of *negative geotropism* bends about and eventually begins to grow upward, in the direction opposite the pull of gravity and, which is ultimately important, toward the light. The root, contrariwise, beginning its growth upward, curves about to head downward in the direction of gravity (*positive geotropism*). Geotropism seems also to be mediated by auxins, but how the distribution of auxins can be affected by gravity is not yet understood. To be sure, a root will veer from its downward path if a rich source of water lies to one side. This is in response to positive *hydrotropism* ("water-turning" G).

Tropisms all involve slow turning through differential growth, but not all plant responses are tropisms. Some are quick responses that are almost animal-like in their resemblance to muscle action (and yet not involving muscles but, rather, such mechanisms as controlled turgor by alteration of the quantity of water present at key spots). And so there are plant species whose leaves fold by night and open by day; there are species with leaves that close at a touch; insect-digesting species with traps that close when certain sensitive trigger-projections are touched, and the like.

There are animal responses that resemble tropisms. An amoeba will move away from the light but a moth will fly toward it.* Nevertheless, the responses of even very simple animals are generally more complicated than those of plants, and to call those responses tropisms would be wrong. For one thing, a tropism involves the movement of only a portion of an organism — such as the root or the stem — whereas an animal is likely to move as a whole. Such movement of a whole organism in response to a stimulus is a *taxis* ("arrangement" G, since the position of an organism is rearranged, so to speak, in response to the stimulus). Thus, the amoeba displays a *negative phototaxis* and a moth possesses a *positive phototaxis*.

Micro-organisms, generally, display a *negative chemotaxis*, which enables them to respond to a deleterious alteration in the

* We think with sardonic amusement of the moth who seems so stupidly to fly into a flame that kills it, but movement toward the light is generally adaptive behavior. The hundreds of millions of years that developed this response did so under conditions in which man-made lights did not exist and therefore posed no danger. Unfortunately for the moth, it cannot modify its response to suit the modified situation.

chemical nature of their surroundings by swimming away, and a *positive chemotaxis,* which is an adaptive response to the type of chemical change brought about by the presence of something edible. There is also *thigmotaxis,* a response to touch, *rheotaxis,* a response to water currents, and a number of others.

The nature of the response may not be a simple movement toward or away. A paramecium, on encountering an obstacle, will back off a certain distance, turn through an angle of 30 degrees, and then move forward again. If it encounters the obstacle (or another obstacle) again, it repeats the process. In twelve attempts it will have made a complete turn and, by then, unless completely ringed by obstacles, it will have found its way past. But there is no true "purpose" to this, either, and however clever the little creature may seem to be in the light of our own anthropomorphic judgment, this "avoidance behavior" is a purely blind course of action developed by the forces of natural selection.

THE REFLEX ARC

The tropisms of plants and the taxis of simple animals are generalized responses of an entire organism or of a major portion of one to a very generalized stimulus. Such a generalized response to a generalized stimulus can be mediated through a nervous system, as in the case of the phototaxis of the moth, but with the development of a specialized nervous system both stimulus and response can be refined.

Special nerve-receptors can be stimulated by feebler changes in the environment than ordinary cells can be. In addition, the presence of a forest of nerve endings can make it possible to distinguish between a touch on one part of the body and a touch on another, and the two might elicit different responses. Where a nervous system is involved, in fact, a stimulus need not elicit a generalized response at all. A definite motor neuron might carry the signal required to bring about the response of a restricted portion of the body, of one set of glands, or of one set of muscles.

Where a particular stimulus quickly and automatically produces a particular response through the action of the nervous system, we speak of a *reflex* ("bending back" L). The name is a good one, because the nerve impulse travels from a sense organ along a sensory nerve to the central nervous system (usually to the spinal cord but sometimes to the brain stem), and there the nerve impulse "bends back" and travels away from the central nervous system again, along a motor nerve, to bring about a response. The nerve cell connections along which the nerve impulse travels from initial sensation to final response is the *reflex arc*.

The simplest possible reflex arc is one consisting of two neurons, the sensory and the motor. The dendrites of the sensory nerve (see illustrations, pp. 462 and 640) combine into a fiber that leads toward the cell body located just outside the posterior horn of the spinal cord. The axon of this nerve cell is connected by way of a synapse to the dendrites of a cell body in the anterior horn of the spinal cord. The axon of this second cell leads outward by way of an appropriate peripheral nerve to the muscle, gland, or other organ that is to give the response. Since the first neuron receives the sensation it is the *receptor neuron,* and since the latter effects the response it is the *effector neuron.* The region within the central nervous system where the two make the connection is the *reflex center.*

This two-neuron reflex arc is rare, but examples of it exist even in so complicated a creature as man. More common is the three-neuron reflex arc, in which the receptor neuron is connected to an effector neuron by means of an intermediate neuron called the *connector neuron.* The connector neuron lies wholly within the central nervous system. Even the three-neuron reflex arc is simple as far as such arcs go in highly organized creatures. In mammals the typical reflex arc is likely to have a number of connector neurons, a whole chain of them, that may lead up and down the nerve cord from one segment to others.

A complex reflex arc with numerous neurons taking part allows ample opportunity for branching. A specific receptor neuron may

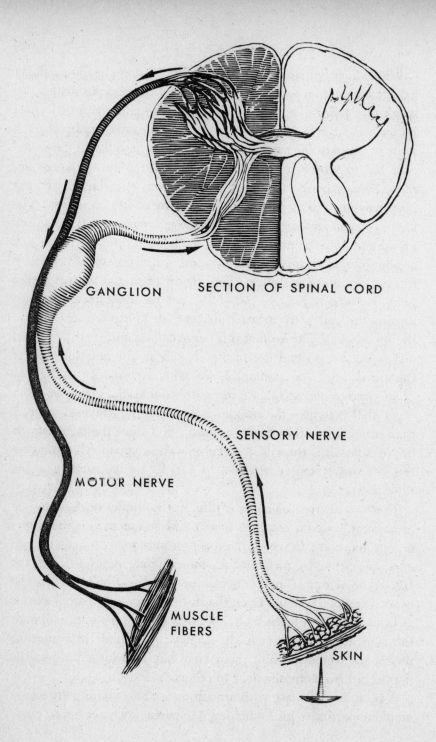

GANGLION

SECTION OF SPINAL CORD

SENSORY NERVE

MOTOR NERVE

MUSCLE
FIBERS

SKIN

end by transmitting its nerve impulse via the various connector neurons to a number of different effectors. For instance, a painful stimulus on the hand may evoke a quick removal of the hand through the contraction of certain muscles. But for this to happen (a *flexion reflex*) there are opposing muscles that must simultaneously be made to relax so as not to hamper the withdrawing motion. In addition, there may be a sudden turning of the head in the direction of the painful stimulus, a sharp uncontrolled outcry, and a contortion of facial muscles. The whole variety of responses may be produced by a simple pinprick that in itself stimulates a very small number of effectors.

At the same time that a flexion reflex takes place in one limb, a *crossed extensor reflex*, sparked by the same stimulus, will take place in the other, stiffening and extending it. So, if we lift a leg in sudden reflex action because we have stepped on a sharp pebble on the beach, we do not usually fall over, as we might expect to since our weight is suddenly unbalanced. Instead, in equally quick reflex, the remaining leg stiffens and our weight shifts.

Another important muscular reflex is the *stretch reflex*. When a muscle is stretched, the proprioceptive nerve endings within it are the receptors of a reflex arc of which the effectors act to bring about a contraction that tends to counteract whatever force is bringing about the stretching. This helps keep us in balanced posture, for one thing. The balance depends upon the equal pulls of opposing muscles. If for any reason a muscle overcontracts, its opposing muscle is stretched, and that opposing muscle promptly contracts in response to the stretch, restoring the balance. If it overreacts, the first muscle is stretched and contracts in its turn.

We are not usually aware of either stimulus or response in this connection. To our conscious selves we seem only to be standing or sitting, and are completely unconcerned with the complex system of reflex arcs that must all cooperate delicately to keep us doing (in appearance) nothing. However, if we suddenly lose our balance seriously, we "catch ourselves" quite without a voluntary decision, and may indulge in violent involuntary contortions in an effort to regain our balance. If the stretch reflex is set off during sleep, the contracting response may again be quite sudden and violent, arousing us and giving us the impression that we "dreamed of falling."

A familiar example of the stretch reflex is the *patellar reflex*, or, as it is commonly called, the "knee jerk." A person being tested for the knee jerk is usually asked to cross his leg and let the crossed leg hang limply. The muscle along the top surface of the thigh has its tendon attached to the bone of the lower leg. If the area just below the kneecap ("patella") is tapped lightly, that tendon is struck and the thigh muscle is momentarily stretched. This initiates a stretch reflex (this one by way of one of the rare two-neuron reflex arcs) and the muscle contracts sharply, bringing the lower leg up in a kicking motion. Because it is only a two-neuron reflex arc, it is a rapid reaction indeed.

The patellar reflex is not important in itself, but its nonappearance can mean some serious disorder involving the portion of the nervous system in which that reflex arc is to be found. It is so simple a reflex and so easily tested that it is a routine portion of many medical checks. Sometimes damage to a portion of the central nervous system results in the appearance of an abnormal reflex. If the sole of the foot is scratched, the normal response is a flexion reflex in which the toes are drawn together and bent downward; but if there is damage to the pyramidal tract the big toe bends upward in response to this stimulus and the little toes spread apart as they bend down. This is the *Babinski reflex*, named for a French neurologist, Joseph F. F. Babinski, who described it in 1896.

Just as a single receptor may in the end elicit the action of a large number of effectors, it is also possible that a particular effector or group of effectors may be brought into play by a large variety of receptors. Small individual painful stimuli over a large area of one side of the body may all cause a reflex motion of the head toward that side, and sudden pain anywhere in the body may elicit an involuntary outcry.

The reflex arc does not involve the cerebrum, so the element of will does not ordinarily enter. The reflex is automatic and involuntary. However, in many cases, the sensation that brings about the response is also shunted into an ascending tract and brought to the cerebrum, where it is then experienced as an ordinary sensation, usually after the reflex response is complete. If, for instance, we inadvertently touch a hot object with our hand, the hand is instantly withdrawn; withdrawn before we are consciously aware of the fact that the object was hot. The awareness follows soon enough, nevertheless, and with physical damage averted (or at least minimized) by automatic reflex action, we can then take the reasoned long-range response of moving the hot object to a safe place, or covering it, or putting a warning sign on it, or cooling it, or doing whatever seems the logical thing to do.

In many cases we are completely unaware of the response we may make to a stimulus. Strong light causes the iris to expand and reduce the size of the pupil. The taste of food will cause the salivary glands to secrete fluid into the mouth, and the cells of the stomach lining to secrete fluid into the stomach. Temperature changes will bring about alterations in the diameter of certain capillaries. We are more a mass of reflexes than we ordinarily realize.

INSTINCTS AND IMPRINTING

The various reflexes I have been talking about are, like the tropisms of plants and the taxis of simple animals, examples of *innate behavior* — behavior that is inborn and does not have to be learned. You do not have to learn to withdraw your hand from a hot object, or to sneeze if your nasal passages are irritated, or to blink if a sudden gesture is made in the direction of your eyes. An infant can do all these things, and more besides.

Such innate behavior can be quite elaborate. One can visualize chains of reflexes in which the response to one stimulus will itself serve as the stimulus for a second response, which will then in turn serve as the stimulus for a third response, and the like. Examples of this are the elaborate courtship procedures among the sexes of some animal species: nest-building, web-building, hive-building, and the intricate patterns of care for the young.

Regrettably, the slow development of such complicated behavior patterns through evolutionary processes is lost to us. Could we trace it, we might easily see how each further link in the chain of reflexes was developed, and how each served to improve the survival chances of the next generation. Behavior patterns do not leave fossil remains, so we can only accept what we find. The necessity of accepting the end-product complications lead the overly romantic to read into the behavior of relatively simple animals the complex motivations of man. The bird in building her nest and the spider in spinning her web completely lack the forethought of the human architect and are not really suitable as subjects for little moral homilies.

Such chains of reflexes give rise to *instinctive behavior* (a term that is falling out of fashion). Instincts are complicated patterns of responses that share the properties of the reflexes out of which they are built. Instinct is usually viewed as a behavior pattern that is fixed from birth, that cannot be modified, that is present in all members of a designated species in an unvarying manner, and so on. Thus, a species of spider builds a certain type of elaborate web without being taught to do so, and may do so, in full elaboration, even if kept in isolation so that it never has an opportunity to see any other example of such a web. Young birds may migrate at the proper time, going to a far-distant place they have never seen and without the guidance of older members of the species.

Nevertheless, this is not absolutely characteristic of all behavior patterns usually termed as instinctive. Some birds may sing characteristic songs without ever having had the opportunity to hear other members of the species do so; but other species of birds may not. In recent years it has come to be realized that there are some patterns of behavior seemingly innate but actually fixed at some time after birth in response to some specific stimulus.

After all, what we call birth is not actually the beginning of life. Preceding it is a period of development within an egg or womb, during which a nervous system develops to what at the time of birth is already a high pitch of complexity. Different reflexes originate at different periods in the course of this development as reflex arc after reflex arc is laid down. In the chick embryo, for example (which is easy to study), the head-bending reflex can be detected 70 hours after fertilization but the head-turning reflex only at 90 hours. Beak-movement reflexes are detectable only after 5 days, and the swallowing reflex does not make itself shown until 8 days after fertilization.

In the human embryo (less easy to study by far) there is also a progressive development. A reflex movement of the head and neck away from a touch around the mouth and nose can be detected in an 8-week human embryo, but such important reflexes as grasping and sucking do not appear until the embryo is at least double that age. To be sure, birth is an important turning point in the developmental process, and by the time it occurs enough reflexes must be developed to make independent life possible, or else the infant will not survive. That is self-evident. Yet there is room for more beyond bare survival.

Such continuity is taken for granted in structural development, where processes sweep past the moment of birth without a pause. The ossification of the skeleton begins before birth and continues after birth for years. The myelinization of nerve fibers begins before birth and continues afterward. Why should this not be true of behavioral development, too? The situation after birth does introduce one radical change. Before birth, the total universe is that of the egg or womb and it is therefore relatively fixed, with limited possibilities of variation. After birth, the environment expands and much more flexibility and variety in the way of stimuli are possible. The "instincts" developed after birth therefore may well depend upon such stimuli in a way that truly innate instincts do not. Chicks and ducklings fresh out of the shell do not follow their mothers out of some innate instinct that causes them to recognize the mothers. Rather, they follow something of a characteristic shape or color or faculty of movement. Whatever object provides this sensation at a certain period of early life is followed by the young creature and is thereafter treated as the mother. This may really be the mother; almost invariably is, in fact; but it need not be!

The establishment of a fixed pattern of behavior in response to a particular stimulus encountered at a particular time of life is called *imprinting*. The specific time at which imprinting takes place is a *critical period*. For chicks the critical period of "mother-imprinting" lies between 13 hours and 16 hours after hatching. For a puppy there is a critical period between three and seven weeks during which the stimulations it is usually likely to encounter imprint various aspects of what we consider normal (and instinctive) doggish behavior.

There is the example of a lamb raised in isolation for the first ten days of its life only. It was restored to the flock thereafter, but certain critical periods had passed and certain imprintings had not taken place. The opportunity was gone. It remained independent in its grazing pattern, and when it had a lamb of its own, it showed very little "instinctive" behavior of a pattern which we usually tab as "mother love." The loss of a chance at imprinting can have a variety of untoward effects. Animals with eyes deprived of a chance for normal stimulation by a variegated pattern of light at a particular time of early development may never develop normal sight, though the same deprivation before or after the critical period may do no harm.

It seems almost inevitable that such imprinting takes place in the human infant as well, but deliberate experimentation on such infants, designed to interfere with any imprinting procedures that may exist, is clearly out of the question. Knowledge concerning human imprinting can only be gained through incidental observations. Children who at the babbling stage are not exposed to the sounds of actual speech may not develop the ability to speak later, or do so to an abnormally limited extent. Children brought up in impersonal institutions where they are efficiently fed and their physical needs are amply taken care of but where they are not fondled, cuddled, and dandled become sad little specimens indeed. Their mental and physical development is greatly retarded and many die for no other reason, apparently, than lack of "mothering" — by which may be meant the lack of adequate stimuli to bring about the imprinting of necessary behavior patterns. Similarly, children who are unduly deprived of the stimuli involved in the company of other children during critical periods in childhood develop personalities that may be seriously distorted in one fashion or another.

But why imprinting? It is as though a nerve network designed to set up a behavior pattern were complete at birth except for one missing link. Given an almost certain stimulus, that final link snaps into place, quickly and irrevocably, with a result that, as far as we know, can neither be reversed nor modified thereafter. Why, then, not have the final link added before birth and avoid the risks of having imprinting fail?

A logical reason for imprinting is that it allows a certain desirable flexibility. Let's suppose that a chick is born with the prescribed behavior of following its true mother, a mother it can "instinctively" distinguish, perhaps through some highly specific odor it inherits and which mother and offspring therefore share. If the true mother is for any reason absent (killed, strayed, or stolen) at the moment of the chick's birth, it is helpless. If, on the contrary, the question of motherhood is left open for just a few hours, the chick may imprint itself to any hen in the vicinity and thus adopt a foster-mother. Clearly, this is an important and useful ability.

We are faced with two types of behavioral patterns, therefore, each with its own advantage. Innate behavior is certain in that it prescribes responses and avoids error, provided the environment is exactly that for which the innate behavior is suited. Noninnate behavior (or "learned behavior") is risky in the sense that if anything goes wrong with the learning process the proper pattern of response is not developed; but it offers the compensation of flexibility in adjusting the pattern to changes in the environment.

Imprinting is only the most primitive form of learned behavior. It is so automatic, takes place in so limited a time, under so general a set of conditions, that it is only a step removed from the innate. There are, notwithstanding, other forms of learning more clearly marked off from innate behavior and designed to adjust responses more delicately and with less drastic finality to smaller and less predictable variations in the environment.

CONDITIONING

A baby is equipped with functioning salivary glands and the taste of food will cause the secretion of saliva by those glands. This is an example of a reflex. It is developed before birth and is thereby innate. It is universal and unvarying in the sense that all babies respond to stimulation of the taste buds by salivating. And it is involuntary. Under ordinary circumstances a baby can't help salivating in response to the taste of food; and, for that matter, neither can you. This is, therefore, an *unconditioned reflex*. There are no conditions set for its occurrence. It will occur under all normal conditions.

The sight or smell of food will not in themselves bring about salivation at first. After an interval of experience in which a particular sight or smell always immediately precedes a certain salivation-inducing taste, that sight or smell comes to elicit salivation even in the absence of the taste. An infant has learned, one might say, that the smell of food or the sight of food means that the taste of food is about to come, and it salivates (involuntarily) in anticipation. Once this association of sight or smell with taste is set up, the response is automatic and resembles a reflex in all ways. However, it is a reflex that is dependent upon one condition; that of association. If feeding always took place in darkness, the sight of food alone would never elicit salivation, since its appearance would never have been associated with its taste. If a certain item of food were never included in the diet its odor would not induce salivation, even though it be a "natural" dietary item for that species. A puppy that has never been fed meat will not salivate in response to the odor of meat.

The reflex that develops in response to an association is therefore a *conditioned reflex*. It is as though the body is capable of hooking neural pathways together to achieve a shortcut. If faced with a situation of "particular smell means particular taste means salivation," a nerve pathway is eventually set up that will give results equivalent to "particular smell means salivation." (This somehow resembles the mathematical axiom that if $a = b$ and $b = c$, then $a = c$.)

This has clear value for survival, since a response that is useful for a specific stimulus is very likely to be useful for other stimuli invariably or almost invariably associated with it. An animal seeking food and guided only by its unconditioned reflex is reduced to sampling everything in its environment by mouthing it. The animal will starve or poison itself, in all likelihood. An animal that conditions itself into recognizing its food by sight and smell will get along far better.

A conditioned reflex can be established for any associated stimulus, even one that does not "make sense." Conditioning is not a logical process — it works only by association. The first to experiment with artificial associations that did not make sense was a Russian physiologist, Ivan Petrovich Pavlov. Pavlov began the important phase of his career by working out the nervous mechanism controlling the secretion of some of the digestive glands. In 1889, he carried on rather impressive experiments in which he severed a dog's gullet and led the upper end through an opening in the neck. The dog could then be fed, but the food would drop out through the open gullet and never reach the stomach. Nevertheless, the stimulation of the taste buds by the food caused the stomach's gastric juices to flow. Here was an unconditioned reflex. Pavlov went on to show that, with appropriate nerves cut, the reflex arc was broken. Though the dog ate as heartily as before, there was no flow of gastric juice thereafter. Pavlov obtained a Nobel Prize for this work in 1904.

By that time, however, something new had developed. In 1902 Bayliss and Starling (see p. 340) had shown that the nerve network was not the only means of eliciting a response by the juice-secreting digestive glands. As a matter of fact, they showed that the action of the pancreas was *not* interfered with by cutting the nerves leading to it, but that there was a chemical connection by way of the bloodstream. Pavlov thereupon struck out in a new direction, with even more fruitful results. Suppose a dog were offered food. It would salivate as a result of the taste through an unconditioned reflex; and would salivate in response to the sight and smell alone through early conditioning. But suppose, further, that each time it was offered the food a bell was rung. It would associate the sound of the bell with the sight of the food, and after this had been repeated from 20 to 40 times salivation would take place at the sound of the bell alone.

Pavlov spent the remaining thirty years of his life experimenting with the establishment of conditioned reflexes. Such conditioning can be established for almost any combination of stimuli and response, though flexibility is not infinite. Experimenters have discovered that certain experimental conditions are more efficient in producing conditioning than others. If the stimulus for which conditioning is desired is presented just before the normal stimulus — that is, if the bell is rung just before the food is presented — then conditioning proceeds most rapidly. If the bell is rung after the food is presented, or at too long an interval before food is presented, then conditioning is more difficult.

Some responses are more difficult to force into line with conditioning than others. Salivation is an easy response to adjust and an animal that salivates copiously can be made to salivate in response to almost anything associated with food. On the contrary, the response of the iris to intensity of light is extremely hard to condition to any stimulus but light. (This seems to make sense.

The response to food needs to be highly flexible, because food can appear in a variety of guises and under a variety of conditions; but light is light, and little flexibility in response to it is either needed or desired.)

Different species vary in the ease with which they can be conditioned. In the main, animals with a more highly developed nervous system are easier to condition. They make the association of bell and food more easily. Or, to put it another way, the fact that more neurons are available in the nervous system, and that these are more complexly interrelated, makes it easier to set up new pathways.

Conditioning is distinguished from imprinting by the fact that the former is more flexible. A conditioned reflex can be established at any time and for a wide variety of stimuli and responses, whereas imprinting happens only during a critical period and involves a specific stimulus and response. Conditioning is a much slower process in general than imprinting is, and, unlike imprinting, it can be reversed.

Suppose that a dog had been conditioned to salivate at the sound of a bell and then over a period of time the bell was repeatedly rung without food being presented. The salivary response would grow weaker, and eventually the dog would no longer salivate when the bell rang. The conditioning will have been extinguished.

As is not surprising, the longer and more intensively a particular piece of conditioning has been established, the longer the time required to extinguish it. As is also not surprising, a conditioning that has been established and then extinguished is easier to establish a second time than it was the first. The nervous system, one might say, has made the new connection once, and it remains there ready to hand.

The conditioned reflex has proved to be an invaluable tool in the study of animal behavior; it can be made to yield answers that would otherwise have required direct communication with a lower creature. In the previous chapter, I said that a bee could

not see red, but could see ultraviolet. How can this be established, since the bee cannot bear direct witness to the fact?
The answer lies in conditioning. A creature cannot be conditioned to respond to one stimulus and not to another unless it can
distinguish between the two stimuli. This would seem self-evident. Suppose, then, that bees are offered drops of sugar solution placed on cards. They will fly to those cards and feed.
Eventually, they will be conditioned to those cards, and will fly
to them at once when they are presented, even when food is
not present upon them. Suppose that two cards are used, alike
in shape, size, glossiness, and in every controllable characteristic,
except that one is blue and one is gray. Suppose further that the
sugar solution is placed always on the blue card and never on
the gray. Ultimately the bee will be conditioned to the blue card
only, and will fly to any blue card presented but not to any gray
card. From this it can be deduced that the bee can tell the
difference between a blue card and a gray card when the only
known difference is color. Hence, the bee can see the color blue.

Suppose the experiment is then changed and a red card and
a gray card are used, with the food always present on the red
card. Finally, when enough time has elapsed to make it reasonable to assume that conditioning has taken place (on the basis
of results in the blue-gray experiment), the bees are tested with
red and gray cards that do not carry food. Now it is found that
the bees fly to the red and gray cards indiscriminately. It would
follow that the bee cannot differentiate red and gray. In short,
it cannot see red.

On the other hand, the bee will differentiate between two
cards that to ourselves seem to be identical in color but differ
in that one reflects more ultraviolet than the other. If food is
placed only on one of these cards and never on the other, this
leads to successful conditioning of the bee. It will distinguish
between the two cards even in the absence of food, though we
with our own unaided eye cannot. In short, it can see ultraviolet.

In the same way, we can test the delicacy with which a dog

can distinguish the pitch of a sound or the shape of some object, by conditioning it to that pitch or shape and then noting to what other pitches or shapes it remains indifferent. A dog will distinguish between a circle and an ellipse, for instance. Also, it will distinguish between a circle in which two perpendicular diameters are each ten units in length and an ellipse in which two perpendicular diameters are nine units and ten units in length, respectively. It will further distinguish between sounds varying in frequency by as little as three vibrations per second. Yet it can also be shown that the dog is completely color-blind, because it cannot be conditioned to any differences in color.

14

OUR MIND

LEARNING

Men have in the past sometimes tended to set up a firm and impassable wall separating the behavior of man from that of all creatures other than man and to label the wall "reason." Creatures other than man we might suppose to be governed by instincts or by an inborn nature that dictates their actions at every step; actions which it is beyond their power to modify. In a sense, from such a viewpoint animals are looked upon as machines; very complicated machines, to be sure, but machines nevertheless.

Man, on the other hand, according to this view, has certain attributes that no animal has. He has the capacity to remember the past in great detail, to foresee possible futures in almost equal detail, to imagine alternatives, to weigh and judge in the light of past experience, to deduce consequences from premises — and to base his behavior upon all of this by an act of "free will." In short, he has the power of reason; he has a "rational mind," something, it is often felt, not possessed by any other creature.

That man also has instincts, blind drives, and, at least in part, an "animal nature" is not to be denied; but the rational mind is supposed to be capable of rising above this. It can even rise superior to the reflex. If prepared, and if there is a purpose to be served, a man can grasp a hot object and maintain the grasp although his skin is destroyed. He can steel himself not to blink if a blow is aimed at his eyes. He can even defy the "first law of nature," that of self-preservation, and by a rational act of free will give his life for a friend, for a loved one, or even for an abstract principle.

Yet this division between "rational man" and "irrational brute" cannot really be maintained. It is true that as one progresses along the scale of living species in the direction of simpler and less intricately organized nervous systems innate behavior plays a more and more important role, and the ability to modify behavior in the light of experience (to "learn," that is) becomes less important. The difference in this respect between man and other animals is not that between "yes" and "no" but, rather, that between "more" and "less."

Even some of the more complicated protozoa — one-celled animals — do not invariably make the same response to the same stimulus as would be expected of them if they were literally machines. If presented with an irritant in the water, such a creature might respond in a succession of different ways, 1, 2, 3, 4, each representing a more strenuous counter. If the irritant is repeated at short intervals, the creature may eventually counter with response 3 at once, without bothering to try 1 or 2. It is as though it has given up on halfway measures and, in a sense, has learned something.

And, of course, more complex animals are easily conditioned in such a fashion as to modify their behavior, sometimes in quite complex manner. Nor must we think of conditioning only as something imposed by a human experimenter; natural circumstances will do as well or better. The common rat was alive and flourishing long before man was civilized. It lived then without reference to man and his habitations. It has learned, however, to live in man's cities and is now as much a city creature as we are; better in some ways. It has changed its "nature" and learned as we have; and not with our help, either, but in the face of our most determined opposition.

To be sure, a lion cannot be conditioned, either by man or by circumstance, to eat grass, since it lacks the teeth required to chew grass properly or the digestive system to handle it even if it could be chewed and swallowed. It is, one could say, the lion's inborn nature to eat zebras and not grass, and this cannot be changed. This sort of physical limitation enslaves man too. A man cannot "by taking thought" add one cubit unto his stature, as is stated in the Sermon on the Mount. Nor can he by mere thought decide to become transparent or to flap his arms and fly. For all his rational mind, man is as much bound by his physical limitations as the amoeba is.

If we confine ourselves to behavior within physical limitations, does the fact that behavior can be modified even in simple animals wipe out the distinction between man and other creatures? Of course it doesn't. That the gap (only man can compose a symphony or deduce a mathematical theorem) exists is obvious and incontrovertible. The only question is whether the gap exists by virtue of man's exclusive possession of reason. What, after all, is reason?

In the case of simple organisms, it seems quite clear that learning, in the sense of the development of behavior not innate, takes place through conditioning, and we are not trapped into believing that anything resembling human reason is involved. A bee has no innate tendency to go to blue paper rather than gray paper, but it can be "taught" to do so by conditioning it to associate blue paper, but not gray paper, with food. The new behavior is as mechanical as the old. The machine is modified by a machinelike method and remains a machine.

In mammals, with more complicated nervous systems than are possessed by any creatures outside the class and with, therefore, the possibility of more complex behavior patterns, matters are less clear-cut. We begin to recognize in mammalian behavior a similarity to our own and consequently may begin to be tempted to explain their activity by using the word "reason." A cat trapped in an enclosure from which an exit is possible if a lever is pushed or a latch is pulled will behave in a manner so like our own under similar circumstances as to convince us that it is disturbed at being enclosed and anxious to be free. And when it finds the exit we may say to ourselves, "Ah, she's figured it out."

But has she? Or is this an overestimate of the cat's mental powers? Apparently the latter. A trapped cat makes random moves, pushing, jumping, squeezing, climbing, pacing restlessly. Eventually, it will make some move that will by accident offer a way out. The next time it is enclosed, it will go through the same random movements until it once again pushes the lever or raises the latch; the second time, after a shorter interval of trial and error, the cat will do the same. After enough trials, it will push the lever and escape at once. The simplest explanation is that it has conditioned itself to push the lever by associating this, finally, with escape. However, there would seem to be also a matter of memory involved; a dim process that makes the cat discover the exit more quickly (usually) the second time than the first.

Animal memory has been tested by experiment. Suppose a raccoon is conditioned to enter a lighted door as opposed to an unlighted one. (It will get food in the first and an electric shock in the second.) Suppose it is barred from entering either door while the light is on and is allowed to make its choice only after the light has gone out. It will nevertheless go to the door which *had been* lit, clearly remembering. If the interval between the light's going out and the liberation of the raccoon is too great, the raccoon sometimes does not go to the correct door. It has forgotten. A raccoon can be relied on to remember for up to half a minute; this interval increases as animals with a more complex nervous system are chosen. A monkey may sometimes remember for a full day.

The English biologist Lloyd Morgan took the attitude that in interpreting animal behavior as little "humanity" as possible should be read into the observations. In the case of the cat in the enclosure, it is possible to avoid humanity just about altogether. A combination of trial-and-error with dim memory and conditioning is quite sufficient to explain the cat's behavior. The question is: How far up the scale of developing nervous system can we safely exclude humanity altogether? Memory improves steadily and surely that has an effect. We might conclude that it does not have too great an effect, since even in man, who certainly has the best memory in the realm of life, trial-and-error behavior is common. The average man, having dropped a dime in the bedroom, is very likely to look for it randomly, now here now there. If he then finds it, that is no tribute to his reasoning powers. Nevertheless, let us not downgrade memory. After all, a man does not have to indulge in trial-and-error only, even in searching for a dropped dime. He may look only in the direction in which he heard the dime strike. He may look in his trousers-cuff because he knows that in many cases a falling dime may end up there and defy all attempts to locate it on the floor. Similarly, if he were in a closed place, he might try to escape by beating and kicking on the walls randomly; but he would also know what a door would look like and would concentrate his efforts on that.

A man can, in short, simplify the problem somewhat by a process of reasoning based on memory. In doing so, however (to jump back to the other side of the fence again), it is possible that the trial-and-error method does not truly disappear but is etherealized — is transferred from action to thought. A man doesn't actually look everywhere for a lost dime. He visualizes the position and looks everywhere mentally, eliminating what his experience tells him are unlikely places (the ceiling, a distant room) and shortening the actual search by that much.

In moving up the scale of animal behavior we find that modification of behavior goes through the stages of (1) conditioning by circumstance, (2) conditioning after trial-and-error, and (3) conditioning after an etherealized trial-and-error. If it seems fair to call this third and most elaborate form of modification "reason" it next remains to decide whether only human beings make use of it.

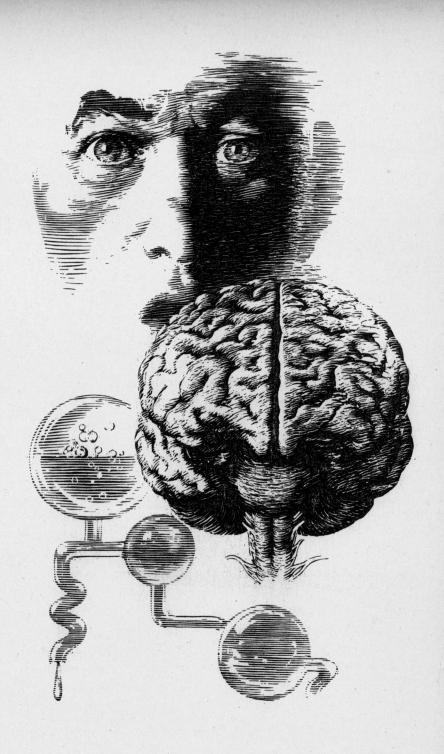

Monkeys and apes remember accurately enough and long enough to make it seem unlikely that they can be thoroughly bereft of such etherealization, and indeed they are not. A German psychologist, Wolfgang Köhler, trapped in German southwestern Africa during World War I, spent his time working with chimpanzees and showed that they could solve problems by flashes of intuition, so to speak. Faced with a banana suspended in air and two sticks, each of which was too short to reach the banana and knock it down, a chimpanzee, after a period of trial-and-error that established the shortness of the sticks, would do nothing for a while, then would hook the sticks together to form a combined tool that would reach the banana. Chimpanzees will pile boxes or use a short stick to get a large stick, and do so in such a fashion as to make it impossible to deny that reason is at work.

At what point in the animal kingdom, trial-and-error is etherealized to a sufficient degree to warrant the accolade of "reason" is uncertain. Not enough animals have been tested thoroughly. If the chimpanzee can reason, what about the other apes? What about the elephant or the dolphin?

One thing is sure. Reason alone does not explain the gulf that lies between man and other animals.

REASON AND BEYOND

But is it fair to compare man and animals on the basis of so relatively simple an act as finding an escape route or a lost object? Can we generalize from finding a dime to reading a book? (The latter no animal other than man can do.) Some psychologists have rather believed that one could. The behaviorists, of whom the American psychologist John Broadus Watson was most prominent, tended to view all learning in the light of conditioned reflexes.

The conditioned reflex differs from the ordinary reflex in that the cerebrum is involved. The cerebrum is not completely essential, to be sure, for a decerebrate animal can still be conditioned. Nevertheless, a decerebrate animal cannot be conditioned as specifically as can one with its cerebrum intact. If an animal is given a mild electric shock on one leg while a bell is sounded, the intact animal will eventually be conditioned to raising its leg when the bell is sounded, even without an electric shock; the decerebrate animal will respond by generalized escape attempts.

If the cerebrum is involved, then it is reasonable to suppose that as the mass and complexity of the cerebrum increases, so will the complexity and intricacy of the conditioned reflexes increase.* More and more neurons can be devoted to "hooking up into circuits" that represent combinations of conditioning. More and more storage units for memory can be set aside, so that trial-and-error can take place among the storage units rather than within the physical world itself.

Given enough storage units for memory and enough room for conditioning, one need look nowhere else to explain human behavior. A child looks at the letter *b* and begins to associate it with a certain sound. He looks at the letter-combination "bed" and begins to associate it with a given word which a few years earlier he had already succeeded in associating with a given object. Speaking and reading become complex conditioned responses, as does typing or whittling or any of a myriad other mechanical skills; and man is capable of all this not because he has something lower animals do not have, but because he has what they all have — only far more of it.

One might insist that the highest attributes of the human mind — logical deduction and even scientific or artistic creativity — can be brought down to hit-and-miss and conditioning. The poem *Kubla Khan,* written by Samuel Taylor Coleridge, was carefully analyzed in a book by John Livingston Lowes called *The Road to Xanadu.* Lowes was able to show that virtually

* In fact, in mammals, the conditioned reflex can easily become too complex to be considered a reflex, and many psychologists prefer to refer to the phenomenon as a *conditioned response.* A collection of conditioned responses will form a *habit.*

every word and phrase in the poem stemmed from some item in Coleridge's past reading or experience. We can visualize Coleridge putting together all the word fragments and idea fragments in his mind (quite automatically and unconsciously) after the fashion of a gigantic mental kaleidoscope, picking out the combinations he liked best and constructing the poem out of them. Trial-and-error, still. As a matter of fact, by Coleridge's own testimony, the poem came to him, line after line, in a dream. Presumably, during the period of sleep his mind, unhampered by waking sensations and thought, played the more freely at this game of hit-and-miss.

If we imagine this sort of thing going on in the human brain, we must also expect that there would exist in the human brain large areas that do not directly receive sensation or govern response, but are devoted to associations, associations, and more associations. This is exactly so.*

Thus, the region about the auditory area in the temporal lobe is the *auditory association area*. There particular sounds are associated with physical phenomena in the light of past experience. The sound of a rumble may bring quite clearly to mind a heavy truck, distant thunder, or — if no associations exist — nothing at all. (It is usually the nothing-at-all association that is most frightening.) There is also a *visual association area* in the occipital lobe surrounding the actual visual area, and a *somesthetic association area* behind the somesthetic area.

The different sensory association areas coordinate their functioning in a portion of the brain in the neighborhood of the beginning of the lateral sulcus in the left cerebral hemisphere. In this

---

* It is the existence of such association areas, without obvious immediate function that gives rise to the statement, often met with, that the human being uses only one fifth of his brain. That is not so. We might as well suppose that a construction firm engaged in building a skyscraper is using only one fifth of its employees because only that one fifth was actually engaged in raising steel beams, laying down electric cables, transporting equipment, and such. This would ignore the executives, secretaries, filing clerks, supervisors, and others. Analogously, the major portion of the brain is engaged in what we might call white-collar work, and if this is considered as representing brain use, as it certainly should be, then the human being uses all his brain.

area, the auditory, visual, and somesthetic association areas all come together. This overall association area is sometimes called the *gnostic area* (nos'tik; "knowledge" G). The overall associations are fed into the area lying immediately in front, the *ideomotor area*,* which translates them into an appropriate response. This information is shunted into the *premotor area* (lying just before the motor area in the frontal lobe), which co-ordinates the muscular activity necessary to produce the desired response, this activity being finally brought about by the motor area.

When all the association areas, the sensory areas, and the motor areas are taken into account, there still remains one area of the cerebrum that has no specific and easily definable or measurable function. This is the area of the frontal lobe that lies before the motor and premotor areas and is therefore called the *prefrontal lobe* (see illustration, p. 508). Its lack of obvious function is such that it is sometimes called the "silent area." Tumors have made it necessary to remove large areas of the prefrontal lobe without particularly significant effect on the individual, and yet surely it is not a useless mass of nerve tissue.

There might be a tendency, rather, to consider it, of all sections of the brain, the most significant. In general, the evolutionary trend in the development of the human nervous system has been the piling of complication upon complication at the forward end of the nerve cord. In passing from the primitive chordates, such as amphioxus, into the vertebrate subphylum, one passes from an unspecialized nerve cord to one in which the anterior end has developed into the brain. Also, in passing up the classes of vertebrates from fish to mammals, it is the forebrain section of the brain that undergoes major development, and the cerebrum becomes dominant. In going from insectivores to primates and, within the primate Order, from monkey to man, there has been

* Both the gnostic area and the ideomotor area are functional only in one cerebral hemisphere (usually the left, but in about 10 per cent of the cases the right). As I said earlier in the book, this existence of a dominant hemisphere is to prevent two separate sets of association-interpretations from arising, as conceivably might happen if each hemisphere were provided with its own "executive."

a successive development of the foremost section of the cerebrum, the frontal lobe.

In the early hominids, even after the brain had achieved full human size, the frontal lobes continued development. Neanderthal man had a brain as large as our own, but the frontal lobe of the brain of true man gained at the expense of the occipital lobe, so if the total weight is the same, the distribution of weight is not. It is easy to assume then that the prefrontal lobes, far from being unused, are a kind of extra storage volume for associations, and the very epitome of the brain.

Back in the 1930's, it seemed to a Portuguese surgeon, António Egas Moniz, that where a mental patient was at the end of his rope, and where ordinary psychiatry and ordinary physical therapy did not help, it might be possible to take the drastic step of severing the prefrontal lobes from the rest of the brain. It seemed to him that in this fashion the patient would be cut off from some of the associations he had built up. In view of the patient's mental illness, these associations would more likely be undesirable than desirable and their loss might be to the good. This operation, *prefrontal lobotomy,* was first carried through in 1935, and in a number of cases did indeed seem to help. Moniz received the Nobel Prize in 1949 for this feat. However, the operation has never been a popular one and is not likely ever to become one. It induces personality changes that are often almost as undesirable as the illness it is intended to cure.

Even granted that the behaviorist stand is correct in principle and that all human behavior, however complex, can be brought down to a mechanical pattern of nerve cells (and hormones)* the further question arises as to whether it is useful to allow matters to rest there.

---

* Actually, it is difficult to deny this since nerves and hormones are the only physical-chemical mediators for behavior that we know of. Unless we postulate the existence of something beyond the physical-chemical (something like abstract "mind" or "soul") we are reduced to finding the answer to even the highest human abilities somewhere among the cells of the nervous system or among the chemicals in the blood — exactly where we find the lowest.

Suppose we are satisfied that Coleridge constructed the poem *Kubla Khan* by trial-and-error. Does that help us much? If it were merely that, why can't the rest of us write the equivalent of *Kubla Khan?* How could Coleridge choose just that pattern out of the virtually infinite numbers offered by his mental kaleidoscope which was to form a surpassingly beautiful poem, and do so in such a short time?

Clearly we have much farther to go than the distance the pat phrase "trial-and-error" can carry us. Briefly, as a change progresses there can come a point (sometimes quite a sharp one) where the outlook must change, where a difference in degree suddenly becomes the equivalent of a difference in kind. To take an analogy in the world of the physical sciences, let us consider ice. Its structure is pretty well understood on the molecular level. If ice is heated, the molecules vibrate more and more until at a certain temperature, the vibrations are energetic enough to overcome the intermolecular attractions. The molecules then lose their order and become randomly distributed; in a fashion, moreover, that changes randomly with time. There has been a "phase change"; the ice has melted and become water. The molecules in liquid water are like the molecules in ice and it is possible to work out a set of rules that will hold for the behavior of those molecules in both ice and water. The phase change is so sharp, however, as to make it more useful to describe ice and water in different terms, to think of water in connection with other liquids and ice in connection with other solids.

Similarly, when the process of etherealized trial-and-error becomes as complicated as it is in the human mind, it may well be no longer useful to attempt to interpret mental activity in behaviorist terms. As to what form of interpretation *is* most useful, ah, that is not yet settled.

The concept of the phase change can also be used to answer the question of what fixes the gulf between man and all other creatures. Since it is not reason alone, it must be something more. A phase change must take place not at the moment when reason is introduced but at some time when reason passes a certain point of intensity. The point is, one might reasonably suppose, that at which reason becomes complex enough to allow abstraction; when it allows the establishment of symbols to stand for concepts, which in turn stand for collections of things or actions or qualities. The sound "table" represents not merely this table and that table, but a concept of "all table-like objects," a concept that does not exist physically. The sound "table" is thus an abstraction of an abstraction.

Once it is possible to conceive an abstraction and represent it by a sound, communication becomes possible at a level of complexity and meaningfulness far beyond that possible otherwise. As the motor areas of the brain develop to the point where a speech center exists, enough different sounds can be made, easily and surely, to supply each of a vast number of concepts with individual sounds. And there is enough room for memory units in a brain of such complexity to keep all the necessary associations of sound and concept firmly in mind.

It is speech, then, rather than reason alone that is the phase change, and that fixes the gulf between man and nonman. As I pointed out on page 582, the existence of speech means that the gathering of experience and the drawing of conclusions is no longer a function of the individual alone. Experience is shared and the tribe becomes wiser and more knowledgeable than any individual in it. Moreover, experience unites the tribe throughout time as well as throughout space. Each generation need no longer start from scratch, as must all other creatures. Human parents can pass on their experience and wisdom to their children, not only by demonstration but by verbalized, conceptual explanation. Not only facts and techniques, but also thought and deductions can be passed on.

Perhaps the gulf between ourselves and the rest of living species might not seem so broad if we knew more about the various prehuman hominids, who might represent stages within that gap. Unfortunately we don't. We do not actually know at what stage of development, or in what species of hominid, the phase change took place.*

PSYCHOBIOCHEMISTRY

The study of the human mind is carried on chiefly by psychologists and in its medical aspects by psychiatrists. Their methods and results are mentioned but fleetingly at best in this book, not because they are unimportant, but because they are too important. They deserve a book to themselves. In this book I am concentrating, as best I can, on anatomy and physiology, plus a bit of biochemistry.

The study of the mind by every means is of increasing importance in modern civilization. There are diseases of the mind as well as of other portions of the body — mental disease, in which the connection between the body and the outside environment is distorted. The message of the senses may be perceived in such a fashion as not to correspond with what the majority are willing to accept as objective reality. Under these conditions a person is said to be subject to hallucinations ("to wander in mind" L). Even where sensory messages are correctly perceived, the interpretation of and responses to those messages may be abnormal in intensity or in kind. Mental disease may be serious enough to destroy the ability of an individual to serve as a functioning member of society; and even if mild enough not to do so may nevertheless put him under an unnecessary burden of emotional gear-grinding.

As scientific advance succeeds in checking the ravages of many physical diseases, the mental diseases become more noticeable

* If it is true that dolphins have a faculty of speech as complex as that of man, then we are not necessarily the only species to have passed the phase change. The environment of the ocean is so different from that of land, however, that the consequences of the phase change would be vastly different. A dolphin might have a man-level mind, but in the viscous and light-absorbing medium of sea water a dolphin is condemned to the flipper and to a dependence on sound rather than vision. Man is not man by mind alone, but by mind plus eye plus hand, and if all three are taken into consideration we remain the only species this side of the phase change.

and prominent among the medical problems that remain. It has been estimated that as many as 17 million Americans, nearly 1 in 10, suffer from some form of mental illness. (In most cases, of course, the illness is not severe enough to warrant hospitalization.) Of those mental illnesses serious enough to require hospitalization, the most common is *schizophrenia* (skiz′oh-free′nee-uh; "split mind" G). This name was coined in 1911 by a Swiss psychiatrist, Paul Eugen Bleuler. He used the name because it was frequently noted that persons suffering from this disease seemed to be dominated by one set of ideas (or "complex") to the exclusion of others, as though the mind's harmonious working had been disrupted and one portion had seized control of the rest.

Schizophrenia may exist in several varieties, depending on which complex predominates. It may be *hebephrenic* (hee′bee-free′nik; "childish mind" G), where one prominent symptom is childish or silly behavior. It may be *catatonic* ("toning down" G), in which behavior is indeed toned down and the patient seems to withdraw from participation in the objective world, becoming mute and rigid. It may also be *paranoid* ("madness" G), and characterized by extreme hostility and suspicion, with feelings of persecution. At least half of all patients in mental hospitals are schizophrenics of these or other types. An older name for the disease was *dementia praecox* (dee-men′shee-uh pree′koks; "early-ripening madness" L). This name was intended to differentiate it from mental illness affecting the old through the deterioration of the brain with age ("senile dementia"), since schizophrenia usually makes itself manifest at a comparatively early age, generally between the years 18 and 28.

One common view of mental diseases is the "environmental theory," which looks upon them as unintelligible if considered in terms of the individual alone. The disorders are considered, instead, to involve the ability of the individual to relate to other individuals and the environment, and the effect of interpersonal stresses on this ability. The disease is hence a function of the individual plus society. In favor of this view is the fact that there is no known physical difference between the brain of a mental patient and that of a normal individual. Favoring it in a more subtle fashion is the ancient view of the fundamental distinction between mind and body — the feeling that the mind is separate and apart from the body, not governed by the same laws and not amenable to the same type of investigation. The physical and chemical laws that have proved so useful in dealing with the rest of the body may be inadequate for the mind, which then requires a more subtle form of analysis.

Opposed to this is the "organic theory," which supports the biochemical causation of mental disease. This holds that what we call the mind is the interplay of the nerve cells of the body, and the mind is therefore, at the very least, indirectly subject to the ordinary physical and chemical laws that govern those cells. Even if a mental disorder arises from an outside stress it is the neurons that respond to the stress either well or poorly, and the varying ability to respond to the stress healthfully must have its basis in a biochemical difference. Favoring the organic theory is the fact that some forms of mental disease have indeed been found to have a biochemical basis. *Pellagra*, a disease once endemic in Mediterranean lands and in our own South, was characterized by dementia as one of the symptoms. It was found to be a dietary-deficiency disease, caused by the lack of nicotinic acid in the diet. As simple a procedure as the addition of milk to the diet prevented pellagra and its attendant dementia, or ameliorated it if already established.

The disease *phenylpyruvic oligophrenia* (ol'ih-goh-free'nee-uh; "deficient mind" G) is characterized by serious mental deficiency. Evidently it is the result of an inborn error in metabolism. In the normal individual, the amino acid phenylalanine, an essential constituent of proteins, is routinely converted in part to the related amino acid tyrosine, also an essential constituent of proteins. This reaction is governed by a particular enzyme, phenylalaninase. In the case of those unfortunates born without the ability to form this enzyme, phenylalanine cannot undergo the proper conversion. It accumulates and is finally converted into substances other than tyrosine, substances not normally present in the body. One of these is phenylpyruvic acid, whence the first half of the name of the disease. The presence of excess phenylalanine, and of its abnormal "metabolites," adversely affects brain function (exactly how is not yet known) and produces the mental deficiency. Here, unfortunately, the situation cannot be corrected as simply as in the case of pellagra. Although it is easy to supply a missing vitamin, it is as yet impossible to supply a missing enzyme. However, some improvement in mental condition has been reported among patients with the disease who have been kept on a diet low in phenylalanine.

This offers a pattern for the possible understanding of the cause of other mental disorders, especially that of schizophrenia. There is always the possibility of an accumulation (or deficiency, perhaps) of some normal constituent of the body, particularly one that manifestly affects brain function and is therefore likely to be found in the brain. In addition there is the possibility of the existence of abnormal metabolites of such substances, metabolites that would themselves interfere with brain function.

The hope that some such solution may exist for schizophrenia is bolstered by genetic data. In the general population the chance of a particular individual developing schizophrenia is about 1 in 100. If, however, a certain person is schizophrenic, the chances that a brother or sister of his will also fall prey to the disease is about 1 in 7. If one of a pair of identical twins is schizophrenic, the chances that the other will become schizophrenic as well is very high, 3 out of 4, or even better. Even allowing for the greater similarities of environment in the case of brothers or sisters than in the case of unrelated persons, there would seem to be a hereditary factor involved. This would mean, according to our present understanding of heredity, an inherited abnormality in one or more enzyme systems and a metabolism that is therefore disordered in some specific manner.

The middle 1950's saw the beginning of a concerted effort to locate a biochemical cause of schizophrenia. For instance, nerve endings of the sympathetic system secrete norepinephrine (noradrenalin), as I pointed out on page 554, and this is very similar to epinephrine (adrenalin), which I discussed on pages 376–379. Adrenalin is an attractive target for suspicion because its function is to rouse the body to react more efficiently to conditions of stress. If mental disease is considered to result, in part at least, from the failure of the body to respond properly to conditions of psychological stress, might it be that the fault lies somewhere in the body's handling of adrenalin?

In the test tube, it is easy to change adrenalin to a compound called "adrenochrome." This is an abnormal metabolite, since it does not seem that adrenalin in the body normally passes through the adrenochrome stage. Interestingly enough, when adrenochrome is injected into normal human subjects, temporary psychotic states resembling those of mental illness are produced.

This is true of other adrenalin-like substances as well. For example, a compound called mescaline, much like adrenalin in molecular structure, is found in a cactus native to the American southwest. The mescaline-containing portions of the cactus are chewed by Indians during their religious rites in a deliberate attempt to achieve hallucinatory episodes. To the Indians, innocent of modern psychiatry, such hallucinations seem to be a window into the supernatural.

Here, then, we have a situation that could be directly analogous to the connection between phenylalanine and phenylpyruvic oligophrenia. Could it be that abnormal metabolites of adrenalin produced by people who happen to be born with a deficient supply of some enzyme or other eventually produce schizophrenia? However, since 1954, when this suggestion was first made, all attempts to locate adrenochrome or other abnormal metabolites of adrenalin in mental patients have failed.

Interest was also aroused in a chemical called *serotonin*. This is closely related to the amino acid tryptophan, which is an essential component of proteins (see p. 346). This relationship is clear in the formulas given here, even for those not familiar with chemical formulas.

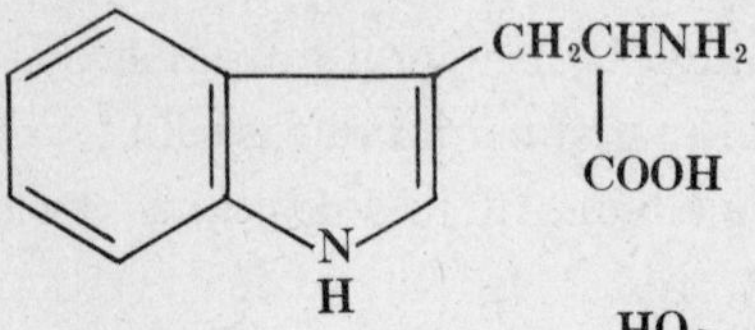

CH_2CHNH_2

$COOH$

SEROTONIN

N
H

TRYPTOPHAN

HO — $CH_2CH_2NH_2$

N
H

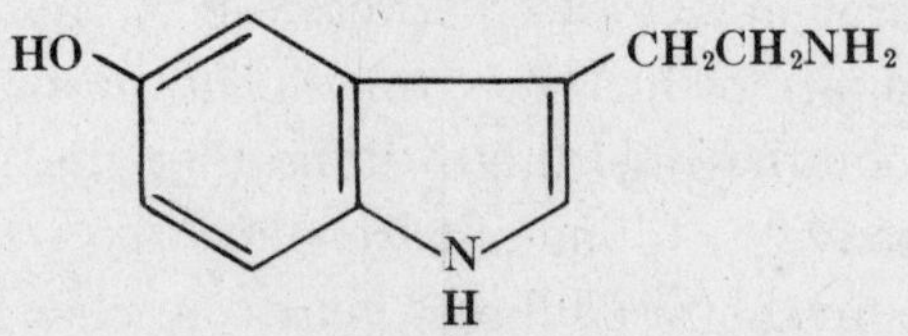

Serotonin is found in numerous organs of the body, including the brain (only about 1 per cent of the body's supply is found in the brain), and it has a number of functions. Some of these, such as its ability to bring about the constriction of small blood vessels and the raising of blood pressure, have no direct connection with brain function, but it seems likely to have some connection with it in other respects.

This was brought home sharply in 1954 when it was discovered (accidentally) that a drug called *lysergic acid diethylamide* could be used to produce hallucinations and other psychotic symptoms. Lysergic acid diethylamide has the same two-ring system that serotonin has (but with a considerably more complicated molecule otherwise) and appears to compete with serotonin for the enzyme *monoamine oxidase*. Ordinarily, monoamine oxidase brings about the oxidation of serotonin into a normal metabolite, one in which the nitrogen atoms have been removed. In the presence of lysergic acid diethylamide, the monoamine oxidase molecules are taken up by the intruder and are unavailable for the oxidation of serotonin. Serotonin accumulates and may finally produce abnormal metabolites. One abnormal metabolite looming as a possibility is bufotenin, a "toad poison" — that is, one of a group of toxic substances found in the parotid glands of toads. This is similar to serotonin in molecular structure and is known to induce psychotic states.

The possibility that serotonin in excess produces schizophrenia is greatly weakened, nevertheless, by the fact that a compound very closely related to lysergic acid diethylamide interferes with serotonin oxidation even more and yet produces no hallucinations. Furthermore, no abnormal metabolites of serotonin have been detected in schizophrenics.

So far, then, the various leads that have arisen in the search for a biochemical basis for schizophrenia (including some I have not mentioned) have led to a series of dead-ends. The search continues, however, and some important byproducts have resulted. There is, for instance, the development of *tranquillizers*. These are drugs that exert a calming effect upon an individual, relieving anxiety and inducing relaxation. They differ from older drugs used for the purpose in that they do not diminish alertness or induce drowsiness. The first tranquillizer to be introduced to the medical world (in 1954) was *reserpine,* a natural alkaloid found in the dried roots of a shrub from India. It seemed significant that part of the complex molecular structure of reserpine consisted of the two-ring combination present in serotonin. This significance was weakened by the introduction that same year of another and even more effective tranquillizer, *chlorpromazine,* which does not possess this particular two-ring combination. The tranquillizers are not cures for any mental illness, but they suppress certain symptoms that stand in the way of adequate treatment. By reducing the hostilities and rages of patients, and by quieting their fears and anxieties, they reduce the necessity for drastic physical restraints, make it easier for psychiatrists to establish contacts with patients, and increase the chances of release from the hospital.

The 1950's also saw the development of *antidepressants,* drugs which, as the name implies, relieve the severe depression that characterizes some mental patients; depression which in extreme cases leads to suicide. It may be that such depression is caused by, or at least is accompanied by, a too-low level of serotonin in the brain. At least the antidepressants all seem to be capable of inhibiting the action of the enzyme monoamine oxidase. With the enzyme less capable of bringing about the oxidation of serotonin, the level of that substance would necessarily rise.

A FINAL WORD

More and more it is becoming fashionable to look upon the brain as though it were, in some ways, an immensely complicated computer made up of extremely small switches, the neurons. And in one respect at least, that involving the question of memory, biochemists are coming to look to structures finer than the neuron, and to penetrate to the molecular level.

Memory is the key that makes possible the phase change I spoke of earlier in the chapter. It is only because human beings (even those not especially gifted) can remember so much and so well that it has been possible to develop the intricate code of symbols we call speech. The memory capacity of even an ordinary human mind is fabulous. We may not consider ourselves particularly adept at remembering technical data, let us say, but consider how many faces we can recognize, how many names call up some past incident, how many words we can spell and define, and how much minutiae we know we have met with before. It is estimated that in a lifetime, a brain can store 1,000,000,000,000,000 (a million billion) "bits" of information.*

In computers, a "memory" can be set up by making suitable changes in the magnetic properties of a tape, changes that are retained until called into use. Is there an analogous situation in

---

* A "bit" is short for "binary digit" and is either 1 or 0 in computer lingo. It represents the minimum unit of information, the amount gained when a question is answered simply "yes" or "no." All more complicated kinds of information can in theory be compounded of a finite number of bits. A face, for instance, or any other object can be built up of patterns of black and white dots, as in a newspaper photograph, each dot being a "bit," either "yes" for a white dot, or "no" for a black one. Our vision consists of such bits, each cell of the retina, responding "yes" for light and "no" for darkness, representing a bit. Our other senses can be analyzed similarly.

the brain? Suspicion is currently falling upon *ribonucleic acid* (usually abbreviated *RNA*) in which the nerve cell, surprisingly enough, is richer than almost any other type of cell in the body. I say surprisingly because RNA is involved in the synthesis of protein and is therefore usually found in those tissues producing large quantities of protein either because they are actively growing or because they are producing copious quantities of protein-rich secretions. The nerve cell falls into neither classification, so the abundance of RNA within it serves as legitimate ground for speculation.

The RNA molecule is an extremely large one, consisting of a string of hundreds or even thousands of subunits of four different kinds. The possible number of different arrangements of these subunits within an RNA molecule is astronomically immense — much, much larger than the mere "million billion" I mentioned above. Each different arrangement produces a distinct RNA molecule, one capable of bringing about the synthesis of a distinct protein molecule.*

It has been suggested that every "bit" of information entering the nervous system for the first time introduces a change in an RNA molecule contained in certain neurons reserved for the purpose. The changed RNA molecule produces a type of protein not produced hitherto. When further "bits" of information enter the nervous system, they can presumably be matched to the RNA/protein combinations already present. If the match succeeds, we "remember."

This is, as yet, only the most primitive beginning of an attempt to analyze the highest functions of the human mind at the molecular level, and to carry it further represents the greatest possible challenge to the mind.

It seems logical, somehow, to suppose that an entity that un-

* The detailed structure of nucleic acids and proteins that makes such immense variability possible, and the manner in which a given nucleic acid can dictate the formation of a particular protein, is a subject of prime importance to biochemists today. There is no room here for even the beginnings of a discussion of these matters, but you can find the details in my book *The Genetic Code* (1963).

derstands must be more complex than the object being understood. One can therefore argue that all the abstruse facets of
modern mathematics and physical science are but reflections of
those facets of the physical universe which are simpler in structure
than the human mind. Where the limit of understanding will be,
or whether it exists at all, we cannot well predict, for we cannot
measure as yet the complexity of either the mind or the universe
outside the mind.

However, even without making measurements, we can say
as an axiom that a thing is equal to itself, and that therefore the
human mind, in attempting to understand the workings of the
human mind, faces us with a situation in which the entity that
must understand and the object to be understood are of equal
complexity.

Does this mean we can never truly grasp the working of the
human mind? I cannot tell. But even if we cannot, it may still
be possible to grasp just enough of its workings to be able to construct computers that approach the human mind in complexity
and subtlety, even though we fall short of full understanding.
(After all, mankind was able in the 19th century to construct rather
complex electrical equipment despite the fact that the nature of
the electrical current was not understood, and earlier still, working steam engines were devised well before the laws governing
their workings were understood.)

If we could do even so much we might learn enough to prevent
those disorders of the mind, those irrationalities and passions, that
have hitherto perpetually frustrated the best and noblest efforts
of mankind. If we could but reduce the phenomena of imagina-
tion, intuition, and creativity to analysis by physical and chemical
laws, we might be able to arrange to have the effects of genius
on steady tap, so to speak, rather than be forced to wait for nig-
gardly chance to supply the human race with geniuses at long
intervals only.

Man would then, by his own exertions, become more than man,
and what might not be accomplished thereafter? It is quite cer-

tain, I am sure, that none of us will live to see the far-distant time when this might come to pass. And yet, the mere thought that such a day might some day come, even though it will not dawn on my own vision, is a profoundly satisfying one.

INDEX

INDEX

A bands, 93
Abdomen, 116, 118
Abdominal wall, 116
Abducens nerve, 543
Absorption, 235, 237
Accessory nerve, 544
Acetabulum, 67
Acetylcholine, 468
  autonomic nervous system and,
    554
Achilles tendon, 108
Achlorhydria, 227
Achromatism, 633
Acne, 289
Acoustic area, 513
Acoustic nerve, 543, 599
Acromegaly, 80, 431
ACTH, 418
  autonomic nervous system and,
    555
Adam's apple, 138
Addison, Thomas, 412
Addison's disease, 412
Adenoids, 209
Adipose tissues, 239
Adrenal glands, 376
Adrenalin, 377
  schizophrenia and, 671
Adrenergic nerves, 554
Adrenochrome, 671
Adrenocorticotrophic hormone, 418
Afferent arteriole, 254
Afterbirth, 305
Agnatha, 19, 43
Air, alveolar, 146, 147
Air bladder, 125
Alanine, 346

Albinos, 274
  eyes of, 612, 613
Alcohol, 234
Aldosterone, 416
Alimentary canal, 213
Allergies, histamine and, 379-380
All-or-none law, 473
Alopecia, 285
Alpha waves, 514
Alveolar air, 146, 147
Alveolus, 144
Amine group, 345
Amino acids, 74, 186, 344
  abbreviations of, 347, 348
  arrangements of, 350, 351, 372
  corticotropin and, 419
  glucagon and, 376
  insulin and, 373, 374
  MSH and, 420
  oxytocin and, 400
  secretin and, 350
  structure of, 345
  vasopressin and, 400, 401
Ammonia, excretin of, 250
Amoeba, 91
  feeding of, 211
Amoeboid movement, 91
Amphibia, 24, 125
  heart of, 155
  lungs of, 143
Amphioxus, 16, 43
  heart of, 154
  nervous system of, 480
Amygdaloid nucleus, 520
Amylase, salivary, 218
  pancreatic, 229
Amylopsin, 229

Analgesic, 564
Anal sphincter, 244
Androgens, 436
Androsterone, 437
Anemia, 191
    iron-deficiency, 196
    pernicious, 198, 227
    post-hemorrhagic, 192
    sickle-cell, 197
Anesthesia, 565
Aneurysm, 181
Angina pectoris, 180
Angstrom, Anders J., 630
Angstrom units, 630
Animal Kingdom, 2
Anisotropic bands, 93
Ankle, 67
Annelid superphylum, 12
Annelida, 7
Annularis, 63
Anteaters, 52, 217
Antelope, legs of, 109
Anthropoid apes, 490
Anthropoidea, 488
Antibodies, 100, 202
    thymus and, 433, 434
Antidepressants, 673
Antidiuretic hormone, 499
Anus, 244, 284, 311
Aorta, 162, 163, 181
    blood flow in, 174
Apes, 70, 71, 100
Aphasia, 509
Aponeurosis, 108
Apoplexy, 179
Appendectomy, 243
Appendicitis, 243
Appendix, vermiform, 243
Appestat, 528
Appetite, 528
Aqueous humor, 619
Arachnoid membrane, 498
Arachnoid villi, 502
Arch of the aorta, 163
Areola, 280
Arginine, 347
Arginine phosphate, 10
Aristotle, 3, 339
Armadillos, armor of, 267
Armpits, 284
Arms, 58
    movement of, 86, 110, 115, 116

Arrectores pilorum, 283
Arterial blood, 191
Arterioles, 160
Arteriosclerosis, 176
Artery(ies), 159
    rupture of, 178
Arthritis, 88
    cortisone and, 416, 417
Arthropoda, 7
Articulation, 84
Artificial respiration, 150
Arytenoid cartilages, 136
Ascending colon, 242
Asexual reproduction, 294
Asparagine, 347
Aspartic acid, 347
Aspirin, 564
Assimilation, 236
Asthma, 142
Astigmatism, 623
Astragalus, 69
Ataxia, 538
Atherosclerosis, 179, 405
Athlete's foot, 289
Atlas, 34
Atmosphere, 120
Atomic weight, 388
Atrioventricular valves, 162
Atrium, 154
Atrophy of muscles, 105
Auditory area, 513
Auditory association area, 662
Auditory canal, 587
Auditory meatus, 587
Auditory nerve, 544
Auricle, 154, 585
Auricular fibrillation, 171
Auriculoventricular node, 170
Auto-allergic disease, 467
Autonomic nervous system, 550-55
Auxins, 426
A-V node, 170
A-V valves, 162
Aves, 24
Axial skeleton, 56
Axillary hair, 284
Axis, 34
Axolotls, thyroid hormone and, 391
Axon, 463
    giant, 465

Babinski, Joseph F.F., 642

Babinski reflex, 642
Baboons, 489
Baby, blood pressure of, 176
    first breath of, 149
    hemoglobin in, 305
    iron supply of, 197
    skeleton of, 39
    skull of, 46
    stomach capacity of, 222
Baby teeth, 53
Backbone, 28
Bacteria, intestinal, 223
    leukocytes and, 202
    lymph nodes and, 208
Balanoglossus, 14
Baldness, 285
Ball-and-socket joint, 86
Banting, Frederick G., 364
Barnum, Phineas T., 430
Basal ganglia,, 520
Basal metabolic rate, 386
Basilar membrane, 593
Basophils, 200
Bats, forelimbs of, 57
    echolocation and, 599, 600
Baumann, E., 383
Bayliss, William M., 340
Beard, 284
Bears, 31, 71
Bees, color vision of, 631n, 651, 652
    communication of, 139
Behavior, innate, 643
    instinctive, 644
    trial-and-error, 656-58
Bekesy, Georg von, 595
Berger, Hans, 514
Best, Charles H., 364
Beta waves, 515
Betz, Vladimir, 509
Betz cells, 509
Biceps brachii, 106
Bicuspids, 51
Big toe, 69
Bilateral symmetry, 6, 36, 42, 477
Bile, 231
    cholesterol in, 405
    duct, common, 232
    gallstones and, 402
    hormones and, 355
    pigment, 233
    salt, 233, 407
Bile acids, 406
Binary fission, 292

Bipedal maladjustment, 40, 66, 68, 69
    103, 116, 129
Birds, 24, 31
    bones of, 78
    cervical vertebrae of, 33
    clavicle of, 59
    feathers of, 268
    heart of, 155
    limbs of, 57
    musculature of, 115
    nitrogen excretion of, 251
    reproduction of, 300
    respiration of, 147
    scales of, 267
    sound production by, 139
    teeth of, 52
Birth, 46
Birthmark, 290
Blackhead, 288
Blacktongue, 218
Bladder, air, 125
    gall, 232
    urinary, 259
Bladder stone, 264
Bleeding, 161
Bleuler, Paul E., 368
Blind spot, 626
Blindness, 161
Blood, 153
    agglutination of, 193
    cholesterol in, 405
    circulation of, 158 ff.
    clotting of, 204
    distribution of, 177
    formed elements in, 184
    glucose in, 356
    life and, 337, 338
    oxygen absorption by, 155
    oxygen transport and, 184 ff.
    plasma of, 184
    pressure of, 175, 178, 255
    quantity of, 182
    transfusion of, 193
    types of, 193 ff.
    velocity of flow of, 174
Blood-brain barrier, 503
Blood dust, 189
    serum, 204
    vessels, 154
Blowholes, 127
Blubber, 240
"Blue blood," 270
Blushing, 177

BMR, 376
Body odor, 278, 279
  segmentation, 36
  temperature, 278
Boil, 203
Bolus, 219
Bone(s), 20, 21, 61
  cartilage in, 79
  cartilage replacement, 44
  growth of, 79
  hollow, 78
  joints of, 84
  number of, 28, 37, 38
  sound-conduction and, 590
  structure of, 76
  water content of, 183
Bowels, 227
Bowman, Sir William, 255
Bowman's capsule, 255
Brachial plexus, 448
Brachiocephalic artery, 164
Brachiopoda, 5
Bradykinin, 358
Braid, James, 567
Brain, 21, 324, 579
  association areas in, 661, 662
  biochemistry of, 667-75
  cerebral lobes of, 507
  chemical barriers in, 503
  cholesterol in, 405
  convolutions of, 485, 506
  damage to, 499
  early conceptions of, 338, 339
  electric potentials and, 513-19
  emotions and, 523, 524
  glucose and, 504
  hormone control by, 525
  hormones and, 554, 555
  low temperature and, 527
  oxygen and, 504
  size of, 492, 494
  sleep and, 529
  spinal, 484
  ventricles of, 499, 500
  visceral, 524
  white matter of, 506, 519
Brain/body ration, 494, 495
Brain stem, 533
Brain tumors, 504
  EEG and, 517
Brand, Erwin, 347
Breastbone, 34
Breasts, 280
Breath, life and, 337

Breathing, 146
Bright, Richard, 255
Bright's disease, 255
Bristle, 282
Broca, Pierre P., 508, 524
Broca's convolution, 509
Bronchial arteries, 164
Bronchial tree, 141
Bronchioles, 142
Bronchitis, 141
Bronchus, 141
Buccinator, 217
Budding, 293
Bufotenin, 372
Bursitis, 88
Butenandt, Adolf, 436, 437
Buttocks, 117
  fat store in, 240

Caecum, 243
Caesar, Julius, 518
Calcaneus, 68
Calciferol, 80
Calcitonin, 397
Calcium carbonate, 5
  ions, 99, 205, 395
  phosphate, 20
Calf muscle, 108
Callus, 270
Canary, respiration of, 146
Cancellous bone, 77
Cancer, 425
  blood, 203
  lung, 145
  skin, 273
Canines, 51
Canthus, inner, 614
Capillaries, 160
  blood flow in, 174
  fluid leakage from, 205
  lymph, 206
Capitate bone, 62
Capsule, synovial, 85
Carbohydrates, 211
  oxidation of, 246
Carbon atom, bonds of, 403, 407
Carbon dioxide, 246, 247
  in lungs, 146
  solubility of, 247
Carbon monoxide, 198
  tetrachloride, 234
Carboxylic acid group, 345
Cardiac glycosides, 409
Cardiac muscle, 156

Caries, 83
Carotene, 274
Carotid arteries, 164
Carpal bones, 62
Cartilage(s), 18, 21, 39, 43, 75, 79
 joints and, 85
Casein, iodine and, 387
Castor oil, 245
Castration, 313, 435
Cat(s), hair of, 282
 limbs of, 70
 toes of, 61
 tongue of, 217
Cataract, 624
Catarrhina, 488
Caterpillar, 298
Cattle, small intestine of, 228
 stomachs of, 222
 teeth of, 52
 toes of, 61
 udder of, 280
Cauda equina, 547
Caudal anesthesia, 547
Caudal vertebrae, 38
Celiac arteries, 164
Celiac plexus, 452
Cell membrane, 72, 122
Cell(s), 5, 71
 contraction of, 92
 glucose and, 366
 motion in, 90
 number of, 73, 322
 specialization of, 333, 334
Cell body, 463
Cellulose, 223
Cementum, 83
Central nervous system, 476
 weight of, 506
Central sulcus, 507
Cephalization, 43, 478
Cephalochordata, 17
Cercopithecidae, 489
Cerebellar hemispheres, 533
Cerebellum, 481, 533
 feedback and, 537, 538
Cerebral hemispheres, 516
 dominance in, 519, 520
Cerebral hemorrhage, 179
Cerebral palsy, 538
Cerebrospinal fluid, 498
 circulation of, 500, 501
Cerebrum, 481
 motor area of, 509

weight of, 506
Cerumen, 588
Cervical nerves, 546
Cervical plexus, 548
Cervical vertebrae, 33
Cervix, 311
Chalones, 356
Chameleons, tongue of, 217
"Cheekbones," 48
Chemical senses, 571
Chemotaxis, 637
Chest, 116
Chewing, 86
Child, heartbeat of, 167
 teeth of, 53
Chimpanzee, 139
 brain of, 490
 brain/body ratio of, 494
 longevity of, 321
 reasoning of, 660
Chitin, 7
Chloride ion, 452
Chloroform, 234
Chlorpromazine, 673
Cholecystokinin, 355
Cholesterin, 402
Cholesterol, 232, 402
 formula of, 404
 myelin sheath and, 466
Cholinergic nerves, 554
Cholinesterase, 469
 inhibition of, 471
Chondrichthyes, 21
Chondrocytes, 75
Chondroitin sulphate, 75
Chordata, 14, 479
 larvae of, 15
Chorea, 522
 hereditary, 525
Chorioid plexus, 500
Choroid, 612
Chyme, 227
Chymotrypsin, 231
Cilia, 91
 respiration and, 129
Ciliary body, 619
Ciliary muscle, 619
Circulatory system, 154
Circumcision, 317
Cirrhosis, 234
Cisterna magna, 500
Clairvoyance, 569
Clavicle, 59

Clitoris, 312
Cloaca, 302
Clostridium tetani, 100
Clotting factors, 204
Cocaine, 564
Coccygeal nerves, 546
Coccygeal vertebrae, 39
Coccyx, 38
Cochlea, 592
Cochlear canal, 593
Cod-liver oil, 272
Coelenterata, 11
  feeding of, 212
Coelenterates, nervous system of,
  475, 476
Cold, common, 131
Cold-bloodedness, 24
Cold perspiration, 277
Cold-receptors, 558
Coleridge, Samuel T., 661
Colic, 241
  renal, 264
Colitis, 241
Collagen, 74
Collarbone, 59
Colloid, 385
Colon, 241
Color(s), wavelength of, 630, 631
Color-blindness, 632
Color vision, 628, 630-33
Coma, 528
Compact bone, 77
Competitive inhibition, 441
Compound eye, 609
Conchae, nasal, 47
Concussion, 499
Conditioned reflex, 649-53
Conditioning, 648-53
Condyle, 42
Cones, 625
Conjugation, 294
Conjunctiva, 614
Conjunctivitis, 615
Connective tissue, 73
Constipation, 245
Consumption, 145
Contraceptives, oral, 444
Convergence, 10
Convolutions, 485
Copulation, 298
Corals, 5
Cori, Carl F., 370
Cori, Gerty T., 370
Corn, 270

Cornea, 611
  transplantation of, 623
Coronary arteries, 163, 180
Coronary thrombosis, 180
Corpus callosum, 519
Corpus luteum, 307, 311, 442
Corpus striatum, 521
Cortex, adrenal, 377, 412
  kidney, 254
  sex hormones and, 442
Cortex, cerebellar, 533
Cortex, cerebral, 482, 506
  mapping of, 509
  sense perception and, 512
  sensory area of, 511
Corti, Marchese Alfonso, 593
Corti, organ of, 593
Corticoids, 413
Corticospinal tract, 510
Corticosterone, 414
Corticotropins, 419
Cortin, 413
Cortisone, 415
  clinical uses of, 417
Costal cartilages, 39, 75
Cough, 134
Cranial nerves, 541-44
Craniosacral division, 553
Craniotabes, 81
Cranium, 40, 46
Creatine, 261
Creatine phosphate, 9
Creatinine, 261
Cretins, 390
Cricoid cartilage, 135
Cro-Magnons, 492
Cross-eyes, 618
Crossopterygii, 22
Crusoe, Robinson, 332
Cryptorchidism, 314
Crystalline lens, 619
Cuboid bone, 69
Cud, 224
Cuneiform bone, 69
Curare, 471
Curd, 224
Cushing, Harvey, 419
Cushing's disease, 419
Cutaneous senses, 557
Cuvier, Georges Leopold, 4
Cyanide ion, 228
Cyanocobalamin, 198
Cyclosis, 90
Cystic duct, 232

Cystine, 264, 347
  structure of, 348
Cystitis, 260
Cytoplasm, 73

2,4-D, 427
Dandruff, 289
Dark adaptation, 609
Darwin, Charles, 586
Davy, Humphry, 565
Dead space, 146
Death, 322
Deciduous teeth, 53
Deer, legs of, 109
Defecation, 244
Defoe, Daniel, 331
Deglutition, 219
Delta waves, 515
Deltoid muscle, 115
Dementia praecox, 668
Demyelinating disease, 467
Dendrites, 463
Dental formula, 51, 52
Dentine, 82
Deoxycorticosterone, 415
Dermatitis, 288
Dermis, 268
Descartes, Rene, 421
Descending aorta, 163
Descending colon, 242
Detoxication in liver, 234
Deviated septum, 128
Diabetes, 257
  insipidus, 257, 401
  hypothalamus and, 525
  mellitus, 262, 362
Diapedesis, 202
Diaphragm, 118, 133, 163
  nerves of, 548
  respiration and, 127
Diaphysis, 79
Diarrhea, 245
Diastole, 173
Diastolic pressure, 176
2,4-dichlorophenoxyacetic acid, 427
Diencephalon, 531
Diffusion, 122
Digestion, 213
  summary of, 236
Digestive canal, 213
Digit, 61
Digitalis, 171, 409
Digitigrade mammals, 70
Dionne, Oliva, 310

Discs, intervertebral, 39, 40
Dislocation, 87
DOC, 415
Dogs, limbs of, 70
  longevity of, 320
  panting of, 276
  tongue of, 217
Dolphins, 139
  brains of, 495, 496
  echolocation and, 600
Dorsal cord, 13
  vertebrae, 34
Dostoyevsky, Fyodor, 518
Cropsy, 207
Duodenum, 228, 229
Dura mater, 497
Du Vigneaud, Vincent, 400, 401
Dwarf, 80

Ear(s), 75, 284
  evolution of, 584, 585
  external, 587
  internal, 592
  middle, 588
  motions of, 119
  movement of, 586
Eardrum, 587
Earthworm, 7, 186
  heart of, 154
  reproduction of, 296
Earwax, 588
Ecdysis, 431
Ecdysone, 432
Echinoderm superphylum, 11
Echinodermata, 6, 10
Echolocation, 598-601
Eczema, 289
Edema, 207
EEG, 514
  epilepsy and, 518
Efferent arteriole, 254
Egg cell, 72, 293
Einthoven, Willem, 172
Ejaculation, 318
Ejaculatory duct, 316
Elastic cartilage, 75
Elastin, 74
Elbow, 85
Electric eel, 460
  cholinesterase and, 469
Electric organ, 460, 461
Electricity, 450
Electrocardiogram, 172
Electrocution, 171

Electroencephalography, 514
Electromotive force, 457
Electrons, 452
Elephant(s), 322
  brain of, 495
  ear of, 282
  heartbeat of, 168
  longevity of, 320
  skull of, 78
  trunk of, 127
  tusks of, 52, 82
Elephantiasis, 207
Embryo, 304
  gill pouches in, 26
  heartbeat of, 168
  notochord in, 18, 19
  tail in, 39
Emetics, 226
EMF, 457
Emotions, 523, 524
Emulsion, 233
Enamel, 83
Encephalitis, 479n
Encephalitis lethargica, 530
Encephalon, 479n
Endocrinology, 360
Endoderm, 11
Endometrium, 309
Enema, 245
Enterogastrone, 356
Enzymes, 212, 344
  hormones and, 352
Eosinophils, 200
Epidermis, 269
Epididymis, 316
Epiglottis, 133
Epilepsy, 517
Epinephrine, 377
  effect of, 378, 379
  formula of, 379
Epiphysis, 79
Epsom salts, 245
Erythroblast, 188
Erythrocyte(s), 187
  breakdown of, 189
  formation of, 188
  hemoglobin content of, 190
  number of, 189
  overproduction of, 199
  size of, 188
Erythropoiesis, 188
Esophageal arteries, 164
Esophagus, 220

ESP, 569
Estradiol, 440
Estriol, 440
Estrogens, 440
Estrone, 440
Ethmoid bone, 45
17-ethynylestradiol, 440
Eunuch, 314, 435, 436
Eustachian tube, 591
Eustachio, Bartolommeo, 591
Eutheria, 303
Excretion, 247, 342n
Excretory system, 247
Expiration, 126, 146
External ear, 587
Exteroceptive sensations, 557
Extra-pyramidal system, 510, 521, 549
Extrasensory perception, 569
Eye(s), 284
  color of, 612
  compound, 609
  lids of, 614
  light focusing and, 620-23
  movement of, 618, 619
  nerves to, 542
  watering of, 615
Eyeball, 611
  interior of, 619, 620
Eyelids, 614
Eye teeth, 51

Face, 47
Facial nerve, 543
Fallopian tube, 307, 318
Fallopio, Gabriello, 307
"False ribs," 35
Farsightedness, 622
Fascia, 107
Fat(s), 183, 211
  bile and, 407
  digestion of, 224, 233, 407
  oxidation of, 246
  polyunsaturated, 406
  storage of, 239
Fatigue, 101
Fatty acids, 236
Feathers, 26, 268
Feces, 244
Fechner, Gustav T., 563
Feedback, 343
  cerebellum and, 536-38
Femur, 67, 86

Fertilization, 295, 308
Fertilized ovum, 295
Fetus, 304n
Fever, 278, 526
Fibrillation, 171
Fibrin, 204
Fibrinogen, 204
Fibroblasts, 74
Fibrocartilage, 75
Fibula, 68
Fimbria, 307
Fingerbones, 63
Fingernails, 267
Fingerprints, 269, 270
Fingers, 86
    tendons in, 108
Fins, 21
Fish, hearing of, 584
    heart of, 154
    heartbeat of, 169, 170
    jaws of, 48
    lungs in, 125
    musculature of, 114
    nostrils of, 126
    oxygen absorption by, 124
    reproduction of, 299
    scales of, 267
    skull of, 44
Fission, binary, 292
Fissure of Rolando, 507
Fissure of Sylvius, 507
Fissures, cerebral, 506
Fixation muscles, 106
Flagellum, 91
Flamingo, 33
Flat feet, 71, 88
Flatus, 244
Flatworms, nervous system of, 476
"Floating rib," 35
Fluoridation, 83
Fluoride ion, 76
    teeth and, 83
Fluoroapatite, 76
Follicle, hair, 285
    ovarian, 442
    primitive Graafian, 306
Follicle-stimulating hormone, 444
Fontanelles, 46
Food, 211 ff.
    canal, 213
    vacuole, 211
Foot, 69
    arch of, 71, 88

Foramen, 37
    magnum, 42, 523
Forebrain, 480
Forehead, 45
Foreskin, 317
Fossil bones, 76
Fourth ventricle, 580
Fovea centralis, 626
France, Anatole, 494
Franklin, Benjamin, 450
Freckles, 274
Freud, Sigmund, 564
Fritsch, Gustav, 509
Frog, 126
    heartbeat of, 168
    nitrogen excretion of, 251
    respiration of, 127
    water excretion of, 256
Frölich, Alfred, 446
Frölich's syndrome, 446
Frontal bone, 44
Frontal lobe, 507
Fructose, 236
FSH, 445, 446
Fundus, 222
"Funny bone," 60n

Galactose, 236
Galen, 449
Gall, 231
    bladder, 232, 355
    stone(s), 232, 402
Galvani, Luigi, 451
Ganglion(ia), 520n
    collateral, 552
    prevertebral, 552
Gas, intestinal, 241, 244
    stomach, 222, 225
Gastrectomy, 228
Gastric juice, 224
    ulcer, 227
Gastrin, 356
Gastroenemius, 108
Gel, 91
General senses, 557
Genitalia, 305
Geotropism, 636
Giant, 80
Giants, pituitary gland and, 430
Gibberellin, 427
Gibbons, 490
Gill(s), 124
    arches, 18

bars, 124
cover, 124
"pouches," 26
slits, 14, 26, 124
Gingivitis, 216
Giraffe, 33, 217
Gland(s), 207, 359
    adrenal, 376
    ductless, 360
    endocrine, 360
    intestinal, 235
    lacrimal, 614
    mammary, 279
    parathyroid, 395
    pineal, 421
    pituitary, 392
    prostate, 316
    prothoracic, 432
    salivary, 219
    sebaceous, 287
    sex, 435
    suprarenal, 376
    sweat, 276
    tear, 614
    thyroid, 381
Glans penis, 317
Glaucoma, 620
Glia cells, 503
Glossitis, 218
Glossopharyngeal nerve, 544
Glottis, 132
Glucagon, 375
Glucose, 236
    blood content of, 366
    in urine, 262
Glucose threshold, 368
Glucose-tolerance test, 32
Glutamic acid, 347
Glutamine, 347
Gluteus maximus, 117
Gluteus medius, 117
Glycerol, 236
Glycine, 346
    bile acids and, 407
Glycocorticoids, 415
Glycogen, 238
    corticoids and, 414
    epinephrine and, 378
Glycosides, 409
Gnostic area, 663
Goblet cells, 129
Goiter, 383
    exophthalmic, 385
    iodine and, 383

iodine-deficiency, 384
Gonadotrophins, 444
    human chorionic, 446
Gonads, 305, 435
Gooseflesh, 283
Gorilla(s), 31, 39
    brain of, 570, 574
    hair of, 283
    longevity of, 321
Gout, 264
Graaf, Regnier de, 306
Grand mal, 517
Grandma Moses, 319, 320, 321
Graves' disease, 385
Graves, Robert J., 385
Gray matter, brain and, 562
    spinal cord and, 540
Greater multangular bone, 62
Grinders, 51
Ground substance, 75
Growth, 423-30
Growth hormone, 428-30
Gullet, 220
Gums, 216
Gut, 213
Gyri, 508

H disc, 93
Habit, 661n
Hair, 26, 45, 128, 268, 281 ff.
    cells, 593
    graying of, 285
    growth of, 286
    sensations and, 560
Hairlessness, 268, 282
Hallucinations, 667
Hallux, 69
Hamate bone, 62
Hamstring, 109
Hand, 61
Hard palate, 134
Havers, Clopton, 77
Haversian canals, 77
Hay fever, 131
HCG, 446
Head, 115
    evolution of, 478
    headache, 568
Hearing, binaural, 599
    pitch and, 593-95
    pressure and, 584
    range of, 596, 597
    sight compared with, 579-81
Heart, 153

blood flow in, 157
hypertrophy of, 168
life and, 338
location of, 156
murmur in, 173
refractory period of, 171
size of, 156
valves in, 159
Heart attack, 180
Heart block, 170
Heartbeat, 167 ff
ions and, 169
sound of, 172, 173
total number of, 320, 321
Heartburn, 225
Heat, body, 275
detection of, 576
sexual, 308
Heat-receptors, 558
Hedgehog, heartbeat of, 168
Heel, 68, 69
Height, 57
Helmholtz, Hermann von, 463, 631
Hematocrit, 184
Heme, 187
Hemichordata, 17
Hemiplegia, 521
Hemoconia, 189
Hemocyanin, 186
Hemoglobin, 186
A, 305
abnormal, 197
breakup of, 233
carbon dioxide and, 247
F, 305
oxygen absorption by, 190
Hemolysis, 198
Hemophilia, 205
Hemorrhage, 192
Hench, Philip S., 416
Henle, Friedrich, 257
Henle's loop, 257
Hensen, Victor, 93
Hensen's disc, 93
Heparin, 205
Hepatic duct, 232
vein, 238
Hernia(s), 117, 118
Hexokinase, insulin and, 339, 340
HGF, 345
Hibernation, 168, 527
Hiccup, 133
Hindbrain, 480
Hinge joint, 85

Hip joint, 86
Hipbone, 64
Hippocrates, 518
Hips, 117
Histamine, 379
Histidine, 347
formula of, 379
Hitzig, Eduard, 509
Hives, 207
Holmes, Oliver W., 565
Hominidae, 491
Homogentisic acid, 263
Homo sapiens, 492
Hoofs, 61, 70
Hooke, Robert, 71
Hormone(s), 342
adrenocorticotrophic, 418
anterior pituitary, 393
antidiuretic, 399
destruction of, 342
enzymes and, 352
female sex, 439
follicle-stimulating, 444
gastrointestinal, 357
growth, 80, 429
interstitial cell-stimulating, 445
juvenile, 432
lactogenic, 445
larval, 432
luteinizing, 445
luteotropic, 445
male sex, 436
melanocytepstimulating, 420
membrane diffusion of, 349
molting, 432
nerves and, 469
ovarian, 439
parathyroid, 395-98
plant, 426-28
polypeptide, 350
posterior pituitary, 398-401
precursors of, 351, 352
pregnancy and, 443, 444
protein, 350
sex, 450
somatotrophic, 429
steroid, 420
synthesis of, 401
termination of action of, 343
testicular, 446
thyroid-stimulating, 393
wounds, 426
Horn, 271
Horse(s), 54

leg of, 109
longevity of, 320
respiration of, 146
toes of, 61
Hottentots, 240
Housemaid's knee, 88
Howler monkeys, 138
Humerus, 60
Humidity, 277
Humming, 136, 137
Hummingbird, brain of, 495
Hunger pangs, 223
Huntington, George S., 523
Huntington's chorea, 523
Huygens, Christian, 606
Hyaline cartilage, 75
Hyaluronic acid, 75
Hydra, 293
Hydrocephalus, 502
Hydrochloric acid, 224
Hydrotropism, 637
Hydroxyapatite, 76
Hyoid bone, 49
Hyperacidity, 225
Hyperglycemic-glycogenolytic factor, 375
Hyperopia, 622
Hyperparathyroidism, 397
Hypertension, 178
Hyperthyroidism, 384
Hypertrophy, 103
Hypnotism, 567
Hypoglossal nerve, 544
Hypophysis cerebri, 392
Hypopituitarism, 393
Hypothalamus, 524, 525
Hypothermia, 527
Hypothyroidism, 385
Hysterectomy, 313
Hysteria, 313

I band, 93
IAA, 426
ICSH, 445
Ideomotor area, 663
Idiopathic hypertension, 179
Ileocolic sphincter, 242
Ileum, 235
Iliac arteries, 165
vein, 165
Impetigo, 289
Imprinting, 646
Incisors, 50
Incus, 49, 588

Index finger, 63
Indolyl-3-acetic acid, 426
Inferior vena cava, 167
Influenza, 131
Insect(s), eyes of, 609
molting of, 431
Insectivora, 485
Insomnia, 530
Inspiration of air, 126, 146
Instincts, 644
development of, 644-48
Insulin, 261
differences in, 374
glucose level and, 367, 368
isolation of, 364
mechanism of action of, 369-71
molecular weight of, 371
structure of, 343
Insulinase, 367
Intercellular cement, 75
Intercostal arteries, 164
muscles, 116
Intercourse, sexual, 298n, 318
Intermedin, 420
Internal ear, 592
Interoceptive sensations, 557
Interstitial cell-stimulating hormone, 445
Interstitial fluid, 205
Invertebral disc, 39, 40
Intestinal glands, 235
juice, 235
Intestines, 227, 243
membrane about, 241
Invertebrates, 3
Involuntary muscles, 98
Ions, 76, 169, 365n, 366n
Iris, 612
Iron deficiency, 196
lung, 105, 151
Ischium, 64
Islets of Langerhans, 361
cell groups of, 345
Isoleucine, 346
Isotropic band, 93
Ivory, 82

Jaundice, 234
Java man, 492
Jaw, 20, 115
bones of, 48
Jejunum, 235
Jellyfish, 152
Joints, 84

Jugular vein, 165
Juvenile hormone, 432

Kallidin, 357
Kallikrein, 357
Kangaroo(s), 31, 57, 302
Kendall, Edward C., 357, 413
Keratin, 268
Ketone bodies, 261
Kidney stones, 264
Kidneys, 252
Kinesthetic sense, 558
Kinins, 358
Kiwi, 57
Knee, 68, 86
  water on, 88
Knee bone, 68
  jerk, 99, 642
Köhler, Wolfgang, 660
Koller, Carl, 564
Krause, Wilhelm, 558
Krause's end bulb, 558
Kupffer's cells, 237

Labia majora, 312
  minora, 312
Lacrimal bones, 48
Lacrimal glands, 614
Lactase, 236
Lacteals, 237
Lactic acid, 102
Lactogenic hormone, 445
Lactose, 236
Laënnec, Rene T. H., 173
Lamarck, Jean Baptiste, 3
Lamprey, 19
  nervous system of, 480
  semicircular canals of, 604n
Lancelet, 16
Langerhans, Paul, 361
Large intestine, 227, 243
Larva, 12
  retention of, 16
Larval hormone, 432
Laryngitis, 140
Larynx, 137
Lateral lines, 584
Lateral sulcus, 507
Lateral ventricles, 500
Laxatives, 245
Learning, 660
Left ventricle, 182
Legs, 63 ff.
  motion of, 111

Lemurs, 486
Lens, 608
Lens, crystalline, 619
  accommodation of, 621
  transparency of, 623, 624
Lentiform nucleus, 520
Leo XIII, 436
Lesser multangular bone, 62
Leucine, 346
Leukemia, 203
Leukocytes, 199 ff.
Leukocytosis, 203
Leukopenia, 203
Leyden jar, 450
LH, 445
Ligaments, 87
Light, 605-7
  colors of, 630
  focusing of, 620-37
  reaction of, 607
  refraction of, 608
  spectrum, 631
  wave nature of, 606
Light adaptation, 629
Lilly, John C., 506
Limbic lobe, 524
Limbic system, 524
Limbs, 56
  distal end of, 60
  joints in, 85
Linea alba, 116
Linnaeus, Carolus, 4
Lipase, 224
  pancreatic, 229
Lipids, 211
Lips, 215
Liver, 207, 231
  cirrhosis of, 234
  glycogen and, 366
  life and, 338
  sugar and, 238
Lobes, cerebral, 517
  prefrontal, 663
Lockjaw, 100
Lowes, John L., 661
Lumbar arteries, 165
  vertebrae, 36
Lumbar nerves, 546
Lumbar plexus, 548
Lumbar puncture, 514
Lunate bone, 62
Lung(s), 125, 142
  collapse of, 150
  lobes of, 142

residual volume in, 147
surface area of, 144, 145
tidal volume in, 146
vital capacity of, 147
Lung unit, 144
Lungfish, 125
lungs of, 143
Luteinizing hormone, 445
Luteotrophic hormone, 445
Lymph, 205 ff
capillaries, 206
glands, 207
nodes, 207
Lymphatics, 206
Lymphocytes, 201, 208
Lymphoid tissue, 209
Lysergic acid diethylamide, 672
Lysine, 347
Lysozyme, 615

Macrophages, 189, 209
Macula lutea, 625
Magnus-Levy, Adolf, 386
Malleus, 49, 588
Malocclusion, 51
Maltase, 236
Mammalia, 24
Mammals, 24
cerebrum of, 483
heart of, 155
longevity of, 320
nitrogen excretion of, 252
number of teeth in, 50
placental, 305
reproduction of, 301 ff
respiration of, 126
Mammary gland, 279
lines, 279
Mandible, 49
Mandibular nerve, 543
Manganese, 186
Marine, David, 354
Marrow, 78
erythrocytes and, 188
Marsupialia, 302
Masseter, 115
Maxilla, 48
Maxillary bones, 48
Maxillary nerve, 543
Meatus, 129
Medial nuclei, 566
Medius, 63
Medulla, adrenal, 347
autonomic nervous system and,
554-55

Medulla of kidney, 254
Medulla oblongata, 481, 531
Megakaryocytes, 204
Megaloblast, 188
Meissner, Georg, 558
Meissner's corpuscle, 558
Melanin, 273
Melanocyte-stimulating hormone, 430
Melatonin, 432
Membrane, cell, 409
depolarized, 458
hormones and, 454
polarized, 457
semipermeable, 553, 554
Membrane, tympanic, 587
Memory, 661
RNA and, 674
Menarche, 312
Meninges, 497
Meningitis, 498
Menopause, 312
Menstruation, 312
anemia and, 196
Mescaline, 671
Mesenteric artery, 164
Mesmer, Friedrich A., 567
Mesoderm, 11
Metabolism, 465
Metacarpal bones, 62
Metamorphosis, 431
Metetarsus, 69
Metatheria, 302
Methionine, 347
Methyltestosterone, 439
Micron, 188
Midbrain, 480
human, 531
Middle ear, 588
Midgets, pituitary gland and, 430
Milk, cow's, 281
human, 280
production, 445
Miller, Jacques, F.A.P., 434
Millimicron, 72
Mineral ions, hormones and, 415
Mineralocorticoids, 415
Mineral oil, 245
Minimus, 63
Mitral valve, 161
Molars, 51
Molecular weight, 349
Moles, 127, 290
Mollusca, 5
Molting, insect, 431

Molting hormone, 432
Moniz, Antonio Egas, 664
Monkeys, 70
  brains, 488, 494, 495
  New World, 488
  Old World, 489
Monoamine oxidase, 672
Monocyte(s), 201, 209
Monotremata, 302
Morgan, Lloyd, 657
Morton, William, G.T., 565
Moths, phototaxis of, 639n
Motion, 89 ff.
Motor area, 509
Motor unit, 471
Mouse, 167, 168
Mouth, 213, 215 ff.
  respiration through, 132
  roof, 48
MSH, 420
Mucin, 218
Mucopolysaccharide, 74
Mucous membrane, 129
Mucus, 74, 129, 221
Müller, Johannes, 464
Multicellularity, 333
Multicellular organisms, 5
Multiple fission, 292
Multiple sclerosis, 467
Mumps, 219
Murmur, heart, 173
Muscae volitantes, 620
Muscle(s), 93
  combinations of, 110
  contraction of, 93
  fatigue of, 101
  insertion of, 106
  lever action of, 112
  nerves and, 470
  origin of, 106
  reflex responses of, 641
  tone of, 103
  weight of, 114
Muscle cells, 98
  "twitch," 99
Mustache, 128, 284, 285
Muzzle, function of, 53
Myasthenia gravis, 471
Myelin sheath, 465
Myeloblasts, 200
Myelocytes, 200
Myoneural junction, 470
Myopia, 622
Myxedema, 386

Narcotic, 564
Nares, 127
Narses, 436
Narwhal, teeth of, 52
Nasal bones, 47
  conchae, 47, 128
Nausea, 226
Navel, 305
Navicular bone, 62, 69
Neanderthal man, 492
Nearsightedness, 622
Neck, 30
Neopallium, 483
Neoteny, 16
Nephritis, 255
Nephrons, 254
Nephrosis, 255
Nerve(s), 449
  abducens, 543
  accessory, 544
  acoustic, 544, 601
  adrenergic, 554
  ancient theories, 449, 450
  auditory, 544
  cervical, 546
  cholinergic, 554
  coccygeal, 546
  cord, 13, 21, 42
  cranial, 541-44
  facial, 543
  glossopharyngeal, 544
  hypoglossal, 544
  lumbar, 546
  mandibular, 543
  maxillary, 543
  mixed, 541
  motor, 541
  muscles and, 470
  myelinization of, 467
  oculomotor, 542
  olfactory, 541, 542
  ophthalmica, 543
  optic, 542
  pancreas and, 339, 340
  refractory period of, 474
  regeneration of, 472
  sacral, 546
  sciatic, 547
  sensory, 541
  spinal, 545-49
  stato-acoustic, 544
  stimulation of, 472-74
  thoracic, 546
  threshold stimulus of, 473

trigeminal, 542, 543
trochlear, 542
vagus, 544
Nerve cell(s), 463
    number of, 503
Nerve cords, 13, 21, 42, 476
Nerve fibers, 461
    afferent, 541
    efferent, 541
    motor, 541
    postganglionic, 551
    preganglionic, 551
    sensory, 541
    sheath around, 465
    somatic, 550
    visceral, 550
    width of, 464
Nerve gases, 471
Nerve impulse, 463
    chemicals accompanying, 468, 469
    speed of, 463-65, 467
Nervous system, 475
    autonomic, 551
    bony protection of, 497
    central, 476, 506
    peripheral, 476
Neural arch, 32
    canal, 32
Neuralgia, 543
Neurilemma, 465
Neuroglia, 493
Neurohumor, 493
Neuromuscular junction, 470
Neuron(s), 463
    connector, 639
    effector, 639
    interconnection of, 468
    receptor, 639
Neutrophilia, 203
Neutrophils, 201
Newton, Isaac, 606
Nictitating membrane, 614
Night blindness, 629
19-nortestosterone, 439
Nipples, 279, 280
Nodes, lymph, 207
Nodes of Ranvier, 465
Noradrenalin, 554
Norepinephrine, 554
Normoblast, 188
19-nortestosterone, 439
Nose, 127 ff.
Nostril, 127
Notochord, 13, 17

    in embryo, 18, 19
Novocain(e), 464
Nuclear membrane, 72
Nucleus, 72
Nyctalopia, 629

Obliquus externus abdominis, 117
Obturator foramina, 64
Occipital bone, 45
Occipital lobe, 507
Occiput, 45
Ocean water, 121, 185
Oculomotor nerve, 542
Odor, body, 278, 279
Old age, 291
Olfactory lobes, 481
Olfactory nerve, 541, 542
Omentum, 241
Oocyte, 306
Ophthalmic nerve, 543
Opossums, fecundity of, 303
Opsin, 628
Optic lobes, 481
Optic nerve, 542
Orangutan, brain of, 490
Orbicularis oris, 215
Orbit (enclosing eye), 44, 48
Organic molecules, 73
Orgasm, 318
Os coxae, 64
    innominata, 64
Ossicles, 49, 588
Osteichthyes, 21
Osteoblasts, 78
Osteoclasts, 78
Osteocytes, 76
Osteomalacia, 81
Osteomyelitis, 81
Osteon, 77
Ostracoderms, 20
Ostrich, legs of, 56
Otoconia, 602
Otocyst, 602
Otoliths, 602
Oval window, 588
Ovarian hormones, 439
Ovaries, 306, 311
Overweight, 528
Oviparous creatures, 301
Ovoviviparous creatures, 301
Ovulation, 307
Ovum(a), 293, 306
    fertilized, 295

Oxygen, absorption of, 123, 124, 152
  blood and, 183 ff.
  energy and, 211 ff.
  life and, 120 ff.
  lungs and, 145, 146
Oxygen debt, 102
Oxygen-drunk, 149
Oxyhemoglobin, 191
Oxytocin, 400

Pacemaker, 169
Pacini, Filippo, 559
Pacinian corpuscle, 559
Pain, 563
  internal, 567, 568
  referred, 569
Pain-receptors, 558
Palates, 48, 134
Palatine bones, 48
Pallium, 482
Palm, 107
Palmar fascia, 107
Palmaris longus, 107
Palsy, 522
Pancreas, 229
  diabetes and, 362
  glandular nature of, 360, 361
  nerves and, 339, 340
  secretin and, 343
Pancreatic amylase, 229
  juice, 229
  lipase, 229
Pancreozymin, 355
Papilla(e), 217, 571, 572
Papillary muscles, 157
Paralysis, 521n
Paralysis agitans, 522
Paramecia, response of, 638
Parasympathetic division, 553
Parathyroid glands, 395
Parathyroid hormone, 395-98
Parietal bones, 45
Parietal lobe, 497
Parkinson, James, 522
Parkinson's disease, 522
Parotid glands, 219
Parrots, longevity of, 320
Parthenogenesis, 295
Pasteur, Louis, 281
Pasteurization, 281
Patella, 68
Patellar reflex, 642
Pavlov, Ivan P., 649

Pectoral girdle, 59
Pectoral muscle, 115
Peking man, 492
Pellagra, 218, 669
Pelvic girdle, 66
Pelvis, 66, 67
Penguin, walk of, 31
Penis, 90, 259, 316
  circumcised, 317
Pepsin, 224
Peptic ulcers, 229
Peptidases, 235
Peptides, 235, 349, 350
Perfusion of organs, 169
Pericardium, 157
Perineum, 311
Peripatus, 9
Peripheral nervous system, 476
Peripheral vision, 526
Peristalsis, 221, 318
Peritoneum, 241
Permanent wave, 286
Pernicious anemia, 198, 227
Perspiration, 276
Petit mal, 507
Phagocytosis, 202
Phalanges, 63
Pharynx, 132
Phenylalanine, 346
  mental deficiency and, 669, 670
Phenylpyruvic acid, 670
Phenylpyruvic oligophrenia, 669
Phenylthiocarbamide, 474, 475
Phosphenes, 617
Phospholipid molecules, 409
Photopic vision, 617
Photoreception, 608
Photoreceptors, 608, 624, 625
Photosynthesis, 120
Phototropism, 628
Phrenic arteries, 165
Phrenology, 508
Phylum (a), 4 ff.
  development of, 8
Pia mater, 498
Pigs, hair of, 282
  nose of, 127
  longevity of, 320
  teeth of, 51
Pineal gland, 421
Pinna, 585
Pisces, 19
Pisiform bone, 62

Pitch, perception of, 593-98
Pitt-Rivers, Rosalind, 389
Pituitary gland, 80, 257, 392
    adrenal cortex and, 417-18
    growth and, 428-31
    hypothalmus and, 525
    lobes of, 392, 393
    sex hormones and, 444, 445
Pituitrin, 399
Placenta, 303
    pregnancy and, 443, 448
Placental mammals, 305
Placodermi, 20, 43
Plant(s), food and, 211
    growth of, 426-28
    motion of, 89
    responses of, 625-27
    symmetry and, 477
Plant hormones, 426-28
Plantigrade mammals, 70
Plant Kingdom, 2
Plasma, blood, 184
    color of, 234
    transfusion of, 195
Platelets, 203
Platypus, duckbill, 279, 302
Platyrrhina, 488
Pleasure center, 524
Pleura, 149
Pleurisy, 150
Plexus, 548
Pneumonia, 145
Poliomyelitis, 105
Pollex, 63
Polycythemia, 199
Polymorphonuclear leukocytes, 200
Polypeptide, 350
Polyuria, 257
Pongidae, 490
Pons, 531
Porcupine, quills of, 282
Pore, 276
Portal vein, 276
    glucose and, 386
Position sense, 558
Posterior pituitary hormones, 398-401
Postganglionic fibers, 551
Post-nasal drip, 134
Potassium ion, 169, 462
    distribution of, 465-67
Potbelly, 116, 241
Potential, electric, 467
Pouch, marsupial, 302

Precognition, 569
Prefrontal lobe, 653
Prefrontal lobotomy, 654
Preganglionic fibers, 361
Pregnancy, 197
    hormones and, 443-48
    testing for, 457
Premolars, 51
Premotor area, 653
Prepuce, 317
Presbyopia, 622
Pressure-receptors, 559
Primates, 485-92
Progesterone, 453
Progestin, 453
Prolactin, 455
Proline, 346
Proprioceptive sensations, 557
Prosecretin, 351, 352
Prosencephalon, 541
Prosimii, 486
Prostate gland, 316
Protein(s), 74, 211
    iodinated, 387
    molecular weight of, 349
    structure, 346
Prothoracic gland, 442
Protoplasm, 72
    movement of, 91
Protoplasmic streaming, 90
Prototheria, 301
protozoa, 5
    feeding of, 211
Pseudopods, 91
Psoriasis, 289
Psychomotor attacks, 517
PTC, 575
Ptyalin, 218
Puberty, 279
Pubic hair, 64, 284
    symphysis, 65
Pubis, 64
Pulmonary artery, 160
    circulation, 164
    vein, 161
Pulp, tooth, 82
Pulse, 159
Pupil, 613
Pus, 202
Pyloric sphincter, 225
Pylorus, 222
Pyorrhea, 217
Pyramidal cells, 499

Pyramidal system, 500
Python, ribs of, 36

Quadrumana, 70, 153n
Quadrupeds, 23
Quadruplets, 310
Quinine, taste, 573
Quintuplets, 310

Rabbit, caecum of, 243
    heartbeat of, 167
    longevity of, 320
Rachitis, 81
Radar, 601
Radial symmetry, 6, 477
Radius, 60, 86
Rami, spinal nerve, 547
Ranvier, Louis A., 465, 466
Rat(s), longevity of, 320
    respiration of, 146
    scales of, 267
Rectum, 244
Rectus, abdominis, 116
    femorus, 118
Red blood corpuscle, 187
Reflex, 639
    Babinski, 642
    conditioned, 649-53
    crossed extensor, 641
    flexion, 641
    patellar, 642
    stretch, 642
    unconditioned, 648
Reflex arc, 638, 639
Reflex center, 639
Refractory period, 459
Regeneration, 269, 424
Regurgitation, 173
Reichstein, Tadeus, 413
Renal arteries, 165, 254
    colic, 264
    hypertension, 179
    pelvis, 258
    threshold, 262
    vein, 165, 254
Renin, 255
Rennin, 224
Reproduction, 292 ff
Reptiles, cerebrum of, 482
    heart of, 155
    jaw of, 49
    lungs of, 143
    nitrogen excretion of, 251
    reproduction of, 300

respiration of, 126
    ribs in, 36
    skull of, 44
Reptilia, 24
Reserpine, 673
Respiration, 127
    rate of, 145
Respiratory bronchioles, 144
    pigments, 186
Response, 634
Reticular activating system, 501, 524
    sleep and, 519
Reticular area, 519
Reticulocyte, 188
Reticulo-endothelial system, 210
Retina, 620
    structure of, 624
Retinene, 628
Rheotaxis, 638
Rheumatism, 88
Rheumatoid arthritis, 88
Rhine, Joseph B., 569
Rhinoceros, 61, 282
Rhodopsin, 628
Rib cage, 35
Ribonucleic acid, 675
Ribs, 34, 35
Rickets, 81
Rigor mortis, 101
Rima glottidis, 135
Ringer, Sidney, 169
Ringer's solution, 169
RNA, 675
Rodents, 52
Rods, 624
Root, hair, 286
Roughage, 244
Round window, 594
Ruffini, Angelo, 558
Ruffini's end organ, 558
Rugae, 222
Rupture, 117
Rutting season, 308
Ruzicka, Leopold, 437

S-A node, 170
Saccharin, 574
Saccule, 584
Sacral nerves, 546
Sacral plexus, 548
Sacral vertebra, 37
Sacroiliac, 65
Sacrum, 37, 65
Saint Vitus's dance, 523

Salivary amylase, 218
    gland, 219
Salivary secretion, 528
Salt, 277
Sanger, Frederick, 372
Saponins, 409
Sarcolemma, 460
Scales, 267
Scapula, 59
Scar, 269
Schizophrenia, 568
Schlemm, Friedrich, 619
Schlemm, canal of, 619
Schwann, Theodor, 475
Schwannoma, 475
Schwann's cells, 475
Sciatic nerve, 547
Sciatica, 548
Sclera, 611
Scotopic vision, 627
Scrotum, 314
Sea cow, 38, 57
Sea squirt, 15
Seasickness, 226
Sebaceous gland, 287
Seborrhea, 288
Sebum, 287
Secretin, 342
    amino acids of, 350
    molecular weight of, 349
    structure of, 344, 350
Secretinase, 344
Secretion, 342n
    endocrine, 354
    exocrine, 354
Segmentation, 7
    human, 36
    nervous system and, 545
Selkirk, Alexander 331
Semen, 316
Semicircular canals, 603
Semilunar valves, 159
Seminiferous tubules, 314
Sensation, intensity of, 562
Sense(s), chemical, 571
    cutaneous, 557
    general, 557
    kinesthetic, 558
    position, 558
    special, 557
    vestibular, 584, 601-4
Sense deprivation, EEG and, 515
Sense perception, 546
Sensory area, 511

Septum, 47
    deviated, 128
Serine, 347
Serum, blood, 204
117-ethynylestradiol, 450
Sexes, 293
Sex glands, 445
Sex hormones, 450
    action of, 451, 452
Sexual intercourse, 298n, 318
    reproduction, 293, 294
Sharks, 48, 50
Sheep, 282
Shell, 5, 19, 20, 266
Shinbone, 67
Shoulder blades, 59
    joint, 87
Shrew, 320, 322
Sickle-cell anemia, 197
Side-chain, amino acid, 345
Sight, depth perception in, 616, 617
Sigmoid colon, 243
Simmonds, Morris, 393
Simmonds' disease, 393
Sinew, 107
Singing, 137
Sinoauricular node, 170
Sinus venosus, 170
Sinusoids, 237
Skeletal muscles, 96
Skeleton, 27 ff
    calcium ion and, 396
Skin, 264 ff
    blood supply of, 177
    color of, 273
    cutaneous receptors on, 549
    darkening of, 430
    heat radiation by, 275
    muscles in, 119
"Skipping a beat," 171
Skull, 34, 40 ff, 481
    bones in 44
Sleep, 105, 149, 529
Slipped disc, 40
Sloths, neck of, 33
Small intestine, 227
    absorption through, 235
Small lymphocytes, 201
Smell, 575-578
    delicacy of, 578
Smell-receptors, 577
Smooth muscles, 93
Snake(s), 217, 267
Sneeze, 130
Snoring, 134

Sodium bicarbonate, 225
  ion, 169
Sodium ion, 462
  distribution of, 465-67
Sodium pump, 466
Soft palate, 134
Sol, 91
Solar plexus, 552
Somatic fibers, 550
Somatotrophic hormone, 439
Somesthetic area, 511
Somesthetic association area, 662
Sonar, 601
Soul, 337
Sound, 135
  communication and, 580-82
  detection of source of, 598, 599
  speed of, 583
Sound waves, 582, 583
  audible, 596, 597
  frequency of, 583
  wavelength of, 583
Sparrow, neck of, 33
Special sense, 547
Spectacles, 623
Spectrum, light, 631
Speech, brain damage and, 509
Sperm cell(s), 92, 295
  motion of, 297
  number of, 318
  size of, 315
Sperm whale, teeth of, 52
Spermatozoon, 295
Sphenoid bone, 45
Sphincter, 215
  cardiac, 221
  ileocolic, 242
  pyloric, 225
  urethral, 259
Sphincter ani, 244
  oris, 215
Sphygmomanometer, 175
Spider monkeys, 489
Spinal column, 28
  cartilage in, 39
  length of, 57
  number of bones in, 37
  shape of, 29
Spinal cord, 518
  ascending and descending tracts in, 529
  central canal of, 499
  weight of, 506
Spinal nerves, 545-49

Spine, 28
Spinous process, 32
Spleen, 28, 338
Splenius muscle, 115
Splintbone, 68
Sprains, 87
Square-cube law, 123, 282
Squids, giant axon of, 474
Squirrel-shrews, 486
Standing, muscle balance in, 543, 544
Stapes, 49, 588
Starch, 218, 229
Starfish, symmetry of, 6, 487
Starling, Ernest H., 340
Stato-acoustic nerve, 544
Statocyst, 602
Statolith, 602
Steapsin, 229
Steatopygia, 240
Stegosaur, nervous system of, 494
Stenosis, 173
Stereoscopic vision, 617
Sternocleidomastoid muscle, 115
Sternum, 34
Steroid(s), 403
  adrenocortical, 413
Steroid hormones, 410
Steroid nucleus, 403
Sterol(s), 271, 402
Stethoscope, 173
STH, 429
Stilbestrol, 441
Stimulus, 634
Stomach, 221
  rumbling of, 223
  secretions of, 355, 356
Strabismus, 618
Stratton, Charles S., 430
"Strawberry mark," 290
Stress, ACTH and, 419
Stroke, 179
Stroma, 198
Strychnine, 100
Subclavian arteries, 164
Subcutaneous layer, 240
Sublingual glands, 218
Submaxillary glands, 218, 219
Subphylum, 17
Subsonic waves, 597
Succus entericus, 235
Sucrase, 236
Sucrose, 236
Sulci, 508
Sunburn, 272

Sunlight, 271
Sunstroke, 284
Superior vena cava, 165
Suprarenal glands, 376
Suspensory ligament, 619
Suture, 47
Swallowing, 133, 138, 219
Swan(s), 33, 320
Sweat, 276, 278
  glands, 276
Swim bladder, 125
Sydenham, Thomas, 522
Sydenham's chorea, 522
Symmetry, 487
  bilateral, 6, 12, 36, 42
  radial, 6, 12
Sympathetic division, 553
Sympathetic trunks, 552
Sympathin, 554
Synapse, 468
  acetylcholine and, 470
Syncytium, 156
Synovial capsule, 85
  fluid, 85
  joints, 85
Syrinx, 139
Systemic circulation, 167
Systole, 173
Systolic pressure, 175, 176

Tadpoles, thyroid hormone and, 390
Tail, 38
Takamine, Jokichi, 377
Talus bone, 69
Tapetum, 625
Tapeworms, 152
Tarsier, spectral, 487
Tarsus, 68
Taste, 571-75
  classification of, 572
  delicacy of, 573
Taste-blindness, 575
Taste buds, 218, 572
Taurine, bile acids and, 407
Taxis, 637
Tear glands, 614
Tears, 614, 615
Teeth, 49 ff., 216
  children's, 53
  decay of, 83
  structure of, 82
Teething, 53
Telencephalon, 531
Temperature, body, 278, 525

Temporal bones, 45
Temporal lobe, 507
Temporary teeth, 53
Tendon, 107
Testes, 313
Testicles, 313
Testicular hormones, 446
Testosterone, 447
Tetanus, 100
Tetany, 99, 395
Tetrapoda, 23
  limbs of, 56
Thalamus, 481, 521
  emotion and, 523, 524
  pain and, 566
  sense perception and, 523
Thales, 450
Theria, 305
Theta waves, 515
Thigh, 67
  motions of, 117
Thighbone, 67
Thigmotaxis, 638
Third ventricle, 500
Thirst, 249
Thoracic duct, 206
  vertebrae, 34
Thoracic nerves, 635
Thoracicolumbar division, 553
Thorax, 118
Threonine, 347
Throat, 132
Thrombocytes, 203
Thrombosis, 179
Thumb, 63
  Tom, 440
Thymus gland, 443, 444
Thyroglobulin, 387
Thyroid cartilage, 135, 381
Thyroid gland, 381
  BMR and, 386
Thyroid-stimulating hormone, 393
Thyronine, 388
Thyrotrophic hormone, 393
Thyroxine, 387, 388
Tibia, 67
Tic douloureux, 533
Tiger, fangs of, 52
Tinnitis, 591
Tissue, connective, 73
Toad poisons, 409, 672
Toad, tongue of, 217
Toadstools, 471
Toe(s), 69, 86

Toenails, 267
Tone, muscle, 103
Tongue, 217
    taste and, 571
Tonsillectomy, 209
Tonsillitis, 209
Tonsils, 209
Tortoises, giant, 319
Touch, delicacy of, 561
    hairs and, 560
Toxin(s), 100, 526
Toxoid, 100
Trachea, 140
Trachoma, 616
Tranquilizers, 673
Transfusion, 193
Transport, active, 445
Transverse colon, 242
Transversus abdominis, 117
Trapezius muscle, 115
Taumatic acid, 428
Trees, evolution and, 486, 487
    life span of, 319
Tree-shrews, 485
Triceps brachii, 110
Tricuspid valve, 159
Trigeminal nerve, 532, 533
Tri-iodothyronine, 389
Triplets, 310
Triquetrum bone, 62
Trochlear nerve, 532
Tropism, 636
"True ribs," 35
Trypanosomiasis, 530
Trypsin, 231
Tryptophan, 348
    formula of, 426, 672
TSH, 393
Tuberculosis, 145
Tubule(s), convoluted, 256, 257
    convoluted seminiferous, 314
    uriniferous, 254
Tumor, 425
Tunicates, 15, 186
Tunnel vision, 626
Tupaiidae, 486
Turbinates, 128
Turgenev, Ivan, 494
Turtles, armor of, 267
Tusks of elephants, 82
Twins, 310
2,4-D, 427
Tyrosine, 263, 346
    formula of, 378, 388

Udder, 280
Ulcer(s), 226, 227, 229
Ulna, 60, 86
Ultrasonic sound, 597
    echolocation and, 600
Ultraviolet light, 271
Umbilical cord, 304
Umbilicus, 305
Unstriated muscles, 93
Urea, 251, 260
Uremia, 258
Ureter, 258
Urethra, 259, 311
Urethral sphincter, 259
Uric acid, 251, 263
Urinary bladder, 259
    calculi, 264
Urination, 259
Urine, 257
    color of, 234
    diabetes and, 362
    glucose, 262, 368
    urea in, 260
    uric acid in, 263
    volume of, 401
    water control and, 399
Urochordata, 17
Uterus, 309
Utricle, 584, 601
Uvula, 134

Vagina, 311
Vagus, nerve, 534
Valine, 346
Valves, heart, 159
    disorders of, 173
    sound of, 173
Vanadium, 186
Varicose veins, 181
Vas deferens, 316
Vasoconstriction, 178
Vasodilation, 177
Vasopressin, 400
Veins, 161
    dilation of, 181
Vena cava, 165
    blood flow in, 175
Venous blood, 191
Ventilation, 277
Ventral cord, 13
Ventricle(s), 155, 162
    brain, 499, 500
Ventricular fibrillation, 171

Venules, 161
Vermiform appendix, 243
Vermis, 533
Vertebrae, 18
    specialization among, 33
    structure of, 32
Vertebral column, 29
Vertebrata, 18
Vertebrates, 3, 480
Vestibular canal, 593
Vestibular sense, 584, 601-4
Vestibule, 584
Vestigial organs, 119
Vibrissae, 560
Villi, 235
Virilism, 420
Viscera, 96, 450
Visceral brain, 514
Visceral fibers, 450
Visceral muscles, 96
Visceral sensations, 457
Vision, alpha waves and, 504, 505
    color, 628, 630-33
    peripheral, 626
    photopic, 627
    scotopic, 627
    stereoscopic, 617
    tunnel, 626
    vitamin A and, 629
Visual area, 503
Visual association area, 662
Visual pigments, 607
Visual purple, 628
Vitamin A, vision and, 629
Vitamin B$_{12}$, 198
Vitamin D, 80, 272
    bone formation and, 397
    formation of, 408
Vitreous body, 619
Vitreous humor, 619
Vocal cords, 135
    false, 140
Voice, 137, 138
    box, 136
Volta, Alessandro, 451
Voluntary muscles, 96
Vomer bones, 47
Vomiting, 225
Vulva, 312

Wadlow, Robert 430
Waistline, 36
Walking, muscular control in, 535, 536
Walrus(es), 52, 282
Warm-bloodedness, 24, 143, 267, 300, 320

Water, absorption of, 243
    body content of, 398, 399
    carbon dioxide and, 247
    evaporation of, 275
    formation of, 246
    hypothalamus and, 525
    kidney reabsorption of, 257
    loss of, 247, 248
    organ content of, 182, 183
    oxygen and, 185
Watson, John B., 660
Weber, Ernst Heinrich, 563
Weber-Fechner law, 563
Whales, 30, 38
    brain of, 495
    cervical vertebrae in, 33
    fat of, 240
    limbs of, 57
    respiration of, 127
    teeth of, 52
Whey, 224
Whispering, 140
White blood corpuscles, 200
White ligaments, 87
White matter, 540
White meat, 102, 103
Whole blood, 184
Windpipe, 140
Wisdom teeth, 53
Wishbone, 59
Woman, brain of, 494
Womb, 303, 309
Women, blood of, 182
    erythrocytes of 189,
    fat storage in, 240
    heartbeat of, 167
    sacrum of, 38
    size of, 114
    urethra of, 259
    voice of, 137
Wool, 282
Wound hormones, 428
Wrist, 61, 62, 107

Yawn, 149
Yeast, 293
Yellow ligaments, 87
Yolk, 296
Young, Thomas, 606, 631

Z line, 93
Zinjanthropus, 491
Zygomatic bones, 48